YALTA

YALTA

THE PRICE OF PEACE

S. M. Plokhy

VIKING

VIKING

Published by the Penguin Group

Penguin Group (USA) Inc., 375 Hudson Street, New York, New York 10014, U.S.A. · Penguin Group (Canada), 90 Eglinton Avenue East, Suite 700, Toronto, Ontario, Canada M4P 2Y3 (a division of Pearson Penguin Canada Inc.) · Penguin Books Ltd, 80 Strand, London WC2R 0RL, England · Penguin Ireland, 25 St. Stephen's Green, Dublin 2, Ireland (a division of Penguin Books Ltd) · Penguin Books Australia Ltd, 250 Camberwell Road, Camberwell, Victoria 3124, Australia (a division of Pearson Australia Group Pty Ltd) · Penguin Books India Pvt Ltd, 11 Community Centre, Panchsheel Park, New Delhi–110 017, India · Penguin Group (NZ), 67 Apollo Drive, Rosedale, North Shore 0632, New Zealand (a division of Pearson New Zealand Ltd) · Penguin Books (South Africa) (Pty) Ltd, 24 Sturdee Avenue, Rosebank, Johannesburg 2196, South Africa

Penguin Books Ltd, Registered Offices: 80 Strand, London WC2R 0RL, England

First published in 2010 by Viking Penguin, a member of Penguin Group (USA) Inc.

ISBN 978-0-670-02141-3
Printed in the United States of America
Maps by Jeffrey L. Ward
Designed by Carla Bolte · Set in Scala

Book Club Edition

For

ANDRII

and

OLESIA

The work, my friends, is peace. More than an end of this war—
an end to the beginnings of all wars.

FRANKLIN D. ROOSEVELT

CONTENTS

MAPS

THE RED ARMY WINTER OFFENSIVE, JANUARY 1945

FINLAND

HELSINKI ★

OSLO ★

NORWAY

★ STOCKHOLM

TALLINN ★

ESTONIA

Baltic Sea

0 Miles   300

0 Kilometers   300

COURLAND

RIGA ★

SWEDEN

LATVIA

DENMARK

COPENHAGEN ★

North Sea

Königsberg

3RD BELARUSIAN FRONT (CHERNIAKHOVSKY)

Danzig

EAST PRUSSIA

Landsberg

Masurian Lakes

Hamburg

Stettin

POMERANIA

2ND BELARUSIAN FRONT (ROKOSSOVSKY)

NETHERLANDS

AMSTERDAM ★

Elbe

PRUSSIA

BERLIN ★

Küstrin

Vistula

1ST BELARUSIAN FRONT (ZHUKOV)

Rotterdam

Arnhem

Poznań

WARSAW ★

Antwerp

Eindhoven

RUHR

Oder

SAXONY

Łódź

Lublin

BELGIUM

Cologne

Bonn

Remagen

Dresden

Breslau

SOVIET UNION

RHINELAND

Frankfurt am Main

PRAGUE

SILESIA

LUXEMBOURG

SAAR

GERMANY

Kraków

1ST UKRAINIAN FRONT (KONEV)

Rhine

BADEN

Danube

FRANCE

WÜRTTEMBERG

BAVARIA

Munich

Salzburg

VIENNA ★

★ BUDAPEST

★ BERN

SWITZERLAND

HUNGARY

ROMANIA

Ljubljana

Milan

ITALY

Trieste

YUGOSLAVIA

Adriatic Sea

Mediterranean Sea

ROME ★

↓ to Caserta

© 2009 Jeffrey L. Ward

German-occupied areas

Allied and liberated areas

Neutral countries

Front lines

Country borders

Red Army winter offensive (January 12–31, 1945)

THE ALLIED OCCUPATION OF GERMANY

DENMARK

Baltic Sea

North
Sea

SCHLESWIG-
HOLSTEIN

Hamburg

Danzig/Gdańsk

Stettin/Szczecin

POMERANIA

HANOVER

PRUSSIA

Elbe

NETHERLANDS

GERMANY

BERLIN

POLAND

WESTPHALIA

Vistula

RUHR

SAXONY

Oder

Leipzig

BELGIUM

Cologne

Dresden

Breslau/Wrocław

HESSEN-
NASSAU

SILESIA

RHINELAND

Frankfurt am Main

PRAGUE

LUXEMBOURG

SAAR

CZECHOSLOVAKIA

Rhine

FRANCE

BADEN

Danube

WÜRTTEMBERG

BAVARIA

Munich

American Zone

British Zone

Soviet Zone

French Zone

0 Miles   200

0 Kilometers   200

AUSTRIA

Boundaries of the
American Zone
proposed by
the United States
in 1944

SWITZERLAND

ITALY

© 2009 Jeffrey L. Ward

NEW BOUNDARIES OF POLAND

SWEDEN

Baltic
Sea

Königsberg/
Kaliningrad

Wilno/Vilnius

Danzig/Gdańsk

Curzon Line

GERMANY Stettin/Szczecin

SOVIET UNION

Western
(Lusatian)
Neisse

Vistula

Poznań

WARSAW

**1947 Soviet-
Polish border**

Oder

POLAND

Brześć/Brest

Elbe

Łódź

Breslau/Wrocław

Lublin

Oder

Chełm/Kholm

Bug (Buh)

Eastern (Glatzer) Neisse

**Molotov-
Ribbentrop Line**

Curzon Line B

Kraków

Przemyśl/Peremyshl

Lwów/Lviv

CZECHOSLOVAKIA

Drohobycz/Drohobych

Territories transferred to the USSR

Territories transferred to Poland

Curzon Line—suggested by the Supreme Council of the
Allied Powers in December 1919 as administrative boundary
between Eastern Galicia and the rest of the Polish state.

HUNGARY

Curzon Line B—suggested by the Council as eastern limit of
Polish governmental authority in case the Ukrainian-
populated Eastern Galicia refused to join the Polish state.

ROMANIA

0 Miles   200

0 Kilometers   200

© 2009 Jeffrey L. Ward

SOVIET SPHERE OF INFLUENCE IN EASTERN EUROPE AFTER 1945

FINLAND

NORWAY

SWEDEN

Baltic Sea

North Sea

Leningrad

Tallinn

ESTONIA

RUSSIAN FEDERATION

Riga

LATVIA

DENMARK

LITHUANIA

Vilnius

Dnieper

Minsk

Elbe

BERLIN ★

EAST GERMANY

POLAND

WARSAW

BELARUS

SOVIET UNION

Rhine

WEST GERMANY

Kyiv

★ PRAGUE

UKRAINE

Lviv

CZECHOSLOVAKIA

Dnister

Danube

VIENNA ★

MOLDAVIA

Chișinău

SWITZER-LAND

AUSTRIA

★ BUDAPEST

HUNGARY

ITALY

ROMANIA

BUCHAREST ★

BELGRADE ★

Danube

YUGOSLAVIA

SOFIA ★

0 Miles 300

0 Kilometers 300

BULGARIA

Adriatic Sea

TIRANA ★

ALBANIA

Soviet Union before 1939

Territories annexed by the USSR in the course of the war

Soviet sphere of influence in Eastern Europe after 1945

© 2009 Jeffrey L. Ward

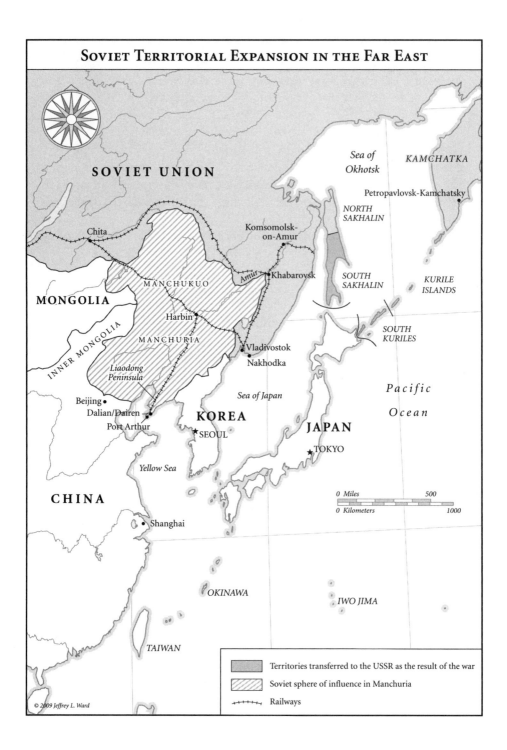

SOVIET TERRITORIAL EXPANSION IN THE FAR EAST

SOVIET UNION

Sea of
Okhotsk

KAMCHATKA

Petropavlovsk-Kamchatsky

NORTH
SAKHALIN

Chita

Komsomolsk-
on-Amur

MONGOLIA

MANCHUKUO

Amur Khabarovsk

SOUTH
SAKHALIN

KURILE
ISLANDS

INNER MONGOLIA

Harbin

MANCHURIA

Vladivostok

Nakhodka

SOUTH
KURILES

Liaodong
Peninsula

Pacific

Ocean

Beijing

Sea of Japan

Dalian/Dairen

KOREA

JAPAN

Port Arthur

SEOUL

TOKYO

Yellow Sea

CHINA

Shanghai

0 Miles   500
0 Kilometers   1000

OKINAWA

IWO JIMA

TAIWAN

Territories transferred to the USSR as the result of the war

Soviet sphere of influence in Manchuria

Railways

© 2009 Jeffrey L. Ward

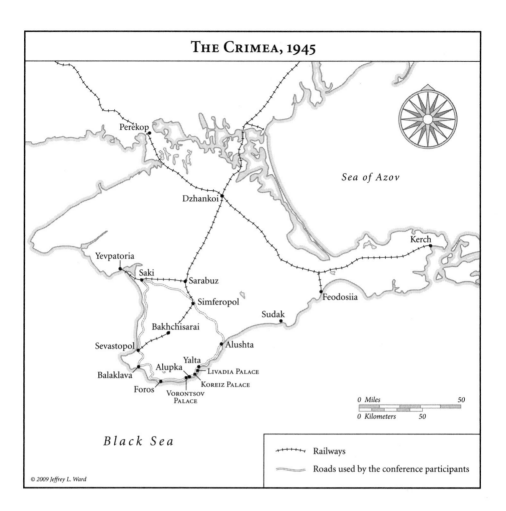

THE CRIMEA, 1945

Perekop

Sea of Azov

Dzhankoi

Kerch

Yevpatoria

Saki

Sarabuz

Simferopol

Feodosiia

Sudak

Bakhchisarai

Sevastopol

Alushta

Yalta

Alupka

LIVADIA PALACE

Balaklava

KOREIZ PALACE

Foros

VORONTSOV
PALACE

0 Miles 50

0 Kilometers 50

Black Sea

┿┿┿┿┿┿ Railways

Roads used by the conference participants

© 2009 Jeffrey L. Ward

INTRODUCTION

The time and location of the meeting were among the most heavily guarded secrets of the whole war. On the evening of February 3, 1945, under cover of darkness, a fleet of Packards brought the two most powerful leaders of the democratic world, Franklin Delano Roosevelt and Winston Leonard Spencer Churchill, to their destination—a group of villas formerly owned by the Russian tsar and prominent aristocrats near the Black Sea resort of Yalta. They called themselves the Argonauts, a reference to the ancient warriors who had traveled to the Black Sea coast to recover the Golden Fleece from a dragon who never slept. Their prize was a settlement to the war that had engulfed the world; their dragon was their host, Joseph Stalin, once a promising Georgian poet and now a ruthless dictator.

Together the three men conducted the most secretive peace conference of the modern era. They moved armies of millions and dispensed victors' justice as they saw fit, deciding the fate of nations and sending millions of refugees east and west because they believed it would promote a lasting peace. They created an institution to guard that peace and the interests of the victors. They left Yalta satisfied but anxious. Behind them lay thirty years ravaged by two world wars that had cost tens of millions of human lives. Before them was the uncertainty of the postwar world.

The contest of geopolitical aspirations, the clash of egos and value systems, and the jockeying for power among the most astute negotiators their nations could produce all played out in eight days at Yalta in February 1945. The three leaders wondered about one another's trustworthiness and readiness to compromise. Would the alumni of the best private schools of Britain and America reach an understanding with the son of a Georgian shoemaker who had dropped out of an Orthodox seminary? Would the two democratically elected leaders know how to handle the godfather of the Gulag? The conference confronted its participants with endless moral dilemmas. It was an emotional roller coaster that involved not only the leaders of the Grand Alliance but also their various subordinates, who fought for their countries' interests and for the favor of their masters.

Within a few short years of the end of the conference, the high hopes of its authors were dashed, their decisions condemned by friend and foe alike. The surviving participants went on the defensive or preferred to forget their involvement. Feelings of disappointment and regret dominated on both sides of the Cold War divide. Yalta became a symbol of lost opportunity, however differently perceived. In the West, it came to be regarded as a milestone on the road to the "lost peace," to cite a 1950s headline in *Time* magazine. In the mainstream discourse of the McCarthy era, the word "Yalta" became a synonym for betrayal of freedom and the appeasement of world communism.

Who was responsible? That became a central question with the onset of the Cold War in the late 1940s, when the two sides blamed each other. There were also heated domestic debates. In the United States the decisions taken at Yalta divided Republicans and Democrats. President Roosevelt and his advisers were accused not only of selling out Eastern Europe and China to Stalin but also of promoting communism at home. The highly publicized trial of Alger Hiss, a member of the U.S. delegation at Yalta who was accused of spying for the USSR, raised the temperature of the debate. Interviewed after his retirement for a book about his life, General George C. Marshall declined to make any substantive comment about his role at Yalta, certain that whatever he said would be turned against him.

Even today, public debate continues to revolve around the 1950s-era questions of who sold out Eastern Europe and whether it was in America's interest to persuade the USSR to join the war on Japan—a fact attested by the reaction of American foreign-policy pundits to a statement made in May 2005 by President George W. Bush, who compared the Yalta agreements to the Molotov-Ribbentrop Pact of 1939. Public debate on the Yalta Conference has so far failed to take account of two major developments: the end of the Cold War and access to formerly unavailable Soviet documents. It has also largely ignored the progress made by professional historians of the Second World War and the Cold War in the last two decades.

The opening of the Soviet archives—the "archival revolution" that followed the collapse of the USSR and coincided with the first years of Boris Yeltsin's rule—made available vast quantities of new documents, including many pertaining to foreign policy. Although many aspects of Soviet history have been reassessed in light of these documents, the Yalta Conference has not. There has been no major Western study of the Yalta Conference since the end of the Cold War, and the cursory treatment of the conference in the more recent surveys of U.S. foreign policy and histories of the wartime alliance cannot do justice to the subject. This new book on the Yalta Conference takes into account the archival discoveries of the last two decades, reevaluates previously known Western sources, and considers the conference and its outcome from a new historical perspective.

Previously inaccessible Soviet documents make it possible to revisit old questions and pose new ones. They confirm some of the hypotheses advanced by previous generations of scholars, who worked without access to the Soviet archives, and refute others. Most important, the new Soviet documents reveal the mind-set of the Soviet leaders at the time of the Yalta Conference. If Stalin and his strategists did not entirely abandon their plans for world revolution, they significantly postponed them and were interested in peaceful relations with the West for at least twenty years. That would give them enough time to recover from the devastation of the world war and prepare for the next stage in the conflict between communism and capitalism, which they considered ineluctable. For the time being they were prepared to sacrifice the communist movements in Western Europe and wanted a quid pro quo from the West that would ensure their domination of Eastern Europe. In Central Europe, despite Stalin's statements to the contrary, the Soviets planned to divide Germany into a number of smaller states, but their intention came to nothing because of Western opposition. There are, however, indications that in Germany the Soviets might have agreed to a demarcation line farther east than the one proposed by the British, which later served as the border between East and West Germany.

The new Soviet documents shed light on by far the most controversial question related to the Yalta Conference, that of the espionage activities of Alger Hiss. In the late 1940s and early 1950s it was alleged not only that Hiss spied for the Soviets but also that he had influenced some of FDR's decisions, which were later regarded as a sellout of American national interests. New evidence from the Soviet archives supports the thesis that Hiss was a Soviet spy at the time of the Yalta Conference, but it also suggests that while he was working for the military branch of Soviet intelligence, he remained virtually unknown to its political branch until after the conference. His military handlers showed little interest in the political information that he could provide, and his performance at the Yalta Conference on political matters, including Soviet participation in the United Nations, did nothing to advance the Soviet agenda. Owing to the activities of the Cambridge Five in Britain and the United States, the Soviet intelligence services were able to supply their masters with copies of most secret American and British documents related to the Yalta Conference. Stalin's spymasters scored a number of impressive coups on the eve and in the course of the summit, but the handling of Hiss was not one of them.

Points on which the new Soviet sources are silent are as important as their revelations. They offer no evidence that Joseph Stalin or his entourage sought to take advantage of the poor health of the American president, or that FDR's uneven performance at the conference table helped the Soviet side achieve its objectives. Nor is there any indication that a tougher Western policy on Poland would have saved that country and the rest of Eastern Europe from Soviet domination. Despite some apparent disagreements among the Soviet leaders on tactical issues, the new archival findings leave no doubt that the Soviets were determined to establish control over their western neighbors, with Poland as the keystone in the arch of their security structure. Stalin was prepared to do whatever it would take to ensure his control over Poland, and Western diplomacy, whether hard or soft, could do little to change that.

Judging by formerly classified materials, the Soviets were as happy with the results of the conference as their American counterparts and no less optimistic with regard to future cooperation. But each side misjudged the other's intentions. What followed was a period of mutual distrust and suspicion that helped bring about the Cold War. Yalta was an important step on the road to that divided and dangerous world, but it did not cause the Cold War or make it inevitable. The Cold War came later, as a result of decisions made by individuals many of whom, at least on the Western side, never set foot on Crimean soil.

Taking the Yalta Conference out of the historical and intellectual context of the Cold War helps establish its proper place in history. Yalta was not the first conference of the Cold War, nor was it the concluding conference of the Second World War (that designation belongs to the Potsdam Conference, which was held in July and August 1945). It was a wartime summit conducted at a time when the common enemy was not yet defeated and victory was close but not yet achieved. This recontextualization brings out the simple but essential realization that its participants helped end the war and established the conditions for a negotiated peace, however imperfect that peace turned out to be. We now know that this peace was not just an armistice leading to a nuclear disaster. Both by design and by default, the Big Three managed to put together elements of an international system that helped preserve the longest peace in European history.

There was a price to pay for ending the war in this way. It involved the sacrifice of publicly declared principles and the compromise of values not only officially professed but also deeply held by Western leaders. And then there was the price exacted from half of Europe, which was subjected to a new totalitarian regime, as the world was too soon engulfed in the Cold War. How did it happen? Could the Western leaders have achieved more while sacrificing less? And, finally, are there lessons for the future? This book engages these questions by telling the story of the negotiations at Yalta and by examining the expectations and disappointments of those involved.

As the narrative focuses on the eight days that Roosevelt, Churchill, Stalin, and their delegations spent at Yalta, the protocols of the meetings became my principal source for reconstructing events. The absence of an official conference record was both a curse and a blessing for the writing of this book. While it was often difficult to piece together the actual substance of debates, combing through records of the same conversations set down by note takers from different delegations made it possible to provide a fuller account of what happened than would have been possible if there had been only one official record. Words and exchanges missed by the Americans were caught by the British or the Soviets, and vice versa. In some instances it was clear that important nuances were missed by the note-takers or lost in translation.

I have quoted liberally from all available records of the conference proceedings and of the private meetings that took place on the side. It should be borne in mind, however, that the words put into the mouths of Roosevelt, Churchill, Stalin, and others are in some instances only approximations (sometimes very close ones) of what was actually said. I have sought to reconstruct them to the best of my ability, using all the sources at my disposal and relying not only on conference records but also on the memoirs of participants, who give invaluable insight into the atmosphere of the meetings. Where possible I used American records to quote FDR's words, British records to render Churchill's comments, and Soviet records to convey Stalin's thoughts, on the assumption that the note-takers understood and recorded their own leaders best. To avoid overwhelming the reader with endnotes, I have grouped all sources used to reconstruct a given debate or conversation in a note at the end of my account of that particular episode.

The Soviet documents published after the collapse of the USSR were my most important source for reevaluating the Yalta Conference, but unpublished American accounts of the summit, especially those of Anna Roosevelt Boettiger and Kathleen Harriman, as well as the papers of Averell Harriman's embassy in Moscow, provided the basis for describing the atmospherics of the conference and its immediate political and geostrategic context. My own findings in the former Soviet archives (especially the State Archive of the Russian Federation) helped document the role played by the People's Commissariat of Internal Affairs (the notorious NKVD) in the conference preparations. Among the most interesting finds was the photo album of the Yalta Conference prepared by commissariat officials for Joseph Stalin. Some of the photos from this album are published here for the first time. Most of the conference photos available today are not dated or bear incorrect dates attributed to them at some later point. Where possible, I have done my best to provide dates for the photos reproduced in this book and to link them to specific events.

Among the major political changes produced by the Yalta Conference was the alteration of place-names. As borders moved, so did peoples, further complicating the shifting patchwork of cultures and languages brought about by the disintegration of the Habsburg, Ottoman, and Russian empires in the wake of the First World War. The fall of the world order known as the "Yalta system" in the late 1980s, and the disintegration of the Soviet Union into a number of independent states, added yet another layer of complexity. Many of the places mentioned in this book had different names before the Second World War. In some instances multiple names are in use even now. In this book, place-names have usually been given in the language of the country in which they are currently located. Thus, the city known in Polish as Lwów, in German as Lemberg, and in Russian as Lvov is called Lviv, as it is now part of Ukraine. Alternative names are usually given on first mention, or when a change in jurisdiction is specifically discussed.

The book focuses on the motivations, thoughts, and actions of the Big Three and their aides at Yalta, with Franklin Roosevelt as its main protagonist. The narrative begins with FDR's journey to the Crimea. It continues with a close look at the opening days of the conference, when the participants discussed military affairs and presented their political agendas, setting the stage for the subsequent debates. It then offers an account of the moves, countermoves, and complex maneuvering of the Big Three on February 7 and 8—the most productive days of the conference, when most of its successes were achieved. This is followed by the debates of the closing days of the conference, when Roosevelt's main task was to secure what he could in areas of disagreement, such as the government of Poland and the treatment of Germany, without threatening the results achieved in the previous two days.

The last two parts of the book, "The Spirit of Yalta" and "The Coming Storm," examine the high expectations following the conference and the profound crisis in East-West relations that began in the weeks leading to FDR's death, which marked the end of the era of close cooperation with the USSR. The book ends with President Roosevelt's death and President Truman's first attempts to reevaluate American foreign policy. Roosevelt was both admired and hated in his day, but it was generally recognized that his inspirational leadership had helped guide the United States out of the depths of the Great Depression and that he had skillfully steered his country to victory. His death, a mere two months after the end of the conference, turned Yalta into a symbol of his foreign policy and ensured that debates on the significance and legacy of the conference would often come down to disputes about his own political legacy.

While the plot of this book is complex and the narrative rich in detail, its main moral argument is quite simple: no matter how much effort is put into the preparation and conduct of an international conference, however skillful and resourceful its participants, and however promising its outcome (and the Yalta Conference was perceived at the time as a great accomplishment), democratic leaders and societies should be prepared to pay a price for close involvement with those who do not share their values. The only way to reduce this price is to know one's ally at least as well as one knows the enemy. As the Yalta Conference and its aftermath show, in the absence of common values binding allies together, the difference between friend and foe can simply be a matter of time.

PART I

OPERATION ARGONAUT

No more let us falter. From Malta to Yalta. Let nobody alter.

WINSTON S. CHURCHILL

I

THE PRESIDENT'S JOURNEY

They began to assemble in the late morning—senators and congressmen, government officials, diplomats and members of their families. By noon there were close to eight thousand of them gathered near the South Portico of the White House. Three thousand onlookers stood at a distance, beyond the fence, in overcoats and galoshes—the snow that had begun to fall the previous night had turned into sleet, but the crowds were not about to leave before they saw what they had come to witness. The occasion was unprecedented in American history. On January 20, 1945, the president of the United States would take the oath of office for the fourth time. Those in the crowd who had heard persistent rumors about Franklin Delano Roosevelt's failing health could finally judge for themselves whether the president, only ten days shy of his sixty-third birthday, was fit enough to lead the nation for four more years.

At noon, when the inauguration ceremony finally began on the White House balcony, the president, bareheaded and dressed in a blue suit, rose to his feet and walked to the podium with the help of his eldest son, James, a thirty-seven-year-old marine colonel on leave from duty in the Pacific. FDR was welcomed with enthusiastic applause. Only those on the balcony could see how difficult it was for him to stand up and walk even a short distance in his heavy full-leg braces. The president's whole body was shaking. James later told his father that he looked like hell.

When the applause subsided and Roosevelt began to speak, his focus was not on the war that his nation was fighting on two fronts in Europe and Asia, nor on the victory yet to be won. It was on the peace that would follow. "In the days and in the years that are to come we shall work for a just and honorable peace, a durable peace, as today we work and fight for total victory in war," declared the president, steeling himself against a brisk winter wind. "We can and we will achieve such a peace. We shall strive for perfection," he promised the nation. Then Roosevelt struck a more cautious note: "We shall not achieve

3

it immediately—but we still shall strive. We may make mistakes—but they must never be mistakes which result from faintness of heart or abandonment of moral principle." He believed he knew how to reach his goal. "We have learned the simple truth, as Emerson said, that 'The only way to have a friend is to be one.' We can gain no lasting peace if we approach it with suspicion and mistrust or with fear. We can gain it only if we proceed with the understanding, the confidence, and the courage which flow from conviction."

It was Roosevelt's shortest inaugural address, consisting of only 573 words. The president's health and the inclement weather did not allow him to speak longer, but the brevity of the address helped emphasize his overriding goal as he assumed office for the fourth and final time. His thoughts were concentrated on peace—one that would be just and durable, not a mere prelude to another war. Privately he was also concerned as to whether he would be around long enough to ensure that the peace was achieved. "Early in January," Eleanor Roosevelt remembered later, "realizing this would certainly be his last inauguration, perhaps even having the premonition that he would not be with us long, Franklin insisted that every grandchild come to the White House for a few days." It was the last time that three generations of the family would be together.

After the ceremony, the president talked to his son James. He wanted to discuss his will. He told James that he should take the family ring and wear it if anything happened to him. His funeral instructions were in the safe. In a few days the president would embark on a long trip that would take him thousands of miles from home. Health concerns aside, it was a dangerous trip to undertake in wartime, but the prize was the kind of peace that Roosevelt had described in his inaugural address. He was prepared to take the risk. No one could say whether he would return alive.[1]

Late in the evening of January 22, a special train with the president and members of his entourage left Washington. Roosevelt was traveling in his private car, which was fitted with bulletproof windows, armor-plated sides, and a reinforced concrete floor, a product of the Pullman Company built for the president after the start of the war. His departure for Yalta was nothing like that of his Democratic predecessor, Woodrow Wilson, for the Paris Peace Conference on December 4, 1918. There were no gun salutes and no crowds wishing him bon voyage. The war was still on, and the Secret Service took every possible measure to conceal the president's departure for the conference, whose venue could not be announced until it was over and all participants had safely left the "undisclosed location." People on the team who were new to the routine of the president's trips abroad were impressed by the level of security that surrounded their boss.

"After taking leave of Mrs. Roosevelt," wrote Edward J. Flynn, the chairman

of the Democratic National Committee and a member of Roosevelt's delegation, the president and his entourage "climbed into the car and we were off,
surrounded by a crowd of secret service men. Our destination was the station
where the special train was waiting. Here again were crowds of secret service
men and other people who were to see that everything went off on schedule."
The president's train reached Newport News, Virginia, on the morning of January 23 under cover of darkness. At 8:30 a.m. USS *Quincy* set out with its precious cargo. The heavy cruiser was headed across the Atlantic to Malta, from
where the American delegates, along with their British counterparts, were to
fly to the Crimea.[2]

Throughout January, public attention in the United States and Britain was
focused on the upcoming meeting of the Big Three, as the wartime leaders
of the United States, Great Britain, and the Soviet Union had come to be known.
The time and place of the meeting were shrouded in mystery. No one doubted
that it would take place soon, but the question of when and where mesmer-
ized the press. Allied correspondents scoured the world for the smallest clue
that would allow them to solve the puzzle. American and British government
officials expected to take part in the summit were under constant watch, and in
January the American press started to report the disappearance from the Washington social scene of some of the leading figures in President Roosevelt's
administration and his personal entourage.

Roosevelt made no secret of his intention to attend a conference after his
inauguration, and on January 26 the *Washington Times-Herald* wrote that "it
now seems unlikely he will linger long in Washington, not even to await Senate
action on a couple of recent appointments." The newspaper also noted the
absence of Secretary of State Edward R. Stettinius Jr. In a few days the *Washington Star* alerted its readers to the absence of the former Supreme Court
justice James F. Byrnes, White House press secretary Stephen T. Early, and
White House officials Samuel I. Rosenman and Lauchlin Currie. The press also
interpreted the mission to Europe of Harry Hopkins, Roosevelt's closest adviser,
the absence from Washington of FDR's only daughter, Anna Roosevelt Boettiger, and the failure of Winston Churchill and his foreign secretary, Anthony
Eden, to appear in the House of Commons on January 23 as signs that the
"long-heralded meeting was about to begin."[3]

As Roosevelt sailed for Europe aboard the *Quincy*, the American security
services were busy dealing with leaks. In Washington they paid a visit to Dr.
Constantine Edward McGuire, a local economist who had learned about the
president's trip in advance from friends, one of whom was a U.S. senator, and
had rushed to tell the news in letters to at least three of his correspondents. Approached by security agents, he promised not to do so again. More
dangerous was the breach of security by U.S. Navy personnel. "Loose lips sink
ships" went a popular saying of the day, and rumors about what ships would

take the president overseas at what time were rampant throughout the East Coast.

On January 10, the FBI informed the Secret Service of rumors circulating in Pennsylvania to the effect that USS *Savannah,* a light cruiser docked at Norfolk, Virginia, was waiting to take the president on a trip to meet Churchill and Stalin immediately after Inauguration Day. On January 22, the day when Roosevelt left Washington for Newport News, Margaret Windler of the Intelligence and Security Division there reported that five days earlier, while attending a dance at the American Legion, she had overheard crewmen of the *Savannah* bragging that their ship would escort the *Quincy* as it took the president overseas. Ms. Windler believed that this was common knowledge among the crew. By the time she filed her report, the *Savannah* with its talkative crew was already at sea.[4]

The *Quincy* was well equipped for its ocean crossing. A heavy cruiser built in Quincy, Massachusetts, and commissioned on December 15, 1943, it was inspected by General Dwight D. Eisenhower in May 1944 and was the first ship to fire at the enemy during the invasion of Normandy that June. It also took part in the invasion of southern France in August 1944. In preparation for the president's trip, the *Quincy* was equipped with a special ramp leading from the main deck to the first superstructure deck. There were also two elevators, one going from the main deck to the first and another reaching the second deck. The president, who was now able to maneuver his wheelchair around the ship, was housed in the captain's quarters.

When Edward Flynn went on deck on the morning of January 30, he saw eight destroyers and nine cruisers protecting the president's ship. Forty minutes after its departure from Newport News, the *Quincy* was joined by USS *Satterlee,* a destroyer that went ahead of the president's ship. An hour later, the light cruiser *Springfield* took a position behind the *Quincy.* Two more destroyers were soon added to the original group, with more to follow as the cruiser approached the Strait of Gibraltar. At night, the ships ran without lights. If a cable had to be sent, one of the ships would leave the group to transmit a radio message. It would then proceed on a different course and be replaced by other ships.

Planes from aircraft carriers and U.S. bases in North Africa would provide air coverage for the small flotilla. The pilots were ordered to shoot even at Allied planes if they headed toward the president's ship and did not respond to warning signals. Warning shots were fired at a Royal Air Force plane, whose pilot was quick to change course. But the main danger came from German submarines. When the *Quincy* intercepted an SOS signal from a small craft near Gibraltar, it did not respond, suspecting that the source could be a German decoy.

Anna Boettiger, who joined her father on the trip to the Crimea, noted in her diary that German submarines were spotted by radar just a day before the

Quincy's arrival in the sector of the Atlantic between Casablanca and Gibraltar. "Only danger apparently lay in possibility that the subs were part of a 'pack' of indeterminate size which was awaiting instructions from . . . shore," she wrote. "Anyway, nothing happened—and I can't say I lost any sleep over it as we were a pretty good task force in our right."[5]

Roosevelt preferred to undertake overseas trips in the company of a family member, as he needed emotional support on long and exhausting journeys. This time there was a rumor that he would go overseas with his wife, Eleanor, who had joined him on his rendezvous with Churchill in Quebec in September 1944. She had asked him whether she could accompany him this time. White House maids hoped that the high seas would reignite their former romance and repair the strains brought on by decades of separation. Roosevelt refused. He wanted to take along their daughter, Anna, who jumped at the opportunity to go overseas with her father.

Anna was thrilled at the prospect of meeting foreign dignitaries, including Stalin, and tried not to think that in fulfilling her father's wish, she was also hurting her mother. As her husband and daughter prepared for their overseas trip, the ever stoic First Lady engaged in the usual rounds, representing the president at inaugural balls and social events in Washington. Their marriage had never recovered from the crisis of 1918, when Eleanor had found love letters from her social secretary, Lucy Mercer, in her husband's suitcase. Confronted by his wife, who offered a divorce, and assailed by his mother, who threatened to disinherit him if he agreed, FDR promised not to see Lucy again. The marriage survived, but the former trust and intimacy were gone.

In the 1930s a married Lucy, now Lucy Rutherfurd, had returned to the president's life. On January 23, 1945, as the *Quincy* left the shores of Virginia, Roosevelt pointed to a distant spot on the coastline and told his daughter that that was the place where "Lucy grew up." On the morning of January 30 it was a package with gifts from Lucy and from his cousin Margaret Suckley that reminded Roosevelt of his birthday. Eleanor tried to send a birthday telegram but failed—the *Quincy* was observing radio silence. The letter he received from her that day had been written a few days earlier and dealt with political matters: it annoyed FDR, who apparently did not hide his feelings from his entourage. Anna confided in a letter to her husband that her father would refer to her mother only when he "griped about her attitudes toward things he's done or people he likes."[6]

To the annoyance of many of FDR's advisers, Eleanor had a strong influence on his political sympathies and executive decisions. She was a demanding partner rather than the protective and forgiving assistant whom Roosevelt needed on his long trip overseas. Anna, on the other hand, was an ideal choice: she could both comfort him and protect him from unnecessary conversations, ensuring that he got enough rest and sleep on the voyage. In the last year of Roosevelt's life, the thirty-eight-year-old Anna took over the functions of the First Lady during Eleanor's frequent absences from the capital. With her second husband, Lieutenant Colonel John Boettiger—a newspaper publisher and, from 1943, a War Department employee—stationed in Seattle, Anna lived at the White House with her five-year-old son, Johnny. She acted as FDR's private secretary: according to the Washington rumor mill, she virtually controlled "access to the throne."

Anna's disappearance from Washington in late January was one of the signs for the news-hungry media that the long-rumored meeting of the Big Three was around the corner. White House officials refused to comment on Mrs. Boettiger's whereabouts. In State Department documents she was referred to only as "lady private secretary," while security services gave her the code name "Topaz" for purposes of internal communication. On the *Quincy* she occupied flag quarters, and her presence initially caused some concern to crew members who thought it bad luck to have a woman on board in wartime. They had little choice but to follow their orders and keep quiet. At the end of the trip, Anna was charged $32.50 for "subsistence in the President's Mess." Only after the conference, in a BBC newsreel released on February 15, was she shown on Malta with Winston Churchill's daughter Sarah Oliver. In March 1945 *Life* published a feature article on the "long-legged, energetic and handsome" Mrs. Boettiger, accompanied by a photo showing her seated at a typewriter at the Livadia Palace near Yalta.[7]

Not unlike President Wilson on the eve of the Paris Peace Conference, Roosevelt chose to surround himself with people with whom he felt comfortable, as opposed to those who might have been most helpful in preparing for the conference. Wilson only reluctantly included his own secretary of state, Robert Lansing, in the peace delegation. Roosevelt, who had gone to Teheran in 1943 to meet Stalin and Churchill without his secretary of state, Cordell Hull, now sent Hull's successor, the forty-four-year-old Edward Stettinius Jr., to North Africa—in Stettinius's words, "to spend a few days reviewing the American position on the various problems to be discussed in the Crimea"—and then to Malta to start consultations with the British before the president's arrival.

As companions on the sea voyage Roosevelt brought his chief military adviser, Admiral William D. Leahy, and two heavyweights in the Democratic establishment: his close associate James F. Byrnes, a former congressman, senator, and Supreme Court justice who, at the time, was the director of the Office of War Mobilization and Reconversion, and his longtime political ally Edward J. Flynn. They were joined by a group of presidential assistants and Vice Admiral Ross T. McIntire, the U.S. surgeon general, who doubled as Roosevelt's personal doctor and usually accompanied the president on his trips.[8]

The only one with any foreign-affairs experience was Admiral Leahy, who had served briefly as U.S. ambassador to Vichy France. Approaching his seventieth birthday, but still healthy and erect, Leahy, whom Roosevelt had known since 1913, had enormous influence on the president. His discretion, loyalty, and ability to get along with people made him indispensable to Roosevelt. He successfully competed for the president's ear with his more liberal advisers and allies, including FDR's vice president in 1941–45, Henry A. Wallace, and Eleanor Roosevelt, whose attitudes he found "idealistic" and "impracticable." Leahy's quiet power, like Anna's, increased during the months leading up to the conference, helped by Eleanor Roosevelt's frequent trips and the virtual absence from the White House of the ailing Harry Hopkins, who was suffering from stomach cancer.

Apart from being the president's chief military adviser, Leahy served as chief of staff to the commander in chief of the U.S. Army and Navy, presiding over the top echelon of the American military—the committee of the chiefs of staff, which would eventually become known as the Joint Chiefs of Staff. He briefed the president on military affairs, turning FDR's conferences with General Marshall into relatively infrequent occurrences. He also provided advice on foreign policy and drafted many of the president's responses to telegrams received and deciphered in the Map Room, the White House communications center. Leahy had a special mission in the Crimea. After FDR's death, the admiral recalled the president's words addressed to him at Yalta: "Bill, I wish you would attend all these political meetings in order that we may have someone in whom I have full confidence who would remember everything that we have done."[9]

A different motive may have been behind the inclusion of Justice Byrnes in the Yalta delegation. Dubbed "Assistant President" in Washington circles, he was indispensable to Roosevelt on the home front, managing the expanded wartime bureaucracy and spearheading the war effort of numerous and feuding government institutions. But there was a dark secret to their relationship. In the summer of 1944 Roosevelt made Byrnes believe that he was supporting his candidacy for the vice presidential nomination at the Democratic Party convention, while in fact he threw his support behind Harry Truman.

FDR apparently decided to make it up to Byrnes by taking him to Yalta. He also counted on his support in selling the decisions to Congress. Byrnes, who was a good stenographer and took detailed notes of the Yalta deliberations, was a reluctant passenger on the *Quincy*. He was invited to join the delegation during Christmas week and refused twice, the second time on the day of departure, noting that he had pressing problems to deal with at home. FDR eventually persuaded him to come, citing his useful expertise in economic issues. After Roosevelt's death, Byrnes would become secretary of state.

Edward Flynn was another last-minute and quite unexpected addition to the group. He had no passport, and on arrival in Malta Roosevelt asked Stettinius to secure one for him, as "he did not want Flynn to spend the rest of his days in Siberia." This turned out to be quite a problem, even for the secretary of state. Flynn eventually crossed the Soviet border with a simple letter indicating his status as a member of the U.S. delegation. He was issued a passport only in Moscow, where he went immediately after the conference. As the head of the Democratic National Committee, Flynn had been involved in the process of selecting Truman over Byrnes as Roosevelt's running mate at the party convention in 1944. A Catholic of Irish descent, Flynn was asked by FDR to address the treatment of the church in Soviet-occupied Eastern Europe.[10]

Byrnes took his role as a member of the president's party most seriously. Along with Leahy, he would stay up to discuss conference-related matters with Roosevelt after dinner. There were four or five such meetings, but it was only the day before the *Quincy* docked at Malta that FDR showed his guest the State Department position papers on issues to be discussed at the conference. The after-dinner chats took place without much input from the State Department or any U.S. agency, and that bothered Byrnes. He attributed Roosevelt's scant preparations on board the *Quincy* to his failing health. But when Byrnes expressed his concerns, Anna assured him that it was nothing more than the combination of a cold and sinus problems.

On January 30, at a distance of some 3,500 miles from the U.S. coast, Franklin Roosevelt celebrated his sixty-third birthday. On that day the *Washington Star* informed its readers that the president's whereabouts were "undisclosed." According to the newspaper, the president "was spending moments of both seriousness and gaiety with close friends and advisers and was receiving the usual congratulations from other chiefs of state." Churchill sent a wire: "Your birthday finds us on the threshold of great decisions and great events."

"The anniversary," wrote the *Washington Star*, "finds the President leaner by 5 or 10 pounds but his physician, Vice Admiral Ross T. McIntire, reported him in excellent shape when he took the oath of office for a fourth term 10 days ago." That was not the impression the president made on his secretary of state. Stettinius believed that FDR's health had deteriorated significantly between mid-December and the inauguration. As Eleanor Roosevelt later wrote, "After the inauguration it was clearer every day that Franklin was far from well. Nevertheless, he was determined to go to Yalta, and when he made up his mind that he wanted to do something he rarely gave up the idea."

The president himself seemed to be in denial of the seriousness of his health problems. Since 1921, when he was diagnosed with polio and lost command of his legs, Roosevelt had refused to be held back by his physical limitations. He never believed that the paralysis was irreversible. The doctor who first diagnosed him with polio had suggested that the first attack of the disease had been a mild one and complete recovery was possible. But years passed with no improvement. Making the best of a bad situation, FDR learned to move in public without crutches, with his legs in metal braces, a cane in one hand, and the other hand often on the arm of one of his sons. He refused to leave politics and was twice elected governor of New York, in 1928 and 1930, and then four times president of the United States.

Admiral McIntire, who became FDR's doctor in 1932, was largely concerned with the president's sinus problems through most of his first three terms. The president's health began to deteriorate in the spring of 1944. Anna, who had moved into the White House by that time and was concerned about her father's sickly appearance, insisted on a thorough medical examination. Dr. Howard G. Bruenn of the Bethesda Naval Hospital diagnosed Roosevelt with bronchitis and hypertension: he had an enlarged heart, with cardiac failure in the left ventricle, resulting in a reduced blood supply to his vital organs. Bruenn recommended reduced smoking and a low-fat diet. There was little else he could do: medication for such problems would not be developed for years.

As time went on, FDR's health problems piled up at an alarming rate, making it more and more difficult for him to execute the duties of his office. Hypertension was his doctors' main concern as his blood pressure steadily rose between March and November 1944 from 186/108 to 260/150. He suffered from occasional abdominal pains and frequent headaches, had trouble sleeping at night, and developed a chronic cough. He was always tired, and his doctors attempted to limit his working day to four hours, a regimen they failed to impose. After giving him virtually a clean bill of health on the eve of the presidential campaign of 1944, there was little they could do.[11]

As the guests gathered on the deck of the *Quincy* on January 30 to celebrate Roosevelt's birthday, Anna "made the birthday dinner a gala occasion." The crew presented the president with a brass ashtray made from the casing of a shell fired from the *Quincy* during the D-Day landing. The commissioned and warrant officers made him birthday cakes, as did the enlisted men. With a cake baked by the president's own chef and another brought by his entourage, there were five in all to celebrate FDR's birthday. Four cakes symbolized his four terms in office. The fifth one had a question mark: would there be a fifth term?[12]

If one set aside his health, then it was not so difficult to imagine that there might indeed be a fifth term for one of the most popular presidents in American history. A few months earlier, FDR had won reelection with 432 electoral votes against 99 for his Republican opponent, Thomas E. Dewey, carrying thirty-six states out of the forty-eight then making up the Union. Admittedly, it was his poorest result, but one that would still have made many of his predecessors jealous. At the start of his fourth term, FDR still generated optimism and hope among the millions of Americans he had led into war and now hoped to lead into peace. His optimism was irrepressible and contagious.

FDR had made a career of defying odds and achieving things deemed impossible by others. Who could have predicted that an East Coast patrician denied membership in the Porcellian, the most prestigious of the Harvard finals clubs, for being "priggish" in the estimation of his classmates would become not only the most admired political leader in the land but also the champion of the masses? Back in 1921, when the thirty-nine-year-old Roosevelt had contracted a debilitating disease, few would have foreseen that in twelve years this man, paralyzed from the waist down, would enter the White House as the next president of the United States. Overcoming obstacles became his modus vivendi.

Roosevelt's readiness to make use of modern communications technology and address the people directly in radio "fireside chats" moved American politics into a new era. Americans felt that they knew him better than any of his predecessors or competitors. An affable public speaker and a witty conversationalist who was equally adept at captivating the imagination of the American people and foreign dignitaries, FDR also remained an enigma, at once friendly and distant, charming and detached even from his closest aides and associates. A master of political compromise, he was regarded as unprincipled and insincere by many members of his own class when he put the "forgotten man" of American politics—the people at the bottom of the social hierarchy—at the center of his rhetoric and many of his political initiatives. In doing so he saved his country from the worst excesses of class struggle.

Assuming office in the midst of a financial crisis that saw most states close their banks, Roosevelt injected hope into the struggling economy by declaring in his first inaugural address: "[L]et me assert my firm belief that the only thing we have to fear is fear itself—nameless, unreasoning, unjustified terror which paralyzes needed efforts to convert retreat into advance." He placed the blame on Wall Street and promised a new approach to fixing economic and social problems: "[T]he money changers have fled from their high seats in the temple of our civilization. We may now restore that temple to the ancient truths. The measure of the restoration lies in the extent to which we apply social values more noble than mere monetary profit."

FDR's recipe for recovery was enhanced federal spending designed both to provide relief to those in greatest distress and to stimulate the stagnant economy. He also stuck to his campaign promises to cut the budget, and his spending increase was accompanied by budget cuts that reduced the salaries of federal employees, veterans' benefits, and military spending. Even so, Roosevelt managed to attract into the civil service a most impressive team of young and idealistic professionals who reformed the government and thus the fabric of American society for generations to come. The recovery, however, was slow, and the American economy struggled in the 1930s, but Roosevelt outdid his rivals in convincing the American public that he was the right man to lead America through its most tumultuous economic and social ordeal. He managed to win reelection three times in an era that laid the basis for subsequent prosperity, but he saw little of it himself.

In the international arena, Roosevelt watched with concern the rise of the Nazi threat and growing Japanese ambitions in the Pacific. He eventually led the United States into a war that Congress and the nation were reluctant to join, one that he considered not only just but essential to the future prospects of his country and the entire world. The national debt shot up from 50 percent of GDP in 1941 to roughly 120 percent in 1945, but the economy was back on track, almost booming, and the country was winning the most terrible war in human history. FDR was an early proponent of a second front in Europe and instrumental in formulating American military policy in the Pacific. In early 1945, as American and British forces fought Hitler's divisions in Belgium and, on the other side of the world, Americans made a successful return to the Philippines and closed in on Manila, he saw it as his main task to create an international system that would make a new global war impossible.[13]

When the president boarded the *Quincy* on the morning of January 23, the end of the war that had dragged on for more than four years was clearly in sight. But news from the battlefields of Europe was not all positive. The Allied invasion of Europe, which began on June 6, 1944, and progressed with success through most of the summer, had lost its impetus by the fall. American and French troops took Paris on August 25, and the British entered Brussels and Antwerp on September 3. Rotterdam was the next target of the Allied strategists, and the supreme Allied commander in Europe, General Dwight D. Eisenhower, appealed to the Dutch to save the city and its industrial infrastructure from German destruction. The expectation was that the city would be taken by the Allies relatively soon, and its port would provide them with a much-needed supply point for Allied troops. But Rotterdam remained in German hands until the end of the war.

Allied plans were further frustrated by continuing German resistance on the northern approaches to Antwerp, which could serve as a new supply center for the Allies only if they gained control of the river Scheldt, linking Antwerp with the sea. Taking the city turned out to be a difficult and lengthy effort. Then came Operation Market Garden, which decimated British and Polish airborne units. As the commander of the British forces in Western Europe, Field Marshal Bernard Montgomery found himself under pressure to speed up the advance of his troops through the Netherlands into Germany. He proposed a bold plan, dubbed Market Garden, the largest airborne operation of the entire war. It was supposed to result in the capture of bridges in Eindhoven, Nijmegen, and Arnhem, deep in the German rear, by an airborne assault, but was poorly planned and ended in a resounding defeat.

Winter brought new problems. On December 16, 1944, on Hitler's orders, three German armies began a counteroffensive in the Ardennes in Belgium, aiming at Antwerp and creating a "bulge" in the Allied defenses. Bad weather precluded the use of Allied aviation, and it took Eisenhower a few days before he and his commanders realized that they were dealing with a major strategic operation of the Wehrmacht, not a local counterattack. They ordered reinforcements into the area to rescue the American 101st Airborne Division, which was surrounded by German panzer divisions. By December 22, with the weather improving and the German panzers starting to run out of gas, the Allies were finally able to take advantage of their air superiority and inflict major damage on the enemy. But fighting continued into the new year. In the course of January 1945, the Allies finally managed to prevail over the German forces. The battle cost the U.S. Army nineteen thousand lives and raised questions about the pace of the advance on Germany.[14]

As the Western Allies tried to recover after the unexpected German counteroffensive and recapture the strategic initiative in the Ardennes, the Red Army began its major winter offensive. After suffering devastating defeats in 1941 and 1942, the Soviet forces had won two crucial battles in 1943. They destroyed the German Sixth Army at Stalingrad in February and then crushed a host of German panzer divisions in the Battle of Kursk in July. By the fall of 1944, the Red Army had liberated the entire territory of the USSR and begun the conquest of Eastern Europe. It had even entered the Third Reich, breaking through German defenses in East Prussia. A country that had seemed to be on the verge of extinction only two years earlier now emerged as the most formidable military power in Europe.

On January 12, 1945, Stalin ordered his armies to attack along a front exceeding 700 kilometers. The offensive, which caught the Germans by surprise on many sectors of the front, was a success. By January 17, German troops had been forced to abandon Warsaw and to withdraw behind the Danube in Budapest; on January 18 they left Kraków, and on the next day the Red Army captured Łódź in western Poland. On January 23, as the *Quincy* set off for Europe, Soviet tanks entered Elbing, in East Prussia. On the president's birthday, the Red Army advance units crossed the Oder. In the next few days they established bridgeheads a mere 70 kilometers from the German capital. The road to Berlin seemed to be open. U.S. military experts predicted a German counterattack from the north against the flank of the advancing Soviet armies, but no one knew whether the Germans would manage to stabilize their defenses.[15]

The Soviet offensive was met with relief by the Allies, and its successes were welcomed in both Washington and London. However, in early January, rumors began circulating in Washington about the possibility of a separate peace between Stalin and Hitler. It seemed that Stalin might be in a position to end the war in Europe on his own terms without reference to the Allies. Roosevelt would have to hurry, or it would be too late to negotiate any aspect of the settlement in Eastern and Central Europe. There was no definite agreement on Poland's borders; the occupation and possible dismemberment of Germany, a role for France in Europe, and important questions about the membership and functioning of a future world peace organization remained unresolved.[16]

It was Roosevelt's tactic throughout the war to postpone agreement on major territorial issues until its end. Like Wilson before him, FDR preferred to speak in terms of principles and generalities while the war was going on. Making backroom deals smacked of the corrupt politics of the past, harking back to the discredited principles of balance of power and spheres of influence. Besides, why recognize the Soviets' right to acquire new territories even before they gained control of them? Roosevelt made a special effort to avoid formal agreements and to hide informal ones from the public. Now, with Soviet troops approaching Berlin, an agreement could no longer be delayed. A deal had to be made as soon as possible, or there might be no deal at all.

On FDR's initiative the forthcoming meeting would address military matters. The eastern and western fronts in Europe were moving ever closer, and FDR wanted the military to coordinate its actions. Also on the president's mind was Soviet entry into the war with Japan. By January 1945, the American army and navy, helped by their British allies, were far advanced toward victory over the Japanese Empire. The shock and humiliation of Pearl Harbor were long gone. The victory of Admiral Chester Nimitz in the Battle of Midway in June 1942 had reversed the fortunes of war in the Pacific. In October 1944 General Douglas MacArthur's troops began the liberation of the Philippines. U.S. aircraft were conducting massive raids on Japan.

"I was of the firm opinion," wrote Admiral Leahy, commenting on the state of the Pacific war on the eve of the Yalta Conference, "that our war against Japan had progressed to the point where her defeat was only a matter of time and attrition." It was the beginning of the end, but the battle for the Japanese islands and mainland China, occupied by the Japanese, still lay ahead and by most conservative estimates would cost the U.S. Army and Navy hundreds of thousands of lives. The atomic bomb was still only a theoretical possibility, and those like Admiral Leahy who believed that the United States could end the war without the bomb or Soviet assistance were outnumbered by military brass who wanted to end the war as soon as possible, with minimal loss of American lives. In this scenario, the USSR would take on the Japanese Kwantung Army in China, while the United States would focus on Japan.[17]

Admiral Leahy believed that one of Roosevelt's principal objectives at Yalta was to secure Soviet cooperation in the creation of the world peace organization that he and Churchill had pledged to establish in 1941. President Wilson had left the United States for Europe in December 1918 believing himself capable of delivering a just peace secured by an international organization that would prevent all future wars. The Paris Peace Conference gave birth to the League of Nations, but Wilson's dream never materialized and, to the embarrassment of its American supporters, the United States never joined the League. Wilson's legacy was very much on Roosevelt's mind before his trip to Yalta: at the last cabinet meeting before his departure Roosevelt even referred to his predecessor. He was determined to make Wilson's dream work.

FDR was a reluctant convert to the United Nations idea promoted by committed Wilsonians like his long-serving secretary of state, Cordell Hull, who left office in November 1944 because of failing health after more than a decade at the helm of American foreign policy. Once Roosevelt's original vision of world peace guarded by four policemen—the United States, Britain, the USSR, and China—was incorporated into the UN project, the president embraced the concept fully and unconditionally. He would have to overcome two main hurdles: to convince Stalin to join and to rally support among the American public and its representatives in Congress. The Soviets had committed to joining the organization in the autumn of 1944, but questions about the location of its headquarters and voting procedure in the Security Council, the exclusive club of the great powers controlling the organization, were left undecided. FDR had to hurry to get firm commitments on the issue before the end of the war, while Stalin was still in a cooperative frame of mind and Americans were still interested in world affairs.[18]

To achieve his objectives, the president had outmaneuvered his own experts in the State Department and the U.S. embassy in Moscow. Roosevelt's decision to recognize the USSR back in 1933 had been made against the will of the State Department's top officials, who were reluctant to extend formal recognition to a communist regime that refused to repay Russia's First World War debts, sponsored international communism, supported subversive and revolutionary activities outside its borders, and generally, in the opinion of Henry L. Stimson, the secretary of state in Herbert Hoover's outgoing Republican administration (and, later, FDR's secretary of war), did not "behave according to fundamental principles of the family of nations."

The president prevailed over his State Department experts by establishing diplomatic relations with Moscow through personal emissaries, bypassing State Department officials. Recognition of the USSR brought American foreign policy into line with that of Britain and the Continental powers, which had recognized the Soviet government back in the 1920s. FDR's decision was supported by many in Depression-stricken America. Some hoped for improved trade; others took Soviet rhetoric at face value and considered the planned Soviet economy a model for solving America's own economic and social problems. It did not work as expected. Trade actually diminished in the years following recognition, and the USSR turned out to be a difficult partner in international affairs.

Stalin's alliance with Hitler in August 1939 and Soviet aggression against Finland later that year helped convince Roosevelt that reciprocity was the most effective, if not the only, way of dealing with the Soviets: they would be treated well only if they cooperated with the Americans. FDR suggested retaliation in kind when the Soviet government imposed restrictions on long-distance telephone calls from the American embassy in Moscow. But the Nazi invasion of the USSR in June 1941 suddenly turned the Soviet Union into a difficult but valuable ally. Roosevelt was determined to help the USSR avoid collapse and then emerge victorious from its prolonged struggle with the Wehrmacht. He pushed legislation through Congress that made Moscow a recipient of American Lend-Lease supplies and was a strong proponent of the opening of a second front in Western Europe.

Still, more often than not, the president would find himself in a state of undeclared war with his ambassadors to Moscow and Soviet experts in the State Department, trying to root out opposition to his generally friendly policy toward the Soviet Union. He regularly shuffled diplomatic personnel and circumvented government bodies, but each new shift eventually went the way of its predecessors, repulsed by the culture of secrecy, suspicion, and duplicity that characterized Soviet dealings with the West.

In the fall of 1943, once the Soviet Union emerged victorious from the battlefields of Stalingrad and Kursk, Roosevelt decided to change his "no questions asked" policy of assistance to the USSR and switched to bargaining tactics, which he considered more appropriate now that Soviet-American relations had taken on the character of a partnership. He also changed the personnel in both Washington and Moscow, sending to the Soviet capital his personal friend Averell Harriman, the heir to a railroad empire, who initially seemed to get along well with the Soviets. By the autumn of 1944 even Harriman, shocked by Stalin's refusal to help the Polish insurgents during the Warsaw uprising, when the Germans slaughtered the flower of the Polish resistance as the Red Army stood idle on the outskirts of the city, had turned into a proponent of a "get-tough policy" toward the USSR. He and his staff in Moscow were taking an increasingly belligerent stand, appalled by the Soviet treatment of Eastern European nations freshly liberated from Nazi control.

Roosevelt generally tried not to be distracted by Soviet behavior on issues that he considered secondary. Harry Hopkins, Roosevelt's close adviser, was echoing the president's views when he stated in the fall of 1944 that Stalin's refusal to help the Warsaw insurgents could not get in the way of negotiations on the future peace organization. Soviet cooperation in the international peace organization was crucial to Roosevelt's vision of the future world order. In return, he would treat the Soviets as equals in world affairs, recognizing their security concerns—which meant accepting their territorial acquisitions of the early war years, when they had sided with Germany—and assisting in postwar reconstruction. The president was optimistic that postwar loans to the Soviet Union would ensure the stability of Soviet-American relations. His opinion was backed up by experts from the Research and Analysis Branch of the Office of Strategic Services, the forerunner to the CIA, who, unlike diplomats, were shielded from day-to-day contacts with Soviet officials and tried to focus on the big picture.[19]

Roosevelt banked on his personal relationship with Stalin, considering it the best way to circumvent or cut through his own bureaucracy and the imaginary hard-liners around the Soviet leader, who were customarily blamed for problems in Soviet-American relations. A product of American political culture, FDR believed in the power of personal relations, including those between heads of state. He made his relationship with Stalin the centerpiece of his policy toward the USSR. "Franklin had high hopes that at this conference he could make real progress in strengthening the personal relationship between himself and Marshal Stalin," wrote Eleanor Roosevelt, commenting on her husband's expectations of the Yalta meeting. This was the meaning of his words in his fourth inaugural speech: "We have learned the simple truth, as Emerson said, that 'The only way to have a friend is to be one.'" Roosevelt was offering his friendship to Stalin and hoping for friendship in return.[20]

On board the *Quincy*, Roosevelt relaxed by watching movies before going to bed. *Our Hearts Were Young and Gay* was the first movie shown to the president and his entourage. The plot of the movie, released in 1944 and based on a bestselling book published two years earlier, was not entirely inappropriate to the occasion. It is a story of two fun-loving and naive college girls traveling to Europe in the early 1920s who meet two eligible men on board their ship and get themselves into troublesome but amusing situations as they try to act grown-up in London and Paris. No one aboard the *Quincy* seems to have drawn parallels between the movie plot and their own European journey.

On the morning of February 2, the voyage across the Atlantic came to an end. Eleven days after leaving American soil, having covered close to 5,000 miles, the *Quincy* entered Valetta harbor in Malta. For most of the trip Roosevelt suffered from a bad cold. By the time the *Quincy* reached Malta, he was feeling better, but that was only a relative improvement, and most of those who met Roosevelt on Malta thought him gravely ill. The British foreign secretary, Anthony Eden, noted in his diary that he looked older and gave "the impression of failing powers." Members of the U.S. delegation who had not seen their president for some time were also quite shocked by his appearance.[21]

Roosevelt left the United States in secret, but no one seemed to care about secrecy on Malta. Both sides of the harbor were lined by local crowds, creating the impression that the island's whole population had come to welcome the American president. FDR enjoyed a reception not unlike the one given to President Wilson by the people of Brest in December 1918 as he made his way to the Paris Peace Conference. On that warm, sunny morning it was difficult not to be impressed by the beauty of the Mediterranean island. "It would be hard not to fall in love with this spot. The universally used, local limestone has a softness of texture which takes away the impression of glare which I remember as typical of other Mediterranean towns I have seen," Anna Boettiger wrote in her diary.[22]

As the *Quincy* entered Valetta harbor, Roosevelt sat on the captain's deck, dressed in a brown coat and a tweed cap, enjoying the view. Spitfires flew back and forth over the harbor as the bands on the U.S. light cruiser *Memphis* and HMS *Sirius*, with marines lined up on their decks, played "The Star–Spangled Banner." As the president's ship passed the light cruiser *Orion*, with Churchill on board, the British crew stood at attention, and their band also played "The Star-Spangled Banner." The *Quincy's* band responded with "God Save the King." "It was quite an emotional moment," wrote Edward Flynn to his wife. Even Anthony Eden was overcome. "While the bands played and amid so much that reeked of war, on the bridge, just discernible to the naked eye, sat one civilian figure," he remembered later. "In his sensitive hands lay much of the world's fate. All heads were turned his way and a sudden quietness fell. It was one of those moments when all seems to stand still and one is conscious of a mark in history."[23]

2

MEETING ON MALTA

There was no person on Malta as anxious to see the American president as the prime minister of His Majesty's government, Winston Leonard Spencer Churchill. On New Year's Day 1945, upon learning of Roosevelt's plans for a stopover on the Mediterranean island, then part of the British Empire, Churchill wrote: "We shall be delighted if you will come to Malta. I shall be waiting on the quay." In fact, the prime minister awaited on board a British warship. That sunny morning, Churchill was recovering from a sudden bout of fever. When his plane reached Malta in the early hours of January 30, Churchill was too weak to get up and spent the first half of the day in bed on the plane, moving to his quarters on the *Orion* only at noon.[1]

Churchill had turned seventy in November 1944, and the stress of war was taking its toll on him. He blamed his fever of 102 degrees on the tablets he was taking on advice of his physician, Lord Moran, who later noted in his defense that his patient had developed a bad habit of running a high temperature on diplomatic missions. The prime minister's principal private secretary, John Martin, confided to Lord Moran prior to the Yalta Conference that Churchill's work had deteriorated. He had become wordy and obsessively preoccupied with one subject or another, to the frustration of his cabinet.[2]

At half past eleven on February 2, an hour after the *Quincy* docked at Valetta harbor, the prime minister felt well enough to pay a visit. He was soon joined by his thirty-year-old daughter, Sarah Oliver, a section officer in the British Women's Auxiliary Air Force. Back in Washington, Roosevelt had explained to his wife his choice of Anna as companion by reminding her that Churchill would also be accompanied by his daughter. Unlike Roosevelt, Churchill had an affectionate relationship with Clementine, his wife of thirty-six years, who was more than ten years his junior. He adored and respected her and wrote long and substantive personal letters on his numerous trips abroad.

Sarah was the couple's third child and second daughter. A talented actress and dancer whose photo appeared on the cover of *Life* magazine in June 1945, she was married to the Vienna-born Jewish actor and musician Victor Oliver. The marriage had its problems, and Sarah had joined the military in September 1941, bringing about an effective separation without going through the ordeal of an actual divorce. She had asked only one favor of her father—to help her join the military—and later wrote that her choice of the Women's Auxiliary Air Force "was influenced by the colour of the uniform." The light blue color of the uniform swayed more than one British woman. It was in this WAAF uniform that she appeared at her father's side in front of the cameras at Teheran. Sarah also wore her uniform to the lunch meeting with Roosevelt on Malta, where she met the president's daughter, Anna Boettiger, for the first time. "I thought at once how amazingly like her mother she was although of course so *much* better looking," Sarah wrote to her mother. "She is very easy and I like her," she continued, "but I think she is quite nervous about being on the trip."[3]

The two leaders and their daughters spent the next hour enjoying the sun and chatting on the deck of the *Quincy* as they waited for lunch to be served. Roosevelt and Churchill had not seen each other since September in Quebec City, where their wives had accompanied them and made a joint radio address to the Canadian people. Relations between the two seasoned statesmen were complex, but a strong bond of mutual respect and even admiration had kept them together through the most difficult years of the war. The prime minister, older than the president but the junior partner in their alliance, had more invested in the relationship, but despite his occasional snide remarks, Roosevelt appreciated Churchill's leadership during the first, most difficult years of the Second World War, and valued his friendship.

Churchill was convinced that personal meetings were essential to keep their friendship intact for the sake of both countries, and he said as much in his address at McGill University in Montreal in September, when both were awarded honorary doctorates. "What an ineffectual method of conveying human thought correspondence is—telegraphed with all its rapidity, all the facilities of our—of modern intercommunication," said Churchill. The crowd laughed, and he continued: "They are simply dead, blank walls compared to personal—personal contacts." This meeting on Malta would give him another chance to reinforce their personal bonds, for his partner appeared increasingly remote as British contributions to the war effort diminished, while America's had grown substantial after D-Day.[4]

As Roosevelt and Churchill met on the deck of the *Quincy*, there was no shortage of topics for conversation. When lunch was served around one o'clock, Churchill was pleased to see at his end of the table a candle and a cigar, placed there, he imagined, on request from the president. "He must have noticed the candle by my bed when we were at the White House," Churchill told Lord Moran later that day, referring to his visit to Washington in May 1943. These small tokens of attention went a long way: the prime minister told his doctor twice that the president was being "very friendly." They were joined for lunch by Edward Stettinius, William Leahy, and James Byrnes on the American side and Anthony Eden from the British delegation. Leahy later recalled that the conversation "was, as usual, well monopolized by the Prime Minister, who spoke about English problems in wartime, the high purpose of the so-called Atlantic Charter, and his complete devotion to the principles enunciated in America's Declaration of Independence."[5]

Churchill was lucky to reach Malta alive. Part of his entourage did not make it, and news of their deaths came on the morning of Roosevelt's arrival. The prime minister left Northolt air base on the evening of January 29. Snow was expected, and he decided to beat the weather. His party consisted of three planes—his daughter, two private secretaries, and Lord Moran joined him on his Skymaster—but only two reached their destination: in the predawn mist, the third overshot the island and crashed into the Sea of Lampedusa, killing most on board, including three Foreign Office officials, the aide-de-camp to the chairman of the chiefs of staff, a lieutenant colonel assigned to Churchill's Map Room, and Anthony Eden's bodyguard. "Such are the strange ways of fate," mused Churchill in his memoirs. "It's the devil," wrote Sir Alexander Cadogan, permanent undersecretary of state, in a letter from Malta: he lost his private secretary in the crash.[6]

Churchill's life had often been in danger before. He first came under fire on his twenty-first birthday in 1895, when he visited Cuba to report for a British newspaper on the Spanish counterinsurgency there. His first experience of battle took place two years later, in a military operation against Pashtun tribes-men in Pakistan. The next year he took part in a British cavalry charge at the famous Battle of Omdurman in Sudan. Released from active service, Churchill traveled in 1899 to South Africa to cover the Second Boer War as a newspaper correspondent. He showed personal bravery when the enemy ambushed the scouting expedition he had joined. What followed gained him national fame and helped launch his political career. Churchill was caught, but he escaped from the prison camp and made his way back to the British after a trek of 300 miles across enemy territory. He rejoined the army and was among the first to enter Pretoria and accept the surrender of the local prison guards.

The future prime minister was first elected to the British Parliament in 1900, beginning a career that would take him to the battlefields of a new century. As First Lord of the Admiralty during the First World War, he had advocated the invasion of the Ottoman Empire through the Dardanelles and was blamed, and took responsibility, for the disastrous Battle of Gallipoli, which cost the British more than twenty thousand lives and left more than fifty thousand wounded, while failing to achieve its main objective—the capture of Istanbul. Humiliated, Churchill rejoined active service, this time as a battalion commander, and spent the end of 1915 and the first months of 1916 on the western front in France, commanding a battalion of Royal Scots Fusiliers.

A rebel by nature and a man of strong convictions, he was subsequently in and out of favor with the leadership of the Conservative Party and the British public. In the first half of the 1930s, during his "wilderness years," Churchill devoted most of his time to writing, a talent he would put to good use during periods out of government or active political life. His views and positions often changed, but some things remained constant. Throughout the 1930s he was a staunch anticommunist, as he had been in 1919–21, when as secretary of state for war he had become a driving force behind the military invasion of Soviet Russia. He also retained an absolute loyalty to the British Empire, for which he had fought in his youth, becoming one of the leading opponents of granting India dominion status. His opinions of Hitler and Mussolini might change, but he constantly worried about German rearmament and tirelessly warned of the rising Nazi threat.

In the late 1930s, Churchill and his small group of parliamentarians joined those criticizing the policy adopted by the Conservative government of Neville Chamberlain. With the outbreak of the Second World War, Churchill was re-instated as First Lord of the Admiralty, the position he had held during the First World War. He became prime minister on May 10, 1940, the day Hitler invaded France. Churchill refused to negotiate with Germany and prepared the nation and the empire for a prolonged and difficult war. In his first address as prime minister, he said that he had "nothing to offer but blood, toil, tears, and sweat." There would be much of that in the months and years to come, but in the fall of 1940 the Royal Air Force managed to repel the German air assault on Britain and derail Nazi plans for the invasion of the island. Britain survived, but it had no resources to challenge German rule on the Continent. Instead, the war was fought in the Mediterranean and North Africa.[7]

Churchill often traveled to remote theaters of war by ship or plane. Recognizing the dangers this entailed, he sent a letter to King George VI designating the forty-seven-year-old Anthony Eden as his successor. Eden had served as foreign secretary in the government of Neville Chamberlain, but he had resigned in February 1938 over policy toward Italy. In September of that year he opposed the Munich agreement, which handed part of Czechoslovakia to Hitler in a failed attempt to satisfy his expansionary ambitions. Eden was a leader of the antiappeasement opposition to the government, whose members became known, partly because of Eden himself, as the "glamour boys." When Churchill took over as prime minister, he first appointed Eden to the post of secretary of state for war and then moved him to the Foreign Office, where he played an important role in building what became known as the Grand Alliance with the United States and, later, the Soviet Union.

The two men had been rivals. Although they worked quite well together, and Eden would eventually marry Churchill's niece, the prime minister preferred to portray his second-in-command as weak and indecisive. Eden remained completely loyal to Churchill throughout the war, although he allowed himself to disagree with the prime minister more than once. He also cherished every moment on trips abroad when he could escape from Churchill's shadow and take well-deserved credit for his role in the war effort. Despite the inherent tension in their relations, Eden declined to take advantage of numerous wartime crises to replace Churchill, while Churchill never cast doubt on Eden's status as heir apparent. In January 1945 the king asked Churchill to submit a new letter in case neither he nor Eden returned from Yalta. Churchill did so in consultation with Eden, and they left for Malta at different times and on different planes. The precaution was by no means unnecessary.[8]

The prime minister first raised the possibility of a Big Three summit in a letter to Roosevelt on July 16, 1944. He proposed that it take place in Casablanca, Rome, or Teheran toward the end of August. A few days earlier the Red Army had taken Vilnius, the capital of Lithuania. Its commanders had launched a major offensive in the direction of Lviv in Western Ukraine, and Soviet troops had crossed the prewar border, advancing into Eastern Europe, whose future lay in the balance. The prime minister was hoping to convince the president to cancel planned military operations in southern France and launch an offensive in the Balkans instead, cutting off Soviet troops from Central Europe. He also felt that a deal had to be struck with Stalin on the future of Eastern Europe. Whether there would be two separate meetings or one involving all three heads of state was still up in the air, but Churchill believed that something had to be done, and soon.

Roosevelt accepted the idea but favored scheduling the conference for the second week of September. Both men wrote to Stalin proposing a September meeting in northern Scotland, to which Stalin could travel by sea or air. "Things are moving so fast and so successfully that I feel there should be a meeting," Roosevelt wrote, betraying the main reason for their concern. Stalin declined the invitation, citing the need to be in Moscow at the time of a major Red Army offensive. By the end of July his armies had entered Poland and were close enough to Warsaw to spark an anti-Nazi uprising that began on August 1 and was drowned in blood by the Germans.

The Soviet offensive was only one reason for Stalin's refusal to go to Scotland. After the Allied landing in Normandy, there was little strategic assistance he wanted from the leaders of the Western democracies, and he had everything to gain from postponing the conference until his forces had captured as much of Eastern Europe as possible. That in any event was the opinion of Harry Hopkins, which he shared with the president. "As to Uncle Joe," wrote Hopkins, using the wartime nickname for Stalin, "he obviously wants to postpone his next meeting with you until after Germany collapses." Stalin was not eager to go to a conference on territory that he did not control. He disliked flying (the flight from Teheran in December 1943 apparently caused him an earache that lasted two weeks), and, always paranoid about his personal security, would not consider a plane trip above enemy territory or by ship through the submarine-infested waters of the Barents Sea.

Roosevelt continued to push for a summit. He offered to meet in Alaska, which Stalin could reach without crossing enemy lines. The meeting would take place in late November, following the U.S. presidential elections. Stalin again refused. He told Averell Harriman that he could not travel far for health reasons but was prepared to dispatch Viacheslav Molotov, the fifty-four-year-old people's commissar for foreign affairs and Stalin's right-hand man, wherever Roosevelt and Churchill decided to have their next meeting. This was not what the two Western leaders, who counted on their good relations with the "malleable" Stalin as opposed to the "tough" Molotov, wanted to hear. The idea was dropped for the time being. It seemed that Hopkins was right: Stalin would avoid meeting his partners face-to-face until the end of the war.[9]

Roosevelt and Churchill met on their own in September 1944 in Quebec City, where they discussed the future occupation of Germany; Lend-Lease supplies of war materials to Britain, which would exceed $31 billion by the end of the war; and British naval participation in the war with Japan. Eastern Europe was not on the agenda in Quebec, as it could be discussed and resolved only with Stalin. Meanwhile the Soviet armies were swiftly taking one Eastern European country after another. By then, Romania and Bulgaria had been overrun by the Red Army. The need for a meeting with Stalin was so urgent that Churchill decided to take the matter in his own hands. Less than two weeks after returning from Quebec, he headed for Moscow, where he spent ten days, from October 9 to 18, trying to make a deal with Stalin on Eastern Europe. The results were mixed—Churchill secured Britain's dominance in Greece, but Stalin appeared determined to install puppet governments in most countries of the region.

Roosevelt was represented in Moscow by Harriman, who attended most but not all of the meetings between Churchill and Stalin. With the presidential campaign in the United States reaching its climax, FDR could not leave the country. The race was close, as the polls showed Roosevelt leading his Republican opponent by only a few percentage points. Running against the energetic forty-two-year-old governor of New York, Thomas E. Dewey, FDR had to put to rest persistent rumors about his own poor health, and in October 1944 he embarked on a vigorous campaign, at one point traveling for hours in an open car under persistent rain through the New York boroughs. The campaign swing was a success, but the president apparently felt bad about his inability to take part in the all-important discussions with Stalin.

The president wrote to both Stalin and Churchill suggesting that the talks in Moscow be considered preliminary to an upcoming Big Three summit. On the last day of Churchill's stay in Moscow, Stalin cabled the president not only agreeing to another summit but suggesting a time and place for it: late November in one of the Soviet Black Sea ports. Having made a deal with Churchill on the fate of the Balkans, where the two leaders had defined their respective spheres of interest, Stalin assumed that his allies were prepared to bargain on the future of the rest of Eastern Europe.

Although Stalin and later Churchill claimed that the Black Sea region was the president's idea, this came as a surprise to most people in Washington. In his cable to the president, Stalin spoke of a conversation between Harry Hopkins and the Soviet ambassador to Washington, Andrei Gromyko, in which the president's adviser had allegedly made the suggestion. He added that he had discussed the proposal with Churchill, who had supported it. Churchill soon wrote to Roosevelt that he was prepared to go to any location acceptable to the president and Stalin. The president, however, was not about to travel to an area so remote from the United States. Members of Roosevelt's inner circle blamed Hopkins for suggesting a journey that would require their ailing chief to travel thousands of miles over enemy territory.

Hopkins was guilty as charged. The whole idea was his own creation. Convinced that a Big Three conference was badly needed before Germany's defeat and that Stalin could not be persuaded to travel outside the USSR, he had proposed the Crimea to Roosevelt, counting on the president's curiosity and desire to visit new places. Roosevelt had not been opposed to the idea so long as it was after the elections. Hopkins took the initiative and asked Gromyko whether a suitable place could be found in the Crimea. Hopkins later remembered that when Roosevelt's advisers "descended on the President to urge him not to go, the President wavered again and cooked up a lot of counter proposals, none of which made any sense." Without rejecting the Soviet suggestion out of hand, Roosevelt tried to convince Stalin to meet at a Mediterranean location.[10]

In his correspondence with Stalin and Churchill in October and November 1944, Roosevelt discussed no fewer than ten possible alternatives: Athens, Piraeus, Salonika, Jerusalem, Istanbul, Rome, Alexandria, Cyprus, Malta, and the French Riviera. On November 18, the president wrote to Stalin, noting that he had reservations about the Black Sea because of the need to bring ships through the Aegean Sea and the Dardanelles. FDR suggested that Stalin could go to the Adriatic coast by rail and from there by ship to Italy or Sicily, with the idea of having the conference either in Rome or in Taormina. He also proposed that the conference be postponed until after his inauguration on January 20, 1945.

As might be expected, Stalin had no objection to postponing the conference. In his cable of November 23 he accepted the late January–early February date, but, citing his doctors' advice, refused to discuss any venue other than the Black Sea coast. The Soviet leader was in no hurry: things were going his way. On the day he wrote to Roosevelt his troops were deep in Czechoslovakia and Hungary, capturing the town of Tokaj with its famous vineyards. Roosevelt all but abandoned hope that Stalin would fulfill the promise given to him at Teheran—to have the next meeting closer to American territory. Back then, after looking curiously at the president's crippled legs, the Soviet leader had promised that next time he would come to the president, not the other way around.[11]

Roosevelt had little choice but to ask Harriman about locations in the Black Sea region. On December 6, he reported to Washington: "Two of our naval officers visited Yalta and Sevastopol during last summer. They report that Yalta has a number of large and well built sanatoriums and hotels undamaged by German occupation. By Russian standards the town is extremely neat and clean. The harbor is small and it is doubted that it is adequate for protected anchorage for a large naval vessel. The winter climate is reasonable. Average temperature in January and February 39 degrees Fahrenheit. The town has good southern exposure and it is protected from the north winds by high mountains."

This was the first time that Yalta was suggested as a meeting place. The information on the level of the destruction in the area was later shown to be wrong, but for those who read Harriman's telegram in Washington, the city looked like a good choice. That was certainly Roosevelt's impression. On the basis of Harriman's report, he wrote to Churchill on December 9, referring to Yalta as a place where the Allied delegations could be accommodated onshore.

A last halfhearted attempt to persuade Stalin to meet closer to American shores was made by Harriman in person on December 14. Stalin promised to consult his doctors but later informed Harriman through Molotov that they were still opposed to a long trip. Clearly, they were going around in circles. Stalin asked Harriman why Hopkins's suggestion to meet in the Black Sea region had been discarded. Harriman explained that Hopkins had merely inquired about such a possibility. The Soviet leader gave Odesa as his first choice for a meeting place, stating that he had already made preparations for the conference there. He noted, however, that if the president preferred, they could meet either in the Crimea or on the east coast of the Black Sea.

Roosevelt, meanwhile, was getting more accustomed to the idea of meeting in the Crimea. On December 19, he cabled Harriman: "We have talked with Captain Frankel who reports weather conditions for flying at Odesa uncertain in winter and weather very cold." Then he added, "I am particularly interested in Sevastopol and Yalta." On December 21, Harriman sent a report to Washington favoring Yalta. The weather in Odesa was "bleak and cold," he wrote. The southern Crimea would be warmer. There was an airport within two or three hours' drive of either Sevastopol or Yalta. As Sevastopol had been completely destroyed, shore accommodations were better in Yalta. On the basis of reports from U.S. Navy officers who had been in the area, Harriman wrote, "without question the living conditions ashore in one or more of the several first class sanatoria and hotels would be more than adequate."[12]

Two days later, Roosevelt cabled Harriman, giving his approval for a meeting in the Black Sea region if Stalin could not go to the Mediterranean. His choice was Yalta, "which appears to be the best place available in the Black Sea having the best accommodations ashore and the most promising flying conditions." Roosevelt decided to fly to Yalta from the Mediterranean, to which he would travel by sea. Molotov was informed of that decision on December 27. At the meeting with Harriman, he still mentioned Odesa and Batumi, but the American ambassador had fixed on Yalta.[13]

If Roosevelt chose the venue for the conference, Churchill came up with a code name, "Operation Argonaut," on December 31. Roosevelt wrote back: "Your suggestion of 'Argonaut' is welcome. You and I are direct descendants." Always at home with the classics, Churchill was able to find a literary parallel that reflected better than anything else the feelings and expectations of the two leaders who were about to embark on a long and dangerous journey to the Black Sea in search of their own Golden Fleece. Stalin, no devotee of the classics, accepted the code name without hesitation. On New Year's Day 1945, after learning of the president's plan to stop over on Malta, Churchill sent Roosevelt a cable that included one of the few lines of poetry he ever wrote: "No more let us falter. From Malta to Yalta. Let nobody alter."[14]

Roosevelt devoted the entire afternoon of February 2, his only day on Malta, to sightseeing. After lunch, accompanied by the governor-general of Malta and his wife, Anna Boettiger, and Sarah Oliver, Roosevelt took a tour of Valetta and traveled to the island's ancient capital, Medina. Bombed by the Axis in a non-stop campaign of air raids that lasted 154 days, Malta was a clear reminder of the recent battle for control of the Mediterranean. Altogether, about fourteen thousand bombs were dropped on "Fortress Malta" between 1940 and 1942. Local residents were evacuated to the center of the island, away from the port, industrial areas, and airfields, but still suffered heavy casualties. The air and naval blockade intended to starve Malta's population and garrison was finally broken in August 1942, when five of the fourteen vessels that left Gibraltar with supplies for the besieged island managed to reach the Grand Harbor of Valetta. The blockade was totally lifted only in the summer of 1943.

"[T]he immense amount of destruction hit me between the eyes because it was my first glimpse of mass destruction of this war," Anna noted in her diary. In Valetta she saw a stone replica of the scroll presented by Roosevelt to the citizens of Malta on his return from Teheran in December 1943, in recognition of their bravery during the Nazi siege of the island. It was mounted on one side of the door leading to the palace; on the other side was a citation from King George VI, who awarded the George Cross to the people of Malta in April 1942 at the peak of the Axis bombing of the island.[15]

Roosevelt's preference for sightseeing was a major disappointment to the British delegation. Charles E. Bohlen of the State Department noted later that the "British were concerned by Roosevelt's refusal to discuss either tactical or substantive questions regarding Yalta." Anthony Eden complained to Harry Hopkins that they "were going into a decisive conference and had so far neither agreed what we would discuss nor how to handle matters with a Bear who would certainly know his mind." Eden's frustration was shared by Churchill. "The President was so unpredictable that the Prime Minister and I became uneasy at this void," Eden wrote in his memoirs.[16]

When the prime minister first learned of the president's plan for a stopover, he asked if they could use the occasion to discuss a common strategy. "Would it not be possible for you to spend 2 or 3 nights at Malta and let the staffs have a talk together unostentatiously?" Churchill wrote on January 5, 1945. If Roosevelt wanted to spend only one night on Malta, Churchill wrote again the next day, would he consider sending the military chiefs there a few days earlier? Roosevelt initially rejected the idea, but Churchill continued to insist and suggested adding Foreign Office representatives. Roosevelt eventually yielded, agreeing to send delegations led by Edward Stettinius and General George Marshall to Malta ahead of time, but he refused to change his own schedule.[17]

The prime minister's insistence was the subject of jokes among the president's entourage on the *Quincy*, and Anna later remembered someone saying that a telegram had come from Stalin declaring: "I said Yalta, not Malta." Roosevelt made every effort to prevent Stalin from suspecting that the two Western leaders had "ganged up" on him. He believed that having no preconference meeting was the best strategy under the circumstances. But Churchill was eager to maneuver the president into committing himself to a common strategy. It appeared that Churchill had won the battle but lost the war: Roosevelt arranged his schedule in such a way as to leave no time for substantive discussion. Bohlen believed that more important than his concern about Stalin was his "general desire to avoid fixed positions and to improvise on the spot, drawing from his information and the mood of the other side."[18]

Churchill was effectively on his own. The main goal of British foreign policy at Yalta was the same as it had been since the Napoleonic wars: to prevent the domination of Europe by a single power that, taking control of the western part of the continent, would pose a mortal threat to Britain. In numerous speeches, Churchill presented this policy in terms of the British struggle against tyranny and aggression. The power with all-European aspirations in the first decade of the twentieth century was Germany, and Britain found itself allied with Germany's eastern neighbor, tsarist Russia. With the defeat of Germany in the First World War and the rise of communism in the former Russian Empire, Soviet Russia took Germany's place as a threat to European stability, and Churchill embarked on a vigorous anticommunist campaign at home and abroad; he now considered the "red menace" much more dangerous to Europe than German imperialism.

The Nazi regime revived the German threat, and Churchill was among the first to alert his compatriots to the growing power of Germany. "[W]e have passed an awful milestone in our history, when the whole equilibrium of Europe has been deranged," he declared after Munich. Churchill never changed his view of communism as a dangerous threat, nor did he underestimate the menace of its transnational appeal to the European status quo, but he put his anticommunist rhetoric on hold after the Nazi invasion of the USSR in June 1941. At stake was not only the defense of British interests abroad but Britain's very survival. Fighting one tyranny with the help of another seemed the right thing to do.[19]

By the time of the Yalta Conference the war against Germany seemed all but won, thanks in large part to Soviet victories, but another possible master of Europe was emerging from the east, and Churchill was not going to leave the diplomatic battlefield without a fight. For the British, the future of Poland emerged as the issue of primary importance, and not only because Poland was the country in whose defense Britain had officially gone to war against Germany. In the vision of postwar Europe shared by Churchill and his foreign-policy advisers, Poland was to serve as a bulwark against Soviet westward expansion. Another important element in Churchill's strategy was a strong France: together with a strong Poland, it would keep a revived Germany in check. To maintain the balance of power in Europe, Germany had to be weakened but not completely destroyed or dismembered. It was a complex game, but Britain had been prepared for it by centuries of involvement in Continental politics. Nevertheless, Britain was now too weak to win the game on its own: American help was essential.[20]

The U.S. government was not eager to become involved in the byzantine politics of Europe, as Americans had little experience of diplomatic games of that kind and despised the very idea of an international order based on a balance of power. Their country was not an island near the European coast; hence they could afford a less utilitarian strategic outlook. After the end of hostilities, went the conventional wisdom of the time, the American public would not tolerate the posting of American troops in Europe for a long period. Britain was regarded as a formidable competitor in the international arena, and Churchill's continuing efforts to carve Europe into spheres of influence were looked upon with suspicion.

Roosevelt and his advisers considered the defeat of Germany their top priority in the war, but the struggle with Japan in the Pacific was no less significant to a nation that had entered the war in the wake of Pearl Harbor. If there was an ally that could offer substantial help in the Pacific theater, it was Stalin's Soviet Union, not Churchill's Britain. Soviet cooperation was also required in the future world peace organization. American and British interests were simply too diverse to allow their leaders to reach a complete meeting of minds on their policies toward the USSR.

Supporters of the New Deal in Roosevelt's administration did not see the growing Soviet power as a threat—at least not an immediate threat. For them, the leader of the British Conservatives was not only an embodiment of selfish capitalism but also a champion of imperialism and a practitioner of old-style diplomacy, with its reliance on secret protocols and spheres of influence. Many in Roosevelt's administration believed, like Wilson before them, in a new world order in which there would be no empires, and newly independent nations would offer equal access to resources and markets to all world powers, not Britain alone. They were suspicious of the imperial aspirations of their former colonial overlords, against whom America's founding fathers had waged their war of independence.

"The President shared a widespread American suspicion of the British Empire as it had once been," wrote Eden, with obvious regret, in his memoirs. "Roosevelt did not confine his dislike of colonialism to the British Empire alone, for it was a principle with him, not the less cherished for its possible advantages. He hoped that former colonial territories, once free of their masters, would become politically and economically dependent upon the United States, and had no fear that other powers might fill that role."[21]

Roosevelt and Churchill differed not only in their worldviews and political agendas but also in their way of dealing with their foreign-policy experts. If Roosevelt preferred to avoid too much contact with his foreign-policy advisers, Churchill sought as much communication as possible, imposing his vision and will on his subordinates. The prime minister's experts were running away from him, trying in vain to avoid long dinners and even longer nocturnal discussions. Churchill, who suffered from fits of depression, did not go to bed until he was completely exhausted. Like Stalin, he held a captive audience at his dinner table well into the early hours of the morning. When Harry Hopkins arrived in London on January 21 for preconference discussions with the prime minister, the talks lasted long into the night. Anthony Eden felt lucky when he got to bed at 1:15 a.m. one night. "I was so tired most of the week," wrote Eden in his diary, "that I made very little sense in the House."

Churchill's routine did not change on Malta. Alec Cadogan wrote to his wife on January 31, "Anthony [Eden] got back from the P.M. about 7 yesterday evening with orders for me and him to dine with P.M. But we were promised we might go to bed at a reasonable hour, as he was going to play bezique with Harriman." That promise was insufficient to reassure Cadogan, who concluded, "Most of us have to go and dine with the P.M. tonight, and fear we shan't see our beds for *hours.*" In the event, Churchill did order cards before midnight and began to play bezique, a French card game that had become popular in Britain, with the U.S. ambassador. Edward Stettinius, who dined with Churchill the following evening, recalled that the prime minister was greatly depressed that evening about the future of the world.[22]

Stettinius came to Malta on January 31 with Harry Hopkins to take part in preconference consultations with his British counterparts, Anthony Eden and Alec Cadogan. The U.S. secretary of state made a startling impression on anyone encountering him for the first time. Only forty-four years old, he had a thick mass of silver-gray hair that contrasted sharply with his youthful looks and energetic style. When he landed on Malta, Stettinius was just completing his second month in office. A former senior executive at General Motors and U.S. Steel, he was no foreign-policy novice, having managed the Lend-Lease program for Roosevelt and served as undersecretary of state before his promotion to the post of secretary in December 1944.

Stettinius's appointment was not without controversy. His predecessor, Cordell Hull, had recommended James Byrnes as his replacement, but the president, concerned that Byrnes might challenge his control over foreign policy, had chosen Stettinius instead. The president's strategy worked. Senator Arthur Vandenberg, admittedly a Republican critic of Roosevelt's foreign policy, reflected the impression of many when he noted in his diary on the day of FDR's death that Stettinius "has been only a presidential messenger. He does *not* have the background and experience for such a job at such a critical time—although he is a *grand person* with every good intention and high honesty of purpose."[23]

The new secretary of state was indeed amiable, and negotiations on Malta went well; both parties were happy with the outcome. Over the course of the war, British-American disagreements covered a broad range of issues, from the conditions of Lend-Lease to military operations in Europe. By the time of the Yalta Conference, most of the disagreements that came within the purview of the foreign ministers had been either resolved or superseded. The main issue by now was one of emphasis. As Anthony Eden noted, "They seemed to me to give rather too much weight to World Council and too little to Poland."

He believed that there could be no true cooperation in the future world peace organization unless Stalin treated Poland "with some decency."[24]

Even the usually critical Cadogan appeared satisfied with the results. He wrote to his wife: "We got on very well and I do not think we are going to have any serious problems with *them*." Stettinius too was happy with the outcome of the talks and had a high opinion of his British counterparts. He praised Eden in his memoirs, stating that his "courageous break with the Chamberlain government over the prewar appeasement policy and his fine intellectual capacity had won him the respect of the Foreign Office personnel and of the average British citizen." There was an unprecedented level of understanding between the foreign ministries of the two allied states. What was missing was an understanding between their leaders.[25]

Most of the limited time Roosevelt devoted to diplomatic consultation on Malta was taken up with a review of the Combined Chiefs of Staff's reports on the Allied military operations in Europe. Roosevelt clearly considered it more important to coordinate military affairs than diplomatic ones. And in the final analysis, coordination meant subordinating British military planning to American priorities. At the meeting with the Allied brass that the two leaders convened on the *Quincy* after Roosevelt's return from his sightseeing trip, the president fully backed his commanders in the dispute over Allied military strategy in Europe. As they had done many times before, the British demanded that the main offensive against Germany be launched on their section of the western front. They also insisted on a major offensive in the Mediterranean theater in addition to the one in Western Europe. The goal was not only to beat the Red Army to Berlin and Central Europe but also to put their own people in charge of the principal military operations.

The Americans, especially General George Marshall, vehemently opposed both plans, considering them useless and, indeed, harmful dispersions of troops. The usually polite Marshall vigorously resisted British attempts to undercut Eisenhower's authority, requesting a closed session, without stenographers, with his British counterparts and telling them exactly what he thought of their demands to switch control of the future offensive from General Eisenhower to Field Marshal Montgomery. He also responded to accusations that the Americans had too much influence on Eisenhower, who as supreme Allied commander was supposed to be independent in his decisions. "Well, Brooke," Marshall told Sir Alan Francis Brooke, the chief of the British General Staff, "you're not nearly as much worried as the American chiefs are worried about the immediate pressures and influence of Mr. Churchill on General Eisenhower. The President practically never sees General Eisenhower and never writes to him—that is on my advice—because he is an *Allied* commander. But we are deeply concerned by the pressures of the prime minister. I think your worries are on the wrong foot."[26]

Marshall's forceful intervention convinced the British that they had no choice but to accept the American strategy of a broad offensive on the western front. All Churchill could do under the circumstances was suggest to Roosevelt that in case of a German surrender in Italy, the Allies should occupy as much of Austria as possible: it was "undesirable that more of Western Europe than necessary should be occupied by the Russians." But the whole argument was hypothetical. For the time being, Churchill had to agree (not without reservations) to remove part of the British forces from Italy and Greece and send them to Western Europe in order to strengthen Allied efforts in the main theater of operations. After the meeting with the Combined Chiefs of Staff, he informed Roosevelt of his intention to transfer the Allied commander in Italy, Field Marshal Harold Alexander, to Western Europe to serve as deputy to General Dwight Eisenhower (making Alexander the senior British military commander in the European theater).[27]

As the British saw it, the dinner before their departure for the Crimea was their last chance to reach an understanding with the president. This turned out to be one more disappointment. Arrangements for lunch, afternoon tea, and dinner on the *Quincy* were taken over by Anna Boettiger, and her main concern was to protect her father from too much exposure to the members of the American and British delegations. She was upset that the same members of the British delegation (she called them "Britishers") who had attended lunch were also invited by her father to dinner. As a result, she had to make separate arrangements for her own guests, such as Churchill's son Randolph, who flew to Malta from Yugoslavia. The relatively small rooms of a naval vessel were not designed for grand receptions. To Anna's further displeasure, Stettinius and Eden, whom she had asked to stay in her own cabin while she prepared drinks, "sneaked to FDR's cabin and discussed with him business until Churchill showed up after his bath 45 minutes later."[28]

Since the dinner was attended by Anna and Sarah, it became more a social event than the business meeting that the British had in mind. Stettinius later wrote that the discussions on the *Quincy* "served again to clarify the American and British attitudes" on a wide range of questions. If one considers Stettinius's list of topics discussed by the two leaders at formal and informal sessions, it looks impressive indeed, covering everything from the war effort in Europe to the future of Germany, Poland, and Romania; policies toward Iran and China; and the world peace organization. There is little doubt, however, that most of these issues would have been mentioned only in passing. Eden, who attended both lunch and dinner on the *Quincy*, complained in his diary: "Pleasant but no business whatsoever done. So a dinner was arranged specifically for this purpose which was no more successful than the luncheon. Impossible even to get near business."[29]

On the night of February 2, the planes carrying members of the American and British delegations left the Luqa airport and headed for the Saki airfield in the Crimea. The exodus from Malta began at 11:30 p.m., with American C-54s and British Yorks and Spitfires taking off at ten-minute intervals. The president's plane, specially equipped for FDR's needs and known to air force personnel as the "Sacred Cow" because it was usually heavily guarded while on the ground, took off at 3:30 a.m. By that time the president was asleep in his compartment. He was leaving Malta without compromising his main objective— his hands were not tied by a preliminary agreement with the British. He was free to adopt any strategy he liked at Yalta.

3

THE TSAR'S PLAYGROUND

The planes carrying the Allied delegations flew over the Mediterranean toward Greece and then turned north, continuing over Turkey and the Black Sea. They were flying at a speed of more than 200 miles per hour at an altitude of approximately 6,000 feet, a height recommended by the president's doctor. It took them nearly seven hours to reach their destination.

Roosevelt and Churchill were escorted by six fighter jets each. The major concern, however, was not enemy planes but possible hostile fire from the remaining German garrisons on islands in the Aegean Sea. A week earlier one of the planes bringing Michael Reilly, the president's chief bodyguard, and his crew on a reconnaissance trip to the Crimea changed course during a storm and encountered German fire over Crete, almost losing its tail. Reilly's plane ascended to 15,000 feet in order to avoid a storm (an altitude considered too dangerous for the president, given his history of high blood pressure), and its wings began icing. He was glad to reach his destination alive.

The German antiaircraft gunners were one problem; Soviet friendly fire was another. After Stalin's personal intervention, the Soviets agreed that one American officer could be stationed at every Soviet antiaircraft installation in the eastern Black Sea region, but that did not guarantee anything. In late January, Soviet antiaircraft gunners had opened fire on a British plane that did not follow Soviet instructions. Approaching Soviet territory, the Allied planes had to execute an identification maneuver, enter a 20-mile-wide corridor, make a prearranged right turn, and then land on a narrow airstrip of the Saki air base. Soviet pilots, who were on high alert in case of enemy attack, were ordered to shoot down any airplane that did not respond to their signals. They were told by their commanders not to bother coming back if they missed an enemy plane, advice they took seriously.[1]

Churchill, whose Skymaster left the Luqa airport five minutes after FDR's, referred in his memoirs to a "long and cold flight." He eventually grew critical of the very idea of holding the conference at Yalta. "If we had spent ten years in our research we could not have found a worse place in the world than Yalta," Churchill complained to Harry Hopkins in January. "It is good for typhus and deadly on lice which thrive in those parts." Hopkins's report, received by the president en route to Malta, was met with outrage by Michael Reilly, who cabled the president: "Conditions not as frightening as Churchill reports and have been adequately corrected by Russians."[2]

The president's Sacred Cow landed at the Saki airfield on February 3 at 12:10 p.m. local time. Everything proceeded without a hitch, except that the Soviets could not understand why FDR's escort planes did not follow instructions: they circled Saki's airstrip instead of landing at the Sarabuz airfield near Simferopol, the capital of the Crimea. Twenty minutes later Churchill's escort planes did the same thing. As Soviet air force commanders tried to figure out what had gone wrong, Anna Boettiger enjoyed the show, impressed with the sight of Churchill's six Lockheed P-38 Lightning fighters circling the air base.[3]

When Roosevelt's and Churchill's planes landed, most members of the American and British delegations were already there, either visiting a tent where champagne, vodka, caviar, and other Russian delicacies had been laid out or on their way to Yalta. The first visitor to the president's plane was Viacheslav Molotov, followed by Churchill. FDR used a specially designed elevator to disembark from his plane and was then carried to a Lend-Lease Jeep supplied by the Soviets. Together with the prime minister and Molotov, Roosevelt inspected the Soviet guard of honor.

Churchill's doctor, Lord Moran, was clearly unhappy to see him following Roosevelt's Jeep on foot. "The P.M. walked by the side of the President, as in her old age an Indian attendant accompanied Queen Victoria's phaeton," noted the ever-critical observer in his diary. His description of Roosevelt was not flattering. "The President looked old and thin and drawn," he wrote; "he sat looking straight ahead with his mouth open, as if he were not taking things in." Anna was also concerned and admitted that he "did look tired after his hard day yesterday and a short night's sleep on the plane." The Soviet doctors brought to the Saki airfield to observe Roosevelt concluded that he was exhausted and in poor health.[4]

The Americans and British boarded a fleet of Lend-Lease Packards and ZiS's—armored Soviet VIP vehicles—and left Saki with an entourage of Soviet officials and security personnel shortly after 1:00 p.m. local time. The hope was to reach Yalta before nightfall. They headed toward Simferopol and then turned south, taking a mountain road to the seaside town of Alushta. On reaching the Black Sea, they turned west and took the "Romanov Road" to Yalta. On orders of the NKVD, the People's Commissariat of Internal Affairs, which was in charge of security, the road was cleared not only of snow but also of most traffic, including pedestrians. The entire route to Simferopol was guarded by Soviet troops, with armed soldiers spaced about 50 feet apart. A peculiar feature of the Soviet guard of honor was that a significant number of soldiers along the road to Yalta were women.

The guests were amused by the special salute given as the motorcade went by. "As the presidential car passed," recalled Charles Bohlen, "the soldiers, many of them girls, snapped to the Russian salute—an abrupt move of the arm to put the rifle at a 30-degree angle from the body. Repeated thousands of times, the salute was impressive." Anna Boettiger found the soldiers "smart and erect," but Michael Reilly, the chief bodyguard, traveling in the same car as the president and his daughter, was not impressed with what he saw. "Some of the Russian troops," he wrote in his memoirs, "were so tiny that their ancient 'Springfields' were bigger than the warriors who carried them. On closer inspection these fierce soldiers proved to be girls still in their teens, but nevertheless fighting components of the Red Army."[5]

From the windows the travelers saw the road, the troops, and the landscape— flat steppes, then mountains—which showed clear signs of the war waged there only a few months earlier. "The rolling countryside was littered with burned-out tanks, gutted buildings, and destroyed German freight trains that had been abandoned and burned by the Nazis in their retreat from the Crimea," wrote Reilly, echoing the account given in the presidential travel log and almost every other memoir of the conference participants. Roosevelt was so affected by the scenes of destruction that during his first meeting with Stalin he stated that "he was more bloodthirsty in regard to the Germans than he had been a year ago."

When the cavalcade reached Simferopol, the travelers finally got a chance to take a closer look at the locals. "On the whole everyone looks extremely well fed and healthy," Anna Boettiger wrote in her diary. Anna's observations were shared by Kathleen Harriman, the twenty-seven-year-old daughter of the U.S. ambassador to Moscow, who had reached Yalta earlier by train. She found "[t]he Ukrainian peasants . . . far more prosperous than those around Moscow." The president's daughter described in detail the appearance of the Soviet citizens she could see from the window of her car. "Men, women and children, alike, wear the drabbest of clothing, in color and style," she wrote. Then she added: "But their clothes are very utilitarian and warm—even though some-times worn looking." What most struck Anna was the virtual absence of men (other than soldiers). "Many children's faces," she wrote, "look much older than their years. The women also look much older than their years and their faces have deep wrinkles very often." She then continued: "This is not strange when you see how hard these women work. They carry terrific burdens on their backs."[6]

It was a long trip, nearly six hours from Saki to Yalta, with the cars proceed-ing at 20 miles per hour. Churchill was bored with the car trip. "Christ! Five more hours of this," he complained to his daughter Sarah Oliver. Anna was protective of her father and insisted on riding with him so that he would not be forced to "make a conversation" with other members of the delegation. They ate sandwiches on the road, and Anna refused to make a stopover for lunch in Simferopol. (She eventually agreed to stop for a few minutes only to use restrooms.) "When we arrived there I found to my horror that Molotov had preceded us and had a table all set up with vodka, wines, caviar, fish, bread, butter—and heaven knows what was to follow," Anna wrote in her diary. The Americans left without eating lunch, but the British were more accommodating. Lord Moran looked "doubtfully" at the caviar, smoked salmon, suckling pig, and champagne. "But the P.M.," wrote Moran, "likes good food and he soon got into form, making some rather daring remarks."[7]

The president was the first to reach his destination, Livadia Palace, but the prime minister was a happier man when he finally arrived at Vorontsov villa, located several miles away. After lunch, the trip did not seem quite so trying. "We still had another two hours to go, but these were enjoyable," Sarah Oliver wrote to her mother. "Papa recited practically all 'Don Juan' and had about 30 minutes sleep." In his memoirs Churchill described "brilliant sunshine" greeting his party as it crossed the mountains. By other accounts, it was a "gummy" day with "lowering clouds that spat rain and a little wet snow." Sarah wrote that on the way from Simferopol to Yalta, "darkness fell, but our headlamps picked out our sentinels still lining the road." On reaching Vorontsov villa, the headquarters of the British delegation, at a quarter to eight, Churchill insisted on having a conversation with Lord Moran and Anthony Eden. "He was in great form," wrote Moran, "protesting that he could easily make the same car journey now, and—raising his voice—make a speech at the end of it."[8]

Livadia Palace, assigned as the headquarters of the American delegation, was not actually in the town of Yalta, which Reilly described as "ground to rubble," but in a settlement 7 kilometers from the city. "Situated more than 150 feet above the sea," noted the author of FDR's travel log in February 1945, the palace "commands a striking panorama of the mountains and the sea to the east and north." "The three palaces lived in by the 'Big Three' are the only buildings left intact," Anna wrote in her diary. "The Tsars and the wealthy used to come by train to Sevastopol, board their yachts there and come to Yalta. Local people remember Joe Davies' stops there on his and Marjorie's yacht!" This was a reference to the visit of the U.S. ambassador stationed in Moscow from 1936 to 1938, who was well acquainted with FDR and his whole family.[9]

Livadia acquired its name from a town in central Greece—a distant echo of the Greek project that preoccupied Empress Catherine II for a significant part of her reign. The annexation of the Crimea in 1783 was only one step in the realization of that project, which envisioned the restoration of the Byzantine Empire and the establishment of Russian control over the Bosporus and the Dardanelles. Catherine even named one of her grandsons Constantine, preparing him to take over the throne of the new Byzantium. She also renamed dozens of Crimean towns and settlements in the Greek manner. Simferopol, the new regional capital; Sevastopol, the base of the Russian Black Sea Fleet; and Livadia, the future site of the tsars' summer residence, all bore witness to ambitious plans that never came to fruition.

Not only did the Crimea fail to become a bridge to Constantinople, but Russian claims to the peninsula and other territories acquired in the late eighteenth century were challenged during the Crimean War, which was fought between Russia and a coalition that included Britain, France, and the Ottoman Empire. The war began in 1853 with a conflict between France and Russia over the control of Christian shrines in Palestine. At stake were the future of the Ottoman Empire and the influence of the great European powers in the region. Tsar Nicholas I misjudged the intentions of the British, who joined the French after some hesitation in an attempt to prevent Russian advances in the Balkans. In 1854, the three powers launched a military intervention in the Crimea.

The allies besieged Sevastopol, but the garrison and the sailors of the sunken imperial fleet refused to surrender and defended the city for almost a year, inflicting heavy casualties on the attackers. The Crimean expedition turned out to be anything but a success, costing the British the flower of their cavalry, which had been recruited from some of the empire's most prominent aristocratic families. It was also a public-relations disaster, as the development of the telegraph made the Crimean War the first international military conflict to be covered by the press as events took place. The British and French did worse than they expected, but so did the Russians, who eventually abandoned Sevastopol. Hopes for the creation of a pro-Russian coalition, including plans to bring the American fleet to the Black Sea in order to offset British and French sea power, never materialized. The new Russian tsar, Alexander II, was obliged to end the war and conclude a peace treaty in Paris in 1856.[10]

The Paris treaty upset the existing balance of power in Europe and was a major setback to Russia's attempts to gain control of Constantinople and the Black Sea Straits. The treaty deprived Russia of its role as protector of Christians in the Ottoman Empire, declared the neutrality of the Black Sea, and prohibited any power, including Russia, from building fortifications on its shores. Although fortifications were not allowed, there was nothing in the peace agreement to prevent Russian aristocrats, and indeed the tsar himself, from building summer palaces on the Black Sea coast. In 1860 Alexander II bought an estate on the shore of the Black Sea known as Livadia, to which he sent his architect Ippolito Monighetti. During the 1860s Monighetti con-structed two palaces there—one large, the other small—and a church. Livadia soon became a favorite summer destination of the imperial family, especially adored by Alexander's wife, Maria of Hesse, who was advised by doctors to spend as much time as possible in a warm climate.

Roosevelt must have remembered the tsar's palaces from the most popular work of his beloved author Mark Twain. In *The Innocents Abroad* Twain described his visit to Livadia in 1867, the first year that the imperial family spent its summer in the Crimea. "We anchored here at Yalta, Russia, two or three days ago," Twain wrote.

> To me the place was a vision of the Sierras. The tall, gray mountains that back it, their sides bristling with pines—cloven with ravines—here and there a hoary rock towering into view—long, straight streaks sweeping down from the summit to the sea, marking the passage of some avalanche of former times—all these were as like what one sees in the Sierras as if the one were a portrait of the other. The little village of Yalta nestles at the foot of an amphitheatre which slopes backward and upward to the wall of hills, and looks as if it might have sunk quietly down to its present position from a higher elevation. This depression is covered with the great parks and gardens of noblemen, and through the mass of green foliage the bright colors of their palaces bud out here and there like flowers. It is a beautiful spot.

Twain, whose Mediterranean and Black Sea tour on the *Quaker City* was sponsored by a San Francisco newspaper, was equally impressed by the recep-tion offered him and his traveling companions by the emperor and by mem-bers of the imperial family, whom he found both polite and genuine (unlike the French, whose hospitality struck him as largely ceremonial). Alexander II said that "he was very much pleased to see us, especially as such friendly relations existed between Russia and the United States," wrote Twain. "The Empress said the Americans were favorites in Russia, and she hoped the Russians were similarly regarded in America."

It was indeed a good time in Russo-American relations, as Twain was visiting Livadia in the year of Russia's sale of Alaska to the United States. Nego-tiations began during the Crimean War, which was covered in American news-papers and followed with great interest by some of the future participants in the American Civil War, who learned from British and French tactics in the Crimea. Aside from financial considerations, the Russians were driven by a desire to undermine the British Empire and get rid of territory that St. Peters-burg could hardly protect in the event of a British attack. The tsar's advisers feared that Alaska might become another Crimea, and there was no Sevastopol-like fortress or significant military installation to protect the territory from foreign encroachment.

Twain, an inveterate foe of autocracy, appeared to have been charmed by the tsar and was fascinated to find himself in the presence of such an all-powerful individual. He wrote:

> It seemed strange—stranger than I can tell—to think that the central figure in the cluster of men and women, chatting here under the trees like the most ordinary individual in the land, was a man who could open his lips and ships would fly through the waves, locomotives would speed over the plains, couriers would hurry from village to village, a hundred telegraphs would flash the word to the four corners of an Empire that stretches its vast proportions over a seventh part of the habitable globe, and a countless multitude of men would spring to do his bidding. I had a sort of vague desire to examine his hands and see if they were of flesh and blood, like other men's.[11]

At the time of Twain's visit, Alexander II was in the midst of transforming his huge empire. A few years earlier, in 1861, he had done what his father, Nicholas I, considered unthinkable and emancipated the serfs. He also spearheaded reforms that eventually affected most Russian social and economic institutions, from the army to the judiciary. Like many Russian reformers, he had a hard time mitigating the forces he unleashed. The tsar's liberalism emboldened the Poles, who rose in rebellion in 1863. The Polish national revival in turn inspired the Ukrainians, to whom the Crimea would eventually belong. Young Russian radicals believed that they could bring about social revolution by killing the tsar. Alexander survived a number of assassination attempts, including one on the way from Livadia to Moscow, but on March 13, 1881, his luck ran out, and he was killed in a suicide bombing by members of a radical populist organization, the People's Will. The young radicals wanted a social revolution: what they got was a lengthy period of reaction and a twenty-five-year postponement of plans to introduce an elective parliament in Russia.

The tsar's son and successor, Alexander III, who undid many of his father's reforms, had little of his father's activist zeal and died peacefully in his bed at the Livadia Palace in 1894. Alexander III probably spent more time at Livadia than any other Russian tsar and even gave the name of his favorite retreat to a steamboat built for him in Scotland in 1880. The imperial family bought Massandra Palace and vineyards, not far from Yalta, and in 1886, after being caught in a storm and spending a night at sea, built the first breakwater in Yalta harbor. In 1891 Alexander III celebrated his twenty-fifth wedding anniversary in Livadia, with fireworks and royal guests from all over Europe. Among them were Albert Edward, the Prince of Wales, who later became King Edward VII, and his wife, Alexandra, the sister of the tsar's consort, Empress Maria.

It was Nicholas II, Alexander III's son, who, together with his wife, Alexandra, built the palace assigned to the American delegation. The old palaces at Livadia reminded Nicholas of his father's death, and he was eager for a new design. In 1909, after a trip to Italy, the tsar commissioned the Russian architect Nikolai Krasnov, who also served as his children's drawing teacher, to build a brand-new palace in Renaissance style. Construction began in 1910, and the palace was finished the following autumn, an impressive feat. The two old palaces were torn down, and only the small church built by Ippolito Monighetti remained as a reminder of the tsars' former residence.

The new palace, built of local Inkerman white stone, was a product of the uneasy interaction of a number of architectural styles. It was decided from the very beginning that the palace would feature four different facades. The billiard hall, where a private dining room would be arranged for President Roosevelt, was built in the Tudor style. There were two courtyards—one Italian, modeled on the convent of San Marco in Florence, the other Arab, with a fountain in the center and elements of Tatar architecture. The new design incorporated some existing elements, including a sarcophagus brought from Pompeii by the original owner of the estate, Count Potocki, who had also planted exotic trees in the adjoining gardens.

Every detail of the architectural plan was approved by the imperial family. According to the history of the palace distributed to members of the American delegation, in order to get back at his difficult clients Krasnov "used lion head caricatures of the Tsar as armrests on the two marble benches outside the main door." The memo went on to say that "the likeness to the Tsar becomes striking when a cap is placed atop the lion's head."[12]

The imperial family vacationed in the new Livadia Palace every year until the outbreak of the First World War. "In St. Petersburg we work, but at Livadia, we live," wrote one of the tsar's daughters, expressing the feelings of the whole family. Upon his abdication in February 1917, Nicholas asked the revolutionary government for permission to retire to Livadia. The request was turned down. Instead, the new government of Alexander Kerensky designated Livadia Palace as a rest home for victims of tsarism. A longtime political exile known as the "grandmother" of the Russian Revolution, Ekaterina Breshko-Breshkovkaia, became its first revolutionary resident in the spring of 1917. Later the Bolsheviks turned the tsar's villa into a sanatorium for tuberculosis patients, according to some accounts, or a mental asylum.[13]

After the capture of Yalta by the Nazis in the autumn of 1941, the palace was turned into the headquarters of the Wehrmacht's Twenty-second Infantry Division, and other units were stationed there in preparation for the German assault on Sevastopol. According to the Ukrainian interpreter assigned to the division's headquarters, the new inhabitants "behaved like animals, getting drunk and sometimes throwing their wineglasses and plates off a balcony overlooking the Black Sea." Hitler eventually gave the palace as a gift to Field Marshal Gerd von Rundstedt, the commander of Army Group South, which had captured the Crimea. In February 1945 Livadia Palace must have been the last thing on Rundstedt's mind: as commander in chief of the German troops on the western front, he was busy trying to stabilize the German defensive line after the Battle of the Bulge.[14]

When the Soviets recaptured Yalta in April 1944, Rundstedt was already on the western front. In the last days of their occupation, the Germans did a good job of stripping the palace of everything of value. According to Soviet reports, the retreating Germans burned down the small palace, destroyed furniture in the large one, damaged its rooms, and chopped down trees in the garden. Only nineteen houses were left standing in the Livadia settlement, with ninety-one partially or completely destroyed. Yalta was not in much better shape.

"Yalta looked like a town on the French Riviera," wrote Major Arthur Herbert Birse, an interpreter with the British embassy in Moscow. "The streets, flanked by small villas with gardens, led to the promenade on the shore. Higher up, nestling among the cypresses and vineyards, stood more imposing houses. The mountains in the background were well wooded and their tops covered with snow. Before us lay the expanse of the sea. But though the town looked attractive as we approached it, a closer look revealed its tragedy. Each house was a roofless shell, the destruction had been systematic, and before the evacuation the Germans had left no house untouched."[15]

Work on the restoration of Livadia and other palaces in the area began in November, soon after references to the Crimea started to appear in correspondence between Roosevelt and Stalin. The pace picked up tremendously after a special directive was issued in Moscow on January 8. The man who signed the directive and put himself in charge of the preparations was Lavrentii Beria, then people's commissar of internal affairs, the agency that ran the Gulag. Beria, who later became responsible for the Soviet nuclear bomb project, was an adept communist manager who freely used terror to mobilize the cumbersome centralized Soviet system. He confirmed his reputation as Stalin's ultimate troubleshooter in the weeks leading up to the Yalta Conference.

Beria signed his directive two days before Stalin received formal confirmation from Churchill of the time and place of the conference. It was supposed to begin on February 2, 1945. He had slightly more than three weeks to prepare the grounds of Livadia and two other Crimean palaces—Vorontsov Palace in Alupka (assigned to the British) and Yusupov Palace in Koreiz (reserved for the Soviet delegation)—for their VIP occupants. What followed was a small miracle that could have been worked only by a combination of terror, rapid mobilization of the state-run economy, shock-work tactics, and the use of slave labor.

Beria's deputies, Sergei Kruglov, a secret-police general, and Leon Safrazian, a construction boss, were put in charge of security matters and the restoration effort. Colonels and majors of state security working under them became responsible for a variety of tasks, ranging from the installation of communication systems to supplying buildings with furniture and bedding. They were supposed to provide two thousand bed sets for the construction workers and guards alone—a gross underestimate, given the number of people actually involved in the reconstruction of the palaces. Altogether more than fifteen hundred railway carriages were sent to the Crimea with building materials, equipment, furniture, and food supplies.[16]

The work was conducted by construction crews from Sevastopol and Yalta, engineer battalions of the Black Sea Fleet and the Red Army, and, as Anna Boettiger later noted, "a small army of Rumanian POWs." Thus, twelve plumbers from Sevastopol working on one of the buildings of Livadia Palace were assisted by 150 prisoners of war. The work was conducted around the clock in two twelve-hour shifts. At midnight the managers would listen to their subordinates' reports and make plans for the next day. The workers from Yalta were at a particular disadvantage, for after every shift they had to walk 7 kilometers to reach their homes. The locals were impressed with the level of organization and discipline ensured by NKVD supervision of the project. They were also happy to receive two meals a day. And they were proud of their accomplishments. The construction crews were given drawings only for the design of the president's toilet and bathroom: as for the rest, they had to come up with their own construction solutions. They organized a small shop for the production of marble elements. The restoration of the floors in Livadia Palace presented a special challenge, as Michael Reilly alerted his NKVD counterparts that they had to be in good shape so that the president could use his wheelchair.[17]

The American and British advance parties that came to the Crimea from Moscow to advise their Soviet hosts on their delegations' requirements witnessed the final stages of Soviet shock-work. Furniture, china, and cutlery taken from Moscow hotels were placed in the rooms immediately after the completion of reconstruction work. The painting and decoration of VIP rooms presented a particular challenge. Kathleen Harriman, charged by her father with overseeing the effort, wrote in one letter: "The rugs for the President's suite have been changed four times. Each time all the furniture had to be moved out—and it's big and heavy and Victorian. The Soviets just couldn't make up their minds which oriental colors looked best."

E. L. Sergeeva, supervisor of the plumbers working on one of the buildings at Livadia, later recalled that the completed work was inspected by NKVD officials, accompanied by Americans led by a woman who proved unusually demanding. The walls of the president's toilet and bathroom were repainted seven times on orders from the woman. Each time she would point to the sea, indicating what color she wanted the walls to be, and, as the color of the sea kept changing, the walls had to be repainted again and again. Whether the story is apocryphal or not, there can be no doubt that the American woman who made such a lasting impression was Kathleen Harriman.[18]

Averell Harriman was quite satisfied before he left Livadia for Malta. On January 25, he asked George F. Kennan, a thirty-nine-year-old rising star in the U.S. diplomatic service and his right-hand man in Moscow at the time, to convey a message to Molotov that began as follows: "I find on arrival to Magneto [the code name for Yalta] all arrangements are progressing expeditiously and satisfactorily. The President will be most comfortably taken care of." Roosevelt began with a delegation of thirty-five, but as the date approached, that number was increased almost tenfold. The Americans suggested that they bring more ships to accommodate additional personnel, but the Soviets pointed to the threat presented by floating mines: as an NKVD official noted, the Germans had decamped "without leaving a map." Livadia Palace was turning into a base camp. "[O]nly full generals and admirals and chiefs of state get rooms to themselves. The rest are packed like patients in a ward," wrote Kathleen Harriman from Livadia. "I never quite realized that so many things could go wrong so many ways," she informed one of her friends. "It's lucky that Averell isn't here to fret, but I guess at the last moment everything will suddenly become smoothed over." And indeed it was.[19]

On January 27, Beria reported to Stalin and Molotov that preparations for the conference were complete. At the Saki airfield a dormitory capable of housing five hundred people was ready for Allied air force personnel. In the main palace of the Livadia complex, forty-three rooms had been renovated. An additional forty-eight rooms were prepared for guests in a second palace. The two buildings were furnished with electrical and heating systems. There was hot water in the restrooms. A bomb shelter capable of withstanding the collapse of the building had been constructed in the basement. A telephone system with twenty outlets had been installed for the American delegation. The Soviet support staff was to be housed in a dormitory that could accommodate sixty people with its own kitchen. The American and British delegations were provided with forty cars, mostly of American make. A bakery and a fishing operation were established on the spot to supplement food products brought from other parts of the USSR. Beria reported that on January 20 the Saki airfield and the premises at Livadia had been inspected and approved by U.S. officials.[20]

"Livadia palace has been completely renovated during the past three weeks since the selection of headquarters for the US delegation," announced the information bulletin issued for incoming members of the American delegation. "No one coming in today can visualize fully the gigantic task the Soviets have accomplished in less than a month to accommodate this conference. The buildings naturally were not built for hotel service. The Soviets have done their best to adapt them to the needs of the large party we have brought in."[21]

When Roosevelt's motorcade reached Livadia Palace on the evening of February 3, the president and his entourage were greeted warmly. "When we arrived," wrote Anna Boettiger in her diary, "fires were blazing merrily in all the downstairs rooms—and were most welcome as we were pretty frozen after our five hour drive." A dinner was served for twelve, featuring caviar, sliced fish "uncooked but cured in some way," game, *shashlyk*, which Anna called "meat and skewer," and potatoes. There were two kinds of dessert and coffee. Champagne, wine, and liquor were plentiful. Kathleen Harriman told Anna that "the maitre d'hotel and his two helpers have set and unset that table 3 or 4 times a day for the past week—experimenting with glassware and china effects." Each place setting featured five glasses. Anna was "appalled" to see so many but found the glassware "lovely." She liked the food but was surprised that "each time anything was refused the maître d'hotel looked either like a thunder cloud or mortally wounded."

The president was singled out for special treatment. The maître d'hôtel greeted FDR with multiple bows, addressing him as "Your Excellency." He had a three-room suite all to himself, with his office located in what used to be the tsar's audience room, his dining room in the former billiard hall, and sleeping quarters in the tsar's former office. He also had the luxury of a private toilet and washroom in a building where, according to Kathleen Harriman, "washing facilities are practically nil." On taking a look at the accommodations, President Roosevelt said, "I can't understand Winston's concern. This place has all the comforts of home."

Kathleen was prepared to share a room with Anna Boettiger, but the president's daughter preferred to have her own small room. "It has a funny old iron bed in it, with a thin mattress which is a foot shorter than the springs, one round table and no chairs," Anna wrote in her diary. "However, I'm promised a bit more furniture tomorrow! Two rooms away is a big room housing a toilet and a basin with cold running water, and nothing else. This room has two doors and one has no lock. For hot running water I have a good block to walk. But, there are three bathrooms (complete ones) on this floor, for about 2 dozen of us, so there should not be too great a jam-up. Father has his own. It's quite a way from his room, but he thinks I may use it as it's only an extra half block away from my cubicle!"[22]

The first floor of Livadia Palace was reserved for the president, his daughter, and principal members of his party, including Secretary of State Stettinius and Ambassador Harriman. The second floor, which had provided quarters for the tsarina and her four daughters before the revolution, was assigned to the chiefs of staff of the armed forces and their aides. General Marshall's lodging was in the former imperial bedroom, while Fleet Admiral Ernest King took the tsarina's boudoir, a source of jokes among members of the delegation. The third floor housed secretaries and clerks. Military and navy personnel were in the second palace, with a Secret Service room, a sick bay, a canteen, and a barbershop located on the third floor. The former guards' residence served as a communications center.

Senior members of the delegation dined on the second floor of the main palace, while junior officers took their meals on the second floor of the residential quarters. Soviet maids made the beds and cleaned the rooms. The services of the barber and manicurist provided by the hosts were free of charge. The members of the delegation were advised to avoid walking around the main entrance of Livadia Palace or any Soviet military installations at any time and to stay away from the parks and seashore at night. "When a guard asks for your 'documente,' 'propusk,' 'passport' or 'bumagy,' show him your identification card without hesitation. If he challenges you for any reason whatsoever, produce your card. Do not try to bulldoze the guards—they have strict orders," read the instructions issued to members of the American delegation.[23]

Churchill grew to like Vorontsov Palace in nearby Alupka, which he believed to have been built by an English architect for a Russian prince who had served as imperial ambassador to London. "The setting of our abode was impressive," he wrote in his memoir, for which he dictated fourteen pages of anecdotes and impressions of his stay in the Crimea. "Behind the villa, half Gothic and half Moorish in style, rose the mountains, covered in snow, culminating in the highest peak in the Crimea. Before us lay the dark expanse of the Black Sea, severe, but still agreeable and warm even at this time of the year."

Churchill was pleased to find portraits of British aristocrats hanging by one of the fireplaces—he recognized them as the Herberts of Wilton, whom he believed to be relatives of the Russian ambassador's British wife. Other members of the British delegation were considerably less impressed. In a letter to her mother, Sarah Oliver characterized the premises as "a bit like a Scottish baronial hall inside and a Swiss Chalet plus Mosque outside." Alec Cadogan, writing to his wife, praised the location but was more than critical of its architectural style. "It's a big house of indiscernible ugliness—a sort of Gothic Balmoral—with all the furnishings of almost terrifying hideosity," he wrote on February 4 from his "small but reasonably comfortable room in the villa."[24]

The palace had been built between 1830 and 1848 by Mikhail Vorontsov, a hero of the Napoleonic Wars, commander of the Russian forces in Wellington's army in 1815, conqueror of the Caucasus and Varna, and governor-general of

New Russia—the imperial province that included the Crimea. Contrary to Churchill's belief, Vorontsov never served as ambassador to London. But his father had. His wife, Countess Elzbieta Branicka, had inspired some of Alexander Pushkin's best poems. His sister Catherine had married into the Herbert family, whose portraits Churchill recognized.

Mikhail Vorontsov spent his childhood and youth in England, where he was educated and served as his father's secretary. The elder Vorontsov wanted his son to master not only the humanities and sciences but crafts as well. He thought that sooner or later a revolution of the kind that had taken place in France would come to Russia, and he wanted his son to be prepared for that eventuality. His son, not expecting a revolution anytime soon, made a brilliant career in the Russian imperial service. He did not rely on his own craftsmanship when he decided to establish a piece of England on the shores of the Black Sea.

Vorontsov Palace was designed by an English architect, Edward Blore, who never visited the construction site. Built over a period of eighteen years with the help of Vorontsov's serfs, who were brought from central Russia, the castle combined Gothic and Arab styles. The southern entrance had a Moorish appearance, and its interior featured Arabic inscriptions, including one that read "There is no conqueror but Allah." The construction of the castle in Alupka did much to persuade the Russian tsars to build their own summer retreat in neighboring Livadia. Nicholas I bestowed a princely title on Mikhail Vorontsov for devoted service to the empire, and the prince lived long enough to see the end of the Crimean War, during which the British forces were supervised by his own nephew, the British secretary of state, Sidney Herbert. The old prince died in November 1856, by which time it was no longer possible to be both a Russian patriot and an Anglophile.[25]

The palace remained in the family's possession until the Revolution of 1917. When the prophecy of the old ambassador was finally fulfilled, the new generation was not prepared to join the victorious class of manual laborers and emigrated instead. The palace's new Bolshevik owners first turned it into a museum and then into a resort. The museum's collection was evacuated during the Second World War, but only a small portion of it survived. By the time the Germans left, it was in the same state of disrepair as Livadia Palace.

Beria reported to Stalin and Molotov that construction workers under NKVD supervision had repaired twenty-two rooms in the main building of the palace and twenty-three rooms in the so-called Shuvalov Building. They also prepared two other buildings, located 2 kilometers away, for members of the delegation and refurbished a Red Army resort in the area. Altogether there were sixty-eight rooms, with a total of 1,545 square meters of living space, as well as a dormitory that could house up to a hundred people. As in Livadia, the repairs included installing electrical and heating systems, and a telephone network with twenty outlets, but there was no bomb shelter; Roosevelt was given special treatment.[26]

"Destruction in Crimea almost complete. Russians in two weeks have rebuilt and furnished only possible accommodations left standing," read the cable of January 31 from the British advance party to the heads of the British delegation on Malta. "Everyone except VIPs will have to share two and four, some six to nine in room, bathrooms few and far between. In Vorontsov three will have to cover up to thirty people." Alexander Cadogan rejoiced that he could use the one specifically assigned to Anthony Eden, while Sarah Oliver was extremely glad that her father allowed her to use his private bathroom. "[B]ut if you were a spectator along the bedroom corridors here about 7.30 in the morning," she wrote to her mother, "you would see 3 Field Marshals queuing for a bucket! And really some Field Marshals will not go into a bucket!"[27]

The guests at Yalta encountered a new culture that they found difficult to grasp. "The place is heavily guarded with Russian soldiers, and we have to carry our identification cards everywhere," wrote Anna Boettiger in her diary on the day after her arrival. "We were asked to produce them every 25 feet and Kathy [Harriman] would explain in Russian where we were going and why. We found we could not go all the way to the beach. One excuse given us was that mines still wash up on the beach and sometimes explode. . . . Then we found we could not go to the little village which adjoins to the palace and where the people lived who looked after the grounds." The president's daughter might have been surprised to learn that this was also how the Muscovite court treated foreign ambassadors back in the sixteenth and seventeenth centuries.[28]

When the first American and British ships sailed into Sevastopol harbor in the last week of January 1945, they were virtually quarantined by Soviet officials. Five Soviet ships staffed by NKVD officers were deployed in the area. Two NKVD agents dressed as sailors were added to the signals group that maintained communication with the Allied ships. Shore visits by Allied naval personnel were allowed only in small groups between 8:00 a.m. and 6:00 p.m., and a checkpoint was established on Graf Square, to which Allied sailors were taken on Soviet ships. There were twenty-five shore patrols, each consisting of two soldiers. The American and British officers must have felt themselves more prisoners than visitors. That was certainly true of the Allied air force personnel, who were kept in virtual imprisonment at the Sarabuz air base until they complained to their hosts: to defuse the situation, they were treated to a Russian opera in Simferopol.

In Sevastopol Allied sailors asked for the location of places of entertainment and liquor stores. "The female agents from among the support staff were instructed with special care," noted the report submitted to Beria (and later forwarded to Stalin and Molotov) on January 27 by General Sergei Kruglov, the commanding NKVD officer of the Crimean "special zone." Kruglov listed three main goals of his operation in Sevastopol: to stop the Allies from planting agents on Soviet territory; to identify intelligence officers among the Allied naval personnel; and to prevent "provocations and other anti-Soviet manifestations on the part of hostile elements" during shore visits by Allied sailors.[29]

Encounters with open-minded and, by wartime standards, well-equipped and well-dressed Allied soldiers might have provoked questions among ordinary Soviet citizens. Official propaganda offered ready explanations for apparent Soviet inadequacies, including wartime destruction and the exploitative nature of the capitalist West, whose elites prospered at the expense of ordinary workers and peasants. But that was the official line: any contact with the West could sow doubt among impoverished Soviet citizens. This threat had to be dealt with, and security measures for the Yalta Conference had as much to do with concern for preventing free communication between Allied personnel and ordinary Soviet citizens as it did with the actual security of conference participants.

If the guards who policed the border between Soviet citizens and their government's guests were visible, those guarding the boundary between Soviet reality and the pre-Soviet past in the minds of Soviet citizens were harder to detect. "We're having a hell of a time finding out about the pre-revolutionary history of this part of the coast, as the Soviets seem very reticent on the subject," Kathleen Harriman wrote from Yalta. Before the conference began and security was tightened, she had a chance to travel to the city of Yalta to meet the sister of Anton Chekhov, who had spent the last years of his life in Yalta. Kathleen was impressed by the eighty-three-year-old lady, "charming and full of life" and "thrilled to be meeting some Americans." But even Maria Chekhova shied away from talking about the pre-Soviet past. She preferred not to discuss what had happened during the German occupation. Kathleen was puzzled: "The natives who work around the place here at Livadia don't seem to know anything either—they are certainly old enough!" They were also old enough to know better than to talk about the past with foreigners: an unguarded comment might easily lead to arrest and imprisonment.[30]

On the road to Yalta, looking at the "guard of honor" lining the road, members of the Western delegations did not know what to make of it. Why waste manpower on theatrics when the Soviets were engaged in a major struggle on the German front? The soldiers belonged to the 290th Novorossiisk special rifle regiment of the NKVD, one of four regiments of internal troops sent to the Crimea to guard the conference. Before being assigned to guard the road, the NKVD troops were used to clear the area of "anti-Soviet elements." Altogether, according to secret-police reports submitted to Stalin, the security forces and NKVD troops checked the identity of 74,000 inhabitants of the area and arrested 835 suspicious-looking individuals.

The members of the Allied delegations were unaware of these extensive preparations. Nor did they realize that the idea of a "guard of honor" was not necessarily of Russian provenance. The Soviets were in fact copying their former allies, the Nazis. Molotov later remembered that when he had visited Hitler in Berlin in 1940, "a guard of honor stood along the rail line all the way from the [German] border to Berlin."[31]

4

THE RED HOST

When Viacheslav Molotov boarded the Sacred Cow to greet the president, he informed him that Stalin regrettably could not meet him personally, as he was not yet in the Crimea. As was so often the case with Soviet pronouncements, this was not in fact true. Stalin was already settled in his residence near Yalta, and Molotov routinely reported to him by telephone on the arrival of the Allied delegations. For now, the dragon was watching the Argonauts from a distance, without betraying his own location or intentions.[1]

On the eve of the conference, Lavrentii Beria informed his boss that a special train had been prepared for his journey from Moscow to the Crimea. It was rare for Stalin to travel even within his own country, and on this occasion special arrangements were made to ensure the security of the train. High-frequency telephone lines were made available to the head of the Soviet state in Kharkiv, Zaporizhia, and Simferopol, the major cities through which the train would pass on its way to the Crimea. Stalin's eleven-carriage armored train followed a route that had been devastated by recent fighting. From his window he saw what any traveler would have seen at the time: near-total destruction of the land and depletion of its human resources.

Major Arthur Herbert Birse of the British military mission in Moscow, who took the same route a few weeks before, wrote in his memoirs: "Stations all down the line consisted of temporary log cabins; towns and villages had been particularly wiped out; whole forests seemed to have been mown down by gunfire. I wondered where the people who crowded round the train at wayside stations lived." "We saw enough war damage to last me a lifetime," wrote Kathleen Harriman, who also traveled by train. "My God, but this country has a job on its hands just cleaning up," she added in a letter home.[2]

Outbound trains were routinely delayed in stations for long periods until incoming trains had passed. Two-track lines were reduced to a single track, so that the whole journey took three days and nights, with most of the time spent at bombed-out stations. Naturally, Stalin did not have to endure the privations of other travelers on the Moscow-Crimea route. Ensconced in one of four carriages inherited from the tsar's train, he avoided the inconveniences of run-down trains with no food service or even tea—an experience to which high-ranking Soviet officials and foreign diplomats were not immune.

Ivan Maisky, the deputy people's commissar for foreign affairs and former Soviet ambassador to London, who had a compartment of his own in a diplomatic coach headed for the Crimea, had to survive on a food package handed to him in Moscow by a Foreign Ministry official. The attendant could offer only boiling water, but no tea, and the bedding he got was gray—a tradition that persisted on Soviet trains until the fall of the USSR. One of the two restrooms was closed, and there was no water in the sink in Maisky's compartment. It was cold, and on the last night before his arrival in Simferopol, the electricity failed, forcing Maisky and his colleagues to light candles.[3]

If these were the conditions of travel for foreign diplomats and high Soviet officials, one can only imagine how ordinary Soviet citizens fared. It was not the war alone that created such difficulties. Two decades of the Soviet experiment had left the country with little more in the way of rail transportation for its leader than the tsar's old carriages.

Stalin had chosen as his headquarters Yusupov Palace in Koreiz, a village between Livadia and Alupka. In Soviet times it was generally known as Koreiz Palace. Under Beria's supervision construction workers built a bomb and gas shelter with a concrete ceiling 2 meters thick and a 1-meter sand cover. It could withstand the direct hit of a 500-kilogram bomb and was much stronger than Roosevelt's bomb shelter at Livadia.

The Soviet dictator had at his disposal two Red Army Air Force airplanes and ten aircraft for delivering mail. A high-frequency telephone system and a Baudot telegraph connected him with the military fronts and various locations in the Soviet Union, and an automatic telephone station of the type that had been installed at Livadia provided communications with the heads of the Allied delegations and Crimean airports and seaports. The maintenance and security of telephone communications was the responsibility of eight companies of special communications units of the NKVD, which assigned one soldier to every kilometer of telephone cable. The airspace above the Crimea was protected by 244 airplanes and antiaircraft units stationed around Yalta, which had at their disposal 300 antiaircraft and machine guns.[4]

Stalin probably chose Yusupov Palace as his residence because of its convenient location between the British and American headquarters, but there was an interesting symbolism in that choice. It was from the dock at Koreiz that the last representatives of the tsar's family had left Russia for exile in April 1919, most likely with the help of Winston Churchill.

Before the Bolshevik revolution, the palace had belonged to Prince Felix Yusupov, an alumnus of Oxford, a St. Petersburg playboy and benefactor of the poor who was the heir to an immense fortune. He was fantastically rich and well connected. Yusupov was married to one of the tsar's nieces, Irina, and allegedly had a long-lasting homosexual relationship with another member of the royal family, the tsar's cousin, Grand Prince Dmitrii. It was together with Dmitrii that Yusupov had assassinated one of the most hated symbols of the old regime, Grigorii Rasputin, the monk-confidant of Tsarina Alexandra. Yusupov had killed Rasputin in December 1916 at his other palace, on the Moika River embankment in St. Petersburg, in order to save the tsar's family from further discredit and Russia from imminent collapse. Only a few months later, in February 1917, Nicholas II had abdicated the throne, and Russia as Yusupov knew it had ceased to exist. Yusupov and his wife gathered up Rembrandt paintings and family jewels from their palace in St. Petersburg and found a temporary safe haven at their villa in the Crimea.

After the Bolshevik takeover of St. Petersburg in October, even the Crimea was unsafe. Prince Yusupov later recalled a visit to his palace by revolutionary sailors: "They called themselves 'naval cavalry,'" he wrote in his memoirs. "A terrified servant came to tell me that they were demanding food and wine. I went into the courtyard. Two of the sailors dismounted and came to meet me. They had degenerate and brutal faces; one wore a diamond bracelet, the other a brooch. Their uniforms were stained with blood. They said they wanted to speak to me in private, so I took them to my room after sending the rest of the band to the kitchen for refreshments. . . . Suddenly one of them asked me if I was really the man who had murdered Rasputin, and on receiving my reply they both drank to my health, declaring that that being the case neither my family nor I had anything to fear from them."[5]

If Yusupov's role in Rasputin's assassination won him a brief reprieve, his Romanov relatives had no such protection. Headed by the family matriarch, the Dowager Empress Maria, Nicholas II's mother, numerous members of the extended Romanov family found refuge in their Crimean palaces of ai-Todor, Dulber, and Harax. With the arrival of the Bolsheviks, they were placed under house arrest. The tsar, together with his immediate family, was executed in Yekaterinburg in July 1918, and the arrival of the Germans in the spring of that year may well have saved the lives of the remaining Romanovs. By the end of the year, the Germans had left, and the Bolsheviks were slowly but surely approaching the imperial family's safe haven in the Crimea. By the spring of 1919, it was obvious that the remaining Romanovs could survive only by fleeing.

They were helped in that enterprise by their relative King George V of England, who acted on the initiative of his mother, Queen Alexandra, a sister of Empress Maria and a frequent guest at Livadia. The British government sent

HMS *Marlborough* from Constantinople to Yalta to collect the empress and other members of her family. Winston Churchill, then secretary of state for war and a strong promoter of military intervention against Soviet Russia, must at the very least have been aware of the plan.

On April 7, 1919, the dreadnought *Marlborough* picked up Empress Maria, members of the Romanov family, and Felix and Irina Yusupov at the pier near Koreiz. A few days later in Yalta harbor the passengers last heard the Russian imperial anthem sung publicly in their honor. "Another ship," Yusupov wrote in his memoirs, "left Yalta just before we did; on board her were the Crimean officers, en route to join the White Army. The *Marlborough* had not yet weighed anchor; standing in the bow, the Empress watched the ship pass by. Tears streamed down her cheeks as these young men, going to certain death, saluted her."[6]

In February 1945 Yusupov Palace became the headquarters of a new Russian ruler who possessed powers that the tsars could only have dreamed of. The path to power followed by Joseph Dzhugashvili, who adopted the revolutionary alias Stalin (man of steel), could hardly have been more different from those of its former owners. He was by turns an aspiring Georgian poet, a young seminarian, a disciple of clandestine Marxist circles, a conspirator and mastermind of acts of revolutionary violence, a Siberian political prisoner, a virtuoso of bureaucratic maneuvering, the organizer of the Great Terror, and, finally, the iron dictator who managed to mobilize his country in the face of imminent annihilation by the Nazi military machine.

Born in 1878 to a cobbler who wanted his son to follow in his footsteps, Stalin gained an education thanks only to the persistence and devotion of his mother. Ketevan Dzhugashvili enrolled her son at the age of ten in a theological school in his native town of Gori. A peasant woman born into serfdom, she wanted her son to become an Orthodox priest. The decision cost her dearly, as Stalin's alcoholic father withdrew all financial support from his wife and son. The schooling was in Russian, a language that the young Joseph learned extremely well but spoke with a strong Georgian accent to the end of his life.

Dzhugashvili graduated first in his class, obtaining a scholarship to the Orthodox Theological Seminary in Tbilisi. He excelled there as well, even becoming a published poet, but quit the seminary after five years before final exams, as neither he nor his mother could afford the increased tuition fee. Instead of becoming an Orthodox priest or a Georgian nationalist poet—his verses, written in Georgian, protested the obligatory use of Russian in a Georgian seminary—Stalin embarked on the road of Marxist revolution, adopting internationalism as an article of his Bolshevik faith.

Stalin was attracted to Marxism by the writings of Vladimir Lenin, and in

1898 he joined the Russian Social Democratic Labor Party—the precursor of the Bolsheviks. His first arrest by the authorities came in 1902, at the age of twenty-three, after he organized mass strikes and riots at the Rothschild-owned oil refinery in Batumi. He was sent to Siberia but escaped soon after arrival—a pattern that would be repeated—and returned to conduct revolutionary activities in the Caucasus. Stalin joined the Bolshevik faction of the Social Democrats, led by Lenin. His specialty became bank robbery and protection rackets, with the proceeds going to the party coffers. To this he added journalism, switching from Georgian to Russian and becoming the first editor of the Bolshevik newspaper *Pravda* in 1912.

In the same year Lenin, whom Stalin had known since 1906, suggested that he write a programmatic article outlining Bolshevik policy on the question of nationalities in the Russian Empire. Stalin, who occasionally traveled abroad on party business but did not know any foreign languages, accomplished the task with the help of one of his future victims, the Bolshevik publicist and propagandist Nikolai Bukharin. *Marxism and the National Question* appeared in print in 1913, turning Stalin overnight into a Bolshevik authority on the issue and making him a natural choice for people's commissar for nationalities in Lenin's first Bolshevik government, formed in November 1917.

Stalin assumed more power in the last years of Lenin's life, as the Bolshevik leader needed him to offset the influence of Leon Trotsky on party and state affairs. In the long and complicated intraparty feud of the 1920s, Stalin emerged victorious, first removing Trotsky from the Politburo, the ruling body of the Bolshevik Party, and exiling him and then turning on his former allies in the struggle with Trotsky, beginning with Bukharin. He became a master of intrigue, displaying characteristics that help explain his subsequent achievements in the international arena. Stalin had enormous power over people. He could charm them when necessary and shower them with gifts and attention when his plans required it. He excelled at pitting one group against another, with neither suspecting him of anything but good intentions. By 1934, having eliminated opposition in the Politburo, Stalin emerged as sole leader of the Communist Party.

Switching from intrigue to brute force, Stalin unleashed a wave of terror against party officials associated in one way or another with his former opponents in the Politburo. The rule of terror as an instrument of the revolutionary struggle had been close to Stalin's heart since his days as a Bolshevik bank robber and racketeer in the Caucasus, but mass terror was not his invention. It had been encouraged and freely practiced by Lenin, who unleashed repressions against the "enemies of the revolution" and representatives of the "hostile classes." Stalin's contribution was to turn the terror against his own party and dramatically enlarge its scope. Like Ivan the Terrible, who massacred rival aristocratic clans, Stalin went after what he perceived as political clans, arresting party and government officials and members of their families on suspicion of having colluded with purged members of the establishment.

Stalin's rule of terror culminated in the Great Purge of 1937–38, which claimed hundreds of thousands of innocent lives. Millions ended up in the Gulag, the system of "correctional labor camps" established by decision of the Politburo in the summer of 1929 and expanded dramatically during the Great Purge. Most of the political prisoners in the vast empire of concentration camps were not former party, government, or secret-police officials. Instead, they were people who had belonged to non-Bolshevik political parties before and during the revolution, well-to-do peasants, former officers and soldiers of the imperial army, and representatives of non-Russian ethnic groups, whose loyalty to the regime Stalin considered questionable. This was his way of preparing for the coming European war and getting rid of the "fifth column," the perceived enemy agents in the revolutionary ranks who, in his opinion, had sealed the fate of the Spanish Civil War.[7]

Like any dictator, Stalin was obsessed with his own personal safety, especially when he had to leave Moscow. In his report on conference preparations, Beria informed him that his security detail, headed by General Nikolai Vlasik, would be reinforced by 100 additional agents and a 500-man special regiment of NKVD troops—this on top of 4 NKVD regiments, 1,200 agents, a motorcycle detachment of 120 men, and 50 specially selected officers already assigned to provide security for conference participants. The buildings housing heads of delegations were encircled by two lines of patrols during daylight hours and three at night.[8]

Whom did Stalin have to fear so deep behind Soviet lines? His victims, whom he regarded as potential enemies of the regime, were many. In the Crimea Stalin had good reason to be vigilant. By the late 1930s he was no longer satisfied with targeted repressions of political leaders and members of particular social and ethnic groups that he suspected of disloyalty. After the German invasion, he ordered forced deportation of entire nationalities that he thought capable of collaborating with the enemy. After the return of the Red Army to temporarily lost territories, the deportations were extended to those ethnic groups that Stalin considered guilty of collaboration with the Germans. The Crimean Tatars—the indigenous inhabitants of the Crimea, who made up close to a quarter of its population—became one of the main victims of that policy.

The deportation of "anti-Soviet elements" from the Crimea began immediately after the Soviet recapture of the peninsula in the spring of 1944. In April and May of that year, Beria informed Stalin and Molotov of the results of the NKVD hunt for German collaborators in the Crimea. The numbers of those arrested in NKVD sweeps were unusually high, reaching six thousand by early May 1944. This was due to the extremely high incidence of "spies" and "anti-

Soviet elements," designations applied to members of the Tatar self-defense units that were formed by and collaborated with the German occupation regime. Beria reported that some twenty thousand Crimean Tatars had deserted the Red Army and joined German military formations. These figures were false, as the report multiplied the actual number of deserters by forty, but they served as the basis for wholesale accusations of collaboration. They were concocted in order to justify a decree, signed by Stalin on May 11, 1944, ordering the deportation of all Crimean Tatars, including women and children, to Uzbekistan and other remote parts of the USSR.

The order was executed on May 18–20, 1944, when close to 200,000 Crimean Tatars were herded onto railway cars and deported. Much smaller numbers of Crimean Greeks, Armenians, Bulgarians, and Germans, also accused of collaboration with the Nazis, followed the Tatars into exile. Altogether Stalin deported more than 225,000 residents of the Crimea, many of whom did not survive the ordeal. Close to 28,000 of the Crimean Tatars deported to special settlements in Uzbekistan, Kazakhstan, and remote parts of Russia died of hunger and disease within the first eighteen months after deportation. The rest were not allowed to return to the Crimea until after the collapse of the Soviet Union. The devastation witnessed by Roosevelt and Churchill on their way to Yalta was not only the result of German barbarism, but there is no evidence that they knew that at the time—the official Soviet announcement of the deportations came more than two years after the event.[9]

The question of resettling the Crimea after the expulsion of the Tatars gave Stalin a tool to punish one more nationality: Soviet Jews, who found themselves victims of a fierce anti-Semitic campaign in the last years before the dictator's death. One of the accusations leveled against the leaders of the Jewish community in the USSR was that of conspiring to take over the Crimea. On February 2, 1944, a year before the Yalta Conference and a few months prior to the Soviet recapture of the peninsula, Solomon Mikhoels, a prominent Jewish actor and head of the government-sponsored Jewish Anti-Fascist Committee, signed a letter to Stalin and Molotov proposing the creation of a Soviet Jewish republic in the Crimea. Traumatized by the Holocaust and facing hostility toward Jewish returnees in recently liberated areas of the USSR, Soviet Jewish leaders were looking for ways to establish a Jewish state in the European part of the Soviet Union.

The Crimea was one possible location of the new autonomous polity. Another was the Saratov region on the Volga River, from which the communist authorities had deported the Soviet German population back in 1941. When Mikhoels and other members of the committee first approached Molotov with their proposal, he advised them to put their ideas in writing and opted for the Crimea, considering it unsavory to settle Jews in former German areas. The

Crimean Tatars had not yet been deported from the peninsula, but that, apparently, was only a matter of time, as the Soviets had begun resettling Tatars from the Black Sea regions as early as 1942. Back in the 1920s Stalin had himself promoted the idea of Jewish settlement in southern Ukraine and the Crimea, where a number of Jewish enclaves were established at the time. Before the war there were close to sixty-five thousand Jews in the Crimea. Those who did not leave the peninsula before the German advance shared the fate of their brethren in other parts of the USSR occupied by the Nazis and perished in the Holocaust.

Plans to create a "Jewish California," as the Jewish Crimean project was occasionally referred to at the time, given the unusually warm (by Soviet standards) Crimean climate, were used by the Soviet authorities to rally support for the Soviet war effort in the United States. Mikhoels discussed the idea with representatives of American Jewish organizations during his trip to the United States in the latter half of 1943, and Soviet intelligence services mentioned the plan in their effort to gain the confidence of Jews working on the Manhattan Project. Some proposed that the Crimean Jewish project should be invoked to obtain U.S. funds for postwar reconstruction of the Crimea, but Stalin found the idea ridiculous and would not discuss it with Roosevelt at Yalta.

During the Great Purge of 1937, Jews were not specifically targeted as an ethnic or religious group. Unlike Poles, Germans, Ukrainians, and other Soviet nationalities whose major cultural centers were outside the USSR, their loyalty to the Soviet regime was not questioned by Stalin, despite his deep-seated anti-Semitism. That changed completely with the creation of the state of Israel in 1948 and its support by the Jewish community in the United States. With the Germans exiled, the Poles resettled, and the Ukrainians and Belarusians "reunited" within the borders of the USSR, the Jews emerged in Stalin's imagination as a new fifth column in the coming war with American imperialism.

The "Crimean affair," a criminal investigation directed against the main promoters of Jewish settlement in the Crimea, was used to unleash an unprecedented attack on the Jewish community in the USSR. The media campaign went hand in hand with the arrest and trial of Jewish activists, and with summary executions. In January 1948 secret-police officers killed Solomon Mikhoels, staging the assassination as a motor accident. Solomon Lozovsky, a deputy people's commissar for foreign affairs at the time of the Yalta Conference, was accused of advising Mikhoels on the Crimean issue. He was arrested, put on trial, and executed along with thirteen members of the Jewish Anti-Fascist Committee in August 1952. "No one is untouchable," one of Stalin's interrogators told his victim in the Crimean affair.[10]

Terror had become a prime instrument in establishing Stalin's power over people, including members of his closest entourage. Even Molotov, Stalin's right-hand man at Yalta, had to pay a high price for his original support of plans for a Jewish Soviet Socialist Republic in the Crimea. In December 1948, at the outset of the anti-Semitic campaign, Stalin ordered the arrest of Molotov's wife, an ethnic Jew and old Bolshevik, Polina Zhemchuzhina. She was accused of assisting Mikhoels with his Crimean project, which was now deemed a manifestation of Jewish nationalism and a brainchild of Zionist circles in the United States. Among other accusations leveled against Zhemchuzhina was her presence in a Moscow synagogue on March 15, 1945, at a service for victims of what would later become known as the Holocaust. Molotov was forced to divorce Zhemchuzhina, who was sent to the Gulag, from which she was released only after Stalin's death in 1953.

Molotov was the last member of Stalin's entourage who would dare to disagree with the Soviet dictator. By the end of the war, he had reached the limit of what Stalin would tolerate in terms of independent thinking. In early December 1945, while on vacation in the Caucasus, Stalin sent a telegram to Beria and select members of his inner circle, stating that "Molotov does not cherish the interests of our state and the prestige of our government; all he wants is to achieve popularity in certain foreign circles." Stalin added that he did not trust people close to Molotov (clearly hinting at Zhemchuzhina) and could not regard him as his first deputy. It was a dramatic fall from grace, and one that Western participants in the Yalta Conference could hardly have imagined ten months earlier, when he was regarded as a powerful hard-liner who was preventing a more liberal Stalin from taking a more sympathetic position.[11]

The Tatars were deported from the Crimea for alleged collaboration with the Nazis, while the Soviet Jews in the USSR who survived the Holocaust were decimated on the pretext that they had tried to take the Tatars' place on the Soviet Riviera. Stalin was reluctant to leave any borderlands in the possession of ethnic and religious minorities—a major feature of his nationality policy. By now, Stalin's youthful allegiance to Georgia was long gone, replaced by imperialist instincts and logic. He therefore considered the southern borders of the USSR much safer after the deportation of the Crimean Tatars and hoped to apply the same technique of forced resettlement and deportation to secure his western borders.

The new Soviet borders, whose legitimacy Stalin wanted the Allies to recognize at Yalta, came into existence as a result of the Molotov-Ribbentrop Pact, signed by the Soviet foreign commissar with Germany's Joachim von Ribbentrop in Stalin's presence in Moscow on August 23, 1939. The Molotov-Ribbentrop Pact unleashed the Second World War by giving Hitler the green light to attack Poland without having to fear a war on two fronts. In exchange for Soviet neutrality, Hitler was prepared to consign significant parts of Eastern Europe to the

Soviet Union, allowing Stalin first to annex Western Ukraine and Western Belarus, which were part of the Polish state, and then to take over Lithuania, Latvia, and Estonia, as well as the Romanian province of Moldavia.

By the fall of 1940, Stalin found himself in possession not only of sizable new territories but also of a multiethnic and multicultural population that he was eager to terrorize and move around in order to secure social and national cohesion. He began mass deportations of potentially "harmful" political and social elements soon after taking control of the area, but the German invasion of June 1941 interrupted his plans. Now, with the Red Army firmly in control of the temporarily lost territories, he could return to his original ideas.

Stalin's push, in the months leading up to Yalta, for recognition of the Soviet borders established by the Molotov-Ribbentrop Pact, his plans to recover Russian imperial losses in the Far East, and his desire to secure a Soviet sphere of influence in Eastern Europe were presented to the Allies as part of a search for security. His thinking was influenced not only by geostrategic considerations, which his Western counterparts regarded as legitimate, but also by a complex brew of the most incendiary ideas shaping world politics in the first half of the twentieth century—those of empire, nationality, and social revolution.

Stalin's insistence that the Allies recognize the new borders created by the Soviet Union's annexation of Western Ukraine, Western Belarus, and the Baltic states had clear strategic underpinnings, but it also reflected a desire to recover territories lost by the Russian Empire during the revolution. The same was true of Soviet territorial demands in the Far East, where Stalin was determined to recover southern Sakhalin, which the imperial regime had lost in the Russo-Japanese War of 1904–5, and establish control over the Kurile Islands, some of which had belonged to Russia before 1875. At the time of the revolution, the Bolsheviks managed to avoid the complete disintegration of the Russian Empire only by recognizing the importance of the national factor in revolutionary politics and restructuring the former empire along ethnic lines. By creating what some historians have called an "empire of nations," the Soviet leadership was able to present its drive for the return of lost territories, and even the expansion of the former empire, as a defense of the right of its constituent nations to live in one state with their brethren.

If after the revolution the Bolsheviks had supported the national awakening in the non-Russian republics, by the time of the Second World War ethnic Russians had resumed their dominant role in the hierarchy of Soviet nations, and non-Russian nationalism was persecuted at home. In the international arena, however, the "age-old" desire of the Ukrainians and Belarusians to live in one state was used as justification for the Soviet annexation of parts of prewar Poland, Romania, and Czechoslovakia. Indeed, on the surface there was no more devoted supporter of Woodrow Wilson's principle of national "self-determination" than Joseph Stalin, who justified the annexation of new territories in the course of the Second World War in terms of the self-determination of national minorities in Eastern Europe.

Stalin's "national" thinking was congruent with his revolutionary vision and rhetoric. The idea of world revolution advanced by the Bolshevik regime in the early 1920s never materialized, but the Soviets continued to encourage the development of local cultures in their parts of Ukraine, Belarus, and Moldavia, hoping that the example of national revival under their rule would encourage irredentist tendencies among national minorities in the young states of Eastern Europe and inspire proletarian revolutions. By the 1930s the Soviets had abandoned such hopes and curtailed or even crushed national revivals in their border republics, but the outbreak of the Second World War presented Stalin with an opportunity to once again export proletarian revolution across the Soviet borders.[12]

Since the time of Napoleon, the political and social status quo in Europe had never been so seriously challenged by a single revolutionary power as it was in the final stages of the Second World War. In the years leading up to Napoleon's invasion of Russia in 1812, Russian journals were full of anecdotes about the French emperor's uneducated and uncultured generals. Now it was the turn of the Western Allies to be shocked by the manners of those who ruled the new revolutionary empire. The palatial venue of the negotiations at Yalta underscored the difference between Joseph Stalin and his forebears.

Not only did the Romanovs, Hohenzollerns, and kings and queens of the British royal house of Saxe-Coburg-Gotha belong to the same educationally, culturally, and politically exclusive club of European royalty, but many were related by blood. They knew perfectly well what each stood for and had in mind when they exchanged notes or met for conferences. That was not the case at Yalta in 1945. If in Britain in 1917 the royal family merely changed its name from Saxe-Coburg-Gotha to Windsor, the transformation in the former realm of the Romanovs was much more profound.

At the time of the Yalta Conference, both Britain and the United States were ruled by their own brand of aristocrats. Winston Churchill was a descendant of the famous Spencer family, which gave England a number of prominent public figures and politicians. Like Churchill, Franklin Delano Roosevelt was a descendant of Henry Spencer, the first Earl of Sunderland—a fact not lost on either of them. More important in the American context was FDR's distant relation to President Theodore Roosevelt and his marriage to the president's niece, whom he had met at a White House reception. At Yalta, Roosevelt and Churchill, alumni of Massachusetts's Groton and London's Harrow boarding schools, respectively, were about to meet the son of a drunken Georgian shoemaker who had dropped out of an Orthodox seminary.

Differences in upbringing, educational background, and political experience of the leaders at Yalta were also reflected in their delegations. Anthony Eden was the very image of a British gentleman in appearance, speech, and manners. A graduate of Eton and Oxford, where he studied Oriental languages, Eden was a descendant of an ancient landowning family and the son of a baronet. Edward Stettinius was typical of the breed of American entrepreneurs who made it big in Roosevelt's administration. The son of a partner in the J. P. Morgan and Co. banking house, he attended the exclusive Pomfret School in Connecticut before going to the University of Virginia, where he studied for four years but did not bother to get a degree. Viacheslav Molotov was the son of a provincial shop clerk. Young Molotov's subversive activities and exile in Siberia prevented him from graduating from the St. Petersburg Polytechnic, where he spent two years before the revolution. A skillful party bureaucrat, Molotov did not speak any foreign languages. He became people's commissar for foreign affairs in 1939, replacing the polished diplomat Maxim Litvinov, whose Jewish background made him unfit in Stalin's eyes to negotiate with Hitler.

The experienced "Russia hands" in the U.S. and British diplomatic services who accompanied their bosses to Yalta had a long tradition of treating cultural differences between the two sides as proof of the former's inferiority. Most British diplomats and Foreign Office experts could not see the Soviets as fully European—it was customary to suggest that they displayed Oriental features, torn between extremes of humanity and cruelty. They presumably inclined toward tyranny, possessed a peasant mentality, were disorganized, and could work only in short bursts of frantic activity. "The Russian temperament," wrote Sir Archibald Clark Kerr, the British ambassador in Moscow, "still finds sustained exertion distasteful." Occasionally the treatment of the Soviets as inferior Slavs gave way to their castigation as Jews, resulting in a curious blend of Orientalism, anticommunism, and anti-Semitism. Alexander Cadogan, for example, offended by Soviet accusations that the British were involved in secret negotiations with Germany, noted in his diary in January 1944: "This is quite monstrous. We tell the Russians everything and play square with them. They are the most stinking creepy set of Jews I've ever come across."

Even lower on the British (or, for that matter, American) list of inferior peoples were the non-Slavic nationalities of the Soviet Union. Averell Harriman, upset by the form of Molotov's request for American loans on the eve of the Yalta Conference, attributed it to the doings of a member of the Soviet State Defense Committee, Anastas Mikoyan, "who had not divorced himself from his Armenian background." "He starts negotiations on the basis of 'twice as much for half the price,'" Harriman cabled to the State Department, "and then gives in, bit by bit, expecting in the process to wear us out." He later recalled that the Soviets became furious when they bugged the British embassy in Moscow and heard comments about their inferiority. He noted: "[I]f we had been tapped they would have known that [the head of the U.S. military mission in Moscow, General John] Deane and I were saying the same things about them. . . . Stalin was particularly touchy on that subject." As it turns out, the American embassy was bugged too.[13]

If the British and American diplomats explained differences in racial or cultural terms, the Soviets did so in class terms. They viewed the American and British politicians and diplomats as representatives of a single imperialist group. For Stalin, Molotov, and Andrei Gromyko, the young Soviet ambassador to Washington, they were first and foremost class enemies—capitalists looking for ways to outsmart naive and honorable representatives of the working class. The Allied leaders' political culture and democratic rhetoric were nothing but a cover for their criminal intentions. Gromyko commented on the style of Western diplomats: "They may strangle one, but they will do so wearing kid gloves, with a smile, almost gently."

Molotov found it easier to deal with the Nazi functionary Rudolf Hess, whom he teased during his visit to Berlin in November 1940 about the Nazi Party's lack of a political program and membership rules—the Bolsheviks had theirs officially published and disseminated—than with representatives of the Western democracies. The Soviet leadership distinguished between the Americans and the British, but only on a personal level, not on that of ideology or culture. "I knew them all, the capitalists," Molotov remarked in conversation with an acquaintance in the late 1960s, "but Churchill was the strongest, the smartest among them."

Stalin also considered Churchill the most dangerous, and saw both Churchill and Roosevelt as representatives of the same imperialist camp. In conversation with Milovan Djilas of the Yugoslav Communist Party on the eve of the Allied invasion of Normandy, Stalin said: "Perhaps you think that just because we are the allies of the English we have forgotten who they are and who Churchill is. They find nothing sweeter than to trick their allies. During the First World War they constantly tricked the Russians and the French. And Churchill? Churchill is the kind who, if you don't watch him, will slip a kopeck out of your pocket. Yes, a kopeck out of your pocket! By God, a kopeck out of your pocket! And Roosevelt? Roosevelt is not like that. He dips in his hand only for bigger coins. But Churchill? Churchill—even for a kopeck."[14] In Stalin's mind, there was a degree of difference between Churchill and Roosevelt, but they were both capitalist thieves.

PART II

A WARRIORS' SUMMIT

It is the Russian Army that has done the main work of ripping the guts out of the German Army.

WINSTON S. CHURCHILL

5

REUNION OF THE BIG THREE

It was close to midnight on February 3 when Averell Harriman and Charles Bohlen, having made their way across three cordons of Soviet security patrols, one with specially trained dogs, finally reached their destination—Koreiz Palace. At ten minutes past midnight they were received by Viacheslav Molotov. The meeting that had been so long in preparation had no prearranged agenda, even for the first day. The goal of the midnight visit was to agree at least on the first agenda item and to make plans for the day ahead. It turned out to be an unexpectedly easy task.

When Harriman informed his host that President Roosevelt wanted to begin with a discussion of military affairs, he was told that Marshal Stalin intended to start with Germany, looking first at military and then at political issues. Harriman asked whether Stalin could visit Roosevelt at Livadia the following afternoon before the start of the official session, which was scheduled to begin at 5:00 p.m. Molotov consented—Stalin had proposed that all conference sessions be conducted at Livadia "for the convenience of the president." Molotov said he thought the conference should go on for about five or six days, and Harriman concurred. He invited Stalin to dinner at Livadia on Roosevelt's behalf the next evening. It was probably the shortest notice ever given by one head of state to another, but it was accepted with gratitude.

From the American perspective, the conference was starting on a high note, with the wishes of the two main actors fully coinciding. The British would go along, as Harriman knew from conversations on Malta. He could go to bed fully satisfied. On January 18, before leaving Moscow for the Crimea and then Malta, he had met with Molotov and told him that, in his opinion, the president would want to discuss at the forthcoming conference the treatment of Germany, the formation of the United Nations, the situation in Poland, and the war in the Pacific. It appeared that on the first question, at least, the Soviets were prepared to accommodate their guests.[1]

Molotov's meeting with Anthony Eden, who visited his Soviet counterpart at noon on the following day, did not proceed quite so smoothly. Eden accepted the understanding reached by Molotov and Harriman the night before on the length of the conference, the location of the meetings, and the first item on the agenda—military affairs and the treatment of Germany. He added that the international peace organization and the situation in Poland should also be discussed. Both items were on the American agenda as well. Molotov had no objection to adding the United Nations to the conference agenda, but Poland was a different matter. Now that the country had been liberated, he said, it should be left alone. This was his way of conveying the message that Poland was already under Soviet control, and British interference was not welcome.

Eden had little choice but to drop the matter for the time being. The conversation turned tense again when Molotov mentioned matter-of-factly that the Western Allies had of course already consulted with one another, which would make the work of the conference much easier. According to the Soviet protocol of the meeting, Eden hastened to assure Molotov that there had been no negotiations on Malta, and that the president and the prime minister had only had a car trip together, a distinction that was lost in translation. One can only imagine Eden's frustration. Not only had meaningful discussions been sabotaged by the president, but Molotov was convinced they had actually taken place.[2]

A few hours after Eden left the Soviet compound, Stalin paid Churchill a visit at Vorontsov villa. The meeting went well: in the words of the British interpreter, both leaders "seemed glad to meet again, and they talked like old friends." "[W]e had an agreeable discussion about the war against Germany," Churchill wrote in his memoirs. They did not discuss contentious political issues, focusing instead on the situation in the theater of war. The meeting was a prelude to the discussion of military affairs, with each man sending out feelers to understand the other's position.

The game of deception and diplomacy had begun. With million-strong armies finally closing in on Nazi Germany, the stakes could hardly have been higher. Churchill was eager to find out the main goal of the Soviet winter offensive, which had begun along the entire eastern front on January 12. He asked what the Soviet strategy would be if Hitler left Berlin and moved to a place such as Dresden. Stalin said that his armies would follow him there. Churchill's objective was probably to learn whether the Soviet commanders would treat the capture of Berlin, which the British regarded as an ultimate war prize, as their main objective even if the German leadership left the capital.

Stalin was upbeat about the offensive, which had brought Soviet forces to the Oder and situated them a mere 70 kilometers from the Nazi capital in less than three weeks. He was dismissive about the quality of Hitler's strategists and did not think much of the German troops his armies had faced in the course of their advance on Berlin. This patronizing treatment of Hitler and his generals may well have been intended as a warning that if the Allies did not act quickly and decisively, the Soviets would finish off the Third Reich on their own, and the spoils of war would go to them. Stalin told Churchill that the Soviet leadership wanted decisive Allied action on the western front to stop the eastward transfer of German divisions. He thought it desirable for the Allies to capture the Ruhr, cutting off Germany's last source of coal to trigger an economic collapse ahead of the military one.

Churchill invited Stalin to the Map Room his team had set up at the villa. It was the object of the prime minister's pride. Before the conference, the British embassy informed the Soviet hosts that "Mr. Churchill hopes that this map room may be adjacent to his private quarters at Yalta, and it should be so placed as to be accessible to President Roosevelt when wheeled in his chair." The Soviets were asked to install electric outlets at intervals of 4 to 6 inches in order to provide power for special lamps that the British would bring to Yalta. An officer flew in ahead of the main delegation to set up the room, and everything was now ready for the briefing.

The prime minister would not travel without his Map Room. The first time he brought it to Washington, in December 1941, it so impressed the president that FDR ordered a similar room to be set up on the ground floor of the White House. In the months leading up to Yalta, the president's deteriorating health reduced the frequency of his visits to the Map Room, which also served as a communications center. His daily briefings on military affairs would now take place in Admiral McIntire's office, while the president's doctor worked on his sinus problems. Churchill, however, as a former army officer, remained deeply involved in the day-to-day business of the war and was clearly happy to show off his mastery of the situation to Stalin. He reported personally on the situation on the western front.

Field Marshal Harold Alexander, the British commander of Allied troops in Italy, briefed Stalin on the situation in the Mediterranean. Major Arthur Herbert Birse, who interpreted for Churchill and Alexander, thought that Stalin was impressed by the report. He was clearly interested in what he heard, and he commented that a German offensive in Italy was highly unlikely. Stalin suggested outflanking the German defenses in the Apennines and sending Allied divisions from Italy through the Ljubljana Gap to Central Europe, where they could join the Soviet armies near Vienna. At this point, Churchill must have regretted his insistence on military consultations on Malta. An attack on the Ruhr, located in the British sector of the western front, had long been advocated by the British military in preference to the American plan of a coordinated attack along the entire front. An offensive from the south toward Austria was another British obsession.

Now, with Stalin advocating an attack on the Ruhr and proposing an offensive through the Ljubljana Gap, Churchill might well have been able to convince the Americans to go along, but it was too late to reopen the debate. After stormy discussions on Malta, both British plans were rejected, and Churchill had been forced to concede defeat. Field Marshal Alexander remarked to Stalin that he did not have the troops to undertake such an operation, and that it was too late in any case. Churchill had to agree with his military commander. "It cost him nothing to say this now, but I made no reproaches," wrote the prime minister in his memoirs about Stalin's proposal. Churchill simply said, "The Red Army may not give us time to complete the operation."

Stalin must have known from his numerous agents in the West about the British position; otherwise it would be hard to explain why he suggested these assaults at the meeting with Churchill but made no mention of them to Roosevelt an hour later. All that Churchill could say concerning Allied intentions on the western front was that an offensive was planned for February 8 along the northern sector. Stalin, who later told Marshal Georgii Zhukov that his main military goal at Yalta was to convince the Allies to start an offensive on the western front, did not show his feelings. He was hoping for a major offensive along the entire western front to be undertaken as soon as possible, not a small-scale attack on one of its sectors.[3]

The opening of the Yalta Conference took place at 5:00 p.m. on February 4 in the rectangular ballroom of Livadia Palace. The room had witnessed its first public function in the fall of 1911, a full-dress ball given by the tsar in honor of the sixteenth birthday of his eldest daughter, Grand Duchess Olga. It was an emotional moment for the young princess, who entered the ballroom on the arm of Nicholas II. She wore a pink silk and chiffon dress and was surrounded by members of the tsar's immediate family, grand dukes and duchesses, foreign royalty, and officers of the guard in their splendid epaulets. Having turned sixteen, Olga was eligible for marriage, and plans were discussed for her to marry a Romanian prince so as to strengthen Russian influence in the Balkans. There were no royalty in evidence on February 4, and the military brass gathered in the ballroom did not wear epaulets. Stalin's gilt marshal's shoulder pieces and his gold Hero of the Soviet Union medal were the only echoes of tsarist finery in the room.[4]

Stalin, as host, was the first to speak, but he used the occasion to ask Roosevelt to open the conference. The president accepted the honor, stating modestly that there was nothing in law or tradition that allotted him that role, and that it was only by chance that he had opened the meetings in Teheran. A rumor circulated in the American delegation that the president got a "great kick" out of the invitation, as he was the youngest of the three leaders gathered at Yalta. Once again Roosevelt managed to maneuver himself into a leading position as chair of the plenary sessions, which allowed him to influence the conference agenda and the course of the discussions, and to assume the role of arbiter and judge in relations between Churchill and Stalin.[5]

This first American success was no accident. It resulted from the strategy that Roosevelt adopted in his correspondence with Stalin after the Teheran Conference of 1943 and the position he took at his first preconference meeting with the Soviet leader, which ended only a few minutes before the start of the plenary session. Stalin had gone to Livadia for a private meeting with Roosevelt immediately after visiting Churchill. Film footage shot by a U.S. Army Signal Corps cameraman shows his party arriving in two cars and the marshal in his greatcoat, accompanied by men in military uniforms, saluting the guards before entering the palace. He was greeted at the entrance by a crowd of photographers.

President Roosevelt sat on a plush couch behind an inlaid table, awaiting his guest in what used to be the tsar's audience room. Stalin was accompanied by Molotov and Vladimir Pavlov, Stalin's favorite interpreter; Roosevelt by Charles Bohlen, who served as his interpreter and adviser. Bohlen later recalled that the meeting reminded him of a reunion of old friends. "Smiling broadly the President grasped Stalin by the hand and shook it warmly. Stalin, his face cracked in one of his rare, if slight smiles, expressed pleasure at seeing the President again." The two leaders sat together on the couch for a discussion that lasted almost an hour instead of the planned thirty minutes. It was there that Robert Hopkins, the son of Roosevelt's principal adviser, took the famous picture of the two men in discussion behind an inlaid table.

Stalin basically had the same message for the president as for the prime minister: the Red Army was fighting the Germans on the Oder; it had captured Silesia, and if the Allies took the Ruhr and the Saar region, cutting off the Nazis' coal supplies, the economic collapse of Germany could actually precede its military demise. Stalin clearly wanted an Allied offensive on the western front. He made no mention of a possible Allied attack from the south to join the Red Army near Vienna (as he had with Churchill), aware that the Americans opposed the idea.[6]

Roosevelt's immediate goal at the meeting was to secure Stalin's approval for establishing direct communications between the headquarters of General Dwight Eisenhower and the Soviet military command. With the Allied armies getting ever closer and some Anglo-American aviation bombing targets in the Red Army's zone of operations, American military commanders had asked Roosevelt to raise this question directly with Stalin. This turned out not to be a problem. Stalin acknowledged the importance of a military-to-military liaison. He showed no dissatisfaction with the president's response to his question about military plans on the western front: a modest offensive was scheduled for February 8, to be followed by another one four days later, but the real blow was to be delivered in March, when Allied troops would cross the Rhine.

In his first meeting with Stalin since December 1943, Roosevelt wanted more than to solve specific problems of military coordination. He wished to renew their personal relationship and revive the atmosphere of trust established in Teheran. He shared with Stalin his disgust at the German barbarism he had witnessed on his journey to Yalta. He supported the return to the Soviet Union of everything that had been stolen by the Germans. He was also in favor of letting the Soviets absorb some German territories and proposed that others could also be annexed by the Netherlands. Roosevelt said he wished Stalin would repeat the toast from Teheran about executing German officers. Churchill had been outraged by the toast, in which Stalin had proposed a mass execution of fifty thousand members of the German officer corps in order to prevent the revival of German militarism.[7]

FDR was trying to win the trust of his host by reminding him of an episode where he had deliberately distanced himself from Churchill. Roosevelt made no secret of their disagreements over strategy on the western front. He told Stalin that the British were insisting on an offensive on their section of the front in Holland, but the Americans, with four times as many divisions in Europe, were entitled to formulate alternative plans. FDR also mentioned differences over zones of occupation in Germany: the British were insisting that the Americans take the southwestern part of the country, where they would have to establish lines of communication through France, while the Americans wanted northwestern Germany with its Baltic ports, through which they could supply their troops. "The British," remarked Roosevelt, "were a peculiar people and wished to have their cake and eat it too." That statement would probably have surprised many of Roosevelt's compatriots, especially readers of *Time* magazine, which claimed in its issue of February 5 that on his way to the Big Three meeting the president had taken a book of essays, *The English Spirit*, by Alfred L. Rowse, who declared "something more than pride in, a deep love for, English things." "It is likely to inspire much the same emotion in President Roosevelt," stated the *Time* article.[8]

Over the first few days of the conference, in order to mollify Stalin and gain a free hand at later negotiations, Roosevelt avoided personal meetings with Churchill, as he had done on Malta. The British, horrified, enlisted the help of Harry Hopkins. But even Hopkins had a hard time getting through to the president. On the evening of February 3, when Anna Boettiger visited his room, Hopkins was "in a stew." "He gave me a long song and dance," she wrote in her diary, "that FDR must see Churchill in the morning for a longer meeting. . . . [He] made a few insulting remarks to the effect that after all FDR had asked for this job, and that now whether he liked it or not, he had to do the work, and that it was imperative that FDR and Churchill have some prearrangements before the Big Conference started." The scene had little impact on Anna, who pointed out that "this course might stir up some distrust among our Russian brethren," a line often taken by the president himself.[9]

Roosevelt's efforts to gain Stalin's trust did not translate into blanket opposition to British initiatives. On the contrary, during their first meeting, he tried to convince Stalin to accept an idea strongly advocated by the British—the creation of a separate zone of occupation for France in Germany. Roosevelt portrayed himself as a reluctant convert who wanted to restore French power so that in a possible future conflict the French army of two hundred thousand could hold back the Germans until the British had had a chance to mobilize their own forces. The president was playing a double game, trying to sell Stalin on a British project even as he ridiculed the British and their protégé General Charles de Gaulle. "De Gaulle compared himself with Joan of Arc as the spiritual leader of France and with [Georges] Clemenceau as the political leader," Roosevelt ironically told Stalin. The Soviet leader remained skeptical with regard to French participation in the occupation of Germany, but he agreed on de Gaulle and could not help noticing Roosevelt's anti-British remarks. The president's reference to the British wanting to "have their cake and eat it too" made it into the Soviet protocol of the meeting.[10]

Stalin appreciated the cordial reception that Roosevelt offered him at Livadia. He demonstrated his own brand of grand gesture with the delivery the next morning of a lemon tree bearing two hundred lemons. This was his response to Roosevelt's comment during their meeting that a good martini had to have a twist of lemon (the president treated Stalin to a dry martini). Stalin was playing host and clearly enjoying the role. Later in the conference, he would seek to enhance his negotiating power by denying gifts and attention to some guests while showering them on others. Roosevelt remained in his good books to the end, but Churchill, the thief who would "slip a kopeck out of your pocket," did not.[11]

The opening session of the conference established a routine for subsequent plenary sessions: unlike the meetings of foreign secretaries and other working groups, they were always attended by the Big Three and served as a forum for their discussions. They began late in the afternoon, generally at four, and continued into the early evening, and they were always chaired by Roosevelt.

The round table that had been placed at the end of the long rectangular room gave more or less equal space to each of the three delegations. The first echelon of delegates, seated around the table, was backed by second and often third echelons of advisers, who sat behind their leaders. Although different people occasionally took seats around the table, depending on the agenda of a particular session, places were always reserved for the foreign ministers and interpreters. The interpreters were the State Department's old "Russia hand"

Charles Bohlen, Major Arthur Herbert Birse of the British military mission in Moscow, and Deputy People's Commissar for Foreign Affairs Ivan Maisky, who was assisted on occasion by Molotov's aide and interpreter, Vladimir Pavlov.

Also usually present were Admiral Leahy, Justice Byrnes, Alexander Cadogan, and Andrei Vyshinsky, another Soviet deputy people's commissar for foreign affairs; Andrei Gromyko and Fedor Gusev, the Soviet ambassadors to Washington and London, respectively; Sir Archibald Clark Kerr, the British ambassador to Moscow; and Averell Harriman, the American ambassador to Moscow. The ambassadors also took part in the foreign ministers' luncheons. Starting on the second day of the conference, these were held before the plenary sessions and dealt with the tasks referred to the foreign secretaries by the Big Three.

The interpreters, along with other members of the delegations, took notes of the plenary sessions, foreign secretaries' meetings, and private conversations between the leaders, but there was no official record of the Yalta Conference. Attempts to coordinate the records of various delegations were minimal, amounting only to agreement on the recorded time of the beginning and end of sessions. Most of what we know today about the conduct of the conference and the actual words spoken by participants comes from the extensive records of conversations prepared by Charles Bohlen, Alger Hiss, and H. Freeman Matthews, which were first published in 1955. The Soviets began to publish their much less detailed records in the 1960s, while British records still remain in manuscript, although an abridged version of the transcripts was published in a limited number of copies after the conference. A comparison of records compiled by members of various delegations not only gives one a better grasp of what actually happened at Yalta but also frequently reveals misunderstandings on the part of the interpreters and their superiors.

As the Big Three gathered in the ballroom of Livadia Palace, members of their delegations had an opportunity to assess their capabilities as diplomats and their styles as negotiators. The British were eager to find out how much FDR's deteriorating health was affecting his leadership capabilities. President Roosevelt was among the first to enter the ballroom, brought in by wheelchair. The transfer to the chair behind the conference table was a cumbersome procedure, and he made a conscious effort to be done with it before most of the participants had entered the room. The cameramen had an unspoken agreement not to take pictures that would betray his physical deficiency, and the world had no idea how badly handicapped the leader of the most powerful country on earth really was.[12]

"There was a good deal of talk after dinner about the conference at the President's house," wrote Lord Moran in his diary that first night. "Everyone seemed to agree that the President had gone to bits physically. . . . He intervened very little in the discussions, sitting with his mouth open. If he has sometimes been short of facts about the subject under discussion his shrewdness has covered this up. Now, they say, the shrewdness has gone, and there is nothing left." Cadogan, on the other hand, found the president in better shape physically than the last time he had seen him, but "woollier than ever."[13]

Churchill, by contrast, seemed as active and energetic as ever. By the beginning of the first session, he had fully recovered from his illness on Malta. Throughout the afternoon, he was an active participant in the discussions, often taking the initiative to present the joint American-British position on a number of issues. He was prepared to plunge into discussion, putting to use his extraordinary rhetorical skills, polished by decades of parliamentary debate. His frequent interventions made a strong impression on some members of the British delegation, such as Admiral Andrew Cunningham, who referred in his memoirs to one of Churchill's long speeches during the first day of negotiations as a "brilliant discourse."

Others were less enthusiastic. Kathleen Harriman wrote that members of the American delegation thought the prime minister was going on too long. "At Checkers," she wrote, "the P.M. holds forth and everyone else listens, but here there's just general conversation." Charles Bohlen, noting that Churchill's arguments were "always well reasoned," pointed out that they were "often based on emotional appeal" and had little impact on Stalin. Cadogan told Churchill's doctor, Lord Moran, after the first day of deliberations that Stalin apparently disliked the prime minister's "theatrical style" and looked at him with disapproval when he gestured grandly "with tears in his eyes." Cadogan's boss, Anthony Eden, was even less kind. "Churchill liked to talk," he noted in his memoirs, "he did not like to listen, and he found it difficult to wait for, and seldom let pass, his turn to speak. The spoils in the diplomatic game do not necessarily go to the man most eager to debate. Stalin sometimes led him on."[14]

Ultimately it was Stalin who emerged as the dominant figure on the first day of the conference. Cadogan found him in good health and even better spirits. "Stalin looks well—rather greyer—and seemed to be in very good form," he wrote to his wife from his room in Vorontsov Palace. Members of the Allied delegations who were meeting him for the first time, like Major General Laurence S. Kuter of the U.S. Army Air Force, were surprised "to hear him speak in a very moderate volume in a voice which while not high, had no forceful tones." Kuter recalled later that Stalin "spoke with simple unquestionable finality. In watching and listening to him, one had no doubt that he was the authority, but also no clue in his stature or deportment to how he obtained that authority."

Kuter's remarks were echoed by those of a more experienced observer of Stalin's negotiating techniques. "He never wasted a word. He never stormed, he was seldom even irritated," wrote Anthony Eden. "Hooded, calm, never raising his voice, he avoided the repeated negatives of Molotov which were so exasperating to listen to. By more subtle methods he got what he wanted without having seemed so obdurate." Eden considered Stalin the toughest negotiator he had ever encountered in his long diplomatic career and claimed that if he had to pick a negotiating team, Stalin would be his first choice.[15]

Stalin certainly cut an impressive figure, but not all credit should be ascribed to his negotiating skills. Thanks to Soviet espionage, he was unusually well prepared for his meeting with his wartime allies. On January 23 and 28, Soviet spymasters had briefed Stalin on the American and British negotiating strategies. The second briefing would have included a discussion of British plans, for on the previous day the People's Commissariat of State Security (NKGB), a body responsible for foreign political intelligence, had forwarded to Stalin a full Russian translation of the British authorities' memo outlining their delegation's strategy at the conference.

The document, obtained by the NKGB station in London, gave Stalin a complete account of Churchill's intentions. It spelled out the British position on all major issues, from the partition of Germany to Poland, as well as the voting formula to be adopted in the United Nations Security Council and the proposed membership of Soviet republics in the UN. If he wished, Stalin could read a memorandum on the partition of Germany, complete with Anthony Eden's covering letter of November 27, 1944, and numerous other documents produced by the British Foreign Office in preparation for the Yalta Conference. Stalin knew what questions the British considered important, what they were planning to raise themselves, and what would be raised by the Americans. The Soviets were also aware of points of agreement and discord between the Western Allies and of their intended line of approach to Stalin on all these issues.

War-era espionage turned out to be the most successful operation ever undertaken by the Soviet intelligence services. Secret documents were stolen by the hundreds, and the perpetrators managed to go undetected for years. One day in 1944 London police officers noticed two suspicious-looking men, one of whom was holding a carryall. The police patrol asked the man to open the bag, which they thought might contain stolen goods. There were no valuables or household items in the bag; instead, it was full of papers that the police found of no interest. Police allowed the men to continue their meeting. The man with the carryall was Guy Burgess, an employee of the Foreign Office press department. His companion was Boris Krotenschield (alias Krotov), an NKGB officer working under Soviet diplomatic cover. The papers were secret Foreign Office documents that Burgess had borrowed from other departments and was now delivering to the NKGB for photoreproduction. In the first half of 1945, he supplied hundreds of such documents to his handlers; of these, 389 were classified as "top secret."[16]

Guy Burgess was one of the "Cambridge Five," a group of idealistic young

Cambridge graduates who believed that by assisting the Soviets they were helping to stop fascism and advancing the cause of world revolution. All members
of the group—Burgess, Donald Maclean, Harold Adrian Russell "Kim" Philby,
Anthony Blunt, and John Cairncross—joined either the British secret services
or the Foreign Office and were well positioned to supply the Soviets with information about British military and political secrets.

In the spring of 1944 Maclean, who had worked for the British Foreign
Office since 1934, was posted to Washington, where he became first secretary
of the British embassy. He offered a gold mine of information to his Soviet
handlers. As de facto secretary of a joint U.S.-British commission on the political and economic future of liberated Europe, Maclean had access to some of
the most sensitive documents pertaining to the closing phases of the war. He
was able to deliver to his handlers a summary of the discussions between
Roosevelt and Churchill in Quebec City in September 1944 and provided copies of correspondence between Roosevelt and Churchill on issues of keen interest to Stalin. He also reported on disagreements between American and British
commanders about military strategy on the western front.[17]

Pavel Sudoplatov, one of the leaders of the Soviet intelligence effort during
the Second World War, later remembered that the information acquired by the
secret services prior to the Yalta Conference allowed the Soviets to conclude that
the Allies had neither a comprehensive plan for postwar Europe nor a joint
position on the matter, aside from demands (which Sudoplatov considered
naive) that the Polish and Czechoslovak governments in exile be returned to
power. The Soviets therefore assumed that a flexible position on their part,
allowing some of the leaders of the London-based governments in exile to
return to their countries and obtain posts in the Soviet-formed governments,
would ensure a "fair division of influence" in liberated Europe. Stalin's spymasters were busy assessing the personal characteristics of Soviet counterparts
at the negotiating table—the kind of material that, according to Sudoplatov,
interested Stalin more than intelligence information per se. The Big Three
arrived in Yalta with very different ideas and goals, assumptions about one
another's objectives, and information.[18]

6

THE WINTER OFFENSIVE

F ranklin Delano Roosevelt was upbeat and optimistic in his opening statement on the afternoon of February 4. He started by thanking Stalin for his
hospitality and stressed that trust and understanding were growing among the
Allies. "When the Red Armies advanced into Germany 25 kilometers," he said,
"it was doubtful whether the Soviet people were more thrilled than those of the
United States or those of Britain." A new stage in Allied relations was about to
begin, and Churchill later nostalgically recalled: "We had the world at our feet.
Twenty-five million men marching at our orders by land and sea. We seemed
to be friends."[1]

The first plenary session of the Yalta Conference was unusual in that it
focused exclusively on military affairs. Its participants therefore included military commanders, many for the first and last time. Churchill was accompanied
by his favorite general, Field Marshal Harold Alexander; the competent chairman of the Chiefs of Staff Committee, Field Marshal Alan Brooke (privately
extremely critical of his colleagues); the head of the Royal Air Force and a strong
advocate of the British tactic of bombing Germany by night, Air Chief Marshal
Charles Portal; and the first sea lord, Admiral Andrew Cunningham, who had
overseen the surrender of the Italian fleet in September 1943.

The American military delegation was led by the U.S. Army chief of staff,
General George Marshall, the architect of the dramatic wartime expansion and
modernization of the U.S. Army and chief strategist of the war. He was accompanied by his chief of naval operations, Fleet Admiral Ernest King, always skeptical of his British allies, and by the assistant chief of staff of the Army Air
Force, Major General Laurence S. Kuter, the only U.S. military commander,
apart from Leahy, to write a memoir about his experiences at Yalta. The two
Allied delegations had their formal and informal heads who led their colleagues
in the diplomatic battle. Kathleen Harriman wrote that the rumor was that
Marshall and Portal stood out among the commanders.[2]

The Soviet military delegation did not include any top commanders. Georgii Zhukov, Konstantin Rokossovsky, Ivan Konev, and Aleksandr Vasilevsky, whose names were well known in the West, were busy leading a major Soviet offensive on the German front. The delegation was led by the first deputy chief of the Red Army General Staff, General Aleksei Antonov, a gifted military strategist. Antonov was assisted by the deputy commander of the Soviet air force, Air Marshal Sergei Khudiakov, and the forty-year-old people's commissar of the Soviet navy, Admiral Nikolai Kuznetsov, both of whose careers had benefited from Stalin's purge of the Red Army high command in the late 1930s. The Yalta Conference represented their first and only opportunity to meet and size up their Western counterparts.[3]

Political advisers were excluded from the first meeting of the conference. Churchill had let Roosevelt know that he would bring mostly military commanders, as he "felt that the meeting should be small since military secrets would be discussed." The president decided to exclude Harry Hopkins and James Byrnes, who, though he was director of the Office of War Mobilization, came to Yalta mainly as a political adviser. On the handwritten list of American invitees, Byrnes's name was placed in parentheses with the note "on polit." and marked with a cross. This meant that Byrnes would be invited to join the meeting once the discussion of "military secrets" was over and political matters came to the fore. Forty-five minutes after the start of the meeting Byrnes received a message inviting him to come to the conference room and wait at the door to be asked in. He stood there for forty-five minutes to no avail, then, angry and humiliated, retired to his room.

Later that day Byrnes vented his frustration to the president's daughter. "Fire was shooting from his eyes," Anna wrote in her diary. "At home he could and did consult with the military, but here he was not considered important enough. He had told the president he had come along to work and not for the ride." Byrnes threatened to turn down the president's dinner invitation and order a plane home, but Harriman was able to persuade him to change his mind. "If you go home you'll be a busted man," he warned Byrnes, who harbored presidential ambitions. "The American people will look on you as a man who has behaved badly." Byrnes chose not to mention this episode in his memoir, *Speaking Frankly*. "This was an extreme case of conference fever—as I used to call it," wrote Harriman, "of everyone wanting to go to every meeting because it made them feel important."[4]

In the game of wartime diplomacy, the player with the most troops on the ground had the loudest voice. Stalin was in a particularly strong position at Yalta because of the swift advance of the Red Army. While the Western Allies were recovering from the Ardennes debacle and still planning their crossing of the Rhine, approximately 600 kilometers from Berlin, Soviet forces had launched an impressive winter offensive that brought them within striking distance of the Nazi capital. Since January 12, when the offensive began, the Red Army had broken through German defenses and advanced up to 500 kilometers in some sectors. It had established bridgeheads on the west bank of the Oder, a mere 70 kilometers from Berlin. The Soviets had destroyed forty-five German divisions and captured close to one hundred thousand prisoners.

In his report General Antonov claimed that the Red Army had begun its offensive more than a week ahead of schedule in order to relieve the Allied divisions fighting off the German onslaught in the Ardennes in what came to be known as the Battle of the Bulge. The offensive had originally been scheduled for the end of January, but to help the Western Allies recover from the German counterattack, Soviet troops had begun operations in bad weather rather than wait for better conditions later in the month. Admiral Kuznetsov wrote in his memoirs that "[i]t was appropriate to remind the Allies that our offensive helped save the American armies from defeat." That was the line taken by the Soviets at the negotiating table as they tried to seize the initiative in the deliberations.[5]

When Churchill expressed his gratitude for the "massive power and successes of the Soviet offensive," Stalin was quick to take credit. He said that he "understood that neither Churchill nor Roosevelt was asking him directly for an offensive," and that he "respected that tact on the part of his allies, but he saw that such an offensive was necessary to the allies. The Soviet command had launched the offensive even before the intended date. The Soviet government considered that to be its duty, the duty of an ally, although it had no formal obligations on that score." Stalin added that he "mentioned it only to emphasize the spirit of the Soviet leaders who not only fulfilled formal obligations but went farther and acted on what they conceived to be their moral duty to their allies." Churchill and Roosevelt found themselves compelled to thank their Soviet benefactor and to come up with an explanation for why no request had been made for help.[6]

The Soviet offensive, which the General Staff had begun to prepare in November 1944, was originally planned for January 20, 1945. It actually began on January 12, in extremely bad weather. According to Marshal Ivan Konev, the commander of the First Ukrainian Front, which was preparing to attack from its bridgehead at Sandomierz on the right bank of the Vistula, he received an order on January 9 from General Antonov telling him to start the offensive eight days earlier than planned. The reason given to him was an "Allied request" based on the "grave situation that had taken place in the Ardennes." The same reason was given to other commanders of Soviet army groups deployed against the Wehrmacht. Judging by the memoirs of one of them, the commander of the Second Belarusian Front, Marshal Konstantin Rokossovsky, they were surprised by the sudden change of plan but managed to speed up their preparations and start the offensive without waiting for reserves that were still en route. This entailed greater reliance on heavy artillery than originally planned, but the gamble paid off. Bad weather on some sections of the 700-kilometer-long front actually worked in favor of the attacking troops, as the snowstorm made them almost invisible to the Germans.[7]

The problem with Antonov's order was that there had been no Allied request to speed up the offensive. "The battle in the West is very heavy and, at any time, large decisions may be called for from the Supreme Command," Churchill had written to Stalin on January 6. "You know yourself from your own experience how very anxious the position is when a very broad front has to be defended after temporary loss of the initiative. It is General Eisenhower's great desire and need to know in outline what you plan to do, as this obviously affects all his and our major decisions. . . . I shall be grateful if you can tell me whether we can count on a major Russian offensive on the Vistula front, or elsewhere, during January, with any other points you may care to mention. . . . I regard the matter as urgent."

This was no request for help but an inquiry about plans, and Stalin acknowledged as much at Yalta. By January 6, Allied forces had stopped the German offensive in the Ardennes, and Field Marshal Montgomery had launched his counteroffensive, which was already three days old. By the time Churchill's message reached Stalin on the evening of January 7, Hitler had ordered the withdrawal of his troops from the Ardennes. Stalin told Churchill that the Red Army would begin a major offensive no later than the second half of January. "We are mounting an offensive, but at the moment the weather is unfavorable," he had told Churchill in a cable sent on January 7. "Still, in view of our Allies' position on the Western Front, General Headquarters of the Supreme Command have decided to complete preparations at a rapid rate and, regardless of weather, to launch large-scale offensive operations along the entire Central Front not later than the second half of January."

Stalin was prepared to present the decision to begin the offensive on the planned date of January 20, or even later, as a favor to the Allies. The answer satisfied Churchill. "The news you give me will be a great encouragement to General Eisenhower because it gives him the assurance that German reinforcements will have to be split between both our flaming fronts," Churchill wrote back, noting that "the battle in the west goes not badly." The matter seemed closed. But the exchange of messages turned out to be the beginning of an elaborate propaganda campaign on Stalin's part.[8]

Judging by the memoirs of Soviet commanders, sometime between January 7 and 9 Stalin decided to advance the date of the offensive to January 12. Scholars continue to disagree on the reason for his decision. Hypotheses range from his desire to capture as much territory as possible before the start of the Yalta Conference to a forecast of warm weather and rain that would make unpaved roads impassable and slow the Red Army's advance. Some believe that the Red Army was basically ready for the offensive by January 10, pointing out that while commanders like Rokossovsky complained bitterly about the change of plan, others, like Konev, later wrote that they had "no intention either to minimize or exaggerate the difficulties this created for us." Zhukov mentioned no difficulties whatever in launching the offensive on the earlier date. It may be that some fronts were prepared before others, and, taking all things into consideration, Stalin decided to pick up the pace. To silence those who might complain about the new date and to boost the morale of his troops, he lied to his generals, citing an Allied cry for help.

It was more than Churchill's telegram that prompted his decision. In the summer of 1944 Stalin had refused to take Warsaw and had allowed the Germans to slaughter the Polish insurgents there despite numerous requests from the Western Allies to help the Poles. He may well have seen an opportunity in the prime minister's request to improve his standing with the Allies, which had been shattered by his failure to support the Warsaw uprising. Three days after the start of the offensive, Stalin explained the logic behind his actions to British Air Chief Marshal Arthur Tedder, Eisenhower's deputy, who was visiting Moscow. "We have no treaty, but we are comrades. It is proper and also sound selfish policy that we should help each other in times of difficulty. It would be foolish for me to stand aside and let the Germans annihilate you; they would only turn back on me when you were disposed of. Similarly it is to your interest to do everything possible to keep the Germans from annihilating me." This reasoning was repeated years later by Molotov, who told a friend: "We didn't let the Germans destroy our allies when Hitler was smashing them in the Ardennes. It was not to our advantage." It is not impossible that Stalin actually believed he had saved the Western Allies. It is beyond any doubt that he now wanted payback.[9]

At the first plenary session of the Yalta Conference, Stalin asked the Western leaders and their commanders what else he could do to help. He referred to the request made to him by Air Chief Marshal Tedder, who had asked whether "it would be possible to keep the Hun [Hitler] anxious . . . from mid-March to mid-May." At the time, he had promised tactical attacks by a limited number of Soviet troops. Now he modified that answer, saying that the offensive would continue as long as the weather permitted. That was the Red Army's original strategy, but now it was presented as a favor to the Allies.

Stalin was pushing for more requests. Eventually Admiral Cunningham took the bait. "He went on to say that the Allies had only to ask and the Russian Army would do all in its power to help," Cunningham wrote in his memoirs. "But nobody really took up the point that we had only to ask Russia for what we needed, so when it came my turn to speak on the U-boat situation, I finished by telling Stalin that he would make a striking contribution to the war at sea if the gallant Red Army would push on and capture Danzig." "This suggestion," Cunningham naively continued, "seemed to cause general hilarity, and the Prime Minister laughed heartily." To Roosevelt's follow-up question of whether Soviet artillery could reach Danzig, Stalin responded that it was not yet in range, but he hoped that it soon would be. He was prepared to take the credit for another favor to the Allies once the city fell into Soviet hands. It accounted for 30 percent of German submarine production, a major concern for Allied sea operations.

By portraying himself as a faithful ally prepared to sacrifice his own troops, if not his strategic interests, to help his Western partners, Stalin was establishing a position from which he could ask them for concessions in return. His main goal at the meeting remained that of inducing the Allies to launch a major attack on the western front as soon as possible. This objective was explicitly stated in General Antonov's report. Antonov had also requested that the Western Allies prevent the transfer of German divisions from Italy to the eastern front and that they bomb the German communication centers of Berlin and Leipzig in order to disrupt German supply lines and troop movements.

This gave Churchill an opening for one last attempt to revive the idea of a joint Anglo-American offensive from the Adriatic in the direction of Vienna through the Ljubljana Gap. He suggested that "it was important to find out . . . whether the Allies could be of more help by reinforcing the Eastern Front or by leaving the divisions in Italy, or by moving across the Adriatic into the Balkans." No military commander, including Field Marshal Alan Brooke, followed up on his question. After the bitter fight on Malta over the direction of the next major offensive on the western front, the British military brass decided to toe the line. Stalin, despite raising the possibility of an Adriatic operation at his preconference meeting with Churchill, remained silent. The prime minister was left on his own. The idea of opening a new front on the Adriatic was now officially dead.[10]

The big strategic question that Stalin had to decide at Yalta was whether the Soviet armies should continue their advance to Berlin or stop at the Oder and consolidate their gains. General Antonov gave an impressive account of the Red Army's achievements, but he was short on detail regarding future plans. Field Marshal Alan Brooke recorded in his diary that Antonov "gave an excellent and very clear talk, but not much we did not know." The same impression was shared by Alec Cadogan.

The reality was that even if the Soviets had wished to reveal their plans, they would have had little to say, as they were improvising on the march. Stalin and his commanders continued to debate the issue during their long nightly sessions after the end of conference proceedings. Admiral Kuznetsov recalled that he would arrive at Yusupov Palace at 10:00 a.m. to report on navy operations to

General Antonov, who in turn briefed Stalin on developments on the front at 11:00 a.m. His second daily report would follow around 9:00 or 10:00 p.m. Stalin would then meet with his commanders to discuss the situation and issue orders.[11]

The main problem confronting the Red Army planners was the continuing resistance of the German armies in East Prussia and Pomerania. Before their offensive, the Soviets had managed to deceive the Germans into thinking that the main thrust of their attack would be directed against East Prussia and Hungary, while in fact the main Soviet forces were concentrated on the central sector of the front and attacked in the direction of Berlin. Zhukov became both the beneficiary and the victim of the success of that strategy. Because the Second Belarusian Front, led by Rokossovsky, encountered stiff resistance in East Prussia and Pomerania, it could not continue the offensive with the same speed as Zhukov's First Belarusian Front. On January 25, Stalin had called Zhukov on the secure high-frequency telephone line and urged him to stop his offensive and wait for Marshal Rokossovsky's troops, positioned on Zhukov's right flank, to catch up. But Zhukov had insisted on continuing the offensive, as that would allow him to take the Germans by surprise and cross the Oder without giving them a chance to establish defensive lines along the river. Stalin agreed.

In the course of the war Stalin, who as commander in chief of the Soviet armed forces bore direct responsibility for the successes and failures of the Red Army, learned to listen to Zhukov and his other generals and take their suggestions seriously. His initial disregard of their advice had cost him and the country dearly during the first years of the Soviet-German war. In September 1941, the Red Army lost more than forty divisions and close to half a million men trapped in a German encirclement near Kyiv when, contrary to Zhukov's advice, Stalin had insisted on the continuing defense of the city. He had learned his lesson. Zhukov, who began the war as chief of the Red Army General Staff but was dismissed after the Soviet defeats of June and July 1941, regained the ruler's favor by October of that year. Stalin placed his outspoken commander in charge of the defense of Leningrad and then of Moscow.

As Stalin's deputy and a plenipotentiary of the Soviet high command, Zhukov played a leading or significant role in all the major battles of 1943: the lifting of the siege of Leningrad, the encirclement of the German Sixth Army at Stalingrad, and the Soviet victory at Kursk. In 1944 he conducted a brilliant operation that liberated Belarus and brought Soviet troops into eastern Poland. The next objective was Berlin, and both Stalin and his most trusted military commander wanted the assault to come off without a hitch. On January 27 and 29, before leaving for Yalta, Stalin approved his commanders' plans for an attack on Berlin. The First Belarusian Front under Marshal Zhukov was instructed to cross the Oder on February 1–2, just as the conference was about to begin, and to continue its advance on Berlin, encircling the German capital from the north. The First Ukrainian Front, led by Marshal Konev, was to reach the Elbe by February 25–28 and, attacking from the south, to take Berlin together with Zhukov's forces. The whole operation might be over by the first week of March, before the thaw made the unpaved country roads impassable for the Red Army's armored divisions.

By the time Stalin reached Yalta, he had received a cable from Zhukov begging him for help. On January 30, Zhukov's advance troops had reached the Oder. They crossed it on the march and established a bridgehead on its west bank. The problem was that Zhukov's right and left flanks were exposed to possible German counterattack. His right flank extended 150 kilometers and remained virtually unprotected. Zhukov asked Stalin to order the commanders of the neighboring fronts, Marshals Konev and Rokossovsky, to speed up their advance. But Stalin did not rush to answer this cry for help. There was little he could do to hasten the advance of the Soviet armies in East Prussia. Both the Second Belarusian Front, led by Rokossovsky, and the Third Belarusian Front, led by General Ivan Cherniakhovsky, a thirty-eight-year-old rising star of the Soviet military establishment, were mired in East Prussia, unable to crush German resistance there.[12]

On the first day of the Yalta Conference Soviet newspapers published Stalin's order congratulating the troops of the Third Belarusian Front on capturing the cities of Landsberg and Bartenstein in East Prussia. Landsberg, situated at the crossroads of railway and automobile routes, was an important German defensive bastion. For centuries it had been on the route of Russian armies fighting their Western competitors for control of Eastern Europe. In February 1807 the city witnessed a fierce struggle between Napoleon's Grand Army and Russian imperial troops. In August 1914, at the beginning of the First World War, it was captured by the Russians only to be abandoned a few days later after they suffered a major defeat in the Masurian Lakes region.

In January 1945 the soldiers of the Third Belarusian Front avenged the defeat of 1914 by breaking through German defenses near the Masurian Lakes. That put an end to Hitler's hopes of stopping the Soviet advance where Kaiser Wilhelm's forces had managed to repel the imperial Russian army. The outraged führer fired General Friedrich Hossbach, who was in charge of the Masurian defensive line, but that did nothing to improve the situation. On the night of February 2 the troops of the Soviet Thirty-first Army, led by General Petr Shafranov, captured Landsberg, making headlines by the time the Yalta Conference opened.

Landsberg quickly disappeared from the papers, but the battle for the city was only about to begin. Soon after the surprise capture, the Germans counterattacked, encircling and besieging the city. For the next seven days, through most of the conference, Soviet troops held the city, beating back the German counteroffensive. On some days they had to withstand up to eight successive

German attacks. The besieged Red Army commanders mobilized every soldier at their disposal, including female medical personnel, to fight the enemy. Every German tank destroyed by gunners gained them a military decoration. Young army nurses picked up rifles and fought with particular resolve, less afraid of being killed than of being taken alive by the Germans. After a week of fierce fighting, the German troops were thrown back, ending the siege of the city, but the battle continued in the vicinity.

With the Soviet tank armies concentrated on the central sector of the front, the troops in Prussia had to innovate, using their artillery guns as assault weapons. The casualties were enormous. A gunner from Ukraine, Vasyl Burlay, who had been awarded a military order for destroying a German tank in February, was not so lucky in an open duel with another tank in the following month. On March 4, as he and his crew were rolling their cannon toward the German defenses, they were hit by a shell from a German tank. Burlay was wounded but survived. Many of his comrades did not. This duel took place on the outskirts of Landsberg a month after the newspapers announced the fall of the city. By that time the Soviet supreme commander of East Prussia, General Cherniakhovsky, was dead, killed by enemy fire near Königsberg on February 18. The capital of East Prussia would not fall to the Red Army until April 9. With the Germans continuing to fight on the shores of East Prussia and Pomerania well into the spring, Soviet plans for the winter offensive had to be revised more than once.[13]

After Antonov's presentation, General Marshall described the situation on the western front and outlined Allied plans for the upcoming offensive. Marshall was the first American general to be promoted to five-star rank, becoming General of the Army on December 16, 1944, two weeks before his sixty-fourth birthday. He had been the planner and driving force behind the spectacular expansion of the U.S. Army from a mere two hundred thousand to more than eight million men. Marshall was considered the obvious choice to lead the Allied invasion of France, but Roosevelt wanted to keep him close to the White House. "I didn't feel I could sleep at ease if you were out of Washington," the president told him.

A highly respected military commander whom even the president did not dare to address by his first name, Marshall projected an image of power and competence. "The German bulge in the Ardennes has now been eliminated and the Allied forces have advanced in some areas beyond the line originally held," Marshall reported. "During the last week General Eisenhower has been regrouping his forces and conducting operations designed to eliminate enemy pockets in the southern part of the line north of Switzerland." He outlined the Western Allies' military plans: there would be two smaller operations in February, but no major offensive or crossing of the Rhine before March. "A crossing will be attempted as soon as the river is reached, but it is recognized that ice will make hazardous any crossing prior to March 1," he said.

Marshall's report made a favorable impression on the Western military commanders, but their Soviet counterparts were unimpressed. They could not help but compare their own successes with the modest achievements of their allies. Admiral Kuznetsov later wrote: "He said that the German bulge in the Ardennes was being eliminated and that the Allied forces had reached the line they had held. This meant that they were holding their initial positions and not advancing." Kuznetsov's skepticism echoed the tone of the Soviet press at the time. One newspaper went so far as to suggest that "the Soviet operations at Budapest alone overshadowed in scale everything that had occurred to date on the western front."

Soviet propaganda aside, General Marshall's report convinced Stalin that the Allies were serious about launching their first attacks on the German lines in February but lacked resources for a major offensive until March. He put aside his request that they invade the Ruhr or transfer troops from Italy to the northern coast of the Adriatic and graciously remarked that the Soviet delegates "had explained their desires to the Allies, but that they had learned from the discussions that their desires had already been met."[14]

Stalin called Zhukov on February 6 and told him to halt the offensive and turn his divisions north. Bridgeheads across the Oder were to be extended and protected, but Berlin would have to wait. The decision to stop Zhukov's armies on the Oder was controversial. General Vasilii Chuikov, the hero of Stalingrad and commander of one of Zhukov's armies, later attacked his former superior for not trying to convince Stalin to continue the advance on Berlin. The Germans had no troops to protect the capital, and its fall would have ended the war sooner and saved hundreds of thousands of lives. In his memoirs, Chuikov compared the Soviet operation in East Prussia in January and February 1945 with the actions of Russian forces in the Masurian Lakes region in August and September 1914 but argued that better coordination of the Soviet troops would have ensured their success.

Chuikov's assessment was not shared by Marshal Zhukov, who in turn drew a parallel in his memoirs between the Soviet march on Berlin in 1945 and the Red Army's assault on Warsaw in 1920, when the Red cavalry had advanced too quickly, and lack of coordination between the two Soviet fronts had brought about the defeat of the revolutionary army, with the consequent loss of Western Ukraine and Belarus. Zhukov thought that history might have repeated itself if the Red Army had continued its march on Berlin in February 1945.[15]

It is quite possible that the bitter experience of 1920 informed not only Zhukov's thinking but also Stalin's. The "Miracle on the Vistula," as the Poles called their successful defense of Warsaw, had a direct bearing on Stalin's early career as a military strategist. Serving as political commissar of one of the two

Red Army fronts advancing toward Poland, he ordered his troops to attack Lviv instead of concentrating all his forces on Warsaw, as suggested by the plan approved by the young up-and-coming Soviet commander Mikhail Tukhachevsky. Stalin's desire to earn his laurels as conqueror of Lviv led to military and political disaster, as the Poles seized the initiative and drove back the Soviet troops, first from the gates of Warsaw and then far to the east. Stalin never forgot the humiliation of 1920. In July 1937, at the beginning of the Great Terror, he had Tukhachevsky shot, but he apparently learned his lesson. His army would not make the same mistake twice.

Although Stalin halted his armies' westward offensive in February, Berlin was still ultimate prize. Members of the Soviet military delegation at Yalta made no secret of their plans to take Berlin. At the first plenary session, General Antonov made it quite clear that the main thrust of the Soviet offensive would be in that direction, although he did not mention the city by name. When Roosevelt greeted Stalin on February 4 with the news that he had placed a bet on whether the Russians would take Berlin before the Americans took Manila, Stalin assured him that the Americans would be first, but he did not deny the Soviet desire to reach Berlin.

With the Allies still recovering from the Ardennes debacle, there was no question in anyone's mind as to who would take the German capital first. When Robert Hopkins approached Stalin during the conference and asked permission to join one of the Soviet units so that he might be the first American cameraman to enter Berlin, Stalin agreed. General Marshall had no objection, but the plan fell through because of strong protests from Robert's father, Harry Hopkins. No one doubted that Red Army troops would be the first to enter Berlin. Everyone at Yalta believed that the Soviet capture of the Nazi capital was just a matter of time. It was only later, when General Eisenhower's armies finally crossed the Rhine on March 7, that Stalin tried to deceive his allies, assuring Eisenhower that Berlin had lost its strategic importance. In the meantime he ordered his generals to speed up preparations for the final assault on the German capital.[16]

Stalin may not have achieved his main objective on the first day of the conference—the promise of a major western offensive in February—but his efforts were not entirely in vain. He was active in discussions, asking pointed questions about Allied operations in the west, demonstrating his knowledge of military strategy and tactics, which was far superior to that of either Roosevelt or Churchill, and offering his advice on military issues. Even General Marshall found himself on the spot: he had to engage in guesswork to answer Stalin's question about the number of Allied armored divisions that were to be involved in the upcoming western offensive. While dominating the discussions, Stalin managed to do so in a way that seemed neither pretentious nor obtrusive. He scored quite a few public-relations points with members of the Western delegations.

Cadogan confided to Lord Moran after the meeting that "he feared Stalin would say: we've done our bit, we can't do much more, but that was not what happened. Stalin said the allies had not asked him to commit himself to any military plan. He had done this offensive in a comradely spirit. He meant it for the end of January, but had put it forward because of events on the Western Front. In spite however of the putting forward of the date the offensive had gone better than he expected. Now he wanted the allies to tell him how he could help." For his part, Stettinius was prepared to take Stalin's claims at face value, but he was not sure how to make sense of Stalin's remark that he had started the offensive without a direct request or pressure from the Allies. He eventually assumed that the Soviet leader had been speaking for the record and responding to criticism within the Politburo that he was giving in too frequently to Roosevelt and Churchill.

Stalin's popularity in the West was never higher than at the time of the Yalta Conference. The February 5 issue of *Time* magazine ran his portrait on its cover in homage to the success of the Red Army's winter offensive. "In December, when Rundstedt broke through in the Ardennes, gloom lay heavy on the western Allies," said the article. "Last week, as Joseph Stalin's armies thundered into the eastern Reich, the pendulum was swinging back to rosy optimism. Perhaps once more it was swinging too far."[17]

7

THE GERMAN QUESTION

When the second session of the conference began at four o'clock on the afternoon of February 5, Roosevelt was determined to turn his so far ceremonial chairmanship into something more substantial. He sought to establish the agenda for the upcoming discussion. Since the Big Three had addressed military questions on the previous day, he suggested that the first order of business be approval of the zones of occupation in Germany. What he really had in mind was French participation, an issue that he had introduced during his private meeting with Stalin the day before.

Before anyone could react, Roosevelt passed Stalin a map of Germany with zones of occupation marked on it. Stalin ignored the map and, without directly rejecting Roosevelt's proposal, offered his own agenda. The issues he wanted to be "added" to the president's list included the possible dismemberment of Germany, the establishment of a new government, an understanding of the practical meaning of the term "unconditional surrender," and the payment of reparations. This agenda conformed to what Molotov had presented to his Western counterparts a few hours earlier; it left no room for discussion of the French desire to join the Big Three in the control machinery for occupied Germany.

Roosevelt proposed what looked like a compromise, noting that Stalin's concern could be addressed in the context of a discussion of the occupation zones. But the Soviet leader was not prepared to compromise. He interjected that he wished to find out whether the Allied leaders stood by their earlier statements on the dismemberment of Germany. Stalin now claimed that Roosevelt and Churchill had initially proposed such dismemberment and suggested specific plans: the president had proposed a partition into five states, while the prime minister had suggested two. Stalin noted that at the time he had sided with the president. He also found "feasible" the tripartite division of Germany suggested by Churchill in Moscow in October 1944.

Stalin had in his files proposals submitted by his foreign-policy experts for the division of the country into four, five, and seven states. The Soviet leader was apparently flexible in this regard. What mattered to him was the principle of dismemberment. In the discussion that followed, Stalin manifested his skill as a negotiator. By asking whether "the president or prime minister still adhered to the principle of dismemberment," he presented the Western leaders with the choice of either committing themselves to dismemberment or admitting that they had changed their previous positions and then explaining why they had done so—an embarrassing exercise under any circumstances. Both Roosevelt and Churchill found themselves involved in the discussion of questions that they would have preferred to leave outside the conference room.[1]

On March 5, 1945, exactly one month later, *Time* magazine published a political fable, "The Ghosts on the Roof," written by Whittaker Chambers. In it the former communist sympathizer turned anticommunist crusader claimed that the former owner of Livadia Palace, Tsar Nicholas II, would have complimented Stalin on his accomplishments at Yalta. Indeed, quite a few elements of Stalin's policy toward Europe at the end of the Second World War seemed to have been taken directly from his imperial predecessor. Stalin's territorial changes and acquisitions corresponded closely to the strategic goals formulated by the tsar at the beginning of the First World War.[2]

"[I]t is primarily in Germany that the great changes will take place," the Russian emperor confided to the French ambassador, Maurice Paléologue, on November 21, 1914.

> As I have said, Russia will annex the former Polish territories and part of East Prussia. France will certainly recover Alsace-Lorraine and possibly obtain the Rhine Provinces as well. Belgium should receive a substantial accession of territory in the region of Aix-la-Chapelle; she thoroughly deserves it! As for the German Colonies, France and England will divide them as they think fit. Further, I should like Schleswig, including the Kiel Canal zone, to be restored to Denmark. . . . And Hanover? Wouldn't it be wise to revive Hanover? By setting up a small independent state between Prussia and Holland we should do much towards putting the future peace on a solid basis. After all, it is that which must guide our deliberations and actions. Our work cannot be justified before God and History unless it is inspired by a great moral idea and the determination to secure the peace of the world for a very long time to come.[3]

While Stalin would not have had much time for God, he would have agreed that the proceedings at Yalta should stand the test of history. He too was keen to strive for world peace, and wanted to ensure that Germany would not threaten his dominance of Eastern Europe. To achieve that goal he looked to the same set of instruments as his Romanov predecessor. Nicholas never had a chance to realize his plans, but in 1945 Stalin found himself in complete command of the battlefield. After having lost the First World War, Russia was now a victor, and Stalin fully intended to redress the balance.

Stalin had come to the Crimea in the tsar's carriage, and he had brought a good deal of the tsar's baggage with him. The Russian Revolution was a direct outcome of the First World War, and there was much in Stalin's thinking, and even in his appearance, that originated in that era. The first Soviet song of the Second World War, "The Sacred War," had numerous textual parallels with one of the patriotic songs of the Great War period. Like the tsar, Stalin called himself "supreme commander" and his headquarters *Stavka*, or supreme command, although unlike the tsar, he rarely left his capital. The reintroduction of epaulets and officer ranks in the Red Army was also a throwback to the First World War.

Despite numerous claims to the contrary, it was Stalin who first put the idea of dismembering Germany on the Allied agenda. It was at a most unlikely moment, in November 1941, when German troops were rapidly approaching Moscow, forcing both Allied missions and Soviet ministries to leave the Soviet capital for the city of Kuibyshev (Samara) on the banks of the Volga. On November 21, 1941, with the Germans only 65 kilometers from Moscow, Molotov telegraphed Ivan Maisky, then the Soviet ambassador to London, with the following message: "Stalin thinks that Austria should be separated from Germany as an independent state and that Germany itself, including Prussia, should be divided into a series of more or less independent states so as to provide a guarantee for the peace of European states in the future."

The message was intended for the British communists, but in the same month, on orders from Moscow, Maisky discussed the question of Germany's dismemberment with Anthony Eden. The British foreign secretary did not rule out such a possibility but doubted whether dismemberment alone would solve the problem, as it would inspire German desire for reunification. Churchill turned out to be more open to the idea than his foreign secretary. On December 5, 1941, with the Germans only 25 kilometers from Moscow, Molotov received a telegram from Maisky indicating that Churchill was in favor of the separation of Prussia from the rest of Germany. Like Eden, however, he wanted to avoid any publicity on the matter so as not to strengthen Nazi fighting resolve. The Allies were clearly warming to Stalin's idea.[4]

The battle for Moscow reached a turning point the day Molotov received Maisky's telegram. On December 5, 1941, with the help of fresh divisions brought in from the Far East, where they had been deployed against Japan, the Soviets launched a counteroffensive against the exhausted and freezing German troops. By the time Anthony Eden arrived in Moscow on December 15 to discuss wartime cooperation and a future peace settlement with Stalin, the Red Army had driven the Germans back from Moscow and liberated the cities of Klin and Kalinin (Tver), 85 and 150 kilometers, respectively, from the capital. As Eden was about to learn, Stalin was growing bolder by the minute. For starters, he suggested the transfer of the western part of East Prussia to Poland and a twenty-year Soviet occupation of its eastern part, as a guarantee of German payment of war reparations. Austria was to be restored as an independent state, and the Rhine region would become a separate entity, as would Bavaria. All these measures would weaken Prussia, which would be turned into a "Berlin state."

Eden replied that he was not personally opposed to the transfer of East Prussia to Poland, and he thought it possible to separate the Rhine region and Bavaria from the other German territories. He believed, however, that dismemberment would be sustainable only if achieved by separatist movements on the ground, which should be encouraged; otherwise, an irredentist movement would reunite the country sooner or later. The British government was prepared to consider the possibility of the dismemberment of Germany, but Eden was not in a position to make any commitments until the issue had been discussed by the cabinet. Stalin tried to pressure his guest into accepting the Soviet proposal, but Eden refused to budge. Stalin had no choice but to wait.[5]

The Soviets continued to make plans for the dismemberment of Germany but avoided thrusting the issue on the Allies. It was included on a list of issues to be studied by a special commission created in September 1943 under the leadership of Maxim Litvinov, Molotov's predecessor as people's commissar for foreign affairs and a recent ambassador to Washington. Later that month the commission received a long paper presenting scenarios for Germany's dismemberment into three, four, or seven parts prepared by a group of economists led by a Soviet academic luminary, Evgenii Varga. In subsequent months Litvinov bombarded Molotov with memos advocating dismemberment as the most effective way to prevent future German aggression. He believed, however, that the idea had only limited support in Britain and the United States.

That assessment probably contributed to the Soviet decision not to raise the question at the Moscow Conference of foreign ministers in October 1943. At the time of the conference, Roosevelt and Churchill strongly supported the idea. So did Stalin and Molotov, but they played a different game. At the meeting Molotov indicated that the USSR was open to discussion: he agreed that Soviet public opinion favored dismemberment. Judging by the instructions to the Soviet delegation and Molotov's own remarks at the conference, his main concern was secrecy. The release of any information on negotiations about Germany's dismemberment or the payment of reparations would, in Molotov's opinion, "merely serve to unite the German people further in their war effort and would play into the hands of Hitler."[6]

Most likely it was not Hitler from whom Stalin wanted to keep his plans secret but the German officers in Soviet captivity, whom he used in the propaganda war against the Nazis from the summer of 1943. If the Soviet position became public, there was little chance that the League of German Officers, which began its activities in the fall of 1943 and included some prominent German commanders among its leaders, would continue its collaboration. The league used imperial German symbols in its propaganda, which was directed toward the officers of Hitler's army and called for the reestablishment of the pre-1937 German borders. Stalin did not plan for a socialist Germany at that point in the war and was satisfied for the time being with the conservative ideology of the league's leadership. But the members of the league would have been surprised to learn that their "ally" was planning the dismemberment of their country. The league was a trump card in the game with Hitler and the Allies that Stalin was not prepared to give up.

"As the Big Three faced the supreme question—what to do with Germany?— Joseph Stalin had an ace which Winston Churchill and Franklin Roosevelt could only look at and admire," wrote *Time* magazine on February 12, 1945. "They had nothing like it: a complete organization of German civilians and army officers, known to the German people and ready to move into the conquered Reich if Stalin so wills." It would appear that by the fall of 1943 Stalin had decided on a policy of encouraging Allied plans to dismember Germany without showing his own hand.[7]

In Teheran it was Roosevelt, not Stalin, who had raised the question of the dismemberment of Germany. But once the question was raised, Stalin immediately declared himself in favor. He left it to Roosevelt and Churchill to come up with specific plans. Since Roosevelt had no secretary of state in Teheran to restrain him, and Churchill would not allow Eden to control him, the two leaders gladly indulged themselves in redrawing the map of Europe.

Roosevelt, recalling the German travels of his youth, said that the country had been much happier when it was divided into 107 principalities. Churchill insisted on the need to separate Prussia, the root of all evil, from the rest of Germany. Stalin set about picking winners and losers. He supported Roosevelt's plan of dividing Germany into five states, although he hinted that he would prefer more drastic measures. He did not like Churchill's idea of a Danubian confederation consisting of Bavaria, Austria, and Hungary, which he regarded as a step toward the re-creation of a greater Germany. The issue was eventually referred to the European Advisory Commission, a tripartite body created in London in January 1944 with the task of preparing solutions for the political problems of postwar Europe.[8]

In the late winter and spring of 1944, Maxim Litvinov worked around the clock in Moscow to prepare detailed plans. Litvinov was in favor of dividing Germany into seven parts, with the southern provinces of Saxony, Bavaria, Württemberg, and Baden comprising separate states. Should it prove impossible to convince the Allies to turn those lands into independent polities, Litvi-nov said in a memo to Molotov, they could be united into a federal state with broad autonomy.[9]

In October 1944, during Churchill's visit to Moscow, Stalin decided that the time had come to reintroduce the issue. His strategy remained the same: not to come up with proposals of his own, but to encourage Western deliberation. This time around, the British seemed reluctant to address the question. Anthony Eden pointed out the complexities involved and outlined in broad terms three possible ways of dividing Germany: drawing new boundaries, fol-lowing historical ones, or placing the industrial areas under international con-trol. Churchill was now in favor of the plan proposed in September 1944 by the American treasury secretary Henry Morgenthau, which envisioned not only the political dismemberment of Germany but also its transformation into an agricultural country. He thought this would open European markets to British industrial goods and advocated that German heavy equipment be moved to the USSR, especially Western Ukraine, which in his opinion had suffered most.

Stalin must have been glad to obtain British support on German reparations, but he wanted Churchill to stay focused on the question uppermost in his mind—that of dismemberment. Churchill, for his part, was willing to discuss the transfer of German territory to Poland and the USSR, as well as international control of German industry, but he said that he had not given sufficient thought to the question of how to carve Germany into separate states. He repeated his support for the isolation of Prussia but would not give details. Stalin kept asking pointed questions, and eventually Churchill and Eden caved in.

On a map produced by their Soviet host they showed how they proposed to divide Germany into three parts: Prussia; a zone of international control that would include the industrial heartlands of the Rhineland, the Ruhr, and the Saar region; and the Austro-Bavarian state, which would include the provinces of southern Germany. Stalin praised the plan and even said that three parts was a better idea than five, which Roosevelt had suggested in Teheran. This was of course a complete reversal of the position that Stalin had taken there. The Brit-ish plan ran counter to the advice of Stalin's own experts, who suggested a seven-state model, and one can only conclude that his new priority was to encourage the British to push ahead with dismemberment, since any plan was better than no plan at all.[10]

It worked only to a degree. After leaving Moscow, Churchill got cold feet. On the eve of the Yalta Conference he was of two minds. On the one hand, the dismemberment of Germany and especially the separation of Prussia was his long-standing objective, one that not coincidentally had also been British gov-ernment policy since the Teheran Conference. On the other hand, he was fac-ing increasingly vocal opposition from members of his own cabinet. Eden had always been cautious, if not outright skeptical. In the summer of 1944, those opposing dismemberment found a strong advocate in the person of the secretary of state for war, Sir P. James Grigg, who argued that forced dismemberment could provoke resistance and require the British to make a commitment of additional manpower and resources that they could not afford.

Churchill wrote to Eden on January 4, 1945, that he doubted "whether any final decisions will be reached" at the upcoming conference. He believed that the consequences of the policy and the reaction of the British public were unpredictable. In view of the upcoming parliamentary election—general elections had been suspended for the duration of the war and would have to be conducted as soon as it was over—he did not want to make himself a hostage to changing circumstances. "It is a mistake to write out on little pieces of paper what the vast emotions of an outraged and quivering world will be either immediately after the struggle is over or when the inevitable cold fit follows the hot." The election was very much on Churchill's mind as he headed for Yalta, and the treatment of a defeated Germany might well become an issue on which it would be fought. The prime minister was hedging his bets.[11]

By the time of the Yalta Conference, Roosevelt no longer had to worry about Polish, Baltic, or other minority votes. Still, he remained cognizant of broader public opinion. When the press picked up the story in the fall of 1944 that he supported the Morgenthau plan, which envisioned not only the dismemberment of Germany but also its "pastoralization" through the destruction of its industries, the president dissociated himself from his trusted secretary of the treasury. If in March 1943 he was happy to discuss with Eden the details of his plan for a tripartite division of Germany, and in December he proudly announced in Teheran that a five-way partition of the country was the product of his own thinking on the issue, by mid-1944 Roosevelt had curbed his enthusiasm, mainly because of opposition from the State Department. Partition would require the long-term occupation of Germany and a commitment of American troops—too high a price to pay, even in Roosevelt's opinion. At the time of his departure for Yalta, the State Department recommended that he support decentralization but not partition, a plan that would impede the government's ability to deal with the country's social and economic problems and "would provide a ready-made program for nationalistic agitators."[12]

Stalin's demand on February 5 that the Western leaders state their positions put them in a tight spot. "In principle all were agreed on the dismemberment of Germany," declared Churchill, according to the British protocol of the meeting, "but the actual method was much too complicated to settle here in five or six days. It would require a very searching examination of the historical, ethnographical and economic facts and would need prolonged consideration by a special committee, which would have to go into the different proposals put forward and advise on them." The comprehensive study of the issue would naturally go on until the end of the war and, more important, long past the parliamentary election.

"We are well prepared for the immediate future, both as to thought and plans concerning the surrender of Germany," he added, according to the American protocol. But Stalin was not satisfied. He used the ensuing discussion of unconditional surrender to turn the debate back to dismemberment. Should the Allies "bring up dismemberment at the time of the presentation of the terms of unconditional surrender?" he asked innocently. "Would it not be wise to add a clause to these terms saying that Germany would be dismembered, without going into any details?"

Churchill refused. He wanted more time. This was Roosevelt's cue to intervene. Immediately before the start of the second plenary session, while the foreign ministers were lunching at Vorontsov villa, the president met for an hour and a half with Harry Hopkins, accompanied by two representatives from the State Department. Hopkins and FDR went over the issues to be discussed in the next few days, including zones of occupation, reparations, and the possible dismemberment of Germany. On this last point, Hopkins advised Roosevelt to adopt the British position and postpone a decision, but he also suggested that the Ruhr and the Saar region could be divided from the rest of Germany and placed under Allied control. Roosevelt liked the idea. Despite the State Department's advice, he favored German dismemberment. His intervention in the debate left little doubt on that score.[13]

Roosevelt proposed a compromise: the prime minister and Marshal Stalin were talking about the same thing! As at Teheran, Roosevelt recalled his trips to Germany and the contentment of small German states forty years earlier. He also mentioned his original proposal to divide Germany into five or seven states. Churchill interrupted him with the words "or less." Roosevelt was certainly flexible on the number of states: it was the idea of dismemberment that he found irresistible. Churchill had been forced to retreat; all he had asked was not to "inform the Germans of our future policy." Roosevelt agreed: "[I]t would be a great mistake to have any public discussion of dismemberment of Germany." Stalin did not comment. The three leaders agreed that the specifics would be discussed by the foreign ministers, who were asked to report the next day on the results of their deliberations.

The president's attempt to reconcile Stalin and Churchill by pretending that there was no difference in their positions confused some people. When Roosevelt cited the trips he had made to Germany in his youth, even his advisers were shocked by the incoherence of his argument. According to Bohlen, Roosevelt's "rambling and inconclusive statement, which did not hang together, was greeted with polite indifference by the Soviet leaders and by slight signs of boredom by the British. Churchill fiddled with his cigar and Eden looked off into the distance." The British had little reason to be enthusiastic about Roosevelt's intervention. But in this case the president's focus was on Stalin, not Churchill. And the Soviets, despite Bohlen's remarks to the contrary, fully appreciated the meaning of his statement. Judging by their transcript of the discussion, they believed that FDR, like Stalin, wanted an immediate decision on dismemberment.[14]

The foreign ministers debated the question over lunch on February 6 in the sunroom of Livadia Palace. Stettinius was responsible for hosting the meeting and for selecting the lunch menu, which turned out to be a challenge. The Americans had to rely on Soviet cooks who supplied French-language menus translated into dubious English. "Caviar with *Blenie* and Cream," for example, was followed by the explanation "*blenie* are very light pancakes and in this form are a great Russian delicacy, especially when served with caviar." Explanations were required even for dishes that the cooks considered to be American. "Fillet of Sturgeon à l'Américaine" was rendered as "broiled sturgeon with some kind of souse." "Tambole à la Californie" was Englished as "a creamy apple dessert."[15]

The greatest problem discussed over lunch involved the choice and meaning of words. Stettinius proposed that the existing formula for the German surrender be amended to include the word "dismemberment." Molotov agreed, but Eden insisted on the word "dissolution." Since the Soviets were pushing for a clear statement that would commit the Allies to the dismemberment of Germany, Molotov now objected. Eden's "dissolution" of the "German unitary state" could mean its mere federalization. The Soviet foreign minister proposed a new formula linking dismemberment to peace and security in Europe. Eden objected. He was finally prepared to accept Stettinius's formula, but Molotov refused to withdraw his new proposal. He wanted it to be reported to the plenary session.

"I had wrangle with Russians," Eden noted in his diary that day. "Stettinius not appearing to seize the points very quickly. Molotov wished to tie us hand and foot to dismemberment before enquiry was made. I refused to do this and stuck to my point." Eden was clearly upset, and when one of Molotov's deputies, Ivan Maisky, approached him, saying that he did not understand the foreign secretary's attitude, Eden could no longer contain his frustration. "I bit him," he wrote in his diary, "reminding him that we were still an independent power."

Maisky was rebuked unjustly. It was not the Soviets but the Americans in relation to whom the British were losing their great-power status. Nevertheless, the Soviets got the message and decided to compromise. Molotov had been made to abandon his plan. That afternoon Stalin greeted Eden warmly. "You have won again," he said. Eden was clearly happy. "My obstinacy," he wrote, "did good, I think." The Soviets got what they wanted and made the British feel good about it. Churchill thanked Molotov for withdrawing his proposal and said that although he had not had a chance to discuss the addition of the dismemberment provision to the terms of surrender with his war cabinet, he would accept the amendment on behalf of the British government.[16]

The battle was over, or so it seemed. Who won and who lost? Stalin and Molotov had demonstrated their tactical brilliance but got only a commitment in principle from their allies, not a detailed plan of action. In the long run it was the American president who gained most from the debate, establishing his reputation as an honest broker at the conference. Stalin and Churchill emerged as the main adversaries on most issues, making Roosevelt the mediator between them. By throwing his weight behind Stalin or Churchill, depending on the nature of the issue and direction of the debate, Roosevelt managed to make himself a far more effective negotiator than his rambling statements suggested.[17]

8

SPOILS OF WAR

"A big day!" Ivan Maisky noted in his diary on February 5. Maisky's area of expertise was German reparations, and Stalin alerted him that the question might come up for discussion later that day. In Stalin's agenda, reparations would follow a discussion of dismemberment. But Stalin had to take the Allies' wishes into account. Once they had come to terms on the partitioning of Germany, Roosevelt put the issue of French participation in the occupation back on the agenda. Maisky had to wait.[1]

As he "understood from Marshal Stalin," Roosevelt said, "the French did not wish to annex outright the German territory up to the Rhine." That was the complete opposite of what Stalin had telegraphed Roosevelt on the results of his negotiations with Charles de Gaulle in December 1944 and what he had told the president during their preconference meeting the previous day. Stalin did not fail to point out the president's faux pas: de Gaulle had told him in Moscow that in fact the French did want that territory for themselves. The president expressed surprise. Although the Big Three were not yet aware of it, on that very day de Gaulle made a radio address to the nation demanding the separation of the left bank of the Rhine from Germany and the stationing of French troops along the river. Even without this information—it would appear in the American news bulletin at Yalta the next day—the opening salvos were hardly promising.

Churchill rushed in to help, shifting the discussion away from the borders to zones of occupation. He offered a formula for solving the problem that would satisfy the Soviets: the French zone would be carved out of the British and, perhaps, the American zones, so it would not affect the Soviet zone. All he asked was that the Soviet government agree that the British and the Americans could work out the details with the French. Stalin objected, but Churchill continued. He claimed that the discussion "brought up the whole question of the future role of France in Europe and that he personally felt that France should play a very important role."

The Allies would need French assistance if the occupation were to last for a substantial period of time; the French had considerable experience in dealing with the Germans, and their army had to be built up as a bulwark against possible future aggression. The Soviets could have Poland as an ally against Germany in the East, and the British wanted France in the West, Churchill argued. Stalin asked whether the British were suggesting a separate zone and a place in the control machinery for Poland. "No," Churchill said carefully, backing down from a British proposal made a year earlier: with two Polish governments, one pro-Western and the other pro-Soviet, competing for the right to rule Soviet-occupied Poland, Churchill was not eager to give the Poles a zone of occupation. But he wanted one for France.[2]

Following the traditional British policy of maintaining a balance of power in Europe to prevent the rise of a single hegemonic state, Churchill did all he could to promote the revival of a strong, independent France. As he saw it, France would keep Germany's economic and military revival in check. To promote his strategy, Churchill made an alliance with General Charles de Gaulle. He was an early supporter of the French military commander turned politician, with whom he shared a determination to stand up to German aggression, whatever the cost. It was at de Gaulle's insistence that in June 1940 the newly appointed prime minister issued a declaration of union offering the French government temporary unification with Britain to help it continue the war against Germany. Churchill also facilitated de Gaulle's radio broadcasts to occupied France and supported his efforts to create the nucleus of a future French army in Britain, to which the general fled after the French surrender.

Charles de Gaulle had much to recommend him. A veteran of the First World War, part of which he spent in German captivity, de Gaulle distinguished himself in the Soviet-Polish war of 1919–21, in which he served as an adviser to the Polish army and earned a Polish military decoration. A professional soldier, he became a strong proponent of the mechanization of the French army during the interwar period and a leading theoretician of mechanized warfare. After the German invasion of France, he organized one of the few successful counterattacks against the advancing Wehrmacht. He continued to resist the German occupation, first from Britain and then from Algeria, to which he moved in May 1943 to lead the French Committee of National Liberation and build up his Free French military forces. De Gaulle's First French Army helped the Allies liberate France after D-Day.

De Gaulle became president of the French provisional government in September 1944 and was relentless in his defense of French sovereignty in his dealings with the Allies. His actions, as well as his obtrusive personality, annoyed many Americans, especially Roosevelt. The British prime minister had his own misgivings: "Remember that there is not a scrap of generosity about this man," he warned his foreign secretary. Churchill was opposed to inviting de Gaulle to Yalta, as he believed that the French leader's presence "would have wrecked all possible progress, already difficult enough." But Churchill saw no alternative to de Gaulle and, more important, no alternative to the policy of rebuilding the French state, army, and standing in the world.[3]

To promote his vision of the French role in postwar Europe, Churchill masterminded the inclusion of France in the European Advisory Commission and the Security Council of the future United Nations organization. The next step was allotting the French a zone of occupation in Germany and including French representatives in the occupation administration. That goal could not be achieved without American support, and Churchill managed to get Roosevelt on board. By the time of Yalta, having tried and failed to establish special relations with some elements of the Vichy government and then to support de Gaulle's rival, General Henri Giraud, Roosevelt concluded that the United States had no choice but to throw its support behind de Gaulle. It was also in the American interest to back British attempts to reintroduce France to the club of great powers.

Before leaving for Yalta, Roosevelt sent Harry Hopkins to Europe to placate not only Churchill, who was upset by anticolonial statements in the American media, and Pope Pius XII, who was not happy about Soviet treatment of the Catholic Church, but also de Gaulle, who was offended that he had not been invited. The French minister of foreign affairs, Georges-Augustin Bidault, told Hopkins before his meeting: "General de Gaulle believes that Frenchmen always try to please the man to whom they are talking. The General thinks they overdo it and he adopts a different attitude. He makes no effort to please." That was if anything an understatement. De Gaulle told Hopkins that the United States had not stood by France in 1920 or at the time of the German assault in 1940; it was now providing assistance, but "grudgingly, under pressure and only at the last minute." If France failed to reassert itself as a great nation, then the American policy was correct, he reasoned. However, "if she does rise again, does stand on her own feet again and does eventually resume her place in the great nations, you are wrong."[4]

The Americans were prepared to help the British restore France as a major European power, but it was a daunting task for a number of reasons. In military terms France was a virtual pygmy, as Charles Bohlen discovered when he accompanied Hopkins on his trip to Paris in January 1945: at best, the country could muster three fighting divisions. Roosevelt told Stalin that he was arming eight additional divisions. That would enable France to perform its duty as an occupying power, but it was not enough to convince Stalin that France had the right to sit at the same table as the Big Three.

Stalin despised the French for their military collapse in 1940, which, in his eyes, made possible Hitler's attack on the USSR a year later. He found de Gaulle an "awkward and clumsy man." Although he liked his independence, seeing a promise of future cooperation, that prospect disappeared in December 1944, when de Gaulle came to Moscow to sign a Franco-Soviet treaty and refused to recognize the Soviet-backed government in Poland. Stalin tried to humiliate the French leader at a reception for him in the Kremlin, proposing toasts to Roosevelt and Churchill but pointedly omitting his guest of honor. He then summoned de Gaulle to the Kremlin at 6:30 a.m. to sign the treaty, which did not take French proposals into account. When de Gaulle refused, the half-drunken dictator produced a revised text on which both parties managed to agree. By Yalta, there was no love lost between them.[5]

The debate between Stalin and Churchill concerning the French zone revealed differences not only in their agendas but also in their political culture. Stalin's argument that France had no right to a place on the Allied Control Commission was based on his assumption that the defeated country was to be run "by those who have stood firmly against Germany and have made the greatest sacrifices in bringing victory." According to the British protocol, Churchill admitted that France "had gone under and not been able to do much to help subsequently," but he argued that British public opinion would not understand the exclusion of France. "The destiny of great nations," he said, according to the American record, "was not decided by the temporary state of their technical apparatus." In a word, whether France was a victor or a loser in the war, it was a great nation in the eyes of its neighbors and could not be treated as a second-rate power. Churchill was protecting the old world order against a revolutionary newcomer who had no respect for it. Was he also thinking about the future of Britain?[6]

The task of convincing Stalin to allocate a separate occupation zone to the French was complicated by the fact that the existing map of occupation zones, on which all three parties had agreed, was of British provenance and did not include a separate zone for France. When the British submitted their plan in January 1944, the Soviets hastened to accept it with relatively minor changes. The British were apparently pleased with the results. Some Western members of the European Advisory Commission, which was charged with allocating occupation zones to the three powers, believed that, given the Soviet war effort, Stalin was entitled to ask for more territory than was allocated by the British proposal.

The Soviets had their own reasons to be satisfied. Unknown to the British, one variant of the Soviets' original proposal asked for less territory than they actually got. The proposal would have established the border between the Soviet and Western zones at the Elbe River, with the Soviet zone extending no farther than Dresden in the south. It was the British who suggested a boundary farther to the west that later became the border between the Federal Republic of Germany and the German Democratic Republic. The British proposal gave the Soviets more territory than they might have expected but, perhaps more important, located their zone of occupation in the East, leaving them in control of East Prussia and the future German-Polish border, wherever they decided to draw it.

The one problem with the British proposal, from Stalin's point of view, was its treatment of the zones of occupation as areas of primary rather than exclusive responsibility. This arrangement would allow American and British troops on Soviet territory and vice versa. To make the idea of exclusive control more attractive to their Western allies, the Soviets agreed that Berlin and Austria could be zones of joint occupation. Another irksome element of the British proposal was the allocation of East Prussia to Poland. "Given existing relations between the USSR and Poland," Molotov wrote in February 1944 to the Soviet ambassador in London, "it is unacceptable to us that any German territory, especially that of East Prussia, be occupied by Polish forces." He did not want an enclave controlled by the London-based Polish government. The British conceded on this point—after all, most of their proposal had been accepted by Moscow at a time when the Soviets were in a position to demand more.[7]

The Americans found themselves ill prepared to object to any deal reached by London and Moscow. In the spring of 1944 U.S. military strategists believed that the Allies would meet the Red Army on the Rhine and felt it was naive to expect that the Soviets would cede any conquered territory to Anglo-American forces. When the U.S. Joint Chiefs of Staff finally submitted their proposal to the European Advisory Commission in London, everyone was taken by surprise. The proposed American zone included northwestern Germany up to Berlin. It accounted for more than half of the country's population and covered 46 percent of German territory, as opposed to 22 percent for the Soviets.

The proposal was not accompanied by an explanatory letter. George F. Kennan, then a member of the American delegation to the commission, was appalled and refused to submit the proposal for discussion. Others in the U.S. delegation were no less skeptical but felt that they had no choice but to present it. General Cornelius W. Wickersham told the disheartened Kennan, "We have to fight for it, my boy, we have to fight for it." "How does one fight," Kennan retorted, "for something which makes no sense and which one does not understand oneself?" Kennan and Wickersham flew to Washington to get more information.

When Kennan finally got to see Roosevelt himself on the matter, the president laughed it off. "Why that's just something I once drew on the back of an envelope," he said. The president, wrote Kennan in his memoirs, had an "aversion to anything that might commit him in advance or restrict his freedom of action, with regard to post-war settlement in Europe." He "would obviously have preferred, in fact, that there be no such commission at all." It was only after Kennan's intervention that the original instructions to the American delegation were revoked and the British-sponsored boundaries of the Soviet zone of occupation approved.[8]

It was at this point in the long and complex negotiations that the French factor entered the picture. It fell to Roosevelt to introduce the idea to Stalin at their preconference meeting on February 4. Did "the president think France should have a zone of occupation, and for what reason?" Stalin asked. Roosevelt admitted that he thought it would not be a bad idea. There was no reason to do it, he offered, but "out of kindness." Molotov objected, but Stalin agreed that the matter could be discussed at the conference.

The next day Roosevelt put the question on the agenda and ensured its positive resolution by claiming, to the surprise of Churchill and Stalin, that U.S. troops would not stay in Europe for more than two years. This was not a negotiating position. The president believed that Congress would not agree to a longer posting of American troops overseas. Churchill was shocked. This meant that the British would need French help more than ever to police occupied Germany; otherwise the situation there might spin out of control. It may well have been the crucial argument that changed Stalin's position. Shortly after Roosevelt's interjection, the Soviet leader agreed to the creation of a separate occupation zone for France "within the British and American zones." Germany was too big to be handled by any one country, even one as large as the USSR. The withdrawal of the Americans would leave a vacuum in the center of Europe that would have to be filled, and de Gaulle was better than nothing.

The Allied Control Commission was a different matter, and Stalin was not prepared to yield on it. He hedged his acceptance of a French zone of occupation with the emphatic proviso that he would not like to see France as a participant in the control machinery for Germany. Churchill saw Stalin's concession as an opening and pushed on, downplaying the commission's significance. "The control commission will be an extraordinary body under the orders of the governments," he said. "[T]here was no reason to fear that basic policy in regard to Germany would be made by the commission." Stalin was unconvinced. He already had to deal with two capitalist countries that occasionally sided against him, despite his best efforts to play one against the other. The addition of France, no ally of the USSR, would make future negotiations even more difficult.

Roosevelt decided it was time to intervene. Harry Hopkins had forwarded him a note stating: "1. France is on the European Advisory committee now. That is only body considering German affairs now. 2. Promise a zone. 3. Postpone decision about Control Commission." Roosevelt followed this prescription to the letter. He reminded his colleagues that the European Advisory Commission included France and declared that he "favored the acceptance of the French request for a zone, but . . . agreed with Marshal Stalin that France should not take part in the control machinery, otherwise other nations would demand participation." Churchill must have been furious, but he made no direct objection. Instead he enlisted Eden's support. Then Molotov joined on Stalin's side. The best Churchill could do was to refer the question of the administration of the French zone to the foreign ministers' committee for consideration.[9]

And so the debate ended with one more compromise brokered by Roosevelt. His power was growing, as was his capacity to influence Stalin on issues that the Soviet leader considered secondary. French participation in the occupation of Germany apparently belonged to that category. Not so German reparations.

With the zones of occupation settled, Stalin turned to Ivan Maisky, who was sitting to his left, and said "rather offhandedly," as the people's deputy commissar for foreign affairs wrote in his diary: "Report." Maisky was caught off guard. He thought Stalin would be the main speaker and that he would take part in the discussion afterward. He had a detailed proposal on German reparations in hand, but its final version had not been approved by either Molotov or Stalin. Like anyone working for Stalin, Maisky knew that this was a dangerous situation. His superior had recently reprimanded him without just cause. When Maisky showed up at the plenary meeting that day, Stalin asked him with visible irritation, "Why didn't you show up for the first session?" Maisky replied that he had not been invited. Stalin was not satisfied. "You weren't notified? What do you mean, you weren't notified? You're just undisciplined. You're taking liberties."[10]

Like quite a few members of Stalin's leadership, Maisky was not an ethnic Russian. Born Jan Lachowiecki in 1884 to an ethnic Polish family living in the Russian Empire, he joined the Russian Social Democratic Labor Party in 1903. His "sin" was that until the revolution he belonged to the wrong faction of the party—the Mensheviks, who were often at odds with Lenin's Bolsheviks. Maisky's other "shortcoming" was that, unlike Stalin and most of his entourage, he had received a good education, graduating with a degree in history from Moscow University. He spent almost a decade before the revolution as a political refugee in Western Europe, where he mastered English and French. Those were dangerous skills to have in Stalin's USSR. In 1953 Maisky would be arrested by Stalin's secret police on charges of espionage. After the dictator's death he was accused of conspiring with the "British spy" Lavrentii Beria, who was arrested in June 1953 and shot as a result of a Kremlin coup. Maisky was cleared of all charges and finally released in 1955. He was lucky to have survived.[11]

Maisky began his career as a Soviet diplomat in 1922, eventually landing postings as Soviet ambassador to Finland, Japan, and, finally, the United

Kingdom. He served in London for eleven years. After his recall from London in the fall of 1943, Maisky was appointed deputy people's commissar for foreign affairs and put in charge of one of the commissions planning the aftermath of the war. Since reparations were his domain, his inclusion in the Yalta delegation may have seemed natural, but it actually came as a pleasant surprise. Maisky was not close to Stalin, and his reports to Molotov often went through another deputy—also an ethnic Pole and a former Menshevik—Andrei Vyshinsky. The invitation to Yalta came after Maisky reminded his superiors of his existence with a report on his meeting with Averell Harriman on January 20, 1945. Harriman visited Maisky because, as he put it, Maisky was "more ready to exchange preliminary views than any other member of the Soviet Foreign Office."

Maisky proved to be a mine of information. On the future of Germany, he said that it should be broken up, with the Rhineland and the Catholic south becoming separate polities, and stripped of its heavy industry so as to prevent the revival of its military power. Reparations should be taken over a period of ten years, in goods and labor. He suggested that the Soviets were planning to deport millions of German workers—mostly men, but also women—to the USSR as forced laborers. The first to be enlisted would be minor criminals, Nazi activists, and the unemployed. Work in the USSR would be both a punishment and a form of social rehabilitation. Maisky's memoirs, which had just appeared in print, came up in the discussion, and Harriman offered to take a copy to Malta to give to the president. That sounded like a good idea, since Maisky did not expect to be at Yalta. The next day he sent his memoirs with a note. "Of course your yesterday's suggestion in this matter accepted," he wrote. "Bon voyage and good luck. Yours sincerely, Ivan Maisky."[12]

In the report he drafted for Molotov and his deputies on the meeting, Maisky did not mention the gift of the book. He explained Harriman's interest in him by stressing the importance to the Americans of reparations, which he presented as one of the two main points on the American agenda at Yalta, the first being the creation of the United Nations. Harriman may have said something of the kind in order to explain his "fishing expedition" in the deputy commissar's office, but it is clear that it was in Maisky's interest to stress the importance of the issue, which fell within his sphere of responsibility. Maisky bent over backward to ingratiate himself with his superiors, presenting his own views on reparations and describing Harriman's reaction. The report cried out: "Comrade Stalin, please take me to Yalta!"

On January 25, five days after Harriman's visit, the excited Soviet deputy people's commissar wrote in his diary: "Today was an excellent day for me." Molotov had invited him to serve as a host and an interpreter during Stalin's meeting with the British parliamentary delegation—evidently a sign of trust— and to join the Soviet delegation at Yalta. When Molotov asked whether he had anything against the trip, the elated Maisky said, "No, I do not. I am entirely at your service." In his diary, he remarked, "How could I possibly have objected?" Three days later, on January 28, he boarded a train for the Crimea.[13]

Maisky was carrying a detailed proposal on reparations, which he continued to polish after leaving Moscow and submitted to Molotov on the first day of the conference. He suggested that 75 percent of German industrial equipment, with an estimated value of $10 billion, be dismantled and shipped off to the countries that had suffered most from German aggression. That task was to be accomplished within the first two years, while the payment of reparations would continue for ten years. The Soviets were to ask for 75 to 80 percent of all dismantled equipment, with the goal of obtaining 65 percent of it. As for forced labor, the Soviets would ask for five million German workers. Total damages inflicted on the USSR by German aggression were roughly estimated at $50 billion.

Maisky had discussed these figures with Molotov and Stalin in Moscow, but no final decision was made with regard to the Soviet share of German reparations or its monetary equivalent. When reparations came up for discussion on February 5, neither Molotov nor Stalin had had a chance to read the final version of Maisky's proposal. "But you have not seen my formula," the frightened Maisky said quietly. "That does not matter," Stalin said; "report. Just avoid touching on the issue of labor." Even Molotov was worried. That night Maisky noted in his diary: "Molotov, sitting to Stalin's right, leaned over to him and asked in alarm: 'Should a figure be given?' 'Yes, give the figure,' Stalin shot back. 'Which one?' Molotov continued, alluding to our disputes in Moscow about the figure for Soviet claims. 'Five or ten?' 'Ten!' replied Stalin. And so it was all settled in an instant." The "figure" in question was the amount of reparations to be demanded by the Soviet Union. Stalin had decided on the spot that it should be $10 billion.[14]

When Roosevelt began with a question about the Soviet request for manpower, Stalin responded that he was not prepared to discuss the matter. Maisky was puzzled. Why? It was not lack of preparation. Stalin probably smelled danger and preferred to remove the issue of "slave labor" from the agenda. He could not know that before the plenary session Hopkins had suggested that if the question came up, "we should readily agree and not reluctantly." The president apparently asked his question not to confront Stalin but to demonstrate his goodwill.

"Will you permit me to speak directly in English?" Maisky asked. "Please go ahead," Stalin replied. Maisky spoke in his fluent but heavily accented English and apparently made a strong impression. Stettinius later wrote: "Maisky, with his clipped, pointed beard and scholarly manner, was an attractive and able person. . . . He delivered his report in a forceful manner and seemed to have the full support of Stalin and Molotov." Maisky himself believed that he had made a good impression on the Allies, given the attention with which Churchill and others followed his presentation. He proposed that the sum of the reparations allotted to individual countries should be based on two factors: the contribution of that country to the victory over Germany and the damage it had sustained as a result of German aggression.

Maisky's presentation was based on his written proposal, but in light of Stalin's decision to ask for $10 billion instead of $5 billion in reparations, he decided to beef up his request for German equipment—from 75 to 80 percent. He also stated that Soviet reparations should amount to "not less than $10 billion," which would cover only an insignificant portion of the direct damage suffered by the USSR as a result of German aggression. On the issue of reparations, the "attractive and able" Maisky was a "hawk." In fact, in December he had proposed a figure of no less than $15 billion.[15]

During Maisky's presentation, Churchill "cast cunning glances" at the Soviet deputy commissar. He then stated that the figure of $10 billion was fantasy. The victors had managed to extract only £1 billion from Germany after the last war, and that only because of money lent to Germany by the United States. Britain had also suffered heavy losses during the Second World War; its war debt had reached £3 billion, argued the prime minister. A British note-taker summarized Churchill's words: "[I]f he could see any way in which our economy could be substantially benefited by reparations from Germany, we would be very glad to follow it. But once bit, twice shy; and he felt great doubts on the matter."

The prime minister was concerned that the British would have to pick up the bill for saving the Germans from starvation if the burden of reparations became excessive. "If you want a horse to pull your wagon," he said in closing, "you have to give him some hay." Stalin responded that "care should be taken to see that the horse did not turn around and kick you." Churchill offered that his horse metaphor was perhaps inept, and suggested that if one took the example of a car, it would have to be supplied with gasoline. This is a poor analogy, as the Germans are not machines, Stalin shot back. He was clearly on a collision course.[16]

Once again, Roosevelt stepped in. And again he seemed to favor the Soviet position. The difference between FDR's stand on reparations at Yalta and that of Woodrow Wilson in Paris could not have been greater. Wilson, bound by his Fourteen Points and his promise that there would be no annexations, contributions, or punitive damages at the end of the war, fought the British prime minister, David Lloyd George, but ultimately succumbed to his demands for indemnities. Now the situation was diametrically reversed: it was the British, citing the lessons of the First World War, who opposed excessive reparations, while the Americans were prepared to go along with the Soviets. They did not want reparations for themselves but were not opposed to others taking them in nonmonetary form.[17]

The Americans, Roosevelt said, did not want German capital or equipment, nor did they want the Germans to starve, but he did not see why the Germans should emerge from the war with a better standard of living than Soviet citizens. This was a dangerous route to take. In fact, Hopkins had warned FDR against adopting Stalin's argument, noting that the Americans would have to find out exactly what the Soviets meant by it. Even after his trip through the war-torn landscape of the Crimea, Roosevelt could hardly imagine actual living conditions in the USSR, which had undergone the traumas of collectivization, terror, and total war. The Red Army soldiers who stormed into East Prussia at the time of the Yalta Conference were shocked by the high standard of living of farmers and city dwellers in Germany. Thinking that they had entered a capitalist paradise made possible by the imperialist exploitation of all Europe, they had made haste to "rob the robbers," plundering the terrified population.[18]

Stalin allowed Maisky to counter Churchill's arguments. Once again he made a strong impression with his mastery of facts and figures. When he said that $10 billion was not such a large sum, as it represented only 10 percent of the U.S. budget for the 1944–45 fiscal year, Stettinius said, "Absolutely right!" When he went on to note that the German military budget during the war approached $6 billion per annum, Churchill exclaimed, "Yes, this is a very important consideration!" Still, despite Maisky's performance, Churchill remained opposed to unrealistically large reparations.

Now it was Stalin's turn. First, he wanted to limit the number of countries qualified to receive German reparations. He pointed out that France had contributed little to the Allied war effort, furnishing fewer divisions than either Yugoslavia or Poland. Contribution to the war effort should be the deciding factor in establishing reparations. Churchill protested. He favored the socialist principle "To each according to his needs, and from each according to his abilities." Stalin was not about to be outplayed on his own turf. "To each according to his deserts," he said curtly. Still, the British resistance alarmed him. Late in the evening, in conversation with his advisers, Stalin proposed that the Soviet share be reduced to $7 billion; the Western Allies could then demand $8 billion in reparations. He wished to avoid antagonizing his allies and wanted to interest them in a deal. Maisky argued against this but noted in his diary: "Nevertheless, Stalin had his say, and that had to be reckoned with."[19]

The plenary session ended with no agreement on the amount in question. As with many other issues, further discussion would be referred to the foreign ministers. It was, however, agreed that a special reparations commission should be set up in Moscow. If the Soviets saw this as an instrument for extracting reparations from the Allied zones of occupation, the British and Americans saw it as a mechanism to keep the Soviet appetite for reparations in check. Stalin's tactics had so far proved less than successful. If, as some scholars have argued, he wanted to present his position on dismemberment as a concession to the Allies and to demand in return their agreement to huge reparations payments, he clearly failed. With the decision on reparations postponed, Stalin's record for February 5 was mixed at best. He had convinced his allies to add the word "dismemberment" to the German surrender formula but had agreed to an occupation zone for the French, even though he did not want France to recover great-power status.[20]

Soviet historians would later be at pains to cover the tracks of Stalin's failed initiatives in the first days of the Yalta Conference. There were two main areas where Soviet editors doctored their edition of the minutes of the conference by removing some of Stalin's comments and remarks: one was the discussion on the dismemberment of Germany; the other was the debate on zones of occupation and the inclusion of France. In the 1960s, when the Soviet minutes were first published, the Soviet leadership was eager to blame the West for the partition of Germany and to exploit anti-American tendencies in French foreign policy to its own advantage. Under these circumstances, Moscow did not want to be seen, even in retrospect, as opposing the revival of a strong French state. The Soviets kept meticulous records, but they "corrected" them to suit their needs.[21]

PART III

A NEW WORLD ORDER

[The Crimean conference] ought to spell the end of the system of unilateral action, the exclusive alliances, the spheres of influence, the balances of power, and all the other expedients that have been tried for centuries—and have always failed.

FRANKLIN D. ROOSEVELT

9

THE SECURITY COUNCIL

On Tuesday, February 6, Sarah Oliver sat down to write a letter to her mother. She described Vorontsov villa, then turned to a scene that had clearly made an impression on her. "As we stood on the terrace overlooking the sea," she wrote, "we saw an amazing sight. A great shoal of fishes were being attacked by air and sea. From the sea by a school of porpoises, from the air by hundreds of gulls—the poor silly fish just huddled together closer and the mass slaughter went on for nearly 3 hours." Sarah told Field Marshal Harold Alexander, who was with her, that "they were surely idiotic not to disperse," to which he responded, "[I]t is much better they should stick together."

Sarah's father was of her view. Winston Churchill was no great believer in the advantages of collective action, thanks to his own checkered political experience. That morning, he was preoccupied by what he had come to see as the inevitability of a future war. "The next war will be an ideological one," he told his doctor while having breakfast in bed in his quarters. Having disagreed with Stalin on almost every point of substance the previous day, the prime minister was not optimistic about future relations between the communist East and the capitalist West.[1]

The future of the world was also on Franklin Roosevelt's mind that morning, but his thoughts had taken a more hopeful turn. He wanted to put the United Nations organization on that day's agenda and called in his secretary of state to propose that he be the main speaker on the issue. Stettinius was delighted. "It was to be a most important moment for me," he wrote later. "I had devoted many days and nights to the problem of building a world organization, ever since I left the Lend-Lease Administration for the State Department. If we could now persuade the Russians to accept our voting proposal, a United Nations conference could be called and our plans for a world organization for peace and security would be nearer realization."[2] Stettinius had inherited his enthusiasm for the United Nations from his predecessor, Cordell Hull, the leader of the State Department's "Wilsonians."

The first outline of the United Nations was drafted by Undersecretary of State Sumner Welles on the basis of the covenant of the League of Nations. A creation of the Paris Peace Conference, the League convened its first general assembly in Geneva in November 1920 and its last in April 1946, when representatives of the member nations voted to dissolve it. The League's activities had in fact come to a virtual halt in 1939, the first year of the war that it had failed to prevent and for whose outbreak it was universally blamed. The problem was that the League could neither adopt nor enforce its decisions: all resolutions had to be passed with the unanimous approval of its council, an executive body that included great powers as permanent members and smaller powers as temporary ones, as well as its assembly. The principle of unanimity was enshrined in the League's covenant, whose fifth chapter stated that "decisions at any meeting of the Assembly or of the Council shall require the agreement of all the Members of the League represented at the meeting." This was virtually impossible to achieve, especially when matters under discussion involved the great powers.

The United States did not join the League. Woodrow Wilson received the Nobel Peace Prize in 1919 for his role in its creation, but he failed to overcome Republican opposition and persuade an increasingly isolationist Congress to ratify the Treaty of Versailles, which would have led to American membership in the League. The American drafters of the United Nations Charter were mindful of the inevitable opposition that any international organization whose decisions would be binding on the United States would encounter in Congress. They also had to overcome a baleful precedent—the League's inability to influence the conduct of Germany and Japan after their departure from the organization in 1933. Italy would follow suit in 1937. The formation of the Axis by these three countries in 1940 met with no effective response.[3]

If the new peace organization was to do better, it would have to learn from its predecessor's mistakes. The drafters of its charter had the daunting task of reconciling what struck many as irreconcilable. Since August 1943, the principal drafter of the document at the State Department had been Leo Pasvolsky, the head of the department's Informal Agenda Group and Hull's former personal assistant. A fifty-year-old Jewish émigré from Ukraine, Pasvolsky was no stranger to the subject of international peace organizations. Back in 1919 he had covered the Paris Peace Conference for the *New York Tribune*, and later he had campaigned for the admission of the Soviet Union, whose brand of socialism he rejected, to the League of Nations.

Pasvolsky's appointment as principal drafter of the charter was a testament to the triumph of Secretary of State Cordell Hull's vision over an alternative model championed by Sumner Welles. Hull favored a centralized structure, while Welles wanted the great powers to bear primary responsibility for security in their respective regions. Welles's model followed FDR's thinking on the role of the "four policemen"—the United States, Britain, the Soviet Union, and China—in the postwar peace arrangement. By the fall of 1943, with Welles resigning in the midst of a homosexual scandal, Roosevelt had opted for the centralized model. FDR's decision was aided by the fact that his "four policemen" would be permanent members of the UN Security Council.[4]

After rejecting Welles's idea that the great powers should exercise regional responsibility, Pasvolsky had to find a way of making membership in the new organization attractive to the great powers without impairing its capacity to arrive at binding decisions. The key to resolving this dilemma would lie in the rules of the United Nations' main executive body, the Security Council. Pasvolsky did away with the principle of unanimity. The right of veto would be granted only to the permanent members of the council and would not apply to all issues. In the months leading up to Yalta, the right of the permanent members of the Security Council—the United States, Great Britain, the Soviet Union, China, and, later, France—to veto issues that directly involved them had become a stumbling block to an agreement. It was one of the few unresolved issues left over from the Dumbarton Oaks Conference, which had taken place in Washington between August 21 and October 7, 1944: most of the problems associated with the creation of the new peace organization had been resolved there.

The American proposal, submitted by Pasvolsky at Dumbarton Oaks, held that all the permanent members of the Security Council should abstain from voting, and thus from exercising their veto power, on most issues directly involving their countries. Both the British and the Soviets objected. When Churchill informed Roosevelt of his concerns before his October trip to Moscow, the president pleaded with him not to mention his objections to Stalin. Churchill promised but reneged on his promise in the first hour of their meeting. In December Roosevelt proposed a compromise formula, according to which the members of the Security Council would have the right to veto all decisions involving their countries except for procedural issues or recommendations on the peaceful resolution of conflicts. The Americans were afraid that if smaller nations were not given the right to raise their grievances against the great powers at the United Nations and, at a minimum, to initiate discussion of measures that should be taken to resolve conflicts peacefully, the organization would have no future. Stalin was unmoved, and so was Churchill.[5]

Stalin gave his formal reasons for objecting in a letter to Roosevelt on December 27. He claimed that the president's "attempt to prevent, on a certain stage, one or several permanent members of the Council from participating in voting . . . can have fatal consequences for the cause of preservation of international security. Such a situation is in contradiction with the principle of agreement and unanimity of decisions of the four leading powers and can lead to a situation when some great powers are put in opposition to other great powers and this may undermine the cause of universal security." In the principle of unanimity, Stalin saw a guarantee of future peace that would ultimately benefit the smaller nations as much as the great powers.

In a letter he sent to Washington the next day, Harriman looked deeper for an explanation. He reminded the president of the Soviet Union's bitter experience in the interwar years, when "the nations of the world have been hostile to or suspicious of them and their objectives." And he noted that the Soviets had a more limited understanding of the role of the peace organization. If Churchill and Roosevelt believed its purpose was to mediate future conflicts, Stalin wanted it simply to stop future aggression, not trusting other nations to resolve disputes once they had flared into violence.

"The court they believe is packed against them," Harriman wrote. And in this Stalin was not wrong. Both the United States and Britain expected to have proxies on the Security Council. The British were pushing for France to be given a seat, and the Americans for China, even though it was occupied and internally divided. They also wanted to add Brazil to the exclusive club of great powers. Stalin had reason to be suspicious of the president's intentions. Harriman believed that the Soviets had made up their mind and that the only way to change their position was for the United States and the United Kingdom "to take a firm and definite stand" and solicit support from the smaller nations.[6]

On Malta, Stettinius convinced Eden to support the American proposal, but Churchill remained uncommitted. With the distinct possibility of the French joining the Security Council and the clear prospect of the British dominions of Canada, India, Australia, and New Zealand joining the General Assembly, Churchill was all for the rights of the smaller nations, but he was afraid that if the British were not protected by the veto power, the smaller nations, assisted by the United States, might rob London of its imperial possessions. He came to Yalta undecided as to what stand to take on voting procedure in the Security Council. His government informed Washington in January that it was in favor of the president's compromise proposal but still had doubts about some of its provisions.

At the White House on January 8, Stettinius had told the president that the issue of veto power for the permanent members of the UN Security Council would have to be resolved at the Big Three meeting. "Otherwise," he said, "the United Nations conference might be delayed for a long time to come, with resultant slackening of interest and possible growth of opposition." The president was eager to avoid delay and said he would press for a solution at Yalta. But he also began to wonder whether the proposal he was promoting would not harm the interests of the United States. The president admitted that he was still worried about what might happen under the American formula if a conflict arose between the United States and Mexico. Given Stalin's objections, he was willing to look for a different formula that would satisfy the Soviets.

Leo Pasvolsky, who was present at the meeting, assured Roosevelt that neither the Soviets nor the Americans had any reason to worry about the protection of their interests under the current plans. "We would abstain from casting our vote only in such decisions as might be involved in the investigation of the dispute, in calling upon the parties to settle it peacefully, and in making recommendations as regards methods and procedures of settlement," Pasvolsky told the president. "No decision for action could be made without our affirmative vote." Roosevelt was unconvinced. He asked a follow-up question about Security Council procedures in the case of a possible U.S.-Mexico dispute over oil and was assured that American interests would be protected. Pasvolsky told him that the UN Security Council would not be able to take action against the United States without American consent.[7]

At Yalta Stalin was the first to raise the question of great-power prerogatives. "It was ridiculous to believe," he said at the dinner hosted by FDR on the opening day of the conference, "that Albania would have an equal voice with the three great powers who had won the war." He continued, according to the American transcript, with the assertion that "some liberated countries seemed to believe that the great powers had been forced to shed their blood in order to liberate them and they were now scolding these great powers for failure to take into consideration the rights of these small nations."

When Stalin spoke of the great powers, he had in mind the Big Three, not the permanent members of the UN Security Council, where he could face opposition not just from the United States and Britain but from France and China as well, and could thus be outnumbered four to one. In defining the role to be played by the great powers, Stalin used the yardstick of the war effort: three great powers had contributed most to the defeat of the enemy, and many smaller states had benefited from their sacrifices. The president seemed to be in agreement: "[T]he great powers bore the greater responsibility and . . . the peace should be written by the Three Powers represented at the table."

Churchill thought differently. For him, it was not a question of "the small powers dictating to the big powers but that the great nations of the world should discharge their moral responsibility and leadership and should exercise their power with moderation and great respect for the rights of the smaller nations." The prime minister rephrased a line from Shakespeare's *Titus Andronicus:* "The eagle should permit the small birds to sing and care not wherefor they sang." (In the original, Tamora, the wife of the Roman emperor Saturninus, tells her husband, who fears a revolt of his own citizens, "The eagle suffers little birds to sing, / And is not careful what they mean thereby, / Knowing that with the shadow of his wings / He can at pleasure stint their melody.")

Ironically, despite the polemics, Churchill felt more at home with the Soviet stand. He shared his thoughts with Eden after dinner, provoking a sharp response from his foreign secretary. Fresh from his talks with Stettinius on Malta, Eden claimed that accepting Stalin's proposal would give the smaller nations no reason to join the international organization and would be poorly received at home. He even threatened to put the matter to a vote in the House of Commons. Churchill then turned to Charles Bohlen, the State Department's Russia expert, who escorted him to the door. "Growling in his customary fashion," he admitted that he had not had time to read the American proposal carefully and asked whether Bohlen could explain its main idea to him.

"Having absorbed a good dinner with the customary libations," Bohlen wrote in his memoirs, "I was emboldened to tell the Prime Minister that our compromise proposal reminded me of a story of a Southern plantation owner who asked a Negro whether he liked the whiskey given him for Christmas. When the Negro replied that it was perfect, the master asked what he meant. The Negro answered that had the whiskey been better, the master would not have given it to him, and had it been any worse, he could not have drunk it." Bohlen's "Negro" was the smaller nations.[8]

On February 6, Roosevelt had his task cut out for him. Without the formula he had proposed, he and his advisers believed that there would be no United Nations organization. But the president was going into what was to him one of the most important meetings of the conference without having secured the support of his principal ally. To be sure, after giving qualified support to Stalin on German dismemberment, reparations, and French participation in the Allied Control Commission, which would be in charge of occupied Germany, he was entitled to hope for some reciprocity on the part of the Soviet leader. But would Stalin come through on the issue that mattered most to the president?

Another concern was Roosevelt's failing health. There were at least six different categories of issues that would be voted on by the Security Council. Would the president be able to present those in a simple but comprehensive manner? Some had their doubts. "'He was irascible and became very irritable if he had to concentrate his mind for long,'" Lord Moran recorded in his diary, quoting a letter from Dr. Roger Lee, the president of the American College of Physicians. "'If anything was brought up that wanted thinking out he would change the subject.'" The outcome of the debate was hard to foresee.[9]

The plenary meeting began at 4:00 p.m. with a photo session. The president was in the driver's seat. He wore his usual jacket and tie, while Stalin sported his marshal's uniform, and Churchill appeared in a colonel's outfit. The highest rank attained by the prime minister in the active military service was lieutenant colonel, but he became honorary colonel of the 4th Hussars, his old regiment, in 1941 and was proud of that distinction. Behind the president were the usual suspects: Stettinius (to his right) and Harry Hopkins; H. Freeman Matthews, the head of the State Department's Division of European Affairs; and, immediately behind the president, the State Department's expert on the United Nations, Alger Hiss. A fire was blazing in the grand ballroom, and Stettinius was ready to speak. The photographers were asked to leave, and it was time to turn to business.[10]

First up on the agenda was a report by the foreign ministers on the matters referred to them the previous day. Stettinius, who chaired the present ministers' meeting, gave a brief presentation, and Roosevelt finally got an opportunity to turn to the issue of the day, the United Nations organization. But Churchill wanted to discuss France. The prime minister pointed to France's increased importance in light of Roosevelt's statement that American troops would not stay in Europe for long. He said that Britain would need a strong French army to keep Germany in check. Roosevelt then backpedaled. American public opinion, he said, was prepared to support the creation of a world peace organization, and with such an organization in place, it might well shift toward supporting the larger deployment of troops in Europe. Since both the British and the Soviets were interested in an American military presence in Germany, this was a good way of changing the subject to the United Nations.

Roosevelt asked that they turn to the American proposal on voting procedure in the UN Security Council. Neither Stalin nor Churchill objected. Noting that the question of voting power was central to the future of the United Nations organization, he linked it with the main goal that had brought the Big Three to Yalta—ensuring a stable world peace. "All nations of the world," he said, according to the American record, shared "a common desire to see the elimination of war for at least fifty years." He was "not so optimistic as to believe in eternal peace, but he did believe fifty years of peace was feasible and possible." These words were certainly welcome to Churchill. They must also have appealed to Stalin, who was uneasy about the possibility of a new war. Ivan Maisky estimated that the Soviets would need ten years to recover from the war. Stalin's aim was a settlement that would ensure peace for twenty to fifty years so as to give the Soviet Union time to become the most powerful state in Europe and Asia and continental Europe time to embrace socialism. There was thus a consensus among the Big Three, each for his own reasons, on the need for a fifty-year peace.[11]

Now it was Stettinius's turn. The secretary of state read the American proposal on voting procedure and explained its main provisions. The U.S. government recognized the special role of the great powers in keeping the peace and therefore favored the principle of unanimity on the Security Council for all decisions involving military or economic measures, he said. That meant permanent members could use their veto power to prevent any action against themselves or their allies. But the principle of unanimity would not extend to measures intended to bring about the peaceful resolution of conflicts. This would allow free discussion in the Security Council of grievances against any of its permanent members but halt any decision directed against them. "We believe that unless this freedom of discussion in the Council is permitted, the establishment of the World Organization which we all so earnestly desire in order to save the world from the tragedy of another war would be seriously jeopardized," Stettinius said, trying to impress on his audience the seriousness of the situation. He did a thorough job. Charles Bohlen considered his presentation the best by anyone at the conference. But it was a long and tiresome exposition that delved into every detail.

Roosevelt asked Stettinius to explain how the American proposal would affect decision making in the Security Council. The secretary of state obliged with another long excursus, made even longer by the need for simultaneous translation. To clarify their position, the Americans released a memorandum listing its main points. According to the memo, the original proposal had been modified to include suggestions made by Stalin and Churchill. That created an unforeseen problem, as the ever-suspicious Stalin wanted to know what changes had been made. Stettinius did his best to explain that the changes were trivial. Then the interpreters became confused, adding to the general sense of uneasiness. Stettinius later recalled the incident as an "unpleasant moment when the Russians thought we were trying to slip something over on them." Andrei Gromyko, who was more familiar with the document than any other member of the Soviet delegation, came to the rescue, convincing Stalin that the changes were indeed of no consequence. During the recess he privately told Alger Hiss that even he did not fully understand the references to the United Nations Charter and had found it difficult to explain them to his superiors.

The momentum was lost. Molotov said that the Soviet delegation would need more time to study the drafting changes introduced to the American proposal. He proposed that the discussion continue on the following day. It became clear that the presentation on which Roosevelt had counted so much, that Stettinius had worked on for so long, and that Bohlen had considered so polished had failed to produce the desired effect.[12]

Help suddenly came from the most unexpected quarter. Churchill, who had shown little interest in the subject, entered the debate on the side of the president. After a private lunch with FDR, he had taken advantage of his host's hospitality and enjoyed his afternoon nap in one of the rooms of Livadia Palace. He now seemed in great fighting form. His decision to take part in the discussion came as a complete surprise not only to the Americans but also to his own delegation. "I was terrified of what P.M. might say," Alexander Cadogan wrote to his wife, as "he does not know a thing about it—he has always refused to look at it—and here he was plunging into debate!"

Churchill said that he had had his doubts about the original voting formula floated at Dumbarton Oaks, but after studying the president's new proposal he had concluded that it adequately protected the interests of the United Kingdom. Peace would indeed depend on the great powers, but it would be unjust not to allow smaller states to present their grievances. "If no such provision was made, it might look as if the three great powers were seeking to rule the world, whereas their desire was to serve the world and to preserve it from any renewal of the frightful horrors which had fallen on the mass of its inhabitants," he said, according to the British record. Cadogan was relieved: the prime minister had taken the line that the Foreign Office wanted him to take and had done so most effectively. "After floundering he did fairly well," the always critical permanent secretary told his wife.[13]

Stalin was drawn back into the discussion as Churchill produced a specific example of how the American formula would protect the interests of the great powers. The prime minister's argument was best summarized in the American record of the proceedings. "If China should raise the question of the return of Hong Kong under the President's proposal, both China and Great Britain would be precluded from voting in regard to the method of settlement of the controversy," he said, to illustrate how the system would work. Stalin found this unconvincing. A few months earlier, in Moscow, Churchill had raised the example of Hong Kong in conversation with Stalin to show why he opposed the American proposal. "If in the discussion of that question Britain and China are asked to go out of the room, and the question is decided by Russia and the United States, Britain will not be pleased," Churchill had told Stalin on October 9. Now he seemed to have no problem with that scenario, having been persuaded by the Americans that he could veto any decision he would not tolerate.

The Soviet leader inquired whether Egypt would be a member of the UN General Assembly and proposed that they discuss the Suez Canal. Churchill preferred to tie up his Hong Kong example first. Britain would be able to use its veto power to stop any action against it by the Security Council and "would not be required to return Hong Kong unless they felt that that should be done. China should however have the right to speak and the same considerations would apply for Egypt if that country had a complaint in regard to the Suez Canal." In the debate that followed, no one seemed to notice that China was not a small nation and, unlike Egypt, was being considered for membership in the Security Council.

Stalin said he did not question the right of smaller nations to voice their grievances, but he believed that Churchill was wrong to assume that China or Egypt would be satisfied with a mere discussion of the issue: they would want a decision in their favor. He mocked Churchill's rhetoric about the danger of creating an impression that the great powers wanted to rule the world. Was it the United States that wished to do so? Stalin asked, to the accompaniment of laughter. The president gesticulated that it was not. Was it the United Kingdom? No. The Soviet Union? Perhaps China? The laughter continued. Churchill tried to explain that he did not mean to single out any one power, but Stalin paid no attention. He continued ironically, "It looks as though two great powers had already accepted a document which would avoid any such accusation but the third has not yet signified its assent." Stalin promised that the Soviets would further study the document. He was convinced that the United States and Britain were ganging up on the Soviet Union and all but accused them of doing so.[14]

If Stettinius's presentation ended in confusion, Churchill's intervention turned Stalin completely hostile. Now the Soviet leader was intent on telling the gathering that there was a more important issue than the right of smaller nations to express their opinions. That issue was the unity of the three great powers, which alone could assure continuing peace. As the American protocol of the meeting recorded Stalin's words: "They all knew that as long as the three of them lived none of them would involve their countries in aggressive actions, but after all, ten years from now none of them might be present. A new generation would come into the present not knowing the horrors of the present war." The Soviet dictator was all but echoing what Churchill had told his doctor that morning. It is hard to say whether that was a coincidence or proof of the effectiveness of Soviet eavesdropping. James Byrnes later considered that statement so uncharacteristic of Stalin that in his memoirs he attributed it to Churchill.

"We are apparently making it our goal to establish world security for at least the next fifty years, or perhaps [I only think] so because of my naïveté?" Stalin offered provocatively. Then he reminded all assembled that "a covenant must be worked out which would prevent conflicts between the three great powers." He was allegedly concerned with the great powers' capacity to prevent the revival of German militarism, but few in the room failed to grasp how dangerous those conflicts could be in their own right, irrespective of the possible revival of the German threat. Suspecting Roosevelt and Churchill of being in league against him, Stalin reminded his counterparts that no peace settlement could last without Soviet participation. After delivering this implicit threat, he apologized for not having had time to study the American proposal in detail.

Stalin's words were a reminder that the peace being negotiated at Yalta was not one between the Allies and the Axis but between the victors themselves. Roosevelt had this in mind when he promised in his fourth inaugural address to work for "a just and durable peace," as did Churchill when he predicted that the next war would be ideological, and Stalin when he thought about the lonely future for the USSR in the American-sponsored United Nations organization. His outburst may have been triggered by a concern that the United States and

Britain would use their client states to launch a diplomatic offensive against the USSR. Stalin hinted at this when he said that the president's proposal could create a dangerous situation for Great Britain: "If China or Egypt raised complaints against England they would not be without friends or protectors in the assembly," he said. Churchill tried to allay Stalin's concerns.

The debate came to an end when Roosevelt finally intervened. He had sat silently through most of the discussion, allowing his unexpected ally to do all the work. Now he entered the fray. He supported Churchill in assuring Stalin that the expulsion of a UN member would require a unanimous decision of the Security Council, something that succeeded in pacifying Molotov, who said this was the first that the Soviet delegation had heard of it. Then Roosevelt explained that the unity of the three great powers was the first goal of his government, but if conflicts were to arise between them, they would become known to the world regardless of voting procedure in the Security Council. "Full and friendly discussion in the Council would in no sense promote disunity, but on the contrary, would serve to demonstrate the confidence which the Great Powers had in each other and in the justice of their policies," he concluded. Stalin showed no sign of softening his position and proposed that the discussion continue on the following day. The president had little choice but to agree. He knew that without Stalin's consent there would be no United Nations, and without that organization he believed there would be no lasting peace.[15]

The Americans were disappointed. "I was deeply disturbed by the clear evidence that Stalin had not considered or even read our proposal on voting in the Security Council even though it had been sent to him by diplomatic air pouch on December 5," Byrnes wrote in his memoirs. Lord Moran recorded Hopkins's reaction to Stalin's position: "That guy can't be much interested in this peace organization." The disappointment was shared by some members of the British party. "Stalin," wrote Lord Moran, "can see no point in vague sentiments and misty aspirations for the freedom of certain small nations. He is only concerned with the borders of Poland, with reparations and with what he can pick up in the Far East. Roosevelt would like to prescribe for the world, Stalin is content to make clear what the Soviet Union will swallow."[16]

10

IN THE FÜHRER'S SHADOW

On February 6, the Big Three approved the first communiqué of the Yalta Conference, which was to be released on the following day. "There is a complete agreement for joint military operations in the final phase of the war against Nazi Germany," the communiqué announced. It also made reference to the future occupation of Germany and the creation of the United Nations: "Discussions of problems involved in establishing a secure peace have also begun. These discussions will cover joint plans for the occupation and control of Germany, the political and economic problems of liberated Europe and pro-posals for the earliest possible establishment of a permanent international organization to maintain peace."[1]

Stalin's suspicion of the United Nations was largely informed by the Soviet Union's sour experience of the League of Nations. Stalin told Roosevelt and Churchill that his "colleagues in Moscow could not forget the events of Decem-ber 1939, during the Finnish war, when, at the instigation of England and France, the League of Nations expelled the Soviet Union and mobilized world opinion against it, even so far as to speak of a crusade." He was referring to the last decision of the League's Security Council, enacted on December 14, 1939. It came at the height of public outrage against the Soviet invasion of Finland, which began on November 30, three months after German troops invaded Poland.

The Soviet attack on Finland resulted from Stalin's attempt to extend his power over the region designated as his "sphere of influence" by the Molotov-Ribbentrop Pact of August 1939, which divided Eastern Europe between Ger-many and the USSR, setting off the Second World War. At the last dinner of the Yalta Conference, which was hosted by Churchill, Stalin ventured something of a backhanded apology for his earlier cooperation with Hitler, although he placed part of the responsibility on the Western Allies. "The Soviet government would never have signed a treaty with Germany in 1939," he said, "had it not been for Munich and the Polish-German treaty of 1934." Stalin regarded the Munich agreement of 1938 and the normalization of Polish-German relations four years earlier as encouragements to German eastward aggression that led up to Hitler's attack on the USSR. The issue of the Soviet-German alliance never came up in any detail during official conference sessions, but the Soviet leaders were persistently haunted by Hitler's shadow in the corridors and conference rooms of the Yalta palaces.[2]

February 6 was the first day since the beginning of the Soviet winter offensive that Adolf Hitler was actually able to enjoy himself. Eva Braun celebrated her thirty-third birthday. There was a party, guests, and dancing. Hitler, according to Martin Bormann, his private secretary and head of the Nazi Party apparatus, was in a "radiant mood." Three days earlier during a heavy Allied bombardment of Hitler's Berlin apartments, the buildings of the New Chancellery, the People's Court, and the Nazi Party headquarters were all hit and damaged. Close to three thousand Berliners died in the inferno, but Hitler and his entourage escaped unscathed in the bunker he had built for himself more than 8 meters beneath the ground.[3]

Hitler had moved to the complex under the garden of the Old Chancellery on January 16. This would be his last home. The Nazi leaders were already considering suicide and looking for supplies of poison. With the collapse of the counteroffensive in the Ardennes and the German defenses in the east, the visibly shaken and worn-out führer took refuge in dreams of postwar retirement in his hometown of Linz. As the town had been destroyed by Allied bombing, Hitler ordered the architect Hermann Giesler to speed up his reconstruction work. The model was finally delivered to Hitler's bunker on February 9. From then on, the führer would spend hours studying it and dreaming.

Speculation about an impending split among the Allies provided another psychological refuge for the disheartened führer. His propaganda minister, Joseph Goebbels, continued to remind him of the "Miracle of the House of Brandenburg," which featured Frederick the Great, Hitler's favorite historical figure, whose portrait hung on the wall of his underground study. In 1762, when Prussia was on the verge of failure in its struggle against a powerful coalition including France and the Russian Empire, Frederick's stubborn resistance was rewarded: Empress Elizabeth of Russia suddenly died, and the anti-Prussian coalition collapsed. Goebbels, who had presented Hitler with a copy of Thomas Carlyle's biography of Frederick the Great, convinced himself that there would be a repetition of history. Hitler and Goebbels pinned their hopes on the incompatibility of Stalin's communism with the values of the Western democracies. The Yalta communiqué gave no indication that a split, if there was to be one, would come anytime soon.[4]

Nazi propaganda declared the already lost war a struggle not only for Germany but for European civilization as a whole against the Red menace and

Asiatic barbarism. It was silent about the fact that the führer had unleashed the Second World War by concluding an alliance with the leader of the very "hordes" now approaching Berlin. Nor would Soviet propaganda make any mention of Moscow's previous alliance with the "German barbarians." The Soviet leaders did not like to be reminded of their deal with the Nazis. In Teheran, when Anthony Eden had referred to the pre-1941 Soviet boundary as the Molotov-Ribbentrop Line, Molotov had interrupted to say that it was the Curzon Line. Eden shot back that there was no difference between the two. "Call it what you will," Stalin said curtly. "We still consider it right and just."[5]

Molotov was only a few months into his new job as foreign commissar when he signed the nonaggression pact that made his name notorious for generations to come. In Stalin's eyes, the man Molotov had replaced in May 1939, Maxim Litvinov, had a number of "shortcomings," including the respect he commanded in London and Paris and the fury he aroused in Berlin.

Litvinov was born in 1876 into a wealthy Jewish family in the Polish-Belarusian border town of Białystok, then part of the Russian Empire. Meir Henoch Mojszewicz Wallach-Finkelstein, as Litvinov was known at birth, joined the Russian Social Democratic Labor Party at its inception in 1898. He became a Bolshevik in 1903 and was forced to leave the Russian Empire after his arrest and spectacular escape from a Kyiv prison. He became an arms trafficker, supplying guns for Russian revolutionaries. He was again arrested in France in 1908 on charges of money laundering: he had attempted to exchange a large amount of currency appropriated by Stalin and his gang of revolutionaries in the Caucasus in the summer of 1907. The whole operation was conducted on Lenin's orders, and it was the first time that Litvinov and Stalin worked together. During the decade before the Russian Revolution of 1917, Litvinov lived in Britain, where he met his future wife, Ivy Lowe, also a descendant of a wealthy Jewish family. When the Bolsheviks took power in Russia, he became the first representative of the revolutionary government to Britain.

As Soviet foreign commissar from 1930 to 1939, Litvinov was instrumental in establishing diplomatic relations between the Soviet Union and the United States. He became a symbol of Soviet commitment to the policy of collective security and to good relations with Britain and France. His dismissal in the months following Munich reflected a deliberate distancing of the Soviet Union from England and France—Stalin was disappointed in the Western democracies' attitude toward the USSR and did not want a Jewish foreign commissar to represent him in dealings with Hitler. Molotov was appointed in Litvinov's place and ordered to purge the Foreign Commissariat of Jews.[6]

The road to cooperation with Hitler was now open. The Molotov-Ribbentrop Pact contained a secret protocol that divided Eastern Europe between Germany and the USSR. "In the event of a territorial and political rearrangement of the areas belonging to the Polish state, the spheres of influence of Germany and the U.S.S.R. shall be bounded approximately by the line of the rivers Narev, Vistula and San," stated article 2 of the secret protocol to the pact. Hitler triggered such a "territorial and political rearrangement" on September 1 by attacking Poland from the west. The Soviets crossed the Polish eastern border on September 17. The new Soviet-Polish border established on August 23 was fine-tuned during Ribbentrop's second visit to Moscow on September 28, with final changes introduced by the secret Soviet-German protocol of January 10, 1941. That protocol increased Soviet deliveries of raw materials, including petroleum products, manganese, copper, and grain, to Nazi Germany, which had begun in the previous year. All these documents were signed for the Soviet side by Viacheslav Molotov.[7]

As was often the case in the conduct of Soviet foreign policy during the war, Stalin was hiding behind his foreign commissar. The Yugoslav communist leader Milovan Djilas, who met with both Molotov and Stalin on more than one occasion, wrote that "with Molotov not only his thoughts, but also the process of their generation was impenetrable. Similarly, his mentality remained sealed and inscrutable. . . . Molotov was almost always the same, with hardly a shade of variety, regardless of what or who was under consideration." Djilas preferred Stalin, who "was of a lively, almost restless temperament." So did Western diplomats, who were more likely to hear the answer they hoped for from Stalin than from Molotov.

But this was little more than a game that Stalin liked to play. The Soviet leader preferred to say no through his chief foreign-policy adviser and to deliver good news himself. The telegrams Molotov sent to Stalin when he was out of the country show quite clearly who was in charge of Soviet foreign policy. Molotov's interpreter, Valentin Berezhkov, believed that his boss had more freedom of action than any other foreign commissar under Stalin, but he was clearly under his boss's spell. "I often had occasion to observe," Berezhkov wrote in his memoirs, "how nervous Molotov became whenever some proposal of his did not meet with Stalin's approval. He would be gloomy and irritable for several days."[8]

The division of Eastern Europe into "spheres of influence" between Germany and the USSR was a peculiar phenomenon. To be sure, the establishment of spheres of influence by large states that dominated their weaker neighbors was a well-established practice in European and world diplomacy of the nineteenth and early twentieth centuries, but the Molotov-Ribbentrop Pact used that concept to denote what eventually became zones of occupation. The two parties were not interested in working with local governments: they wanted to occupy the territories themselves. The Germans took the lead, invading Poland a mere week after signing the Molotov-Ribbentrop agreement. The Soviets followed suit, first taking over eastern Poland and then, once the fall of

Paris signaled a shift in the European balance of power in favor of Germany, occupying countries in their sphere of influence—first in the summer of 1940 the three Baltic states of Estonia, Latvia, and Lithuania, and then Bessarabia (Moldavia) and northern Bukovyna, which had hitherto belonged to Romania.

The only state in the Soviet sphere that remained independent was Finland, simply because it offered resistance. Finland emerged from the Winter War of 1939–40 with reduced territory, shattered but sovereign, and ready to fight for its continued existence against the Red giant to the south. Soviet losses were enormous. Stalin learned his lesson and did not try to introduce socialism in Finland after the war. Hitler saw the results of the Winter War as proof that the USSR was a colossus with feet of clay. He would not make any more deals as favorable to the Soviet Union as the Molotov-Ribbentrop Pact.

Molotov got an opportunity to sense the new mood in Berlin on his short visit to the German capital in November 1940. The main purpose of his trip was to complain about German violations of the nonaggression pact. Stalin was upset about the presence of German troops in Finland, which the pact assigned to the Soviet zone of influence, and by the conclusion in August 1940 of a German-Romanian treaty about which the USSR had not been consulted. The Soviets wanted the Germans out of Finland and urged them to revoke their signature to the treaty of mutual assistance with Romania.

Stalin also had his eye on the Black Sea Straits, a centuries-old obsession of Russian foreign policy. The Eastern Question, as the European diplomatic wrangle over the division of Ottoman possessions became known in the nineteenth century, may have been considered largely settled in London and Paris, but Russia never got what it wanted most from the failed empire—the Straits. Without controlling the Bosporus and the Dardanelles, the Soviets could not feel entirely secure in the Black Sea, and their southern fleet would be locked out of the Mediterranean. After dividing Eastern Europe with Germany, Stalin was prepared to take part in the division of southeastern Europe. He was eager to establish Soviet military bases in the vicinity of the Straits and (now that Romania was in Germany's camp) to bring Bulgaria into the Soviet sphere of influence.

In their negotiations with Germany, as later with the Western Allies, the Soviets argued the case for the creation and expansion of their sphere of influence by appealing to their security needs. The Straits, Molotov claimed, had served as "England's historic gateway for attack on the Soviet Union." This was a veiled reference to the Crimean War and foreign intervention immediately after the Russian Revolution. "The situation was all the more menacing to Russia as the British had now gained a foothold in Greece," he continued. "Russia had only one aim in this respect," he told Hitler. "She wanted to be secure from an attack by way of the Straits and would like to settle this question with Turkey; a guarantee given to Bulgaria would alleviate the situation," continued Molotov, referring to Soviet plans to include Bulgaria in their sphere of influence by concluding a treaty of mutual assistance against possible aggression. "As a Black Sea power Russia was entitled to such security and believed that she would be able to come to an understanding with Turkey in regard thereto."

If Stalin and Molotov were interested in establishing secure Soviet borders in Eastern Europe and enhancing Russian influence in the Balkans, Hitler wanted the Soviet Union to help him defeat the British Empire. He tried to downplay Soviet-German tensions in Eastern Europe and sought to maneuver the Soviets out of the region, diverting them against the British Empire in Asia. He invited Molotov to join the tripartite Axis Pact, signed less than three months earlier by Germany, Italy, and Japan, and help divide the entire world into spheres of influence. In the grand scheme he laid out, Italy would get North Africa, Germany would recover its former colonies in sub-Saharan Africa, Japan would take over Southeast Asia, and the USSR would be given freedom of action in Iran and India.

Molotov showed no interest in expanding into Asia, but as the talks went on, Soviet demands concerning Eastern Europe increased. Molotov not only insisted on the removal of German troops from countries bordering the USSR but also made implicit threats against Finland. At his last meeting with Ribbentrop in Berlin, Molotov indicated that the USSR was interested in developments in a number of countries outside its sphere of influence. "The fate of Romania and Hungary was also of interest to the Soviet Union and could not be immaterial to her under any circumstances," he said. "It would further interest the Soviet government to learn what the Axis contemplated with regard to Yugoslavia and Greece, and, likewise, what Germany intended with regard to Poland." Farther north he expressed his country's interest in the continuing neutrality of Sweden and strategic passages: the Store Belt, the Lille Belt, Oresund, Kattegat, and Skagerrak. This was the agenda contained in Stalin's telegrams: Molotov sometimes repeated his arguments verbatim.[9]

The negotiations in Berlin went nowhere. If Molotov was met with great pomp on his arrival, he was sent home with minimal attention. Hitler was outraged by Molotov's arrogant demeanor and lack of flexibility. He might have agreed with Churchill's later remark that Molotov was a modern robot. But Molotov, misreading the signals he was getting from his hosts, returned to Moscow convinced that Germany was interested in strengthening its relations with the USSR. Ten days later he summoned the German ambassador and handed him the Soviet conditions for joining the Axis powers. They were nothing more than a recapitulation of the demands he had made in Berlin. Some would later serve as a basis for the position taken by the Soviet leadership in its negotiations with Britain and the United States at Teheran and Yalta.

The USSR agreed to join a quadripartite alliance with Germany, Italy, and Japan on condition that German troops be removed within the next few months from Finland, Soviet land and naval bases be established in the Black Sea Straits, Bulgaria sign a mutual-assistance agreement with Moscow, the Soviet Union be given a free hand south of the Caucasus as far as the Indian Ocean, and Japan renounce its interests in northern Sakhalin. The Germans never responded. The idea of directing Soviet expansion toward the Indian Ocean was Hitler's, but he found the rest of the Soviet agenda outrageous. Riding high on the easy territorial acquisitions of the previous year, Stalin had overplayed his hand, asking too much and offering very little in return.[10]

The alliance with Hitler offered Stalin a hope of realizing the grand imperial vision of the tsars. In November 1914, not long after the outbreak of the First World War, Nicholas II shared his vision of a new Balkan order with the French ambassador, Maurice Paléologue. Constantinople should become a neutral city, with the Turks expelled from Europe. Former Turkish territories on the European continent should go to Russia and Bulgaria. "Western Thrace to the Enos-Midia line should be given to Bulgaria," the emperor offered. "The rest, from that line to the shores of the Straits but excluding the environs of Constantinople, would be assigned to Russia." Nicholas considered the whole Balkan Peninsula a Russian sphere of influence and confidently planned territorial changes there: "Serbia should annex Bosnia, Herzegovina, Dalmatia and Northern Albania. Greece should have southern Albania with the exception of Valona, which must be assigned to Italy. If Bulgaria behaves properly she should receive compensation in Macedonia from Serbia." Such was imperial policy at its height.[11]

Stalin inherited a shattered empire whose territorial losses he was now trying to recover. But if he inherited the ruins of an empire, he also embraced imperial dreams. The goal of controlling Constantinople and the Straits would inspire both the tsars and their communist successors. Even younger Soviet officials like Valentin Berezhkov, who interpreted Molotov's conversation with the German ambassador, Friedrich von Schulenburg, concerning Soviet conditions for joining the Axis, were susceptible. "Can Stalin actually realize that age-old dream of the Russian autocrats? There will indeed be reason to exalt him as wise and great," Berezhkov thought as he escorted Schulenburg from the Kremlin. "I was overcome by some kind of great-power intoxication," he wrote many years later, in the last days of the USSR. "I gave no thought at all to how much grief, blood, and tears the realization of those plans would bring."

Molotov's visit to Berlin left Stalin with the illusion that within a few short months he could be in possession of the Straits. Stalin's relations with the British, who were courting the Soviet dictator even as he was courting Hitler, offered no prospect of anything of the sort. The British had learned about the timing of Molotov's visit in advance; they expressed their attitude toward what they saw as a deepening of the Soviet-German alliance by bombing Berlin on the night when Molotov had his last meeting with Ribbentrop. If anything, the bombing complicated the German task of convincing Molotov to take part in the division of the "defeated" British Empire. In response to Ribbentrop's claim that Britain was finished, Molotov allegedly asked whose bombs were falling on Berlin.[12]

The bombing of the German capital was coordinated with the release of sensitive information on a British diplomatic offer to the Soviets. In October the British ambassador in Moscow, Sir Stafford Cripps, proposed an agreement whereby the British Empire would recognize the Soviet territorial acquisitions of 1939–40, including the annexation of the eastern Polish provinces, in exchange for neutrality vis-à-vis Britain and noninterference in the affairs of Indian Ocean countries. The proposal was not remotely as attractive as Hitler's offer, nor did it address the main Soviet concerns of the day. "The truth is that it was not so much Sir Stafford who failed as the British Government in London," claimed an article in the November 25, 1940, issue of *Time*, "which understands Russian sensitivity less than its Ambassador. While Sir Stafford was earnestly assuring Moscow of Britain's friendship, the Government froze the Baltic States' bank balances in England, refused to surrender Lithuanian, Latvian and Estonian ships in British ports, and last month requisitioned several of those ships. All this served to deepen Joseph Stalin's Oriental distrust of the Occidental Britons." Indeed it did![13]

Hitler tried to play on that distrust. During his meeting with Molotov, he allegedly said, "What's happening? An England, some miserable island, owns half the world and they want to grab it all—this cannot be tolerated. It's unjust!" "This cannot be considered normal," Molotov said in response. As he remembered later, Hitler "cheered up." "He wanted to win me over and almost did," Molotov remarked with an ironic smile to one of his acquaintances in the early 1970s. In his later years, Molotov was proud that the Nazi leader got nothing from him. "He wanted to involve us in risky business," said Molotov. "And he'd be better off after we got stuck in the south. We'd depend upon him there when England went to war with us. You had to be too naïve not to realize that." Neither Stalin nor Molotov considered himself naive. Their anti-imperial indoctrination led them to reject visions of faraway colonial acquisitions, but they were willing participants in the partition of Europe into spheres of influence, which they considered an imperative of Soviet security.[14]

The negotiations in Berlin had convinced Hitler that he would have to move against his former ally: the Soviet Union refused to embark on a military campaign against Britain in Asia and had become too greedy for its own good in Europe. On December 18, 1940, less than a month after Molotov's visit to Berlin, Hitler signed plans for the invasion of the USSR. Operation Barbarossa, named after the twelfth-century Holy Roman Emperor who led the Third Crusade but died before reaching the Holy Land, was scheduled for May 1941.

Its authors planned a surprise attack on a front almost 3,000 kilometers in length, involving 410 divisions, or more than four and a half million men. It was postponed for a number of reasons, including bad weather and the previously unplanned German invasion of Greece and Yugoslavia in April, and it began in the early hours of June 22, taking the Soviet leadership by surprise.

Over coffee at one of Molotov's meetings with Hitler in November 1940, Joachim von Ribbentrop, a former wine merchant, had regaled Molotov and Hitler with a discussion of wine labels and peppered his guest with questions about the Massandra vineyards on the outskirts of Yalta. Less than a year after the kaffeeklatsch in Berlin, the Germans were in full possession of the Massandra vineyards. By November 1941 they controlled the Crimea, where Red Army formations had been cornered in Sevastopol, and had taken Kyiv, besieged Leningrad, and approached Moscow.

The German invasion dramatically altered the dynamic in Europe. Britain, which had fought Nazi Germany alone after the surrender of France in June 1940 (the United States remained officially uninvolved), gained an unexpected ally. Churchill was quick to put aside his anticommunism and take advantage of the new situation. "If Hitler invaded Hell," he said later, "I would make at least a favourable reference to the Devil in the House of Commons." On July 8, he wrote to Stalin. Four days later Molotov sat down in Moscow with Sir Stafford Cripps to sign an agreement on a new military alliance with Great Britain. In late July Stalin received Harry Hopkins, who flew to Moscow through Arkhangelsk to size up the Soviet leader. In late September Averell Harriman and Lord Beaverbrook, representing the American and British governments, came to Moscow to negotiate with Stalin on the delivery of military supplies in order to keep the Soviet Union fighting. A new alliance was born. Leaders of countries that had begun the war on opposing sides were now partners.[15]

At Yalta neither Stalin nor Molotov was eager to remind his guests of his dealings with Hitler and Ribbentrop on the eve of the war. But their experience of negotiating with the Nazis and the territory they seized could hardly have failed to influence their current tactics and ambitions. When they switched sides, the Soviets' greatest preoccupation was to reclaim what they had obtained as a result of the Molotov-Ribbentrop Pact and to get as much as possible of what had been on Stalin's agenda during Molotov's trip to Berlin in 1940. In the course of negotiations with Anthony Eden in December 1941, Stalin insisted not only on the recognition of the new Soviet borders with Poland but also on the right of the USSR to have "mutual-assistance" treaties with Finland and Romania. The idea of gaining control over the Black Sea Straits and establishing a protectorate over Bulgaria was dropped, given that Turkey was neutral, and one had to be careful not to provoke it into joining the war on Germany's side. Romania, as a neighboring country, carried more weight for Moscow than

Bulgaria, whose strategic importance was mainly related to control of the Straits.

Soviet diplomatic language was adjusted to fit the requirements of their new alliance. Rather than formulating demands in terms of spheres of influence, Molotov now spoke of "collective security" and treaties of "mutual assistance." As a trade-off for the military bases in Finland and Romania, they proposed that the British establish a similar relationship with Holland and Belgium. The rationale was that both countries needed such outposts to ward off future aggression from Germany. The Soviets would propose the same quid pro quo again in May 1942, and again without success.

In the fall of 1943 they turned down a British proposal to issue a joint declaration renouncing spheres-of-influence diplomacy. The proposal was put forward on the eve of the conference of foreign ministers that took place in Moscow in October and November 1943. The British, who had abandoned hope of convincing the Americans to launch an Allied invasion of the Balkans, were now keen to prevent the Soviets from establishing a sphere of influence in that part of the world. A puzzled Molotov commissioned Maxim Litvinov to explain what the British had up their sleeve. Litvinov's diplomatic career had been saved by the German attack on the USSR. His connections with the Western democracies were at a premium again. He was brought out of semiretirement and dispatched to Washington as Soviet ambassador, and in May 1943 he was recalled to Moscow to serve as Molotov's deputy. Molotov, who was suspicious of his intelligent and worldly predecessor, ensured that Litvinov would have little influence in the commissariat. Still, Litvinov's expertise was needed, and his memoranda were certainly read, if not always taken into account, by both Stalin and Molotov.

The best Litvinov could come up with was an analysis of the Western press. In his report to Molotov he noted that an editorial of March 9, 1943, in the London *Times* had proposed to treat Europe as a zone of mutual British-Soviet responsibility. If Britain's borders were to be on the Rhine, the Soviet borders should be on the Oder, the editorial argued. The *Times* editorial aroused protests from representatives of the nations that would be swallowed up by this agreement, most notably the Poles, and Litvinov thought it possible that the British proposal was intended to calm public opinion.

The Soviets wanted no part in whatever game the British were playing by denouncing spheres of influence. "It is to be considered undesirable," read the instructions to the Soviet delegation at the Moscow Conference, "to have our hands tied by the proposed declaration, whose only purpose is to offer satisfaction to the Poles, Turks, and others who fear our influence in Eastern Europe." The conference adopted a four-nation declaration that proclaimed the Allied commitment to work jointly toward the creation of an international organization and included a pledge not to use military force in the liberated areas after the end of the war. There was not a word in the document about spheres of influence. The Soviets could regard this as a victory.

At the conference, Molotov opposed the British idea of forming a set of federations of smaller East European states on the Soviet borders, stating that Soviet public opinion regarded them as a new cordon sanitaire directed against the USSR. He was referring to an appeal made in 1919 by the French president, Georges Clemenceau, to create an alliance of states bordering on Soviet Russia in order to stop the spread of communism. While Molotov rejected plans for East European federations, he stopped short of renouncing spheres of influence as an instrument of Soviet foreign policy. That spheres of influence would help organize a world awaiting the spread of communist revolution was a basic premise of Soviet policy throughout the Second World War. Molotov allegedly told Hitler that "if the socialist and capitalist states want to reach an agreement, there must be a partition—this is your sphere of influence and this is ours."[16]

II

DIVIDING THE BALKANS

" There will no longer be need for spheres of influence, for alliances, for balance of power or any other of the separate alliances through which, in the unhappy past, the nations strove to safeguard their security or to promote their interests," wrote Cordell Hull optimistically in his report on the Moscow Conference of foreign ministers that took place on the eve of the Teheran meeting of the Big Three. Hull's statement was cited in a paper entitled "American Policy Towards Spheres of Influence," which was included in the State Department's Yalta briefing book. The same wording could be found in Roosevelt's report to Congress on the results of the Yalta Conference. It was a classic example of Wilsonian idealism—a mix of good intentions and wishful thinking.

The leaders of the United States began the twentieth century like those of any other great power, strongly believing in the principle of balance of power and the division of the world into spheres of influence. The Monroe Doctrine, which declared the preponderance of U.S. interests in Latin America, was an article of faith in American foreign policy. President Theodore Roosevelt, a strong believer in spheres of influence and the balance of power, had no qualms about the Japanese occupation of Korea in 1908: since Korea was too weak to defend itself, no law or agreement could protect it from its more powerful neighbor.

All this changed with the presidency of Woodrow Wilson, who in the last years of the Great War gave powerful voice to prevailing disappointment with the old principles of international politics that were widely held responsible for the outbreak of the conflict. Wilsonian principles triumphed again with Cordell Hull's defeat of Sumner Welles's model of a regionally based world peace organization. By the fall of 1943, the Wilsonian vision of a new world order free from spheres of influence dominated American thinking on international affairs. The problem was how to convince the world, especially America's partners in the Grand Alliance, that it should be relegated to the past.

The State Department paper in the Yalta briefing book left no doubt that while the United States was working hard on the blueprint of the world security organization, its allies were busy dividing Europe. "The evolution of events in recent months," wrote the authors of the paper, "indicates that the British and the Soviet Governments are in fact operating under such an arrangement [for the division of spheres of influence], as shown chiefly by the Soviet forbearance in Greece and the teamwork in Yugoslavia where the British seem to feel, however, that the odds are against them. In Albania, where, so far as we know, no arrangement was made, the British have tried to keep a little ahead of the Russians. In Hungary the Russian military position has given the Soviet Government a predominant position, which the British have perforce had to accept. With only a somewhat precarious 'lead' in Greece, the British may well feel that the scheme has neither divided in an equitable manner the areas of influence, nor protected the British position in the Mediterranean."[1]

On January 12, 1945, Maxim Litvinov and Ivan Maisky attended a reception at the American embassy, where they watched the American blockbuster *His Butler's Sister*, starring Deanna Durbin. Kathleen Harriman, who was a hostess, later told her sister Mary that three Russian songs performed by Durbin "brought the house down—though there was much laughter about pronunciation." "Both Litvinov and Maisky," she continued, "sitting next to me cried (or at least sniffled) at the sentimental parts, which I thought rather sweet."[2]

The two men sniffling next to Kathleen Harriman were the primary architects of the new Soviet foreign policy. In the spring of 1943, when Stalin decided to take personal control of relations with the Western Allies, appointing the young and inexperienced yes-men Andrei Gromyko and Fedor Gusev as ambassadors to Washington and London, respectively, Maxim Litvinov and Ivan Maisky, who had served in the Allied capitals during the first stage of the war, were brought back to Moscow and put in charge of two commissions responsible for Soviet postwar planning. They wrote scores of memos dealing not only with the partition of Germany and German reparations but also with Soviet strategic interests and aspirations in Europe and beyond.

The victories at Stalingrad and Kursk, and the Teheran Conference, which brought de facto recognition of the 1941 borders, encouraged Soviet strategists to take an optimistic view of their geopolitical prospects. Soviet ambitions in Europe became obvious to American observers after Teheran. In December 1943, in an article entitled "Cordon Insanitaire?" *Time* magazine gave voice to the worries of policy makers in Washington: "Thus Russia once again served notice of her determination to block the revival of the old cordon sanitaire idea of unfriendly buffer states between Russia and the West. What western statesmen had to worry about was whether Russia intended to make this impossible by setting up its own form of cordon 'insanitaire' among the central and eastern European countries."[3]

George Kennan, who returned to the U.S. embassy in Moscow in the summer of 1944 after a seven-year absence, expressed similar concerns in a thirty-five-page memo entitled "Russia—Seven Years Later," which he completed in September. Kennan argued that the USSR was prepared to realize its foreign-policy agenda of 1939, which was heavily influenced by tsarist ambitions. "The program meant," wrote Kennan, "the reestablishment of Russian power in Finland and the Baltic states, in eastern Poland, in northern Bukovina, and in Bessarabia. It meant a protectorate over western Poland and an access to the sea for the Russian Empire somewhere in East Prussia. It meant the establishment of dominant Russian influence over all the Slavs of Central Europe and the Balkans, and, if possible, the creation of a corridor from the western to the Southern Slavs somewhere along the border between Austria and Hungary. Finally, it meant Russian control of the Dardanelles through the establishment of Russian bases at this point." This was more or less the program laid out by Molotov in his conversations with Hitler in Berlin. "It is a matter of indifference to Moscow whether a given area is 'communistic' or not," Kennan continued. "But the main thing is that it should be amenable to Moscow influence, and if possible to Moscow authority."[4]

Would the Soviets continue the policy of the tsars, or would they be fired by visions of world revolution and global communist dominance? That was the question Roosevelt and his advisers asked themselves during the war. It was not easily answered, partly because the master of the Kremlin and his chief strategists were themselves torn by conflicting imperatives: promoting the geostrategic objectives of the USSR and assuming responsibility for the world communist movement.

In January 1944 Maisky composed a long memo that was sent to Stalin, Molotov, Beria, and other members of the Soviet leadership. He proposed that the Soviet Union should seek to establish itself as the dominant land power in Europe and Asia and to promote the triumph of socialism in Europe. The successes of the Red Army and the rise of communist-led resistance movements in Nazi-occupied Europe encouraged him to think big. Socialist revolutions in Europe were a major goal of Maisky's plan, and indigenous communist movements were to help achieve that. Nevertheless, the geopolitical interests of the Soviet Union ultimately defined his strategy. The Soviet-Czechoslovak treaty of mutual assistance, signed on December 12, 1943, provided Maisky with a model. The agreement obliged the two countries to offer each other military assistance in case of German aggression for the next twenty years. Other countries, such as Poland, were invited to join on the same terms. Maisky regarded the signing of the treaty as an indication that Czechoslovakia was "capable of being an important conductor of our influence in Central and Southeastern Europe."

In the Balkans, Maisky proposed that mutual-assistance agreements be signed not only with Romania but also with Yugoslavia, Bulgaria, and Greece. The treaties, while offering protection against foreign invasion, would provide a legal basis for Soviet presence and influence in the region. Maisky linked the conclusion of such treaties with prospects of eliminating the pro-German regime in Bulgaria and the growing influence of Communist parties in Greece and Yugoslavia. Greece gave Maisky pause. Well versed in British foreign policy, he wrote: "The question of Greece is somewhat more complex. The USSR is considerably less interested in Greece than in other Balkan countries, while England, on the contrary, is extraordinarily interested in Greece." The Greeks were not to be turned down if they asked for a treaty, but Britain was to be included as a signatory.

If Britain objected to Soviet treaties with Yugoslavia and Bulgaria, argued Maisky, it could be invited to join them as a third party. Geographic proximity would ultimately strengthen the influence of the USSR. Maisky proposed that every effort be made to weaken Hungary and Turkey. He also wanted to strengthen Soviet influence in northern Iran and gain access to the Indian Ocean through ports in the south of the country. Maisky's program was far more ambitious than the requests that Stalin and Molotov made to Hitler in 1940, or indeed anything that Russian strategists had imagined since the First World War. The transnational ideology that Russia had lacked in 1914 was giving communist Russia an additional edge.[5]

On October 9, 1944, Stalin and Churchill met in Stalin's Kremlin office, accompanied only by their foreign ministers and interpreters. "The Americans would be shocked if they saw how crudely he [the prime minister] had put it. Marshal Stalin was a realist. He himself was not sentimental while Mr. Eden was a bad man," Churchill told Stalin according to a passage in the British protocol that was omitted from the official record of the discussion but fully corroborated by the Soviet protocol of the meeting. The prime minister then offered Stalin a proposal for carving up the Balkans between Britain and the USSR. "So far as Britain and Russia are concerned, how would it do for you to have ninety per cent predominance in Roumania, for us to have ninety per cent of the say in Greece, and go fifty-fifty about Yugoslavia?" Churchill would later write, recalling his conversation with Stalin. It was a proposal to divide the Balkans into spheres of influence, consciously made behind the back of one of the members of the anti-Hitler coalition. Despite Roosevelt's insistence, Averell Harriman was not invited to the meeting. The initiative came from the British: Stalin merely went along.[6]

Britain was an old power, and for generations its leaders had considered spheres of influence the most natural way of organizing the world and securing British interests abroad. In 1938 Neville Chamberlain not only allowed Hitler to make territorial acquisitions in Europe but also was ready to give Germany a sphere of influence in Africa. That outlook did not change when Churchill replaced Chamberlain as head of the British government, but the close relations with the United States favored by Churchill made it necessary to change the language that the British used abroad. In the fall of 1943 they puzzled the Soviets by offering a joint declaration renouncing spheres of influence as an instrument of foreign policy. They clearly did not want the Soviet Union to have a sphere of influence in Eastern Europe, but, like their Soviet counterparts, they hardly considered the principle wrong in itself.

In the spring of 1944, as the Red Army approached the prewar Soviet borders, and the Communist parties and their partisan forces gained ground in Yugoslavia, Greece, and Italy, time was running out for a deal with the Soviets. All three countries bordered the northern Mediterranean, a strategically important region for the British Empire, and all three had strong Communist parties that gained influence and numbers in the course of the war. Their aspirations to power were an obstacle to British plans for the region. Churchill believed that he could solve the problem by dealing directly with Moscow. On May 4, 1944, he wrote to Eden: "Evidently we are approaching a showdown with the Russians about their Communist intrigues in Italy, Yugoslavia, and Greece." Two weeks later Eden summoned to London the Soviet ambassador, Fedor Gusev, to discuss the prime minister's initiative: in exchange for the British giving the Soviets a free hand in Romania, London would get a free hand in Greece.

Britain was keenly interested in controlling Greece: in a letter to the British ambassador to Washington, Lord Halifax, Churchill referred to Greece as Britain's old ally, "for whom we sacrificed 40,000 men in 1941." This was an allusion to Britain's participation in the defense of Greece against the German invasion, which ended in failure and was later severely criticized in Parliament. With its strategic position in the Mediterranean, Greece was the key to the control of transportation routes essential to the British Empire. If Britain was serious about keeping India, it had to prevent other powers from taking control of Greece or, indeed, any other Mediterranean nation. Romania had a coast on the Black Sea, not the Mediterranean, and was thus a mere "paper loss" to the British. Churchill believed that the Soviets would occupy it and impose their rule with or without British approval.

The Soviet leaders were definitely interested in the British proposal, but Stalin insisted that the Americans sign it as well. Churchill had no choice but to go to Roosevelt for approval. In his letter to the president he used language as evasive as possible so as not to alarm Washington. "There have recently been disquieting signs of a possible divergence of policy between ourselves and the

Russians in regard to the Balkan countries, and in particular towards Greece," wrote the prime minister on May 31, 1944. "We therefore suggested to the Soviet Ambassador here that we should agree between ourselves as a practical matter that the Soviet Government would take the lead in Rumanian affairs, while we would take the lead in Greek affairs, each Government giving the other help in the respective countries. . . . I hope you may feel able to give this proposal your blessing. We do not of course wish to carve up the Balkans into spheres of influence, and in agreeing to the arrangement we should make it clear that it applied only to war conditions."

The prime minister's message infuriated Roosevelt's advisers, who had been led to believe by Lord Halifax that the British would discuss their proposal with Washington before offering it to Moscow. Now it turned out that consultations with the Soviets had already taken place! Upon learning of Washington's reaction to his message, Churchill wrote to Halifax saying once again that he was not planning to carve Europe into spheres of influence. At the same time, he pointed out that Washington had its own sphere of influence in Latin America: the British, he noted, were taking their lead from the United States. That message, which Churchill encouraged Halifax to show to the Americans, made things even worse. Roosevelt wrote to Churchill that the proposed measures would lead to "the division of the Balkan region into spheres of influence despite the declared intentions."

Churchill restated the arguments he had made to Halifax, omitting any reference to Latin America. He claimed that there was no other way to deal with the problem, as any consultative machinery would be too cumbersome to permit timely action. Churchill wrote that the British needed to act quickly and decisively to neutralize the communist guerrillas in Greece and save the country from civil war. He also brought up the British sacrifice for the defense of Greece in 1941 and the fact that the king and the prewar Greek government were in exile on British territory. The Soviets, in his opinion, would do as they wanted in Romania without regard to the West. Churchill promised to report to Roosevelt on British actions in Greece.

On June 13, 1944, Roosevelt finally gave his consent. Nevertheless, he kept complaining about British unilateralism, and Churchill promised that the deal would be reviewed in three months. In Roosevelt's eyes, it was Churchill, with his imperial outlook, who was chiefly responsible for bringing back the old and discredited principle of spheres of influence. Churchill would not admit as much in his memoirs. He modestly referred to the spheres-of-interest deal as a "political arrangement with the Russians."[7]

Roosevelt's worst suspicions were confirmed in October 1944, when Churchill and Stalin turned the Eden-Gusev deal, reached in May, into a comprehensive agreement on the division of the Balkans. Churchill did everything in his power to avoid language that would annoy the Americans. He proposed to define each power's influence in a given country in percentages, explaining later to his cabinet that these were not meant to establish a "rigid system of spheres of interest." They were rather intended as "an interim guide for the immediate war-time future." There would be no impenetrable borders obstructing the movement of capital, goods, and political ideas.

Having discussed Anglo-American relations with Roosevelt at Quebec City in September 1944, and not wanting to wait until the next Big Three meeting, now that it had to be postponed to allow for the American elections and the presidential inauguration, Churchill decided to meet with Stalin in Moscow. Poland and the Balkans were at the top of the prime minister's agenda. His main concern was a communist takeover of Eastern Europe. "As the victory of the Grand Alliance became only a matter of time it was natural that Russian ambitions should grow," Churchill wrote in his memoirs. "Communism raised its head behind the thundering Russian battle-front. Russia was the Deliverer, and Communism, the gospel she brought."

Bucharest fell to the Soviets on August 23, 1944. Sofia followed suit on September 8, when the Bulgarians surrendered. On September 24, the Red Army resumed its attack on the southern sector of the German front, aiming at Budapest and Belgrade. All that stood between the Soviets and Greece was the Eden-Gusev deal, made a few months earlier, and by now all but defunct. The Soviets would hardly feel compelled to honor the deal if there were no British troops in Greece. Racing against time, Churchill sent British paratroops to the lower Greek mainland. The invasion was announced on October 5, a few days before Churchill's trip to Moscow.[8]

Few were misled about the motive. "The British 'invasion' of Greece announced yesterday is more properly an 'occupation' for politico-military objectives rather than an assault," wrote Hanson W. Baldwin in the *New York Times*. Still, the optics of the Balkan situation had improved. On October 9, the day on which the British prime minister flew to Moscow, an article in *Time* magazine gave a different snapshot of the situation: "Russia's Red Army lunged last week across the Danube into Yugoslavia. British forces landed on the coasts of Albania, on the islands of Dalmatia, inched into Greece. From two sides of the Balkan massif, Europe's two greatest powers were approaching a junction in the Balkans."[9]

The fate of the whole Balkan Peninsula hung in the balance, and Churchill had no time to lose. His first meeting with Stalin took place at 10:00 p.m. on the day of his arrival. They started with Poland. Then Churchill broached the Balkan question. By now the deal on Romania and Greece had expired— three months had passed, after which, as Churchill had promised Roosevelt, the agreement would be reviewed, and the Soviets, now in full possession of

Romania, could easily disregard its provisions. Given the merely symbolic presence of British paratroops on Greek soil, Churchill had to rely on diplomacy to prevent such an outcome.

The prime minister began by praising the Soviet armistice with Romania, stating that what was happening in that country was a Russian affair. "But in Greece it was different," Churchill said, according to the British protocol. "Britain must be the leading Mediterranean power and he hoped Marshal Stalin would let him have the first say about Greece in the same way as Marshal Stalin had about Romania." Stalin did not object. To Churchill's great relief, the Soviet leader responded like a pragmatic imperial strategist rather than a preacher of the communist gospel. "Great Britain lost a great deal as a result of German seizure of the Mediterranean sea lanes," Stalin began. He understood that "if the security of that route is not ensured, Great Britain will suffer a great loss. Greece is an important point for establishing the security of that route." He agreed that "England should have the right to a deciding voice in Greece."

Churchill could not have hoped for a more positive response. He wrote in his memoirs: "The moment was apt for business, so I said, 'Let us settle about our affairs in the Balkans.'" He told Stalin that he had prepared a table whose main idea should be handled in such a way as not to alarm the United States with the possibility of a division of Europe into spheres of influence. Roosevelt had insisted that Harriman be present at all British talks in Moscow, but Churchill suggested to Stalin that he be invited to most but not all meetings between the two leaders. Stalin could not have been more agreeable: Roosevelt was asking too many things for himself, while leaving too few to Britain and the USSR. Besides, the Soviet Union had a treaty of mutual assistance with Britain but not with the United States.

To cement this new relationship, Churchill confided that he did not like the American proposal for voting procedure in the United Nations Security Council. This was a private remark, and Churchill expressed his hope that Stalin would deny they had ever discussed the question in Moscow. Stalin confirmed it with a smile. The two leaders clarified their positions and swore each other to secrecy. They could now do business behind their partner's back.

Churchill's offer to Stalin was prepared in the form of a table. In Romania the USSR would have 90 percent influence, with 10 percent going to Britain; those proportions would be reversed in Greece, and Yugoslavia would be divided equally. Next on the list was Hungary, also divided 50/50, and Bulgaria, with 75 percent influence for the USSR and 25 percent for Britain. "I pushed this across to Stalin, who had by then heard the translation. There was a slight pause," remembered Churchill. "Then he took his blue pencil and made a large tick upon it, and passed it back to us. It was all settled in no more time than it takes to set down."

Either Churchill's memory was playing tricks on him—he dictated the account of the meeting in November 1950—or the prime minister was playing tricks on the readers of his memoirs. Stalin's tick was placed against the percentage allocation for Romania only, meaning that he was prepared to extend the Eden-Gusev agreement on Romania and Greece but not to accept the rest. In fact, Stalin immediately made a counterproposal: he wanted a 90 percent share for the Soviet Union in Bulgaria as opposed to the 75 percent suggested by Churchill. Eden, who was present at the meeting, intervened, saying that in Romania the British were mere observers, but they wanted a larger role in Bulgaria. Despite Churchill's later statement to the contrary, there was no immediate deal on percentages.

When Molotov joined Churchill and Stalin, he raised an issue that had been on his agenda in Berlin in 1940: were the British prepared to discuss the Turkish question? It became clear that in the minds of the Soviet leaders Bulgaria was still linked to the Black Sea Straits. Churchill said that he was not touching on the Turkish question but was glad that the two sides had reached agreement on the rest of the issues. Then it was Stalin's turn. He pushed Churchill for revisions to the Montreux Convention of 1936, which gave Turkey control over the Straits. The prime minister took a defensive position: he was in favor of Soviet ships having access to the Mediterranean but was not prepared to make a firm commitment at that point.

Churchill did not want to involve Turkey. He did, however, want to protect British positions in Italy, which he considered part of the Western, if not exclusively British, zone of influence. There he was eager for Stalin to rein in the communists, whom he considered troublemakers: their activities in northern Italy might lead to clashes with Allied troops. Stalin was not keen to oblige. He claimed to have no influence over the Italian communist leader, Comrade Ercoli (Palmiro Togliatti). There were no Soviet troops in Italy, and he could not issue orders to communists there, as he could in Bulgaria. "If he were to give any advice to Ercoli, Ercoli could send him to the devil, as he, Comrade Stalin, does not know national conditions in Italy at all," reads the Soviet protocol of the meeting. Stalin seemed open to a deal on Italy in exchange for freedom of action in Bulgaria. He never said so directly, but in response to Churchill's repeated request to rein in the communists in northern Italy, Stalin reiterated that he wanted to change the percentages for Bulgaria. Churchill played for time. He suggested that Molotov and Eden discuss the question first. He did not care terribly much about Bulgaria.[10]

On October 10, Molotov told Eden that the Soviet share of influence in Hungary should be increased from 50 to 75 percent. Eden, for his part, was interested in securing the 75/25 split in Bulgaria that Stalin had challenged the previous day. He proposed the creation of a tripartite commission there on the model of the Allied Control Commission established for Germany—at Yalta the accession of the French to that commission would become a highly controversial issue. Molotov protested, saying that Bulgaria was not occupied by three powers, as Germany would be. He compared Bulgaria to Italy, where the Western Allies were calling all the shots: by the same token, the Soviets should be in charge of Bulgaria. They bargained endlessly over percentages. On the next day, October 11, the two sides finally reached an agreement: 80/20 in Bulgaria and Hungary and 50/50 in Yugoslavia. The Soviets improved their position in Bulgaria by 5 percent and in landlocked Hungary, where the British showed little resolve to fight for their "share," by 30 percent, but Eden was quite happy. He wrote in his diary: "[A]ll was as smooth as it had been rough yesterday and we obtained what we wanted on almost all points. I should say 90 per cent overall."[11]

Churchill and Eden did what they could: Stalin held all the trump cards. The precarious British position in the Balkans on the eve of the meeting was described most vividly by Whittaker Chambers in the October 9 issue of *Time* magazine. "It was sound policy for the Russians to refrain from setting up Communist governments in the Balkan states now occupied by the Red Army," wrote *Time*'s diplomatic observer. "But Britons would be less than empire builders if they were not aware that, in the cold-blooded language of politics, the Balkans had become a Russian sphere of influence. As such, it undid the work of a hundred years of British statecraft, and made Russia a Mediterranean power—poised massively above the artery of Empire at Suez."[12]

The Moscow deal put Churchill's worries to rest, at least with regard to the Mediterranean. Greece would be protected, and the British had secured a 50 percent share in Yugoslavia. At one point in the negotiations Molotov even suggested that if Britain agreed to a predominant Soviet role in the Balkans, the USSR would stay away from the Adriatic coast. From the British viewpoint there were reasons for optimism: the empire would continue in its prewar configuration, its lines of communications intact and secure. The fate of the rest of the Balkans would not directly impact the United Kingdom.

Churchill could see no other way of dealing with the growing Soviet influence in Europe. In Eastern Europe it was the strength of the Soviet armies that worried him; in southern Europe it was the strength of the local Communist parties, which continued to take orders from Moscow despite the formal liquidation in May 1943 (under Western pressure) of the Communist International, the headquarters of the world communist movement, which was based and controlled in Moscow. Churchill assured Roosevelt that he would inform him about the Moscow negotiations, but the Americans were never told about the percentages deal.

On February 6, 1945, the State Department telegraphed Yalta to give Stettinius its position on an article published in December in the Soviet foreign-policy journal *The War and the Working Class*, under the pseudonym G. Malinin. The author tried to reconcile the concept of what he called "security zones" with the idea of an international peace organization. "Malinin" criticized the formation of blocs, claiming that they caused wars. He was also against "spheres of interest," as they presupposed the dominance of one country over another. "Malinin's" solution was to establish "security spheres" within the international world organization. He was in favor of allowing the British to sign agreements with Belgium and Holland, while reserving the right for the USSR to sign agreements with its neighbors.

The article was translated into English and sent to Washington, where it was regarded as a potential threat to the future United Nations organization. The State Department experts did not trust "security spheres." They turned out to be right. The author hiding behind the pseudonym "Malinin" was none other than the Soviet deputy people's commissar for foreign affairs, Maxim Litvinov. In a memorandum he forwarded to Molotov and Andrei Vyshinsky in January, he drew on the ideas expressed in his published article but used the terms "sphere of influence" and "security sphere" interchangeably.[13]

Litvinov made his major contribution to Soviet thinking on spheres of influence in November 1944. A few weeks after the Churchill-Stalin percentage deal, he submitted a memorandum proposing that Europe be divided between the USSR and Britain into two spheres of influence. Litvinov's plan was less influenced than Maisky's by visions of world communist revolution and more by geopolitical thinking. Litvinov was the only consistent supporter of close cooperation with the Western Allies during and after the war. Later, some students of Soviet foreign policy would see in him and his ideas an alternative to the Cold War policies eventually adopted by the Soviets. His disagreement with the direction of Soviet postwar policy was known in the West, and his death under suspicious circumstances in December 1951 was taken to corroborate such assessments. But Litvinov's wartime memos show that he had a most unusual view of postwar cooperation.[14]

Litvinov's memorandum assigned Sweden, Finland, Poland, Czechoslovakia, Hungary, Romania, all of the Balkans excluding Greece, and Turkey to the Soviet "security sphere." The British sphere would include Western Europe, with Denmark, Germany, Austria, and Italy constituting a neutral zone. Litvinov's appetite was bigger than that of Maisky ten months earlier, as shown by his addition of Sweden, Poland, Hungary, and Turkey to the earlier list. It exceeded Kennan's worst expectations and would have given Churchill and Eden a terrible fright. Litvinov was doubtless emboldened by the successes of the Red Army, which by November 1944 was in possession of much of Poland and had entered Hungary. But no Soviet success could explain the addition of Sweden and Turkey, nor were there any plans to invade those countries, as they remained neutral and had no German troops on their territory.

On January 11, 1945, in preparation for the Yalta Conference, Litvinov sent Molotov and Vyshinsky a second memo that repeated major provisions of his earlier memorandum of November 1944 and the article he published later that year in *The War and the Working Class*. He maintained that ideally the Soviet "security sphere" would include Finland, Norway, Sweden, Poland, Hungary, Czechoslovakia, Romania, Yugoslavia, Bulgaria, and Turkey. Litvinov expected the British to oppose the inclusion of Yugoslavia and Turkey in the Soviet sphere. He also thought that it would be unwise to discuss "security spheres" with the Americans, given the negative attitude of the American media to the idea. "Personally, Roosevelt, as a realist," wrote Litvinov, "perhaps sees the inevitability of spheres, zones, and blocs arising in Europe, but, taking account of public opinion, he will not venture to give his agreement to that in any form."[15]

Like the Molotov-Ribbentrop Pact of 1939, Litvinov's plan was a proposal to formally divide the world in two irrespective of the will of the nations in question, which could be coerced into acquiescence once an agreement was reached. It was an ambitious plan, to say the least, but it accepted some limits, as Litvinov had no desire to dominate southern Europe. The Soviets wanted control of the Straits in order to turn the Black Sea into an internal lake, not to dominate the Mediterranean. Greece had a special place in the Russian imperial psyche, given its Orthodox heritage and the Greek project of Empress Catherine II, which was meant to take possession of Constantinople. In the twentieth century, however, Greece was never high on the list of Russian and Soviet geopolitical objectives. The converse was true of Romania, which, along with Bulgaria, offered access to the Straits by land.

Molotov and Stalin followed Litvinov's advice and made no effort to put the question of spheres of influence on the agenda of the Yalta Conference. While there was a fair amount of discussion about Yugoslavia and Turkey at Yalta, spheres of influence were never openly discussed. The American delegation at Yalta would not have entertained it as a legitimate topic of discussion. The only American official who might have, George Kennan, was in Moscow, entrusted by Harriman with running the day-to-day business of the American embassy during the ambassador's absence. By then Kennan had strengthened his conviction that the Soviets were determined to secure control of a sphere of influence in Eastern Europe. He had also decided that it was in America's best interest to accept it. He wanted to bury the idea of the United Nations "as quickly and quietly as possible."

In a letter that Charles Bohlen received on arrival at Yalta, Kennan wrote:

> I am aware of the realities of this war, and of the fact that we were too weak to win it on our own. I recognize that Russia's war effort has been masterful and effective and must, to a certain extent, find its reward at the expense

of other peoples in eastern and central Europe. But with all of this, I fail to see why we must associate ourselves with this political program, so hostile to the interests of the Atlantic Community as a whole, so dangerous to everything which we need to see preserved in Europe. Why could we not make a decent and definitive compromise with it—divide Europe frankly into spheres of influence—keep ourselves out of the Russian sphere and keep the Russians out of ours?

Bohlen considered Kennan's proposals unrealistic. "Foreign policy of that kind cannot be made in a democracy," he wrote to his friend from Yalta. "Only totalitarian states can make and carry out such policies." Nor did he think that formal international agreements could stop Soviet expansion in Europe. "Either our pals intend to limit themselves or they don't. I submit, as the British say, that the answer is not yet clear. But what is clear is that Soyuz [the Soviet Union] is here to stay, as one of the major factors of the world. Quarreling with them would be easy, but we can always come to that."[16]

The exchange between Kennan and Bohlen went to the heart of the moral dilemma that the Western delegations faced at the Yalta Conference. Was it better to accept the reality of Soviet military dominance in Eastern Europe and dissociate themselves politically and morally from what the Soviets were doing there, or, on the contrary, should they try to influence the situation by cultivating the Soviets and thus implicitly legitimizing their rule? Bohlen believed that more could be achieved by remaining on a friendly footing with the Soviet Union. That was also the prevalent mood in the American delegation at Yalta. Roosevelt and his associates were prepared to pay a price for their continuing alliance with the Soviets. Like Bohlen, they probably believed that there would always be time to exercise other options.

I2

THE BATTLE FOR POLAND

"**M**r. President, at this time the fate of many nations rests in your hands and in the hands of Prime Minister Churchill," began a letter telegraphed to Roosevelt at Yalta. It was dated February 3, 1945, and signed by the prime minister of the Polish government in exile, Tomasz Arciszewski. No one knew the exact day of the start of the Big Three conference, but Arciszewski asked the State Department to give the letter "urgently" to the president. Fateful decisions about his homeland would be made soon, and he knew he was running out of time. Arciszewski sent a similar letter to Churchill.

The leader of the London Poles called on the American president to save his nation. "The whole world expects that these important discussions . . . will result in the creation of foundations for a future peace, a peace which should bring to nations the freedom of conscience and speech and secure for them freedom from fear and want," he wrote, invoking the language of the Atlantic Charter, which was dear to Roosevelt's heart. "I trust that these essential freedoms will also be granted to our nation, which has been fighting unflinchingly for their realization at the side of the great American and British democracies. In particular I trust you will not permit any decisions to be taken which might jeopardize the legitimate rights of Poland or her independence and that you will not recognize any faits accomplis with regard to Poland." It was the letter of an ally who knew that his country was about to be betrayed.[1]

At Yalta, all three participants considered the Polish question to be the most difficult one on their agenda. Every major geopolitical sticking point—the relations between the great powers and smaller nations, the tension between the vision of the world peace organization and the practice of spheres of influence, and the legitimacy of territorial acquisitions—came together in the debate on Poland.

On his first night at Vorontsov Churchill, full of energy despite the long flight and the car trip, stayed up late talking to Eden, his doctor Lord Moran, and his daughter Sarah: "If the President is only going to be here for five days, we mustn't waste time like this," he said. "We must begin with the political part of our programme, the Poles in particular. After all, I can't tell the Russians how to advance more quickly in the East. Stalin must realize that the people in England who are keenest on good relations with Russia are most worried over Poland. Our future good relations with our ally are at stake. We can't agree that Poland shall be a mere puppet state of Russia, where the people who don't agree with Stalin are bumped off. The Americans are profoundly ignorant of the Polish problem. At Malta I mentioned to them the independence of Poland and was met with the retort: 'But surely that isn't at stake.'"

Lord Moran, who recorded this impromptu speech, noted that it was not the first time Churchill had presented this argument: "When the P.M. begins to talk of the Poles, I know what is coming. I could prompt him if he faltered in his piece." If Churchill's remark about "ignorant" Americans was not entirely mistaken, it was not entirely fair either. Eden and Stettinius had actually agreed on a common strategy on Poland when they met on Malta. In fact, Churchill was in part repeating what Eden had written to him after the meeting. "If the Russians persist in their present policy," wrote Eden, "that would only neutralize the efforts of all those in our two countries most anxious to work with Russia."[2]

The fate of Poland was one of the few matters on which there was basic understanding between Churchill and Roosevelt. For the Americans, Poland was the acid test of Soviet goodwill and an essential guarantee that their dream of the United Nations could come to fruition. For the British, Polish independence was both a matter of enormous symbolic importance, as they had entered the Second World War on account of Poland, and the last hope of checking Soviet expansion in Eastern Europe. If the Western Allies were determined to address Poland at Yalta, the Soviets were reluctant. On February 4, when Eden suggested during a preconference meeting with Molotov that Poland be put on the agenda, Molotov responded that it would be better to leave the Poles alone.

The Soviets were eager to maintain the territorial acquisitions they had secured with the Molotov-Ribbentrop Pact, which had assigned the Ukrainian and Belarusian provinces of Poland to the Soviet Union. They also wanted control over the Polish government. In the memo he drafted that January, articulating Soviet foreign policy and goals, Litvinov pointedly did not include Poland as one of the countries whose fate the Soviets would decide in concert with their Western Allies. It was not that he was unaware of the British and American stand; rather, the future of Poland had already been decided in the Kremlin—it would be subject to close Soviet control. Any talk of a Soviet sphere of influence would be meaningless if the largest country bordering the USSR was not part of that zone.[3]

"I come from a great distance and therefore have the advantage of a more distant point of view of the problem," Roosevelt told Stalin and Churchill on the afternoon of February 6. In opening the discussion on Poland he was eager to establish his credentials as an impartial observer and disinterested judge. The fate of Poland was the first item on the British agenda, but the Big Three addressed it only after they had talked about Germany and the United Nations organization, which were the main points on the Soviet and American agendas. There were two main components to the "Polish problem": the borders of the future Polish state and the composition of its government.

Roosevelt began his presentation with borders. "He said," according to Charles Bohlen, who recorded his words, "that at Teheran he had stated that he believed the American people were in general favorably inclined to the Curzon Line as the eastern frontier of Poland, but he felt that if the Soviet Government would consider a concession in regard to Lwow and the oil deposits in the Province of Lwow that would have a very salutary effect." What was at stake was the future of the city of Lviv (Polish Lwów, Russian Lvov), a predominantly Polish (and, before the war, Jewish) enclave in a region inhabited largely by Ukrainians, and the oil fields in the Drohobych (Polish: Drohobycz) region. Roosevelt urged Stalin to draw the Soviet-Polish border in such a way as to leave Lviv and Drohobych on the Polish side. FDR said that there were six or seven million Poles in the United States. It would make his position at home easier if the Soviets could give something to their homeland. "Most Poles, like the Chinese, want to save face. . . . I am not making a definite statement," he added, "but I hope that Marshal Stalin can make a gesture in this direction."[4]

Roosevelt was trying to persuade Stalin to make major changes to the borderline to which he and Churchill had all but agreed at Teheran. Back then, Stalin and Molotov had defended the Soviet-Polish border established by the Molotov-Ribbentrop Pact, pointing out that it merely followed the so-called Curzon Line, which in turn was based on the ethnic boundary between the Poles and the Ukrainians. That line was first proposed as the eastern limit of Polish governmental authority in a declaration issued by the Supreme Council of the Allied powers in December 1919. A few months earlier, the Poles had defeated the armed forces of the Western Ukrainian People's Republic and secured control over the former Austrian province of Galicia, whose capital was Lviv. The experts of the Supreme Council prepared two versions of the line, depending on whether Eastern Galicia, which was largely settled by Ukrainians, remained part of the Polish state. One version left Lviv on the Polish side, the other on the Ukrainian.

In the summer of 1920 the British foreign secretary, Lord George Nathaniel Curzon, proposed the version of the line that left Lviv on the Ukrainian side as a line of demarcation between the Polish forces and the Red Army, which was then advancing on Warsaw. The proposed border, known as the "Curzon Line," was destined to play an exceptionally important role in international relations, although both the Soviets and the Poles rejected it at the time. The Soviets had high hopes of igniting world revolution and were not interested in ethnically based lines that would limit their progress. The Poles stopped the Soviet advance at the gates of Warsaw in a battle that came to be known as the "Miracle on the Vistula." They then counterattacked and, after advancing into Soviet territory, moved their border east of the Curzon Line, annexing territories settled by ethnic Ukrainians and Belarusians. Three leaders with key roles in the Second World War were directly involved in those events. Stalin, who served at the time as the political commissar of one of the Soviet military formations, contributed to the defeat of the Red Army by splitting its forces and ordering an attack on Lviv instead of continuing the advance on Warsaw. De Gaulle served as a military adviser to the Polish army, and Stanisław Mikołajczyk, the future prime minister of the Polish government in exile, fought in its ranks.

After their defeat at the Battle of Warsaw and their subsequent retreat deep into their own territory, the Soviets had no choice but to accept the new border at peace talks with the Polish government in Riga in 1921. Even so, they never ceased to assert that the lands east of the Curzon Line had been occupied by Poland in violation of the ethnic principle—by which logic, all Ukrainian and Belarusian lands had to be part of the USSR. The Molotov-Ribbentrop Line was fairly close to the Curzon Line, which gave the Soviets less territory. After the German attack on the USSR, the Soviet leadership was prepared to drop its insistence on the Molotov-Ribbentrop Line, concede some territory, and accept the Curzon Line. Apparently the Soviets believed there was a better chance of getting Western recognition of a line named after a British lord than the Nazi foreign minister.[5]

The tactic worked, largely because no one in the West doubted that the Soviets would eventually come into possession of Lviv and try to retain it at all costs. The Western leaders struggled to come up with a formula that would satisfy the Soviets without antagonizing the Poles. In November 1944, when Harriman visited Washington to discuss a number of urgent issues with the president, he found him in one of his dreamy moods, trying to come up with a solution to the Lviv problem. "The President developed a fantastic idea," wrote Harriman, "that Stalin might agree to have the city, which was a Polish island in a sea of Ukrainian peasants, governed by an international committee, leaving it for future plebiscites to decide the outcome. I tried to tell him that it was impossible to have a Polish, capitalistic city in a Ukrainian, socialist countryside. The President saw no problem with that. He said the peasants could come into Lviv and sell their produce to Poles for rubles." Roosevelt believed that commerce could solve every problem in the world.[6]

The president decided to make a last-minute plea to Stalin at Yalta, but he was careful about the manner in which he presented his request. "He said that he was merely putting forth this suggestion for consideration and would not insist on it," according to Charles Bohlen's record. FDR was especially careful partly because there was no real agreement between the Western Allies on the issue of Lviv. In his memo of February 1, 1945, on the results of his meeting with Stettinius on Malta, Eden told Churchill: "As regards Poland's eastern frontier, His Majesty's Government have already agreed with the Russians and announced publicly that this should be the Curzon Line, giving Lvov to the USSR. The Americans may however still press the Russians to leave Lvov to Poland." Indeed, the State Department memo on the Polish question, drafted around the same time, stated: "We should make every effort to obtain agreement for a Polish frontier in the east, which should run along the Curzon Line in the north and central section, and in the southern section should follow generally the eastern frontier line of the Lvov province."

On February 6, probably to the surprise of the Americans, Churchill supported their position after listening to the president's plea concerning Lviv. The prime minister said that he and Eden had been criticized by members of their own party for supporting the Soviet position on the Curzon Line and Lviv, but he believed that the Soviet claim was based not on force but on right, given Soviet sacrifices in the war with Germany and their efforts to liberate Poland. "If, however," he added, according to the American record of the meeting, "a mighty Power like Russia were to make a gesture of magnanimity to a much weaker Power, and were to make some territorial concession, such as suggested by the President, he need not say how much we should both admire and acclaim the Soviet action."[7]

This was a position similar to the one Churchill had taken on January 22, when British policy on Lviv was raised at a meeting of the war cabinet. One of its members reported rumors that Stalin was prepared to make a grand gesture on the eve of the Big Three meeting: to hand over Lviv to Poland "and build as his own gift to the Ukraine, another great Ukrainian city in its place." Eden was skeptical on the issue of Lviv, but not about the Ukrainian state itself. "He thought," stated the record of the meeting, "that Premier Stalin was genuine when he urged that the Ukraine would be a state of its own, in which case, of course, it would need a capital city as its centre." Churchill cautiously hoped for a grand gesture toward the Poles. "Nothing could have exceeded the stiffness with which Premier Stalin had in earlier conversations refused to concede Lvov," began the prime minister. "He had always thought, however, that Premier Stalin might make a great gesture at the Peace Table, and might then yield Lvov to Poland." He thought that the recent successes of the Red Army might encourage such a gesture, but the best British tactic under the circumstances was to refrain "from maintaining constant pressure on him."[8]

While Roosevelt began his presentation on Poland with the border issue, his principal concern was to maintain Polish independence, which was closely associated with the composition of the new Polish cabinet. The Big Three came to Yalta recognizing two different Polish governments. The United States and Britain recognized the London-based government in exile led by Tomasz Arciszewski, while the Soviets recognized the so-called Lublin government, which began its activity in Chełm (Ukrainian: Khoem), moved to Lublin, and, by the time of the Yalta Conference, had established itself in a suburb of Warsaw. Here was a divisive issue that would test their ability to resolve their differences. Eden and Stettinius, meeting on Malta, agreed that the solution lay in the creation of a new interim government that would pledge to hold free elections "as soon as conditions permit." The formation of a new government and subsequent elections became the cornerstones of Anglo-American policy on Poland.[9]

On February 6, switching from the border question to the future of the Polish government, Roosevelt suggested that a presidential council be formed that would appoint a government composed of representatives of the five main Polish parties, including the communists. Accor3ding to the plan proposed to Roosevelt by Stettinius, this new government would include representatives of the main political camps, starting with Bolesław Bierut, the leader of the Lublin Poles, and Archbishop Adam Stefan Sapieha of Kraków, the mentor of the future pope Jan Karol Wojtyła. Roosevelt liked the idea, though not from any particular knowledge of the Polish situation. "They wouldn't have a king, and they needed a regency council," he told Stettinius at Yalta. In actual fact, the Poles had not had a king since the eighteenth century and had done quite happily without one during the interwar period. Still, the idea of a council had its attraction. In it the communist Bierut would be outnumbered at least five to one.

"One thing must be made certain," said the president, eager to make his proposal more palatable to the Soviets: "Poland should maintain the most friendly and cooperative relations with the Soviet Union." Stalin, who was becoming increasingly agitated, interjected, "Poland should maintain friendly relations not only with the Soviet Union but with the other allies." He clearly had trouble imagining how a coalition government dominated by noncommunist parties could maintain good relations with the USSR. Few noncommunist Polish leaders would forgive or forget the Molotov-Ribbentrop Pact. Roosevelt refused to be distracted. He "had merely put forth a suggestion." He "thought if we could solve the Polish question it would be a great help to all of us."

Churchill was in full agreement with the president when he declared that Poland should harbor no "hostile design or intrigue against the USSR." According to the British record of the meeting, the prime minister said

> that he was more interested to see a strong, free and independent Poland than he was in particular territorial boundaries. He wanted the Poles to be

in a position to live freely and to live their own lives in their own way. That was the object which he had always heard Marshal Stalin proclaim with the utmost firmness. It was because he put his trust in the Marshal's declarations as to the sovereignty, independence and freedom of Poland that he did not consider the frontier question to be one of supreme importance. It was this that was so dear to the heart of the British nation and the British Commonwealth of Nations. It was for this that we had gone to war against Germany—that Poland should be free and sovereign. Everyone knew what a terrible risk we had taken when we had gone to war in 1939 although so ill-armed. This action had nearly cost us our life, not only as an Empire, but as a nation.

Poland should be "mistress in her own house and captain of her soul," declared Churchill, according to the American protocol. He indicated that the British did not "have intimate contact" with the Polish government in London and said he was in favor of forming a new government immediately that could include Stanisław Mikołajczyk, Stanisław Grabski, and Tadeusz Romer, members of the old government with whom the British had good working relations and who were prepared to recognize the new Soviet-Polish boundary. "This Government would be charged with preparing the way for a free vote of the Polish people on their future Constitution and Administration," Churchill argued. "If this could be done, we should have taken one great step forward towards the future peace and prosperity of Central Europe."[10]

The British were prepared to support the idea of a presidential council, but only if it facilitated the rapid creation of a new government, which was their ultimate goal. At a meeting of the British war cabinet on January 26 Churchill told his colleagues that "he anticipated that the Soviet representatives at the forthcoming meetings of Heads of Governments would demand the recognition of the Lublin Committee as the Government of Poland." He was ready for the fight. "We must bear in mind that recognition was the one counter which remained in our hands, and that we should not give it up save in return for something worth having," said the prime minister. If the Soviets refused to form a new government, Eden suggested to Churchill on Malta, "the present deadlock must continue. That would be bad, but a simple recognition of the Lublin Government would be even worse."[11]

The differences between the Allies on the Polish issue went back to the first months of the Second World War, when they were on opposite sides. It was the German invasion of Poland that had compelled Britain to declare war. After the Polish defenses collapsed, London had offered a safe haven to the Polish government in exile. The Soviet Union, by contrast, joined the Germans and embarked on an aggressive program of territorial acquisitions at the expense of the Polish state. This created a problem for all parties once the Soviet Union became the next victim of German aggression and joined the anti-Hitler coalition. The British pushed the London Poles to sign a treaty of mutual assistance with Moscow, but the country's borders remained unresolved, and Stalin came to see the London Poles as the main obstacle to international recognition of the new Soviet borders.

The victories on the front emboldened the Soviet leader in his hostility toward the Polish government in exile. His offensive against its representatives in Moscow began less than ten days after the encirclement of the German Sixth Army at Stalingrad. On November 31, 1942, Stalin abolished thirty-six offices of the Polish embassy in the USSR responsible for Polish citizens deported or evacuated to the Soviet interior from Western Ukraine and Western Belarus. Their employees were accused of spying. On January 16, 1943, Moscow informed the Polish government in exile that it had decided to revoke a provision of their treaty recognizing the Polish citizenship of ethnic Poles who found themselves on Soviet territory after September 1939. From now on they would be treated as Soviet citizens.

The Polish government protested and asked Britain and the United States to intervene. But after the German surrender at Stalingrad, nothing could stop Stalin. On February 17, 1943, the Soviet authorities officially refused to negotiate the issue of citizenship, and two days later Stalin launched a propaganda offensive against the Polish government. As the war of words intensified between Soviet propaganda outlets and the Polish media in exile, the British Foreign Office told its ambassador to the Polish government that he should instruct the Poles not to respond to the Soviet provocations, which would only "start a new exchange of home truths." Diplomatic discussions with Moscow would be more productive. The ambassador agreed, but the Polish government did not. It fired back with a statement on March 5, arguing that the Curzon Line was an armistice boundary, not a state border.[12]

In mid-April German radio announced the discovery of a mass grave of thousands of Polish officers in Katyn Forest, near Smolensk. The officers, taken prisoner by the Soviets in the fall of 1939, had been executed by their captors in the spring of 1940. The Soviets denied the charges and blamed the Germans for killing the Polish prisoners after they had taken the territory in 1941. The Polish government called for an investigation by the International Red Cross. The outraged Soviet leaders claimed that this was proof that the London Poles were siding with Nazi Germany. They used the incident as a pretext to break off diplomatic relations. Molotov, who signed the letter officially terminating relations, claimed that the Polish government was conducting a propaganda campaign in order to force Moscow to make territorial concessions at the expense of Soviet Ukraine, Belarus, and Lithuania.

A new low in Moscow's now officially nonexistent relations with the Polish government in exile was reached in the summer of 1944, when Stalin formed a Polish government of his own. The Polish Committee of National Liberation, hastily formed in Moscow in the second half of July (the name was modeled on the French committee led by Charles de Gaulle), agreed to the new Soviet-Polish border and was fully backed by the Soviet authorities. The committee was headed by the relatively unknown socialist Edward Osóbka-Morawski but in fact controlled by Polish communists, including its deputy head, Wanda Wasilewska, a Red Army colonel, and Bolesław Bierut, a longtime agent of Soviet military intelligence. On July 22, 1944, Moscow radio announced to the world the creation of the new committee. Stalin now had a Polish government of his own in essence, if not in name.[13]

Now the Soviet leader felt secure enough to resume negotiations with the London Poles. On August 3, at Roosevelt's insistence, he received in Moscow the prime minister of the Polish government in exile, Stanisław Mikołajczyk. The stocky, balding forty-three-year-old politician was an influential figure in Polish exile circles. He had fought twice in defense of Warsaw, first in 1920 against the Soviets, and then against the Germans in 1939, when he was head of the Polish Peasant Party and enrolled in the Polish army as a private. He and his comrades had succeeded in beating off the Soviets in 1920 but had suffered defeat in 1939. He became the leader of the Polish government in exile after his predecessor, General Władysław Sikorski, died in an airplane crash over Gibraltar in July 1943. Mikołajczyk possessed little of the charisma or authority of Sikorski, who first served as prime minister of Poland in 1922. Referred to by British leaders and Foreign Office officials as "Mick," the new prime minister struggled to reconcile the demands of his government with British and American interests, and the reality of Poland's defeat with a vision of its future grandeur.[14]

Eager to reverse the unfavorable tide of history, Mikołajczyk knew that the Poles had no one to rely on but themselves. Before leaving for Moscow, he gave his consent to an anti-Nazi uprising in Warsaw led by the underground Home Army, which acted in close cooperation with the Polish government in London. The revolt began somewhat prematurely on August 1, 1944, with Soviet troops approaching the city and Moscow radio calling on the Poles to rise. But no attempt was made to coordinate the Red Army's actions at the approaches to the city with those of the insurgents in Warsaw. Their leaders hoped that they could liberate Warsaw by themselves, establish their own administration, and create conditions for the return of the Polish government in exile. After more than two months of heroic struggle, the uprising was crushed. The Germans almost leveled Warsaw and annihilated potential future leaders of an independent Polish state. Estimates of Polish losses run as high as a staggering 150,000.

When Mikołajczyk green-lighted the uprising, he hoped that its success would strengthen his hand in negotiations with Stalin. By the time he met the Soviet leader, the rebels were already in trouble, as they had failed to achieve their immediate objective of establishing a solid front line in the city. Their forces remained scattered, which made it virtually impossible for them to liberate the whole city on their own. The success or failure of the uprising would eventually depend on Stalin. Faced with the prospect of the London Poles establishing their headquarters in Warsaw a few days after his own Polish government had been established in Chełm, Stalin was not inclined to support the rebels. Ultimately he preferred to leave them with no effective assistance, despite his promises to the contrary to Mikołajczyk.

There were both military and political reasons for this. When Soviet troops reached the outskirts of Warsaw they lacked the resources to continue their advance beyond the Vistula River. (They had encountered stiff resistance from a number of German armored divisions.) But Stalin's refusal to allow Allied airplanes, which supplied the rebels with food and ammunition, to land on Soviet territory for refueling leaves no doubt that he did not want the uprising to succeed. He wanted Poland for himself.[15]

When Stalin met with Mikołajczyk in early August 1944, his immediate goal was to secure the Polish prime minister's agreement to the formation of a new government consisting of selected London Poles together with the leaders of the Polish Committee of National Liberation. He also wanted him to recognize the Curzon Line as the basis for the new Soviet-Polish border. Stalin insisted that Mikołajczyk meet with the freshly minted Committee of National Liberation. With two Polish governments competing for recognition, Stalin could take on the role of proponent of inter-Polish understanding. The Western Allies found themselves backing Mikołajczyk's "unrealistic" London government, which refused to recognize what the Western leaders themselves considered to be in the best interests of the Polish people.

Churchill and Eden spent a good part of 1944 going from one meeting with "Mick" and his colleagues to another, trying to convince them to accept the new realities. Their last attempt was made in the course of Churchill's trip to Moscow in October 1944. Mikołajczyk, who was brought to Moscow on Churchill's insistence, was finally persuaded to accept the Curzon Line as a basis for the new eastern border of Poland. The hope was that Stalin might then be obliged to reach a compromise with the London government, but Mikołajczyk proved unable to convince his colleagues to approve the deal. He was forced to resign, bringing about the fall of the government. Mikołajczyk's resignation in late November 1944 left Churchill and the Western Allies with no one they fully trusted at the head of the Polish emigration. The new government of Tomasz Arciszewski, a socialist leader smuggled out of Poland in July 1944, failed to establish good relations with the Western Allies, who continued to rely on Mikołajczyk in their assessment of the Polish situation.

On New Year's Eve 1944, the Moscow-controlled Committee of National Liberation changed its name to the Provisional Government of the Republic of Poland. The communist Władysław Gomułka was appointed one of the two deputy prime ministers. The new government was officially recognized by the Soviet Union on January 5, 1945, over protests from the Western Allies. By the time of the Yalta Conference the provisional government was in Warsaw, where it controlled local administration in the Soviet-occupied part of Poland.[16]

The Soviets did their best to persuade other countries to recognize the provisional government. Stalin applied enormous pressure on General de Gaulle during his visit to Moscow in December. De Gaulle eventually succumbed, agreeing to an exchange of representatives, although Maurice Dejean, de Gaulle's ambassador to the Allied governments, assured the British Foreign Office on January 3 that he did so "on the understanding that they would have no diplomatic status." The Czechs were next on the Soviet list. On January 29, news reached the British war cabinet that "the Czechoslovak government, as the result of pressure from the USSR, now proposed to grant immediate recognition to the Lublin government. President [Edvard] Benes would advise the Czechoslovak Cabinet tomorrow to accede to the Russian wishes." Churchill told his colleagues, "We could not stop the Czechoslovak Government from recognizing the Lublin Government. Our own position was, of course, that we were determined that freedom, independence and sovereignty, coupled with free elections, should be ensured for Poland."[17]

The Western Allies were initially divided in their response to Stalin's actions. Roosevelt believed that Mikołajczyk and the Lublin Poles could still reach a compromise. "The president seemed still hopeful of getting Mikołajczyk to join up with the Lublin party and form a single government," telegraphed Lord Halifax, the British ambassador in Washington, on the results of his meeting with Roosevelt on January 6. "All Poles," suggested the president, "must be brought to see that they could only exist by the good favor of Stalin. Benes had been wise enough to see this and had therefore managed to get along very well." The British Foreign Office had believed that adding Mikołajczyk to the Lublin committee would not resolve the problem. In a memorandum on the "Polish-Russian Settlement" issued on January 5, they argued: "It is not enough to place Mr. Mikołajczyk and his supporters in a position which would enable them to sign a pact with the Soviets, because such a pact may not have lasting effects, but it is indispensable as far as the Polish side is concerned—to have the responsibility of such agreement shouldered by all shades of Polish politics."[18]

Such a program was much easier to formulate than to implement. For one thing, there was no unity among the different "shades of Polish politics" in exile. Like Roosevelt, Churchill and Eden preferred to deal with Mikołajczyk, who was now out of power, but the legitimate representative of the Poles abroad was now Tomasz Arciszewski. He and his supporters were opposed to any compromise with the Soviets on borders or the composition of the government. Throughout January, Eden and his advisers discussed a variety of scenarios for dealing with the problem. One involved bringing Mikołajczyk back into government and then initiating a compromise between the London and Lublin Poles. The project was eventually abandoned, as it was agreed that there was no ground on which Mikołajczyk and Arciszewski could come together.

Sir Orme Sargent presented the position of many of his colleagues in the British Foreign Office when, on January 8, he argued against building up a new representative government in London. "This would indeed be throwing down the gauntlet to Stalin and I cannot see that it would bring us any nearer a compromise solution, which is what we must look for," he said. He had no illusions regarding the representative character of the Lublin government but believed that with Soviet support and NKVD tactics, it would succeed in attracting new followers. "Instead, therefore, of building up a rival representative Government in London, ought we not to try to 'penetrate' the Lublin Government by arranging for Mikołajczyk and other political leaders and groups who are prepared to work for Polish-Russian entente to join with the Government while the latter are still prepared to welcome them. . . . This would mean that instead of reinforcing the present London government we would be prepared to see it disintegrate."[19]

Mikołajczyk went along with the new plan. On January 22, during his visit to the Foreign Office, he said that "it was no good of thinking of the fusion of the London government and the Lublin Committee." According to the British report on his visit, Mikołajczyk added that he would "not exclude the possibility of his collaborating in a government which would include, and no doubt, be based largely on, the Lublin party as well as Poles from liberated Poland." The previous day he had presented Eden with a memorandum spelling out his views of the situation. In it he argued for simultaneously deciding on the eastern and western borders, meaning that there should be no concession on eastern territories without compensation in the west. He hoped that in the east, the border would be more favorable to Poland than the Curzon Line. On the issue of the future government, which he considered tantamount to the question of Polish independence, Mikołajczyk believed that each of the five major political parties should have 20 percent of the cabinet seats.[20]

A few days earlier, Arciszewski and his colleagues had submitted to the British government a statement declaring that there should be no discussion of the borders of Poland at the impending meeting of the Big Three. With regard to the constitution of the government, they proposed that an inter-Allied commission be formed. The Foreign Office was skeptical if not openly opposed to these proposals. Alec Cadogan told the Polish foreign minister, Adam Tarnawski, on January 26 that "the document was not very realistic and did not in present circumstances advance matters much." Tarnawski responded that he did not think the Polish demands "so unreasonable that they ought not to be put forward." With apparent contempt, Cadogan asked whether the Polish government had any other ideas as to how they should conduct their business. Tarnawski offered no alternative and briefed Cadogan on Polish reports about Soviet arrests and killings of members of the Polish underground, declaring that it "must be stopped."

"I pointed out however," wrote Cadogan in his report on the meeting, "that it was really no use saying 'this must be stopped' when the Russian Army was in occupation of the country and Russian authorities in practical control. We had foreseen all these dangers and it was for that reason that in the past year or eighteen months we had been pressing for a compromise solution of the question, and in doing so we had been conscious of the dangers that a failure to reach agreement might produce." Tarnawski shot back that the previous government had gone too far in attempting to accommodate Soviet demands, without achieving anything. "I had only wished," Cadogan wrote in his report, "to put an end to this line of talk, which seemed designed to show that the Polish government had done all that was possible and to throw the blame on us for everything which Poland and the Polish population might have to suffer."

On the following day Eden instructed the Foreign Office to ask the Polish government in exile to provide a list of names of the leaders of the Polish underground so that the British delegation at Yalta could appeal to the Soviet government regarding their safety. Tarnawski refused to provide a list without consulting the leaders of the underground in Poland. Apparently the London Poles were concerned that the list would end up in Soviet hands. Instead, the Polish ambassador to Britain, Count Edward Bernard Raczyński, wanted the British to intervene on behalf of all members of noncommunist parties active in Poland, and officers and soldiers of the Home Army. The British delegation was leaving for Yalta with two Polish memoranda. The one they were prepared to take into account was Mikołajczyk's, not that of the leaders of the Polish government in exile.[21]

On January 28, Eden wrote to Churchill: "We want . . . a free and independent Poland. Stalin has promised this to us before, but he is not at present fulfilling his promise. Unless we can get a free and independent Poland our future cooperation with him, whether we will or not, is bound to be affected." The experts at the American embassy in Moscow were extremely pessimistic about the prospects of Stalin's delivering on his promise. "In the above circumstances," wrote the authors of the embassy's report, "the Soviet Government's position is that affairs in Poland are a fait accompli and that there is no compromise desirable or possible any longer with the Polish Government in London or its members. It may be expected, therefore, that the Soviet Government will request the American and British governments to recognize or at least send representatives to the Provisional government. If this is not forthcoming, the Soviets are likely to bide their time."[22]

13

"WHAT WOULD THE UKRAINIANS SAY?"

Stalin became increasingly agitated during Roosevelt's and Churchill's presentations on the afternoon of February 6. He interrupted Roosevelt twice, asked for a ten-minute recess, and was the first to speak after the break. "Suddenly Stalin stood up (hitherto he had always spoken seated) and made a broad gesture with his right arm," wrote Ivan Maisky, who knew Stalin quite well and was taken aback by the vehemence of his response. "He wanted to leave the table and start walking from one corner to the other, as he often did during conversations in his office, but he caught himself in time and refrained: at a conference of the 'Big Three' such behavior was not entirely appropriate. Accordingly, Stalin merely pushed back his chair and, gaining some free space, began to speak with unusual fervor."[1]

The Soviet leader started by cynically appropriating Churchill's theme, namely, that the solution of the Polish question was a matter of honor for the British. He said that it was also a matter of honor for the Russians, who in the past had "greatly sinned against Poland," but for them it was in addition a matter of security, not only because Poland bordered on the Soviet Union but also because, in the last thirty years, Germany had twice invaded Russia through Polish territory. Stalin insisted that the Polish corridor "cannot be mechanically shut from outside by Russia. It could be shut from inside only by Poland. It is necessary that Poland be free, independent and powerful. It is not only a question of honor but of life and death for the Soviet State. That is why Russia today is against the Czarist policy of abolition of Poland. We have completely changed this inhuman policy and started a policy of friendship and independence for Poland."

Stalin was actually saying that, unlike the Russian Empire, the USSR was not questioning the right of the Polish state to exist, but neither would it allow Poland complete independence, not because it was trying to establish a sphere of influence on its borders but because Germany threatened the USSR through Poland. The USSR was prepared to create a strong Polish state, but as a matter of security it had to dominate that state completely. In his defense of the Soviet position, Stalin was eager to invoke the origins of the Curzon Line, an argument that he often employed in negotiations with British leaders and the representatives of various Polish groups, including the leader of the Polish government in exile, Stanisław Mikołajczyk, in the course of 1944. The Curzon Line had not been invented by the Soviets, he said, but by the British, French, and American delegations to the Paris Peace Conference in 1919. Lenin had refused to accept it, but now Stalin was prepared to use that line as the basis for the Soviet-Polish border, giving Poland the province of Białystok, the birthplace of Maxim Litvinov, which the Soviets had taken over after being given a free hand by the Molotov-Ribbentrop Pact.

"The Soviet government had already deviated from Lenin's position," reads the Soviet protocol of the meeting. "Stalin asked whether the Allies wanted the Soviet leaders to be less Russian than Curzon and Clemenceau. . . . What would the Ukrainians say if they accepted the Allies' proposals? They might say that Stalin and Molotov had turned out to be less reliable defenders of the Russians and the Ukrainians than Curzon and Clemenceau. In what light would Stalin appear then on his return to Moscow? No, it was better to let the war against the Germans go on a little longer, but the Soviet Union had to be in a position to compensate Poland in the west at Germany's expense." The only concession Stalin was prepared to make was to offer divergences from the Curzon Line up to 8 kilometers in favor of Poland.[2]

Stalin countered Western demands for a new democratic government in Poland by accusing the representatives of the London government of instigating anti-Soviet activities behind Red Army lines. He claimed that the "Warsaw Poles" had trouble talking to the "London Poles," and that the Red Army, which needed stability behind the lines, was being assaulted by agents of the Polish government in London, who had already killed 212 Soviet officers and soldiers. In short, the Warsaw government was helping the Red Army defeat the Germans, while the London government was obstructing its actions. There was no way to check or refute Stalin's statement. Given the fact that Soviet security forces were attacking and disarming units of the Polish Home Army, which owed its allegiance to the London government, the casualties on the Soviet side may well have reached into the hundreds.

Stalin's response amounted to pure demagoguery. He concentrated his attack on Churchill's proposal that a new Polish government be formed at Yalta. "I am afraid it was a slip of the tongue," he said, "for without participation of the Poles it is impossible to create a Polish government. I am called a dictator and not a democrat, but I have enough democratic feeling to refuse to create a

Polish government without the Poles being consulted." He subsequently asked, "Should we ask the Warsaw Poles to come here or perhaps to Moscow?" The question remained unanswered.[3]

The Soviet dictator was at pains to show that although he had not been democratically elected, he was not free to do just as he pleased and had to pay tribute to various constituencies. If Roosevelt acknowledged the limitations imposed on his actions by American public opinion and voters, and Churchill cited the position of the war cabinet and criticism in his own party, Stalin claimed that he was under pressure and could not go back to Moscow with anything less than the Curzon Line. With the last remnants of political opposition to the regime erased in the terror of the 1930s, and with Stalin in full control of the Communist Party Politburo, the Council of Ministers, and the Supreme Soviet—the token Soviet parliament—there was in fact no one in Moscow capable of challenging the dictator's actions. His alleged constituency was made up of the peoples of the Soviet Union, also wholly subordinate to the Communist Party.

Stalin claimed Lviv and the surrounding area on behalf of the Ukrainians, the second-largest nationality in the USSR after the Russians. The city of Lviv was founded by the Rus' prince Danylo in the mid-thirteenth century and named after his son Lev. The environs of Lviv were settled by ethnic Ukrainians, who called themselves Ruthenians, but in the first half of the fourteenth century the region came under Polish control, and the ethnic composition of the city, now known as Lwów, changed dramatically. German, Polish, and Jewish merchants and artisans settled in the city, making Ukrainians a minority. When Maria Theresa of Austria added the region to her possessions in the last decades of the eighteenth century, German-speaking bureaucrats moved into the city, known in German as Lemberg.

The tsars had considered the Austrian province of Galicia part of the ancient Rus' land, and when Russian troops entered the city in the course of the First World War they claimed it for Russia on that basis, changing its name to Lvov. With equal enthusiasm they fought the opposing claims of Poles and Ukrainians, whom they labeled Mazepists, after the eighteenth-century Cossack leader Ivan Mazepa, who "betrayed" Tsar Peter I by siding with the Swedes at the Battle of Poltava in 1709. At that time the Russian army had support in Galicia from the so-called Russophiles, a Ukrainian cultural and political movement that considered Galician Ukrainians part of a larger Russian nation.

In 1920 Stalin moved his cavalry toward the city, seeking to claim it in the name of world revolution and international proletarian solidarity. The Soviet refusal to accept the Curzon Line as the boundary between the revolutionary government in Moscow and the reborn Polish state led to the temporary loss of Western Ukraine. In Eastern Ukraine the Bolsheviks established the Ukrainian

Soviet Socialist Republic (Ukrainian SSR). When they took Lviv in 1939 on the basis of the Molotov-Ribbentrop Pact, they annexed Western Ukraine to the Ukrainian SSR. By that time the Ukrainian political parties had emerged victorious in Galicia, displacing the remaining Russophiles.

The Soviets came back in 1944 as champions of the liberation and reunification of ancient Ukrainian lands. They took a page from the book of the Ukrainian Insurgent Army, which was also fighting for the unification of all the Ukrainian ethnic lands. Like the Ukrainian nationalists, the Soviets were in favor of the development of Ukrainian culture, but unlike their foes, they had in mind a very peculiar form of culture, with no provision for an independent Ukraine or, indeed, any independent political movement at all. Nevertheless, they exploited the Ukrainian-Polish antagonism, encouraging Polish migration from Lviv to the Polish territories in the west.[4]

By the time of the Yalta Conference, the constituent republics of the USSR had gained the right to have their own commissariats of defense and foreign affairs, a step that helped Stalin make a case for their independent membership in the United Nations. The new status of the republics as autonomous foreign-policy actors was achieved as a result of Stalin's constitutional reform of early 1944. Now Ukraine, the second most populous republic of the Soviet Union, on whose behalf Stalin laid claim to Lviv, became an important trump card in his quest for dominance in Eastern Europe. Most Ukrainians lived in the USSR, but there were millions in Poland, Romania, and Czechoslovakia. Ukrainian national feeling, especially the desire of Ukrainians divided by numerous international borders to live in a state of their own, was masterfully exploited by Stalin in his campaign to convince Polish politicians to accept the Curzon Line as the future Soviet-Polish border.

The propaganda war began with a contribution from Stalin's favorite playwright, Oleksandr Korniichuk, the head of the Ukrainian Writers' Union and the author of popular plays. *Mr. Perkins's Mission in the Land of the Bolsheviks*, about an American millionaire visiting the USSR, was first staged in December 1944 at the Moscow Theater of Satire and reviewed in *Time* magazine. Averell Harriman attended a performance with his daughter Kathleen before leaving for Yalta; they both enjoyed the comedy, and Kathleen later befriended the actor who played Mr. Perkins. He had never traveled abroad or met an American before, and he had prepared for the role by studying two newsreels that featured visits of American delegations to the USSR. "He did a damn good job," wrote Kathleen in a letter to her sister Mary.[5]

On February 19, 1943, Ukraine's leading newspaper, *Pravda Ukraïny*, published an article by Korniichuk entitled "The Reunification of the Ukrainian People within Their Own State." The playwright, known for his close association with Stalin, accused the émigré Poles of a desire to restore Poland's seventeenth-century borders, which stretched from the Baltic to the Black Sea.

He reminded his readers of the historical and ethnic grounds for the Soviet claim to Western Ukraine, recalling the Cossack revolt of 1648, the topic of an anti-Polish drama he had written before the war, and the nineteenth-century Ukrainian cultural revival in Lviv. In the next few days the article was reprinted under a slightly different title in *Izvestiia* and other leading Soviet newspapers. It was distributed abroad by the Soviet media monopoly TASS (Soviet Telegraph Agency). The Soviet attack on the Polish government had begun.

Korniichuk was soon named one of Molotov's deputies and put in charge of relations with Slavic countries. The Polish question became his responsibility. An ethnic Ukrainian, Korniichuk was married to a Polish politician and writer, Wanda Wasilewska, which made him a perfect candidate for the job in Stalin's eyes. He was mostly silent at meetings of the commissariat's top officials, and Molotov used to joke that Korniichuk would listen to his colleagues' discussions and then put all of them into a play. In his new post Korniichuk collected enough material to write *Mr. Perkins's Mission in the Land of the Bolsheviks*. With the Kremlin's support, Korniichuk's wife was elected president of the Union of Polish Patriots, a pro-Soviet Polish government in the making. A strong-willed woman who usually dressed in military uniform, she looked manly in her jodhpurs and was a butt of jokes among Red Army officers, who called her "Korniichuk's husband." Together Wanda and Oleksandr Korniichuk were important weapons in Stalin's arsenal.[6]

There was no doubt among the leaders of the Polish exiles as to who was really behind Korniichuk's article. On February 25, 1943, they fought back: "It is absolutely absurd to suspect Poland of intentions to base the eastern boundaries of the Polish Republic on the Dnieper and the Black Sea or to impute to Poland any tendencies to move her frontier farther to the east," they announced. A resolution adopted by the Polish government in exile restated its commitment to the eastern borders of 1939. The Kremlin countered with a TASS statement accusing the London Poles of denying the Ukrainian people their right to join their brethren.

An important new argument surfaced in the TASS statement. For the first time a reference was made to Lord Curzon, who had allegedly understood that the Poles had no right to claim Ukrainian ethnic territory. After Stalingrad, the Soviet dictator decided that he wanted a political dividend for his military success. Casting himself as a responsible statesman (unlike the Polish leaders in exile), he no longer insisted on the Molotov-Ribbentrop borders. Now he was prepared to make certain adjustments in favor of the future Polish state and to draw the new border along the Curzon Line, based on the ethnic principle and sanctioned by one of the leaders of the British Empire.[7]

In the days leading up to Yalta, the British Foreign Office Research Department produced a memorandum entitled "Poland's Ukrainian Minority." It was drafted by Elisabeth Pares, the granddaughter of Sir Maurice Powicke, daughter of Richard Pares, and future wife of Robert Arthur Humphreys, all eminent Oxford historians. Elisabeth Pares argued that "the problem of Poland's eastern frontiers presents not simply a Russo-Polish issue, but a triangular situation in which Poland's national minorities constitute the third party; and the record of Polish relations with the most important of those minorities—the Ukrainians—has been anything but a happy one. It would perhaps be unfortunate if our strong concern for Poland's interests were allowed to obscure these facts."

In her report, Elisabeth Pares wrote about the growth of animosity between Ukrainians and Poles during the German occupation and noted that Poles living east of the Curzon Line were moving to territories under the control of the Lublin government in anticipation of official transfers of population. She warned against believing Polish claims that most Ukrainians would like to stay in Poland, pointing out that there was no evidence of such a preference among them. The only possibility of uniting all Ukrainians in one political unit was, in her opinion, the incorporation of Western Ukraine into the Ukrainian Soviet republic. She considered the creation of an independent Ukrainian state "quite inconceivable . . . at this late stage in East European history."

One of Elizabeth Pares's superiors amended her memorandum with his own comments, pointing to Lviv as a Ukrainian cultural and national center that was home to a Ukrainian educational society (*Prosvita*) and the Shevchenko Scientific Society, as well as a base for the activities of Mykhailo Hrushevsky, "the greatest Ukrainian historian" and head of the Ukrainian government in 1917–18. Hrushevsky, who chose to live in Soviet Ukraine in the 1920s rather than stay in Polish-controlled Lviv, was presented as an example of the preference of Ukrainian nationalists for the Ukrainian SSR over Polish-controlled Eastern Galicia. That preference could only be strengthened by the creation of separate Ukrainian commissariats of defense and international affairs.[8]

In a telling slip of the pen, the Foreign Office expert spelled Hrushevsky's name in a way that resembled the English spelling of the surname of the communist leader of Ukraine, Nikita Khrushchev—"Khrushchevsky." That also happened to be the name used by Stalin when he accused Khrushchev, only half-jokingly, of being a Polish spy. The fifty-year-old Khrushchev, already bald and notably overweight but full of energy, was in fact nothing if not a major anti-Polish force in Stalin's employ. Born in southern Russia, he spent most of his early life in Ukraine, where the family moved when Khrushchev was fourteen years old. He went to work in the Donbas coal mines and joined the Bolsheviks during the revolution. His party career took him first to Kyiv and then to Moscow, where he was sent to obtain his higher education. Among his classmates was Svetlana Allilueva, the wife of Joseph Stalin. The connection turned out to be crucial for Khrushchev's career and, indeed, the future of the USSR.

In 1935, six years after coming to Moscow as a provincial party functionary in search of higher education, Khrushchev, who never completed his studies, became first secretary of the Moscow city committee of the Communist Party, where he supervised the construction of the Moscow subway system. In 1938 he was sent to Ukraine as first secretary of the republic's Communist Party and Stalin's viceroy. His responsibilities extended to the Sovietization of Lviv and other parts of Western Ukraine after the Red Army crossed the Polish border and took over the region in 1939. After the German surprise attack in June 1941, Khrushchev joined the Red Army's retreat from Ukraine. He served as the political commissar of the Stalingrad front during the Battle of Stalingrad and resumed his responsibilities as Stalin's viceroy in Ukraine when Soviet forces took the offensive and began the recapture of Ukraine in 1943. Stalin valued Khrushchev's organizational talent and leadership skills but often treated him as a court jester, forcing him to perform Ukrainian dances and belittling him with nicknames like "Khrushchevsky."[9]

Like everyone else in the Politburo, Stalin underestimated Khrushchev. After spending years as virtually his own master in Kyiv, away from Stalin's day-to-day control, Khrushchev managed to develop his own power base, playing the intermediary between the center and the local party and Soviet elites. Those elites, though virulently antinationalist in their rhetoric, inherited from their opponents a vision of a greater Ukraine encompassing all ethnically or historically Ukrainian territories from Brest and Pinsk in the north to Przemyśl (Ukrainian: Peremyshl) and Chełm (Kholm) in the west. In 1939, after the Soviet takeover of the eastern Polish provinces, Khrushchev tried to attach to the Ukrainian republic not only Lviv but also Brest and Pinsk, which went to Belarus on Stalin's orders. In March 1944, in a speech to the Ukrainian Supreme Soviet, Khrushchev laid claim to Lviv and other areas east of the Curzon Line, and to the Chełm region and adjoining territories beyond the line. "The Ukrainian people will seek to include in the Ukrainian Soviet state such primordial Ukrainian lands as the Kholm [Chełm] region, Hrusbeshiv [Hrubieszów], Zamostia [Zamość], Tomashiv [Tomaszów], [and] Iaroslav [Jarosław]." The claim was met with stormy applause.

There was a personal connection in Khrushchev's claim to the region. His wife, Nina Kukharchuk, was an ethnic Ukrainian from the lands west of the Curzon Line. As it happened, she came from the Chełm region, which was now being claimed by her husband. A Ukrainian-Polish borderland that had belonged to the Russian Empire before 1918, the region was claimed by the Ukrainian state in 1917. It was not, however, part of the Ukrainian SSR during the interwar period, nor was it included in the Soviet zone of occupation established by the Molotov-Ribbentrop Pact. The population was ethnically mixed, and local Ukrainians were divided between those who believed that they were part of a larger Russian nation and those who had a distinct Ukrainian identity.

In July 1944 Khrushchev sent Stalin a proposal for the creation of a Kholm province within the Ukrainian republic, noting that "historically those lands adjoined Ukraine, and in the past some of those lands were part of the Russian state." Khrushchev's memorandum, dated July 20, 1944, reached Stalin in time for him to use the "Kholm card" in his negotiations with the Polish Committee of National Liberation, the future "Lublin Poles," over the Soviet-Polish border. Stalin informed the Poles of Khrushchev's request on July 25. The next day they signed a border agreement with the USSR based on the Curzon Line that assigned Lviv to the USSR and Kholm to Poland. Kholm, now recognized by the Soviets as Polish Chełm, became the first seat of the pro-Soviet Polish government.

Lviv was a different story. It soon became a stumbling block in negotiations between the Soviets and the Polish government in exile. Khrushchev stated in his memoirs that because ethnic Poles were an absolute majority in the city, the Soviet authorities rushed to Lviv in July 1944, immediately after it fell into the hands of the Red Army, to establish their administration there before the Polish government in exile could do so. "We had to make haste," he said, "so that our people could take charge of the city." Polish inhabitants of the city who eagerly awaited Soviet liberation from the Germans would soon be disappointed.[10]

According to British diplomatic reports from Moscow, Lviv's Polish elite could not reconcile itself to the fact that the city was to become Soviet—this at a time when, after the extermination of the Jews in the Holocaust and the departure of many ethnic Ukrainians to the countryside because of harsh wartime conditions, the city's ethnic composition had become more Polish than ever before. The Poles were now desperate. There were rumors of a coming revolution in Russia, an approaching Soviet-British war over Lviv, or, alternatively, of Britain abandoning Poland to the Bolsheviks. Lviv's Polish elites placed their hopes in the Western Allies. They prayed for a generous gesture by Stalin, although they feared that he was determined to win over the Ukrainians by giving them the city. Sir Frank Roberts of the British Foreign Office, a participant at Yalta and a future ambassador to the Soviet Union, agreed with the conclusion of a professor from Lviv interviewed by the British in Moscow that "Poland will not now get Lvov back." He concluded that Stalin's policy toward the Ukrainians "seems to be a mixture of appeasement (the offer of Lvov) and repression (shootings and deportations) on a large scale."

British Foreign Office reports in May 1945 portrayed the city as a besieged fortress. Fighters of the Ukrainian Insurgent Army were active at night, assassinating Soviet officers and soldiers. By day, their captured colleagues would be put to work cleaning city streets under the guard of NKVD troops. Lviv became the headquarters of one of the Soviet fronts and was full of soldiers recovering from their wounds in local hospitals. Members of the Red Army high command who were killed in action were buried there as well.[11] A British military mission that visited the city that month noted the progressive de-Polonization of its cultural life: plays were performed in either Russian or Ukrainian. As the Soviets encouraged Poles to leave, they settled Russians in their place. They were prepared to dismantle and ship to Poland monuments to Polish historical figures such as King Jan Sobieski, as well as Polish manuscripts and cultural artifacts from the collections of not only Lviv but also Kyiv.[12]

In the fall of 1944 the Ukrainian communist authorities signed an agreement on population exchange with representatives of the Polish government in Lublin. The ethnic cleansing practiced during the war by Ukrainian and Polish militias on both sides of the Curzon Line made civilians run for the cover of friendly regimes once the Red Army occupied the region and initiated population transfers. Elisabeth Pares of the British Foreign Office knew about Poles fleeing the Soviet zone, while Soviet reports noted acts of violence against Ukrainians west of the Curzon Line and observed the willingness of Ukrainians to spend weeks at railway stations waiting to be evacuated to territory under the control of the Ukrainian Soviet republic.

By the time of the Yalta Conference, there seemed to be growing recognition on the Polish side that deportations and transfers of population would take place one way or another. Ralph Parker, the correspondent of the London *Times* and the *New York Times* in Moscow and unofficial adviser to the Soviet Relations Section of the British Ministry of Information, who visited the Lublin area in January, told Harold Balfour, the head of the consular section of the British embassy in Moscow, that the "consensus of opinion at Lublin was that one million Poles would eventually be repatriated from eastern Poland and that Ukrainians and Belorussians would migrate from Poland leaving her as a homogeneous state in which minorities including Jews would be assimilated into indigenous population." "Polish soldiers of peasant stock from Tarnopol and Lwów regions with whom Parker spoke," telegraphed Balfour from Moscow, "expressed no enthusiasm for inclusion of their land in USSR but declared the attitude of the Ukrainians in these regions was so hostile that Polish villagers were as a rule anxious to transfer themselves to the West."[13]

There was also resistance to forced resettlement on both sides of the Curzon Line. As late as May 1945, the British Foreign Office was receiving reports that the Polish population of Lviv was refusing to leave the city and continued to hope that the founding conference of the United Nations would revisit Yalta and assign the city to Poland. At the same time, Ukrainians west of Lviv in the border town of Przemyśl, the seat of a Ukrainian Catholic bishopric occupied by the Soviets from 1939 to 1941, were refusing to move, hoping that the town would again be included in the Ukrainian republic.

The NKVD was meanwhile helping local Poles make the "right choice" by unleashing a campaign of terror east of the Curzon Line. In 1944 alone, more than 117,000 Poles were forcibly moved from the Ukrainian SSR to Poland. The deportations did not come as a complete surprise to the population of the area, as according to the Soviet statistics close to 400,000 Poles alone had been arrested or deported in the former Polish territories between 1939 and 1941. The Polish government in exile put that figure at 900,000. The Poles constituted the absolute majority of the deported, but they were not the only group targeted by the regime. Significant numbers of Ukrainians, Lithuanians, and Jews went through the same experience.[14]

The Soviet plan was to resettle Poles from the east into the western territories acquired from Germany, but deportations began before the Red Army secured the German territories. Thus, as one dictatorship replaced another, Polish refugees were herded into former German concentration camps not long after their original inmates were liberated by the Red Army: some Lviv Poles found themselves in Majdanek, the former Nazi forced-labor camp on the outskirts of Lublin, where some sixty thousand Polish Jews and twenty thousand ethnic Poles died between October 1941 and July 1944. A report received by the Polish government in London in September 1944 described the situation as follows: "The Lwów district is being rapidly emptied of its Polish population which is being replaced by Soviet nationals. Poles conscripted up to the age of 36 are being sent to Jarosław [west of the Curzon Line] and thence to Majdanek where they exist in indescribable poverty, starving behind wires and under Soviet guard."[15]

The Soviets were eager to move large numbers of people east and west within their zone of occupation and control, but they were determined not to let anyone leave that zone. Even American citizens stranded on the Soviet side of the rapidly moving frontier found it difficult to get out. On February 10, 1945, a Polish woman named Stasia, who was an American citizen trapped by wartime events in her native town of Przemyśl on the Ukrainian-Polish border, sent a letter to her brothers in the United States begging for help. Characteristically, her complaints were not about the Germans but about the Soviets. Her sister's husband, who had been a policeman before the war, had been arrested and deported to Siberia. Then her sister was arrested. Stasia's sister ended up in Iraq, but her husband and son died in Siberia. "Father and mother are no longer owners of our property," Stasia wrote, "because it has been nationalized by the Soviet authorities. . . . There's many a day that I cry that I left America. I never realized what war meant until I have seen it. Have you been asking the American Embassy about my whereabouts, because they've been looking for me? I thought I could leave everything and could go back to America, but the Soviets refused to give me permission saying I belong to them now."[16]

As Stalin tried to persuade the Western leaders on the afternoon of February 6 that the Lublin government enjoyed overwhelming popular support in Poland and that it was the Red Army that was the target of Polish Home Army attacks, not the other way around, those who knew the situation from Polish underground reports were skeptical, if not outraged.

Eden later wrote that Roosevelt and Churchill were very good in their presentations, while Stalin "gave us a very dusty answer." After the end of the debate, Churchill did not refrain from letting the Soviets know exactly what he thought of their policies in the region. "I am very distressed," he told Maisky, who recorded the conversation in his diary. "Stalin is too unyielding. In my last speech I tried to be as delicate and careful as I could. I spoke of 'different information.' . . . But, to speak frankly, every day we receive many reports that cast the internal situation in Poland in an extremely murky light: the Lublin government is unpopular; many detest it; all dissidents are being arrested and exiled to Siberia en masse; everything rests on your bayonets."[17]

Others were impressed by Stalin's speech. His exercise in Soviet patriotism and questionable dialectics was appreciated by the members of the Soviet delegation. Andrei Gromyko, then a young Soviet ambassador to Washington, cited an excerpt from Stalin's speech in his memoirs, which were written more than forty years later. Justice Byrnes was more in agreement with Gromyko than with Eden in his assessment of the effect produced by Stalin's intervention. "Marshal Stalin replied with an impassioned statement," he noted in his memoirs. "It was the only time during the entire conference," according to Byrnes, that Stalin "exhibited his strong feelings in such a manner." The emotional charge of the moment was not lost on other participants. "A sure clue to the gravity of the problem," wrote Bohlen, "was Stalin's getting up and walking up and down behind his chair while expounding his points. His best debating skill stood out on the Polish question."[18]

The closing of what Stalin called the "Polish corridor"—the strategic section of the European plain between Germany and the USSR—was an extremely important matter for the Soviets; in geostrategic terms it outweighed all the other problems discussed at the conference, with the notable exception of the final defeat of Germany. Stalin could not afford to lose on this issue, and yet he was faced with a united front. Roosevelt did not long maintain his facade of impartiality and was not afraid of creating the impression that he and Churchill were "ganging up" on Stalin. The usually implacable dictator apparently decided to resort to a device he rarely used—an emotional appeal. The tactic succeeded. Everyone expected Churchill to speak emotionally, but Stalin's sudden appeal made a strong impression on all present. The incident was exaggerated by members of the American delegation on their return to Washington and took on fantastic details that made their way into the press.

"Advisers who sat at FDR's elbow at Yalta tell a colorful inside story about what happened between Roosevelt, Stalin and Churchill during negotiations over Poland," wrote Drew Pearson, one of America's leading journalists at the time, in the *Washington Post*.

> They were tremendously impressed with Stalin—his simplicity, directness and modesty. Most of the time he remained seated, seldom appearing to become aroused. A big-neck interpreter wearing a No. 17 collar sat beside him, translating with skill and effectiveness. Only during the Polish conversations did Stalin rise from the conference table to argue vigorously.
>
> For three years, Stalin has contended that the Curzon Line, fixed by Lord Curzon, then the Foreign Minister of England, and agreed to by Clemenceau, should be the new boundary between Russia and Poland. He repeated this at Yalta, reminding Roosevelt and Churchill that American geographers had charted the line for Lord Curzon as the best division between the Polish and Russian peoples. Then, rising from his chair, Stalin said dramatically: "Do you want me to tell the Russian people that I am less Russian than Lord Curzon? Do you want me to tell the Russian people that I am less Russian than Clemenceau? Do you want me to accept less than they proposed for Russia?"
>
> Again Stalin rose to talk about the Lublin government. "Are we going to discriminate in favor of the government which fled to England and 're-mained there in safety'?" Stalin said. "Or are we going to recognize the Lublin government, which remained in Poland and risked the danger of fighting underground?" "Did your army liberate Poland, Mr. Churchill?" he asked dramatically. "Did your army liberate Poland, Mr. President?" he asked, pointing to Roosevelt.[19]

Stalin never actually posed those questions, but Pearson captured the spirit of the debate. Stalin was in complete control of the situation where it mattered most—in Poland. He thought that the right of conquest—or, in the language of the time, "liberation"—entitled him to choose the Polish government. After all, he had not interfered in the installation of new governments in Western Europe. "I must say," he noted in response to Roosevelt's and Churchill's remarks, "that the Warsaw government has a democratic base equal at least to that of de Gaulle."[20]

As Stalin spoke, Roosevelt's and Churchill's faces became ever grimmer. The Western leaders were losing a debate on an issue they could not afford to lose, not only because of their democratic principles but also because of the political situation at home. The British government, which had entered the war on account of Poland, was already under attack in Parliament and in the press for its failure to protect the independence of Poland, whose sons were fighting along with the British on the German front. The Americans were also uneasy, given the Polish émigrés' lobbying activities on Capitol Hill, and the country's generally pro-Polish sympathies. Poland was not Romania, Bulgaria, or even Finland, countries they could fairly easily cede to Stalin. It was part of the winning Allied coalition, the country that had first dared to stand up to German aggression.

Harry Hopkins was probably the first to realize that there was no point in continuing a discussion in which there was no way to refute Stalin's data without causing a major scandal. In the middle of Stalin's speech, Hopkins passed the president a note: "Why not let this wind up today when Stalin is thru—say we will talk it over again tomorrow. It is 7:15." Roosevelt followed Hopkins's advice. When Stalin finished, FDR, citing the late hour, suggested that they postpone further discussion of the Polish question until the next day, but Churchill was impatient to respond. The prime minister declared that he "must put on record the fact that the British and Soviet Governments have different sources of information in Poland and therefore they obtain different views of the situation there." As the meeting adjourned, Roosevelt stated that the Polish question had been a headache to the whole world for five centuries, and Churchill and Stalin agreed that something would have to be done to change the situation.[21]

That evening, given the poor prospects for a settlement, Roosevelt decided to appeal to Stalin directly. He would send him a personal note. The letter was drafted by Charles Bohlen, who described the atmosphere prevailing in the Western delegations: "As we left the conference table that day, the Americans and the British faced a formidable task in trying to salvage anything on Poland. We were up against a simple fact: the Red Army held most of the country; Stalin had the power to enforce his will. But the President would not give up so easily." Neither would Churchill. "I am sure that we must come back hard on this," Eden wrote in his diary. "Dined with Winston and we discussed this and line to take tomorrow." When Averell Harriman showed Eden the draft of the president's letter, Eden found it to be "on the right lines but not quite stiff enough" and suggested changes that were accepted by Churchill and Roosevelt.[22]

"I have been giving a great deal of thought to our meeting this afternoon, and I want to tell you in all frankness what is on my mind," read the president's letter. "In so far as the Polish Government is concerned, I am greatly disturbed that the three great powers do not have a meeting of minds about the political setup in Poland. It seems to me that it puts all of us in a bad light throughout the world to have you recognizing one government while we and the British recognize another in London. I am sure this state of affairs should not continue and if it does it can only lead our people to think there is a breach between us, which is not the case. I am determined that there shall be no breach between ourselves and the Soviet Union."

Bohlen believed that the Soviet goal at Yalta was to maintain control over Poland without causing a breach with the Allies. He therefore expected Roosevelt's statement about the possibility of a breach to hit home. "I have had to make it clear to you that we cannot recognize the Lublin Government as now composed," continued the letter, "and the world would regard it as a lamentable outcome of our work here if we parted with an open and obvious divergence between us on this issue." The letter offered a solution. Roosevelt dropped Mikołajczyk's idea of a presidential council, opting instead for Churchill's proposal that a new Polish government be formed at Yalta.

To counter Stalin's objection that it would be undemocratic to form such a government without consulting the Poles themselves, Roosevelt took the dictator at his word and suggested that Polish politicians be brought to the conference. They were to include not only members of the Lublin government but also leaders from London and Poland. The list included the British candidates Mikołajczyk, Grabski, and Romer, as well as Archbishop Sapieha and other Polish leaders originally suggested by Roosevelt as members of the presidential council. The task of the new government would be to hold free elections in Poland. Roosevelt went out of his way to assure Stalin that he would never support a government "inimical to your interests."

Eden was trying to strengthen the president's language, as may be judged from his penciled remarks on the draft of the letter preserved in the Foreign Office archives: "I have had to make it clear to you that we cannot recognize the Lublin Government as now composed, and the world would regard it as a lamentable outcome of our work here if we parted with an open and obvious divergence between us on this issue." He also added Mikołajczyk's name as a candidate for the Polish government and changed the president's formula regarding the future obligations of the British government. If the president's request was met, the British government "would be prepared to examine with you conditions in which they would dissociate themselves from the London government." The original draft of the letter made British abandonment of the Polish government in exile directly dependent on Stalin's agreement to FDR's proposals.

The letter suggested that an understanding on Poland would serve as a test of the possibility of more important agreements in the future. Here was Stalin's chance to convince the American people that he could be trusted. "You must believe me when I tell you," wrote the president, "that our people at home look with a critical eye on what they consider a disagreement between us at this vital stage of the war. They, in effect, say that if we cannot get a meeting of minds now, when our armies are converging on the common enemy, how can we get an understanding on even more vital things in the future." Bohlen later said that the passage was added to impress the seriousness of the situation upon

Stalin. "In retrospect," he wrote in his memoirs, "I believe it was perhaps a mistake to include this sentence, since Stalin considered references to American public opinion in the same category of nonsense as his references to the will of the Supreme Soviet."[23]

Stettinius told Eden on Malta that "failure to find the solution would greatly disturb American public opinion and might prejudice the whole question of American participation in the World Organization." Thus the questions of Poland and the United Nations turned out to be closely linked in the minds of the Western conference participants. They were also discussed on the same day. On neither question did the Western leaders achieve any progress. Roosevelt badly needed a deal on Poland, but at the end of a long and difficult day he could do little else than pin his hopes on a personal appeal to Stalin. It was now a matter of waiting for Stalin's response.[24]

PART IV

THE DIPLOMATS' CHESSBOARD

A sincere diplomat is like dry water or wooden iron.

JOSEPH STALIN

14

COUNTING VOTES IN THE
UNITED NATIONS

Those who play the variant of chess known as "Yalta" know how valuable (but tricky) temporary alliances can be. The game was created following the Yalta Conference and named after it. In this game for three players, the contest takes place on a six-sided board. Standard chess rules apply, but there are some important exceptions. All disagreements are decided by majority vote: thus, when one player is placed in check by another, the third player can help him out if his own position permits it. Alliances are made for strategic advantage, but, as those who have played the game can attest, they are invariably broken. The creators of the Yalta game grasped the basic rules of engagement at Yalta better than many historians who have studied the conference. At no time were these shifting allegiances more apparent than on February 7 and 8. The United Nations; the fate of Poland and, by extension, of Eastern Europe as a whole; and Soviet participation in the war with Japan—all these big-ticket items were up for discussion during those two crucial days.

From the American perspective, February 7 dawned with little hope of positive development. There was a crisis over Poland and no sign of agreement on the United Nations, despite Stettinius's detailed report the previous day. And this was day four of a conference that was planned to last no more than five or six days! Immediately after breakfast, Harry Hopkins and James Byrnes called a meeting with representatives of the State Department to discuss the situation. They advised Stettinius that the approval of the American voting formula in the UN Security Council was the most important question at the moment and should be resolved before any other at that day's meeting of foreign ministers, slated to begin at Koreiz Palace at noon. ·

Molotov was presiding, but Stettinius seized the initiative by asking the first question: was there any aspect of his presentation on the United Nations the previous day that required additional explanation? He was prepared to entertain questions now. Molotov responded, in his capacity as chairman, that the

United Nations was not on the agenda, since it had not been referred to the foreign ministers for discussion. Stettinius's attempt to hijack the agenda failed, deepening American desperation. It would be a major political and public-relations disaster if the talks ended with no agreement on the United Nations.

One can imagine Stettinius's surprise when, just minutes before the start of the plenary session at Livadia, Churchill sat down on the edge of a chair between Roosevelt and his secretary of state, and said, "Uncle Joe will take Dumbarton Oaks." This could only mean that the Soviets would accept the American voting formula. But how did Churchill know, and why was he the one delivering the message? Was it true or just wishful thinking? After all, only a few hours earlier Molotov had refused even to discuss the issue with Stettinius. The president and the secretary of state had no choice but to wait and see what would ensue.[1]

The president opened the meeting with a statement on Poland. He emphasized that he "was less interested in the tracing of the frontier lines than he was in the problem of the Polish Government." That was where the discussion had left off the previous day, but Poland would have to wait. According to established practice, the first item on the agenda was the report of the foreign ministers. Once Molotov concluded his presentation, which dealt with various aspects of the German question, from the planned partition of the country to German reparations, Roosevelt suggested that they return to Poland. There was no objection, but an intervention from Stalin postponed the discussion once again.

The Soviet leader said that he had received the president's letter and that he had been trying to reach the representatives of the Polish government in Warsaw, to no avail. Then he said that Molotov had prepared a proposal addressing the president's concerns, but it still had to be typed. While this was being done, Stalin suggested that they switch to another topic, perhaps the United Nations. The delegates readily agreed. It must have been extremely gratifying to Hopkins and Byrnes to hear Stalin himself raise the question that they considered so important.[2]

Stalin invited Molotov to speak. "After hearing Mr. Stettinius's report and Mr. Churchill's remarks, which had clarified the subject," Molotov said, "the Soviet Government felt that these proposals fully guaranteed the unity of the Great Powers in the matter of preservation of the peace." The Soviets were accepting the voting formula in the Security Council in its entirety and "had no comments to offer." "A sigh of relief passed through the British and American ranks," Ivan Maisky noted in his diary. "There were smiles on many lips." This was a major victory for Roosevelt—one as complete as it was unexpected.

But that was not the end of Molotov's presentation. He wanted to return to a question that had been discussed but not resolved at Dumbarton Oaks—that of the membership of Soviet republics in the United Nations organization. Molotov no longer insisted that all sixteen republics should become members, as the Soviets had suggested at Dumbarton Oaks, but he hoped that three or, at a minimum, two republics would be admitted. Bewildered, Roosevelt asked whether Molotov meant that the republics should be admitted as members of the General Assembly. Molotov said yes. He went on to observe that "the Dominions of the British Commonwealth have gradually and patiently achieved their place as entities in international affairs. . . . [I]t was only right that three, or at least two, of these Soviet Republics should find a worthy place among the members of the Assembly. Their sacrifices and contributions to the war earned them this place." He then reminded the president of the concession just made by the Soviet side on the voting formula.[3]

The Soviets felt that they would be grossly outnumbered, if not entirely sidelined, both in the Security Council and in the General Assembly, unless they could secure additional votes. Britain and its dominions were about to get six votes. The Americans were pushing for the inclusion of "associated nations"—six Latin American countries, plus Ireland and Egypt—which had avoided formal declarations of war on Germany or Japan but were loosely associated with the Allied cause. With the Latin Americans as de facto clients, and China as a proxy in the Security Council, the United States could feel secure without violating the principle of one nation, one vote. Not so the Soviets. First they objected to the "associated nations" being founding members of the UN, and then they insisted on membership for their sixteen republics, which no one believed were more independent than American states. The question remained unresolved at Dumbarton Oaks, and the briefing book issued to members of the U.S. delegation at Yalta predicted that it would resurface once agreement had been reached on voting procedure in the Security Council.[4]

The Soviet leaders knew that their main stumbling block was the complete lack of sovereignty of the republics. In his speech to the plenary session Molotov noted that constitutional reforms had been undertaken in February 1944. After the Teheran Conference, commissariats of foreign affairs had been formed in every constituent republic of the USSR, which allowed them to participate individually in international affairs. Molotov explained that Ukraine, Belarus (White Russia, according to English usage of the time), and Lithuania had been chosen as candidates for admission to the United Nations because "these three republics had borne the greatest sacrifices in the war and were the first to be invaded by the enemy." He also pointed out that "it was superfluous to explain the size, population, and importance of Ukraine."

After Russia itself, Ukraine was by far the best-known Soviet republic in the West, and the Soviets considered the case for Ukraine to be the strongest. They also believed that they had an additional clinching argument. Either during the recess or after the end of the meeting, Stalin communicated to the president that he "felt his position in the Ukraine was difficult and insecure. A vote for the Ukraine was essential . . . for Soviet unity." Stettinius, who was told about this conversation by FDR and recorded it in his memoirs, was prepared to take the argument at face value. "No one was able to determine the extent of the Ukrainian difficulty," he wrote a few years after the conference, "but we in Washington, of course, had heard talk during the German advance that the Ukraine might leave the Soviet Union."[5]

The situation in Ukraine was indeed a problem for Stalin. In the months leading up to Yalta, Lavrentii Beria's intelligence reports were full of information about the activities of the Ukrainian Insurgent Army in Western Ukraine and the operations of the NKVD against the insurgents. Stalin had little problem in controlling the leadership of Soviet Ukraine, led by Nikita Khrushchev. If anything, the appointment of Stalin's favorite playwright, Oleksandr Korniichuk, as Ukrainian commissar of foreign affairs in February 1944 after his tenure as Molotov's deputy in Moscow showed how purely symbolic the reform had been.

According to secret-police reports, few people in the USSR had any illusions on the matter. Oleksandr Dovzhenko, a leading Soviet filmmaker who was under NKVD surveillance at the time, was highly critical both of Korniichuk and of the Soviet "constitutional reform." "From Moscow's viewpoint, Korniichuk is an ideal figure as people's commissar of foreign affairs, since any Russian is more of a Ukrainian than he is," he told an acquaintance, according to a report filed by Beria's agents. "Everything basically remains as before," he remarked on another occasion. "The Ukrainian People's Commissariat of Foreign Affairs will not be able to make any independent decisions, as all decisions and directives will be delivered by Moscow. It's a fiction."[6]

In the year leading up to Yalta, Ukraine's alleged independence had been used to strengthen the Soviet position in negotiations with Polish political factions over the future Soviet-Polish border. The tactic appeared to have succeeded on more than one occasion. Not only were Polish procommunist circles obliged to drop their claim to Lviv when faced with the Ukrainian government's concurrent claim to Chełm, but some Western observers came to believe in the relative independence of the Soviet government in Kyiv. On the day of Moscow's recognition of the Polish government, the British correspondent Ralph Parker asked his companion, who happened to be a Soviet secret-police informer, "But do Ukraine and Khrushchev recognize the Polish provisional government?"

The effect was probably greater than Stalin had originally expected, and in the summer of 1944 he decided to change the leadership of the Ukrainian commissariat, replacing Korniichuk with an experienced hand in international affairs, the former secretary of the Communist International Dmytro Manuilsky. The emphasis shifted from propaganda actions, where Korniichuk was an expert, to international politics, in which Manuilsky had more experience than his boss, Molotov. Stalin was clearly anxious to ensure that Ukraine become a member of the United Nations, and for that to happen its foreign office would have to be led by a professional who could fully exploit the republic's new position to Moscow's benefit.[7] Oleksandr Dovzhenko believed that the whole affair was engineered by Stalin under pressure from the United States. "What does America think of these measures?" he asked his acquaintance. "After all, everything is perfectly obvious."[8]

No one at Yalta believed in the independence of the Soviet republics, but Roosevelt was in a difficult position: a major breakthrough had been made with regard to voting procedure in the Security Council, but the bill for that concession was now being presented. As Molotov made his plea for inclusion of the republics, the president passed a note to Stettinius: "This is not so good." Even one additional vote for the USSR was one too many, as it contravened the fundamental principle "one nation, one vote." The president decided to begin by securing Soviet agreement to the voting formula in the Security Council. It "was a great step forward which would be welcomed by all the peoples of the world," he said. The next task would be to convene a conference to set up the world organization. Roosevelt wanted it to take place by the end of March, or perhaps even earlier, within the next four weeks.

FDR tried to shelve Molotov's request for additional votes. He embarked on a long and somewhat confusing excursus on differences in tradition and state structure in various countries, trying to undermine Molotov's comparison of Soviet republics to British dominions. He suggested that the question be studied by the foreign ministers as they discussed the time and place of the UN founding conference. Previously, questions had been referred to the foreign ministers only after detailed discussion by the Big Three had yielded no consensus. This time, he tried to pass the issue off to the foreign ministers before a discussion had even begun.

James Byrnes, who vehemently opposed giving any country more than one vote, was satisfied with the president's response. Before leaving for Yalta, at a meeting with members of the Senate Foreign Relations Committee, Roosevelt had ridiculed the original Soviet proposal that all the Soviet republics independently join the United Nations, telling the senators that he would insist on the admission of all the American states. The revised Soviet position would not change the balance of power either in the General Assembly or in the Security Council, but it would undermine the integrity of the assembly. The semi-independent British dominions, which were well on the way to complete independence, had legitimate grounds for representation, but the Soviet republics were at best autonomous units of a highly centralized state.[9]

If he had unexpectedly entered the UN debate on the side of the president the previous day, this time Churchill threw his support behind Stalin. Unlike the Americans, the British were prepared to close their eyes to the realities on the ground. According to the British record of the meeting, Churchill "expressed his heartfelt thanks to Marshal Stalin and the Soviet Government for the great step forward which they had taken to meet the views put forward by President Roosevelt as to voting on the Security Council of the World Organization. The agreement of the three great powers which had been reached round the table that afternoon would give relief and satisfaction to people all over the world. As regards membership of the World Organization, the suggestion just put forward by M. Molotov differed greatly from the previous suggestion made by the Soviet Government. Everyone must feel that here, also, a remarkable advance had been made towards general agreement."

"We could never agree to any system which excluded self-governing Dominions from the position they had held and justified for a quarter of a century," said Churchill, having noted that the British Empire differed from America in having four self-governing dominions that had participated in the League of Nations. "For these reasons we could not but hear the proposals of the Soviet Government with a feeling of profound sympathy." Churchill's appeal was getting more and more emotional. "His heart went out to mighty Russia, bleeding from her wounds, but beating down the tyrants in her path," the British note-taker recorded. "He recognized that a nation of 180 million might well look with a questioning eye at the constitutional arrangements of the British Commonwealth which resulted in our having more than one voice in the Assembly." Churchill thanked the president for not giving Molotov a negative answer and apologized to Stalin, saying that he could not support his request outright, as he had not yet had a chance to consult his war cabinet.[10]

Roosevelt made one more attempt to shelve the question. He repeated his earlier proposal that the matter be referred to the foreign ministers, but Churchill would have none of it: there was already too much for the foreign ministers to do. He also attacked Roosevelt's proposal to hold the founding conference of the United Nations in March. The war would still be under way, which would put pressure on the British government to attend to both international and domestic issues. Other countries, especially in Europe, would find it difficult to participate, and their delegations might not be fully representative.

FDR tried to calm his British partner, noting that the conference would only establish the United Nations in principle, while organizational work would be done three to six months later. This made little impact on Churchill, who repeated his argument against calling the conference in March. Churchill apparently found a sympathetic ear in Stettinius, who passed the president a note stating that Secretary of War Henry Stimson was of the same opinion as Churchill. Hopkins was much less sympathetic. "There is something behind this talk," he wrote on a piece of paper that he passed to the president. "Perhaps we'[d do] better to wait till later tonight [to find out] what is on his mind." Roosevelt repeated one more time his proposal that the issue be referred to the conference of foreign ministers. Churchill finally agreed. Stalin, who had sat silent throughout, gently backed the president: "The foreign ministers will not make decisions but merely report to the Conference." The immediate impasse was resolved, and the negotiators took a short break.[11]

This was the first time that tensions between Roosevelt and Churchill came to the surface. Quite a few members of the American delegation were upset by Churchill's intervention. "Such long addresses were tedious," noted Admiral Leahy in his memoirs, "because of their necessity of being translated into Russian, if not for many other good reasons." Churchill's stand on the Soviet republics was not completely unexpected, as Stalin had linked them to the membership of the British dominions, and as Charles Bohlen put it, the Americans "knew of his desire to get India into the United Nations." But his opposition to an early conference on the UN came as a surprise even to his own delegation.

"The P.M. got rather off the rails," Alec Cadogan wrote to his wife. "Silly old man—without a word of warning to Anthony or me, he plunged into a long harangue about World Organization, knowing nothing whatever of what he was talking about and making complete nonsense of the whole thing. The worst of it was that what he said was completely contrary to the line already agreed with the Americans! However, I was able to explain privately to them that they needn't take it too tragically, that it didn't really mean anything and that we could clean up the mess afterwards." Anthony Eden also noted in his diary the surprise and frustration of the American delegation.[12]

As Churchill spoke, the president wrote to Hopkins, "All this is rot!" He then crossed out "rot" and replaced it with "local politics." Hopkins agreed. He wrote back, "I am quite sure now he is thinking about the next election in Britain." In an exchange that did not make it into the American or British protocols of the meeting but was recorded in the Soviet one, the president tried to appeal to the prime minister along these terms. He observed that, like Churchill, he had his share of difficulties at home, and said he thought it would be easier to get the necessary two-thirds majority in the Senate if the conference took place during wartime. It was a plea for assistance. Churchill admitted that the coming parliamentary elections were indeed on his mind.[13]

There were a number of reasons for Churchill's unexpected rebellion. The American and British positions on the United Nations were far from identical. In the letter that he sent his deputy prime minister, Clement Attlee, in the early hours of the morning on February 8 to ask for approval of his position from the war cabinet, Churchill explained that the Soviets had reduced their claim for membership in the UN General Assembly from sixteen republics to two, Ukraine and Belarus—he rightly considered demands for a third, Lithuania, to be little more than a negotiating ploy. These republics, argued Churchill, had suffered most in the war and had "fought well." The American position, continued the prime minister, was to delay a solution to this question until the United Nations Conference was convened in March. "Our position appears to me to be somewhat different," he wrote. "For us to have four or five members, six if India is included, when Russia has only one is asking a great deal of an Assembly of this kind. In view of other important concessions by them which are achieved or pending I should like to be able to make a friendly gesture to Russia in this matter. That they should have two besides their chief is not much to ask, and we will be in a strong position, in my judgment, because we shall not be the only multiple voter in the field."[14]

Churchill thus clearly intended to oppose the president. He was justifiably unhappy with Roosevelt's refusal to coordinate their positions at the start of the conference. "Winston is puzzled and distressed," wrote Lord Moran in his diary on February 7. "The President no longer seems to the P.M. to take an intelligent interest in the war; often he does not seem even to read the papers the P.M. gives him. Sometimes it appears as if he has no thought-out recipe for anything beyond his troubles with Congress."[15]

But why did Churchill push back at this point and publicly disagree with the president? Stalin, who barely participated in the discussion but stood to benefit most from Churchill's outburst, might well be credited with provoking it. The previous day Stalin had clearly been disturbed by the united British-American front not only on Poland but also on veto power in the Security Council. On the United Nations the Soviet position was closer to that of the British, and Stalin appears to have decided to split the united front by favoring Churchill, who was being shunned by the president and felt increasingly isolated.

The prime minister was singled out for special treatment by Stalin when he was informed about the coming Soviet concession. Molotov's statement at the plenary session that Churchill's remarks on the voting procedure had been essential in helping the Soviets grasp the essence of the American plan was also not lost on the prime minister. In a letter to Attlee, penned early the next day, Churchill wrote: "All the American proposals for the Dumbarton Oaks constitution were accepted by the Russians, who stated that it was largely due to our explanation that they have found themselves in a position to embrace the scheme wholeheartedly." Stalin, who liked to play off his unsuspecting subordinates against one another at the Kremlin, appears to have succeeded in doing the same to the two Western leaders.[16]

After the break, when Roosevelt delivered a long speech on Iran, Churchill could hardly conceal his frustration. Churchill was struggling, caught between true admiration for a close friend and ally and the disappointment that he felt increasingly after Teheran, when Roosevelt began to shift toward Stalin at the expense of the prime minister. "[T]hough we have moved a long way since

Winston, speaking of Roosevelt, said to me in the garden at Marrakesh, 'I love that man,' he is still very reticent in criticism," Moran noted in his diary that evening. "It seems to be dragged out of him against his will. And with half a chance he will tell over dinner how many divisions the Americans had in a particular show against our handful, and how their casualties in that engagement dwarfed ours, and things of that kind." The days of easy intimacy between Churchill and Roosevelt were gone.[17]

The gap that emerged between Roosevelt and Churchill during the plenary session was afterward skillfully exploited by Stalin. He was silent through the exchange but later approached the president privately, making his case for the addition of the Soviet republics and complaining not only of troubles with the Ukrainians but also of opposition in Moscow, where he claimed that the Politburo would agree to Soviet participation in the United Nations on condition that the USSR get additional votes. Stettinius, who had a chance to talk privately with Roosevelt later that day, found him in a conciliatory mood. "It had been a most fruitful day, and we were all thoroughly gratified that we were now a step further along the difficult path to a world organization of nations," wrote Stettinius in his memoirs. Roosevelt told Stettinius that "from the standpoint of geography and population he did not believe there was anything preposterous about the Russian proposal for two extra votes."

Despite fierce opposition from Byrnes and Hopkins, the feeling was growing in the American delegation that a concession was in order. Harriman later recalled, "We all realized that Stalin would feel very much outnumbered, and were greatly relieved that he had reduced his demand from sixteen to two additional votes." Harriman was prepared to put aside the question of how much independence Ukraine and other Soviet republics actually had to shape their own foreign policy. After all, Molotov never claimed that they were fully independent, raising instead the example of the British dominions, which were gradually finding their place in the international arena. Besides, there would be some fifty seats in the General Assembly—what practical difference would two or three extra Soviet republics make to the success or failure of the United Nations? "The actual power," Roosevelt reminded his secretary of state, "would rest in the Security Council, and each country in this body, large or small, would have only one vote." It was Stettinius's understanding that the president had all but made up his mind.[18]

On February 8, when Stalin arrived at Livadia Palace shortly after lunch for his appointment with FDR, the president was with Stettinius reviewing the results of the foreign ministers' meeting that morning. As Stettinius was preparing to leave, the president turned to Stalin and said, "The foreign ministers have met and have reached agreement on today's agenda." Stalin immediately asked whether this was about the admission of the two Soviet republics to the United

Nations. The president said yes. His timing could not have been better, as the meeting that day would be devoted to one of the two most important questions on FDR's agenda, that of Soviet participation in the war on Japan. Stalin had arranged for Molotov to time his announcement on Soviet acceptance of the American voting formula in the Security Council so as to soften the president's stand on Poland. Now Roosevelt timed his announcement on the admission of two Soviet republics to the UN with a view to influencing Stalin's position on the Far East.[19]

The problem with the president's yes was that the foreign ministers had not in fact agreed on the admission of the two Soviet republics. The main obstacle to their agreement, interestingly, was the position taken by the American secretary of state. Stettinius had said that the issue "should be given sympathetic consideration" at the future United Nations Conference and indicated that this was the president's new position. The problem, in his opinion, was the Dumbarton Oaks decision on "one nation, one vote." Molotov was dissatisfied. He indicated that if the USSR was not accommodated, it would make trouble on the question of membership in general. "Which Polish government . . . should be invited?" was his first question. Would nations that did not have diplomatic relations with the USSR be invited as well? "If agreement could not be reached on the membership of the organization it should be reported accordingly," Molotov concluded, threatening the Allies with public exposure of problems with the United Nations.

The threat hit home. Stettinius said he "was trying to find a way to arrange for consideration of the Soviet request before the first meeting of the assembly." Eden proposed that the issue be reinserted on the agenda of the conference. Molotov saw an opening and pushed harder. He proposed an "amendment" to Eden's proposal to the effect that the foreign ministers "had agreed that it would be advisable to grant admission to the assembly to two or three Soviet republics." It was not accepted. Stettinius decided to play for time. He said he "had not had an opportunity to discuss this matter with the President this morning and it was, therefore, impossible for him to make any firm commitment." He was, however, quite optimistic and "hoped and expected that the United States would be able to give a favorable reply by the end of the day."[20]

This left many of the participants confused. Had he said yes or no? The Soviet protocol concluded that the issue had been resolved. But Alger Hiss, the American note-taker at the session, thought differently. When the British, who were responsible for typing the official protocol of the meeting, arrived at the plenary session that day with a text that suggested that all the foreign ministers supported their proposal, Hiss raised the alarm. He was brushed off by Eden: "You do not know what has taken place." On the previous day Hiss had written and distributed to members of the American delegation a memorandum entitled "Arguments against the Inclusion of Any of the Soviet Republics among the Initial Members." He was now surprised to learn that his advice was being ignored. Eventually the British told the bewildered Hiss that they had obtained approval for the change in the protocol from none other than Stettinius.[21]

The secretary of state denied ever having given explicit agreement to alter the notes. Stettinius found himself in a difficult position, as he was caught between Roosevelt, who was evidently prepared to compromise, and his advisers, who were vehemently opposed. Stettinius left for the foreign ministers' meeting on February 8 with a copy of Hiss's "Arguments." It noted that the republics had never signed the United Nations Declaration; that, unlike the British dominions, they were not yet ready for membership; and that they were not sovereign states under international law. Stettinius did not use the memorandum or its recommendations in the discussion but ultimately blocked the Soviet proposal. "Although the President, the night before, had stated that he thought the Soviet request 'was all right,' I desired to reserve the United States' position at the Foreign ministers' meeting until I had an opportunity to check again with the President," Stettinius wrote in his memoirs. Just before Roosevelt's meeting with Stalin later that day, Stettinius had a chance to discuss the issue with the president again. Roosevelt indicated that they would have to accept the proposal.[22]

Stettinius was at pains to explain in his memoirs, which appeared in 1949, that responsibility for the decision to admit two Soviet republics to the United Nations lay with the president and not with him. He was in fact responding to the suggestion in Byrnes's memoirs, published two years earlier, that Stettinius first gave his agreement to the Soviet request at the foreign ministers' conference and only then advised the president. Stettinius denied the charges. Ironically, in July 1945, Isaac Don Levine, a renowned journalist and early anticommunist crusader, accused Hiss of persuading President Roosevelt to admit Ukraine and Belarus into the United Nations during a private meeting between Roosevelt and Stalin at which Hiss was allegedly present. But there is no indication that this meeting ever took place. Hiss in fact was rallying forces against the Soviet proposal.[23]

The plenary session on February 8 started a quarter hour later than usual, at 4:15 p.m.: Roosevelt and Stalin had been discussing the war in the Far East. The president opened the afternoon session by announcing that there had been a breakthrough on the membership of the Soviet republics in the UN General Assembly. It was his understanding that "the foreign secretaries could report complete success and he wished to congratulate them on their work and to ask Mr. Eden to report to the Conference." Eden reported that two Soviet republics would be invited to join the United Nations, but the invitation would be issued not by the Big Three but by the delegates of a future UN founding conference. The announcement came as a shock to Byrnes and other opponents of the

Soviet proposal in the American delegation. "I was surprised at the agreement which, in my opinion, was very unwise," wrote Byrnes in his memoirs. But what Byrnes saw as an imprudent concession on the part of the president was seen by Stalin and Molotov as a half measure that they had trouble accepting.

Stalin opened the debate by pointing out that among the states invited to the UN founding conference there were ten countries with no diplomatic relations with the USSR. How could the USSR participate with them in a conference that would entail discussing issues of world security? Then came the question of why countries such as Argentina and Turkey, which had never declared war on Germany or fought in the war, should be invited. The president smelled trouble and quickly intervened. He blamed his own former acting secretary of state, Sumner Welles, for the failure of the Latin American countries to declare war on Germany: Welles had advised them that it would be enough to break off diplomatic relations with the Nazi regime, and that had been a mistake. Recently he had written to the presidents of the Latin American countries urging them to declare war on Germany, and he was sure that they would follow his advice. Turning to the United Nations Conference, the president suggested that only those nations that had declared war by the end of February should be invited.

Stalin agreed, but that was not the end of the story. He switched to the question of Ukraine's and Belarus's admission to the UN General Assembly. Could they be mentioned by name in the protocol of the foreign ministers' meeting? Yes, that was acceptable. A crack in the president's defenses was opening up. Molotov stepped in to widen it: "Would it not facilitate the admission of these two Soviet republics as members of the assembly if they signed the United Nations Declaration before the first of March?" Hiss had proposed in his memo to Stettinius that the republics' failure to sign the UN Declaration be used as an argument against their membership in the assembly. Now Molotov was trying to take care of that "formality."

Again Churchill stepped in on the Soviet side. He did not raise the issue of the timing of the UN founding conference—that had been settled to general satisfaction by the foreign ministers earlier that morning, and the conference would take place in San Francisco in late April—but he wanted to talk about the two Soviet republics. It did not seem "quite right," he said, according to the American protocol of the meeting, "to take in small countries who had done so little, simply by the expedient of their declaring war and to exclude the two Soviet republics from the meeting." He "had very much in mind the martyrdom and sufferings of the Ukraine and White Russia." He was in favor of limiting the list of countries invited to the conference to Allies, but if others were to be added, then why not include the two Soviet republics as well?

"I don't want to embarrass the President," said Stalin, seeing an opening, "but if he will explain his difficulties we will see what can be done." Roosevelt was boxed in, but he remained undeterred. What was at stake, in his opinion, was not just the issue of adding new countries to the list but that of "giving one of the Great Powers three votes instead of one." He wanted to put this question before the conference. Stalin continued his offensive: "[W]ould it not be all right if the Ukraine and White Russia signed the United Nations Declaration?" The president stood firm: it would not overcome the difficulty. Stalin finally withdrew his proposal.[24]

If Roosevelt derived any satisfaction from his achievement, it was short-lived. After the meeting he encountered rebellion in his own camp. Admiral Leahy warned the president of possible difficulties at home. James Byrnes reminded Roosevelt of his promise to American senators that he would ask for all American states to join the UN if Stalin pushed for the admission of the Soviet republics. He pointed out that opposition to the League of Nations twenty-six years earlier had been fueled by the concession of voting rights to the British dominions. Now, Byrnes warned, the same argument could be used by opponents of the UN.

Byrnes mobilized Harry Hopkins, and both men urged Roosevelt to withdraw his support for the British proposal unless the United States also got three votes in the General Assembly. The president reluctantly agreed to raise this question with Stalin on some other occasion. Roosevelt was under attack from both sides. "The President seems to have no mind of his own," Hopkins complained to Lord Moran later that day. "He came to Yalta apparently determined to oppose any country having more than one vote, but when the P.M. came out strongly in favour of Stalin's proposal Roosevelt said he, too, would support Stalin at San Francisco."

Not all members of the American delegation agreed with Hopkins's judgment. Stettinius, for one, saw in Roosevelt's flexibility proof that the president was in good physical and mental shape. "There had been no briefing of the President by the State Department on this particular question," he wrote in his memoirs. "Throughout this give-and-take, his mind functioned with clarity and conciseness, furnishing excellent proof that he was alert and in full command of his faculties." Hopkins was concerned with policies, Stettinius with politics. Roosevelt, meanwhile, was trying to steer a course midway between his desire to remain united with Stalin and Churchill and his need to placate his own advisers. On this particular issue, he made no one happy. But he got what he wanted most: the United Nations organization was about to be born.[25]

15

STALEMATE ON POLAND

On the morning of February 7, Roosevelt anxiously awaited Stalin's response to his letter proposing that representatives of Polish political parties be invited to Yalta to set up a new government. At the foreign ministers' session at noon, Molotov acted as if there had been no letter, but Roosevelt was in no mood for delay. He opened the plenary session by proposing that they "take up the Polish question."

"When we concluded our meeting yesterday," he said, "Marshal Stalin had explained his views. I have nothing special to add to what I said yesterday. I think it is particularly important to find the solution of the governmental question." He said he thought it would be necessary to disregard the existing Polish governments in London and Warsaw and form a new government. "I think we want something new and drastic—like a breath of fresh air," he concluded.

Stalin spoke only after Roosevelt asked him directly whether he had anything to add to his statement of the previous day. He began by acknowledging that he had received the president's letter "an hour and a half ago," and said, "I immediately gave instructions to find Bierut and Morawski so that I could talk with them on the phone. [A]t the moment they are outside of Warsaw at Łódź or Cracow but they will be found and I must ask them how to find the representatives on the other side and what they think of the possibility of their coming. I can then tell how soon they will arrive. If [the former prime minister Wincenty] Witos or [Archbishop Adam Stefan] Sapieha could come here it would facilitate a solution but I do not know their addresses. I am afraid we have not sufficient time."[1]

This amounted to a rejection of Roosevelt's proposal. Not willing to turn it down directly, Stalin prevaricated. He had nothing against bringing the leaders of the Lublin (now Warsaw) government, who could be located by NKVD officers in no time, to Yalta, but he wanted to avoid the involvement of other Polish leaders at all costs. For the moment, he decided to play for time. The Soviet protocol of the meeting quoted him as saying, "[T]he participants in this meet-ing will not have time to await the arrival of the Poles in the Crimea."[2]

Stalin knew that stalling without offering concessions on another front would only increase Roosevelt's frustration. "Molotov has prepared a draft to meet in a certain extent the President's proposal," he said. "Let us hear it when it arrives as the translation is not yet finished. Meanwhile, we might discuss Dumbarton Oaks." This was when he indicated his willingness to accept the American formula on voting procedure in the Security Council. The new pro-posal on Poland, spelled out by Molotov in six points, also seemed promising. Aside from an effort to delineate the country's eastern and western borders, it suggested that the existing provisional government be augmented with "some democratic leaders from Polish émigré circles." Its composition would be decided in Moscow in consultations between Molotov and the American and British ambassadors. The provisional government, to be recognized by the Allies, would call a general election as soon as possible. Molotov said that his colleagues had been unable to reach the Polish politicians by telephone and there would not be enough time for them to come to Yalta. He added that the proposal "went far toward meeting the president's wishes," so perhaps their presence was no longer necessary.

Molotov's proposal looked like a step in the right direction: the Soviets were finally prepared to talk about the composition of a new government and to include representatives of non-Communist parties in it. The president was pleased but not yet prepared to declare victory. Harry Hopkins passed him a note: "Why not refer to foreign ministers for detailed discussion and report tomorrow or next day?" Roosevelt did just that, saying that progress had been made and asking for time to study the proposal.

What made the president bristle was the word "émigré": he said that there were plenty of Poles to choose from in Poland. This made Churchill, who had supported the London Poles, very uncomfortable. As the prime minister began to speak, Roosevelt passed a note to Stettinius: "Now we are in for 1/2 hour of it." Churchill began by trying to prevent the London Poles from being excluded from the future government. He agreed with the president that the term "émi-gré" was badly chosen: it had been coined after the French Revolution, and in Britain it was taken to mean people driven out of their country by their compa-triots. The London Poles were not émigrés but "Poles temporarily abroad." Churchill's next theme was Poland's western border. After a long exchange with Stalin on the subject, he asked for time to study Molotov's proposal. "He agreed that it would be well to sleep on this problem and take it up tomorrow, but he did feel that some progress had been made," Charles Bohlen noted. It appeared that an imminent breach had been avoided.[3]

That night Churchill celebrated and prepared for battle at the next session. "This has been a much better day," he cabled his wife. He was more explicit in a telegram to Clement Attlee. "An answer [to Roosevelt's letter] was put forward by the Russians to-day, Wednesday," he wrote. "It does not challenge in principle any of the broad issues. . . . This matter is by no means settled. It is our plan to fight hard for a government in Poland which we and United States can recognise and to which we can attract the recognition of all the United Nations. In return for this we require real substantial and effective representation from the Polish element with whom we have at present been associated, especially Mikołajczyk, Grabski, and Romer, as well as from a number of Poles still in Poland, Witos, Sapieha, etc., whom the Americans have listed. If it can be so arranged that eight or ten of these are included in the Lublin Government it would be to our advantage to recognize this Government at once." He asked the war cabinet to give him full freedom of action in that regard. The cabinet complied.[4]

Churchill's optimism was shared by Alec Cadogan, who wrote his wife the next day: "We made some progress yesterday, and Uncle Joe showed signs of being accommodating both in regard to Dumbarton Oaks and Poland." Eden wrote more cautiously in his diary: "Then came Poland and Russians again made some concessions, which give hope though we are still far from where we want to be." His caution, as it turned out, was amply warranted.[5]

The next morning the British and the Americans circulated their counterproposals. Eden believed that the British counterproposal was better, but the American one provided a basis for discussion at the plenary session on the afternoon of February 8. The Americans returned to the idea of a presidential council, now to consist of three members, including one communist. Its task would be to form a new government in consultation with Poles in Poland and abroad. They would all be brought to Moscow, where they would take part in deliberations chaired by Molotov and the two Western ambassadors. The government thus formed would be responsible for organizing free elections in Poland.[6]

Churchill quickly expressed his willingness to accept the American proposal with minor amendments. But if the Allies hoped that the Soviets would follow suit, they were soon to be disappointed. Molotov, who spoke on behalf of the Soviet delegation, defended the existing Warsaw government, to which they were prepared to admit Poles recommended by the Western Allies, but he would not hear of dissolving it in favor of an entirely new government. Molotov rejected the notion of a presidential council, claiming that the existing government "stands at the head of the Polish people and enjoys great prestige and popularity in the country."

Churchill could not leave this statement unanswered. He used all his powers of oratory in an effort to convince Stalin of the need to form a new democratic government in Poland. Churchill said that "they were at the crucial point of this conference," according to the British protocol of the meeting. "This was the question for the settlement of which the whole world was waiting. If they departed still recognizing different Polish governments, it would be accepted all over the world that fundamental differences still existed between Russia and their British and American allies and the consequences would be most lamentable. It would stamp this conference with the seal of failure." According to the American protocol, Churchill added, "and nothing else we did here would overcome it."

As a British note-taker recorded, the prime minister did not conceal his distrust of Soviet claims concerning the popularity of the Lublin Poles:

> They took different views about the basic facts in Poland, or at any rate some of them. According to the information of His Majesty's Government the new Lublin (now Warsaw) Government did not commend itself to the great majority of the Polish people, and they could not feel that it would be accepted abroad as representing them. If the conference were to brush aside the existing London Government and lend all its weight to the Lublin Government, there would be a world outcry. As far as could be foreseen, the Poles outside of Poland would make a virtually united protest. There was under British command a Polish army of 150,000 men gathered from among all those who had been able to come together from outside Poland. This army had fought and was still fighting very bravely.

Churchill stated that he "did not believe that this army would be at all reconciled to the Lublin Government, and it would regard Great Britain's action in transferring recognition from the Government which they had recognized since the beginning of the war as a betrayal of that Government."

The prime minister noted the impossible situation in which recognition of the Lublin government would put him and his cabinet colleagues:

> As Marshal Stalin and Mr. Molotov well knew, he himself did not agree with the London Government's actions, which had been foolish at every stage. But the formal act of transferring recognition from those whom they had hitherto recognized to this new government would cause the gravest criticism. It would be said that His Majesty's Government had given way completely on the Eastern frontier (as they in fact had) and had accepted and championed the Soviet view. It would also be said that they had broken altogether with the lawful Government of Poland, which they had recognized for these five years of war; and that they had no knowledge of what was actually proceeding in Poland. They could not enter the country. They could not see and hear what opinion was. It would be said that they could only accept what the Lublin Government proclaimed about the opinion of the Polish people, and His Majesty's Government would be charged in Parliament with having forsaken altogether the cause of Poland.

The prime minister was in this instance not overstating the case. He had heard many such accusations during his meetings with Mikołajczyk and Arciszewski, as well as from members of his own party. He warned Stalin that even if he were to accept the Soviet proposal, the debates in Parliament "would be most painful and embarrassing to the unity of the Allies." Molotov's proposals "went nearly far enough," he believed. "If they gave up the Polish Government in London," argued the prime minister, "a new start should be made from both sides on more or less equal terms. Before His Majesty's Government could abandon their present position of continuing to recognize the London Government, they would have to be satisfied that the new Government was truly representative of the Polish nation."

Churchill's appeal did not move Stalin. He backed Molotov, stating that it would be better to reconstruct the existing government than to create a new one. He refused to discard the Warsaw government on the grounds that it was extremely popular in Poland. Stalin insisted that the Polish people sympathized with leaders who had stayed with them during the occupation. According to the American protocol, Stalin declared that "it was his impression that the driving out of the Germans by the Red Army had been received by the Poles in the light of a great national holiday. The people had been surprised that the Polish Government in London had not had any part in this great holiday. They enquire, 'We of the National Council and Provisional Government participated in this holiday, but where are the London Poles?'" This cut no ice with the Western leaders, especially Churchill, who was well aware that the regime the Soviets had established in occupied Poland was no holiday.

But this was not Stalin's main point. He raised the case of France, where the Western powers had acted without consulting the Soviets. In early January Molotov, upset with negative Western reaction to the transformation of the Polish Committee of National Liberation into a provisional government, made a note for his subordinates: "Poland is a big deal! But we do not know how governments were organized in Belgium, France, Greece, and elsewhere. No one asked us, although we do not say that we are displeased with one or another of those governments." Now Stalin compared the position of the Warsaw government to that of General de Gaulle: "Neither had been elected, and he could not say which one enjoyed the greatest degree of popularity—yet we all had dealt with de Gaulle and the Soviet Government concluded a treaty with him. Why should we be so different with regard to the Polish Government, and why could we not deal with an enlarged Polish Government." The discussion was entering dangerous territory.

Roosevelt decided that it was time to move on. He asked Stalin about the timing of elections in Poland and, after being told that they could be arranged within a month unless the situation on the front precluded it, suggested that the Polish issue be discussed by the foreign ministers and then reported to the

plenary session. Everyone agreed. But Stalin was not prepared to drop the subject of Western involvement in Western Europe and the Balkans. Now he
wanted to know "what is holding back the formation of the united government
in Yugoslavia" and "what was going on Greece." He added that he "had no
intention of criticizing British policy there but he would merely like to know
what was going on."

Clearly unhappy with the Western Allies' position on the question of Poland,
Stalin was now "contextualizing" the Polish case. He reminded Churchill that
a few weeks earlier the Soviets had turned a blind eye to the British crackdown
on procommunist forces in Greece. In so doing, he was observing his earlier
agreement with Churchill, which had recognized British predominance in
Greece. Before the meeting was adjourned, Churchill was obliged to acknowledge that he was in debt to his host. The British, he said, "had rather a rough
time in Greece and they were very much obliged to Marshal Stalin for not having taken too great an interest in Greek affairs."[7]

Molotov's six-point plan contained provisions for Poland's future borders. The
Curzon Line had already been accepted by the Allies as Poland's eastern fron-
tier. Molotov's proposal for the western border was even more controversial.
According to the Soviet draft, ". . . [T]he Western frontier of Poland should be
traced from the town of Stettin (Polish) and farther to the south along the river
Oder and still farther along the river Neisse (Western)."[8]

Stalin was eager to show that he was not just taking from Poland but giving
to it as well. Ever since the German attack on the USSR in 1941, he had been
prepared to compensate Polish territorial losses in the East with acquisitions at
Germany's expense in the West. In fact, he was prepared to give Poland more
than the Western Allies were comfortable with. The establishment of the western border of Poland along the Oder and Neisse rivers had been discussed in
general terms at Teheran. The understanding at that time was that the border
would follow the Eastern Neisse. But at Yalta Stalin suggested the Western
Neisse as the new boundary, which would mean moving the southern part of
the Polish-German border 200 kilometers west.

After Teheran, Stalin maintained his support for the Oder–Eastern Neisse
Line, which corresponded to Russia's war aims in 1914, when both Nicholas II
and his foreign minister, Sergei Sazonov, were prepared to give Poland Silesia
and the eastern part of Poznań province, which then belonged to the German
Reich. Polish claims to Silesia were largely historical, as the territory had been
controlled by a Polish state back in the tenth century. By the twentieth century
most of the population there was either German or heavily Germanized, especially in Lower Silesia, whose principal city was Breslau (Polish: Wrocław). Nevertheless, it served Stalin's interests to offer Poland compensation at Germany's
expense so that he could keep the Soviet territorial acquisitions of 1939 intact

and claim Königsberg and adjoining territories of East Prussia for himself. In the summer of 1944 he personally drew an Oder–Eastern Neisse border between Germany and Poland on one of the maps preserved in the Russian archives. The map leaves no doubt that the Neisse River Stalin had in mind was the Eastern Neisse.

Stalin switched to the Western Neisse sometime during the summer or possibly the fall of 1944, once he had managed to create a Polish government of his own. For him, as for the British, the location of Poland's western boundary depended on the composition of the Polish government. From Stalin's perspective, adding new territories would make the future Polish government more loyal to Moscow, and putting a loyal government in control of as much Western territory as possible would strengthen the Soviet position in Central Europe and further weaken Germany, Stalin's main security concern at the time. Besides, his position would make him appear to be a defender of Polish interests, and Stalin was quick to point out at Yalta that Mikołajczyk had been delighted to hear that Poland's frontier would extend to the Western Neisse.[9]

The change in Stalin's position did not come as a complete surprise, as the idea had been promoted by the Lublin government for some time. On January 2, 1945, according to the war cabinet minutes, Eden informed his colleagues that he "was disturbed at the extent to which the Lublin Poles were opening their mouths." He elaborated on this statement at a cabinet meeting on January 22: "The Lublin government were now opening their mouths still wider, and were asking for additional territories in Pomerania, together with Lower Silesia." On the next day he submitted a memo on the Polish western frontiers in which he argued against the Western Neisse line. The war cabinet approved that position at its meeting on January 25. "If, as now seemed more probable," went the argument, "we had to deal with the claims of the Lublin Poles who were ready to accept the Curzon Line anyhow, there was no longer any need for H. M. Government to support any more extensive transfers of territory than we thought convenient and proper on other grounds. . . . Our line might be that H. M. Government must not be considered as having accepted any definite line as a Western Frontier of Poland."[10]

During their consultations on Malta, Eden and Stettinius had agreed to oppose any further westward shift of the Polish borders if it was proposed at Yalta, as they were alarmed by the sheer number of people who would have to move. Churchill gave voice to those concerns in a letter to his wife from Malta. "I am free to confess to you," he wrote, "that my heart is saddened by the tales of the masses of German women and children flying along the roads everywhere in forty-mile-long columns to the West before the advancing Armies. I am clearly convinced that they deserve it; but that does not remove it from one's gaze. The misery of the whole world appals me and I fear increasingly that new struggles may arise out of those we are successfully ending."

According to British estimates, allocating parts of East Prussia and Upper Silesia to Poland would create 2.5 million German refugees. Establishing the new frontier on the Oder would add another 2.5 million displaced persons. These changes had been discussed at Teheran. Moving the border to the Western Neisse would mean resettling another 3.25 million ethnic Germans on top of that. The Americans were particularly cautious, refusing to transfer anything more than East Prussia, a small portion of Pomerania, and Upper Silesia. "We should resist vigorously efforts to extend the Polish frontier to the Oder Line or the Oder-Neisse Line," read the U.S. State Department memorandum prepared on Malta.

The British were somewhat more accommodating. They had already agreed to the Oder Line during talks with the Soviets and representatives of the London Polish government in Moscow in October 1944. They decided, however, to oppose the Western Neisse Line, and after consultations with the Americans on Malta, Eden suggested that Churchill drop even his earlier support for the Oder Line. The British had accepted the Oder Line in order to help Stanisław Mikołajczyk convince his colleagues to make their peace with territorial losses in the East, but they were not eager to do a similar favor for the "Lublin Poles."[11]

"It would be a great pity to stuff the Polish goose so full of German food that it died of indigestion," Churchill told Stalin, taking it upon himself to present the Western position. He was in favor of moving the Polish boundary westward and thought that the Poles should take in compensation for their eastern losses as much German territory as they could handle, but no more. According to the British protocol of the meeting, "He was conscious of a large body of opinion in Great Britain which was frankly shocked at the idea of moving of millions of people by force. He himself was not shocked, but it was certainly a view which would come very much to the fore in Great Britain. A great success had been achieved in disentangling the Greek and Turkish populations after the last war and the two countries had enjoyed good relations ever since; but in that case under a couple of millions of people had been moved. If Poland took East Prussia and Silesia as far as the Oder, it would mean moving six million Germans back to Germany. That might be managed subject to the moral question, which he had to settle with his own people."

Churchill's knowledge of history or, rather, his memory may have been quite selective. The "disentanglement" of Turks and Greeks after the First World War, which the Greeks remembered as part of the "Asia Minor Catastrophe," was hardly a "great success" in humanitarian terms—but his reference to British public opinion was not a sham. Back in London the war cabinet expressed its concern: "Vast transfers of population would be involved. It was uncertain whether Poland would be able to populate and develop territories so extensive, and Germany's dependence on food imports would be greatly increased. Moreover, public opinion, both in the parliament and in the country, was increasingly critical of the exaggerated territorial demands which had been put forward by the Lublin Poles."

Churchill did his best to prepare the British public for the coming shift of the Polish borders. In a speech to Parliament on December 15, 1944, he had stressed the benefits of expulsions and transfers for the future European peace. "The transference of several millions of people would have to be effected from the east to the west or north, and the expulsion of the Germans . . . from the area to be occupied by Poland in the west and north. For expulsion is the method which, so far as we have been able to see, will be the most satisfactory and lasting. There will be no mixture of populations to cause endless trouble as in Alsace-Lorraine. A clean sweep will be made. I am not alarmed by these large transferences, which are more possible than they ever were before through modern conditions."

At Yalta, Churchill dissociated himself from the large segment of British public opinion that would be "shocked at the idea of moving of millions of people by force." The discussion reached a new low when Stalin joined the debate. He indicated that there would be no need to transfer Germans from the future Polish territories: "There will be no more Germans there for when our troops come in the Germans run away and no Germans are left." Churchill acknowledged that "this, of course, simplified the problem." He felt that it had been simplified even further by the fact that, in killing between six and seven million Germans in the course of the war, the Allies had created space in Germany for those who would be resettled from the West. Churchill expected that German casualties would grow by a million more before the end of hostilities. When Stalin asked whether he meant one or two million, the prime minister responded, according to the American protocol of the meeting, "Oh, I am not proposing any limitations on them."[12]

As supreme commander of the Red Army, Stalin spoke with confidence when he assured Churchill that German refugees were leaving the territories about to be captured by Soviet troops en masse. Arbitrary killing, rape, and looting became part of everyday life for those who did not manage to escape. In the spring of 1945 the Soviet authorities in East Prussia reported to Moscow that the suicide rate was increasing among Germans in general, and women in particular, in Soviet-occupied territory. Stalin was in no hurry to restore discipline in his occupying army.

When, in the fall of 1944, the Yugoslav communist leader Milovan Djilas went on record criticizing Red Army soldiers for rape and murder in Yugoslavia, unfavorably comparing the behavior of Soviet soldiers with that of their British counterparts, he got into trouble with Stalin. "Does Djilas, who is himself a writer, not know what human suffering and the human heart are? Can't he understand it if a soldier who has crossed thousands of kilometers through blood and fire and death has fun with a woman or takes some trifle?" If this was Stalin's response to complaints about the crimes of the Red Army in Yugo-slavia, then what hope might there be for the Germans?[13]

In January 1945 the Soviet press took an extremely aggressive approach toward German war criminals, and the German population in general. The best Soviet propagandist of the period, Ilya Ehrenburg, led the charge. "The embit-tered German-hating Ehrenburg," stated the survey of the Soviet press com-piled by the American embassy in Moscow, "writing with more precision than usual, outlined his program: restore devastated Soviet areas with German labor squads, hang the criminals, spare the children."

Ehrenburg was the only Soviet journalist who, in Stalin's opinion, needed no editors. "Now we understand the Germans are not human," he wrote in August 1942 in the Red Army newspaper *Krasnaia zvezda* (Red Star). "Now the word 'German' has become the most terrible curse. Let us not speak. Let us not be indignant. Let us kill. If you do not kill a German, a German will kill you. He will carry away your family, and torture them in his damned Germany. If you have killed one German, kill another." With the Wehrmacht deep in Soviet territory, this was an appeal to fight the German army, but with the Soviets entering Prussia it turned into a call to annihilate the Germans as a people.

"What would you do if you found a German beside a Christmas tree?" Ehrenburg asked a Western guest at the reception hosted by Averell Harriman on January 12, 1945. When a British general responded, "Shoot him," Ehren-burg said, "That is too good to him. You should hang him from the Christmas tree." He then stated that he had gone on record against child murder and would ensure that Germans be hanged only from the age of sixteen.[14]

On February 6, the day before Molotov proposed that Poland's western bor-der extend to the Western Neisse, the Soviet occupation authorities in Germany issued an order to form labor battalions of Germans aged seventeen to fifty. Those who did not escape and were not shot were now being sent east to the Soviet Union. Stalin was not too far from the truth when he told Churchill that there would be no Germans left in the territory he proposed to give to Poland. It was only in April 1945 that the Soviets introduced measures to stop mass murder, rape, and looting in Germany, despite numerous earlier reports. Stalin decided that the time had come to edit Ehrenburg: he was officially repri-manded in *Pravda* for inciting senseless violence.[15]

Churchill was prepared to match Stalin in talking brutal realpolitik, but he would not give up his opposition to the Soviet proposal to move the Polish border farther west. The British counterproposal accepted the Polish border on the Oder but not on the Western Neisse. It called for the forced resettlement of Germans then living east of that line and the voluntary resettlement of Poles from Germany to the east of the line. The American proposal also accepted the Oder but not the Western Neisse. At the plenary session of February 8, Molotov tried to sway the Allies by playing the democrat and offering to ask the Poles what they thought. He had no doubt that both the London and Warsaw Poles would prefer the Soviet proposal to the one suggested by the Western Allies.[16]

During the heated discussion of the Polish question at the plenary sessions on February 7 and 8, the Western Allies refused to yield on the country's western boundaries, while the Soviets refused to form a new Polish government. Since the two issues were related, it is quite possible that if Stalin had agreed to compromise on the government, enlarging it with eight to ten political leaders from Polish democratic parties (as Churchill hoped), Roosevelt and Churchill would have been more responsive to Soviet proposals on the western boundary. But Stalin refused to accommodate Western requests, and Roosevelt and Churchill were not prepared to countenance the moral and logistical problems involved in the transfer of great numbers of Germans in order to give more territory to a communist-controlled government in Warsaw.

The chess game that began with Roosevelt's letter to Stalin on the evening of February 6, followed by Molotov's proposal on February 7 and the Western counterproposal made on the morning of February 8, now seemed headed for a draw. Someone would have to back down, but neither side was prepared to do so. "Not such a good day," Eden wrote in his diary on February 8. "Stuck again over Poland."[17]

16

THE BOMBLINE

In the early afternoon of February 7, Sarah Oliver drove with her father to Livadia for the plenary session. "It was a lovely day again, the sun did its best for the scene—it tried hard to warm the granite peaks—it shone so hard on the sea that the reflection made one blink," she wrote in a letter home. "Papa and I looked solidly out on the scene and presently he said, 'The Riviera of Hades!'" The rain that everyone had expected the previous evening never came, and the British military commanders decided to take a break from their discussions to tour the battlefields of the Crimean War. "All the Chiefs of Staff have taken a holiday to-day to look at the battlefield of Balaclava. This is not being stressed in our conversations with our Russian friends," Churchill wrote that evening to his deputy prime minister, Clement Attlee.[1]

Officially the purpose of the trip was to visit Sevastopol, also the site of a more recent struggle between the Red Army and the Wehrmacht. "We left at 9 am," Field Marshal Alan Brooke recorded in his diary, "and drove by what is known as Vorontsov's Road, namely the road constructed by the former owner of the house we are in, when he was Viceroy of the Crimea. This is a most lovely road winding high up on the mountains above the sea." Brooke, the foremost British military strategist and Churchill's candidate for overall command of the Allied invasion of Europe, who was passed over in favor first of General Marshall and then of General Eisenhower, kept a diary in which he recorded some not very flattering comments about his colleagues and superiors, including Churchill, whom he considered a most difficult person to deal with.

An avid admirer of nature who enjoyed hunting and fishing and would later serve as head of the Zoological Society of London, Brooke was glad of the opportunity to take part in a field trip. He brought along sketches of the battlefields of Balaklava. Once the group reached the area, he got busy locating the battle sites and was excited to find the site of the famous Charge of the Light Brigade. His companions were suddenly distracted by signs of a more recent struggle.

They located the remains of a human skeleton on the ground. "Can you tell if it is a Russian or a German skull?" someone asked Lord Moran, who was part of the group. The doctor could not tell. Brooke noted the signs of recent warfare: "A grave beside a wrecked aeroplane here, a broken down tank there, rows upon rows of shell and bomb craters, twisted iron cheveaux-de-frise, tangled basket wire, odd graves, and the usual rubbish of a battlefield. It is very strange how history can repeat itself under a different guise."[2]

If on the fourth day of the conference the British commanders could relax and engage in sightseeing, their American counterparts were growing ever more desperate over the lack of progress on their main objective: negotiating the entry of the Soviet Union into the war with Japan. The planning of joint operations against the Japanese in the Pacific theater was one of the main reasons why Roosevelt had invited his military commanders to join him at Yalta. But the U.S. military's attempts to raise the war in the Pacific at the first tripartite meetings of General Staff representatives were repeatedly undermined by the Soviets. On February 7, American persistence finally paid off. The U.S. military commanders may have missed the sightseeing tour, but they managed to ensure that a Soviet-American military meeting was on the agenda for the next day. They also finally reached agreement on the bombline—the boundary between the operational zones of Soviet and Allied aviation in Central Europe. The direct outcome of that agreement was the destruction of Dresden by Allied bombing a few short days after the end of the Yalta Conference.

Military relations between the Western Allies and the Soviets turned out to be as challenging as political ones. At first the Americans were largely concerned with the problems that they encountered with their British partners. On Malta, General Marshall had been drawn into a major debate with the British commanders over the direction of the offensive on the western front. Marshall told Roosevelt on the morning of February 4 that the British military's new bone of contention was liaison with the Soviet commanders. The British objected to any direct communication between commanders on the western front and the Soviet General Staff, partly out of fear that the Americans would bypass them and deal with the Soviets on their own.

When General Eisenhower was planning his actions in the Ardennes in January, he had no way of finding out from the Red Army General Staff when they were planning to launch their offensive, as he lacked the right to communicate directly with his counterparts in Moscow. Under the new arrangement envisioned by the Americans, Eisenhower would have the right to communicate directly with the Red Army General Staff through the American military mission in Moscow. The British were afraid that this would leave Churchill and the whole British military command largely out of the picture. They preferred that communication be established between the Combined Chiefs of Staff, that is, both British and American commanders, and the Soviet General Staff. The Americans considered this arrangement cumbersome and ineffective.[3]

Marshall, who was fully aware of what problems the British might cause the Allied effort, was less attuned to problems that might arise from the peculiar nature of Soviet political and military culture. Averell Harriman sought to explain some of these at the president's meeting with his military advisers on the morning of February 4. He pointed out that it would be impossible to have meaningful discussions with representatives of the Soviet General Staff unless they received approval for such discussions from Stalin. On that, as on many other issues pertaining to Soviet political culture, Harriman was in full agreement with the head of the U.S. military mission in Moscow, General John R. Deane.

Before the Yalta Conference, Deane had prepared a memorandum on "the methods, procedures and characteristics of the Soviet military authorities" for the military members of the U.S. delegation. "Thus far it has been impossible to induce the Soviet military authorities to conduct thorough discussions of questions which we raise prior to receiving a government decision on the main issues involved," stated the memorandum. "There is only one person in Russia from whom a foreigner can sometimes obtain a decision at the first meeting— Marshal Stalin." The U.S. commanders asked the president to raise directly with Stalin the possibility of establishing a liaison between General Eisenhower and the Soviet General Staff. They also wanted him to ask Stalin to let his General Staff conduct "free and open" discussions with their Western counterparts.[4]

Roosevelt raised both points during his preconference meeting with Stalin on February 7. He gave the Soviet leader a memo on the agenda for negotiations between the Allied commanders and suggested that, as the western and eastern fronts were drawing ever closer, Eisenhower should be allowed to establish direct contact with the Soviet military instead of going through London and Washington. Stalin agreed, saying that the military staffs "would work out the details of this suggestion." The president had every reason to be satisfied with Stalin's response, but it would certainly have raised suspicions among more experienced Soviet hands. As Deane had learned the hard way, agreement "in principle" meant very little, for in the process of "working out the details" the Soviets could easily render it meaningless.[5]

The next day, Soviet commanders were eager to discuss both the details of their ongoing offensive and their requests for Allied actions on the western front. But the scope of the discussion was strictly defined by Stalin's comments the day before. Whenever a new question was raised or a new proposal made, they would stall, first trying to come up with an excuse as to why they could not agree to the new proposal, and then stating that they would have to discuss it with Marshal Stalin. When Admiral Leahy proposed that direct liaison be established between Eisenhower's headquarters on the western front and Moscow, Field Marshal Alan Brooke, always suspicious that his American counterparts were trying to cut off British access, proposed that liaison could be established instead between the American, British, and Soviet chiefs of staff. He also suggested that contacts be extended to lower-level commanders. That would have given Field Marshal Alexander, the Allied commander in the Mediterranean, the right to communicate with commanders of Red Army units in the Balkans.

The idea made perfect sense, given that the fronts were moving closer together, and accidents were beginning to happen: on one occasion, Soviet troops in the Balkans were mistakenly bombed by U.S. airplanes. The Americans embraced it, but now the Soviets objected. The man entrusted with putting forward the Soviet position was the first deputy chief of the Red Army General Staff, General Aleksei Antonov, whom Allied commanders considered a competent strategist. After his presentation to the first plenary session, General Laurence S. Kuter of the U.S. Army wrote that he "spoke, acted, and reacted very much as we would expect a top-flight conservative American chief of staff to do in the absence of his commander."

Now Antonov divided the question into two parts: liaison between the General Staffs and between commanders in the field. He said that the first could be conducted through the Allied military missions in Moscow, while the second could be reviewed once the fronts drew closer. The original American proposal, forwarded by the U.S. Joint Chiefs of Staff to Moscow on January 18, called for establishing direct lines between Eisenhower and the Red Army General Staff through the U.S. military mission in Moscow. Stalin had approved this, assuming that it would add one more channel of communication entirely subject to his control.[6]

General Marshall was stunned. He said he could not understand the reason for limiting communication. Antonov said that the issue would be resolved in due course, effectively indicating the limits of his authority. Marshall pushed again. He reminded everyone of the mistaken American bombing of Soviet troops in the Balkans, to which Antonov responded that it had been the result of a navigational error. Marshall pointed out that the Allied air forces could not bomb the retreating Germans even in good weather, since the bombline was supposed to be agreed upon in Moscow and the formality made effective action on the front impossible. Field Marshal Alan Brooke supported him. Antonov stuck to his guns, saying that the Soviet air force operations were decided in Moscow and had to be coordinated there.

At this point British Air Marshal Charles Portal intervened. He said that strategic air force operations should indeed be coordinated at the highest level, but Field Marshal Alexander and the Allied air forces in the Mediterranean theater had to have direct contact with Soviet armies in the Balkans and in Hungary. Antonov had run out of excuses. Marshal Sergei Khudiakov of the Red

Army Air Force finally told the conference that in his opinion, "with regard to direct liaison between Field Marshal Alexander and the Russian left wing . . . this was a matter that should be reported to Marshal Stalin." At last everyone understood that the Soviet commanders had no authority to make decisions on matters not preapproved by Stalin, and the question was temporarily dropped.[7]

General Kuter later summarized his impressions of the "free" exchange of views: "The meeting was in general a satisfactory one, since this was the first time that the Russians themselves advanced any views of their own. In presenting individual views, however, and always in replying to questions, the Russians normally prefaced their observations and replies with the statement that they were speaking for themselves, informally and unofficially. After giving such informal and individual replies, they would state that they would see 'the Marshal' later that day and could then present a firm and official reply at the next meeting."

Acceding to the Allied proposal would have run counter to the Soviet policy of concentrating decision-making processes in Moscow. Behind that policy lay the traditional Russian suspicion of foreigners, a reluctance to engage in collaboration with the West unless absolutely necessary, and fear of exposing Soviet citizens to Western influences—all features of Soviet political and military culture described in General Deane's memo. At the next tripartite meeting of military commanders, Antonov reported Marshal Stalin's belief that as long as there was no direct contact between Soviet and Allied troops, there was no need to establish liaison on lower levels. That was the end of the discussion.[8]

The Soviet commanders' lack of authority to make even minor decisions came as a surprise to most members of the Allied military delegations, who enjoyed much more freedom. General Deane's memo had explained the reasons, but it took the American and British generals some time to adjust to the new reality. Eventually they grew accustomed to the notion that responses to new ideas or proposals would be forthcoming only on the day after they were presented. The Western military commanders could hardly have imagined the kind of psychological pressure that their Soviet counterparts were subjected to on a daily basis, working under the watchful eye of a paranoid dictator and his secret police.

The fate of one of the most outspoken and likable Soviet commanders at Yalta, Air Marshal Sergei Khudiakov, was especially telling. Round-faced and cheerful, Khudiakov, the chief representative of the Soviet air force command at the conference, made his way into quite a few pictures taken at Yalta. He established a strong professional bond with his American counterpart, General Kuter, who saw in him all the characteristics of a "cocky aviator." Kuter wrote later that Khudiakov opened the first conference of air force chiefs with a "brisk and pleasant statement that it would be no longer necessary for the airmen to confer with the formality of diplomats or in the classical or stilted military terms of Army and Navy commanders." Even when he gave a negative response, he managed to do so in a manner that reinforced the solidarity among the air force chiefs of the three Allied powers. "General Staffs are undoubtedly millstones around the necks of aviators all over the world," Khudiakov concluded at the end of the last and not very successful meeting of air force commanders. Kuter would later write that he "spoke as a pleasant, brusque, direct-dealing" person and "appeared to have more freedom of expression than his colleagues."[9]

Khudiakov was forty-three to Kuter's forty and both had had spectacular careers during the war: Kuter advanced from major to major general in a little more than two years, skipping the rank of full colonel. It took Khudiakov slightly more than three years to jump four ranks, advancing from colonel to marshal of the Soviet air force. After Yalta, both Kuter and Khudiakov were assigned to the Far East, Khudiakov as commander of the Soviet air force during the brief war with Japan and Kuter as deputy commander of the U.S. Army air force in the Pacific. But the parallels between their lives and careers ended there.

Born Armenak Khanferiants, of Armenian parentage, Khudiakov was one of the organizers of the Red Guards in Baku, the future capital of Soviet-controlled Azerbaijan, during the revolution. He changed his name to honor a Russian friend killed in the fighting. His open and independent style was probably too much for Stalin, and it may well have contributed to his downfall less than a year after Yalta. Khudiakov was arrested on December 14, 1945, and later accused of having been recruited as a spy by the British at sixteen, when he was just beginning his revolutionary activities in Baku. His arrest, part of Stalin's attempt to build a criminal case against Marshal Georgii Zhukov, who was accused by party bosses of "Bonapartism," could not have happened without Stalin's personal approval. In the fall of 1949, when the head of Stalin's bodyguards, General Nikolai Vlasik; the head of his personal secretariat, Aleksandr Poskrebyshev; and Marshal Kliment Voroshilov, then Stalin's deputy in the Council of People's Commissars, were discussing Khudiakov's arrest but could not recall his surname, Stalin was quick to come up with it. Khudiakov was shot by a firing squad in April 1950.[10]

It was not the first time Stalin had turned against military leaders. He had destroyed the flower of the Red Army, including its chief strategist, Marshal Mikhail Tukhachevsky, in the purges he conducted between 1937 and 1938. Two of the current top commanders, Marshals Konstantin Rokossovsky and Kirill Meretskov, had been released from prison to lead their armies in the war. Now there was a new crop of commanders to be taken care of. In his postwar assault on his generals, Stalin accused them of stealing art objects and other valuables from parts of Germany occupied by the Red Army. Those accusations were not without foundation, to put it mildly, but the main goal of the campaign was to keep the generals in line and show a new generation who was in charge.

Free expression did not enhance one's chances of survival. But cockiness and a good rapport with the Allies were not the only grounds for victimization in Stalin's terror. The life and career of another Soviet commanding officer at Yalta, Admiral Nikolai Kuznetsov, commander of the Soviet navy, further attest to the risk of a military career under Stalin. Unlike Khudiakov, Kuznetsov was not highly regarded by his Western counterparts. Kuter considered him a "political admiral" and concluded that "his knowledge and interest in naval operations was rudimentary." Admiral Leahy had an equally low opinion of him. "He was a great big man dressed in a handsomely tailored admiral's uniform. He spoke French well enough for us to talk together and I found him thoroughly informed, although I had doubts that he was a very good sea commander," wrote Leahy in his memoirs.

When he was appointed people's commissar of the Soviet navy in 1939, at the age of thirty-four, Kuznetsov had had less than three years' experience as a cruiser commander and had spent little more than a year as commander of the Soviet Pacific Fleet. Stalin's purges of the high command before the war had made Kuznetsov's spectacular career possible, but the terror unleashed against the generals after the war almost put an end to that career. In 1947 Kuznetsov was removed from his post and demoted to the rank of vice admiral. He was accused of supplying the British with documentation about a "secret" Soviet torpedo in 1944—a ridiculous charge, given that the license for its production had been purchased by the USSR from Italy in 1935.

By 1951 Stalin had reappointed the frightened and humiliated Kuznetsov to his old post, but he never regained his rank of admiral. Still, he was lucky. His downfall after Yalta, like Khudiakov's, shows plainly what was behind the Soviet commanders' reluctance to take on responsibility in negotiations with their Western allies. On February 8, at dinner in Yusupov Palace, Stalin proposed a toast to "those to whom we all look in war for our security, those on whom our very security depends, the heroes of all the women, and the centre of all things as long as hostilities continue, only to be forgotten and lapse into oblivion as soon as hostilities cease—our soldiers."[11]

A few years after the end of the war, General Deane wrote that joint Soviet-American planning of the Pacific war was hampered by their different understanding of the functions of a military alliance. The Americans thought in terms of joint operations, the Soviets in terms of defining tasks that each party would perform independently. The differences in approach became fully apparent when it came time to "work out the details."[12]

In the absence of effective communication between commanders on the ground, the only solution open to both air forces as the fronts drew closer was to establish a new bombline to determine the limits of aerial operations on both sides. General Antonov suggested that a bombline be established at a distance of some 60 kilometers from the Soviet front lines. The Americans and British asked for time to study the issue. They were not pleased. Field Marshal Alan Brooke noted in his diary that day: "Antonov produced an arbitrary line running through Berlin, Leipzig, Vienna and Zagreb which did not suit us."

After considering the issue overnight, the Western Allies rejected Antonov's proposal. General Kuter presented the American and British position, questioning the need for a bombline at all—a clear reconsideration of the January agenda of the U.S. Joint Chiefs of Staff. Had a new bombline been established, important industrial targets and oil refineries in the East would have become off-limits for Anglo-American bombing. Kuter proposed instead that communication between Allied air force commanders be improved. The Soviets declined. Also discussed was possible coordination of bombing on German territory by American, British, and Soviet aircraft. The Soviets declined again.

At some point it became clear that the Americans and British on the one hand and the Soviets on the other had a different understanding of the term "bombline." Kuter, Portal, and Khudiakov found a solution on February 7, while the British commanders were on their sightseeing trip. They introduced a new term, "zone of limitation," to describe areas open to bombardment by either side. Linguistic adjustments aside, in one form or another the bombline would remain. The Western Allies were now in a hurry to attack German targets before the Soviet front line came too close to the objectives they had already singled out for massive bombing.[13]

The city of Dresden was the primary victim of the "zone of limitation" agreement reached at Yalta—one of the few direct outcomes of the military consultations held there. In early 1945 Dresden was one of the few major German centers to have escaped systematic Allied bombing. Its inhabitants found comfort in the rumor that Churchill's aunt had lived in the city and that it was being protected by the personal intervention of the British prime minister. Unfortunately for the Dresdeners, this was not the case. The city was added to the list of Allied air targets in January 1945 as Churchill looked for ways to assist the Red Army's winter offensive, as well as to demonstrate the power of the Allied bombers, whose destructive potential was far superior to anything the Soviets could produce at the time.

At Yalta the Allied commanders learned, probably to their surprise, that Dresden was directly on the bombline proposed by the Soviets. Within a few short days, if the Soviet offensive continued, the city would be out of reach for Allied bombers. British Air Marshal Charles Portal convinced General Antonov to add Dresden to Berlin and Leipzig as targets that would be bombed by the Allies on Soviet request. On February 7, General Deane was notified by his superiors that Dresden would be bombed by the Allies along with other German centers. The exact day of the raid was not specified at the time, but on February 12, the day after the end of the Yalta Conference, General Deane notified the Soviet General Staff of the coming attack.

On the night of February 13 the Royal Air Force Bomber Command executed the first night air raid on the city. "Florence on the Elbe" was reduced to rubble by Allied bombers in three major raids between February 13 and 15. Altogether 1,300 British and American bombers dropped more than 3,000 tons of bombs. The inner city was completely destroyed, with twenty-five thousand killed outright or burned alive in the firestorm. Ironically, as a result of the bombing, the outlying industrial areas suffered significantly less than the historic city center, and the Nazis were able to restore military production there in a relatively short period.

The bombing of Dresden, which began only two days after the end of the Yalta Conference, became a symbol of the cruelty, horror, and senselessness of "terror bombing" in the Second World War. The memorandum issued to the Royal Air Force pilots prior to their attack on the city read: "[I]ntentions of the attack are to hit the enemy where he will feel it most, behind an already partially collapsed front, to prevent the use of the city in the way of further advance, and incidentally to show the Russians when they arrive what Bomber Command can do." The Soviets did not arrive until May 8, the day of Nazi Germany's capitulation on the western front. They made their way to the city by crossing the Elbe on the "Blue Wonder," a nineteenth-century metal bridge that had miraculously survived not only the Allied bombardment of Dresden but also Nazi attempts to blow it up in anticipation of the Soviet advance.[14]

17

THE FAR EASTERN BLITZ

S talin was pacing in his study at Yusupov Palace, as he liked to do in his Kremlin office. He could not contain his excitement. "Good," he said, "very good." And then he said it again. In his hands he held a letter from President Roosevelt, delivered to his study by a courier. Unable to wait for the official translation, he had summoned the young Soviet ambassador to Washington, Andrei Gromyko, to interpret the contents immediately. Gromyko told him that Roosevelt was prepared to accommodate Soviet claims to southern Sakhalin and the Kurile Islands. "This is an important letter," Stalin told his ambassador. "The Americans recognize the justice of our position on Sakhalin and the Kuriles. Now in return they will try to insist on participation in the war on Japan. But that's another question altogether."

"Tell me, what do you think of Roosevelt? Is he clever?" Stalin asked Gromyko. This time the future Soviet foreign minister decided not to regale Stalin with a class analysis of Roosevelt's capitalist policies, as he had done on an earlier occasion. He recognized his master's mood: Stalin was pleased with Roosevelt's letter and wanted to hear good things about its author. "Comrade Stalin," followed the carefully worded answer, "Roosevelt is a highly intelligent, very capable man. Just the fact that he got himself elected president for a third time and then a fourth term speaks for itself. Of course, he was helped by the international situation. And a lot of it was also due to the capable job the Democrats did in popularizing his name. But his talks on the radio, his 'Fireside Chats,' also made a big impact on millions of Americans."

"That was smart of him," remarked Stalin. "Yes, he got everything right." "He had what I would call a smile of solid satisfaction on his face," Gromyko wrote in his memoirs. "It was an expression I had noticed when he was feeling good, when the discussion was about someone to whom he was well disposed."[1]

Roosevelt's letter was the first official recognition of the "political conditions" that Stalin had put before the Americans as the price for Soviet participation in the war in the Pacific. The "justice" of the Soviet demands, which Stalin now believed to be recognized by Roosevelt, was based as much on historical considerations as on geopolitical ones. In 1905 President Theodore Roosevelt had helped negotiate the Treaty of Portsmouth between the Russian and Japanese empires, ending a year and a half of warfare between the two powers over control of northeastern China and Korea. The American president won a Nobel Peace Prize for his diplomatic effort, but not everyone was happy with the results. For Russia it was a major humiliation, the culmination of months of defeat on land and sea at the hands of "inferior" Asians.

According to the treaty, the tsarist government agreed to turn over to Japan the southern part of Sakhalin and evacuate its army from Manchuria in northeastern China and surrender control of the railroads it had built there. It would also allow Japan to lease the Liaodong Peninsula with the former Russian naval base of Port Arthur and recognize Korea as part of the Japanese sphere of influence. The Russian quest for a warm-water port on the Pacific thus ended in disaster. The government had to agree to the peace conditions mediated by Roosevelt partly because of the Revolution of 1905, which weakened the empire from within. Now Stalin, who had participated actively in that revolution, was trying to avenge the defeat and humiliation he had helped impose on the former rulers of the empire.[2]

Soviet war aims in the Pacific were first formulated in the aftermath of the German defeat in the Battle of Moscow in December 1941. Back then Solomon Lozovsky, Molotov's deputy, had sent Stalin a memorandum suggesting that the USSR should improve its geostrategic position in the Far East, where the Soviet ports of Magadan and Vladivostok were cut off from the Pacific Ocean by Japanese possessions, including the Kurile Islands and southern Sakhalin. "We can no longer endure a situation in which Japanese warships can cut us off at any moment from the Pacific Ocean and from our ports and close Laperuz Strait, the Kurile Straits, Sangar Strait, and Tsushima Strait," wrote Lozovsky. In his opinion, it was time to start thinking about "our Far Eastern boundary and freedom of communication between the ports of the Soviet Union and the ports of the entire Pacific coast."[3]

Whatever the Soviets were thinking in December 1941, they had to keep their thoughts in utmost secrecy. In April 1941 they had signed a five-year neutrality pact with Japan, and it was only the Japanese decision not to attack the Soviet Union immediately after the German invasion in June of that year that had allowed Stalin to move fresh divisions from the Far East to Moscow and repel the German offensive against his capital. American Lend-Lease supplies were coming to the Soviet Union through its Pacific ports, and there again Japanese goodwill was essential to the continuing existence of the USSR's wartime lifeline. The Soviet victory at Stalingrad frightened the Japanese government, which proposed to send an envoy to Moscow in order to improve Soviet-Japanese relations, but Stalin turned down the offer. He preferred that relations remain as they were— neutral.

In October 1943 he told the visiting U.S. secretary of state, Cordell Hull, that after the surrender of Germany the Soviet Union would join the Allies in defeating Japan. In Teheran Stalin suggested that the Allies establish their "strong points" (military bases) around Japan but refused to discuss his territorial demands in Churchill's presence; he listed them in a private meeting with Roosevelt in which he gave the president to understand that Soviet participation in the war on Japan would depend on Allied actions in Europe. His price in territories significantly surpassed Lozovsky's. In January 1944, upon his return from Teheran, Roosevelt informed the Pacific War Council that he had reached an understanding with Stalin on the transfer to the USSR of Japanese-held southern Sakhalin and the Kurile Islands, recognition of Soviet rights to the Chinese port of Dairen (Dalian) and the Manchurian railroads in northeastern China, and participation in a forty-year trusteeship over Korea.

While they were in Teheran, Roosevelt forwarded a letter to Stalin asking for the right to set up U.S. air bases in the Soviet Far East, which would be used against Japan once the USSR entered the war. The Soviets showed little interest in the matter. Stalin assured his counterparts that the Soviet Union would join the war after the end of hostilities in Europe, once the Red Army's numbers in the Far East had been tripled by the transfer of units from the western front. Like many proposals accepted in Teheran, this was an oral understanding, not binding on either party, that would serve as a basis for later negotiations. That was its status in all subsequent discussions between the USSR and the United States on Soviet participation in the Pacific war.

Even Stalin's top foreign-policy advisers were not informed about the Soviet commitment to enter the war in the Pacific. Ivan Maisky showed no knowledge of the agreement in the memorandum on postwar world organization he submitted to Stalin and Molotov in January 1944. He believed that the USSR had to annex the Kurile Islands and southern Sakhalin but felt it could do so even without engaging in warfare with Japan. In fact, Maisky advised against such a war, proposing that Stalin leave the Western Allies to fight Japan alone as a payback for their procrastination in opening the second front in Europe.

In September 1944 Stalin expressed his surprise to Harriman and Archibald Clark Kerr that the Western Allies were proceeding with plans for joint operations in the Pacific without Soviet participation. He confirmed his decision to enter the war. But in the following month, during Churchill's visit to Moscow, when Harriman reminded Stalin of the American request, the Soviet leader told him that political questions should be clarified first. In the late autumn and early winter of 1944, the Soviet press gave some indication of what political questions Stalin had in mind. Reclaiming Port Arthur, a seaport and fortress lost to the Japanese forty years earlier, seemed to be a priority. "A book on the siege of Port Arthur in the Russo-Japanese war, publication of which was withheld for several years, appeared and was favorably reviewed in the press," reported the American embassy in Moscow.[4]

In December, when Harriman, acting on instructions from Washington, finally asked Stalin to enumerate his political questions, Stalin presented a list of demands identical to the one he had discussed with the president at Teheran. The Soviet leader asked for the "return" to the USSR of southern Sakhalin and the Kuriles to allow free passage between Vladivostok and the Pacific Ocean. "[A]ll outlets to the Pacific were now held or blocked by the enemy," said Stalin. He also wanted to lease Port Arthur, Dairen, and the Chinese-Eastern Railway. Harriman, who was familiar with the content of the private talks between Roosevelt and Stalin in Teheran, noted that with regard to a warm-water port on the Pacific, the president had in mind not a lease but an international free port. Stalin responded, "This can be discussed." There was one more request, which had not been discussed in Teheran. Stalin wanted assurances that the status quo would be maintained with regard to Mongolia, the only Soviet client state of the interwar period, meaning that it would remain independent of China.[5]

Roosevelt was clearly in no hurry to resume the discussion. As was often the case, different parts of his administration had different opinions on the issue. While the military was urging the president to ensure the earliest possible entrance of the Soviet Union into the war with Japan, State Department experts opposed territorial concessions. In December 1944 a memorandum on the Kurile Islands prepared by the State Department's Inter-Divisional Area Committee on the Far East argued against their transfer to the USSR. This was followed in January by a memorandum against handing over southern Sakhalin. Both took account of ethnic, historical, economic, and geostrategic factors and suggested an American response to the Soviet demands that included the possibility of establishing an American military base on one of the Kurile Islands.

The Kurile Islands had never belonged to Russia in their entirety: the southern part of the Kurile chain was ethnically Japanese and had belonged to Japan since the early nineteenth century. This was recognized by Russia in 1855. Twenty years later the Russians swapped the rest of the Kurile Islands, which were in their possession at the time, for southern Sakhalin, which then belonged to Japan. Tokyo was able to reclaim southern Sakhalin, and renamed it Karafuto, after its victorious war with Russia in 1905. Fifteen years later, during the Russian civil war, the Japanese also took the northern part of Sakhalin, but they were forced to return it to Moscow in 1925. The importance of the Kuriles was largely strategic. Southern Sakhalin had an ethnic Japanese population of more than four hundred thousand and was integrated into the Japanese Empire economically and administratively.

The State Department experts argued that under no circumstances should either southern Sakhalin or the southern part of the Kurile Island chain be handed over to the USSR. Stalin knew the State Department's position thanks to his spies—a copy of the memorandum on the Kurile Islands was found after the collapse of the USSR in the archive of the president of the Russian Federation. Surprisingly, neither of the State Department's memos on the territorial problems in the Far East made it into the Yalta briefing books, and there is no indication that the president was familiar with their recommendations. Either way, he decided to branch out on his own.

When in a preconference meeting with the president on February 4 Harriman suggested that in return for participation in the war on Japan Stalin would probably demand southern Sakhalin, the Kurile Islands, the Dairen railroad, and maintenance of the status quo in Mongolia, Roosevelt said that he was prepared to "go ahead" on all questions except Mongolia, on which he wanted to consult Chiang Kai-shek. Stettinius was sidelined, and the opinion of the State Department was ignored. When the secretary of state finally learned that Roosevelt and Stalin had begun their discussion of the Far East, using Harriman as an intermediary, he asked the president whether he needed any assistance. FDR said no: it was "primarily a military matter," and he preferred it to "remain on a purely military level."[6]

"I knew at Yalta," Stettinius wrote in his memoirs, ". . . of the immense pressure put on the President by our military leaders to bring Russia into the Far Eastern war." A memo on the Far East that did make it into the Yalta briefing book came, perhaps not surprisingly, from the Joint Chiefs of Staff. It pressed for Russia's entry into the war with Japan at "as early a date as possible": "The objective of Russia's military effort against Japan in the Far East should be the defeat of the Japanese forces in Manchuria, air operations against Japan proper in collaboration with U.S. air forces based in eastern Siberia, and maximum interference with Japanese sea traffic between Japan and the mainland of Asia."[7]

The specific role assigned to the Soviets by U.S. military planners was a direct consequence of the plan for the invasion of Japan approved by the Joint Chiefs of Staff in July 1944. The plan represented an uneasy victory for General Marshall, who considered it essential to invade the Japanese homeland, over Admiral Ernest King and General H. H. Arnold, commander of the Army Air Force, who believed that the war could be won by means of a blockade alone. They eventually agreed on a two-stage invasion of Japan. American casualties for the first stage, the invasion of Kyushu, were estimated at 100,000; for the second—the invasion of Honshu and the Tokyo plain—at 250,000. In November the Joint Chiefs of Staff concluded a study that posited that Moscow's strategic interests would eventually bring it into the war with Japan whether the United States wished it or not. The problem was that the Americans could not wait indefinitely. The study called for the earliest possible Soviet entry into the war: the goal was for the Soviets to tie up a million-strong Japanese army in Manchuria in order to ensure a successful American invasion of the Japanese islands. This was the basis of the memorandum from the Joint Chiefs of Staff that was sent to Roosevelt on January 23 and ended up in the president's Yalta briefing book.[8]

When the Soviets refused to discuss any specifics before their political demands had been met, the American military commanders did not hesitate to remind the president of their needs. They sent their first note to General Antonov, asking him to secure approval from Stalin for negotiations on the Pacific war, on the night of February 3. They received no answer. When, two days later, Admiral King announced that he would make a presentation on the war in the Pacific the following day and would be prepared to entertain Soviet questions, General Antonov said he would be glad to hear the report, "but as far as the discussion of the matter was concerned the Soviet General Staff would prefer that this should take place after the war in the Far East had been considered by the Heads of Government." That same day, Admiral Leahy asked the president to raise two specific questions with Stalin. One had to do with transoceanic supply, the other with the establishment of U.S. air bases on Soviet territory. Both matters were considered urgent, and later that day Roosevelt sent Stalin a letter requesting help on both fronts.

That night, the president hosted a dinner for his close advisers, including his three top military men. General Marshall entertained the company with stories of the fighting against the "Japs." Kathleen Harriman, who was present at the dinner, retold one of them about the American cavalry division that had entered Manila two days earlier. "Their job was to clean up Jap snipers in the hills," she recounted in a letter to a friend. "The soldiers were organized into groups of ten. They'd go out in the hills and, like hunting season, there was a limit strictly enforced, of 3 Japs per G.I. Later the limit was changed to one Jap—one outfit, to make the hunting more sporty, stripped its weapons down to those used by the Japs themselves. But Marshall said that soon had to be stopped. It was going too far!" No racist bragging about American successes in the Philippines could get around the fact that the Americans were facing a formidable opponent: progress was painful and slow. The battle for Manila, which began on February 3, would last a whole month, costing the U.S. military more than a thousand dead and more than five thousand wounded. At that rate the Americans would certainly need Soviet help, and quickly.

The following day brought no change in the Soviet position. King delivered his presentation as promised, and Antonov repeated his statement of the day before. Only Admiral Kuznetsov showed some interest in King's report, asking whether U.S. Navy plans included the capture of an island in the Kurile chain— King had mentioned this as a possibility. Kuznetsov was also interested in plans for U.S. submarine operations in the Sea of Japan. The Soviets indicated that they considered the Pacific an arena of secondary importance. "Would not concentration on the main front hasten the end of the war in Europe and thus hasten the war against Japan by making additional forces available?" General Antonov asked Field Marshal Alan Brooke. There was no discussion of joint operations in the Pacific, and the meeting ended with no plans for another.

Even General Kuter's attempt to engage the most outgoing of the Soviet commanders, Marshal Khudiakov, proved fruitless. Khudiakov implicitly raised the possibility of Soviet participation when he argued for a transfer of C-54 Skymaster transport planes and B-24 Liberator heavy bombers under the Lend-Lease arrangement, but when Kuter asked Khudiakov directly about Soviet entry into the war in the Pacific, he was told that "Marshal Khudiakov was describing only a possibility after Germany had surrendered. As to commitment, nothing more committal than a smile and a shrug was obtained from the Russian."

Stalin did not reply to FDR's letter either. The Soviet dictator was clearly signaling that he would make no decisions until he had received answers on the Kurile Islands, Sakhalin, and northeastern China. By the end of February 6 the president had received another note from Admiral Leahy, asking him to press Stalin. Roosevelt was caught between the demands of his military and Stalin's "political conditions." Further delay was impossible: he would have to speak directly to Stalin, and he knew what his host wanted to hear.[9]

The American military commanders noticed a change in Soviet attitudes on the evening of February 7. As the British toured the battlefields of Balaklava, Admiral Leahy sent General Antonov a note requesting a "secret discussion" between the U.S. and Soviet military commanders to be held at 3:00 p.m. the following day at Soviet headquarters. Antonov agreed.

That evening Antonov invited Admiral Kuznetsov to Koreiz Palace to hear his regular report to Stalin on military affairs. Around midnight, when the report had been delivered, Stalin invited his military commanders to dinner. The discussion at table began with an assessment of the situation on the German front. Stalin then turned to Kuznetsov and asked him to describe the state of the Pacific Fleet. The admiral took advantage of this opening to remind Stalin of his request for American ships. Kuznetsov was the only Soviet commander who could not wait to join the war on Japan: he was eager to negotiate with Admiral King the transfer of American ships to the Soviet Pacific Fleet. At the beginning of the conference he turned to Stalin for help, but he was told that the time was not yet ripe. Now he received a different answer. "I remember that," Stalin said. "I shall speak with Roosevelt today."[10]

When Stalin walked into Roosevelt's study at 3:30 on February 8 for a private talk on the Far East, accompanied by Molotov, Harriman, and two interpreters, he found the president in the middle of a conversation with Stettinius. The secretary of state, who had not been invited to the meeting, knew from his previous conversations that the Far East was the purview of the military and thus outside his domain. He left the room. The two leaders were about to embark on a complex diplomatic game. Roosevelt began from afar. He asked Stalin whether the U.S. Air Force could establish a base in the vicinity of Budapest and conduct bombing surveys in Eastern Europe. Only then did he turn to the Far East. Since Manila had been retaken from the Japanese, he noted, additional air bases were now required to intensify the bombing of Japan so that they might win the war without having to send in ground troops.

Stalin knew where the conversation was heading: Roosevelt wanted to talk about U.S. military bases in the Soviet Far East—a point he had raised in his unanswered letter of February 5. Stalin said he was not prepared to provide the U.S. Air Force with bases on Kamchatka, given the presence of the Japanese consul there. But he could allow two bases in the Amur River region, in close proximity to China. It was a promising beginning. For months the American military had been pressing for bases in the Soviet Far East, and now the issue seemed to be resolved. As always, the response had come from Stalin himself: no one below him would have dared to venture an opinion on such a sensitive matter as allowing foreign troops on Soviet territory.

Roosevelt pressed on. He handed Stalin a memo asking him to instruct his military to start joint planning of Far Eastern operations. Stalin said he would give orders to that effect. A breakthrough had been achieved. Roosevelt had reason to be satisfied: his whole military agenda had been accomplished in a few minutes. He had received a clear indication that the Soviet Union was entering the war with Japan. His second big task at Yalta was all but completed. There was only one unanswered question: what would Stalin want in return?

"All that is good," the Soviet leader said now, "but what about the political conditions on which the Soviet Union is entering the war with Japan?" He had in mind the conditions he had discussed with Harriman in Moscow. Roosevelt said he "felt that there would be no difficulty whatsoever in regard to the southern part of Sakhalin and the Kurile Islands going to Russia at the end of the war." This corresponded to the content of the letter that, according to Gromyko, had given Stalin such cause for elation. This time Stalin showed no sign of emotion.

To the rest of the issues raised with Harriman the response was more ambiguous. Roosevelt recalled their conversation in Teheran, when he had said that he was in favor of allowing the USSR access to a warm-water port at the end of the South Manchurian railroad, possibly in Dairen, but he said that he had not had an opportunity to discuss the issue with Chiang Kai-shek. The president was in favor of declaring Dairen a free port: allowing the USSR to lease it would give Churchill an excuse not to return Hong Kong to China, which Roosevelt wanted him to do.

Stalin decided for the moment to move on to another corner of his chessboard. He wanted to know what the president thought about the status quo in Outer Mongolia. Roosevelt said he believed it had to be preserved, but this was another matter on which he had been unable to speak with Chiang Kai-shek. When Stalin asked about the Soviet rights of control over the Manchurian railroads to Dairen, Port Arthur, and Vladivostok, Roosevelt's response was more or less the same. There were two possible solutions, direct lease or joint operation with the Chinese, but he would have to talk to Chiang Kai-shek.

Roosevelt had resigned himself to handing over Japanese territories to the USSR, but he was opposed to making concessions at the expense of China, a regional ally that he was attempting to build up into a great power and a member of the UN Security Council. Stalin was clearly disappointed. He had promised almost everything the Americans wanted and had received much less than he expected in return. A skillful negotiator, he decided to change tactics. He threatened to revoke his major concession—the promise to enter the war with Japan.

According to the American protocol of the meeting, Stalin said that "if these conditions are not met, it would be difficult for him and Molotov to explain to the Soviet people why Russia was entering the war against Japan. They understood clearly the war against Germany, which had threatened the very existence of the Soviet Union, but they would not understand why Russia would enter a war against a country with which they had no great trouble. . . .[I]f these political conditions were met, the people would understand the national interest involved and it would be very much easier to explain the decision to the Supreme Soviet."

Roosevelt began with his by now standard comment that he had not had a chance to talk to Chiang Kai-shek, but then he said, "[O]ne of the difficulties in speaking to the Chinese was that anything said to them was known to the whole world in twenty-four hours." Bohlen, who served as the president's interpreter, observed in his memoirs, "It was obvious that he was bothered by what he was doing." The president felt he could not afford to lose Soviet military assistance in the war on Japan, but neither could he commit himself publicly to the creation of a Soviet sphere of influence in northeastern China. He would, however, consider a secret deal.

Stalin seized the moment. He told the president that he did not think "[i]t was necessary yet to speak to the Chinese." He assured FDR that there would be no leaks from the Supreme Soviet. Then he added, "[I]t would be well to leave here with these conditions set forth in writing agreed to by the three powers." The president agreed: "[T]his could be done." The deal was struck: Soviet entry into the war with Japan in exchange for territorial acquisitions at Japan's expense and the creation of a Soviet sphere of influence in northeastern China. The Soviet presence in that part of China would ensure the continuing existence of an independent Mongolia.

Aware of Roosevelt's discomfort, Stalin hastened to assure him of his good relations with the government of Chiang Kai-shek: in April a representative of the Kuomintang would visit Moscow, and he would be glad to meet him. Besides, the Chinese could be informed about the deal as soon as he had moved twenty or twenty-five divisions from the German front to the Far East. Also, the USSR would be satisfied with the internationalization of a Chinese port, as opposed to its outright lease.

Roosevelt wanted to capitalize on the agreement to secure Stalin's cooperation for the creation of a new American-led order in Asia. In their first private meeting, he had distanced himself from Churchill even as he advanced a common British-American agenda. On this occasion, he intended to make a deal with Stalin behind Churchill's back. The first item on his Asian agenda was Korea. He reminded Stalin that in Teheran he had proposed trusteeship over Korea. Now he wanted to suggest that the trustees be the United States, China, and the USSR. Stalin did not object but showed little desire to give the Americans de facto control of Korea, a traditional Russian sphere of interest. Their attitudes seemed to have been reversed: Roosevelt was pushing for great-power supremacy, while Stalin was ostensibly concerned with the rights of smaller nations.

Stalin asked whether Korea would become a protectorate. No, it would not, Roosevelt assured him. Stalin then suggested limiting the term of trusteeship. To the president's proposal that twenty to thirty years should pass before trusteeship was removed, Stalin responded, "The shorter the period, the better." He also inquired whether it would be necessary to station troops in Korea and was pleased to hear Roosevelt say that there would be no need for them. Finally, the president said he "personally did not feel it was necessary to invite the British to participate in the trusteeship of Korea, but he felt that they might resent this." Again, Stalin made a show of concern. Yes, the British would be offended; the prime minister will kill us, he joked. He felt that they should be invited. Roosevelt suggested a compromise: initially there would be three trustees, but the British could be invited if they made too much noise. Stalin agreed. The deal on Korea was sealed.

Stalin was on his best behavior. Wanting to thank the president for accommodating Soviet demands on Japan and China, he returned to the questions raised at the beginning of the meeting. Yes, he would instruct his military commanders to provide the U.S. Air Force with bases in the vicinity of Budapest and allow the bombing survey team to operate in Soviet-occupied areas of Eastern Europe. There was now an atmosphere of mutual trust and understanding between the two leaders, and a feeling grew that there were no problems they could not solve.

China? They agreed that the Chinese needed better leadership and that the Kuomintang and the communists had to form a common front against the

Japanese. Indochina? The president was consistent with what he had said in Teheran: over British objections, he wanted to put the region under trusteeship instead of returning it to France. Stalin was in full agreement: the French were not in a position to defend Indochina, and the British would have to go along, unless they wanted to lose Burma again.

The meeting was moving to a close, and Stalin decided to raise one last issue, so dear to his admiral. "Mr. Stettinius had told Mr. Molotov there was a possibility that the United States would have surplus shipping property after the war which might be sold to the Soviet Union." He cautiously inquired whether this was in fact true. The president was more than gracious. He was prepared to change American legislation to make such a sale possible and to transfer the ships on credit, with no interest. He did not miss an opportunity for a dig at the British: They "had never sold anything without commercial interest," he said.

Stalin praised the president not just for the promise of ships but for Lend-Lease in general, "a remarkable invention without which victory would have been delayed." He elaborated: "[I]n former wars some allies had subsidized others but this had offended the allies receiving the subsidies and had led to difficulties. Lend-Lease, however, produced no such resentment." The president was pleased to hear this and quite prepared to take full credit for the Lend-Lease program. He explained that "four years ago, when having a rest on his small yacht, he had thought and thought of a way to help the Allies and at the same time avoid the difficulties inherent in loans, and he finally hit upon the scheme of Lend-Lease."[11]

The meeting was over. All accounts indicate that it lasted no longer than half an hour. They were running late for the plenary session, which had been postponed to accommodate the change in their schedules. They had covered a lot of ground and reached an understanding on more than one issue. It was now up to the military commanders to make more specific plans on the conduct of the war.

Half an hour before Stalin and Roosevelt's private conversation, the American and Soviet military leaders had met for their first discussion of joint action in the Pacific theater. When the American military learned that General Antonov had agreed to the meeting, they were not sure what to make of it. That morning, Admiral Leahy was quite pessimistic, saying that he "entertained little hope of engaging in extended conversations with the Soviet General Staff." Marshall was more optimistic. "[O]ur success in arranging a meeting with the Soviet Army Staff was a good omen as to the Soviets' willingness to discuss the matters in which we are interested," he noted.[12]

When the meeting began at 3:00 p.m. at Koreiz Palace, Admiral Leahy was the first to speak. He went straight to business and announced that he wanted to discuss the Far East and needed information to proceed with the planning of the war. The Soviet commanders were both accommodating and cautious. After making Leahy read aloud the list of American requests, General Antonov stated that what he was about to say was a reflection of his personal views only. He promised, however, to "refer the questions to Marshal Stalin the same day and . . . arrange to provide complete and authoritative answers as quickly as possible."

Antonov explained that there had been no change in Soviet war plans. This meant that the Soviets intended to direct the main thrust of their attack into Manchuria, with the goal of cutting off Japanese forces there from their formations in the rest of China. The Soviets were prepared to occupy southern Sakhalin at the start of hostilities. They might require American help in protecting Kamchatka and eastern Siberia from seaborne attack and would need Pacific supply routes to be open. Aside from American supplies of military equipment, food, and ammunition, which were already pouring into the Far East, they would appreciate American assistance in constructing storage facilities. On the question of American air bases in the Soviet Far East, Antonov was reluctant to offer even his personal view. He promised to refer the question to Stalin.

In the fall of 1944 the U.S. military had dispatched a group of planners to Moscow to prepare for joint operations in the Pacific theater, but the Soviets had dragged their feet and sabotaged the planning. The Soviets wanted to avoid at all costs the presence of foreign troops on their territory, remembering Western military intervention during the Russian Revolution, but they were never shy about securing as much military hardware and supplies as possible from the Americans. The rationale was that Soviet troops were bearing the main burden of the war and paying for Allied achievements with their lives. The least the Allies could do was provide equipment and supplies—this, in any event, was Admiral Kuznetsov's credo. He was prepared to send three thousand crewmen to the United States to man the ships that would be transferred to the Soviet Pacific Fleet.[13]

Despite Antonov's disclaimer, and his refusal to discuss U.S. bases, the American commanders were satisfied with the results of the meeting. Admiral Leahy, who had originally been deeply skeptical, summarized its outcome in his memoirs in highly positive terms: "For the first time we discussed information that was necessary for us to have at the earliest practicable date in order to proceed with detailed plans for the war against Japan, subsequent to the collapse of Germany. These plans involved a principle very important to the Soviets, namely, basing some of the American operations on Russian territory. General Antonov and his colleagues said that our plans seemed excellent and looked good to them. Although considerate and sympathetic, Antonov said he could not reply to any of our questions without getting permission from his Commander-in-Chief, Stalin. 'Well, gentlemen,' I said, 'this is important. We want to get action at once. Will you please get the necessary authority from Stalin?' Antonov promised immediate action." With "political questions" out of the way, the Soviets were eager to cooperate.[14]

Roosevelt had obtained Stalin's all-important commitment to enter the war against Japan, but that commitment had come at a high price. The president had agreed to hand over territories even before the war was over—the very policies he had condemned both publicly and privately on numerous occasions, notably in the Atlantic Charter. As he was well aware, it was one thing to compensate Stalin with territories taken from a common enemy, as was the case with Japan, and quite another to hand over lands of a friend and an ally, as he had done with China. But his concern was with the overriding national interest as he understood it at the time: to shorten the war and save American lives. The Soviet refusal during the first days of the conference to discuss joint operations against Japan convinced Roosevelt that there would be no effective cooperation with the Red Army, and perhaps even no Soviet participation in the war in the Far East, unless Stalin's conditions were met. Many would later wonder whether the cost to China and, eventually, to the United States had been too high.

Awaiting the arrival of President Franklin Roosevelt at Malta on February 2 1945 (left to right): U.S. Secretary of State Edward R. Stettinius Jr., British permanent undersecretary for foreign affairs Alexander Cadogan, and U.S. ambassador to Moscow W. Averell Harriman.

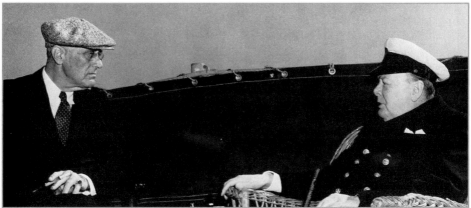

Franklin Roosevelt and Winston Churchill on the deck of USS *Quincy*, moored in Valetta harbor, Malta, on February 2, 1945. Despite the image of close cooperation projected by the photo, FDR managed to avoid any substantive talks with Churchill during his one-day stopover on Malta.

British and American military commanders: Field Marshal Alan Brooke (second from right), flanked by Marshal of the Royal Air Force Charles Portal (to his right) and Admiral of the Fleet Andrew Cunningham (to his left), facing General of the Army George C. Marshall and Fleet Admiral Ernest J. King (with his back to the camera). Their heated three-day consultations on Malta led to the complete victory of American plans for the conduct of the Allied campaign in Western Europe.

Tired but upbeat, President Roosevelt speaks with his chief adviser, Harry Hopkins, on landing at the Saki air base in the Crimea, on February 3, 1945. Soviet foreign commissar Viacheslav Molotov stands to their immediate left, next to Hopkins.

Women were an important part of the work force assembled by Stalin's secret police to prepare for the Yalta Conference. They are shown here carrying a load in front of Livadia Palace, the lodging of the American delegation.

President Roosevelt holds a preconference meeting with his advisers in Livadia Palace, which was bugged by the Soviets. Left to right: Stettinius, King, Marshall, Harriman, Fleet Admiral William D. Leahy, and FDR.

Joseph Stalin pays a visit to FDR at Livadia Palace on February 4, before the official start of the conference. Vladimir Pavlov, Stalin's interpreter, is on the right, with his back to the camera. To the right of Pavlov (obscured from view) is Charles E. Bohlen, translating for FDR.

East meets West. Andrei Vyshinsky, Molotov's deputy and Stalin's ruthless prosecutor during the show trials of the 1930s, is seen here greeting Churchill before the start of the conference. To the right of Vyshinsky is Major Arthur Herbert Birse, interpreting for Churchill. Harriman, Cadogan, and British foreign secretary Anthony Eden (standing) are in the background at left.

Plenary session of the conference at Livadia Palace. Facing the camera (left to right): Molotov, Stalin, Pavlov (obscured from view), Soviet deputy foreign commissar Ivan Maisky, Soviet ambassador to Washington Andrei Gromyko, Leahy, H. Freeman Matthews of the U.S. State Department (in the second row), Stettinius, Alger Hiss of the State Department's Office of Special Political Affairs (in the second row), Roosevelt, Bohlen, and Director of the Office of War Mobilization James Byrnes. Next to Byrnes are members of the British delegation: Cadogan (obscured from view), Eden, Churchill, Birse (with his back to the camera), Edward Bridges of the British Foreign Office (with his back to the camera), and British ambassador to Moscow Archibald Clark Kerr.

Meetings of the foreign ministers and their staffs took place in turn at each of the three headquarters. Here, a Soviet photographer captured a meeting of the foreign ministers at Vorontsov villa, the lodging of the British delegation. Facing the camera (left to right) are Soviet ambassador to London Fedor Gusev, Vyshinsky, Molotov, Sergei Golunsky, interpreting for Molotov, and Gromyko. Stettinius, Hiss, Eden, Birse, and Cadogan are among the members of the Allied delegations with their backs to the camera.

"The girls" (left to right): Sarah Oliver (Churchill's daughter), Anna Roosevelt Boettiger, and Kathleen Harriman, who recorded invaluable behind-the-scenes vignettes of the conference in their diaries and letters home.

Stalin in conversation with Harriman and Molotov, with Pavlov serving as interpreter. It was during one such conversation that Stalin persuaded Harriman to lift his opposition to Soviet demands in the Far East.

Stalin making a joke, possibly at Churchill's expense. Birse serves as interpreter. Harriman is on the far right, behind the prime minister. Churchill's doctor, Lord Moran, was upset by the way Stalin treated Churchill throughout the conference, but Churchill did not seem to mind.

Stalin and Molotov in front of Livadia Palace, waiting for the members of the Western delegations to arrive for a photo session on the afternoon of February 9.

One of the iconic pictures of the conference, taken on February 9. The Big Three, backed by their military commanders (left to right): Cunningham (talking to Churchill), King, Portal, Leahy, Marshall (partly obscured from view by Leahy), Major General Laurence S. Kuter, General of the Army Aleksei Antonov, Marshal of the Soviet Air Force Sergei Khudiakov (immediately behind Stalin), and Lieutenant General Anatoly Gryzlov, who signed the Soviet-American agreement on the exchange of prisoners of war on behalf of the Soviet command. Cadogan is on the far right, behind Gryzlov

The last lunch, on February 11. Stettinius raises a toast. Facing him are Pavlov, Stalin, Roosevelt, Churchill, and Molotov.

The American delegation leaving Livadia on the afternoon of February 11. Stettinius, who would stay at Livadia to finish editing the final documents and then go to Moscow, bids farewell to Roosevelt's daughter, Anna. Sarah Oliver is in the background.

Churchill, with his trademark cigar and wearing a "Russian hat" that became a target for the jokes of Western journalists, is photographed here before leaving Livadia on the afternoon of February 11. Sarah Oliver, seen next to her father, wrote that on the way from Livadia to Vorontsov villa, Churchill suddenly felt lonely and decided to leave the place right away.

Molotov and Eden signing one of the final documents of the conference, possibly the Soviet-British agreement on the exchange of prisoners of war. This is one of the few photos of Molotov smiling.

18

"ALLIES SHOULD NOT DECEIVE"

As the conference moved into its fourth and fifth days, life and work at the villas became distinctly predictable and routine. "Physically," wrote Sarah Oliver to her mother on February 8, comparing Yalta and Teheran, "this conference does not seem as hard as the one last year. They do not meet till 4 in the afternoon, when they have a whacking session of 4 to 5 hours and then they part, returning to their lairs." "We have reduced the Conference to such an orderly procedure that one day is very like another," wrote Alec Cadogan on the morning of the same day. "We work in the morning till 11.30, when we have a meeting of Foreign Secretaries, followed by lunch. Yesterday this took place at the Russian HQ. Today we are acting as hosts. Then follows the meeting of the Big Three, which goes on usually till about dinner time."

People were also getting accustomed to their living arrangements. Cadogan, who was easily irritated as a rule, wrote in a letter to his wife, "We are really very comfortable here." Although the permanent undersecretary complained about the "remote control" lighting system in the British compound, he seemed more amused than upset by the absentmindedness of the Soviet electricians. "The lights in Anthony [Eden]'s room, his bathroom and in the offices all turn on and off from a switchboard at the end of the passage! So that a Russian housemaid or a heavy-fingered Marine either plunge one in darkness or switch on the light at 6 a.m.! However, I think, I'm curing them of that."[1]

The Westerners were getting used to the scarcity of restroom facilities, which they accepted with resignation, if not humor. "In Livadia Palace," remembered General Laurence Kuter, "the subject of bathrooms was never dropped with a casual mention of the chambermaid aspect. Excepting only the war, the bathrooms were the most generally discussed subject at the Crimean Conference." People eventually got used to the long bathroom lines in the morning. They took the opportunity to discuss the events of the previous day and exchange the latest news and views about upcoming items on the conference agenda. "As a result," remembered Kuter, "particularly before breakfast, numerous informal, impatient conferences were held in the halls for extraordinarily long periods of time."

Food was another aspect of everyday life at Yalta to which the Western delegates had to adjust. "The food is quite good though, as usual in Russia rather monotonous," noted Cadogan. "And of course they have to be trained in the matter of breakfast. Caviar and mince pies for breakfast are all very well once in a way, but they pall after a bit. However we have now drilled them into giving us omelets and suchlike." He concluded on an upbeat note: "No lack of eggs and butter." Kuter wrote that apart from cold cuts and goat cheese with hot tea, normally served for breakfast at Livadia, the Soviet hosts began to offer American dishes "with some pride." "There was a choice between Wheatena and Cream of Wheat," noted the general. "A new touch was given by serving them with hot butter lightly spiced with garlic."[2]

It was a welcome change from earlier days, when the British and the Americans struggled to explain themselves to the waiters, who, as Admiral Leahy put it in conversation with Anna Boettiger, spoke "no known language." When Leahy ordered an egg, toast, and coffee for breakfast on February 4, the waiter gestured that he understood the order and, fifteen minutes later, brought a tray of caviar, ham, and smoked fish, accompanied by vodka. "For God's sake, send me someone who speaks English—and get this fellow and his wares out of here!" shouted Roosevelt's chief of staff. The president's daughter found the scene amusing enough to record it in her diary.[3]

Churchill dealt with the problem of Russian-style breakfasts by skipping them. "[H]e awakes rather late," Sarah wrote to her mother, "and there isn't time for breakfast and lunch and work and a little sleep before the 'do' at 4—so now he has just orange juice when he is called and 'brunch' at 11.30—then nothing till 9 o'clock! This seems a very long time, but he really is very sensible and says that is what he likes best." Cadogan noted no complaints from Churchill about the lack of food or drink. "P.M. seems well," he wrote on February 9, "though drinking buckets of Caucasian champagne which would undermine the health of any ordinary man." The Soviets did not skimp on alcohol. Cadogan wrote that, aside from "bowls of fruit and bottles of mineral water," his room was supplied with a "decanter of vodka!"[4]

There was no shortage of vodka or champagne at the dinner hosted by Stalin on the evening of February 8 at Koreiz villa. The menu included whitefish in champagne sauce, as well as traditional Russian caviar and pies, Caucasian *shashlyk* of mutton, and Central Asian pilaf of quails. It was the most impressive reception of the conference, and Sarah Oliver referred to it in her letters home as a banquet. There were thirty people at dinner, including "the girls"—

Anna Boettiger, Sarah Oliver, and Kathleen Harriman—who were thrilled to be there. Alger Hiss, who was not among Stalin's guests, later recalled the positive influence of the three young women on everyday life at Yalta. They "contributed to a mood that at times was almost like that of a country party where the guests good-naturedly put up with overcrowding," he recalled.[5]

Stalin was in a good mood that evening. "The 'Bear' as host was in terrific form and it was very friendly and gay," Sarah wrote to her mother. "He really was terrific," echoed Kathleen Harriman in a letter to her sister. "He enjoyed himself, was a splendid host, and his three main speeches were swell, and meant something more than the usual banalities. In true Soviet fashion, he sat in the middle of a long, long table with the President on his right and Churchill on his left, Molotov, Eden and Stettinius opposite. At times Stalin just sat back and smiled like a benign old man, something I'd never thought possible. Anyway, I was much impressed." Not only the "girls" were impressed. Edward Stettinius also found Stalin in "excellent humor and even in high spirits." Alan Brooke noted in his diary: "Stalin was in the very best of form, and was full of fun and good humour apparently thoroughly enjoying himself." He must have felt the conference was moving his way.[6]

By the fifth day, with the end in sight, the Big Three were in a position to make a preliminary assessment of successes and failures. They came to the dinner party after a long and frustrating day. A few hours before dinner, Roosevelt had obtained a guarantee from Stalin that the USSR would participate in the war on Japan. But the price was high. Besides, there was a continuing deadlock on Poland, despite some encouraging intimations the previous day. Nor was there agreement on French participation in policing Germany or on the scale of German reparations. Earlier that day, Churchill had summarized for Eden the argument of the Foreign Office paper he had just read: "1. The only bond of victors is their common hate. 2. To make Britain safe she must become responsible for the safety of a cluster of feeble states." The prime minister rejected that approach. "We ought to think of something better than these," he concluded.

If the alliance was to hold together, it would have to find common ground. There was some basis for hope in the good personal relations among the Big Three. Even as Churchill complained to Attlee that "we are having hard times here," he also wrote that "all personal relations are excellent." Stettinius attributed the good mood at the conference to the fact that there was no preset formal agenda: the Big Three could easily pass from one question to another if they encountered insuperable obstacles to a particular problem. At the end of a long day full of hard bargaining, they could still relax in one another's company. Dinners played an important part in easing tensions and promoting agendas. Debates initiated in formal sessions continued in more muted fashion: the diplomatic game, once started, did not lose momentum.[7]

"In an alliance the allies should not deceive each other," Stalin declared in a toast at the Koreiz villa dinner. His words were recorded by Major Arthur Herbert Birse, who accompanied Churchill to the party. "Perhaps that is naïve? Experienced diplomats may say, 'Why should I not deceive my ally?' But I as a naïve man think it best not to deceive my ally even if he is a fool. Possibly our alliance is so firm just because we do not deceive each other; or is it because it is not so easy to deceive each other? I propose a toast to the firmness of our Three-Power Alliance. May it be strong and stable; may we be as frank as possible," he concluded.[8]

Was the Soviet leader deceiving his guests and trying to cover his tracks, or was he afraid that they would deceive him? Before dinner was served, Sarah Oliver had a chance to talk to one of the most feared men in the Soviet Union. His name was Lavrentii Beria, and it was the first time that the head of the dreaded People's Commissariat of Internal Affairs made his appearance at the conference. "The head of the OGPU was there!" Sarah wrote, using the old acronym of the Soviet secret police. "I recited to him my five Russian sentences—one of which is 'Can I have a hot water bottle please?' To which OGPU replied 'I cannot believe that you need one! Surely there is enough fire in you!' It looked as if there was a future to this conversation; but at this point dinner was served."

A known womanizer (and a rapist), Beria enjoyed suggestive banter. Later that evening he discussed the sex life of fish with the British ambassador to Moscow, Sir Archibald Clark Kerr. But there was more to Beria than smooth insinuation. Stettinius, who, like Sarah, first met him at Koreiz, found "the strong [man] in the Politburo . . . hard, forceful, and extremely alert." Kathleen Harriman described him the next day as "little and fat with thick lenses, which give him a sinister look, but quite genial."[9]

The Yalta Conference was Beria's debut on the international scene to which he had long aspired. He had attended the Teheran Conference incognito, but this time he was a member of the official delegation. At forty-six, Beria was one of Stalin's top lieutenants, brought by the Soviet dictator from his native Georgia to Moscow in 1938 to replace the architect of the Great Terror, Nikolai Yezhov. Like the previous head of the Soviet secret police, Genrikh Yagoda, Yezhov was accused of being a foreign spy and shot. Beria met the same fate after Stalin's death in 1953. He outlived his master by managing to prove himself not only loyal but indispensable to him.

As people's commissar of internal affairs, Beria was in charge of the giant Soviet security apparatus and the Gulag—the dreaded main directorate of labor camps. He eventually became responsible for Soviet efforts to build a nuclear bomb and for atomic espionage, directly channeling the data gathered by the intelligence network in the United States to Soviet scientists led by the physicist Igor Kurchatov. Stalin tried to keep Beria in check by creating a special People's

Commissariat of State Security (NKGB) under Vsevolod Merkulov, who was responsible for most Soviet intelligence gathering abroad. Nevertheless, in the secretive world of Soviet espionage Beria was the most influential figure.[10]

When Roosevelt first noticed Beria at Stalin's dinner and asked the Soviet leader who was the man in the pince-nez, Stalin identified him as "our Himmler." Roosevelt was upset by the joke and by the fact that Beria overheard Stalin's reply, but the Soviet Himmler offered only a weak smile in return. Sir Archibald Clark Kerr toasted him as the "man who looks after our bodies." Beria again kept silent, but Churchill, apparently upset by the inappropriate joke, walked up to Clark Kerr and, according to Kathleen Harriman, "instead of clinking glasses shook his finger at Archie and said, 'Be careful, be careful'—in other words, 'shut up.'"[11]

Western diplomats had every reason to be careful around Beria. On the eve of the Yalta Conference, one of his assistants, Pavel Sudoplatov, warned Averell Harriman about potentially dangerous liaisons that his daughter Kathleen had allegedly had with some Russian young men in Moscow. Sudoplatov later claimed that it was a friendly warning, an attempt to establish relations of trust with the American ambassador, but it was also a reminder that Beria was watching. Roosevelt, Churchill, and Harriman all invited their daughters to join them at Yalta. Stalin did not travel with either his daughter or his son. Beria was the only Soviet leader whose son, Sergo, was at Yalta, but he was there in a very peculiar capacity. Sergo Beria did not attend dinners or write letters home giving his impressions. His records were of a different kind and were prepared with only one reader in mind—Stalin.

An intelligence officer and a student at a military academy during the war, Sergo Beria knew English and German and was an electronics enthusiast. In 1943 he was handpicked by Stalin, who had known him as a child, to join the group of electronics specialists and interpreters who bugged Roosevelt's quarters in the Soviet embassy in Teheran during the Big Three meeting there. In February 1945 he was again recalled from his studies in Leningrad to perform the same functions at Yalta. Sergo Beria was part of a group that included both military personnel like himself and NKGB operatives. They had had no previous contacts with foreigners and were isolated from other Soviet personnel at the conference. They dined in a separate room and were relatively low in the Yalta pecking order.

The eavesdroppers, some flown in from Moscow to record and transcribe conversations, were not part of the Soviet security detail, whose members were apparently encouraged to make friends with their British and American counterparts. In occasional drinking bouts, representatives of the two Allied secret services tried to outdo one another. Sergo Beria and his colleagues were forbidden to imbibe. He noted in his memoirs, however, that at drinking parties during the conference the American and British guards "often fell under the table and regularly had to be carried to their bedroom." Michael Reilly, the head of FDR's security detail, later bragged that on his arrival in the Crimea, his boys outdrank the Soviets eight to one—eight Americans were still on their feet after a night of drinking, and only one Soviet. The "painful victory" was achieved, according to Reilly, on the basis of "sheer patriotism."[12]

When an advance group of U.S. officers "debugged" Livadia Palace before Roosevelt's arrival, they missed the more sophisticated listening devices. According to Beria, instructions to members of the Allied delegations not to discuss sensitive issues had little effect. The Soviets not only bugged the premises occupied by the Allied delegations but also used directional microphones to listen at a distance to conversations outside the palaces. They turned their microphones on immediately after the two Western leaders landed at the Saki air base, and Beria remembers listening to the brief conversation between Roosevelt and Churchill immediately after their landing, as the British prime minister followed the president's Jeep on foot.[13]

Beria was responsible for recording and transcribing President Roosevelt's conversations at Yalta. The transcripts went to the General Staff of the Red Army. Scholars never saw the transcripts of any of the conversations recorded by the Soviets at Yalta, and Beria did not know how and to whom the information he gathered was reported, nor how it was received. But his account of the Teheran Conference, where he was part of a significantly smaller electronic surveillance team and personally reported to Stalin, makes it possible to reconstruct what was going on behind the closed doors of Stalin's office at Yalta.

On the eve of the Teheran Conference in November 1943, Stalin personally selected members of the eavesdropping team, conducting preliminary one-on-one interviews, during which he portrayed himself as concerned with the moral implications of the whole undertaking. "I have had you brought here," he told Sergo Beria, "along with some other young men who have never had dealings with foreigners, because I want to entrust you with a mission that is delicate and morally reprehensible. You are going to listen to the conversations that Roosevelt will have with Churchill, with the other British, and with his own circle. I must know everything in detail, be aware of all the shades of meaning. I am asking you for all that because it is now that the question of the second front will be settled. I know that Churchill is against it. It is important that the Americans support us in this matter."[14]

The man who had turned his country into a quintessential police state that encouraged children to snitch on their parents and forced spouses to report on each other was also a gifted actor who fooled quite a few of those who came to know him, including his American and British guests. What shocked the young Beria was not the fact of eavesdropping on the Allies but what he heard in the taped conversations. He was especially impressed by the way in which Alec Cadogan spoke to Churchill on the telephone while visiting the British embassy in Moscow. Cadogan apparently chided Churchill for making a decision without consulting with the cabinet.

Beria was shocked. "If any of the deputy people's commissars—forget deputies, even members of the government themselves and members of the Politburo of the Central Committee—had ventured to speak to Stalin in such a tone . . . ," he wrote in his memoirs, leaving the sentence unfinished—he could not imagine what would have happened to such an official in Stalin's Soviet Union. He knew very well what happened to people guilty of much lesser transgressions. When he shared his impressions with his father, Lavrentii Beria allegedly remarked, "But relations among members of government are entirely different there. Any one of them has the right to defend his point of view and contest the premier's opinion."

Every morning in Teheran, for an hour to an hour and a half, Sergo Beria and other members of the Soviet eavesdropping team reported to Stalin on the recordings made the previous day. Dialogues between Roosevelt and Churchill, as well as conversations involving the Joint Chiefs of Staff, were reported first. Stalin relied on the Russian translations of the conversations and often asked Beria and others about the intonation with which this or that phrase had been spoken. "Did he say that with conviction or without enthusiasm? How did Roosevelt react? Did he say that resolutely?" Stalin asked.[15]

At Yalta, Beria forwarded the transcripts of Roosevelt's conversations to his military superiors. His father told him at the time that Stalin was less interested in the results of the eavesdropping, for he assumed that he could get the Allies to go along with his plans in any case. Pavel Sudoplatov, who claims to have been appointed by Beria to head an intelligence group charged with gathering and assessing information on the eve of the Yalta Conference, later remembered that Stalin showed more interest in the personal profiles of Western participants in the conference than in intelligence information.[16]

Alec Cadogan was relieved not to have been invited to Stalin's dinner at Koreiz. "A great mercy, as I am tired of these silly toasts and speeches," he wrote the next day to his wife. Admiral Leahy counted thirty-eight. Field Marshal Alan Brooke was seated at the dinner table between General Antonov, who spoke only rudimentary French, and Averell Harriman, whom he disliked. The incessant toasts irritated Alan Brooke, as they left little time for eating, and the food would get cold before it could be consumed. "The standard of speeches was remarkably low," he noted in his diary, "and most consisted of insincere slimy sort of slush!"[17]

Stalin, for his part, enjoyed the toasts, an ancient Georgian art of which he was a master. The toastmaster at Koreiz was Molotov, who, according to Kathleen, "was quite amusing at times." But he was overshadowed by Stalin. Over dinner "Stalin kept leaping to his feet and once called himself a 'garrulous old man.'" Stalin was a devotee of late-night dinners, to which he usually invited his underlings in order to get them drunk and make fun of them. He could not break the habit even at Yalta. Beria was one of the objects of his jibes at dinner; another was Fedor Gusev, the Soviet ambassador to London. Stettinius remembered later that Stalin "teased Gusev for always being glum and serious" and "carried his jesting almost to the point of extreme ridicule." The guests had mixed feelings about Stalin's way of entertaining himself. "The funniest thing of all," wrote Kathleen Harriman, "was when Stalin started teasing Gusev . . . and ended with saying: 'he is a gloomy man, but sometimes gloomy men are more reliable than likeable ones.'"[18]

Churchill was the recipient of most of Stalin's toasts that evening. "I propose a toast for the leader of the British Empire," he said, according to the British record, "the most courageous of all Prime Ministers in the world, embodying political experience with military leadership, who when all Europe was ready to fall flat before Hitler said that Britain would stand and fight alone against Germany even without allies." He continued: "To the health of the man who is born once in a hundred years, and who bravely held up the banner of Great Britain. I have said what I feel, what I have at heart, and of what I am conscious." Who could resist such flattery?[19]

The prime minister was moved by Stalin's praise. Lord Moran recorded in his diary that after dinner Churchill was "sentimental and emotional," and the prime minister's secretary heard him singing "The Glory Song" on his return from Koreiz. "This place has turned out very well so far, in spite of our gloomy warning and forebodings," Churchill cabled Attlee that evening. Years later, at the height of the Cold War, he was still sufficiently pleased to publish Stalin's toasts in his memoirs.[20]

Churchill was not to be outdone in the art of speech making. When he had a chance to respond to Stalin, he displayed the full power of his eloquence. "It is no exaggeration or compliment of a florid kind when I say that we regard Marshal Stalin's life as most precious to the hopes and hearts of all of us," he began, according to the British record, which he later used in his memoirs. "There have been many conquerors in history, but few of them have been statesmen, and most of them threw away the fruits of victory in the troubles which followed their wars. I earnestly hope that the Marshal may be spared to the people of the Soviet Union and to help us all to move forward to a less unhappy time than that through which we have recently come." He finished on an even more emotional note: "I walk through this world with greater courage and hope when I find myself in a relation of friendship and intimacy with this great man, whose fame has gone not only over all Russia, but the world."[21]

For all his suspicions Churchill believed that he could trust Stalin and that without him the Kremlin hard-liners would have made it impossible to continue the Grand Alliance. Over dinner, Stalin came as close as he ever would to apologizing for his alliance with Hitler in 1939. He told Churchill, who later included his words in his memoirs, that "if the British and French had sent a mission to Moscow in 1939 containing men who really wanted an agreement with Russia, the Soviet Government would not have signed the pact with Ribbentrop." But flattery over dinner was cheap, and not all were equally taken in. "[I]t is typical of Stalin that he does not let his feeling count if it does not suit his book," noted Lord Moran. "During the Conference he has been quite rough with the P.M."[22]

American accounts suggest that Stalin was the first to speak that evening of the dangers awaiting the alliance. "[I]t was not so difficult to keep unity in time of war since there was a joint aim to defeat the common enemy which was clear to everyone," he declared in one of his toasts. "The difficult task would come after the war, when diverse interests would tend to divide the Allies." Stalin was "confident that the present alliance would meet this test," but it would be "our duty to see that it would, and that our relations in peace time should be as strong as they had been in war."

"I must say," Churchill rejoined, "that never in this war have I felt the responsibility weigh so heavily on me, even in the darkest hours, as now during this Conference. But now, for the reasons which the Marshal has given, we see that we are on the crest of the hill, and there is before us the prospect of open country. Do not let us underestimate the difficulties. Nations, comrades in arms, have in the past drifted apart within five or ten years of war. Thus toiling millions have followed a vicious circle, falling into the pit, and then by their sacrifices raising themselves up again. We now have a chance of avoiding the errors of previous generations and of making a sure peace. People cry out for peace and joy. Will the families be reunited? Will the warrior come home? Will the shattered dwelling be rebuilt? Will the toiler see his home?"

This was the beginning of a long toast that Charles Bohlen, the American note-taker at the dinner, summarized as follows: "He said that in the modern world the function of leadership was to lead the people out from the forests into the broad sunlit plains of peace and happiness. He felt this prize was nearer our grasp than anytime before in history and it would be a tragedy for which history would never forgive us if we let this prize slip from our grasp through inertia or carelessness."[23]

Stalin too was concerned about the future of the alliance. He would need a period of peaceful coexistence, a "breathing space," to allow his country to recover from the war. He worried that the Western Allies might make a separate deal with Germany and turn against him. To Stalin, in the final analysis, they were all capitalists. He trusted Roosevelt more than he would ever trust Churchill and was prepared to go along with the president's desire to form the United Nations organization if that was what it took to hold the alliance together. "I propose a toast for the successful conclusion of Dumbarton Oaks, and that our alliance, born under the stress of battle, be made solid and extended after the war," he declared, doubtless for Roosevelt's benefit.[24]

Roosevelt remained silent throughout most of the dinner. When Stalin toasted him at the beginning of the evening, he responded, according to the American record, that the "atmosphere at this dinner was as that of a family" and called upon his counterparts to work together in order to "give every man, woman and child on this earth the possibility of security and wellbeing."[25] These sentiments had little to do with the unity of the alliance addressed by Stalin and Churchill. We do not know Roosevelt's thoughts at the time, but his faithful secretary of state, Edward Stettinius, called the banquet "the most important dinner of the Conference." Next morning the president ordered Stettinius to soften the American position on two of the most contested issues: the Polish government and German reparations. Standing on the crest of Churchill's hill and seeing the prize of the stable peace he had long desired, Roosevelt was prepared to make concessions.[26]

PART V

THE WHEELS OF COMPROMISE

The United States will not always have its way a hundred percent—nor will Russia nor Great Britain. We shall not always have ideal answers—solutions to complicated international problems, even though we are determined continuously to strive toward that ideal.

FRANKLIN D. ROOSEVELT

19

A POLISH SURRENDER

The famous photos of the Yalta Conference featuring Churchill, Roosevelt, and Stalin with their advisers and military commanders in the background were taken on the afternoon of February 9, 1945, in the Italian courtyard of Livadia Palace. Three chairs were placed on Oriental carpets at one end of the yard. Photographers and cameramen took their positions at the opposite end, either on the ground or on the second-floor balustrade. Roosevelt sat in the middle, and Stalin took a seat to the left of him, leaving the one on the right for Churchill, who entered the courtyard when the photographers and cameramen were already assembled.

As the photo session was unfolding, Churchill smoked his ever-present cigar, and Roosevelt indulged in a cigarette. Stalin apparently decided that it was too cold to start his pipe. Churchill wore a Russian-style fur cap, his hands hidden in the pockets of his gray overcoat. Roosevelt looked exhausted. He exchanged comments with people standing behind him, while Stalin apparently cracked a joke or two. The film shot by the Americans showed the prime minister removing his hat as the Soviet interpreter, Vladimir Pavlov, spoke to him. All three leaders were smiling.

At the party hosted by Stalin at Koreiz Palace the previous evening, Roosevelt had said that the atmosphere was "that of a family." Now the time had come to pose for family pictures. "I sensed a kind of euphoria among the principals and members of all three delegations for what had been accomplished," Robert Hopkins later remembered. "Their faces reflected relief from the strain of negotiations, and there was laughter and good-natured banter." Hopkins, then twenty-three and, in his words, "outranked by almost everyone there," unexpectedly found himself in charge of the photo shoot. As Harry Hopkins's son, he already knew the Big Three personally, and in 1943 he had photographed Roosevelt and Churchill during their meeting at Casablanca. He was now recalled from the German front and flew to Malta, where he joined his father and the rest of the American delegation on the way to the Crimea. He seized the initiative at Yalta and was the only photographer allowed to document the beginning of the first private meeting between Roosevelt and Stalin.

"How do you want to handle this, Robert?" Roosevelt asked once he saw Hopkins on the lawn. "First, Mr. President, I'd like to have Mr. Stettinius stand behind you, with Mr. Molotov behind Marshal Stalin, and Mr. Eden behind Prime Minister Churchill. Then I would like the others who participated in the deliberations to move in so that they will be included in the photographic record of the conference." Hopkins later remembered that "the three senior diplomats took their places as I requested, but the others did not move out of the way, as I had hoped." There was a good deal of confusion in the courtyard as diplomats slowly made way for military commanders and vice versa. Field Marshal Alan Brooke noted that the photo session "was a most disorganized procedure with no one getting the people in their places for the various military and political groups."

"As I was taking a picture of Stalin and Molotov under the arcade," Robert Hopkins remembered, "Stalin motioned me to approach. He smiled and shook my hand and asked me what I had been doing since we last met. 'I want to be the first American photographer in Berlin, but this seems unlikely, since your troops are on the outskirts of the city, and we're 125 miles away,'" said the young Hopkins. "'How would you like to be attached to the Red Army?' Stalin asked. 'Then you could be the first American to film the fall of Berlin.' This proposal took my breath away," Hopkins wrote in his memoirs. "Without thinking, I blurted out, 'Could you arrange that?,' momentarily forgetting that he could arrange anything in the Soviet orbit. 'You take care of it from your end, and I'll take care of it from ours,' said Stalin."[1]

While Hopkins recovered from Stalin's unexpected proposal, his Soviet counterpart, the Red Army captain and professional photographer Samary Gurary, was equally breathless, only in his case out of fear. In his excitement following the photo session, Gurary opened his camera without rolling back the film. He immediately closed the camera but was convinced that it was too late. A twenty-nine-year-old photojournalist for the leading Soviet newspaper *Izvestiia,* who had been among the first to take pictures of the Majdanek concentration camp, he was now almost certain that his days were numbered. "During the ten minutes that it took to develop the film, my life hung by a thread," he later remembered. "Stalin personally examined the photographs and decided where each one was to be sent. 'Why are you so pale, Samary?' asked the guard. I answered that I was tired, thinking all the while what would become of me if the film had been exposed." Before the start of the photo session, Andrei Vyshinsky, had warned him, "Be careful, Samary, you are the only one from the Soviet press." Luckily the shot with the three leaders seated in front of Livadia Palace was not exposed—the ruined film started two frames later. Gurary's photo even made it into the main Soviet newspaper, *Pravda*.[2]

The photo session lasted close to half an hour. The delegations returned to Livadia Palace afterward for another round of negotiations. At a quarter past four, a select group of advisers and diplomats joined the Big Three in the tsar's former ballroom. The meeting, which had begun with jokes and smiles in front of the cameras, was about to become one of the hardest-fought contests of the proceedings. It would also become the turning point of the whole conference.

The plenary session began, as usual, with the report of the foreign ministers. Stettinius, who had chaired the meeting that day, announced that the Americans had dropped the idea of forming a Polish presidential council. As he was preparing to move on to the next subject, Churchill interrupted him and suggested that discussion of the Polish question begin right away—Stettinius could conclude his report afterward. What made Churchill so eager to begin discussion of the Polish question was a major development at that day's meeting of foreign ministers. Not only had Stettinius proposed that Americans were prepared to drop the idea of a presidential council, about which Churchill had been skeptical from the beginning, but he had also put forward a new plan for the formation of the Polish government. In more ways than one, that proposal was tantamount to an abandonment of long-standing British and American positions.[3]

The new American strategy was devised by Roosevelt during his morning meeting with Stettinius.[4] The president, with his two main prizes in hand—Soviet membership in the United Nations and participation in the war on Japan—apparently decided that he could not risk them by forcing the Soviets to do what they obviously did not want to do: form a truly democratic and representative Polish government. Unlike Churchill, he did not believe that further negotiations would do anything to advance the Western agenda and did not want to quarrel publicly with the Soviet Union over Poland, as that would defeat his efforts to bring his own country into the United Nations. What he needed was a document on Poland that would satisfy his domestic constituencies but still be acceptable to Stalin. He also probably took to heart the previous evening's comment on the future of the alliance. The last two full days of the conference, February 9 and 10, were spent in search of a compromise that would satisfy public opinion at home and ensure future peace abroad.

The new American proposal presented by Stettinius at the noon meeting of foreign ministers suggested that "the present Polish Provisional Government be reorganized into a fully representative government based on all democratic forces in Poland and including democratic leaders from Poland abroad, to be termed 'The Provisional Government of National Unity.'" The government was to be "reorganized" on the basis of consultations in Moscow between Molotov and the two Western ambassadors. Its main task would be to conduct "free and unfettered" elections "as soon as practicable." The Allied ambassadors in Warsaw were to inform their governments of "the carrying out of the pledge in regard to free and unfettered elections." By using the word "reorganized," the Americans were in effect capitulating to the Soviet demand that the new government be formed on the basis of the existing one. They were also accepting the Soviet request that it be formed in Moscow and not at Yalta, as the British had hoped. The American proposal switched the focus of debate from the shape of the provisional government to future elections. This would now become the key issue in the diplomatic contest over Poland.

Molotov was taken aback by the sudden shift and did not know how to respond. He asked for the American proposal to be translated into Russian, withholding comment for the time being. Privately he must have been gratified, as his tough stand was paying off. There were those in the Soviet leadership, like Lavrentii Beria, who argued for a temporary coalition between communists and representatives of the bourgeois parties, later to be replaced by a communist-dominated government, but Molotov rejected that view. "We were very worried about the Polish question," he later recalled. "We got what we needed, though they tried in every way to encroach on our interests—to impose a bourgeois government in Poland that would certainly have been an agent of imperialism. But we, Stalin and I, insisted on having at our border an independent but not hostile Poland."[5]

Later that day, when Churchill proposed that the Big Three discuss the Polish question, Molotov immediately stepped in and declared that "the Soviet Delegation was very anxious to come to an agreement." He suggested this could be done "with certain amendments to Mr. Stettinius' proposal." It would appear that, having examined Stettinius's formula, Stalin and Molotov felt they had finally worn out their opponents. The amendments they suggested, though minimal, were very telling. Molotov wanted the words "fully representative" to be dropped from the description of the "reorganized" government. He also proposed that the reference to the participation of democratic parties in the forthcoming elections be amended by adding the words "non-Fascist and anti-Fascist." He wanted the reference to ambassadors reporting on the conduct of the elections to be deleted. Overt international supervision would offend the Poles, he argued, and it was self-evident that ambassadors were obliged to report to their governments on developments in the countries to which they were posted.

Molotov presented his amendments as insignificant modifications of the American proposal. He then tried to change the subject to the Yugoslav situation, but Churchill would not be distracted. "[I]n the general atmosphere of agreement, we should not put our feet in the stirrups and ride off," the prime minister said. He clearly did not like either Stettinius's proposal or Molotov's amendments and was prepared to take as much time as necessary to defeat them. Roosevelt suggested that they take half an hour to study the proposal, but Churchill, according to the American protocol, shot back, "I mean more than that. I do not feel that we should hurry away from the Crimea leaving these vital problems unresolved or reach hasty decisions. These are among the most important days that any of us shall live. Of course you could all go away and leave me in this delightful spot but I do urge that we stay a little bit longer to conclude our discussions satisfactorily." Neither Roosevelt nor Stalin responded.

When Roosevelt took the floor after the break, what he said could hardly have satisfied the prime minister. According to the British note-taker, "The President said that they had discussed the document on Poland informally during the interval and had come to the conclusion that the differences between themselves and the Russians were largely a matter of the use of words. They were nearer than ever before, and there was a real chance that they could get this document into a form on which they could all agree, and so reach a solution on the Polish question till an election could be held." After a short exchange with Molotov, Roosevelt said that "he would like to ask on behalf of some six million Poles in the United States for some assurance that the elections really would be honest and free." He wanted the foreign ministers to continue working on the language of the Polish formula later that day.

Churchill did not object to a new meeting of foreign ministers. By now he had given up nearly all hope for the formation of a fully representative Polish government. He focused instead on the Polish elections and was quite prepared to dig in his heels. He was determined to defeat Molotov's amendments. He insisted on the last paragraph of the American proposal, which gave the ambassadors a special role in the elections. On the previous day Eden had told Molotov and Stettinius that he did not believe that the Lublin government could conduct fair elections in Poland. Now that the Western Allies had agreed to "reorganize" the existing government in Poland, arranging for observers seemed their only hope of keeping the vote honest.

The prime minister appealed to Stalin to allow Western ambassadors to observe the elections. "He would like Marshal Stalin, with his patience and kindness, to consider the difficulty of the British position," said Churchill, according to the British protocol of the meeting. "The British Government did not know what was going on inside Poland, except through dropping brave men by parachute and bringing members of the Underground Movement out. They had no other means of knowing, and did not like getting their information in that way." Churchill assured Stalin that he would raise no obstacle to Soviet observance of elections held in other parts of Europe. He "personally would welcome observers of the three powers in any area where they appeared needed," said Churchill, according to the American protocol. It was his understanding that "Tito would have no objection to foreign observers when elections were to be held in Yugoslavia, and the British would welcome observers from the United States and the Soviet Union when elections were held in Greece, and the same would apply to Italy." His was not an idle request: he "knew in Egypt that whatever government held the election, won."

Stalin was looking for weaknesses in his opponent's line of attack. To Churchill's remark about Egypt he responded that as far as he knew, the most prominent Egyptian politicians spent their time buying one another out. He said there were no grounds to compare Egypt with Poland, given the high level of literacy in Poland and the low one in Egypt. His remarks echoed Soviet media coverage of the Egyptian elections that January, which had stressed that the country's political scene was dominated by personalities, not principles, and that the parties had no programs. Churchill withdrew his comparison, but he would not allow Stalin to distract him from his main theme—the fairness of the Polish elections. "Would Mikołajczyk be able to go back to Poland and organise his party for the elections?" he asked Stalin directly. Stalin said that as a member of a nonfascist party, Mikołajczyk would have the right to take part in the election.

When Roosevelt entered the fray, he offered Churchill his full support. "I want this election in Poland to be the first one beyond question," declared the president. "It should be like Caesar's wife. I did not know her but they said she was pure." Stalin, who was at pains to reduce Allied expectations, shot back, "They said that about her but in fact she had her sins." His attack on the elections and on electoral democracy in general was based on a belief, which he happened to share with Goebbels, in the plutocratic nature of democratic governments. The plenary session, which had begun in the friendly atmosphere of the joint photo shoot, ended in deadlock.[6]

Contrary to Roosevelt's expectations, the evening meeting of foreign ministers, the second one that day, did little to resolve the Polish problem. Eden began the meeting by stating that he had received a strong telegram from the war cabinet "indicating that the earlier basis of discussion had not been satisfactory." This last-minute attempt on the part of the British foreign minister to change the course of deliberations failed. Like their superiors earlier that day, the foreign ministers reached no agreement on the role of ambassadors in the future elections. The meeting, convened at half past ten, ended after midnight with no prospect of resolution.

Eden was clearly upset by the day's results. "Found the Russians unprepared even to consider our draft," he recorded in his diary that night, "so I fairly let them have it, told them something of British opinion, said I would far rather go back without a text than be a party to the sort of thing they wanted." He was no less upset by the Americans. "President Roosevelt observed that the differences between ourselves and the Russians were largely a matter of the use of words," he wrote in his memoirs. "He was deluding himself. After much more dogged argument, we finally reached agreement on words, but it was not long before we learned that the difference of intention remained untouched."

Cadogan was of a different opinion. "We really have made some progress," he wrote his wife the next morning. "We have begun night sessions and had a meeting of Foreign Secretaries at the Russian H.Q. last night, which went on till after midnight. But it was worthwhile, as we nearly succeeded in getting quite a decent arrangement about Poland, which I hope we can get over the last hurdle today. That will be the most important thing, if we can get that. Because after all, if we couldn't get a decent-looking Polish settlement, none of our other high-falutin' plans for World Organization and suchlike would make much sense." Like his American colleagues, Cadogan was "thinking big." The real prize was postwar cooperation: all he wanted on Poland was a decent-looking arrangement.[7]

On the morning of February 10 Churchill was not in the best of moods. He stayed in bed, receiving visitors (including Cadogan) and working on his papers until midafternoon. He cabled Mrs. Churchill: "Have been very hard pressed these last few days." Churchill's secretary, Marian Holmes, recorded in her diary, "PM a bit irate." That morning he had made her fuss with the curtain on his bedroom window: "Down a little. No that's too much. A little higher."

Churchill had a problem with his eyes, which were irritated by sunlight, but that was not the only reason for his unhappiness. The conference was not going his way, and as far as he was concerned, the Americans were making new problems with their constant concessions to the Soviets. On the morning of February 10 they agreed to withdraw their proposal that the Polish elections be monitored by Western ambassadors. As Churchill worked on his papers, the foreign ministers were meeting next door in Vorontsov villa. That made it easy for Eden to inform Churchill when Stettinius proposed to drop the paragraph about Western ambassadors reporting on the elections. "Americans gave us no warning and I don't propose to agree to their action," Eden noted. "Certainly do not agree" was Churchill's note back. He was prepared to fight on with or without American support.[8]

The new American concession originated with Roosevelt. On the morning of February 10, FDR met with his secretary of state to review the remaining agenda. "The President had Poland much in mind, and I went over again the American position on the issue of the Polish Government. We were anxious to reach an agreement with the other two governments that day," Stettinius wrote in his memoirs. "[W]e did not wish to prevent a Polish settlement by insisting on the last sentence of our formula," he added, referring to the provision giving Allied ambassadors the right to monitor the elections. "If the statement of this fact in the agreement irritates the Russians," Roosevelt told his secretary of state, "we can drop the statement, but they must understand our firm determination that the ambassadors will observe and report on the elections in any case."

Stettinius followed the president's instructions to the letter. At the foreign ministers' session later that day he presented the new American position, saying that the president would have preferred to leave the Polish formula unchanged but that he was "anxious to reach agreement" and "willing to make this concession." Molotov pushed for more. He proposed an amendment stating that the Western governments would establish diplomatic relations with the Polish government, as the USSR had already done. This implied that the Lublin government and the future Polish government were one and the same. This time around, Stettinius and Eden joined ranks. They said there was to be a new government in Poland and that all three Allies would recognize it.[9]

Informed by Eden of the outcome of the debate, Churchill decided he would now have to act decisively. In a telegram to Attlee composed in the early afternoon, he stated that the resolution of the Polish question depended on future elections and on securing proper information about what was going on in Poland. This was the only unresolved issue and it "will be fought out today." After drafting the telegram, Churchill ignored his previous agreement to meet with the president and left for Koreiz villa. It was Stalin, not Roosevelt, who held the key to the resolution of the Polish problem.[10]

When the prime minister arrived, accompanied by Eden, he was in a combative mood. He told Stalin, according to the Soviet protocol, that he had come to discuss a "highly unpleasant matter." He wanted to speak about the last paragraph of the Polish formula but had just heard from Eden that the Soviets were already making additional demands. Molotov, who was present at the meeting, immediately produced a fresh version of his amendment on the recognition of the Polish government. It did not equate the future Polish government with the existing Lublin one, and Churchill calmed down a bit. He approved the new formula: the immediate tension was resolved.

Churchill could now proceed to a discussion of the role of Western ambassadors in monitoring the elections—the main issue that had brought him to Koreiz. As always, he complained about the lack of independent information from Poland, buttressing his argument on the need for ambassadors' reports. Stalin used the opportunity to attempt to trick the British into establishing diplomatic relations with the Lublin government. "De Gaulle has a representative of his own in Lublin," he remarked. "Perhaps the British government should send the same kind of representative to Poland." Churchill said that that would be possible only once a new government was formed.

The dialogue was going nowhere, and Eden decided to bring the conversation closer to the purpose of the British visit. He told Stalin that he and Churchill wanted to "include in the agreement a condition that there would be Allied representatives in Poland who would report to their governments on how the fulfillment of the agreement was going." "That goes without saying," responded Stalin. "The British government will have an envoy and officials in Poland." Eden pushed further: "Will the envoy have freedom of movement?" "The Red Army command will not interfere with the envoy's movements," Stalin assured his guest. "As for the Polish government, one can negotiate with it." This was a loophole designed to give Stalin freedom of action in the future.

At this point Eden proposed a new formula. Upon the formation of the Polish government, the Allied powers would "exchange Ambassadors by whose reports the respective Governments will be kept informed about the situation in Poland." He dropped the reference to the ambassadors reporting on the elections. Stalin was satisfied. He agreed to the new formula, and according to the Soviet protocol of the meeting, Churchill and Eden thanked him for that. The reference to the ambassadors reporting on events in Poland would appear in the final document, despite the American agreement to drop it, but there would be no reference to the elections. It was the best that Churchill could achieve under the circumstances.[11]

Both Churchill and Stalin were late for the plenary session. Entering the grand ballroom at Livadia Palace, Churchill apologized to the president and then told him, "I believe that I have succeeded in retrieving the situation." It was only partly true. The final draft of the Allied declaration on Poland, approved that afternoon, was in all but form an act of surrender to the Soviets. Its language, open to various interpretations, fully reflected the tension between the Soviet and Anglo-American delegations at Yalta. At Roosevelt's request, the reference to the pro-Soviet government as the "Provisional Government of Poland" was replaced with a reference to the "Provisional Government which is now functioning in Poland." To accommodate Stalin, the reference to "fully representative government" was dropped; a reference to antifascist parties was added, though in somewhat revised form ("anti-Nazi parties"); and the statement on the ambassadors was revised, making them responsible for reporting on the situation in Poland in general as opposed to ensuring "free and unfettered elections." The Soviets agreed to "reorganize" the existing government by adding politicians from Poland and abroad, but who they would be, how many, and in what capacity remained to be decided by Molotov, Harriman, and Kerr in Moscow.[12]

When Eden read out the new resolution at the plenary session, Churchill raised no objection: to counter the inevitable accusations that the British government had abandoned its ally, the British insisted on the inclusion of a short statement to the effect that the complete liberation of Polish territory had created a new situation in the country. The prime minister had no further interest in discussing either the Polish government or the Polish elections. There was, however, one last issue to be decided: that of Poland's western frontiers. With the battle over the government all but lost, Churchill was more reluctant than ever to push the new Poland too far westward. Nevertheless, he wanted some mention of the western frontier in the final document of the conference.

Roosevelt preferred that the final decision be postponed until consultations were held with the new Polish government. He also wanted the statement on the western border to be drafted by Churchill. The Big Three agreed that Poland would receive territories to the north and west of its former boundaries, but that the new borders would be decided later, upon consultation with the new Polish government. When Molotov proposed to add a sentence on the return to Poland of its "ancient frontiers in East Prussia and on the Oder," the president asked how long ago Poland had had those frontiers. When Molotov answered, "[V]ery long ago," Roosevelt joked that Britain could ask for the return of the United States on the same grounds. Stalin noted that the ocean would prevent that from happening, and the question was dropped.

In general, the Americans were quite careful to avoid responsibility for the delineation of new borders. Roosevelt ignored Harry Hopkins's advice not to make a clear commitment on the Curzon Line, but he modified the statement on the western borders in order to present it as an expression of the views of the three political leaders, as opposed to a commitment of governments. This was a prudent approach. The Polish diplomats who were already mounting resistance in Washington were disappointed to learn that in law those decisions amounted to no more than a declaration of intent. As such, they did not require congressional approval.[13]

Negotiations over Poland, which turned out to be the most difficult issue discussed at Yalta, finally came to an end on the evening of February 10. The Western delegates at Yalta had little choice but to accept the fact of preponderant Soviet power. Roosevelt believed that subjecting Stalin to greater pressure would bring no results. Churchill disagreed and wanted further discussions, but there is no indication whatever that Stalin was prepared to compromise on Poland. The country was too important in his scheme of things to loosen his grip on it.

Roosevelt managed to avoid an open breach with the Soviets by finding language to paper over the remaining differences. Stettinius passed the president a note that read: "Mr. President: Not to *enlarge* Lublin but to form a *new* Gov. of some kind." The last three words, "of some kind," turned out to be apt. Charles Bohlen, who helped draft the American proposal on Poland, later wrote, "the agreement, although not what the West had wanted, appeared to us, with some doubts, as acceptable." Others were less optimistic. Averell Harriman later criticized Roosevelt for "accepting Stalin's language that instead of creating a new Polish government, the existing Provisional Government should be reorganized." He also explained the nature of Bohlen's doubts at the time.

"There was an expression we used at the Embassy at that time—that trading with the Russian you had to buy the same horse twice. . . . I had that feeling about the Polish agreement and said as much to Bohlen."

Lord Moran, always the realist, believed that it was too late to worry about Poland after the outcome of Teheran and the Churchill-Stalin meeting in Moscow in the fall of 1944. He wrote in his diary: "It was plain at Moscow, last October, that Stalin means to make Poland a Cossack outpost of Russia, and I am sure he has not altered his intention here." Roosevelt, whom Harriman accused of "accepting Stalin's language" on Poland, was seemingly resigned. When Admiral Leahy, who was not involved in the actual negotiations on the issue, told Roosevelt, "Mr. President, this is so elastic that the Russians can stretch it all the way from Yalta to Washington, without ever technically breaking it," he was told, "I know, Bill, I know it. But it's the best I can do for Poland at this time."[14]

20

THE FATE OF GERMANY

"This is an egg I have laid myself," Churchill told Roosevelt and Stalin on the evening of February 9. He was referring to the Moscow Declaration of 1943, which he had helped draft in the fall of 1943. It called for Nazi war criminals to be extradited to the countries in which they had committed their crimes. Now he wanted to raise the question of the "grand" criminals, as he called them—the leaders of the Third Reich who had committed crimes in more than one country. It was close to eight o'clock, the plenary session had been dragging on for more than three and a half hours, and Roosevelt was eager to end the discussion. He remarked that the question was too complicated to be resolved at Yalta and proposed that it be referred to the foreign ministers, who would present a report in three or four weeks. Churchill persisted. He wanted the Big Three to agree on a list of Nazi criminals who would be shot upon capture and identification.

Stalin showed some interest in the subject. In May 1941 Rudolf Hess, Hitler's close associate, had flown to Britain to negotiate peace but was arrested and had been in British custody ever since. Stalin, apprehensive that the British might use him for separate peace talks with the Nazis, asked whether Hess would be on Churchill's list. He also wondered whether prisoners of war could be put on trial. Hess "would catch up with the others," Churchill told Stalin. Those who "committed crimes against the laws of war had always been liable to be tried," he said, according to the British protocol, but did he understand the marshal correctly that before being shot the main criminals should be put on trial? Was he implying that it should be a "judicial rather than a political act"? Stalin said that indeed this was what he had in mind. The man who had shocked Churchill in Teheran by suggesting that fifty thousand German officers be executed now favored putting the major war criminals on trial.

Disturbed by this sudden turn, Roosevelt expressed his preference that the procedure not be too judicial. Under no circumstances did he want reporters or photographers at the trial. Churchill agreed that the trial should be largely political. Seeking to limit discussion, he dropped his insistence on drawing up a list of major war criminals. "We should merely have an exchange of views here," he said. "There is nothing of course that would be said in public about this because I fear retaliation on our prisoners." He raised no objection when Roosevelt suggested that they refer the question to the foreign ministers.[1]

The two Western statesmen had no experience of show trials and, given their knowledge of the Anglo-Saxon legal system, were reluctant to hand over the fate of the Nazi leaders to rule-bound lawyers. Stalin had a different view. The Soviet show trials of the late 1930s had sent dozens if not hundreds of his political opponents, including such revolutionary heroes as Grigorii Zinoviev and Lev Kamenev, to their deaths and demonstrated the propaganda value of kangaroo courts. Should Roosevelt and Churchill wish for more specific advice, Stalin could easily have called on Andrei Vyshinsky, the former state prosecutor at the Moscow trials of the 1930s, whose short biography, included in Stettinius's briefing book, indicated that he had "made a name for himself in the Metro-Vickers trial in 1933 and the Trotskyist-Zinoviev-Bukharin trials in 1936 and 1938." In the first case, British engineers in the Soviet Union were charged with espionage; in the second, similar accusations were leveled against former leaders of the October Revolution.[2]

For Stalin, there was no difference between political and legal procedures: as he was leaving Moscow for Yalta, Soviet newspapers were full of reports on the public trials of Nazi collaborators in Bulgaria. After the conference, the Soviet information agency TASS issued a poster depicting Hitler and his associates being pushed behind bars with a rifle butt decorated with Allied flags. The inscription beneath the picture read: "An inevitable date. War criminals. A realization of the unshakable decisions of the Allied conference in the Crimea. The din of battle is growing ever louder in Germany—the organizers of fascist crimes are approaching their end." Stalin presented the preliminary and inconclusive discussions on the fate of war criminals at Yalta as an "unshakable decision."[3]

Two "German" questions remained unresolved until the last days of the conference: the composition of the Allied Control Commission and German reparations. The British had not given up hope of making France a full member of the commission, and the Soviets were determined that they should receive $10 billion in reparations. These were conflicting agendas. Churchill wanted more control over Germany and fewer reparations to prevent it from being bled to death as a result of excessive Soviet demands. Stalin, for his part, did not want a British proxy on the control commission, and he believed that the Germans should pay for the reconstruction of the Soviet Union, which had been devastated by the Nazi invasion. Roosevelt did not see either of these as a matter of primary importance. He was quite prepared to change position on both issues to bring about an agreement.

On February 9, France was very much on Roosevelt's mind. Winding up the last joint session of the American and British military commanders, which he had co-chaired with Churchill, Roosevelt jokingly remarked, "This has been a fine conference, Winston, unless you go back to Paris and make another speech and tell the Frenchmen that the British intend to equip twenty-five more French divisions with American equipment." Roosevelt was referring to the speech that Churchill had given on November 11, 1944, when he paid a triumphant visit to the French capital and attended the first commemoration of Armistice Day 1918 in Paris since the liberation. Churchill at first denied ever making such a statement. Then he said, "Whatever I said in Paris, I said in French, and I never know what I'm saying when I talk in French, so pay no attention to it."[4]

Later that day Roosevelt offered his limited support for the British proposal that France be added as a signatory to the Declaration on Liberated Europe. Stalin showed no inclination to compromise. "Three powers are better than four," he said. According to Charles Bohlen's notes of the meeting, Roosevelt remarked that "in earlier drafts France had been included but was now absent." Churchill, taking FDR's comment as evidence of support, suggested that "it might be possible to ask France to associate itself with the Declaration." The president's position was changing, which the British took as a good sign.[5]

This was the doing of Harry Hopkins, whom the British knew to support their view of France's role in Europe. Lord Moran noted in his diary on February 5: "The President sides with Stalin; he likes France, but de Gaulle gets on his nerves. However, Hopkins is backing the P.M.; he has the good sense to see that a stable Europe is impossible without a strong and virile France." Hopkins had supported the British position from the very start of the conference. Backed by State Department staffers Charles Bohlen and H. Freeman Matthews (who had served in the U.S. embassy in France), he urged the president on February 5 to change his position on French participation in the control commission. FDR promised to think the matter through.

"Hopkins," wrote Moran in his diary, "is, of course, a valuable ally, particularly now, when the President's opinions flutter in the wind. He knows the President's moods like a wife watching the domestic climate. He will sit patiently for hours, blinking like a cat, waiting for the right moment to put his point; and if it never comes, he is content to leave it to another time." Hopkins raised the question again on February 8 at a meeting attended by Averell Harriman, James Byrnes, and Charles Bohlen. All three senior advisers took the same position. "France should be represented on the Council," argued Byrnes; "they could not accept a zone without such representation . . . any other action would greatly humiliate them." Faced with this common front and responsive to this last argument in particular, the president agreed to act.[6]

At the plenary session on February 9, when Stalin showed no inclination to compromise, Roosevelt decided not to press the issue any further in the presence of Churchill. He hedged his earlier remark, suggested that for now it would be better to limit the number of signatures to those of the three great powers, and proposed that the issue be referred to the foreign ministers, who were to meet that evening. After the meeting was over, he sent Harriman to inform the Soviet leader in private that he had changed his mind on France and wanted its full participation in the control commission. Stalin now gave in. He said that, given the president's new stand on the matter, he would go along with the American proposal.[7]

Stalin kept his word. When during the plenary session on February 10 Roosevelt announced that he had changed his mind on French membership in the Allied Control Commission, Stalin raised his arms to signal that he would surrender. In the European context at least, France was now recognized as a great power. Stalin's change of mind came as a major surprise to some members of the American delegation, including Bohlen, as well as to many members of the British party. Lord Moran clearly resented the fact that Stalin, who had vehemently opposed Churchill on the French question, readily agreed with the president. "The President has changed his mind again," he wrote in his diary. "But nobody appears in the least surprised. He has now agreed with the P.M. that France should be member of the Control Commission. Stalin made it plain at once that if this was the President's wish he would accept it. One cannot help noticing Stalin's deference to the President's opinions throughout the Conference. This frame of mind does not come naturally to Stalin."[8]

Churchill was not so fastidious. Stalin's concession meant victory for the British on an important aspect of their European policy. On British initiative it was agreed to send a telegram to de Gaulle inviting France to become a member of the commission. It did little to placate the proud Frenchman: according to the U.S. ambassador to France, Jefferson Caffery, he "was in a sulky mood" after the publication of the conference communiqué, "apparently expecting a bigger personal role for himself . . . as well [as] something concrete in regard to France's position in the Rhineland." Roosevelt may have regretted his last-minute support of the French when he heard a few days later that de Gaulle had changed his mind and refused to meet with him in North Africa after the Yalta Conference. He was offended at not having been invited to Yalta. Stalin had little reason to regret his "surrender." He attempted to cash in his French chip later that day by getting the president to take his side on a question of much greater significance to him—that of German reparations.[9]

Final negotiations on reparations began on the morning of February 9. At his meeting with Stettinius Roosevelt said that he had decided to concede not only on Poland but also on reparations. The issue was of secondary importance to the president. With some of his most trusted advisers, such as Secretary of the Treasury Morgenthau, pushing for the "pastoralization" of Germany, Roosevelt saw no reason to turn reparations into another stumbling block that would only prolong the conference.

Stettinius presented both concessions at the foreign ministers' meeting later that day. Like the American formula on Poland, the new language on reparations was styled as a compromise between the British and Soviet positions, while in fact yielding to the Soviets on the major points. It took account of Soviet insistence that reparations should go in the first instance to those who had contributed most to the victory over Germany, and the British proposal that preference should be given to countries that had suffered most from German aggression. It incorporated almost verbatim a paragraph from the Soviet proposal that divided reparations into two categories: those to be extracted in the form of equipment within two years and the remainder, which would include annual deliveries of goods and commodities over a ten-year period. It also instructed the Reparations Commission to take into consideration the Soviet proposal that total reparations should amount to $20 billion.

Ivan Maisky could finally take pride in his achievements. He had been the principal figure on the Soviet side pushing for $10 billion in reparations, and now it appeared that he had managed to persuade not only Stalin but also the Americans to back his claim. On February 5, when late in the evening Stalin decided to reduce Soviet demands to $7 billion, Maisky noted in his diary: "Still, I could not so easily sacrifice 'my' 10 billion." He soon had another chance to press his claim. At the meeting of foreign ministers on February 7, Molotov and Maisky left the Soviet figure at $10 billion, while suggesting that $8 billion be allocated to Britain and the United States, and $2 billion to other victims of German aggression.

When Stettinius informed his colleagues on February 9 that the Americans were prepared to consider $20 billion as a starting point for discussion, Maisky expressed support for the first two paragraphs of the new American formula. He also wanted to revise the last paragraph in order to mandate that the commission should accept (not just consider) the figure of $20 billion as a basis for discussion. Eden strongly objected to specifying any figure. Molotov threatened to ask for more. He mentioned that Maisky and his experts, who had come up with the figure of $10 billion for the Soviet share of reparations, "had done good work—it had only one defect, that of minimalism." Stettinius, fearing an escalation, said that he considered Maisky's figure reasonable. It was a major victory for the Soviets, spoiled only by Eden's recalcitrance. The British foreign secretary stated that he would await instructions from his government.[10]

A letter from the war cabinet arrived on February 10. "We consider it quite inadmissible to state any figure for German deliveries until the possibilities have been properly investigated on the spot," it said. "We consider 20 billion dollars (equals 500 million pounds a year) far too great. It is roughly the equivalent of Germany's pre-war gross exports (i.e. not allowing for any imports) in an average year. It is not to be thought that this should be paid by a Germany which has been bombed, defeated, perhaps dismembered and unable to pay for imports."

At the noon meeting of foreign secretaries that day, Eden sought to postpone a decision on the amount in question by referring it to the Reparations Commission. Molotov vented his annoyance. "Are there no points with which Eden is in agreement?" he asked. "In such a situation there is no basis for the work of the Reparations Commission." When Eden refused to budge, Molotov said that he was disappointed. The Soviet note-taker recorded Molotov's words: "The essence of Eden's statement comes down to taking as little from Germany as possible." Still the foreign secretary would not yield. He read an excerpt from the war cabinet telegram and submitted his own proposal. It stressed that reparations should not jeopardize Germany's economic existence or its ability to export goods in order to pay for imports. The British were prepared to fight to the finish.[11]

Stalin took it upon himself to raise the question of reparations during a private meeting with Churchill before the plenary session later that afternoon. He asked whether the British were "scared" by the Soviet request. Churchill ignored the intimation of cowardice and said that he had a telegram from the war cabinet prohibiting him from mentioning any figures in the reparations agreement. Stalin pressed on: was Churchill taking pity on the Germans? Eden said it was not a question of pity but of British experience with reparations after the First World War. Churchill developed the argument, expressing doubt that the Soviets would manage to collect as much as they expected. He pointed out that British expectations were limited. "For ourselves," he remarked, "we do not want German labor. We might take over part of German trade and certain raw materials, like potash, timber, etc. But we do not want manufactured goods, which would only mean unemployment for us."

Stalin was eager to bribe the Allies with the prospect of German loot and wanted the British to take more. He offered Churchill "shares in German undertakings." Churchill did not nibble. He did not object, however, to the Soviets taking German equipment. "By removing factories and equipment from Germany, Russia would be doing us a service, for it would put an end to German exports which could then be replaced by British exports," he said. Stalin said that the Soviets would happily remove German factories once they got hold of them. The conversation switched to another topic, and the issue remained unresolved.[12]

During the plenary session later that day, Churchill referred once again to his instructions from the war cabinet. Stalin was silent, but Roosevelt unexpectedly joined the debate on Churchill's side. He was afraid that "if any figures were mentioned, the American people would believe that it involved money." Caught off guard, Stalin remarked only that the figure mentioned by the Soviets was a mere expression of the value of reparations, much of which would be collected in materials. He turned to Gromyko and asked him quietly, "What should I make of Roosevelt? Does he really disagree with Churchill, or is it just a ploy?" This was a tricky question. Gromyko's answer deliberately conformed to Stalin's suspicions. "There are differences between them," he whispered, "but one must be aware that he is correct in his behavior towards the British Prime Minister. Even so, that same correctness would never stop him bringing unofficial pressure on Churchill. If he hasn't done this, I hardly think it's accidental."

Stalin made no secret of his displeasure. "This was the only time during the conference that Stalin showed some annoyance," H. Freeman Matthews noted in the American protocol of the meeting. As he had during his emotional speech on Poland on February 6, Stalin rose from the table. Later that evening Hopkins reenacted the entire scene for Lord Moran, who duly recorded it in his diary. "Stalin rose and gripped the back of his chair with such force that his brown hands went white at the knuckles," wrote Moran. Hopkins recalled that the Soviet leader "spat out his words as if they burnt his mouth. Great stretches of his country had been laid waste, he said, and the peasants put to the sword. Reparations should be paid to the countries that had suffered most."

"If the British felt that the Russians should receive no reparations at all," Stalin said, according to the American transcript of the meeting, "it would be better to say so frankly." Churchill denied any such reservations: he simply wanted the commission to study the question. Stalin insisted they agree in principle that Germany had to pay reparations and that the Reparations Commission should take into consideration the American-Soviet proposal that the amount be $20 billion, with half that sum going to the USSR. Stalin finished his emotional plea by asking the president whether the Americans were withdrawing their earlier proposal.

"Were our allies perhaps thinking that the Soviet economy should not be allowed to recover too quickly?" Gromyko later asked, hinting at underlying concerns. It could only have been on Stalin's instructions that, even as the Big Three were debating the question, the cautious Gromyko conveyed his displeasure to the president's right-hand man, Harry Hopkins, who was sympathetic to Soviet demands. "Gromyko just told me," Hopkins wrote in a note that he passed to Roosevelt, "that the Marshall thinks you did not back up Ed [Stettinius] relative to Reparations—and that you sided with the British—and he is disturbed about it. Perhaps you could tell him privately later." The intervention had its effect. The previous evening Stalin had accommodated FDR's request on France; now he was signaling that he needed help on reparations. The president could not say no.[13]

Once Stalin was through, Roosevelt hastened to assure him that he was "completely in agreement" with Soviet demands. He added that his only concern was the word "reparations," as it might make the American public think that the Allies meant cash. FDR suggested replacing "reparations" with "compensation for damages." It seemed like a quid pro quo for the admission of France to the control commission. Stalin cashed in his French chip, and it appeared that he had won the day. The president was back in the marshal's corner, and the prime minister was left on his own to oppose the Soviet demand for $10 billion in reparations.

Churchill returned to the telegram he had received from the war cabinet and read excerpts. He drew on all his rhetorical powers in an effort to persuade Roosevelt to shift the American position once again, and he almost succeeded. "It was always a pleasure to listen to his eloquent sentences," wrote Stettinius. "The beautiful phrases just roll out as water in a running stream." The president began to waver once again. The debate dragged on, and Stalin finally agreed that it would be up to the Reparations Commission to decide on the amount. "We bring our figures before the commission, and you bring yours," he said to Churchill. The prime minister then asked Roosevelt, "How about the United States?" "The answer is simple," said the president. "Judge Roosevelt approves and the document is accepted."[14]

Roosevelt was happy with the outcome. He wanted to play honest broker in relations between Britain and the USSR, but he was being pushed toward the Soviet position by his experts. Hopkins counseled him to "seek agreement by which Germany would not be self-sufficient but be forced to import." Morgenthau advocated the dismemberment of Germany and the complete destruction of its industrial base. Under pressure from the State Department and seeking to placate the media, Roosevelt had abandoned the Morgenthau plan, but he could easily return to some of its provisions in spirit if not in letter, to placate the Soviets.

Although Churchill had prevailed, he was left feeling disappointed. Lord Moran, who saw him later that evening, recorded in his diary that Churchill was upset by the excessive Soviet demands. The Americans could not understand Churchill's stubbornness on the issue. Moran explained to Harry Hopkins that "the P.M.'s mind is full of what happened at the end of the First War. He thinks the Russian demands are madness. Who, he demanded angrily, is going to feed a starving Germany?" This made no impression on Hopkins, who advised the president to accept the Soviet proposal. He told Moran, "The Russians had given way a good deal at the Conference. It was our turn to give something. We could not expect them always to climb down."

The British position on reparations was not unaffected by the upcoming parliamentary elections: public opinion would not tolerate economic policies leading to widespread starvation in Germany. Britain's hopes of economic revival were predicated on increased exports to Western and Central Europe. Its geostrategic interests were pegged to the creation of a West European Union. Both goals required a weakened but not economically prostrate Germany. Churchill and Eden well understood these interests and made a strong stand at Yalta to defend them.[15]

Stalin was the least happy of the three world leaders. As the Western Allies accepted his surrender, he remarked caustically, "And won't you go back on this tomorrow?" At the end of the meeting he mumbled in a voice loud enough to be heard by members of the Soviet delegation, "It is possible the USA and Britain have already agreed in this with each other." Stalin would return to the question of reparations at the dinner hosted that evening by Churchill.[16]

Back in 1917, the Bolsheviks had come to power with a promise to end the "imperialist war" and appealed to the nations of the world to conclude a peace without annexations or reparations. Stalin had set an altogether different agenda. After securing Allied approval for the annexation of German territories, the Soviet leadership went on to claim the lion's share of the reparations imposed on a defeated Germany. Ironically, it was the "imperialist" governments that sought to limit the appetite for spoils of the "proletarian" state. It was in response to American and British concerns voiced at the Moscow Conference in the fall of 1943 that the Soviet leaders first agreed to switch from monetary reparations to those taken in kind—equipment, raw materials, and manpower—and to limit the term of reparations to ten years.

In February 1945 Soviet newspapers were already publishing articles that asserted the Soviet government's right to take possession of German plants and machinery on occupied territory. The government-controlled Soviet press hailed the Yalta agreements as a triumph of historical justice. The only internal challenge came from the ranks of the League of German Officers, formed by the Soviets from German POWs in order to conduct anti-Nazi propaganda across the front lines. According to secret-police reports, the members of the league reacted to the news with "exceptional hostility." The league's leader, General Walther von Seydlitz, stated, "Where now are the unshakable principles and the right of nations to self-determination? The Russians have no right to give the Poles living space if they take it away from us. An occupation would be enough to ensure security. This is a policy of force. We still have much to learn about Leninist-Stalinist humanism."

Others saw in the decisions of the conference manifestations of a new "Red imperialism." A league activist, Colonel Hans Günther van Hooven, predicted that the Yalta decisions would strengthen the German resolve to fight: "I would just like to know where the line is actually to be drawn between enslavement and compensation for damages. It will not be difficult for Hitler to call for resistance to the utmost, as the communiqué of the Crimean conference has nothing positive to say to the German people." Western monitors of German broadcasts noted the "political haranguing motif" in Nazi radio programs produced for troops immediately after the end of the conference.[17]

With victory in sight, Stalin could afford to ignore the effect of his demands on members of the League of German Officers and its counterparts in the ranks of the Wehrmacht. When Churchill asked him on February 10 "whether the German generals now in the hands of the Russians were going to be used for purposes other than propaganda," the dictator replied, "God forbid!" Given the vast destruction caused by the German invasion, the Soviet government wanted to extract as much German wealth as possible. According to Maisky's figures, his ambitious request would correspond to only 20 percent of war losses. Since the Soviet economy was highly centralized, it could absorb unlimited injections of goods and manpower without creating unemployment. Unable to satisfy the demand even of its internal market, the Soviet government was not interested in expanding the buying power of foreign markets like Germany. In geostrategic terms, the revival of Western and Central Europe was not in the best interests of the Soviet Union.

Ultimately, the USSR had fallen into the trap of which Churchill warned Stalin: after the First World War, the Germans had paid reparations to Britain with old ships while building a modern navy of their own. Molotov would later complain that the USSR could not take too many reparations from East Germany at a time when the United States and Britain were helping to rebuild West Germany. He referred to the reparations as "trifles." "Our state was huge. And these reparations were of old, obsolete equipment," he complained. The Soviets continued to use some of the requisitioned German equipment well into the 1980s.[18]

The debates over Germany's future during the last three days of the Yalta Conference produced mixed results. The Big Three agreed in principle that the main Nazi war criminals would be tried, but that decision was left out of the final communiqué of the conference. They agreed that France should be added to the control commission but failed to please the French. They also agreed to set up a Reparations Commission but could not agree on what instructions it should be issued. Roosevelt, who had no serious interest in these issues, was simply trying to reconcile the conflicting demands of his partners. He changed his original position on France and reversed himself twice on the reparations issue, ultimately managing to resume his favorite role of "Judge Roosevelt."

Churchill could congratulate himself on a major victory, although the persistent Soviet demands for more reparations brought on a sense of gloom. The prime minister's stubborn insistence on French participation in the Allied control machinery and his refusal to place any figure on reparations had yielded positive results. The Americans had supported him and compelled Stalin to accept the British position. Faced with the joint opposition of the Western Allies, the Soviet dictator had caved in on French participation and temporarily drew back from his demand for $10 billion in reparations.

Could a joint British-American stand on Poland and Eastern Europe have achieved similar results? The Soviet sources suggest that this is unlikely. The fate of Western Europe was a secondary matter for Stalin: what mattered to him was control of Eastern Europe, which bordered directly on the USSR. He needed Allied cooperation to keep Germany down and extract reparations, but in Eastern Europe, which was completely occupied by the Red Army, Stalin had no need to make concessions. Theoretically, to be sure, Roosevelt and Churchill could have dissociated themselves from Stalin's policies, as Churchill had done on German reparations, but in practice they could not afford to fall out publicly on an issue of such significance as the future of Poland. It would have derailed Roosevelt's United Nations project and compromised Churchill's chances of winning the postwar elections. If the Allies wanted any say in Eastern Europe, they would have to maintain friendly relations with the Soviets.

21

LIBERATED EUROPE AND THE
BALKAN DEAL

On the morning of February 9 the Americans presented a short document entitled Declaration on Liberated Europe. First brought up for discussion by Stalin that afternoon and approved the following day, it was a peculiar document, open to different interpretations. No piece of paper approved by the Big Three became more prominent immediately after the conference or in the course of the long and frosty Cold War, and received less attention during the actual deliberations. The declaration set forth principles to which all three powers agreed to adhere in their treatment of the countries liberated from the Nazis, which, at the time of signing, the British were openly violating in Greece and the Soviets in Poland.

FDR, who proposed this memorandum of good intentions, was not prepared at the time to back them up with U.S. troops. He felt he needed a statement on the democratic commitment of the Grand Alliance to mobilize domestic support for the United Nations organization. The Declaration on Liberated Europe served its purpose at the time, contributing to the general exhilaration that greeted the Yalta agreements and helping to inflate Western expectations of future Allied cooperation. "Later," wrote Henry Kissinger, "when it decided to organize resistance to Soviet expansionism, America did so on the basis of Stalin's failure to keep his word—as given at Yalta and as the American leaders and public had understood it."[1]

The declaration began its life as a preamble to a State Department document calling for the creation of a European Commission aimed at preventing the division of Europe into British and Soviet spheres of influence. The commission, consisting of representatives of the three powers—four, if France was included—would help set up interim governments and conduct free elections in the countries of liberated Europe. Of special concern to its authors was the situation in Greece and Poland, where the liberating powers had created major international problems by aggressively backing one side.

The idea of forming a European Commission for liberated areas had been brewing in the State Department for some time and had the backing of its leading experts. John Hickerson, deputy director of the Office of European Affairs, produced these and other arguments in favor of a special commission in a letter he sent on January 8, 1945, to Secretary of State Stettinius. Hickerson's proposal formed the basis of Stettinius's own recommendation to Roosevelt, dated January 18, which proposed that a European High Commission handle political and emergency economic problems in former German satellites or countries previously occupied by Germany. The proposal was accompanied by two attachments: a Declaration on Liberated Europe, to be signed by the leaders of the four great powers (including France), and the actual blueprint for the commission, spelling out its organizational principles and functions.

Stettinius was a great believer in the idea and secured Eden's backing on Malta. There was, however, one major stumbling block—the president himself. As Stettinius told Eden on February 1, Roosevelt felt the creation of the commission could "prejudice the prospects of the world organization." This was the exact opposite of the opinion held by the ultimate American expert on the world organization, Leo Pasvolsky. Pasvolsky saw the proposed commission as an antidote to emerging domestic opposition to the United Nations. But the president remained suspicious of regional European structures, which, in his view, would effectively deny the United States a position of influence on the subcontinent. He had successfully sabotaged the work of the European Advisory Commission in the past and did not want another European structure that he would have to circumvent in the future.

Roosevelt discussed these issues with James Byrnes on board the *Quincy*, and it fell to Byrnes to confront Stettinius with more arguments against the establishment of the commission. One of those was that Congress would not like the idea of appointing an American commissioner with independent authority. Besides, the American people wanted their troops back from Europe as soon as possible, and the U.S. government was not willing to accept responsibility for internal European affairs. Under these circumstances, American participation in the commission would make little sense. Since Byrnes was obviously speaking on behalf of the president, Stettinius had little choice but to drop the idea.[2]

Nevertheless, the proposal lived on. On February 5, the day after Stettinius's talk with Byrnes, he met with Alger Hiss to discuss what, if anything, could be done with the proposal. Hiss, whose presence at the conference later created such an uproar in the American political establishment and society at large, produced a draft of the declaration that included parts of the former proposal but did not call for a special institution to implement the principles it proclaimed. The new document included 95 percent of the original text verbatim and stated that the governments involved agreed to undertake joint action to achieve their goals. These included helping the newly liberated nations establish internal order, carrying out emergency economic measures, setting up governments broadly representative of all democratic elements, and, last but not least, conducting free elections. Instead of a commission, the ambassadors of the great powers would deal with these issues, but otherwise the two documents were much the same.

The text composed by Hiss underwent further editing and was significantly abridged before Roosevelt presented it to his counterparts on February 9. There were three major changes: the reference to the French government as one of the four powers was dropped; assistance in organizing free elections would be offered only "if necessary"; and the paragraph on ambassadors was replaced with a pledge to establish appropriate machinery for carrying out joint responsibilities. Any teeth in the declaration were now gone, which increased the chances of its being accepted by the Soviets. If that was indeed the strategy, it worked.[3]

When Stalin raised the issue of the declaration at the plenary session on February 9, he praised it for its reference to the need to eliminate vestiges of Nazism and fascism in liberated Europe. A few minutes earlier he had alluded to fascist elements among the Polish political leaders, a comment that had outraged Churchill, who "did not much like the division between Fascists and non-Fascists, on the grounds that anybody could call anybody else anything." As Bohlen observed in his memoirs, "the term 'anti-Fascist' was too broad, since 'Fascist' might easily be interpreted to mean anybody who opposed a Communist government in Poland." As Stalin turned to the text of the declaration, reading a paragraph concerned with the liquidation of the last vestiges of Nazism, FDR saw an opening. "This is the first example for use of the declaration," he said. He pointed out that the excerpt read by Stalin was important and proceeded to read the next paragraph, which dealt with representative governments and free elections. Stalin quickly responded that he approved both sections of the declaration.

It was a promising beginning. When Roosevelt formally introduced the declaration for discussion a few minutes later, the first to challenge its content was unexpectedly Churchill, who was uneasy with the president's comment that the declaration would "apply to any areas or countries where needed as well as to Poland." This meant that the declaration, which contained a reference to the Atlantic Charter with its recognition of the "right of all peoples to choose the form of government under which they will live," could apply to Greece and perhaps even to the territories of the British Empire, raising potential difficulties for British rule abroad.

The prime minister did not object to the text of the declaration, but he wanted to include in the protocol of the meeting an interpretative statement about the Atlantic Charter that he had given to Parliament back in 1941. To buttress his case, Churchill mentioned that he had also sent the text of his statement to Wendell Willkie, Roosevelt's Republican opponent in the presidential elections of 1940, who had become a strong supporter of FDR's foreign policy after his loss. Roosevelt laughed. "Was that what killed him?" He could not resist a joke at the expense of his former Republican opponent, who had died in the fall of 1944. But it was also a joke at Churchill's expense, as the prime minister had never fully accepted the Atlantic Charter's promise of national self-determination.

Churchill found himself on the defensive. He promised to provide the conference with a copy of his interpretation of the Atlantic Charter. The next challenge came with the rejection of Eden's proposal that France be added as a signatory to the declaration. Stalin opposed the change, saying that "three are better than four." Roosevelt supported his host and suggested that for the time being it was better to limit the number of the signatures to three. He also had nothing against Molotov's addendum, which stipulated that "support will be given to the political leaders of those countries who have taken an active part in the struggle against the German invaders," a change that would allow Moscow to legitimize its support for communists in any country under its control. Churchill knew exactly what Molotov had in mind. At one point he even remarked that it was not his fault that communists made the best guerrilla fighters. He asked for time to think matters through.

"[T]he prime minister need have no anxiety that Mr. Molotov's amendment was designed to apply to Greece," Stalin remarked acidly. Churchill shot back that he was not anxious but "merely desired that everybody should have a fair chance and do his duty." He remarked that the British did not want a joint Allied military command in Greece but welcomed observers. He also declared that the British would leave the country once peace was established there. Stalin ended the discussion, declaring his "complete confidence in the British policy in Greece." This was a reminder that Churchill owed him a large debt with regard to Greece and that he expected a free hand in the Soviet-occupied countries of Europe.[4]

Britain's position in Greece was precarious indeed. Greece was the country where British interests were strongest and their power to influence the situation weakest. The Eden-Gusev deal, negotiated in May 1944, had given Britain freedom of action in Greece. On October 13, 1944, while Churchill and Eden were conducting talks with Stalin and Molotov in Moscow, British paratroops entered Athens in a bid to make the summer deal permanent. By that time, the Germans had evacuated most of Greece, which was coming under the control of the procommunist Greek People's Liberation Army (ELAS). With some fifty thousand fighters, ELAS was by far the largest military formation in the country. It was only because of Moscow's insistence that ELAS accepted British involvement in Greece and Greek communist leaders joined the British-sponsored government of Prime Minister George Papandreou.

But even Moscow could not guarantee the voluntary disarmament of ELAS fighters. In early December the communists withdrew from the government, and bloody clashes began on the streets of Athens over efforts to disarm ELAS units. The British intervened on the side of the government forces, bringing in artillery and airpower. The resulting struggle, which lasted more than a month, saw the ELAS forces gain the upper hand in Athens and Piraeus, only to lose the battle to the British. Their defeat was due mainly to a split in the ELAS leadership over relations with Moscow: when representatives of the Greek Communist Party went to Moscow in January 1945 to discuss the situation, neither Stalin nor Molotov found time to meet with them.[5]

On Christmas Day 1944 Churchill and Eden flew into Athens to take charge of the situation. A few weeks earlier Churchill had suggested Athens to Roosevelt as a much better site than Yalta for a meeting of the Big Three. Now he found himself in a city ravaged by urban warfare. "The big plane landed in Athens on a chilly Christmas Day," wrote *Time* magazine in its description of Churchill's visit. "In the streets British troops were blasting and bayoneting ELAS riflemen out of a gasworks. In their homes, Athenians were burning furniture to keep warm. A few Greek civilians recognized and cheered the portly figure in the R.A.F. commodore's uniform as he stepped out of an armored car. Before a pink stucco building Churchill paused, waved and smiled. The fighting continued."

In October 1943 Eden had signed a four-nation declaration renouncing the use of force by occupying powers after the end of hostilities. Now the Germans and Italians were long gone, but British troops were fighting the largest and most popular anti-German resistance group in the country so as to install their own government. Churchill did not waver. In fact, he had been preparing for that struggle all along. On November 7, 1944, when things looked calm and the communists showed every sign of cooperation with the British, he wrote to Eden: "In my opinion, having paid the price we have to Russia for freedom of action in Greece, we should not hesitate to use British troops to support the Royal Hellenic Government under M. Papandreou." Churchill had in mind the "percentage deal," which assigned most of the Balkans to Stalin's sphere of interest.

On December 5, Churchill telegraphed the British military commander in Athens, General Ronald Scobie: "Do not, however, hesitate to act as if you were in a conquered city where a local rebellion is in progress. . . . [W]e have to hold and dominate Athens. It would be a great thing for you to succeed in this without bloodshed if possible, but also with bloodshed if necessary." Churchill later admitted that when composing his message to Scobie he had in mind the telegram sent to the British authorities in the 1880s by the chief secretary for Ireland, Arthur James Balfour. The telegram included the words: "Don't hesitate to shoot." The chief secretary was nicknamed "Bloody Balfour" for the brutality of his measures. In his public pronouncements, Churchill avoided such ruthlessness. Indeed, he did his best to reconcile his imperial instincts with his freedom-loving rhetoric.[6]

"It has fallen to the hard lot of Britain to play a leading part in the Mediterranean. We have great responsibilities and we have made great exertions there," declared Churchill in the House of Commons on January 18, 1945. "We have one principle about liberated countries, or repentant satellite countries, which we strive for according to the best of our ability and resources. Here is the principle. I will state it in the broadest and most familiar terms: government of the people, by the people and for the people, set up on the basis of free universal suffrage, elections with secrecy of ballot, and no intimidation. That is, and that always has been, the policy of this Government in all countries. It is not only our aim and in our interest; it is our only care. It is to that goal that we try to make our way across all difficulties, obstacles and perils of the long road. Trust the people. Make sure they have a fair chance to decide their destiny without being terrorized from either quarter or regimented. There is our policy for Italy, for Yugoslavia and for Greece. No other interest have we than that. For that we shall strive, and for that alone."[7]

The prime minister was not being completely honest. Democracy was indeed high on his agenda, but the interests of empire were even higher. In the Mediterranean, protecting imperial interests also meant waging open or covert warfare against the most popular antifascist organizations of the time, many of which had earlier been supported and armed by the British themselves. Churchill found himself in the hot seat over British actions in Greece and interference in Italian affairs, where the British were trying to rein in communist influence on the government and society at large. In the weeks leading up to the Yalta Conference, the prime minister was grilled by the press both at home and abroad. There was an uproar in Parliament, the U.S. State Department issued a statement questioning British actions in Athens, Churchill's order to Scobie was leaked to the press, and Roosevelt let him know that he could offer no public support. As the British ambassador to the United States, Lord Halifax, informed his government on January 6, Roosevelt, whom he had seen that day, praised Churchill's actions in Greece but said that the British "did not realize his difficulties in bringing American opinion along."

Tacit support came at this stage from an unexpected quarter: there was no word of criticism from Moscow. The "percentage deal" was working. Stalin acted as if he knew nothing about the British suppression of the communist movement in Greece. Eight years later, Churchill expressed his appreciation for Stalin's attitude in his memoirs: "Stalin . . . adhered strictly and faithfully to our agreement of October, and during all the long weeks of fighting the Communists in the streets of Athens not one word of reproach came from *Pravda* or

Izvestiia." Indeed, the Soviet media even published Churchill's statements claiming that the insurgents were planning to set up a communist state. Stalin was punctilious about choosing when to focus public opinion on the matter by way of the media and when to keep his dissatisfaction private. While the Soviets remained silent in public, they did not hold their fire in private meetings and conversations. Developments in Greece finally gave them an opportunity to pay the British back for their criticism of Soviet practices at home and abroad.[8]

At a reception in Spaso House, the residence of the American ambassador in Moscow, on January 12, 1945, Ilya Ehrenburg, one of the leading Soviet journalists of the time, was quick to cite British actions in Greece when the British journalist Marjorie Shaw complained about Soviet censorship. When Shaw said that she was not responsible for what was going on in Greece, Ehrenburg exclaimed, "How can one talk with you English? You blame me when Petrov [the Soviet censor] cuts out two words, but you will never acknowledge actions of your government which embarrass you." The Soviet journalist did not drop the subject and later posed a rhetorical question, comparing Lord Byron, who had died in 1824 in the midst of a struggle for Greek independence, with contemporary British commanders: "There are good Englishmen and bad Englishmen. But which does one choose, Byron or General Scobie?"[9]

By the time of the Yalta Conference, the most acute stage of the Greek crisis was over, and Churchill could happily advise Stalin of its temporary stabilization. On February 8, 1945, when Stalin asked Churchill to describe the situation in Greece, the prime minister dodged the question, saying that he did not want to spoil the marshal's appetite before dinner. But Stalin was eager to remind the British premier about his restraint in Athens and did so more than once during the conference. He clearly expected a quid pro quo with regard to Poland.

Churchill, for his part, would not be intimidated into supporting the Soviets in countries that were not part of the October 1944 percentages deal. At Yalta he and Eden did not address Romania, but in Bulgaria, where they eventually agreed to 20 percent influence, they wanted the Soviets to stop speaking and acting on behalf of the Allied Control Commission without consulting them first. They also wanted the commission's decisions to be adopted on the basis of unanimity once the war was over. In effect, they were asking for the right of veto, which would have made the 80/20 deal useless from the Soviet point of view.

Yugoslavia, where both countries had agreed to split their influence down the middle, was especially tricky. Before Yalta, the British, who had consistently backed the creation of a Balkan federation, reversed themselves and opposed talks between Bulgaria and Yugoslavia that might have led to the creation of a federative structure. The Soviets, who had always opposed federations in

Eastern Europe, now favored a Yugoslav-Bulgarian understanding, hoping to increase their influence in Yugoslavia through Bulgaria, which was under their complete control. It was not this issue, however, but that of the formation of a new Yugoslav government that turned out to be the biggest bone of contention between the British and the Soviets at Yalta.

In Teheran, the Big Three recognized Josip Broz (Tito) and his communist-controlled partisan units as the main anti-Nazi force in Yugoslavia. In June 1944 the British supported the formation of a joint Yugoslav government including Tito's men and members of the London government in exile of King Peter II. They also increased their support of Tito's partisans by making regular airdrops of badly needed supplies. But the Tito-Šubašić agreement (signed by Tito and the head of King Peter II's government, Ivan Šubašić) on the formation of a new government was not fully implemented in the months leading up to the Yalta Conference. Šubašić, who was supposed to become prime minister, remained in Britain. Given his absence from Yugoslavia, Tito's administration lacked full legitimacy in the eyes of the world. The British wanted to amend the Tito-Šubašić agreement in order to reduce communist influence on the government before their man left for Yugoslavia to meet Tito and his subordinates.

On February 8, Anthony Eden proposed several amendments to the Tito-Šubašić agreement. Britain wanted to enlarge the Anti-Fascist Assembly of National Liberation of Yugoslavia, a quasi-parliament controlled by Tito's supporters, by adding members of the prewar Yugoslav parliament. They also wanted the assembly's acts to be ratified afterward by a broadly based constituent assembly. The Soviets did not object to the amendments themselves, but on the next day they blocked the British proposal, suspecting that London was in league with the exiled King Peter II and acting on his behalf. According to that logic, not allowing Šubašić to go to Yugoslavia also meant preventing him and Tito from forming a regency council to replace the exiled king.

The debate on Yugoslavia, short but heated, culminated at the plenary session of February 9. It was resolved to the satisfaction of both sides, given that Soviet suspicions of British collusion with the king were exaggerated, to say the least. Both sides obtained what they wanted. The Soviets received assurances that Šubašić would leave for Yugoslavia as soon as weather permitted. The British accepted Stalin's commitment that amendments to the original agreement would be accepted as soon as the new government began to function in Yugoslavia. On the following day Šubašić was able to leave Britain for Yugoslavia. A statement on Allied support for the Tito-Šubašić government was added to the final protocol of the Yalta Conference. The issue was resolved, but the debate hinted at trouble ahead. When Stalin said that Šubašić should come to Yugoslavia without further delay so as to keep the government in balance, Churchill responded that his absence from Yugoslavia would have no effect on the government, "as Tito was a dictator and could do what he wants." Stalin denied this, but Churchill's remark indicated that he understood who was in charge of Yugoslavia. So much for the 50/50 deal.[10]

In theory, the Declaration on Liberated Europe would put an end to unilateral actions by Allied powers in countries under their control. Greece and Yugoslavia were among the first to which it would apply. More urgent still was Poland. But the document signed at Yalta failed to include a mechanism for the implementation of its principles. The Americans were not prepared to commit themselves to anything. The British, for their part, had little enthusiasm for a declaration that included a dangerous reference to the Atlantic Charter, with its suggestion that all subject people should be free to choose their own government. And Stalin believed in the disposition of forces, not in declarations of principle.

Molotov later remembered that Stalin treated the declaration "warily from the outset." "The Americans submitted the draft," he recalled. "I brought it to Stalin and said, 'This is going too far!' 'Don't worry,' he said, 'work it out. We can deal with it in our own way later. The point is the correlation of forces.'" Molotov followed orders. His amendments, calling for the support of "political leaders . . . who have taken an active part in the struggle against the German invaders," would have given Moscow unlimited opportunities to interfere in the affairs of the occupied countries while ignoring all the other provisions of the declaration. Churchill's opposition prevented that from happening.

Molotov submitted a similar proposal at the foreign ministers' meeting on the evening of February 9, but the amendment was rejected once again, this time by Stettinius. At the foreign ministers' meeting the following day, Molotov proposed another amendment. If Roosevelt's text directed the signatories to create appropriate machinery for carrying out their responsibilities in countries in crisis, Molotov's amendment obliged them merely to arrange for consultations. As Molotov saw it, if the declaration did not reflect the interests of the USSR, there was no need to create machinery to implement its principles. Stettinius and Eden readily agreed to kill the last vestige of what was originally supposed to be the European High Commission. The amendment was eventually accepted.[11]

From an American perspective, the declaration was a success. It committed the United States to nothing, while placing responsibility on the Soviets and the British to behave according to its principles. The declaration was a public-relations insurance policy in case anything went wrong in Europe. Unfortunately, many things did.

22

IRAN, TURKEY, AND THE EMPIRE

"I absolutely disagree," exclaimed Winston Churchill, addressing a surprised Edward Stettinius, who had just begun his presentation of the foreign ministers' recommendations on the afternoon of February 9. Stettinius had proposed that the Security Council hold consultations on territorial trustee-ships and dependent areas before the United Nations Conference, so that a mechanism for dealing with colonial territories would be included in the UN Charter. "I will not have one scrap of British territory flung into that area," protested Churchill, according to notes made by Justice Byrnes. "After we have done our best to fight in this war and have done no crime to anyone I will have no suggestion that the British Empire is to be put into the dock and examined by everybody to see whether it is up to their standard. No one will induce me as long as I am Prime Minister to let any representative of Great Britain go to a conference where we will be placed in the dock and asked to justify our right to live in a world we have tried to save."[1]

Churchill's words echoed thoughts he had shared with his wife in a letter dispatched from Malta on the eve of his departure for the Crimea. Deeply impressed by his reading of Beverley Nichols's *Verdict on India*, he told Clem-entine: "Meanwhile we are holding on to this vast Empire, from which we get nothing, amid the increasing criticism and abuse of the world and our own people and increasing hatred of the Indian population." The prime minister understood the futility of the struggle to which he was committed, but he was determined to persevere as long as he was in office. He continued his letter: "However out of my shadows has come a renewed resolve to go fighting on as long as possible and to make sure the Flag is not let down while I am at the wheel."[2]

Admiral Leahy later wrote that he was pleased with the "courageous state-ment of the British leader," but he was in the minority. Later that day, Harry Hopkins told Lord Moran that the prime minister had spoken "so rapidly that he could hardly follow what he said." For the British delegation as a whole, it was an embarrassing moment. The prime minister's outburst resulted from a complete misunderstanding. The proposal Churchill regarded as a threat to the British Empire actually concerned territories that belonged to or were administered by Japan. Stettinius was simply reporting on the agreement, which had the full support of Anthony Eden and Alec Cadogan, who were present in the room. Churchill calmed down only after Stettinius explained that the provision on trusteeships was not intended to undermine the British Empire. He insisted on a clear statement that the provisions of the agreement did not apply to the empire.

Eden later remembered that the only participant who openly welcomed the prime minister's outburst was Stalin. "He got up from his chair," wrote Eden, "walked up and down, beamed and at intervals broke into applause. This embarrassed Roosevelt and did not really profit anybody, except perhaps Stalin, who was able to please himself and point to the division of his allies at the same time." When Churchill turned to Stalin for moral support and suggested that the Soviet leader would probably oppose the idea of internationalizing the Crimea, Stalin denied him any satisfaction. He was trying to make the most of the prime minister's embarrassment, although Churchill's argument corresponded closely to Stalin's own thinking about the special rights of the great powers over smaller nations. Over dinner on the opening night of the conference, Churchill had strongly disagreed when Stalin had argued that the great powers had won special rights because of their role in the war. Now he was employing the very same argument in defense of the British Empire. In doing so, he was also weakening his position as a critic of Soviet policies in Poland.[3]

Roosevelt was genuinely embarrassed by Stalin's reaction to Churchill's outburst, but he was probably not displeased to see Churchill humiliated on the issue of colonialism. Later that day, at the dinner that he hosted for the U.S. military commanders, he could not forgo the pleasure of making a few jokes at Churchill's expense. "He stated that he had had a great deal of trouble with Winston, who was in very bad form—his midday nap having been interrupted," wrote General Kuter, who attended Roosevelt's reception that night. "[T]he Prime Minister had sat at the table and drifted off into a sound sleep from which he would awaken very suddenly making speeches about the Monroe Doctrine. The President said he had to tell him repeatedly that it was a very fine speech, but that it was not a subject under discussion." The Monroe Doctrine, which served to justify the U.S. sphere of influence in Latin America, would normally be invoked by Churchill to counter American attacks on British imperialism. Roosevelt clearly believed that he had scored a point that day in their ongoing debate.[4]

Churchill's outburst removed any lingering notion in Roosevelt's mind that the British were prepared to relinquish their empire. As Eden put it, "[T]he Prime

Minister's vehemence was a warning signal to the Americans." Churchill was determined to maintain Britain's imperial possessions and, if possible, to extend the British presence in strategically important parts of the world. This applied particularly to Iran, where Britain was in possession of one of the world's largest oil refineries, had deployed troops since the summer of 1941, and was competing for influence and access to oil resources with both the Soviets and the Americans.

Stettinius informed the Big Three in the same report that the foreign ministers had made no progress in their discussion of the situation in Iran. Earlier that day Eden had proposed that British, Soviet, and American troops withdraw from Iran at the earliest possible date and had suggested that they postpone their negotiations on oil concessions. Molotov refused to discuss the proposal on the grounds that Eden's troop withdrawal proposal was new and had to be studied first. None of the Big Three commented on the issue. Iran became one of the irritants in their relationship and had the potential to complicate it even further.[5]

The British considered the Soviets the more dangerous adversaries. Since the nineteenth century, Russia had been competing with Britain for influence in Iran and Central Asia. In 1907 the Russians and the British had agreed to divide Iran, officially known before 1935 as Persia, into spheres of influence: Russia would control the north and Britain the south, with its vital strategic oil city of Abadan. This agreement, soon overtaken by the Russian Revolution, gained a new lease in August 1941, when Soviet and British troops occupied Iran in what might be called the first joint Allied operation of the war. The British moved in from the south and the Soviets from the north, securing oil refineries and the Trans-Iranian Railway. Oil and control of the supply route to the USSR were the main reasons for invading the country, whose leadership was drawing ever closer to Nazi Germany.

The invasion was not only the first successful Allied military action of the war—it was also the first betrayal of the lofty principles of the Atlantic Charter, which Churchill and Roosevelt had released to the general public on August 14, 1941. Eleven days later, on the first day of the Allied invasion of Iran, Reza Shah Pahlavi, the country's ruling monarch, appealed to Roosevelt to intervene in the crisis. He reminded the president of "the declarations which Your Excellency has made several times regarding the necessity of defending principles of international justice and the right of peoples to liberty" and added: "I beg Your Excellency to take efficacious and urgent humanitarian steps to put an end to these acts of aggression."

After a week of procrastination, Roosevelt told the shah that he could not intervene. "Viewing the question in its entirety involves not only the vital questions to which Your Imperial Majesty refers, but other basic considerations arising from Hitler's ambition of world conquest," the president wrote. He promised, however, to work with the British and the Soviets to issue a declaration stating that they would leave Iran when the war was over. In the following year American troops and advisers would in fact join the Soviets and the British in Iran to ensure the smooth functioning of the Lend-Lease route to the USSR, which led from the Persian Gulf ports to Soviet Azerbaijan.[6]

In November 1943, with Iran virtually an Allied protectorate occupied by armed forces of the great powers, its capital, Teheran, was deemed an ideal venue for a meeting of the Big Three. Besides discussing the campaigns against Germany and Japan, the Allied leaders found time to issue Roosevelt's long-promised declaration on Iran, pledging to withdraw their troops at the end of the war. The rhetoric concealed the actual military occupation of the country. "The Governments of the United States, the USSR, and the United Kingdom are at one with the Government of Iran in their desire for the maintenance of the independence, sovereignty and territorial integrity of Iran," stated the declaration. It ended with a peculiar promise: "They count upon the participation of Iran, together with all other peace-loving nations, in the establishment of international peace, security and prosperity after the war, in accordance with the principles of the Atlantic Charter, to which all four Governments have subscribed."[7]

After the Teheran Conference, the president decided to turn Iran into a showcase of American benevolence toward less fortunate countries. At the airport before leaving the country, he discussed his plans for rejuvenating Iran with his special representative there, General Patrick Hurley, who later prepared a memorandum along the lines they discussed on future American policy toward Iran. The president endorsed Hurley's memo in a letter to Cordell Hull, calling for the development of an "unselfish American policy" in Iran. He sent a copy of the memorandum to Churchill despite (or perhaps because of) its open attack on British imperialism in Iran.

Churchill was not pleased. He did not respond for three months and then wrote to the president, stating that Hurley "seems to have some ideas about British imperialism which I confess make me rub my eyes." The prime minister said that there was no conflict between imperialism and democracy. "I make bold, however, to suggest," he wrote, "that British imperialism has spread, and is spreading, democracy more widely than any other system of government since the beginning of time. . . . We are certainly no less interested than the United States in encouraging Persian independence, political efficiency and national reform."[8]

On the eve of the Yalta Conference, Iran became a battleground of the three Allies. The prize of the three-way contest was oil. The British discovered oil in Iran in 1908 and soon established the company that later became British Petroleum. They joined the Soviets in invading Iran in 1941 mainly to protect their foremost oil asset, the Abadan refinery in the south. American oilmen joined the game in 1943. They lobbied the Iranian government for oil concessions of their own, prompting the British to follow suit. Given their combined influence, there was every indication that such concessions would be forthcoming.

The activities of the British and American oil companies alerted the Soviets. In the fall of 1941, at one of the most difficult moments of the war, they refused a British offer to relieve Soviet troops in Iran so that they could join the fighting on the German front. In the autumn of 1944 Stalin sent a delegation to Teheran led by a deputy commissar for foreign affairs, his old acquaintance and former prisoner Sergo Kavtaradze, who had spent years in prison before being released in 1939. Kavtaradze's task was to secure exploration rights and oil concessions for the USSR in northern Iran. The Soviets behaved like the proverbial bull in the china shop, using pressure and threats to achieve their goal; as the Iranians complained to the British and the British to the Americans, they were not eager to pay royalties. The Soviet Union was an occupying power and a member of the Grand Alliance, so the Iranian government had little choice but to cooperate.

The Western Allies were in a position to be more insistent. With American encouragement (to the dismay of U.S. oil companies), the Iranian government announced that it would postpone all negotiations on new oil concessions until the end of the war and the withdrawal of foreign troops. The Roosevelt administration planned to remain in Iran with its economic development assistance programs after the war. The main winners were the British, who got to keep the Abadan oil refinery. The main losers were the Soviets, who would have no chance to take part in the Iranian oil bonanza once their troops were gone.

Kavtaradze tried to save the situation the only way he knew how—by coercion. During his audience with the young shah, Mohammad Reza Pahlavi, who had taken office after his father was forced into exile by the British-Soviet intervention, Kavtaradze resorted to threats. The Soviets used their troops to interfere with the movements of the Iranian army and mobilized their political ally, the procommunist Tudeh Party, to apply pressure on the government, causing the resignation of the Iranian prime minister, Muhammad Sa'ed, in November 1944. Parliament soon adopted a decree prohibiting the government from granting oil concessions in wartime. After months of trying to turn the tide in his favor, Kavtaradze left for Moscow empty-handed.

It was a major defeat for him personally and, as Stalin later told Eden, for Molotov as well. In the months leading up to Yalta, the Soviets did not abandon their plans for obtaining oil concessions in northern Iran. A report based on the Soviet press prepared by the U.S. embassy in Moscow on the eve of the conference summarized the Soviet position: "It was alleged that Sa'ed and his government were fascist in their outlook. . . . At the height of the controversy, *Izvestya* asserted that there was no legal basis for the presence of American troops in Iran."⁹

The Iranian government, caught in an undeclared war between the Allies, looked back to the happier days of the Teheran Conference and hoped that they would return. On January 18, 1945, the Iranian ambassador in Washington visited Stettinius and, on the instructions of his government, invited the Big Three to hold their next meeting in Iran. The ambassador was concerned about Russia's recent actions toward his government and said he hoped that at the next Allied summit the United States would show greater support for a strong and independent Iran. Stettinius assured his guest that "in his forthcoming conversations with Churchill and Stalin, [the president] would constantly keep their interests in mind."¹⁰

Before Yalta, Churchill had urged Roosevelt to put Iran on the agenda of their discussions with Stalin. When Iran first came up for discussion at the plenary session on February 7, Roosevelt delivered a speech that was full of compassion for the sorry state of Iran's economy and the plight of its people. He said that "Persia did not have the purchasing power to buy foreign goods, and if expansion of world trade was to occur measures must be considered for helping those countries like Persia that did not have purchasing power." The president considered Iran an ideal object for the activities of the "new world organization."¹¹

Roosevelt's pitch for Iran, which came in the midst of heated debates on Poland and the United Nations, made no perceptible impression on his counterparts. Churchill, according to Ivan Maisky, "politely listened to the president, but the premier's face registered boredom and hidden irony. Stalin remained silent and drew figures in his notebook." Roosevelt's appeal fell on deaf ears. Maisky himself was extremely skeptical about the issue and wrote in his diary that he could not believe his ears as he listened to the president. For Maisky, the Iranian question was defined by the presence of troops and access to oil resources. He did not doubt that those factors were also uppermost in American minds, even if the president appeared to be making an ingenuous (or naive) appeal on behalf of its poor. The only one who seemed excited about Roosevelt's speech was Edward Stettinius. In his memoirs he praised the president's conviction that the rich powers had an obligation to help less fortunate ones and noted, "It was this kind of vision on the President's part that made it such a privilege for those of us who had a deep interest in improving the lot of the less fortunate to work with him."¹²

The barely disguised irony with which Churchill listened to Roosevelt's pitch for a new Iran might well be explained by his suspicion that the true American agenda was only partly informed by idealism. The president's disdain for empires went hand in hand with his plans to use anti-imperialism and the promotion of free trade as vehicles to expand American power in the world. Roosevelt saw no contradiction between the interests of free peoples and those of the United States: he considered them complementary.

Stalin had his own reasons for skepticism. When, at the Teheran Conference, Roosevelt had approached Stalin with a proposal to create a trusteeship, with American participation, to build a new port in southern Iran and jointly run the Iranian railway, he had politely remarked that it was an interesting idea. He was not interested in turning a two-way contest for Iran into a three-way one. Given British opposition to the idea and the lack of Soviet support, Stettinius and his advisers were convinced that it should be dropped. They favored playing along with British interests in the region.

The British were pushing for the earliest possible withdrawal of all foreign troops from Iran, ahead of the schedule adopted at the Teheran Conference, where it had been decided that troops should pull out within six months of the war's end (by which point there would be no further need for the supply route to the USSR). Stettinius told Eden on Malta that he was prepared to accommodate this and that he would consider rerouting Lend-Lease supplies through the Dardanelles. He also promised American support in convincing the Soviets to withdraw their troops ahead of schedule. That would put the British back in control of southern Iran. State Department experts believed that "the continuance of the British Empire in some reasonable strength is in the strategic interest of the United States."[13]

Stettinius emerged at Yalta as a strong supporter of the British position on Iran. The Soviets showed no sign of following suit. Iran was first considered by the foreign ministers on February 8. Eden led the charge, taking on the role of protector of Iranian sovereignty. He stated that the Iranian government had to be master in its own house, free to make its own decisions. This was followed by an implicit threat: "[O]therwise the Allies might find themselves in competition in Iranian affairs. No one desired that." Eden did not question Soviet rights to obtain concessions but proposed a public declaration to the effect that the Allies would not press for concessions as long as their troops were in Iran. He also suggested that troop withdrawal begin as soon as possible after Lend-Lease supplies ceased to be delivered through Iran.

Molotov was unmoved. He said that the question of troop withdrawal would have to be studied first, which might take some time. It might also necessitate revisions to the agreement with Iran concerning the presence of Allied troops on its territory. As for oil concessions, he claimed that the USSR had sent a delegation to Teheran only after representatives of the Iranian government had expressed interest in granting concessions. The Iranians then changed their mind. Molotov was adamant that the crisis had been resolved: "Kavtaradze had returned and the strong-armed methods he had used have subsided." There was no need to discuss the matter at the conference, he said. The situation would "take its own course."

Stettinius's and Eden's assurances that they did not object in principle to Soviet oil concessions made no impression. Neither did their calls for a joint statement on the withdrawal of troops, which they argued would facilitate the resumption of negotiations. Eden's suggestion that the early withdrawal of troops would require no amendment to the treaty with Iran also fell on deaf ears. Molotov was determined to prevent any formal document on Iran from being adopted at Yalta. The only concession he was prepared to make was to summon Kavtaradze to Yalta to report on his actions in Iran. Unknown to the Western Allies, Kavtaradze was in fact already there, having arrived on January 30.[14]

Eden concluded the discussion on February 8 by undertaking to think about what Molotov had said and to prepare a new formulation. In fact, there would be no new formulation. Eden stuck to his guns and the next day submitted to the Soviet and American delegations a draft declaration that had every appearance of being the original British proposal. He wanted the Allies to issue a joint declaration promising the early withdrawal of their troops from Iran and the postponement of all negotiations on oil concessions until that process was completed. Molotov's statement that he had not had time to study the proposal was reported to the plenary session. Neither Churchill nor Roosevelt reacted to the news.[15]

The Soviets refused to discuss Iran. On February 10, the last full day of the conference, their demurral resulted in the most awkward diplomatic exchange recorded at Yalta. When Eden asked whether Molotov "had considered the British document on Iran," the Soviet foreign commissar responded that he "had nothing to add to what he had said several days ago on the subject." Eden reformulated the question: "Would it not be advisable to issue a communiqué on Iran?" "This would be inadvisable," came the answer. Stettinius tried to salvage the situation by suggesting that a phrase be added to the conference communiqué stating that "Iranian problems had been discussed and clarified during the Crimean Conference." Molotov said he "opposed this idea." Eden was prepared to compromise and proposed a statement to the effect that "the declaration on Iran had been reaffirmed and re-examined during the present meeting." "Mr. Molotov opposed this suggestion," stated the American protocol of the meeting.[16]

After the meeting Stettinius told Eden that he "was getting nowhere with this attempt and only exacerbating things." He wanted to drop the issue. But Eden refused, believing that there was "too much at stake," as he later wrote in his memoirs. Churchill refused to bring up Iran at the plenary session but did not object to Eden's raising it personally with Stalin. The Soviet leader, playing benevolent host, had once invited Eden to come directly to him if he had problems with lower-rank Soviet representatives.

When Eden decided to avail himself of this invitation, Stalin unexpectedly burst into laughter. "You should never talk to Molotov about Iran," he said. "Didn't you realize that he had a resounding diplomatic defeat there? He is very sore with Iran. If you want to talk about it, talk to me. What is it?" Eden softened his message. Instead of insisting on the early withdrawal of Allied troops from Iran, he proposed that all three Allies start planning troop withdrawals to be conducted after the end of the war. "Yes, I understand," Stalin said. "I'll think about it."[17]

It is hard to say whether this conversation had any impact on the Soviet position at Yalta. The conference communiqué was limited to a statement that the three foreign ministers had exchanged opinions on the situation in Iran and would continue their consultations through diplomatic channels. Contrary to Molotov's wishes, the Yalta communiqué mentioned Iran, though not in the way that Eden had wanted. Years later, Eden linked his conversation with Stalin to the withdrawal of Allied troops from Teheran in the summer of 1945.[18]

During the final days of the Yalta Conference, while Churchill and Eden were doing their best to protect their stake in Iran, Stalin made a last-minute effort to secure something that Russian emperors had always dreamed of but never managed to achieve—to take control of Istanbul and the Black Sea Straits. The Straits had been a subject of Molotov's discussions with Hitler in November 1940 and Stalin's conversation with Churchill in October 1944. Both the British and the Americans expected the Straits to come up at Yalta, but that did not happen until the last full day of the conference.

Stalin first expressed interest in discussing the status of the Straits during his private meeting with Churchill in the early afternoon of February 10. It was "intolerable," said Stalin, that the Soviet Union "should be at the mercy of the Turks, not only in war but in peace, and for Russia to have to beg the Turks to let her ships go through the Straits." He wanted to revise the Montreux Convention of 1936, which gave Turkey control over the Straits, and asked his guest what he thought in that regard. Churchill confirmed what he had told Stalin in October: he was not opposed to revising the convention; the Soviets had only to make a reasonable proposal. Stalin still had no written proposal: he wanted to introduce the issue at the forthcoming plenary session and then refer it to the foreign ministers. Churchill promised his support.[19]

Churchill had agreed long ago that the Soviets should be given some control over the Straits, and contrary to Eden's advice, he was not asking favors in return. In late January 1945, before departing for Malta, Eden sent Churchill a note assessing possible Soviet demands and proposing a British counterstrategy. The foreign secretary expected the Soviets to insist on territorial acquisitions in the Far East and a revision of the Montreux Convention. Eden advised

Churchill to insist on a quid pro quo with regard to such demands. The prime minister replied that he was not prepared to object to Soviet requests. Eden was forced to retreat.[20]

When Stalin addressed the plenary session on February 10, raising the question of the Straits, Churchill remarked with a smile, "I tried some time ago to get through the Dardanelles and the former Russian government had two army corps ready to help me at the other end. However, we did not succeed in joining hands. I consequently have some feeling on this question." Churchill was referring to one of the greatest disasters of his political career—the failed British attempt early in the First World War to take control of the Dardanelles by sea and a simultaneous land invasion of the Gallipoli Peninsula. The operation, proposed and tirelessly advocated by Churchill, who was then First Lord of the Admiralty, began in February 1915. The Turks fought back with unexpected rigor. Among their leading officers was an up-and-coming division commander, Mustafa Kemal, who would soon become successively the first speaker of parliament, first prime minister, and first president of the new Turkish state. In 1934 he would be given the honorific name Ataturk—Father of the Turks. After a year's fighting, half a million men had died on both sides.

The memory of the Gallipoli debacle and the desire to avenge it had haunted Churchill ever since. Stalin offered the prime minister his backhanded support. "You were in too much of a hurry to take away your troops," he said now. "Perhaps in another week you would have won as the Germans and Turks were getting ready to withdraw." Churchill did not disagree. "I had nothing to do with that decision," he said. "I was already out of the government." Churchill lost his seat in the cabinet owing to the public outcry about the disastrous course of the battle.[21]

In his presentation, Stalin repeated more or less the same argument for the revision of the Montreux Convention that he had made to Churchill in Moscow in October. "We believe that it is now out of date," he said. "The Japanese Emperor was one of the parties to it. In fact, he plays a greater role in it than the Soviet Union. The treaty was made at a time when relations between Britain and Russia were not very good. Now that is all changed. I do not think that Great Britain would with the help of the Japanese want to strangle Russia." Stalin's long-term goal was to establish Soviet control over the Straits and allow the presence of Soviet military bases in the area, but for now he did not want to alert the Allies to the full scope of his ambitions. "I do not wish to pre-judge future decisions," he said. "The interests of Russia should be taken into account and observed."

Roosevelt was the first to respond. "I only want to say," he remarked vaguely, "that we have three thousand miles of mutual boundary with Canada. There is no fort and no armed ship on this entire distance. If other parts of the world would do the same it would be a wonderful thing." Churchill, the next to speak, was more specific. As promised, he supported Stalin's request that the Montreux Convention be revised, but he wanted a concrete proposal. He also wanted to provide the Turkish government with assurances that its independence would be preserved. In the end, the Soviets made no specific proposal, and on Stalin's suggestion the issue was referred to a future foreign ministers' meeting in London. The Turkish government would be assured that neither the country's independence nor its territorial integrity was at stake.[22]

Control of the Black Sea Straits, the reconciliation of Allied interests in Iran, and the future of colonial possessions were all discussed at the conference, but they were given short shrift, partly because the three leaders knew they had no easy solutions to offer. These issues reemerged at the very center of the international agenda immediately after the end of the war. Turkey and Iran became the first battlegrounds of the Cold War, and former colonial possessions became objects of fierce competition between the two camps in the early 1950s.

First came the crisis over Turkey. The Western Allies' willingness to revise the Montreux Convention was certainly a step forward from Stalin's viewpoint, but it was hardly an indication that Britain and the United States would agree to a Soviet military presence in the area and de facto Soviet control of the Straits. The statements on the independence and territorial integrity of Turkey included in the final document of the Yalta Conference did not bode well. That is probably why the Soviets decided to revert to unilateral action, telling the Turkish government in March 1945 that they wanted to revise the Soviet-Turkish treaty. This came as no surprise to diplomatic observers in Istanbul, who had concluded by January that it was only a matter of time until the Soviets presented their demands.[23]

Turkey's decision on February 23, 1945, to abandon its neutrality and declare war on Germany and Japan did little to change Soviet intentions. Joseph Goebbels commented in his diary on March 21: "The Kremlin has revoked its treaty of friendship and non-aggression with Turkey. The reason given is extraordinarily interesting and original. The Kremlin declares that it is interested in retaining a solid relationship of friendship with Turkey; circumstances have changed with the war, however, and so the relationship between the Soviet Union and Turkey must be revised accordingly. Expressed differently this means that Stalin thinks the moment has now come to lay hands on the Dardanelles. Turkey has therefore reaped no advantage from declaring war on us at the Anglo-American behest and consequently appearing as a belligerent power. The Kremlin has not allowed itself to be affected by this at all." Goebbels was able to read Stalin's mind to a degree that few Western leaders could match.[24]

The Turkish crisis was one of the first sparks of the Cold War. Molotov later sounded almost apologetic in his private reminiscences. He blamed Stalin for committing an error, something that he did with great reluctance and very rarely. "In his last years Stalin got puffed up a bit," Molotov remembered. "In foreign affairs he had to demand exactly what Miliukov had demanded—the Dardanelles! Stalin said 'Go ahead, press them for joint possession!' Me: 'They won't allow it.' 'Demand it!'" Molotov believed that the Soviets could achieve what they wanted only if Turkey were a socialist state. Since it was neither socialist nor occupied by the Red Army, the Soviet foreign commissar was not inclined to repeat the demands for the Dardanelles voiced earlier by the tsar's generals and by Pavel Miliukov, the foreign minister of the Russian provisional government in 1917 and an archenemy of the Bolsheviks. In their official pronouncements the Soviets sought to conceal any link between their foreign policy and that of the Russian Empire. They justified their policies by referring to the will and interests of colonial peoples oppressed by the imperialist West. [25]

On the eve of Yalta, the British claimed that the Soviet push for oil concessions in northern Iran was just a first step toward the annexation of the region. Whether that was indeed the case or a self-fulfilling prophecy we will never know, but by May 1945 Molotov and Kavtaradze were already busy planning the creation of two puppet states on the territory of northern Iran, one for the Azeri minority and the other for the Kurdish one. Both states collapsed once Soviet troops left Iran in late 1946. The British stayed and retained control over the Abadan oil refinery, which became the world's largest refinery by 1950. American advisers also stayed in Iran.[26]

In July 1945 *Time* magazine reported the return from a three-year stint in Iran of the former superintendent of the New Jersey State Police, Colonel H. Norman Schwarzkopf. The colonel, who had become a national figure as a result of his efforts to solve the 1932 kidnapping and killing of the two-year-old son of the celebrated pilot Charles Lindbergh, told journalists that "his 21,000 Iranian cops—scattered over 628,000 square miles—now do their bandit-chasing on foot, wheel, horseback and camelback, dressed in uniforms modeled after the Jersey state troopers'." President Roosevelt's policy was in action. Later that year Schwarzkopf returned to Iran, accompanied by his family, to continue building up the Iranian police force. His involvement there fit perfectly into Roosevelt's vision of an "unselfish American policy."[27]

In Iran, however, as throughout the oil-rich Middle East, it was almost impossible to draw a clear line between unselfish policy and American economic and geostrategic interests. In 1953 Colonel Schwarzkopf was among those U.S. officials who facilitated the American- and British-backed overthrow of the Iranian government of Prime Minister Mohammad Mosaddeq, who had ordered the nationalization of Iran's oil industry in 1951. Thirty-eight years later, in February 1991, Colonel Schwarzkopf's son, General H. Norman Schwarzkopf Jr., led coalition forces against Saddam Hussein's Iraq in the name of the sovereignty of oil-rich Kuwait. He did so with a mandate from the UN Security Council. For the first time since the creation of the United Nations, the Soviet Union supported an American- and British-led military intervention. It seemed that the new international order promised at Yalta had finally arrived.

23

SECRET AGREEMENTS

Roosevelt awoke on the morning of February 10 in his bedroom in the tsar's former office at Livadia Palace determined that this would be his last working day at the conference. With the main objectives of the meeting already achieved, he wanted to conclude negotiations on issues still unresolved and leave as soon as possible. FDR's advance team of security agents was already in the Middle East, preparing his meetings with King Farouk of Egypt, King Ibn Saud of Saudi Arabia, and Emperor Haile Selassie of Ethiopia. Regional development and the creation of a Jewish state in Palestine were on the president's agenda there. Weary of the tough negotiations and convinced that further talks would only bring more of the same, he was ready to leave Yalta for the warmer climate of the Mediterranean.

If the Soviets did not learn of the president's plans through their listening devices, they got a clear indication that he was ready to wrap up when Admiral Ernest King and James Byrnes left Livadia after an early breakfast with Roosevelt and headed first to Simferopol and from there to the Saki airport to board a plane home. There were quite a few things that Stalin wanted to finish up before the president left Yalta, but none was more important than finalizing the deal on the Far East.[1]

At 2:00 p.m., after the meeting of foreign ministers, Molotov summoned Averell Harriman, the president's point man on the Far East, to Koreiz. He presented Harriman with a draft agreement on Soviet entry into the war with Japan. The agreement had been reached in principle between Roosevelt and Stalin, but the devil was in the details. What Chinese ports the Soviets would get, and under what conditions, had been left unresolved, as was Soviet control over the Manchurian railroads. On February 8, Roosevelt had mentioned only one port, Dairen. He was strongly opposed to a lease and had proposed instead that it become a free port. Stalin did not object. As for the Manchurian railroads, Roosevelt had noted that they could perhaps be operated jointly with the Chinese. Stalin left both options—lease and joint operation—on the table. The general notion of keeping the deal secret from the Chinese until the Soviets relocated their troops to the Far East was also open to various interpretations. All these points would now have to be clarified.

Molotov took that task upon himself. The Soviet protocol spoke unequivocally of leasing both the ports and the railroads. There was not a word in the text about consultations with the Chinese government either immediately or afterward. Molotov's proposal also advanced the Soviet claim to two Far Eastern ports, Dairen and Port Arthur. Port Arthur was on Stalin's original Far Eastern agenda, which had been presented to Harriman in Moscow in December. It had special significance for Stalin in both military and political terms, giving the USSR a warm-water seaport on the strategically important peninsula between mainland China and Korea and reaffirming Russia's return to the area after its humiliating defeat in the Russo-Japanese War.

Port Arthur had first become a Russian naval base in 1898. It was assaulted by the Japanese on February 8, 1904, in a surprise attack reminiscent of Pearl Harbor, with the difference that the attackers came by sea, not by air, and inflicted less devastating losses. The Russian navy survived this first attack. It was destroyed almost a year later by Japanese artillery besieging the city. The Russian defenders showed exceptional heroism, surrendering only after the complete annihilation of the fleet in early January 1905. The defense gave rise to a popular historical myth that exalted the heroism and patriotism of ordinary Russian soldiers and seamen. Now, by ensuring the Russian navy's return to Port Arthur, Stalin would revive that imperial myth and avenge the national humiliation suffered forty years earlier.[2]

Harriman was concerned by the extent of the new demands. Invoking the president's name, he promptly suggested amendments. First, he proposed that Port Arthur or Dairen be either leased or turned into an international port. Second, he added the option of joint control of the Manchurian railroads. Finally, he wanted to add a clause stating that the agreement on ports and railroads required the concurrence of the Chinese government. Molotov was prepared to accept the first two amendments but questioned the third. After all, the two leaders had agreed in principle not to inform the Chinese so as to prevent leaks and avoid alerting the Japanese. Molotov asked that the amendments be submitted in writing.

Harriman returned to Livadia to discuss the amendments with the president. Roosevelt approved the corrections, including the one on the need to consult the Chinese government, and the text went back to Molotov. In light of later developments, it was claimed that the agreement's fatal flaw was its failure to list the Kurile Islands, which the Soviet Union planned to annex, but the president never questioned the Soviet right to the whole Kurile chain, nor did

Harriman ever raise the question. At stake was the fair treatment of an ally, the Chinese government, not that of the enemy, which gave neither Roosevelt nor Harriman any pangs of conscience.

Stalin was unhappy with Harriman's additions. Apparently realizing that Harriman, not Roosevelt, was the main obstacle, he approached him later that day, saying he had nothing against internationalizing Dairen but needed a lease on Port Arthur, as he planned to turn it into a naval base. Harriman advised Stalin to raise the question with Roosevelt. Stalin obliged. He saw Roosevelt in his Livadia office together with Harriman and Bohlen. It would appear that Stalin's personal appeal fully neutralized Harriman's opposition to the Soviet proposal. He raised no objections, and the president agreed to the lease of Port Arthur, briefly forgetting his original argument that the lease of a Chinese port would make it more difficult to convince the British to leave Hong Kong.

Stalin was now satisfied and not opposed to making a concession of his own. He announced that he was in favor of jointly operating the Manchurian railways with the Chinese. He also agreed that he and FDR could secure the Chinese government's concurrence, but there was a catch, as he wanted the Chinese to guarantee the status quo in Outer Mongolia. He also wanted the Chinese to recognize the independence of Mongolia, the only Soviet ally in the region. The president did not object. He asked whether Stalin wanted to discuss the matter with Chiang Kai-shek himself. Stalin, who was by no means eager to do so, replied that he was an interested party and would prefer that the president do so himself. Roosevelt had little choice but to agree.

Roosevelt had at last secured Stalin's signature on a document that guaranteed Soviet entry into the war with Japan three months after the German surrender. Thanks to his last-minute bargaining, Stalin cleared the way for a Soviet naval base to be established at Port Arthur. The Soviet military presence there was bound to decide the issue of control of the railroads. The continuing existence of a formally independent Mongolia was another major achievement slipped in at the last moment. At the end of the meeting Harriman asked Stalin whether he would be willing to make the appropriate amendments to the original proposal, a gesture he must have regretted when he saw the final text of the agreement, which contained a new phrase stating that with regard to ports and railroads, the "preeminent interests of the Soviet Union shall be safeguarded." Harriman protested, but Roosevelt was not willing to raise a fuss about a few extra words. He insisted that Molotov's additions simply showed that the USSR was more interested in the area than the Western Allies.[3]

Harriman was unconvinced. He showed the draft to the American military advisers, hoping that if they objected he could raise the issue again with the president. But they were happy with what they were getting: a clear pledge of

Soviet entry into the war. Kathleen Harriman recalled that Admiral King a few days earlier reacted to the news with the words: "We've just saved two million Americans!" Harriman did not raise the question again.[4]

What Roosevelt had chosen to treat as a matter of language became a geopolitical issue when the Chinese government entered into negotiations with Stalin over its sovereign rights to the ports and the railroads. The exact meaning of Molotov's additions was indeed open to interpretation. When, in June 1945, Acting Secretary of State Joseph Clark Grew presented Foreign Minister T. V. Soong of China with the conditions of the secret treaty signed at Yalta, informing him that the U.S. government was committed to support the agreement "as it stands," Soong responded, "The question is as to just what you have agreed to support." Molotov's addition gave the Soviets a legal pretext to impose their will on the Chinese.[5]

When Churchill unexpectedly walked into the president's office on the afternoon of February 10, the conversation between Stalin and Roosevelt was almost over, and the last remaining problems in their agreement on the Far East had been ironed out. The prime minister later presented the whole issue as one of secondary importance to Britain. "In the United States," wrote Churchill— or, rather, one of the members of his "Syndicate," a group of assistants who helped him research and write his memoirs—"there have been many reproaches about the concessions made to Soviet Russia. The responsibility rests with their own representatives. To us the problem was remote and secondary."

This was not entirely true. The British Empire had formally been at war with the Empire of Japan since December 8, 1941, when the Japanese government declared war on both the United States and Britain in the wake of its attack on Pearl Harbor, and Churchill did not want to be "frozen out" of the agreement on the Far East. A day earlier, during discussion of the report from the Combined Chiefs of Staff on the planning of the war in the Pacific, he suggested that "it would be of great value if Russia could be persuaded to join with the United States, the British Empire, and China in the issue of a four power ultimatum" to Japan. He also suggested the possibility of negotiating surrender conditions with the Japanese, believing that this could hasten the end of the war. Roosevelt did not think that an ultimatum would work; he had nothing against mentioning to Stalin the possibility of a negotiated settlement with the Japanese.[6]

During their private meeting that morning, Churchill had asked Stalin directly about Soviet "wishes" with regard to the Far East. The Soviets, Stalin said, wanted a naval base at Port Arthur, while the Americans wanted the ports to be internationalized. Churchill was eager to support the Soviet position and said that Britain would "welcome the appearance of Russian ships in the

Pacific." He was also in "favour of Russia's losses of 30 or 40 years ago being made good." It is unclear whether Churchill realized that the Soviet presence in Port Arthur would make it more difficult for Roosevelt to drive the British out of Hong Kong or whether he had other considerations in mind, but his position obviously encouraged Stalin to make the British party to the agreements on the Pacific.[7]

While Roosevelt wanted to leave the British out of the Soviet-American deal on the Far East, Stalin wanted them in, probably seeing Britain as his main postwar competitor and wanting to secure its acceptance of his territorial acquisitions. The first draft of the agreement, proposed by Molotov on February 10, already listed Britain as a signatory. When Churchill was presented with the final version of the document on February 11, he was prepared to sign it, even though he was seeing it for the first time. Eden was less accommodating. He openly disputed with his boss whether Britain should be a signatory to the agreement. Cadogan was called in and advised against signing, but Churchill was unmoved. In the end he signed the agreement, arguing that failure to do so would undermine British authority in the area and exclude London from all future discussions of the Far East.[8]

"The actual agreement signed by the President and Stalin was entrusted to my care and kept in my secret files at the White House," wrote Admiral Leahy in his memoirs. He explained that "no publicity could be given to the agreement at that time because officially Russia still was at peace with Japan." As the secrecy of some of the Yalta accords came under attack in the American media after the end of the conference, Leahy, Harriman, and others invoked wartime conditions and the need for military secrecy as justification. But to one secret deal reached at Yalta this justification could not apply: it had to do with membership in the United Nations—an organization that was supposed to do away with the old balance-of-power system and all its secrecy.[9]

It was past 8:00 p.m. on February 10 when, before leaving for dinner, Roosevelt dictated his last letter of the conference. The matter he was about to raise was of a delicate nature. Having initially opposed giving UN membership to the Soviet republics on the grounds that one nation should have only one vote in the General Assembly, the president was now about to ask Stalin to increase the number of votes allocated to the United States.

"My dear Marshal Stalin," he began. From the outset he assured the Soviet leader that he would carry out his commitment and support the admission of Ukraine and Belarus to the United Nations. "I am somewhat concerned lest it be pointed out," he continued, "that the United States will have only one vote in the Assembly. It may be necessary for me, therefore, if I am to insure whole hearted acceptance by the Congress and people of the United States of our participation in the World Organization, to ask for additional votes in the Assembly in order to give parity to the United States." Roosevelt dictated a letter to Churchill along the same lines and asked that a copy of his letter to Stalin be sent to the British prime minister. He had postponed writing the letter until the last minute and finally succumbed to pressure from his advisers.[10]

James Byrnes was by far the strongest opponent of giving the USSR two additional seats in the General Assembly, and the main promoter of the idea of counterbalancing Soviet gains by assigning additional seats to the United States. Immediately after the president agreed to admit the two Soviet republics on February 8, Byrnes reminded him of his promise to the Senate Foreign Relations Committee to propose that all U.S. states be given UN seats if the Soviets continued to push for the membership of their republics. On the way back to Livadia from Stalin's dinner at Koreiz on February 8, Byrnes had tried on Edward Flynn the arguments he had used earlier that day in his futile attempt to persuade Roosevelt to oppose UN membership for Belarus and Ukraine. Byrnes believed that the proposal would provoke the same negative reaction as Britain's proposal in 1920 that its former colonies, now autonomous dominions, be admitted to the League of Nations. British insistence had spelled the end of U.S. support for the League. Soviet efforts to bring their proxies into the world organization, he argued, would have the same effect.

Flynn, the Irish Catholic chairman of the Democratic National Committee, could not have been more receptive: it was Irish Americans who had opposed the British proposal in 1920. He told Byrnes that Irish voters in New York and throughout the country would never agree to an arrangement that gave Britain six votes, Russia three, and the United States only one. The Dumbarton Oaks agreement was dead, he declared. Byrnes was probably not inclined to accept all of Flynn's views—a few hours earlier he had assured the president that the American public would now accept the seating of the British dominions in the United Nations, as they had established their autonomy since the end of the First World War—but what mattered was Flynn's general opposition to the Soviet proposal and his support for the parity of all the great powers in the General Assembly.

That was the principle Byrnes advocated over lunch with the president on February 9. Among the guests was Winston Churchill, and Byrnes managed to persuade both leaders that the number of American seats in the assembly should be increased in response to the inclusion of the two Soviet republics. Byrnes favored giving seats to Puerto Rico, Hawaii, and Alaska. No final decision was reached, but Churchill seemed to be on board. Hopkins, who was not present, also backed the plan. Under pressure from Byrnes and Hopkins, the president promised to raise the question with Stalin. He could not ignore political allies of the stature of Byrnes and Flynn.

After the plenary session that afternoon, Alger Hiss, the author of the State

Department memo arguing against the admission of the two Soviet republics, tried to persuade Byrnes to change his mind. Hiss argued that the best way out was to try to persuade Stalin to release the president from his commitment to support admission of the Soviet republics. Byrnes did not budge. He eventually won: the president fulfilled his promise and sent the letter to Stalin at the last possible moment. By that time Byrnes was already on his way back to Washington. It was anyone's guess what he would tell the press on his return. Roosevelt's press secretary, Stephen Early, sent a telegram to Washington warning his colleagues of Byrnes's arrival. The last sentence of Early's message specified that "final communiqué should be published, however, before Justice Byrnes says anything."[11]

Roosevelt was a reluctant participant in the whole undertaking, and it is not clear what he expected the outcome to be, or even whether he cared much. It appears, however, that Stalin saw Roosevelt's letter as an opportunity to obtain from his allies what he had failed to get earlier—a public commitment to the admission of the two Soviet republics. On February 11, when the Big Three gathered for the last time to discuss the communiqué and sign the final documents of the conference, Molotov proposed an addition to the section of the communiqué dealing with the creation of the United Nations: "It was also decided to recommend to the [San Francisco] conference to invite Ukraine and Belorussia as founding members of the international security organization." Roosevelt did not beat around the bush: it would be most embarrassing for him to add those words to the text of the communiqué. He proposed sticking to the original informal agreement among the Big Three: the Allies would support the admission of the two Soviet republics at the San Francisco conference.

Churchill, who had earlier sided with Stalin, now backed the president. He said that three members of his war cabinet opposed the violation of the "one nation—one vote" principle. He also expected protests from the dominions. He needed time to prepare the ground and would have to ask for an adjournment to consult with the dominions, which could take several days. There was a pledge with regard to membership for the two republics in the draft of the final conference documents, he argued, and he preferred that nothing more be said. Stalin decided that he would have to change tactics. "In that case," he said, "the Soviet delegation can withdraw its proposal." He suggested moving on to other issues. Roosevelt was quick to express his gratitude.[12]

After the meeting he received Stalin's answer to his letter. "Dear Mr. Roosevelt," Stalin wrote, "I entirely agree with you that, since the number of votes for the Soviet Union is increased to three . . . the number of votes for the USA should be also increased. I think that the number of votes for the USA might be increased to three." Roosevelt had never mentioned the number of additional seats he wanted for the United States. Stalin was probably calculating that the Americans would not agree to fewer than two additional seats, and that they might decide to seek parity with Britain and its dominions. He was prepared to agree to two additional American votes; two additional votes for the USSR meant much more to him than two votes for the client-rich United States.[13]

24

PRISONERS OF WAR

Churchill had two major questions on the agenda for his private meeting with Stalin on the afternoon of February 10. The first related to Poland: he wanted to ensure that the West would have observers in Poland in the weeks and months leading up to the promised elections. The second concerned Allied prisoners of war. The British prime minister did not get far on the first issue: Stalin refused to allow British officials into Poland until Britain had established diplomatic relations with the new Polish government. He was much more successful on the second.

As the Red Army seized and dismantled German concentration camps, it found itself in the position of liberating tens of thousands of Allied prisoners of war. And as the Western Allies approached German territory, they found themselves in control of tens of thousands and later hundreds of thousands of Soviet citizens. These included men in German uniforms—former Soviet POWs coerced by the Nazis to join their auxiliary formations—and civilians, some deported by the Germans and others fleeing the Soviets. The Western Allies were deeply concerned about the well-being of their prisoners of war and would spare no effort to get them back. They also had to deal with the growing number of Soviet nationals in their custody. Churchill needed Stalin's help to address both problems.

The prime minister began by expressing concern about the British POWs in Soviet custody. He asked Stalin to share information about them, to give British officers access to them, and to permit the Red Cross to send them supplies. He also wanted to send seven thousand of them to Odesa, from where they could be transported home on ships that would bring seven thousand Soviet citizens from camps in Britain. As the British note-taker recorded, "The prime minister spoke of the embarrassment caused us by the large number of Russian prisoners in the West. We had about 100,000 of them. 11,000 had already been transported home, and 7,000 more would leave this month. He wanted to know the Marshal's wishes about the rest."

Stalin promised full Soviet cooperation. He also had a few requests of his own. "The Soviet government would ask," Stalin said, "that those Soviet citizens who find themselves in Allied hands not be beaten or forced to become traitors to their homeland." He told the prime minister that the Soviet government considered both forced laborers and those who had taken up arms against the Allies to be Soviet citizens. "The Soviet government also asks the British government," he continued a few minutes later, "to keep Soviet citizens separate from Germans and not to give them the same treatment as Germans."

Churchill promised the full cooperation of the British government on all points. "The prime minister explained," recorded the British note-taker, "that we were anxious that these [Soviet] prisoners should be repatriated, and the only difficulty arose from a lack of shipping space. As regards segregating them from the Germans, this was difficult in the first instance, but as soon as they were sorted out, they would be kept separate." He did not question Stalin's comment that his government considered all categories of Soviets captured by the Allies to be Soviet citizens. The British government had already decided that Soviet nationals would be returned regardless of their wishes.[1]

If there was anything that Churchill did not understand, it was the reference to "traitors to their homeland," but he did not press for clarification. Yet that designation made all the difference in the world to hundreds of thousands of people who were repatriated to the Soviet Union, willingly or not, as a result of the Yalta agreements. With those words, they were sentenced to death or long imprisonment in the Gulag. One thing Churchill must have known was that Stalin's eldest son, Yakov, was a prisoner of war in Germany. He may also have known that Stalin had refused a German offer to swap his son for Field Marshal Friedrich Paulus. What Churchill did not know was that in the eyes of the Soviet regime, Yakov was a traitor to his homeland, and his wife had been sent to the Gulag to pay for the "sins" of her husband.

Yakov was one of the hundreds of thousands of Soviet POWs who were taken captive during the first months of the war, when the Germans surrounded whole Soviet armies whose commanders were under strict orders prohibiting retreat. As an artillery officer, he followed his orders to the letter, refusing to retreat. His sin was to have preferred German imprisonment to death in battle or suicide. Stalin said to his youngest son, Vasilii, "The fool—he could not even shoot himself!" Yakov made his father proud only when he committed suicide in April 1943 by jumping onto the wire fence of the Nazi concentration camp in which he was being held. Stalin ordered the return of his daughter-in-law from imprisonment. Death was the only act that could make a Soviet prisoner of war, even Stalin's own son, immune to the accusation of having betrayed his homeland.

The sons and daughters of Stalin's leadership cadres were given much the same treatment. Nikita Khrushchev, Stalin's lieutenant in Ukraine, simply adopted his granddaughter as a daughter when his son Leonid, a Soviet air force pilot, was shot down over Smolensk and presumed to be a prisoner of war. With his son allegedly in a POW camp and his daughter-in-law in the Gulag, punished for her husband's alleged betrayal, Khrushchev asked his granddaughter to call him "papa." It later became known that Leonid Khrushchev had died in battle. If that was how members of the Politburo treated their own children who had the misfortune to fall into enemy hands, they could hardly be expected to behave differently toward the sons and daughters of ordinary Soviet citizens who ended up on the wrong side of the Soviet-German front.[2]

It was three o'clock in the morning on January 2, 1945, when Valentin Berezhkov, who had been Stalin's interpreter in Teheran, was awakened by a phone call from his boss, Viacheslav Molotov, who wanted his assistant to report immediately to his office in the Foreign Commissariat. There was nothing unusual in such a call. Like other members of the Politburo, Molotov followed Stalin's example and worked into the early hours of the morning. Besides, the meeting of the Big Three was coming up soon, and Molotov had more to do than ever before. Berezhkov was actually lucky to have had New Year's Day off, as Molotov's other assistant, Vladimir Pavlov, was working that day. Berezhkov ordered a car from the Kremlin garage and soon arrived at the commissariat. He extended New Year's greetings to his colleagues, only to be given an unusually cool reception—their expressions told him that something was terribly wrong.

Molotov was in his office. He invited Berezhkov to take a seat and asked the question Berezhkov most feared: did he have any news from his parents? Berezhkov had grown up in Kyiv; his parents and sister had remained in the city when it was taken by the Germans in September 1941. In November 1943, after the Red Army retook the city, Berezhkov made a hasty trip to the Ukrainian capital to find out what had happened to his family. They were nowhere to be found. Berezhkov told Molotov about his fruitless trip on his way back to Moscow from Teheran, saying that his parents might have been deported by the Germans against their will. Molotov tried to calm him down. He assured him that his parents would eventually be found. This could only have increased Berezhkov's anxiety. He knew from his visit to Kyiv that his parents had worked in German-run institutions, and the Soviet authorities generally regarded such people with the greatest suspicion. Whether his parents had ended up in the West of their own free will or had been deported, his days were numbered. Sooner or later he would be fired, possibly sent to the Gulag, or simply eliminated.

Now Molotov explained to the frightened Berezhkov that Lavrentii Beria had sent a report stating that Berezhkov's parents, his sister, and her husband had willingly left Kyiv in September 1943. According to this report, Berezhkov's father, a former professor at the Kyiv Polytechnical Institute, had worked as an engineer in the department of heavy industry during the German occupation, while his mother had been an interpreter for the Nazi police. By Soviet standards, they were collaborators and traitors. The report went on to claim that Berezhkov's family had been visited by high-ranking German officials, and, concerned about their fate after the return of the Red Army, had left the city in a train provided by the Germans for *Volksdeutsche* (local ethnic Germans) and administrative personnel. Molotov explained that Beria wanted to conduct a further investigation but that Berezhkov could not remain in his position. This was also the opinion of Comrade Stalin. He ordered Berezhkov to surrender the keys to his office and told him to go home and await a decision on his case.

Berezhkov's pass to the Kremlin was taken when he left the complex. He spent two fearful weeks waiting for the midnight knock on the door, well aware that people had been arrested and shot for lesser "crimes." Finally, on January 17, Berezhkov received a telephone call. Molotov had saved his assistant. He was put in charge of producing German and English versions of the leading Soviet foreign-policy journal, *The War and the Working Class*. He was to discontinue all contact with foreigners, to tell no one what work he had performed in the Foreign Commissariat, and to use a pseudonym if he should decide to publish his own work. Berezhkov gladly accepted these conditions.[3]

In the months after his fall from grace, Berezhkov underwent a psychological crisis. "I became particularly upset on reading reports about the Yalta Conference," he wrote later. "It seemed that just yesterday all its participants had been side by side with me. Together with them I was supposed to have gone to the Crimea, entered the Livadia Palace, and interpreted Stalin's conversations with Roosevelt and Churchill. Over four years I had become used to being needed in all such cases. I was offended to tears, even insulted." The system had rejected Berezhkov, but it had also amazingly spared his life. He was lucky. The Soviet authorities never caught up with his family, and the accusations of collaboration remained just that—unconfirmed accusations. He survived not only Stalin, Beria, and Molotov but also the Soviet Union itself to tell his story.

The Berezhkovs did, in fact, leave Kyiv of their own free will. After reaching Bavaria, which became a U.S. zone of occupation, they emigrated to the United States, where they are buried at the Inglewood Park Cemetery in Los Angeles County. Had they found themselves in the Soviet zone of occupation, they would have been hunted down and sent back to the USSR. The NKVD had little difficulty locating people in its zone. At Yalta Churchill asked Stalin to help him locate his niece, Betsy Pongraz, and her family, who had been in Hungary when the war broke out and from whom he had not heard since. Stalin said he would do what he could. On March 3, the NKVD had located the Pongraz family in Budapest and placed it under Soviet protection.[4]

At Yalta the Western allies agreed to return not only prisoners of war but all Soviet citizens in their custody to the USSR, regardless of their will. Had Berezhkov made it to Yalta, he would have witnessed the signing of an agreement creating legal grounds for the forced return of his parents. He would have been well aware of the fate that would have awaited them.

On February 9 a battalion of the Russian Liberation Army, recruited by the Germans from former Soviet prisoners of war, was sent into battle against Soviet troops who had established a bridgehead on the right bank of the Oder in the vicinity of Küstrin, less than 70 kilometers from Berlin. It was the first time the Liberation Army soldiers had been allowed to fight. The battalion fought well, and four of its members, including the commander, Colonel Zakharov, were awarded the Iron Cross. The fate of Zakharov's men was decided not on the battlefield but at the negotiating table.

The Soviets often called Russians in German uniform *vlasovtsy* after Zakharov's superior, the commander of the Russian Liberation Army, General Andrei Vlasov. Like Stalin, Vlasov was a dropout from an Orthodox seminary; unlike Stalin, he joined the Red Army right after the revolution and had a distinguished military career before the Second World War. In the late 1930s he served as a Soviet military adviser to the government of Chiang Kai-shek. After the German invasion of the Soviet Union in June 1941, Vlasov led a successful counterattack that resulted in the temporary recapture of the town of Przemyśl, situated directly on the Molotov-Ribbentrop Line (and, later, the Curzon Line). His corps avoided encirclement at Kyiv later that year, and in December 1941 he distinguished himself in the Battle of Moscow. Soon he would run out of luck. In July 1942 Vlasov led an operation intended to lift the siege of Leningrad. Penetrating too deeply into German-held territory, his forces were surrounded. Vlasov refused to leave his troops and was captured by the Germans. He eventually became the driving force behind the creation of the Russian Liberation Army and had little difficulty in persuading his former subordinates to join the new formation.

Soviet prisoners of war in German concentration camps found themselves in an impossible situation. Outlawed by their own government, they were starved to death and treated as subhuman by their captors. More than three million of them, close to 60 percent of all Soviet prisoners in German custody, died of hunger and disease. The Soviet Union was not a signatory to the 1929 Geneva Convention, which governed the treatment of prisoners of war, and Berlin never responded to the Soviet offer, made in the summer of 1941, to extend the convention to Soviet and German POWs. None of the provisions of the Geneva Convention, which guaranteed that prisoners would be treated honorably, provided with food, clothing, and medical attention, and not forced to work in military-related fields, and which were applied in some measure to the British and American POWs, were observed with regard to the Soviet POWs. But legal niceties were hardly relevant: the Nazis regarded Slavs as *Untermenschen* and treated them with contempt.

When the Germans began to run short of manpower, many Soviet POWs accepted offers to join German auxiliary units—a decision that often made the difference between life and death. Ideological motives were sometimes a factor, especially in the case of the Vlasov units. The Russian Liberation Army declared as its goal the liberation of Russia from communism and the establishment of an independent Russian state. Andrei Vlasov and his soldiers went into battle for the first time during the Yalta Conference, fighting a war that was already lost and knowing perfectly well that nothing could save them from Soviet fury. Three months later, in early May, they turned their arms against SS units in Prague and helped liberate the city from the Germans. They then marched west and surrendered to the Allies on May 10.

Vlasov, who had earlier been offered a chance to escape to Spain, refused and once again stayed with his men. Two days later, on his way back from negotiations with American commanders, he was arrested by the NKVD in front of his American hosts. His men were soon sent back to the Soviet Union to face a military tribunal. Vlasov and eleven of his men were hanged in August 1946. That was the prospect facing every former Soviet citizen in German uniform, of whom there were close to a million. The Western Allies failed to grasp this. Knowing that there were Soviet *Hilfswillige* ("willing helpers") in German units in France, the Allies dropped leaflets promising them speedy repatriation to their homeland if they surrendered to Allied troops. There could hardly have been a greater incentive for the *Hilfswillige* to keep fighting on the German side.[5]

The American and British military missions in Moscow first raised the question of POWs with the Red Army General Staff in June 1944. Their concern was to facilitate the return of their own men, and they assumed that the Soviet POWs, increasing numbers of whom had been falling into their hands since D-Day, also wanted to go home. The Soviets were about to enter Eastern Europe, where most of the camps housing Western POWs were located, and it was high time to make arrangements for their speedy repatriation. The heads of the missions presented the Soviet military with a list of POW camps in the path of their troops and requested assistance in repatriating them.

There was no reply. The first thousand Western POWs were successfully flown out of Romania in early September, but this was done with the help of

Red Army commanders on the ground before Moscow took full control of the situation. It was the last major transfer of that kind. Afterward the Soviets would assure the Western Allies that they were doing all they could to help repatriate their POWs, but they refused to grant Allied officers access to prison camps where their POWs were being held. They would eventually be handed over deep in Soviet territory, in locations such as Odesa. Eastern Europe soon became out of bounds for the West, and the Soviet government was not prepared to make exceptions even on an issue in which it was itself deeply interested.[6]

In July 1944 the British Foreign Office first informed the Soviet ambassador in London, Fedor Gusev, about the growing number of Soviet citizens in British custody. In August the Soviets made their own requests for the return of their prisoners of war. By then there were close to twelve thousand Soviet POWs in Allied camps in Britain. Some had already been sent overseas to the United States and Canada. The majority were *Hilfswillige*, who had been taken captive in German uniforms. Soviet officials protested against giving Soviet citizens in Allied custody the status of POWs, claiming that they had been taken to Germany against their will. They had suffered enough and should be treated as citizens of an Allied state. The Soviets asked that they not be kept together with Germans or subjected to any form of anti-Soviet propaganda and that they be repatriated to the USSR as soon as possible.[7]

This show of concern was in sharp contrast to the Red Army's own treatment of *Hilfswillige:* they were shot on sight without even being court-martialed. Soviet officials had one main goal: to assure the speediest possible repatriation of their citizens. By denying them the status of POWs, who were protected by the Geneva Convention, they sought to remove all legal obstacles to their forced repatriation. And by projecting the image of a government that cared about its citizens, they sought to ease Western anxieties about the treatment of returnees. Moscow was eager to avoid leaving large numbers of former Soviet citizens in the West, as they might provide a basis for a massive anti-Soviet movement like the one that had developed in Europe after the Russian Revolution.

In October 1944 Stalin raised the issue over dinner with Churchill and Eden on their visit to Moscow. Molotov, who took part in the discussion, indicated that the Soviet Union had the right to demand the return of its citizens and said that POWs should be repatriated irrespective of their wishes. Eden agreed. In return he wanted help with the repatriation of British prisoners of war. In his private conversation with Stalin a few days later, Churchill said that the first Soviet POWs would soon be dispatched from Britain, and he tried to obtain assurances that they would be treated fairly.

"Most Soviet citizens were forcibly mobilized by the Germans into their army. Whole battalions surrendered to the British," Churchill remarked. Sensing what Churchill had in mind, Stalin told him more or less what he wanted to hear. "There are also scoundrels among those people, but we will not treat them very severely," he said. And that was the end of the conversation. Churchill noted that he felt himself responsible for their fate, as they had surrendered to the British, but Stalin turned the conversation to another topic.

From the outset, influential members of the British government, such as the minister of economic warfare, Lord Selborne, and the secretary of state for war, Sir James Grigg, opposed forcible repatriation of the Soviet POWs to the USSR. When the British government began to receive reports that Soviet POWs were committing suicide rather than return to the USSR, the policy of forced repatriation became even more controversial. Eden believed that it had to be done to ensure Soviet cooperation on the return of British prisoners of war. His line eventually prevailed. The first shipment of Soviet POWs left for Murmansk on October 31, 1944, less than two weeks after Churchill and Eden's return from Moscow. Ten thousand people were sent home on British ships.[8]

The Americans, who had been pressing the Soviets for months to begin consultations on the repatriation of POWs, finally got their answer at the end of November. Molotov informed the American embassy in Moscow that the Soviets were prepared to discuss the issue but were interested in more than POWs. They wanted to talk about the treatment and repatriation of Soviet citizens forcibly deported by the Germans. "The immediate rendering of assistance and return to their homes of Soviet prisoners and also Soviet citizens forcibly deported by the Germans to Germany and German occupied countries who have been liberated as a result of Allied military operations in the west is of interest to the Soviet Government," the letter stated.

Unlike the British, the Americans decided very early on against the forced repatriation of Soviet citizens. They treated them as they treated the Germans, applying the terms of the Geneva Convention. Doing otherwise, the Americans believed, would provoke German reprisals against U.S. prisoners in their custody. The Soviets did not agree with that approach. Again and again, they protested that their citizens should not be treated as POWs and kept in the same camps as the Germans. On the surface it appeared that they were being overprotective, and that annoyed some Americans. "It was the old question of Russians, captured in German uniforms while in the act of shooting at American soldiers," wrote General John Deane in his memoirs. "We could hardly be expected to put them up at the Ritz in Paris or the Mayflower in Washington—at least not until we found out that they were really our friends."[9]

In the months leading up to the Yalta Conference, the Soviets continually harassed their Western counterparts with complaints about the alleged mistreatment of Soviet citizens in Allied custody. In November 1944 Colonel General Filipp Golikov, a former head of Soviet military intelligence whom readers of *Time* magazine knew as one of the young commanders who had defeated the Germans at Stalingrad, published an article criticizing the Allies for their treatment of Soviet citizens in their custody. Golikov wrote about millions of Soviet nationals brought to Western Europe by the Germans as forced laborers. He also mentioned those who had been forced by the Germans to take up arms and who had deserted at the first opportunity and joined the Allies. Now, complained the general, they were being kept in the same POW camps as Germans, who were being given preferential treatment.[10]

"Great interest was shown in the return of all categories of Soviet nationals or persons who could be claimed as such, particularly those found among German forces by the Allies," the U.S. embassy in Moscow told Washington in its overview of the Soviet press. "Extreme touchiness was shown over reported reluctance of many of these people to return, and over alleged encouragement being given to such sentiments by foreign authorities. Press stories of warm reception accorded repatriates did not check with reports of Embassy observers, and apparently reflected a desire to disarm suspicions of those still abroad."[11]

Soviet complaints about the mistreatment of Soviet citizens in Western camps were designed to counterbalance Western complaints about the Soviet authorities' failure to take proper care of Western POWs in their custody. The more the Soviet side came under attack for its failure to allow British and American officers access to their POW camps and for delaying the transfer of their POWs to points where they could be picked up, the more the Soviets complained about the alleged mistreatment of their citizens in Western custody.

On January 11, in the midst of preparations for his departure to Yalta, Ambassador Andrei Gromyko found time to call Undersecretary of State Joseph Grew to discuss an accident that had taken place at the POW camp in Rupert, Idaho. Gromyko informed Grew, who was unsure of the location of the town and referred to it in his memorandum of the conversation as Rupert, Iowa, that there were close to a thousand Soviet citizens detained in that camp, and some of them had been viciously beaten by the commanding officer, Captain Morton Gwyn. Gromyko demanded that an investigation be held and that Captain Gwyn be removed from his post. "It was extremely distasteful to him to have to inform his Government that treatment of this kind could take place in an American camp," declared the ambassador.[12]

By continually raising complaints about Allied treatment of their POWs, the Soviets tried to harass their Western counterparts into quickly transferring them to Soviet custody. This was the solution Anthony Eden had suggested in Moscow in October 1944. Churchill later endorsed the position that the sooner the British got rid of Soviet POWs in their custody, the better. The question was how to assemble enough ships to send them to the Soviet Union. Repatriation would not only remove a thorny issue from the diplomatic agenda and end the headache of military administrators but also pave the way for speeding the repatriation of Western POWs.

On January 3, 1945, Stettinius cabled Harriman that the first 1,100 Soviet POWs held in U.S. camps had been turned over to the Soviet authorities on the West Coast. The U.S. government was thus prepared to carry out Soviet demands even before negotiations had begun, as long as the returnees agreed to go home. But there was a problem about which Stettinius wanted to warn the ambassador: "Department is extremely anxious that in any discussion concerning the repatriation of American and Soviet prisoners of war and civilians there be no connection between the return of Americans . . . and Soviet nationals." The American embassy in Moscow, which for months had been insisting on a reciprocal agreement, was now told to abandon its own position.

Who was and who was not a Soviet citizen was a murky question in itself. The Americans and the British, who had originally been assured by the Soviet command that there were no Russians in German uniforms, were now faced with the enormous task of separating them from the rest of the prisoners. That task was complicated by the fact that the Soviet POWs claimed German citizenship on the basis of their service in the German army and the rights of POWs according to the Geneva Convention. They insisted on being treated as Germans, not as Russians, and the last thing they wanted was to be put in separate camps and then repatriated to Stalin's USSR.

"Among the persons fighting with the German troops are a few with Slavic names who disclaim Soviet nationality," read Stettinius's telegram. A few weeks later, on January 22, Stettinius informed the American embassy in Moscow that the Soviets had contacted the U.S. Sixth Army to say that they considered natives of the Baltic states and former Polish territories east of the Curzon Line to be Soviet citizens. The U.S. military refused to accept that definition, insisting that "displaced persons are of the particular nationality they claim to be and that their claim for repatriation is accepted by the appropriate Allied liaison officer."

The U.S. administration also decided to stand firm on the issue of Soviet defectors who had asked for political asylum in the United States. On January 5, Stettinius, Attorney General Francis Biddle, and FBI chief J. Edgar Hoover decided to turn down a Soviet request to extradite the most prominent Soviet defector at the time, an employee of the Soviet trade mission in the United States, Viktor Kravchenko. The Americans considered the topic so important that Stettinius's Yalta briefing book began with materials on Kravchenko, but the Soviets never raised the issue.[13]

In January it seemed that after a long period of procrastination the Soviets were beginning to cooperate. They responded positively to a British proposal and met with the Americans. The often critical General Deane was happy with the meeting. "After a few rounds of vodka we parted on a note of cordiality that was never again to be attained," he wrote in his memoirs. Everyone agreed that it would make sense to sign an agreement on prisoner swaps at the meeting of the Big Three. The only problem was how to prevent it from getting lost among all the other important issues.[14]

The first tripartite meeting to discuss prisoners of war took place in the late afternoon of February 9 and included General Deane on the American side, Rear Admiral E. R. Archer for the British, and Kirill Novikov, representing the Soviet Foreign Commissariat. The Soviets did not want the United Nations Relief and Rehabilitation Administration to be mentioned in the agreements as a supplier of food for liberated prisoners and civilians, as that would interfere with their policy of restricting the access of Western representatives to their territory. On the following day, that attitude prompted Churchill to raise the issue of supplies to liberated prisoners of war at his private meeting with Stalin. With Eden by his side, the prime minister not only discussed the fate of Soviet prisoners in British custody but also asked about the British prisoners released during the Red Army's winter offensive. "He begged for good treatment for them," reads the British protocol of the meeting; "every mother in England was anxious about the fate of her prisoner son." He also "said we wanted to send liaison officers to the Red Army to look after our men." Stalin agreed.[15]

Agreement on the repatriation of liberated prisoners of war and civilians was reached on the last day of the conference, February 11. By that time Eden had completely won over Stettinius, who decided to ignore the advice of Joseph Grew, based on the recommendations of the U.S. attorney general, that captured Soviet citizens should be given the rights guaranteed by the Geneva Convention. There would be no reference to the Geneva Convention in the agreements. The Combined Chiefs of Staff endorsed the document, as General Eisenhower urged headquarters to make a decision on the repatriation of twenty-one thousand Soviet POWs in American custody in Western Europe. The State Department formally had nothing to do with the agreement. The American document was signed by General John Deane.

The Soviet-British document was signed by Eden himself. He also signed a number of accompanying documents that put Soviet POW camps in Britain under Soviet command and jurisdiction, evidently in haste, as he had to send Molotov two separate letters from Vorontsov Palace clarifying what the British side had meant with regard to Soviet jurisdiction over the POW camps in Britain, and stating that he had no authority to accept one of the conditions on behalf of Australia. Cadogan was pleased with the result.[16]

The two bilateral agreements provided that each party would immediately inform the other of its citizens in its custody, place them in separate camps, allow access by officers of the respective countries to their compatriots, and prevent the dissemination of propaganda directed against them. Neither the

American nor the British agreement made any mention of forced repatriation. The relevant part of the Soviet-American document read: "All Soviet citizens liberated by the forces operating under United States command and all United States citizens liberated by the forces operating under Soviet command will, without delay after their liberation, be separated from enemy prisoners of war and will be maintained separately from them in camps or points of concentration until they have been handed over to the Soviet or United States authorities, as the case may be, at places agreed upon between those authorities." There was nothing in the Yalta documents that obliged the Western Allies to repatriate Soviet citizens against their will.[17]

That did not stop the Soviets from demanding forced repatriation of Soviet POWs, allegedly on the basis of their agreements. In March 1945 the Foreign Commissariat forwarded a note to the U.S. State Department protesting that the Americans were keeping a group of Soviet citizens in their custody under various pretexts. "The Soviet government insists on the repatriation of all former Soviet prisoners of war remaining in the camps of the USA, and on the transfer of . . . Soviet citizens to representatives of the USSR, in conformity with the agreement of February 11, 1945." The State Department continued to resist Soviet requests for the extradition of those Soviet citizens who had been captured in German uniform and claimed the protection of the Geneva Convention until the end of hostilities in Europe. But then the department's position suddenly changed. As Joseph Grew explained in a letter to Secretary of the Navy James Forrestal, he did not object to extradition "now that Germany has unconditionally surrendered, that all American prisoners of war held by the German armed forces have been liberated and that therefore there no longer exists any danger that the German authorities will take reprisals against American prisoners of war."

On June 29, after learning of the decision to extradite them to the USSR, 154 Soviet prisoners of war in Fort Dix, New Jersey, shut themselves in their barracks and attempted to commit mass suicide. The American guards fired tear-gas grenades into the building, forcing the prisoners to break out of their quarters. Seven POWs were gunned down by the guards as they rushed at them. In the barracks they found three men hanging from the rafters next to fifteen nooses prepared for the next group. News of the revolt of Soviet prisoners who preferred death to extradition leaked out to the press, aborting the next attempt to ship POWs to the USSR. In August, however, James Byrnes, who succeeded Stettinius as secretary of state, authorized extradition "in conformity with commitments taken at Yalta."

A Canadian report on the return to the USSR of one group of Soviet POWs from camps in Britain tells a horrific story about what awaited the returnees upon their arrival:

The disembarkation started at 1830 hrs. and continued for 4½ hrs. The Soviet authorities refused to accept any of the stretcher cases as such and even the patients who were dying were made to walk off the ship carrying their own baggage. Two people only were carried off: one man with his right leg amputated and left one broken, and the other unconscious. The prisoner who had attempted suicide was very roughly handled and his wound opened up and was allowed to bleed. He was taken off the ship and marched behind a packing case on the docks; a shot was then heard, but nothing more was seen. The other 32 prisoners were marched or dragged into a warehouse 50 yards from the ship and after a lapse of 15 minutes, automatic fire was heard coming from the warehouse; twenty minutes later a covered lorry drove out of the warehouse and headed towards the town. Later I had a chance to glance into the warehouse when no one was around and found the cobbled floor stained dark in several places around the sides and the walls badly chipped for about five feet up.

The most notorious case of forced extradition of refugees claimed by the Soviet Union as its citizens took place in late May 1945, in the Austrian city of Linz. There the British authorities forcibly repatriated thousands of Russian Cossacks led by the Cossack generals Petr Krasnov and Andrei Shkuro, commanders of White forces who had fought the communists during the revolution and then emigrated to the West. Krasnov and Shkuro and their closest associates were hanged in Moscow in 1947.[18]

The agreement on the treatment of liberated prisoners of war turned out to be one of the most controversial documents signed at Yalta. Diplomats such as Charles Bohlen subsequently pointed a finger at the military, which was in charge of the execution of the agreements. While Allied commanders knew what was going on, as they had to deal with the refusal of many former Soviet citizens to return home, their freedom of action was restricted by concern about their own POWs. General Deane, who signed the agreement for the American side and was troubled by the lack of progress on the repatriation of Americans, called the winter of 1944–45 the darkest period of his mission to Moscow but never mentioned the forced repatriation of Soviet POWs as a matter of major concern. He was preoccupied with the fulfillment of his principal duty, the return of his compatriots.[19]

The POW agreement exposed a fundamental difference between the Allies, who had joined together to fight a common enemy but took opposing positions on soldiers and civilians who had fallen into enemy hands and on the right of citizens to leave their homeland at will. There was no higher priority for soldiers of the Western democracies at the end of the conflict than to save their prisoners of war. There was no greater crime in the Soviet code than that of falling into enemy hands. In their approach to their subjects, the Soviet author-ities followed the age-old tradition of the tsars of Muscovy. The inhabitants of lands instantly became subjects of the autocrat, and any opposition to his will became an act of treason. Like runaway serfs, they had to be caught and brought back to their master. The fact that the revolution had removed the tsar had changed little in the mentality of the rulers. The erring subjects, now called citizens, were still regarded as traitors.

PART VI

THE SPIRIT OF YALTA

The best friendships are those founded on misunderstandings.

JOSEPH STALIN

25

THE LAST SUPPER

Close to nine o'clock on the evening of February 10, Winston Spencer
Churchill sat in the reception room of Vorontsov villa, waiting for his
guests of honor. He was doing his best to play the genial host. "Churchill, with
his great sense of showmanship and appreciation of military pomp," recalled
Edward Stettinius, "had a regimental guard lined up on the steps of the villa."
The problem was it was not the only guard in place. The prime minister
glanced at the Soviet soldiers who had arrived a few hours earlier and were now
standing near the entrance. "They locked the doors on either side of the reception rooms which were to be used for dinner. Guards were posted and no one
was allowed to enter. They then searched everywhere—under the tables and
behind the walls. My staff had to go outside the building in order to get from
their offices to their own quarters," Churchill recalled a few years later.

Dinner was scheduled for eight thirty, but it was already close to nine, and
not one guest was in sight. It had been a long and difficult day. Churchill had
fought tooth and nail to reduce German reparations: Ivan Maisky, whom he
knew quite well from his years as Soviet ambassador in London, had pushed
for exorbitant terms. "The little man, with his slanting eyes and pointed beard,
asked for his pound of flesh as if he were addressing the students of the London
School of Economics," wrote Lord Moran. "When Winston told me about the
discussion he spoke as if he felt very sad about the greed and folly of the Russians. And I noticed a grey look about his gills which I haven't seen before."

Churchill was so upset by Roosevelt's readiness to accommodate Soviet
demands that after lunch he skipped their prearranged meeting and went
instead to see Stalin. Then there was the president's desire to leave Yalta as
soon as possible. A few hours earlier Roosevelt had suddenly announced that
he would be leaving the conference the next day at 3:00 p.m., which came as a
shock to the British delegation. "It was pointed out by everyone that it would
be quite outside of the limits of possibility to get everything tidied up in time.

But the President remained quite unmoved although he could produce no sort of reason why he should leave today or why at 3:00 p.m.," wrote an irritated Cadogan on the following day, having had to work until 1:30 in the morning to get the documents ready for signing.

When Anna Boettiger told Sarah Oliver that the president would have to leave to keep important appointments, Sarah was far from impressed. "As if," she told Lord Moran, "the Conference isn't so much more important than anything else." The prime minister shared his daughter's view. He was not pleased that Roosevelt was rushing through the end of the conference in order to meet Ibn Saud of Saudi Arabia and other Middle Eastern leaders in the Mediterranean—practically Churchill's own backyard.

The only good news was coming from the western front. Before the Big Three wrapped up their last full session and left for their quarters to prepare for dinner, Churchill announced that "British troops began an attack at dawn yesterday in the Nijmegen area. They advanced about three thousand yards and are now in contact with the Siegfried line." The British were approaching the German fortifications built in the 1930s against the French Maginot Line and preparing to enter Germany itself. They were finally "closing on the Rhine," as Churchill often described their advance toward the river, and that gave him some satisfaction. "The offensive will continue without cessation," he concluded triumphantly.[1]

Finally the guests arrived. The president, who was wheeled in first, loudly apologized for being late. "I could not get something done up," he said, his voice deep and strained. He had just signed his letters to Churchill and Stalin asking for additional seats in the UN General Assembly. Then, almost immediately after Roosevelt, came Stalin. His guards had noticed that one of the British female staffers had left a purse by the window. Stalin would not enter until the lady had been made to remove her purse. The dictator, paranoid about his personal security, arrived, according to Churchill, "in a most cordial mood." "May I escort you?" Churchill asked, and led him into the banquet room.

Compared with Stalin's dinner at Koreiz Palace, where the guests had included military commanders and "the girls"—Anna Boettiger, Sarah Oliver, and Kathleen Harriman—the British reception was a fairly modest event. Stalin came with Molotov and his favorite interpreter, Vladimir Pavlov. Roosevelt was accompanied by Stettinius and Charles Bohlen, Churchill by Eden and Major Arthur Herbert Birse, who interpreted for the British. They had cocktails and were then invited to the dinner table.

The menu, printed on the prime minister's personal letterhead, with the address "10 Downing Street, Whitehall" in the upper right-hand corner, perfectly reflected the situation: the British were playing host, but the Soviets were clearly in charge. Some of the courses were deeply familiar: "Caviare Pies,"

"White and Red Salmon," "Suckling Pig with Horse-radish Sauce," and "Shash-lik of Mutton," a grilled shish kebab. Privately the British complained about the excessive food and alcohol and the limited selection, repeated from one reception to the next. This time they were likely pleased by the addition of "Roast Turkey," "Green Peas," and "Roasted Almonds"—dishes that had not been on the almost identical menu at Stalin's reception two days earlier. The British reception was less formal. As Churchill later recalled, once dinner was over, conversation continued in smaller groups.[2]

The prime minister was first to raise his glass. He proposed a drink to "the health of His Majesty the King, the President of the United States, and President Kalinin of the U.S.S.R., the three heads of the three States." Churchill was delighted to play the gracious host, but the tensions of the day would not subside, and the toast was a slap at Stalin. Two days earlier, Stalin had toasted the health of the king in a backhanded way that had upset Churchill, saying that he was generally on the side of the people, not kings, but that in this war he had learned to honor the British people, who honored their king, and so he was prepared to raise a toast to the king's health. Churchill told Molotov that he would prefer it if future toasts were limited to the three heads of state. He was now introducing this practice and asked the president, as the only head of state present, to respond.

Churchill, who had two distinguished guests at the table, deliberately toasted only one of them, doing so in a way that most probably irritated the other. Roosevelt "seemed very tired," as Churchill later recalled, but sensed the awkwardness of the situation. "The Prime Minister's toast recalls many memories," he began. "In 1933 my wife visited a school in our country. In one of the classrooms she saw a map with a large blank space on it. She asked what was the blank space, and was told they were not allowed to mention the place—it was the Soviet Union. The incident was one of the reasons why I wrote to President Kalinin asking him to send a representative to Washington to discuss the opening of diplomatic relations." Roosevelt concluded his response by stating, "That is the history of our recognition of Russia." As had often happened during the conference, Churchill tried to get back at Stalin, only to have Roosevelt support him.[3]

Stalin apparently decided that the time was right to seize the initiative. He told Churchill that he "feared to have to go back . . . and tell the Soviet people they were not going to get any reparations because the British were opposed to it." The prime minister, who had been upset a few hours earlier by the "greed and folly of the Russians," now found himself on the defensive. "[O]n the contrary," he said, "he very much hoped that Russia would receive reparations in large quantities, but he remembered the last war when they had placed the figure at more than the capacity of Germany to pay." Churchill fell into his own trap and agreed a few minutes later to something he had vehemently opposed:

that reparations could be mentioned in the communiqué, along with the statement that the USSR and the United States had agreed to take the sum of $20 billion as a basis for future discussions, with half going to the Soviet Union.[4]

Stalin could savor his victory. Churchill proposed another toast, this time to Stalin's health. "I have drunk this toast on several occasions," he began. "This time I drink it with a warmer feeling than at previous meetings, not because he is more triumphant, but because the great victories and the glory of the Russian arms have made him kindlier than he was in the hard times through which we have passed. I feel that, whatever differences there may be on certain questions, he has a good friend in Britain. I hope to see the future of Russia bright, prosperous, and happy. I will do anything to help, and I am sure so will the President. There was a time when the Marshal was not so kindly towards us, and I remember that I said a few rude things about him, but our common dangers and common loyalties have wiped all that out. The fire of war has burnt up the misunderstandings of the past. We feel we have a friend whom we can trust, and I hope he will continue to feel the same about us. I pray he may live to see his beloved Russia not only glorious in war, but also happy in peace."[5]

Stettinius, who believed that Molotov and Maisky had pressured Stalin into raising the question of reparations once again, was now eager to assure the Soviet leader of American goodwill. He told Stalin that if their two countries worked together after the war, every home in the Soviet Union would have electricity and plumbing, unconsciously echoing Lenin's famous phrase that communism meant Soviet power plus the electrification of the whole country. Although plumbing was not included in Lenin's package, Stalin presumably would not mind throwing it in as well. He nodded and said, "We have learned much already from the United States."[6]

Roosevelt was happy to elaborate on Churchill's theme of overcoming mutual misunderstandings. He recalled his conversation with the head of the chamber of commerce at a reception in a small town in the American South. His interlocutor, a member of the Ku Klux Klan, was flanked by an Italian and a Jew. Roosevelt asked whether they also belonged to the Ku Klux Klan, hinting at its anti-Jewish and anti-Catholic attitudes. Yes, came the answer. "[T]hey were considered all right since everyone in the community knew them. [I]t was a good illustration of how difficult it was to have any prejudices—racial, religious or otherwise—if you really knew people," concluded Roosevelt, drawing an unexpected moral from his curious story. Stalin agreed.[7]

The tone of the conversation had shifted. The talk centered on the coming elections in Britain, which Churchill was obliged to call immediately after the end of hostilities, with Stalin and Roosevelt trying to encourage him as best they could. The Communist dictator and the Democratic president crossed ideological lines to give political advice to the Conservative prime minister. For a moment, the three statesmen found common ground in their life experiences. Stalin refused to take Churchill's worries seriously. "[T]he people would understand that they needed a leader, and who could be a better leader than he who had won the victory?" he asked rhetorically. The leader of the workers' and peasants' state did his best to convince Churchill that the Labour Party would never be able to form a government in Britain. Stalin's conviction was based on his deep-seated antipathy toward the noncommunist Left, a feeling he had inherited from Lenin. Roosevelt offered his own advice on how to deal with the Left. Recalling his first presidential election in the midst of the Depression, FDR noted that "any leader of a people must take care of their primary needs." At that time, he said, the "United States was close to revolution because the people lacked food, clothing and shelter." He had promised all that and was elected president. "Since then there was little problem in regard to social disorder in the United States."

Stalin had relied on brute force rather than promises of general welfare. Now he chose to remain silent. Nor did he show any visible reaction to Roosevelt's praise of Churchill's service to his country as a member of the opposition. The prime minister "was in and out of the government," Roosevelt said, "for many, many years, and it was difficult to say whether he had been of more service to his country within the government or without." He "had been perhaps of even greater service when he was not in the government since he had forced the people to think." What Stalin, whose policy toward the opposition had been to hunt down and kill such rivals as Leon Trotsky, made of this can only be conjectured.

Churchill said the election would be difficult. He did not know the strategy of the Left and felt vulnerable. Stalin observed that Left and Right were parliamentary terms: in France the prewar socialist prime minister Édouard Daladier had dissolved the trade unions, while Churchill had refused to touch them. "[W]ho, then, could be considered more to the left?" Stalin, to be sure, had no need to worry about enemies on the left: the Soviet regime had done away with independent trade unions during the first years of its rule, and its left-wing opponents—Mensheviks, Socialist Revolutionaries, and others—had been suppressed by means of political trials, executions, and deportations.

The prime minister went on to observe that Stalin "had a much easier political task since he only had one party to deal with." Stalin took this as an expression of admiration. "[E]xperience had shown one party was of great convenience to a leader of the state," he said, according to the American record of the conversation. Churchill later recalled Stalin saying with great conviction that "one party is much better." Whatever the exact wording, the prime minister responded that "if he could get full agreement of all the British people it would greatly facilitate the task."

Churchill warned Stalin that he would have no choice but to "speak very harshly about the [British] Communists," otherwise he could lose the elections. Stalin responded mildly that "the Communists are good boys." "We are against them and we shall have to make our case," Churchill continued. He took care to say that he had nothing against the communists personally. Despite his differences with William Gallacher, the British communist leader and member of Parliament, Churchill had written him a letter of sympathy on the loss of two of his foster children in the war.

The prime minister even suggested that the gulf separating the traditional parties from the communists was not as unbridgeable as one might think. In his opinion, "the British opposition to Communism was not based on any attachment to private property but to the old question of individual versus the state." He was prepared to admit that the war was bringing the British closer to communism. "In war the individual of necessity is subordinate to the state and . . . in England any man or woman between the ages of eighteen and sixty was subject to the government." Stalin did not respond, but he knew perfectly well what Churchill was getting at. The closest the Soviets ever got to their communist ideal was during the civil war in Russia, when they declared the policy of "war communism." They had to retreat after that and allow some private initiative in order to rebuild a starving country.

Stalin felt relaxed enough to recall his communist youth and even criticize his German communist comrades, although, as Churchill later remembered, his main target was "the unreasonable sense of discipline in Kaiser's Germany." Visiting Leipzig before the Russian Revolution, Stalin traveled with two hundred German communists to attend a conference. As Churchill recalled, "Their train arrived punctually at the station, but there was no official to collect their tickets. All the German Communists therefore waited docilely for two hours to get off the platform. So none of them were able to attend the meeting for which they had travelled far."

By this time, an atmosphere of intimacy prevailed in the room. Churchill thanked Stalin for his hospitality to the British parliamentary delegation that had visited Moscow on the eve of the conference, and Stalin responded that he liked young military fighters such as the British commando Simon Fraser (Lord Lovat), one of the members of the delegation. He told the gathering that in recent years he "had acquired a new interest in life, an interest in military affairs; in fact, it had become almost his sole interest."

The discussion shifted toward Roosevelt's forthcoming meetings in the Middle East, where he would be discussing the establishment of a Jewish state in Palestine. "The Jewish problem was a very difficult one," opined Stalin. The Soviets had "tried to establish a national home for the Jews in Birobidzhan, but . . . they had only stayed there two or three years and then scattered to the cities." Stalin did not want to admit that his insistence on creating an autonomous Jewish polity in the Far East, far from the traditional Jewish area of settlement in Eastern

Europe, was largely responsible for the failure of the initiative. "Jews were natural traders," he explained, "but much had been accomplished by putting small groups in some agricultural areas." When Roosevelt said that he was a Zionist and asked whether Stalin also was one, the communist leader responded that he "was one in principle, but he recognized the difficulty."[8]

The evening exemplified what later became known as the spirit of Yalta—the feeling that there were no problems that they could not solve in the future. "I believe that the whole discussion that evening," wrote Edward Stettinius, "as well as the spirit of most of the Conference, furnishes a genuine example to the world that, where objective conditions exist, people with different backgrounds and training can find a basis of understanding." If anything, their readiness to overlook profound political and cultural differences fed their hopes. The Big Three could reach tactical agreements by avoiding the problems that divided them, but that was hardly the same thing as solving them. Roosevelt did not abandon his suspicions of British imperialism, Churchill never ceased to be anticommunist, and Stalin could hardly understand the logic of his capitalist counterparts or the nature of their democracy, which could relegate victors to defeat at the polls, allegedly making them more useful to the country than they would be in power.[9]

As the evening drew to a close, Churchill made one last attempt to dissuade Roosevelt from leaving the conference on the following day. "Franklin," he said, "you cannot go. We have within reach a very great prize." "Winston," came the answer, "I have made commitments and I must depart tomorrow as planned." Ultimately Roosevelt agreed to postpone his departure if necessary, but he did so in order to accommodate a request from Stalin, not because of Churchill's plea. The prime minister had every right to feel excluded from the close relationship that had emerged over the course of the conference.

Churchill became the target of his guests' rhetorical sallies. Roosevelt remarked that Churchill "was always talking about what the Constitution allowed and what it did not allow, but actually there was no Constitution." He then compared the British constitution with the Atlantic Charter, reminding Churchill that he had never signed their first agreement. It was the second time since Malta that Roosevelt had joked about the charter at Churchill's expense, but Churchill did not seem to mind. He told the president that the Atlantic Charter was not a law but a star.[10]

After dinner Churchill took Stalin and Roosevelt to the Map Room he had set up and told them about the success of the British attack on the western front. Canadian troops had reached the Rhine at Cleves. He told Roosevelt and Stalin the story of Anne of Cleves, the fourth wife of King Henry VIII, and sang a couple of bars of the First World War song "When We've Wound Up the Watch on the Rhine." That was not the only song Churchill sang that evening.

When Stalin, betraying his main concern at the time, suggested that the British might want to make a separate armistice with the Germans, Churchill preferred to respond to the insult by singing. According to the British captain Richard Pim, who was present during the Map Room conversation, "the Prime Minister looked hurt and in a corner of the Map Room, with his hands in his pockets, gave us a few lines of his favorite song, 'Keep Right on to the End of the Road.' Stalin looked puzzled. Roosevelt saved the situation with a joke. 'Tell your chief,' he said to Vladimir Pavlov, who as always interpreted for Stalin, 'that this singing by the Prime Minister is Britain's secret weapon.'"[11]

Churchill did not let himself get involved in a major quarrel with Stalin, as he had on the opening night. This time the atmosphere was much less tense. "When the Marshal left," Churchill later recalled, "many of our British party had assembled in the hall of the villa, and I called for 'Three cheers for Marshal Stalin,' which were warmly given." The appeal was sincere. Lord Moran believed that at Yalta Churchill was getting along with Stalin better than ever before. Commenting on the after-dinner conversation, Churchill would write, "In this manner, the evening passed away agreeably."[12]

26

CROSSING THE FINISH LINE

On the morning of February 11, Lord Moran found the prime minister not in the best of spirits. Churchill, he noted in his diary, "was moody" and "gave me a sour look." He was suffering an emotional hangover: thoughts suppressed the night before were coming back to haunt him. "The president is behaving very badly," Churchill told his doctor. "He won't take any interest in what we are trying to do." Lord Moran was of the opinion that the president had lost his grip and was a mere passenger at the conference. The prime minister agreed with the first observation but was not prepared to admit the second. He changed the subject to his concern about reparations. He was also uneasy about the situation in Poland. Lord Moran tried to calm him: "With the Red Army where it is, isn't it too late to try to bargain? Wasn't the damage done at Teheran?" Churchill ignored his comments. He had been much more pleased with the outcome of the Teheran Conference than he was with the way things were turning out at Yalta.[1]

About noon, when Churchill arrived at Livadia, Roosevelt was just concluding a car tour of the grounds in the company of his daughter. An American military cameraman was on hand to film their return. They both looked relaxed and happy as they inspected a U.S. naval guard drawn up outside the palace. Members of the three delegations had worked into the early hours of the morning on documents that were to be reviewed and signed by the Big Three. After breakfast, the documents had been discussed by the three foreign ministers; now it was the turn of the leaders themselves to review them.

The meeting started at a quarter past twelve in the tsar's former billiard hall, which had been turned into Roosevelt's dining room. The formal session lasted a mere forty-five minutes. Roosevelt shared his impressions of the tour of Livadia's grounds, and Stalin told the gathering that he intended to turn all three palaces into spas. He kept his word: after the conference, he transferred the palaces to the NKVD, which transformed them into vacation retreats for the

Soviet elite. Stalin offered to use the draft communiqué prepared by the American and British delegations as a basis for discussion. They went through it paragraph by paragraph, with Stalin saying "OK" and Roosevelt and Churchill expressing their approval with *"khorosho,"* which means "good" in Russian.

Most of the corrections were stylistic. Churchill was especially forthcoming. He requested that all references to "joint" be removed, as the word meant for him "the Sunday family roast of mutton." Admiral Leahy was not amused. As he wrote later: "Most of the modifications were to meet his ideas of correct English. Churchill, of course, preferred British English!" Stettinius, delighted that Churchill was suggesting only minor drafting changes to the text he had helped craft, happily went along, as did Roosevelt. Stalin, whose English was limited to a few phrases such as "You said it" and "The toilet is around the corner," did not object either. Churchill's other drafting correction was replacing the plural "reparations" with the singular "reparation"—a change that did not affect the sum of $20 billion and was thus acceptable to Stalin.

The first disagreement that came up had to do with the United Nations. Stalin tried to sneak in a statement on inviting Ukraine and Belarus to San Francisco as founding members. Roosevelt objected, and this time Churchill gave the president his full support. "If the matter was now brought publicly before the world, it would be a subject of controversy for a long time," declared Churchill. Stalin withdrew, but Molotov proposed another amendment, perhaps in retaliation. He wanted the reference to FDR as author of the proposal on voting procedure in the UN Security Council to be removed from the communiqué. Stalin remained silent, indicating that he agreed. But the Americans would not back down: the reference would allow Roosevelt to claim a major political victory at home, and he told Stettinius that he wanted it in the text. It stayed, at least for the time being.

The next disagreement originated with Churchill, who was clearly concerned with the conference's decisions on Poland and looking for the right language in which to frame them for his domestic audience. He was unhappy with the first sentence of the paragraph on Poland, which said that the three powers wanted to avoid any divergence in their policies, and suggested its deletion. Eden, for his part, proposed amending it to read: "we were impressed by the dangers of any divergence of policy between the major allies toward Poland." Churchill was satisfied with the change, but now it was Stalin's turn to object. He wanted the whole phrase to be removed. "Some may have been impressed, others not," said the dictator. Roosevelt suggested a compromise that sounded much more optimistic: "We came to the Crimea Conference resolved to settle our differences about Poland." While recognizing differences, this formula relegated them to the past.

Everyone agreed, but the prime minister could no longer conceal his mounting dissatisfaction with the essence, not the language, of the decisions they had reached on Poland. The agreements "will be very heavily attacked in England," he told the gathering. "It will be said we have yielded completely on the frontiers and the whole matter to Russia." Churchill may have been hoping that something could still be changed, but Stalin was not receptive. "Is it in earnest? I doubt it," Stalin said, referring to the criticism Churchill claimed he would face at home. "I assure you it is," Churchill shot back; "the London Poles will raise a dreadful outcry." "But the other Poles will predominate," Stalin responded, probably feeling that he was now on firmer ground.

Churchill retreated. "I hope you are right," he said. "We are not going back on it. It's not a question of numbers of Poles but of the cause for which Britain drew the sword. [They] will say you have completely swept away the only constitutional government in Poland. However I will defend it to the best of my ability." Roosevelt was quick to console the prime minister. He told Churchill that there were ten times as many Poles in the United States as in Britain, but he too was prepared to defend the declaration on Poland. The Soviets were satisfied. Pavlov, whose protocol of the meeting omitted the entire debate between Churchill and Stalin, recorded this statement by Roosevelt.[2]

With the United Nations and Poland out of the way, the rest of the communiqué aroused no substantial disagreement. Stalin wanted no mention of the exchanges of prisoners of war in the communiqué, arguing that it was a matter of inter-Allied relations. He may well have been concerned about the impact of the agreement, if publicized, on Soviet prisoners of war and civilians in Allied custody. Churchill did not object to leaving the POW agreement out of the communiqué but wanted it to be published afterward, since it would help him sell the Yalta accords back home. Stalin went along with this.

The last question to be decided was whether the Big Three would sign the communiqué and, if so, in what order. The discussion once again manifested Roosevelt's long-standing policy of allying himself with Stalin and the Soviet leader's tactic of cultivating the American president while making a show of humility, and Churchill's growing insecurity about Great Britain's place in the postwar world. When Molotov asked whether the communiqué should be signed by the heads of government, Roosevelt said yes, pointing to the precedent of the Teheran Conference. He also suggested putting Stalin's signature first, as he had been "such a wonderful host." Stalin objected: "The United States has a sharp-tongued press," he told the president, "that may represent the matter in such a way that Stalin made the president and the prime minister trail after him." He proposed putting the signatures in Cyrillic alphabetical order: first Roosevelt's, then his, and finally Churchill's.

Churchill immediately jumped in. "If you take the alphabet, I'll be first," he said, referring to the Latin alphabet. "If you take age I also come first," he added. Stalin did not object. He actually insisted on being last: no one would then be able to say that he had led the two Western heads of government into adopting decisions that favored the USSR. Thus Churchill signed the conference communiqué first, and Stalin signed last. That was also the order of signatures on the protocol concerning German reparations, which Churchill read and approved in the presence of Stalin and Roosevelt.

The communiqué included a paragraph on Poland that Churchill vehemently opposed, as he did certain provisions on reparations, but he signed it nevertheless. He also signed the secret agreements on the Far East, which allocated the Kurile Islands to the Soviet Union and recognized its special interests in northeastern China, against the advice of his foreign-policy team. Even if his signature appeared last on those documents, it was meant to show that Britain was still a great power involved in major political decisions.[3]

As Allied diplomats were assigned to revise the text of the communiqué and prepare it for signature, the Big Three, their foreign ministers, and their immediate entourage were served the final lunch of the conference. Stalin was clearly in a good mood. As he asked Molotov's deputy, Andrei Vyshinsky, to work on the final version of the communiqué, Stalin joked, "He is not interested in lunch." As always, he was glad to joke about his subordinates at their expense. Vyshinsky's British counterpart, Alec Cadogan, was not only invited to lunch but received special treatment from Stalin. A photo taken by an American photographer shows him sitting across the table from Churchill, flanked by Admiral Leahy and Stettinius. "After lunch," Cadogan wrote to his wife the next day, "I was standing talking to someone. I felt a nudge, turned round and found Joe holding two glasses of brandy, and I had to drink 'no heeltaps' with him." During lunch Stalin preferred not to discuss specific issues. His only noteworthy comment concerned Iran: he said that any nation that kept its oil in the ground, not allowing it to be exploited, was "working against peace." It was startling to hear the head of the communist government talk like a Texas oilman.[4]

Even before the waiters had managed to remove the dirty dishes and clear the table, the communiqué and protocol on reparations were brought in. The Big Three signed the document in the established order: first Churchill, then Roosevelt, and finally Stalin. At a quarter to four on February 11, the last plenary session of the conference formally ended. A few minutes after exchanging gifts and decorations for their military commanders, the Big Three left Livadia. "Well—it's over! Yesterday lunchtime saw the conclusion," wrote Sarah Oliver on February 12 in her letter home. "Stalin, like some genie, just disappeared. Three hours after the last handshake, Yalta was deserted, except for those who always have to tidy up after the party."[5]

Among those who stayed to "tidy up" were the three foreign ministers. They continued editing the text of the communiqué already signed by their superiors and discussed the summary of conference decisions, which they signed on their own. It was the last battle of the conference, and the first battle over its interpretation.

Molotov proposed that the Declaration on Liberated Europe be included in the communiqué rather than published as a separate document. He was probably hoping to diminish its significance. Eden and Stettinius accepted this but were less accommodating on other points. When Molotov proposed removing the formula on UN Security Council voting procedure, which gave special credit to Roosevelt, from the text of the communiqué, Stettinius refused, noting that the issue had been discussed in the presence of Roosevelt and Stalin, and the president had made it clear that he wanted his name to be mentioned. Later, mollified by Molotov's suggestion that the Americans could publicize the president's role once the communiqué had been released, Stettinius relented. "We do not want to hush-hush this fact," Molotov told his American counterpart.

Eden had his own set of issues that he wanted to slip in at the last minute. He suggested adding Saudi Arabia, a traditional British ally and recipient of British assistance in the Middle East, to the list of countries invited to the UN founding conference. To Molotov's surprised "Why?" Eden responded that the Saudis had expressed their desire to declare war on Germany but had been dissuaded by the Allies. "It would be good to have a Moslem or two," he said. "Ibn Saud is having a cup of coffee with the President." Stettinius supported the idea, but Molotov did not, fearing that such an invitation would create an unwanted precedent. At the end of the meeting Eden agreed to drop his proposal.

Molotov, for his part, pushed for a new formula on Iran. He objected to the statement that Stettinius and Eden had "drawn attention to the need to observe the Teheran Declaration" with regard to oil concessions, and proposed its replacement with a neutral formula to the effect that the three foreign ministers had exchanged views on the subject. Molotov indicated that if his proposal was not accepted, the whole section would have to be dropped. The threat worked: Eden and Stettinius capitulated. Molotov's efforts to revise the statement on the Montreux Convention and improve Soviet chances of grasping the Black Sea Straits were less successful. He wanted to introduce a phrase stating that the convention did not correspond to the new situation, but Stettinius objected that it would be premature to make such a statement before the three ministers had studied the matter. Eden's compromise formula was added instead: the ministers would discuss the Soviet proposal and the Turkish government would be informed about the deliberations "at the appropriate moment."

It was past 6:00 p.m. when the "protocol of the proceedings"—by far the most detailed document of the Yalta Conference, which spelled out its decisions on all major issues—was signed by the three foreign ministers. Molotov and Eden also signed Soviet-British agreements on the exchange of prisoners of war. The Soviet-American agreement was signed by representatives of the two military commands. The discrepancy indicated the differing attitudes of the British and American foreign secretaries. Eden endorsed the agreement all along, despite disturbing reports about the Soviet treatment of returnees, while Stettinius took a much more cautious approach once he was informed about the refusal of Soviet POWs to return to their homeland.

When the three foreign ministers walked into the entrance hall of Livadia Palace after signing the final documents, Molotov noticed the lemon tree that had been brought there on Stalin's orders after Roosevelt had remarked that martinis tasted much better with lemon. As there were still many lemons on the tree, Molotov proposed that Eden and Stettinius each take a branch as a souvenir. They did so. Then it was the turn of Allied diplomats and military personnel gathered in the room to do the same until, as one of the Soviet diplomats wrote, all the branches were gone, and only those parts that "could be sawed or chopped with an ax" remained. The Allies returned home from the peace conference with branches of lemon instead of palm. For the time being, they did not see the irony in their gesture.[6]

"We have wound up the conference—successfully I think," Roosevelt wrote to his wife on departure. "I am a bit exhausted but really all right." During the last days of the conference, the president had pushed to bring closure, explaining to Stettinius that he had to apply such pressure in order to prevent it from "dragging on for days." Once he left Livadia, however, he did not rush to the Saki airfield to meet the "three kings" who, as he told Stalin, were waiting for him in the Mediterranean. Instead he went to Sevastopol, where he would spend a night on the USS *Catoctin*, which was moored in the harbor. The idea was suggested by Roosevelt's naval aide, Admiral Wilson Brown, who believed that FDR's presence would boost the crew's morale.

It certainly did. "The *Catoctin* manned the rail and accorded the president full honors as he went on board," stated the president's travel log. "The *Catoctin* served a delicious steak dinner to us," continued the log's author, "which was a real treat for us after eight days of Russian fare." The president's chief bodyguard, Michael Reilly, remembered that they ate Texas steak. But the stopover proved difficult for the president himself. Averell Harriman, who accompanied Roosevelt, later remembered: "It was a three hour drive over twisting roads and when we reached the ship it was so hot on board that I almost collapsed myself. The president had a ghastly night and I think it affected his health. At any rate, he looked tired and worn the next morning."

On the way to Sevastopol, the president's party passed the century-old battlefields of the Crimean War, including the site of the charge of the Light Brigade, but Roosevelt's strongest impressions were of the devastation inflicted on the country by the most recent war. "FDR seemed appalled at the destruction, saying that there was no military reason for it; that Yalta had no military value, no defenses; and that the sight of it now made him want to exact an eye for an eye from the Germans, even more than ever," Anna Boettiger had noted in her diary on February 3, describing their approach to the city. The destruction that FDR saw in Sevastopol made an even greater impression on him. According to the presidential log, "The city was virtually leveled to the ground except for the walls of homes and other buildings which the mines, bombs and shells in recent battles left standing like billboards—mute testimony of the horrorful wanton Nazi vengeance. Of thousands of buildings in the city, the president was told, only six were left intact when the Germans fled."

The president had been told about the destruction by his daughter, but now he saw it for himself. The image of the leveled city was indelible and would strengthen his perception of the Soviet Union as the primary victim of Nazi aggression. "There was little left in Yalta except blank walls, ruins, destruction," he told Congress on March 1. "Sevastopol, that weather-fortified port, about forty or fifty miles away—there again was a scene of utter destruction—a large city with its great navy yards, its fortifications. I think less than a dozen buildings were left intact in the entire city. I had read about Warsaw and Lidice and Rotterdam and Coventry—but I saw Sevastopol and Yalta. And I know that there is not room enough on earth for both German militarism and Christian decency."

Some of the Nazi leaders took offense upon reading Roosevelt's statement. On March 2, Hitler's minister of propaganda, Joseph Goebbels, dictated the following diary entry: "It is mere insolence when Roosevelt says that he has seen the devastation in Sevastopol. His conclusion is that between Christian decency and Nazism there is a great gulf fixed. Of the frightful destruction wrought daily by the American Air Force on unfortified and undefended German towns he naturally says nothing at all." The moral outrage that Nazi aggression aroused in Roosevelt, whose sympathies lay with the Soviet victims, made no impression on Goebbels.[7]

After Roosevelt had left Livadia, Churchill, in his daughter's words, suddenly felt lonely. Stalin, who disappeared "like some genie," showed no interest in a private meeting with the prime minister, nor did he propose anything to occupy him on the following day. On the way from Livadia to Vorontsov villa, Churchill suddenly decided to leave the site of the conference immediately instead of waiting until the next day, as originally planned. "Why do we stay here? Why do not we go tonight—see no reason to stay here a minute longer—we're off!" declared the suddenly energized Churchill. "He sprang out of the car and whirling into the Private Office announced: 'I do not know about you—but I am off. Leave in 50 minutes!' After a second's stunned silence," wrote Sarah, "everyone was galvanized into activity. Trunks and large mysterious paper parcels given to us by the Russians—whoopee—filled the hall. Laundry arrived back clean but damp."

Churchill's decision came as a surprise to everyone in the British party. It was half past four, and Lord Moran was getting ready to go for a walk when Churchill appeared in the villa. "'We leave at five o'clock. Where's Tommy? Sawyers!' His voice rose," wrote Moran in his diary. "'Sawyers! Where is everyone?'" Sawyers, Churchill's valet, was clearly upset. "They can't do this to me!" he declared, surrounded by half-packed bags, literally beating his breast. "He put a sponge bag in and then put it out. He carefully laid out the Lord Warden of the Cinque Ports suit, then changed it for the Royal Yacht Club suit," wrote Sarah Oliver to her mother. "Papa, genial and sprightly like a boy out of school, his homework done, walked from room to room saying: 'come on, come on!'"

Approaching bad weather was given as an excuse for the sudden change of plans. As always, the mercurial Churchill was ready to change his mind at a moment's notice. Within the next fifty minutes he did so repeatedly: they would leave; they would stay; they would leave again. They actually left at half past five and two hours later were already in Sevastopol, where they boarded the British ship *Franconia*. The captain thought that Churchill looked tired, but the prime minister immediately asked for the diplomatic pouch. Churchill was hungry for news from the outside world.

The prime minister was relaxed and happy to be aboard a British ship. First, they would have dinner. "Grand to get back to English fare after the sucking-pig and the cold fatty approaches to all their meals," the prime minister told his guests. He sang "The Soldiers of the Queen." "The P.M., who has been in a vile mood throughout the Conference, irritable and bad tempered, is now in tearing spirits," wrote Lord Moran in his diary. "I'm so relieved to get this bloody thing off," Churchill told his doctor, referring to the Yalta communiqué. "Anyway," he continued, "that's done with and out of the way." Churchill was clearly unhappy with the outcome of the conference but glad to see the end of it. "He is trying to forget that he has achieved little," wrote Moran, who knew his patient better than anyone else. "He is playful, smiling, mischievous."

The more the actual experiences of Yalta receded in memory, the better they would look to Churchill in retrospect. By the next day, he was already prepared to see the communiqué as a success. "I hope you will like communiqué published tomorrow morning," he cabled Clementine from the *Franconia*. "We have covered a great amount of ground and I am very pleased with the decisions we have gained." The Yalta Conference was over; the Yalta myth was about to be born.[8]

Churchill was in no hurry to leave the Crimea. The return trip involved an exhausting and potentially dangerous flight to the Mediterranean, and Britain's seventy-year-old prime minister felt he could use some rest. Besides, he had no immediate appointments. Churchill spent three nights on the *Franconia*, moored in Sevastopol harbor, and, like Roosevelt, got to see the ruins of the city. He had seen destruction before, not least in his native England, and was much less impressed than the president. Before leaving for the Saki airport on the morning of February 14, he received the first report of the bombing of Dresden by 805 British aircraft the previous night. The results of the raid were not yet known, but the report stated that in the previous fifteen hours fourteen V-2 rockets had hit the London area, killing fifty-five people. The ruins of Sevastopol held little novelty.

Thinking back to his first evening on the *Franconia*, Churchill recalled, "From the deck we looked out over the port, which the Germans had practically destroyed, though now it was full of activity again and in the night-time its ruins blazed with light." The next day he asked his Soviet guide whether they were short of glass. Glass was indeed in short supply, and the guide answered that they were using plywood to board up windows. The prime minister said that the British were also short of glass; two million houses had been damaged and 10 percent made uninhabitable.

On the streets of Balaklava, where he stopped on his way to the most famous battlefield of the Crimean War, Churchill told his doctor, "I have been studying their faces, Charles. There is pride in their looks." He added, "They have a right to feel proud." The scene that provoked this remark was by now all too familiar. "Sarah," wrote Moran, "was giving chocolates to some children, when a Russian soldier waved the children away, and, turning to Sarah, said that their children did not need feeding." The General Information Bulletin issued to the American delegation at Yalta specifically warned against presenting gifts to Soviet soldiers. "Under no circumstances may Soviet sentries be offered cigarettes, candy, etc.," read the bulletin. "Under Soviet military law acceptance of any type of gift by a sentry is strictly forbidden and violation is punishable by extreme penalties."[9]

Unknown to the Western delegates at Yalta, these restrictions applied not only to guards but also to Soviet citizens in general. "We must teach our people to assume that every foreigner is a spy," a Soviet official told George Kennan, then a counselor at the American embassy, in July 1944. "It is only in this way that we can train them to exercise the self-control which they should exercise as citizens of a great power." "Our people," he continued, "must not be allowed to forget that they live in a capitalist environment, that a friend may be a friend today and an enemy tomorrow. We cannot permit you to associate closely with them. You will tell them all sorts of things about your countries, about your higher standard of living, about what you consider to be your happier life. You will confuse them. You will weaken their loyalty to their own system."[10]

By means of surveillance and repression, the regime had taught its people to stay away from foreigners. Children alone had not yet learned the lesson. While Kathleen Harriman found it impossible to extract any information from Maria Chekhova, Anton Chekhov's sister, about her wartime experiences, Ivan Maisky, who visited her on February 3, was greeted with the story of how she had saved the Chekhov museum during the German occupation. Maisky left an emotional note in the museum's guest book and later appealed to Molotov, asking him to help Maria Chekhova with food supplies and vitamins.[11]

There was a gulf between the Westerners and their hosts, and their histori-cal memories were very different. Balaklava Field, which meant so much to the British, was of no interest to their Soviet hosts. Churchill and his entourage were somewhat embarrassed at showing so much interest in the history of a war in which British forces had invaded Russian territory, but it soon became apparent that they had no cause for concern. Their NKVD guard had never heard of the Crimean War, and the Soviet admiral who accompanied them on the trip thought that the British wanted to visit the site in order to pay tribute to recent fighting between the Red Army and the Wehrmacht.

Churchill later remembered, "As [Brigadier] Peake pointed to the line on which the Light Brigade had been drawn up the Russian admiral pointed in almost the same direction and exclaimed: 'The German tanks came at us from over there.' A little later Peake explained the Russian dispositions, and pointed to the hills where their infantry had stood, whereupon the Russian admiral intervened with obvious pride: 'That is where a Russian battery fought and died to the last man.' I thought it right at this juncture to explain that we were study-ing a different war, a war of dynasties, not of peoples. Our host gave no sign of comprehension, but seemed perfectly satisfied."[12]

Ironically, the misunderstandings that kept haunting the Soviets and the British until the end of Churchill's stay in the Crimea had a more positive than negative effect on their relations. Kirill Novikov, a high-ranking Soviet diplomat who was in charge of conference logistics, recalled that Stalin continued to treat Roosevelt and Churchill differently until the last moment of their presence on Soviet soil. To show his regard for Roosevelt, Stalin ordered the delivery to his plane, just before his departure, of a few cases of mineral water from the Cau-casus that the president had praised during the conference. There was no such show of benevolence toward Churchill, who was seen off by a party of junior Foreign Commissariat officials. Churchill, Novikov recalled, had to deliver his farewell speech in front of the commander of the guard of honor.

What Stalin intended as an insult apparently went unnoticed. "At the air-field a splendid guard of honour of N.K.V.D. troops was drawn up," Churchill later recalled. "I inspected them in my usual manner, looking each man straight in the eye. This took some time, as there were at least two hundred of them, but it was commented on in a favourable way by the Soviet Press. I made a farewell speech before entering the plane." In the speech he made reference to the "great leader." "I thank you all, and, on leaving the Russian land and the redeemed Crimea, cleansed by Russian valor from the foul taint of the Hun; on leaving Soviet territory, I express to all of you and to your chiefs, especially to your great leader, the Supreme Commander, Marshal Stalin, the gratitude and admiration for the valiant Russian people and its army experienced by the British race scattered throughout the world, on all the oceans and regions of the globe."[13]

27

DAYS OF HOPE

O f all the writers who have been to Yalta, Anton Chekhov has given us the most evocative description of the view from the grounds of Oreanda, the tsar's manor next to Livadia. "Yalta was hardly visible through the morning mist; white clouds stood motionless on the mountain-tops," he wrote in one of his best-known stories, "The Lady with the Dog." "The leaves did not stir on the trees, grasshoppers chirruped, and the monotonous hollow sound of the sea rising up from below, spoke of the peace, of the eternal sleep awaiting us. So it must have sounded when there was no Yalta, no Oreanda here; so it sounds now, and it will sound as indifferently and monotonously when we are all no more. And in this constancy, in this complete indifference to the life and death of each of us, there lies hid, perhaps, a pledge of our eternal salvation, of the unceasing movement of life upon earth, of unceasing progress towards perfection."[1]

This "unceasing progress towards perfection" was something the Western delegates to the Yalta Conference might have hoped to be participating in during those chilly days of February 1945. "The Americans pitch their song on a higher note," wrote Lord Moran in his diary on February 11. "They are leaving Yalta with a sense of achievement, they feel they are on top of the world and that while other conferences had been concerned with proposals of policy, Yalta has been the scene of important decisions that must influence the future of the world."

"We really believed in our hearts that this was the dawn of the new day we had all been praying for and talking about for so many years," Hopkins told his biographer, Robert E. Sherwood, after the war. "We were absolutely certain that we had won the first great victory of the peace—and, by 'we,' I mean *all* of us, the whole civilized human race." Lord Moran recorded in his diary that Hopkins, "lying on his sick-bed, is firmly convinced that a new Utopia has dawned. He says the Russians have shown that they will listen to reason, and the President is certain that he 'can live at peace with them.'"

328

It was Hopkins's excitement rather than Roosevelt's more cautious belief in the possibility of future cooperation with the Soviets that defined the mood of the American delegation. The military had particular reason to be pleased with the outcome of the conference, as Soviet participation in the war with Japan was now an accomplished fact. Admiral Leahy told Harriman that the Pacific deal "makes the trip worthwhile." General Marshall was even more enthusiastic in conversation with Stettinius. "For what we have gained here, I would gladly have stayed a whole month," he said when the secretary of state suggested he must be glad to be going home at last.[2]

American diplomats were not far behind in their endorsement of the results. Stettinius was convinced that, on balance, the Americans had done extremely well. "The record of the Conference shows clearly that the Soviet Union made greater concessions at Yalta to the United States and Great Britain than were made to the Soviets," he wrote in his memoirs. Charles Bohlen recalled that "the general mood was one of satisfaction." He considered the decisions "realistic compromises between the various positions of each country" and thought that "each of the three leaders had achieved his main goals." There were of course concerns—Poland was at the top of everyone's list—but most Americans were confident that what had not been resolved at Yalta would be settled at the "final" peace conference. "In short," recalled Bohlen, "there was hope, as we left Yalta of genuine cooperation with the Soviet Union on political questions after the war."[3]

The Americans were not alone in catching the "Yalta spirit." General Hastings Ismay, Churchill's military secretary, wrote to Admiral Louis Mountbatten, the supreme Allied commander in Southeast Asia, that the conference was "a great success not so much, perhaps, because of the formal conclusions that were reached, but because of the spirit of frank cooperation which characterized all the discussions." Ismay believed that this attitude was shared by all members of the delegation with the exception of the prime minister, "who had been disillusioned by the failure to settle the Polish problem." Ismay was right: even the skeptical Alexander Cadogan left Yalta with a sense of accomplishment. "I think the Conference was quite successful," Cadogan wrote to his wife on the last day of the summit. "We have got an agreement on Poland which may heal differences, for some time at least, and assure some degree of independence to the Poles. We have agreed the Dumbarton Oaks plan, and we have got a number of other things settled, including an important agreement with the Russians about the treatment of our prisoners whom they liberate. I hope the world will be impressed!"

The members of the war cabinet back in London clearly were. On February 12, when they assembled to discuss the text of the communiqué on the results of the Yalta Conference, Deputy Prime Minister Clement Attlee announced that "the results which, in face of great difficulties, have been achieved by the Prime

Minister and the Foreign Secretary were highly satisfactory." The members of the war cabinet were pleased with the decision on the United Nations: "[W]hile we have had to concede founder membership to the Ukraine and White Russia, it was clear that the Americans were wholly with us in that matter." The war cabinet welcomed the agreement "reached on the very difficult matter of Poland" and was pleased that the decision on its western border was to be postponed until the "Peace Conference." On the dismemberment of Germany, "ample elbow room had been retained." France would get its zone of occupation, join the Allied Control Commission, and add its signature to the Declaration on Liberated Europe. The agreements on Yugoslavia and German reparations raised no objections. The conference was hailed as a triumph, and the cabinet agreed to send a telegram congratulating Churchill and Eden on "the skill and success with which they had conducted their discussions and the results they had achieved."[4]

Cadogan was impressed not so much by the immediate results as by the new spirit of cooperation shown by his Soviet hosts. "I have never known the Russians so easy and accommodating," he wrote in a letter to his wife. "In particular Joe has been extremely good. He is a great man, and shows up very impressively against the background of the other two aging statesmen." Belief in Stalin's goodwill underpinned the newfound optimism. "The Russians had proved that they were reasonable and farseeing and there wasn't any doubt in the minds of the President or any of us that we could live with them and get along with them peacefully for as far into the future as any of us could imagine," Hopkins told Sherwood. "But I have to make one amendment to that," he continued: "I think we all had in our minds the reservation that we could not foretell what the results would be if anything should happen to Stalin. We felt sure that we could count on him to be reasonable and sensible and understanding—but we never could be sure who or what might be in back of him there in the Kremlin."

Hopkins's views were shared by quite a few of his colleagues. Stalin "was considered and well mannered," wrote Alger Hiss, "but, more important, he appeared to be genuinely conciliatory in attitude, abandoning with seeming grace his position on a number of points." "He was friendly, and seemed in many instances to compromise in order to reach an agreement," recalled Leahy. "Stalin had made a genuine concession in finally agreeing to France as one of the powers occupying Germany," wrote Bohlen. "Each country altered its position on the United Nations." In his balance sheet of the conference, Stettinius counted four Soviet concessions with regard to the United Nations alone: the acceptance of the American formula for voting in the Security Council, withdrawal of the earlier request for membership of all sixteen Soviet republics in the UN, agreement to invite Latin American countries that had not declared war on Germany by the time of the conference to join the UN, and agreement not to veto free discussion of matters relating to the interests of the great powers.

Stalin's readiness to compromise when his underlings would not give an inch came as a surprise. "It is interesting to speculate as to the reason for Stalin's flexibility and agreeableness at Yalta," wrote Alger Hiss. "It seems to me unlikely that this mood . . . simply masked intransigence. After all, it was we, not Stalin, who came bearing requests." Hiss, whose espionage for the Soviet Union was never proved in court but whose leftist sympathies are not in doubt, struggled like other members of the American delegation to make sense of Stalin's personality and behavior. He knew of Stalin's "monstrous crimes against his people" and had trouble reconciling that fact with the simple, modest image that the marshal successfully projected at Yalta. "He stood in the lavatory line with his aides and the rest of us lesser fry while Churchill was taken to Stettinius' suite and Roosevelt went to his own," recalled Hiss. "We never solved the enigma of Stalin's character," he concluded. Senior members of the American delegation struggled to understand how such a seemingly reasonable and gracious man could be so inflexible and stubborn when it came to German reparations or the government in Poland. Stettinius resolved the contradiction by accepting Stalin's claim that he was not free to make decisions on his own. He believed that Stalin was under pressure from hard-liners in the Politburo and even saw this as the source of problems with Yalta's implementation.[5]

Churchill believed that he had cracked the enigma of Stalin, grasped the logic of his actions, and that he was in a position to predict them. "Stalin isn't going to butt in in Greece," he told Moran. "In return, he expects a free hand in Bulgaria and Rumania. The fifty-fifty plan [for Yugoslavia] arranged at Moscow is working out in his favour. He'll let his people be beaten up in Greece for the sake of his larger plans. I find he does what he says he will do. It isn't easy to get him to say he will do it, but once he says something, he sticks to it." On the last day of the conference, Churchill told his doctor, "Stalin has only referred to Greece once, when he asked me what was happening there. He said: 'I do not want to criticize anything, nor to interfere, I am quite content to leave it to you.'" "Winston's emotional nature," commented Moran, "to be sure, has been deeply touched by the faithful manner in which Stalin has discharged his undertaking not to interfere in Greece."

Churchill thought he could trust Stalin. He also wanted to forget the low points of the conference negotiations and was prepared to brush aside Stalin's adept use of the Greek situation to coerce him into making concessions on Poland and Yugoslavia. "The P.M. spoke once more of the disaster it would be if anything happened to Stalin," recorded Lord Moran on the evening of February 11. "His humour, understanding and moderation, on many occasions, had made a deep impression on him." This impression deepened in the following days, as Churchill found himself increasingly under the spell of the "spirit of Yalta." On February 14, he cabled Attlee in London: "I am profoundly impressed with the friendly attitude of Stalin and Molotov. It is a different Russian world to any I have seen hitherto." Churchill fought to the very end on Poland and German reparations and felt more betrayed by Roosevelt than by Stalin. He would soon regret his faith.[6]

The sense of satisfaction with the level of cooperation achieved at the conference was not limited to the Western delegates. A few days after his return to Moscow, Molotov sent a telegram to Soviet embassies on the results of the conference. "The general atmosphere at the conference was of a friendly nature, and one could feel an effort to come to an agreement on contested questions," said the telegram. Admiral Kuznetsov recalled in his memoirs that "the general tone of the conference was imbued with mutual agreement and a striving for concord." "Everyone at the Yalta Conference knew that the decisions taken in the Livadia Palace had immense significance for the peaceful future of Europe. We felt we were at the focus of history and that Justice was standing by, scales in hand," wrote Gromyko in his memoirs.[7]

For the members of the Soviet delegation, Yalta was about justice: the punishment of the aggressor and rendering of just deserts to the victors—especially the Soviet Union, which had suffered the most and contributed the most to victory. "Stalin often said that Russia wins wars but does not know how to avail itself of the fruits of victory," recalled Molotov years later. "Russians fight magnificently, but do not know how to conclude a peace; they are always passed by, never get their due." This time, they would get their due. "The Americans recognize the justice of our position on Sakhalin and the Kuriles," an excited Stalin had told Gromyko. The Soviet Union was being admitted to the club of great powers after decades of isolation: its just demands were finally being heard.[8]

Ivan Maisky, who drafted the text of Molotov's telegram on the results of the Yalta Conference, spelled out Soviet successes for the benefit of the Soviet ambassadors. Apart from Poland, Yugoslavia, and reparations—the issue for which he bore personal responsibility—Maisky enumerated other Soviet achievements: the Western pledge to recognize Ukraine and Belarus as founding members of the United Nations at the San Francisco conference; the agreement of the Western powers to revisit the Montreux Convention on the Black Sea Straits; and, last but not least, the avoidance of a discussion of Iran. The overall sense of the telegram was that the Soviet Union had achieved its major objectives. In early March, Maisky wrote a private letter to his old acquaintance Aleksandra Kollontai, the Soviet ambassador to Stockholm, in which he stressed the growing international influence of the Soviet Union. "The Crimean conference was very interesting. My basic impression comes down to the view that our influence in general and that of Stalin as an individual is extraordinarily great," he wrote. "Seventy-five percent of the conference decisions are our decisions, particularly on the Polish question, Yugoslavia, and reparations. Cooperation among the 'Big Three' is now very close, and Germany will not fare well either during the war or after it."[9]

Maisky's excitement at the results of the conference reflected a sense of satisfaction at the very top of the Soviet pyramid of power, including Stalin himself. There is no better evidence of this than the list of Soviet security officials and military commanders—more than a thousand—decorated for their role in the preparation and conduct of the conference. The list, prepared by Beria, consisted mostly of officers of the People's Commissariat of Internal Affairs and the People's Commissariat of State Security. Ten of them received Orders of Mikhail Kutuzov, which were normally awarded to the commanders of Red Army fronts for the preparation and conduct of major military operations, not to secret policemen, who never saw front-line duty. Among those who received the highest award were Stalin's personal pilot, General V. G. Grachev, and the commander of his personal security detail, General Nikolai Vlasik.[10]

Marshal Georgii Zhukov, who visited Stalin in Moscow in March 1945, found him happy with the outcome of the conference. Stalin was convinced that at least one of the Western leaders could be trusted. He had been concerned that the Western Allies might conclude a separate peace with Germany at the very end of the war, robbing the Soviet Union of the spoils of its victory. He suspected Churchill but, judging by Zhukov's account, felt confident that he could trust Roosevelt. Stalin needed American help not only to defeat Germany but to rebuild the Soviet Union. Roosevelt had convinced Stalin at Yalta that cooperation with the West and especially with the United States was possible. That realization made the Soviets more open to compromise than ever before and contributed to the atmosphere of hope and mutual trust shared by all participants.[11]

The Yalta agreements marked a high point that would not be recaptured. In the months ahead, the United States and Britain would draw closer, but there would be no such progress in relations with the Soviet Union. In his memoirs, Alger Hiss noted the limits of the spirit of Yalta: "Stalin as well as Churchill spoke frequently and emphatically of the importance of preserving Great Power unity after the war. Perhaps privately each desired such unity only if it could be obtained on his own terms without compromise."[12]

On February 27, Churchill presented the results of the Yalta Conference to his country in a speech at the House of Commons that lasted almost two hours and required a break in the middle. As he had warned on the last day of the conference, there was strong opposition in Parliament to the decisions on Poland, and he did his best in the speech to defend positions that he did not support.

Churchill's main argument was that Stalin had pledged to honor both Polish sovereignty and democracy. The agreement itself was less than satisfactory, but he had come back with Stalin's word.

Privately, the prime minister was struggling. He was haunted by memories of Munich as he considered and reconsidered what had happened. The deal on Poland was now under attack by members of Parliament who had supported the Munich agreement. Churchill recognized the irony and feared that he was repeating the mistake of his predecessor, Neville Chamberlain. "The PM was rather depressed, thinking of the possibilities of Russia one day turning against us, saying that Chamberlain had trusted Hitler as he was now trusting Stalin," wrote Jock Colville, Churchill's private secretary, commenting on the prime minister's mood at dinner on February 23. On another occasion he was more self-assured. "Poor Neville Chamberlain believed he could trust Hitler," Churchill remarked. "He was wrong. But I do not think I am wrong about Stalin." Still, when Colville suggested that Churchill strike a phrase that smacked of Munich out of the draft of his speech to Parliament, Churchill obliged. The phrase read: "Russia seeks not only peace, but peace with honour."

In a letter to Peter Fraser, the prime minister of New Zealand, Churchill openly admitted the limits of what he could do at Yalta. "Great Britain and the British Commonwealth are very much weaker militarily than Soviet Russia, and have no means, short of another general war, of enforcing their point of view. Nor can we ignore the position of the United States. We cannot go further in helping Poland than the United States is willing or can be persuaded to go. We have therefore to do the best we can." "The proof of the pudding is in the eating," continued the prime minister. "We are only committed on the basis of full execution in good faith of the terms of our published communiqué."

Publicly, however, Churchill stuck to his guns, which meant reaffirming his trust in Stalin's word. On the evening of February 19, immediately upon his return to London, he told the war cabinet that Stalin "meant well to the world and to Poland" and that there would be no "resentment on the part of Russia about the arrangements that had been made for free and fair elections in that country." Opposition in his own party would soon force him to concede that there might be a problem with Stalin's word. Two days later, at a meeting of the war cabinet, he stated: "[I]f the terms of the communiqué agreed with Premier Stalin were carried out in full faith, all would be well. If, on the other hand, effective reality were not given to those undertakings, our engagement would be altered." Churchill believed that "the Russians would honour the declaration that had been made, but the acid test of their sincerity in this matter in the immediate future would be whether any objection would be raised to M. Miko-łajczyk returning to Poland."[13]

Always the shrewd politician, Churchill sought as much as possible to shift responsibility for future developments in Poland from himself to the Soviet leader. In his speech to the House of Commons, he said:

> Most solemn declarations have been made by Marshal Stalin and the Soviet Union that the sovereign independence of Poland is to be maintained, and this decision is now joined in both by Great Britain and the United States.... The impression I brought back from the Crimea, and from all my other contacts, is that Marshal Stalin and the Soviet leaders wish to live in honourable friendship and equality with the Western democracies. I feel also that their word is their bond. I know of no Government which stands to its obligations, even in its own despite, more solidly than the Russian Soviet Government. I decline absolutely to embark here on a discussion about Russian good faith.

Churchill admitted, however, that the Yalta agreements were open to interpretation. How will this Declaration be carried out? How will phrases like "Free and unfettered elections on the basis of universal suffrage and secret ballot" be interpreted? Will the "new" Government be "properly" constituted, with a fair representation of the Polish people, as far as can be made practicable at the moment, and as soon as possible? Will the elections be free and unfettered? Will the candidates of all democratic parties be able to present themselves to the electors, and to conduct their campaigns? What are democratic parties?

Churchill's answer to these questions was not very promising. "People always take different views," he admitted, reminding his listeners of British debates on party politics.

Churchill's own presentation indicated that there was more than one way to understand the documents signed at Yalta. He preferred to speak about the creation of a new Polish government, avoiding the Soviet formula, which called for the reorganization of an already existing one. "The agreement provides for consultation with a view to the establishment in Poland of a new Polish Provisional Government of National Unity," Churchill told Parliament. In fact, the Soviets considered it one of their major diplomatic successes that the conference communiqué included their formula on the *reorganization* of the existing Polish government, as opposed to the formation of a new one.

Pressured by his opponents in the House of Commons, Churchill hoped that the spirit of Yalta would prevail. "No one can guarantee the future world," went a paragraph of the speech that was omitted from the final draft. "There are some who fear it will tear itself to pieces and that an awful lapse in human history may occur. I do not believe it. There must be hope. The alternative is despair, which is madness. The British race has never yielded to counsels of despair."[14]

Roosevelt left Yalta far more optimistic than Churchill about the future of the world. "The far reaching decisions we took at Yalta will hasten victory and the establishment of a firm foundation for lasting peace," Roosevelt cabled Stalin from the *Quincy* in the mid-Atlantic on February 23.[15] The speech he delivered to Congress on March 1, the day after the debate on Yalta ended in Parliament, was more measured. The president stressed that what had been achieved at Yalta was just a first step in the right direction and that, like any international agreement, it was the result of compromise. "The United States will not always have its way 100 percent, nor will Russia, nor Great Britain. We shall not always have ideal answers, solutions to complicated international problems, even though we are determined continuously to strive toward that ideal. But I am sure that under the agreements reached at Yalta there will be a more stable political Europe than ever before."

The rhetoric of the rising power was more humble than that of the waning empire. It was also more true to the letter of the Yalta agreements. Facing no significant opposition on the Polish question or any other point discussed at Yalta, the president had no need to declare his trust in Stalin. He was also more explicit than Churchill in saying that the new Polish government would in fact mean a reorganized old one. "Accordingly," stated Roosevelt, "steps were taken at Yalta to reorganize the existing provisional government in Poland on a broader democratic basis, so as to include democratic leaders now in Poland and those abroad. This new reorganized government will be recognized by all of us as the temporary government of Poland."

Roosevelt was not immune to making more of the Yalta agreements than they were. If Churchill wanted them to provide the basis for the creation of a truly sovereign and independent Poland, Roosevelt saw them as heralding a new international order based on liberal institutions and international cooperation. For him, the tripartite agreement on the United Nations and the Declaration on Liberated Europe, in which the Allies agreed to consult one another on the resolution of crisis situations, indicated that such a new world order was coming into existence. "I think the Crimean Conference was a successful effort by the three leading nations to find a common ground of peace," he told Congress. "It spells, it ought to spell, the end of the system of unilateral action and exclusive alliances and spheres of influence and balances of power and all the other expedients that have been tried for centuries, and have always failed."[16]

As Churchill and Roosevelt delivered their speeches, there was probably no more anxious or more critical reader of them than the Reich minister of public enlightenment and propaganda, Joseph Goebbels. He was clearly encouraged by the critique of the Yalta decisions in the British Parliament and the opposing voices in the American press, which focused largely on the Polish problem. At the same time, he was realistic enough not to expect that such criticism would affect the course of the war. "Churchill will emerge from this debate unscathed," dictated Goebbels on February 28. "England is too weak to be able to afford a government crisis, particularly at this stage of the war. She went along with the rest, she will be carried along with the rest and she will hang with the rest. She has started on the downward path and must stew in her great dilemma." The "rest" were the United States and the Soviet Union; Goebbels considered the latter to be in control of the conference proceedings.

Goebbels had been upset by Roosevelt's remark that there was "not room enough on earth for both German militarism and Christian decency." "I now definitely take the view," he reasoned on March 2, "that German publicity should concern itself somewhat less with foreign statesmen's speeches. They deluge the world daily with fresh statements and, if we take issue with them, we are indirectly making propaganda for them. The only interesting point in Roosevelt's speech is that he referred to prolonged war against Japan." A day earlier, Goebbels had found solace in Roosevelt's statement at a press conference that there had been no discussion of Japan at Yalta. Allied deception was working.

Over the next few days, anxiously following British and American criticism of Soviet actions in Eastern Europe, Goebbels was more pessimistic about the prospects of a falling-out between the Allies. On March 6 he dictated to his secretary: "Britain cannot for the present forgo Soviet Russia's friendship and co-operation, cost what it may. This is reinforced by the fact that in no area of foreign policy has America been prepared to support Britain in a firm stand against Moscow." Regarding Soviet-American relations, the Reich minister shared the opinion of Japanese politicians who believed that "America will only revise her attitude to Soviet Russia when the war against Japan has been victoriously concluded or when it is no longer dependent on the good will or possible participation of Soviet Russia." Goebbels's hopes were slim: "[A]t the moment our political prospects are nil," he dictated. "But this can change from day to day, particularly if developments in Soviet-occupied areas proceed at their tempo of the last few days."[17]

Goebbels was referring to a number of very real crises that broke out in the weeks following the Yalta Conference. All of them were related to Soviet actions in Eastern Europe and were as much the result of conflicting political agendas as of differing interpretations of the documents signed at Yalta. There, the Big Three had found language to paper over their differences: now they would pay the price for not resolving them.

PART VII

THE COMING STORM

This war is not as in the past; whoever occupies a territory also imposes on it his own social system.

JOSEPH STALIN

28

SIGNS OF TROUBLE

On February 23, 1945, Joseph Stalin issued Order of the Day, no. 5, congratulating his troops on the twenty-seventh anniversary of the Red Army:

> Within forty days of the offensive in January–February 1945 our troops have ejected the Germans from 300 towns, captured about 100 war plants manufacturing tanks, aircraft, armaments and ammunition, occupied over 2,400 railway stations, and seized a network of railways totaling over 15,000 kilometers in length. Within this short period, Germany has lost over 350,000 officers and men in war prisoners and not less than 800,000 in killed. During the same period, the Red Army has destroyed or seized about 3,000 German aircraft, over 4,500 tanks and self-propelled guns and not less than 12,000 guns. As a result, the Red Army completely liberated Poland and a considerable part of the territory of Czechoslovakia, occupied Budapest and put out of the war Germany's last ally in Europe—Hungary—captured the greater part of East Prussia and German Silesia and battled its way into Brandenburg, into Pomerania, to the approaches to Berlin.

The continuing Soviet winter offensive and the enthusiastic response to news of the conclusion of the Yalta Conference turned the celebration of the Red Army anniversary into a major international event. In Washington, the Soviet embassy threw a reception for more than a thousand guests. In New York, the anniversary was marked with a 6-foot-high cake weighing 500 pounds that was valued at $1,000. The Grand Alliance seemed stronger than at any time previously, and very few people in Washington wanted to give heed to the clouds gathering over the snow-covered fields of Eastern Europe.[1]

The month of March, which began in the United States with Roosevelt's address to Congress, saw an unprecedented worsening of Soviet-Western relations. The impressive achievements of the Red Army meant that with every passing day the Soviets were in control of ever more territories and people. And it was the treatment of those people and territories that aroused great concern in London and Washington. In a few short weeks Soviet-American-British relations sank to their lowest point since 1941, shaking the wartime alliance to its foundations. It started with a letter that Roosevelt sent to Stalin on March 3, two days after his triumphant speech to Congress. The letter addressed a question that had received relatively little attention during the Yalta Conference—the treatment of Allied prisoners of war. An agreement on the matter had been signed by representatives of the U.S. and Soviet militaries, and this was the first time that the question had reached the highest level of political leadership.

"I have reliable information," Roosevelt's letter began, "regarding the difficulties which are being encountered in collecting, supplying and evacuating ex–prisoners of war and American aircraft crews that are stranded east of the Russian lines. It is urgently requested that instructions be issued authorizing ten American aircraft with American crews to operate between Poltava and places in Poland where American ex-prisoners of war and stranded airmen may be located." The president moved on to the public-relations implications of the crisis. "I regard this request to be of the greatest importance not only for humanitarian reasons but also by reason of the intense interest of the American public in the welfare of our ex–prisoners of war and stranded aircraft crews."[2]

The brusque tone of Roosevelt's letter reflected the outrage felt by General John R. Deane, the head of the U.S. military mission in Moscow, on hearing about the experiences of three American officers who had arrived on his doorstep on February 17. Captain Ernest M. Gruenberg, Second Lieutenant Frank H. Colley, and Second Lieutenant John N. Dimmling Jr. had escaped from a German concentration camp when it was relocated farther west, away from the approaching Soviet front. They then hitchhiked all the way to Moscow from Poland, traveling on Soviet railway tracks during the day and staying in peasant homes at night. They relied on the food and supplies provided by the local population and finally got to Moscow by train. A Red Army soldier whom they met at the railway station directed them to the American embassy.

"I do not think any officers ever had a more sincere welcome than those first three bedraggled ex-prisoners did when they came into our headquarters," wrote Deane a few years afterward. "To us they represented the thousands of Americans who we expected would be liberated and for whom we were prepared to do much if only allowed the opportunity." What outraged Deane was that the officers' story indicated that he had been lied to or at best kept in the dark by his Soviet counterparts regarding the number of American prisoners of war in Soviet-controlled Eastern Europe and the conditions in which they found themselves.

It turned out that there were hundreds if not thousands of dirty, hungry, and exhausted Americans, some in urgent need of medical assistance, wandering in the woods of Poland in search of American military representatives. Red Army officers were not interested in them, and some of the former POWs were robbed of their watches at gunpoint by Soviet soldiers. There were dozens of wounded Americans in a Soviet repatriation camp near Warsaw about whom Deane knew nothing. According to the protocol on the exchange of prisoners of war signed by Deane a few weeks earlier at Yalta, his Soviet counterparts were obliged not only to inform him about American prisoners in Soviet custody but also to allow American military and medical personnel access to places of concentration of American POWs behind the Soviet lines.

Armed with the three officers' testimonies, the outraged Deane confronted his Soviet contacts, demanding information on American prisoners of war in their custody and access to the repatriation camps in Poland. What he got in response was conflicting information on the number of Americans in Soviet custody and assurances that an American military mission would be allowed to contact the ex-POWs in the repatriation camp that was being set up in Odesa. Deane wanted his people to fly to Poland on American aircraft to evacuate the Americans there, but he was making no headway.

It was only when Deane enlisted Harriman's assistance that things began to move, albeit slowly. The ambassador appealed to Andrei Vyshinsky, and a small group of American representatives, including a doctor, was allowed to fly to Lublin on a Soviet aircraft. This limited American success was short-lived. Once in Poland, the group was confined to the city. Harriman appealed to Washington, asking for Roosevelt's personal intervention with Stalin. He was desperate to secure permission for American aircraft to fly into Poland to evacuate Americans.[3]

FDR sent his harsh cable to Stalin on March 3. Stalin responded two days later. He assured the president that the Red Army's difficulties involving the transportation of American POWs to transit camps behind the Soviet lines were over. There were 1,200 Americans in Odesa, others were on their way there, and there was no need to send American planes or representatives to Poland. Stalin tried to calm Roosevelt: "I want to assure you that on our part we shall do everything possible for the creation of favorable conditions for them [American POWs], as soon as they will be on the territory which will be taken by the Soviet troops."

Stalin's response was hardly satisfactory. Deane was eager to go to Poland himself, and Harriman again asked Vyshinsky for permission. The reply he received smacked of a diplomatic trap. Vyshinsky wanted Deane to apply for permission to the Polish government, which in Harriman's eyes would have been tantamount to an American recognition of the Moscow-controlled government. Harriman again appealed to the president, who followed up with an even more abrasive message to Stalin. "Frankly I cannot understand your reluctance to permit American officers [to provide] means to assist their own people in this matter," wrote Roosevelt. "This Government has done everything to meet each of your requests. I now request you to meet mine in this particular matter. Please call Harriman [who will be able] to explain my desires in detail."

Parts of the message sounded more like an order than a request. But Stalin remained unflappable. On March 22, he cabled the president that his sources of information were incorrect. There were only seventeen Americans still in Poland, and they were about to be flown to Odesa. The Soviet dictator then switched to a more informal, almost personal tone: "In regard to a request contained in your message I must say that if that request concerned me personally I would readily agree even to the prejudice of my interests. But in this case the matter concerns the interests of the Soviet armies at the front and Soviet commanders, who do not want to have extra officers with them, having no relation to military operations." Stalin was using his military commanders, who had nothing to do with the prisoners of war (POWs were completely within the jurisdiction of the NKVD), as an excuse to say no once again.

He was also prepared to take the offensive. As Soviet officials had often done before, Stalin accused the Americans of ill-treatment of Soviet citizens in their custody: "[F]ormer American prisoners of war liberated by the Red Army are in Soviet prisoner-of-war camps in good conditions, at any rate in better conditions than former Soviet prisoners of war in American camps where they have been partially placed together with German prisoners of war and where some of them were subjected to unfair treatment and unlawful inconveniences up to beating as it was reported to the American Government more than once."[4]

This was the end of the correspondence between the two leaders concerning prisoners of war. Harriman urged Roosevelt to send another message demanding unrestricted access to American POWs in Eastern Europe, but the president declined. There were other urgent issues on the agenda at the time, including Soviet participation in the United Nations Conference. Besides, it was clear by now that the Soviets would not allow American officials into Poland. American pressure had produced some positive results, and the prisoners were indeed promptly transferred to Odesa, where Deane and his people were busy feeding them, attending to their medical needs, and sending them home.

This exchange was the first test of the Yalta agreements. The results were ambiguous at best: the Soviets would stick to the letter of the agreements while disregarding their spirit. They were prepared to give American representatives access to their former prisoners of war, but only in transit camps deep inside Soviet territory, not in the recently liberated areas of Eastern Europe. The Soviets were concerned that the Americans were using the POW issue as a pretext to introduce their military personnel into Eastern Europe so as to gather information on Soviet conduct there. It had been a Soviet policy to seal off the region, and Stalin was not about to change it. The Americans, for their part, thought that the Soviets wanted to trick them into de facto recognition of the Lublin government and refused to take the bait.

The Soviets treated the American POWs fairly well, certainly much better than they would have treated their own. Their living conditions were on par with those of Red Army personnel, a fact fully recognized by Deane and others at the American mission in Moscow. The problem was that those standards were extremely low. Deane found the rations at the Odesa camp sufficient only if supplemented with American supplies shipped from Moscow. After hearing about conditions in the Red Army transit camps, many of the American POWs in Eastern Europe preferred to stay on their own, avoiding Soviet troops by hiding in the woods, and escaping from the camps if they could. This further strained relations, as the Soviets underestimated the number of American POWs behind their lines, while the Americans exaggerated it.

It was on the emotionally charged and culturally loaded issue of prisoners of war that Roosevelt first lost his temper with Stalin and sided completely with his representatives in Moscow, who by now were sick and tired of Soviet ways of doing things. The harsh tone of Roosevelt's messages to Stalin, so different from that of his earlier telegrams, can be explained in part by the fact that they were prepared by Admiral Leahy and inspired by State Department officials like Harriman, who were deeply frustrated by Soviet behavior after Yalta. But this frustration soon extended to the president himself.

On March 13, he summoned to his office one of the administration's top economists, Leon Henderson, to discuss Allied policies in Germany. He told Henderson not to rush things in Germany because of possible surprises on the part of the Soviets. "He said," Henderson later recalled, "that the British, French and ourselves would abide by agreement but the Russians would suit themselves! I asked if they were not meticulous on things they agreed to. I remembered the protocols. He said yes—on protocols, on anything that would show, but anywhere else, they would go their own way." As time passed and the crisis over the treatment of American POWs deepened, the president's frustration grew stronger and stronger. On March 24, Anna Rosenberg Hoffman, Roosevelt's unofficial adviser on labor issues, witnessed his reaction to a cable from Stalin that was brought to him at lunch. After reading the cable, Roosevelt "banged his fists on the arms of his wheelchair and said: 'Averell is right; we can't do business with Stalin. He has broken every one of his promises he made at Yalta.'" The president was referring to more than the clash over American POWs.[5]

On March 8, 1945, Kathleen Harriman wrote to her sister from Moscow: "The war is going wonderfully well again now, what with the offensive on the Western front. Gosh, it's exciting. But the news is slightly dampened here by our gallant allies who at the moment are being most bastard-like. Averell is very busy—what with Poland, PWs and I guess the Balkans. The house is full of running feet, voices, and phones ringing all night long—up until dawn." Averell Harriman, the key figure in the POW crisis, also played an important role in the two other crises that began to develop in Allied-Soviet relations in late February and March 1945. These concerned Soviet conduct in Romania and Poland.[6]

In the fall of 1944, Molotov had promised the American and British ambassadors that consular officers of all countries belonging to the United Nations would be allowed in Romania. This was in line with the practice of the Western Allies in Italy. In January, however, the Soviets refused to admit Lee E. Metcalf, an American delegate to the Allied Control Commission, to Romania. To offset American protests, Molotov complained to Harriman that the "Soviet representatives in Italy had no rights whatsoever. In the beginning they had no work to do. According to the Italian statutes they were there merely for consultations." The message was clear: don't interfere with what we are doing in Eastern Europe, and you will get a free hand in Western and southern Europe.[7]

On February 13, two days after the end of the Yalta Conference, the Romanian communists organized a mass demonstration in Bucharest demanding the removal of the coalition government of General Nicolae Radescu and its replacement by a communist-controlled cabinet. When the American and British representatives on the Allied Control Commission for Romania requested a meeting of the commission on February 24, Stalin sent Andrei Vyshinsky to Bucharest. Judging by the short biography prepared by the State Department on the eve of the Yalta Conference, the Americans regarded Vyshinsky as relatively liberal. They credited him with the Soviet recognition of the Marshal Pietro Badoglio government in Italy and with their conciliatory approach to the Radescu government in Romania. They were soon to be bitterly disappointed.

Vyshinsky arrived in Bucharest on February 27 and immediately requested a meeting with the king. There, he demanded the dismissal of the Radescu government, claiming that it was unable to maintain order. He wanted it to be replaced by a government based on "truly democratic forces," meaning the communists and their allies. The next day Vyshinsky accused the existing government of protecting "fascists" and gave the king two hours to dismiss the government. "In leaving," wrote James Byrnes on the basis of a report from the American representative in Bucharest, "he slammed the door so hard that the plaster around the door frame was cracked badly. It has never been fixed; it remains to testify to the strength of his feeling and his arm." Through a combination of threats (to abolish Romanian statehood) and promises (to attach Hungarian Transylvania to Romania), Vyshinsky eventually managed to install a new government led by the communist Petru Groza.[8]

The Soviet-engineered coup d'état alarmed London and Washington. Since

Churchill, given his percentage deal, was in no position to protest directly, he appealed to Roosevelt. He told the president that "[t]he Russians had succeeded in establishing the rule of Communist minority by force and misrepresentation." Roosevelt agreed but refused to act, believing that "Romania is not a good place for a test case." The Soviets had been in complete control there since the fall of 1944, and given the country's strategic location on the Red Army supply and communications lines, it would be difficult to challenge Soviet claims concerning the military necessity of their actions. Roosevelt knew about Churchill and Stalin's deal on the Balkans and apparently decided to avoid involvement in a potentially embarrassing situation.

In Washington there was a growing realization that something had to be done, but given the president's silence, Stalin felt it safe to ignore the efforts of American diplomats to remedy the situation. On March 17, 1945, Molotov turned down an American request for consultations on the Romanian situation in keeping with the provisions of the Declaration on Liberated Europe—the approach Churchill had suggested to Roosevelt. The Romanian crisis was resolved, Molotov told Harriman, and there was thus no need to invoke the provisions of the declaration, which required joint Allied consultation in case of a crisis.[9]

A much greater and lasting problem surfaced in Poland. At Yalta, the formation of the Polish government was referred to a commission composed of Molotov, Harriman, and Archibald Clark Kerr, the British ambassador to the Soviet Union. This Moscow commission became the main arena in which the future of Polish freedom and independence would be decided. "The Yalta proposal concerning Poland is a 'good façade' and much of the responsibility for working out the details will rest upon American and British Ambassadors at Moscow," the British Foreign Office cabled to the Americans. Harriman later claimed that even before leaving the Crimea, he and Bohlen had agreed that "the whole negotiation we had just completed at Yalta would have to be developed again from the ground up."[10]

While the Allies pinned their hopes on the commission, the representatives of the Polish government in London had no such illusions. "The commission established in Moscow will be controlled by Molotov," the Polish ambassador to Washington, Jan Ciechanowski, told Acting Secretary of State Joseph Grew on February 16. He knew that the battle was lost. Privately he asked Grew how he and his personnel would be treated once the Allies withdrew their recognition of the London government. Grew had no answer.[11]

In the weeks following the Yalta Conference, the Poles were the first to raise questions. Those in the American media and political establishment who questioned the Yalta agreements did so with regard to Poland and on behalf of the Polish electorate. On February 14, the *Washington Post* featured an article entitled "London Poles Flay Big Three's Border Pact. Accuse Conference of Acting Contrary to Atlantic Charter." The *Washington Times-Herald* published a story headlined "Half of Poland Is Given to Stalin." Some commentators referred to the deal on Poland as a "compromise in which Stalin dictated most of the terms." Senators Burton Kendall Wheeler and Henrik Shipstead and Representatives John Lesinski and Alvin O'Konski were critical of the agreement, as were the leaders of the Polish-American community.[12]

Poland was of course a much greater problem for Churchill. As early as February 12 the Polish ambassador to Britain, Count Edward Bernard Raczyński, visited the British minister of state, Richard Law, asking for clarification of the Yalta agreements. He immediately pointed out the weakest points of the settlement on Poland: the continuing existence of the Lublin government; the failure to specify how many members of the reorganized government would come from noncommunist parties; and the reference to anti-Nazi parties, which was open to Soviet interpretation. He also stated that for the first time in the negotiations Poland's eastern and western borders were being considered separately. Nothing that he heard from his British counterparts allayed Raczyński's concerns. He noted the difficulties that the agreements created for Poles fighting alongside the Western Allies in Italy.

Five days later Field Marshal Harold Alexander heard about the concerns of the Polish soldiers from their commander in Italy, General Władysław Anders. "By a conference at which Poland was not represented, not invited to state her views, the Government is displaced, the Constitution annulled and hence all treaties abrogated, what therefore is the position of loyal Poles?" demanded Anders of his commander. "One of the main points he has always made to his troops," argued Anders, "is that they are fighting for Poland. Now they ask what is there to fight for?" Alexander had no satisfactory answer. He said that although he had been at Yalta, he had not attended political meetings, and he counseled patience. He recognized that the Polish corps was in no position to engage in major operations on the Italian front and promised to keep the Poles out of action, asking them simply to hold the section of the front line where they were posted. News of the conference decisions began to create problems at the front—the outcome that Churchill had warned about at Yalta.[13]

On February 21, Churchill met with General Anders and found him distressed, predicting "the end of Poland." Criticism of the Yalta agreements was coming not only from Arciszewski's government and Polish military formations loyal to it but also from Polish allies of the British government—Mikołajczyk and his group. After the publication of the Yalta communiqué Mikołajczyk found himself under attack in the Polish press, which claimed that the Yalta agreements were based on his suggestions. The former prime minister published his protest in both Polish and English. In the English version, which appeared in the *Daily Herald* on February 16, Mikołajczyk stated that he had never suggested separate consideration of Poland's eastern and western borders, had argued for leaving Lviv in Poland, and had never advocated broadening or reorganizing the existing Lublin government.

Concerned that Mikołajczyk's views would influence British public opinion, Foreign Office officials did not wait for Churchill and Eden to return from Yalta before setting up a meeting to calm down their allies. Eden met with Mikołajczyk and Tadeusz Romer, the former Polish foreign minister, upon his return on February 20 and was deeply disappointed by their reaction. "I have taught myself not to expect any thanks for anything we may be able to do for other people, but I must confess that I had not quite expected these gentlemen to be so skeptical of the arrangement reached at the Crimean Conference and by implication so critical of the plan." News of the revolt that had begun in the Arciszewski camp and spread to Mikołajczyk's followers soon reached British political circles.[14]

In Churchill's address to the House of Commons on February 27, it was the settlement of the Polish question that caused the most controversy. Churchill's speech was interrupted more than once, and twenty-five members of Parliament, mostly from the prime minister's own Conservative Party, voted against their leader's motion to approve the Yalta decisions, considering them a violation of Britain's obligations to its Polish ally. The dissent was not lost on Joseph Goebbels, who eagerly followed the debate. "Criticism of the Yalta decisions comes from Tory circles," he recorded in his diary. "The group of Tories forming the inner circle has long been at work either to bring Churchill back onto the right course, or to bring him down. In these circles people talk of Poland when of course they mean Germany."[15]

Goebbels was wrong. The debate concerned Poland and was only entering its early stages. A new phase opened with the proceedings of the Molotov-Harriman-Kerr Commission, which was entrusted with the formation of the new Polish government. Before its first meeting on February 23, 1945, the British, wishing to avoid a repeat of Yalta, insisted on a common strategy with the Americans. They argued that even if the Soviets concluded that the Western Allies were "ganging up" on them, the negative effect of that impression would be significantly outweighed by the realization that the British and the Americans "see eye to eye on many important issues." The Western goal was to ensure adequate representation of noncommunist Poles in the new government and to secure their capacity to influence decisions and their execution.

The British suspected that Molotov would use the facade of the Lublin government to veto noncommunist candidates proposed by the Western ambassadors. They suggested that no candidate should be barred from being invited to Moscow without a unanimous decision. "We should propose therefore," read the Foreign Office instructions to the British ambassador in Moscow, "that the Commission should at once invite representatives of 'Lublin' and an unspecified number of representative Poles from inside and outside Poland to Moscow to discuss among themselves under the Commission's auspices how representative government can be formed, allocation of key posts and how presidential functions should be performed pending elections."[16]

The British were right. Molotov used the Lublin Poles as a foil to veto invitations to some of the leading Polish politicians suggested by the Western Allies, first and foremost Stanisław Mikołajczyk. Molotov wanted to begin by inviting only representatives of the Lublin government, and adding representatives of the noncommunist Poles later. The Western ambassadors were at a major disadvantage in Moscow not only because of the lack of reliable information and poor coordination but also because their security had been breached. The Soviets knew about their plans and disagreements from their numerous agents in the West. As always, their spies did an outstanding job of supplying their handlers with accurate information on British and American strategy and tactics at the negotiations.

According to the official history of the Russian intelligence services, in March and April 1945 the Soviet leaders had at their disposal the Foreign Office instructions to Sir Archibald Clark Kerr, written soon after the Yalta Conference, defining the British position on the formation of the new Polish government and a copy of a Foreign Office letter on the reaction of General Władysław Anders to the Yalta decisions. Copies of those documents came to Moscow directly from London, supplied by members of the Cambridge Five.[17]

In the summer of 1944, Donald Maclean, a member of the Cambridge Five who moved to Washington to take a position in the British embassy, began to supply information on British-American relations through the NKGB's New York station. His documents were often considered so important and time-sensitive that instead of being sent to Moscow by diplomatic mail they were coded and dispatched by cable. That was the case with the correspondence between the Foreign Office and Britain's Moscow ambassador, Clark Kerr, and its Washington ambassador, Lord Halifax, in March 1945.

Through Maclean the Soviets learned that Kerr and Harriman had decided to insist on the inclusion of two of their nominees from London and two from Poland in the future government. They also learned that Harriman's nominees were Stanisław Mikołajczyk and Stanisław Grabski from London and Professor Stanisław Kutrzeba from Poland. Maclean's telegrams also revealed an area of disagreement between the United States and Britain. While the British were prepared to confront Molotov on the issue of Soviet conduct in Poland, the Americans preferred to use more conciliatory language. According to a telegram by Lord Halifax delivered by Maclean to his Soviet handlers, the State Department considered the British draft note to Molotov excessively sharp, showing "too great a distrust of Soviet intentions in Poland." Harriman believed that pressure would have to be applied to make Mikołajczyk issue a statement accepting the Yalta decisions, if not necessarily endorsing them.[18]

The debate on whether to invite the Lublin Poles first centered on the interpretation of one sentence in the Yalta declaration, which read: "M. Molotov, Mr. Harriman and Sir A. Clark Kerr are authorized as a Commission to consult in the first instance in Moscow with members of the present Provisional Government and with other Polish democratic leaders from within Poland and abroad." When, at the first meeting, Molotov suggested that they call in representatives of the Polish government and agree on the names of the other Poles to be summoned to Moscow, Clark Kerr was instructed to respond that "the decision of this question should not await the Warsaw Poles." Molotov then quoted from the Yalta formula on Poland, and both ambassadors eventually agreed that the Warsaw Poles could be summoned first.[19]

They later revoked their consent, suggesting that Molotov had misinterpreted the text of the Yalta agreement. Charles Bohlen, who had helped draft that agreement, was consulted in Washington and he confirmed that the words "in the first instance" referred not to the Warsaw government but to Moscow as the commission's place of meeting—the assumption being that it could later meet in Warsaw as well. While this may well have been the original intent, there is no mention of a possible Warsaw meeting in the document. Molotov was not the first to conclude that the words "in the first instance" referred to the Warsaw Poles. A British embassy document entitled "A Possible Line of Approach to the Setting Up of the Poland Commission to Be 'Sold,' if Possible, to M. Molotov," received in the American embassy in Moscow on February 22, one day before the first meeting of the commission, contained the same interpretation: "It is to be suggested that in the first instance the Commission should see the representatives of the Provisional Government now acting in Warsaw, then the representatives of other Polish democratic political groups, and then the whole bunch together."[20]

Also confronting the commission were their differing interpretations of the words "democracy" and "fascism." The debate started at Yalta, with Churchill and Eden on one side and Stalin and Molotov on the other, and its echoes reverberated in Moscow. On March 6, Molotov suggested that the Western ambassadors' candidates "might not be truly democratic." His target was Archbishop Sapieha of Kraków, who, according to Molotov, "had once opposed, as being a luxury, the increase in public schools." In Soviet eyes, it was a short step from not being entirely democratic to being a fascist. "We might, however, make a mistake," argued Molotov, "and find a fascist in our midst if we do not get Warsaw's advice."

As Churchill warned those present at Yalta, the Soviets were prepared to use the term "fascist" indiscriminately against their enemies. One could easily become a "fascist" simply by criticizing the government. U.S. congressman Alvin O'Konski was accused by *Pravda* on February 18 of spreading "fascist propaganda" concerning the situation in liberated Poland. The Soviet press also vented against the writings of "some pro-Nazi journalists, such as the notorious Brown of the *Washington Post*." The fact that Goebbels's propaganda machine lauded the Polish government in exile's opposition to Yalta made that government an easy target in the Soviet propaganda war. "The political bankrupts of the emigrant 'government' are finally exposing themselves as Hitler's hirelings by daring to call the Crimean decisions the fifth partition of Poland," asserted the Soviet press.

The U.S. embassy review of the Soviet media in the first months of 1945 gives a good idea of the Soviet understanding of democracy at the time of the Yalta Conference. Elections, like those in Egypt, were characterized as games played by corrupt politicians. The Soviet media also attacked the American model of a free press, stating that it could not serve as an example to the rest of the world. The "free press" was not free: it served special interests and was inferior to state-controlled media. For the Soviets, democracy was about the power of the people, which could best be exercised through the rule of the communist vanguard. The Soviets did not deny the right of the Western Allies to call themselves democracies, but neither did they doubt their own democratic credentials. After the conference, the Soviet press hailed the Yalta decisions as an achievement of the "great democratic powers." For a while, the Soviet leaders were prepared to regard the United States and Britain as democratic nations, but they would not give them a monopoly on the use of the term.[21]

Churchill was one Western leader who realized early on the danger represented by demagogic use of democratic terminology by the Soviet leadership and its sympathizers in the West. In December 1944 he found himself obliged to specify his understanding of democracy in the British Parliament. "[W]ho are the friends of democracy, and also how is the word 'democracy' to be interpreted?" he asked, responding to an attack in Parliament on his policy in Greece, where he had authorized a crackdown on communist militias. "My idea of it is that the plain, humble, common man, just the ordinary man who keeps a wife and family, who goes off to fight for his country when it is in trouble, goes to the poll at the appropriate time, and puts his cross on the ballot-paper showing the candidate he wishes to be elected to Parliament—that he is the foundation of democracy." Armed bands wishing to establish a totalitarian regime, as Churchill characterized his communist opponents in Greece, were "the last thing which resembles democracy."[22]

29

SPY WARS

On February 13, 1945, Secretary of State Stettinius and his staff were invited to a reception hosted by Deputy Commissar of Foreign Affairs Andrei Vyshinsky in the commissariat's guesthouse in Moscow. Stettinius and three of his close associates—H. Freeman Matthews, Alger Hiss, and Wilder Foote—had flown to Moscow the day before from Yalta to continue discussions. They spent only one full day in the Soviet capital, but still squeezed in a performance of *Swan Lake* at the Bolshoi hosted by Molotov.[1]

Vyshinsky was the main toastmaster, and his own toast made an impression on the secretary of state. "[T]he Soviet Union [is] doing its best," he declared, "to learn from the United States and [has] already mastered the art of producing many of the things for which America [is] famous." He hoped that "the Soviet Union would eventually not only equal but surpass the United States in production." The toast was about the economy, but it was also about competition and American know-how. Soviet emulation sometimes took a less benign form. Vyshinsky may not have known about the effort to obtain technological information from inside America's top-secret Manhattan Project, but he was no stranger to the world of Soviet espionage.

There is reason to believe that on that day, possibly at dinner, or perhaps later, at the Bolshoi, Vyshinsky met with a Soviet agent who had accompanied Stettinius from Yalta as part of the American delegation. The star prosecutor at the Moscow show trials of the 1930s, Molotov's right-hand man at Yalta, and, a few weeks later, a door-slamming bully in Bucharest, Vyshinsky must have been the picture of gratitude as he expressed the appreciation of the Red Army's Main Intelligence Directorate, the GRU, to its American agent for a job well done. The next morning, he went to the Moscow airport to bid farewell to the American delegation. "It was below zero and a light snow was falling," Stettinius remembered. "Molotov, in a black coat and black fur hat, Vishinsky in his Foreign Office uniform, . . . were awaiting us there. As we stepped from our car the band struck up 'The Star-Spangled Banner,' and we could see the aluminum alloy of the C-54 sparkling in the bright light of the floodlights. . . . It was an impressive occasion." Stettinius was leaving Moscow with a Soviet agent on board his plane.[2]

The future never looked brighter for Soviet spymasters. On March 30, Lieutenant Anatolii Gorsky, the Washington resident of the People's Commissariat of State Security (NKGB), reported to his superiors in Moscow on a meeting earlier that month between one of his officers, identified in the secret cable as "A," and a Soviet agent who had been at Yalta code-named "Ales." The ciphered message, signed with Gorsky's code name, Vadim, read:

> As a result of A's chat with Ales the following has been ascertained: Ales has been working with the neighbors continuously since 1935. For some years past he has been the leader of a small group of the neighbors' probationers, for the most part consisting of his relatives. The group and Ales himself work on obtaining military information only. Materials on the Bank allegedly interest the neighbors very little and he does not produce them regularly. . . . Recently Ales and his whole group were awarded Soviet decorations. After the Yalta Conference already in Moscow Ales was allegedly contacted by a Soviet personage in a very responsible position (Ales gave to understand that it was Comrade Vyshinsky) and on the instruction of the Military neighbors passed on to him their gratitude.[3]

The text of the message, intercepted by American counterintelligence as part of the Venona Project, which was initiated by U.S. military intelligence in 1943 to monitor Soviet intelligence traffic and deciphered years later after the end of the war, indicates that one of the members of the U.S. delegation at Yalta, who went on to Moscow after the conference, was running a network of Soviet spies ("probationers"). He did not work for the NKGB foreign intelligence service but was in contact with "neighbors," which in NKGB parlance of the time meant Red Army Intelligence. Soviet military intelligence was not interested in information about the "Bank"—the U.S. State Department— about which the agent apparently knew a good deal, and that clearly made the NKGB, which wanted such information, envious of its more successful "neighbor." The agent's success was attested by his ten years of service, Soviet decorations, and the commendation from Vyshinsky. But who was the mysterious Ales, and what kind of information could he deliver to the Soviet spymasters?

Few have any doubt today that Ales was none other than Alger Hiss, then deputy director of the Office of Special Political Affairs at the State Department and Roosevelt's point man for the creation of the United Nations. Given that he was a member of the U.S. delegation at Yalta, traveled to Moscow after the Yalta Conference, was a member of the communist movement in the 1930s, and had relatives who may well have been Soviet "probationers"—a brother working at the State Department and a wife who shared his political views—Hiss is by far the most likely suspect. His prominent role in the preparations for the United Nations Conference in San Francisco alerted NKGB officers in the United States to his existence, and they decided to establish contact with a star agent of the competing intelligence service. A cable of March 5 reported that an agent code-named Ruble (identified by the FBI as Harold Glasser), who was asked to provide an assessment of Ales, characterized him as "a strong, determined man with a firm and resolute character" who "is a communist with all the consequences of illegal status. Unfortunately, he evidently understands the rules of security [*konspiratsiia*] as his own [business], as [do] all local communists." Like many other Soviet sympathizers who ended up spying for the USSR for ideological reasons, Hiss apparently considered himself a free agent and ignored his handlers' instructions on the rules of espionage. Whatever his technical shortcomings, he rebuffed Glasser's attempts to put him in touch with the NKGB resident in Washington, Anatolii Gorsky.[4]

Hiss became a media darling when he was appointed secretary-general of the United Nations Conference in San Francisco. *Time* magazine informed its readers about his appointment in its April 16 issue, characterizing him as "lanky, Harvard-trained Alger Hiss, one of the State Department's brighter young men." It was stated that he had been chosen for the post at Yalta. The article suggested that Hiss would be "an important figure" at the founding conference: "As Secretary-General, managing the agenda, he will have a lot to say behind the scenes about who gets the breaks." A *Time* article of May 28, 1945, written with the input of the magazine's founder and publisher, Henry Luce, who was impressed by Hiss's performance in San Francisco, referred to him as "young, handsome . . . a U.S. State Department career man functioning as international secretary-general. Relaxed and alert amid innumerable annoyances, Hiss was master of the incredibly complicated conference machinery."[5]

Not all the editors of *Time* were excited about the Yalta Conference or Hiss's achievements there and in San Francisco. One of them, Whittaker Chambers, wrote a negative piece about the Yalta Conference entitled "The Ghosts on the Roof," in which he portrayed Stalin as determined to continue the imperialist policy of the tsars, a man whom Tsar Nicholas II would have praised for his territorial acquisitions in Eastern Europe. Chambers later claimed that he wrote the essay without knowing about Hiss's role at Yalta. Subsequently, on hearing of Hiss's successes in San Francisco, Chambers grumbled to his colleagues that Hiss was a communist but was getting important jobs nevertheless.[6]

Chambers, a communist activist during the 1920s and most of the 1930s, served as a courier for other activists spying for the Soviet Union. "Invited" to visit Moscow at the height of the Great Terror, he declined the honor, knowing the gruesome fate of other Soviet agents recalled to Moscow by the paranoid

Stalinist leadership. He then turned staunchly anticommunist, launching a one-man crusade against his former party colleagues. On September 1, 1939, the first day of the Second World War, Chambers denounced Alger Hiss and a number of other government officials in Washington as Communist Party members in a letter to the assistant secretary of state in charge of intelligence, Adolf Berle Jr. The case was of low priority at the time, and the FBI did not interview Chambers until 1942. Approached by FBI agents, Hiss denied any involvement in communist activities.

In the spring of 1945, with Hiss's appointment to the top job in San Francisco, the FBI revived its interest in Chambers's accusations. It alerted the State Department's internal security service, which in turn interviewed Chambers, who restated his original accusations. There was little else to go on, and the internal security service had no choice but to leave the department's rising star alone. J. Edgar Hoover, the longtime head of the FBI, refused to give up. His agents interviewed Chambers again in May 1945 and then leaked potentially damaging information about Hiss to friendly members of Congress and to the Catholic priest John Cronin, who had made a name for himself as a ferocious anticommunist crusader long before Richard Nixon and Joseph McCarthy joined the fray.[7]

Hiss's resignation from the State Department in 1946 to direct the Carnegie Endowment for International Peace did not save him from further persecution. In August 1948, at the peak of the Soviet-American confrontation over the Berlin blockade, Chambers and Hiss faced each other in an open session of the House Un-American Activities Committee (HUAC). Chambers accused Hiss of being a communist, while Hiss continued to deny membership in the Communist Party. The major turn in the case occurred in November and December 1948, when, after being sued by Hiss for slander, Chambers produced a microfilm of typed copies of secret State Department documents hidden in a hollowed-out pumpkin at his farm. According to Chambers, the documents had been obtained in 1937–38 from Hiss and his wife, Priscilla, who had retyped them on their Woodstock typewriter, following instructions from the Soviet spymaster Boris Bykov.

The HUAC hearings suddenly took on a new and dangerous significance. From a forum for exposing communist beliefs of some members of Roosevelt's administration they turned into a high-profile denunciation of Soviet penetration of the American government. The growing spy mania created by the dramatic worsening of Soviet-American relations in the first stage of the Cold War helped seal the fate of Alger Hiss. He could not be prosecuted for espionage because of the statute of limitations, but he was eventually convicted in January 1951 on charges of perjury—lying about the nature and the length of his acquaintance with Chambers—and sentenced to five years in prison.[8]

The Hiss trials marked a watershed in American politics. Since Hiss portrayed himself as a staunch supporter of the New Deal, they cast a shadow on the liberal policies of the Roosevelt administration, suggesting a link not only between communist convictions and espionage activities but also between liberalism and the betrayal of national interests. Was Hiss indeed a member of the Communist Party and a Soviet spy, as Chambers maintained and J. Edgar Hoover believed? Or was he the innocent victim of a witch hunt, as claimed by his supporters, including Eleanor Roosevelt and influential political commentator Walter Lippmann, one of the founders of *The New Republic*? For the great majority of present-day scholars, the Venona documents, which contain Anatolii Gorsky's report of March 30, 1945, about the activities of "Ales," constitute the "smoking gun" that Hoover lacked in the 1940s. Soviet intelligence documents that became available after the collapse of the USSR point in the same direction, strengthening the case against Hiss. They leave little doubt that Hiss was a longtime Soviet agent, still active at the time of the Yalta Conference.[9]

Less persuasive are suggestions that Soviet intelligence had daily briefings with Hiss during his stay at Yalta, which have not been corroborated by documentary evidence and are based on recollections of retired Soviet intelligence officers or members of their families. One of the oral testimonies from the Soviet intelligence milieu suggests that at Yalta Hiss had regular meetings with Mikhail Milshtein, a high-ranking officer in Soviet military intelligence, who later recalled that he was at the conference meeting with one of his assets. If that was indeed the case, and Milshtein's contact at Yalta was in fact Hiss, then his Soviet handlers were most probably interested in military rather than political matters. This is the conclusion one draws from what is known about Hiss's espionage activities and the position he took at Yalta on the membership of the Soviet republics in the United Nations.[10]

In 1953, testifying before the U.S. Senate Foreign Relations Committee, Charles Bohlen stated that Hiss had never advised President Roosevelt on any policy issues. He had served as an adviser to Stettinius and had never attended negotiations of heads of state—he was present only at the plenary sessions as a note-taker and at the foreign ministers' meetings. Bohlen also stated that he did not "recall Hiss expressing an opinion on anything about Poland, the Far East or anything. I do recall him expressing his opinion about United Nations matters." In his memoirs, written more than a quarter century after the conference, Bohlen took this one step further. He said that he did not know Hiss personally before Yalta. "At meetings at Yalta, his slightly cavernous face always wore a serious expression. He was not an outgoing person, but one who seemed to regard his associates from a superior distance," he wrote. Bohlen claimed that far from taking a pro-Soviet stand, Hiss had actually led the opposition in the American delegation to Stalin's proposal to give the Soviet Union two additional seats in the UN General Assembly—a claim fully corroborated by State Department documents.[11]

If Hiss was indeed a Soviet spy, as the new evidence suggests, then his performance at Yalta is puzzling. Judging by what we know today, the Soviet spymasters mismanaged their greatest asset at the conference. In a few years, however, Hiss's presence there would become a trump card for those in the United States who wished to denounce not only Yalta but also Roosevelt's New Deal and his foreign-policy legacy.[12]

Stalin never fully trusted his allies and relied heavily on his intelligence networks abroad to keep tabs on them. If anything, he intensified covert operations after Yalta. As tensions grew in the first months after the conference, so did the importance attributed by the Soviet leadership to its intelligence effort. With hundreds if not thousands of undercover Soviet intelligence officers, agents, and informants in the United States alone, the Soviet intelligence services were in a position not only to supply their political masters with detailed information on the Western Allies' plans at Yalta but to follow shifts in their policies after the conference. Soviet espionage helped fuel Stalin's suspicions and contributed specifically to the deterioration of relations after Yalta.

On March 29, Stalin summoned Marshal Georgii Zhukov to the Kremlin to discuss the Red Army offensive against Berlin. He showed the marshal a letter from one of his Western "well-wishers." "It reported," remembered Zhukov, "on behind-the-scenes negotiations between Hitler's agents and official representatives of the Allies, from which it became apparent that the Germans were proposing to end the struggle against them if they would agree to a separate peace on any condition. That report also said that the Allies had supposedly declined the German demands. But the possibility of the Germans' opening the road to Berlin to Allied troops was not ruled out. 'Well, what do you say about that?' asked J. V. Stalin. And, without waiting for an answer, he noted immediately: 'I think that Roosevelt will not violate the Yalta agreement, but as for Churchill, he is capable of anything.'"[13]

What Zhukov read in Stalin's study was an intelligence report on the so-called Bern incident, involving highly secret contacts between the U.S. foreign intelligence service and representatives of the German administration in northern Italy. The key figures in question were Allen Dulles, the Bern station chief of the U.S. Office of Strategic Services (a forerunner of the CIA), and Obergruppenführer Karl Wolff, the former head of Heinrich Himmler's secretariat, who in the last years of the war became the commander of SS forces in northern Italy, responsible for, among other things, antipartisan warfare and the deportations of Jews. The first meeting between Dulles and Wolff took place in Zurich on March 8, 1945. The conversation was held around a fireplace in the library of an apartment rented by the Office of Strategic Services (OSS). A fifty-one-year-old professional diplomat and intelligence expert, Dulles believed that a wood fire made people feel at ease, and that was the atmosphere he wanted to create for his first meeting with the senior SS official. Those taking part in this "fireside chat" were Dulles, his assistant Gero von Gaevernitz, and Karl Wolff.

The general's trip to Zurich had not gone smoothly: an avalanche blocked the train tracks on the Swiss side of the border, and Wolff and his party, consisting of a number of SS officers, had to walk along the tracks to board another train. Among the passengers were some Italians who knew Wolff personally, and the powerful SS general had to duck and stall on his way to the train to avoid detection. Also quite unsettling for him were the hours leading up to the meeting with Dulles. The OSS chief in Switzerland had insisted that the meeting take place on his territory and made the general wait a few hours. Now the burning wood in the fireplace and a drink of Scotch were supposed to relax him, and by all accounts it seems to have worked.

Wolff managed to make a highly positive impression on his host. The consultations continued the following day, now with the participation of SS Standartenführer Eugen Dollmann. In his reports to OSS headquarters in Washington and, later, in his autobiographical book about the events of the spring of 1945, Dulles went out of his way to stress that Wolff did not act as a representative of Himmler or question the principle of unconditional surrender. Dulles was under explicit orders from Washington not to negotiate with the German political leadership or compromise the Allies' demand for unconditional surrender.[14]

For months before this meeting he had turned down offers of just such negotiations from the Germans, but time was passing, the war was nearing its end, and the OSS chief in Bern was under pressure to produce tangible results. Acting in the gray zone offered by his official permission to assist the military in arranging the surrender of German forces on the western front, Dulles had to ensure that the news of his meeting did not leak.

Whether by accident or by design, the first report he cabled on March 8 about the arrival of Wolff's group in Switzerland contained an error, creating the impression that he had been joined by a representative of Field Marshal Albert Kesselring, the German supreme commander in Italy. In reality, all four members of Wolff's party were members of the SS, and Wolff had nothing to offer the Allied military except the cooperation of the German police and SS troops in northern Italy. Wolff said he was prepared to talk with Kesselring, but it was clear he did not represent the German military. Dulles corrected the mistake the following day, but the erroneous information that representatives of the Wehrmacht were "allegedly prepared to make definite commitments in regard to terminating German resistance in northern Italy" entered the information pipeline, inflating the expectations of Anglo-American military commanders and politicians alike. More important for our story, this legitimized further contacts with members of the SS in neutral Switzerland. Allen Dulles code-named these contacts Operation Sunrise.[15]

What Dulles did not know was that Operation Sunrise had been initiated not by him but by the Germans, who were in fact carrying out their own operation, code-named "Wool." The German operation aimed at splitting the Allies. Its first stage was to establish direct contact with Anglo-American representatives in Switzerland through Baron Luigi Parrilli, a former representative of several American firms in Italy. The operation was conceived at a meeting of German SS and security officials in Verona in November 1944. It was then approved by SS intelligence headquarters in Berlin, and in February it secured the support of the SS supreme commander in northern Italy, Karl Wolff.

An experienced Nazi apparatchik, Wolff flew to Berlin to speak with Himmler and on February 4, 1945, the first day of the Yalta Conference, he met with Hitler himself. The führer did not object to Wolff's plan of establishing contact with the Americans in order to split the Allies. This meant, in effect, that Wolff could begin the operation but would become a scapegoat if things went awry. His SS superiors and colleagues, who were looking for their own ways to establish contacts with the West before the collapse of the Nazi regime, would eat him alive. The peculiar mixture of officially stated goals and individual ambition to curry favor and arrange for a soft landing after the war comes across most clearly in the diary of Guido Zimmer, an SS officer who played an active part in the operation and suggested Baron Parrilli as a go-between.[16]

Parrilli's mission proved an unqualified success. In Switzerland, through the intermediacy of the Swiss secret service, the baron met with Dulles's assistant Gero von Gaevernitz, who indicated his readiness to meet with higher German SS and military officials. Parrilli soon returned to Switzerland accompanied by his case officer, Zimmer, and Standartenführer Eugen Dollmann. They met in Lugano with another OSS officer, David Blum. That meeting opened the door to Wolff's personal visit to Switzerland, preconditioned by the release from German captivity of two leading members of the Italian resistance.

Dulles was so impressed by his conversations with Wolff on March 8 and 9 that he suggested that the Allied commander in Italy, Field Marshal Harold Alexander, send representatives to Switzerland to conduct talks with Wolff on the surrender of German troops in Italy or, possibly, on the entire western front. The idea was approved in both London and Washington, and two Allied generals were dispatched to Bern to negotiate with the Germans. They met Wolff on March 19 at a villa near the Italian border, but this time the message from the SS general was less optimistic than it had been ten days previously. Kesselring, on whose support Wolff had counted earlier, had now been transferred from Italy to serve as commander of the whole western front. Wolff temporized as he played on the Allies' hopes for the surrender of all German armies in the West, but it eventually became clear that he could not deliver what they wanted from him.[17]

By mid-March the Bern incident, as the Switzerland negotiations became known in Allied correspondence, even though none of the meetings with Wolff took place in the Swiss capital, had become a bone of contention at the highest levels of Allied diplomacy. Knowing of Stalin's sensitivity to anything that smacked of separate peace negotiations on the part of the Western Allies, the Western leaders agreed that they would have to let the Soviets know what was going on in Switzerland. Churchill ignored American intentions of simply informing Moscow of the preliminary talks and proceeded to ask for the Kremlin's approval. Cables to that effect went to Moscow on March 11, and Molotov responded the next day, demanding the inclusion of Soviet representatives in the talks. Harriman felt this was a terrible idea, and the head of the U.S. military mission in Moscow, General John Deane, pointed out that the Western Allies had not insisted on participating in the Soviet negotiations with encircled German troops on the eastern front. American officials believed that endorsing the Soviet position would mean delaying the talks and jeopardizing them with possible "embarrassing demands."[18]

The British went along with this, and the Soviets were told that the preliminary negotiations could not wait and would start without their representatives, but they were welcome to attend final negotiations at Field Marshal Alexander's headquarters in Caserta. On March 16, Molotov furiously insisted that the Bern negotiations be broken off. He repeated his demand in a letter of March 24, accusing the Western Allies of negotiating behind Russia's back. On the same day Roosevelt wrote to Stalin, presenting the whole incident as a misunderstanding and explaining the secrecy in terms of military necessity (the letter was prepared by Admiral Leahy and signed by the president). There was not a word in the president's telegram about Dulles's meeting with Wolff on March 8; Alexander's dispatch of negotiators to Switzerland was explained by the need to verify "unconfirmed information" concerning the desire of some German officers to arrange a surrender. "Up to the present time the attempts by our representatives to arrange a meeting with German officers have met with no success, but it still appears that such a meeting is a possibility," wrote the president. Roosevelt walked a fine line between half-truth and outright deception, omitting from his letter not only Dulles's "conference" with Wolff but also the meeting of March 19 with Wolff attended by representatives of Field Marshal Alexander, and refusing to apply the term "meeting" to any of the contacts except the planned surrender ceremony in Caserta.

Stalin was unimpressed. He rejected Roosevelt's parallel between the meeting in Switzerland and the negotiations on the surrender of German troops on the eastern front. In the latter case, the troops were encircled and had no choice but to surrender to avoid annihilation, while on the western front the German troops were not encircled and did not face annihilation. "If, nevertheless," wrote Stalin, "the Germans in northern Italy seek negotiations in order to sur-render and to open the front to the Allied troops, then they must have some other, more far-reaching aims affecting the destiny of Germany." Stalin did not hide his concern: he wanted to avoid a situation in which the German command would break off hostilities with the Anglo-American Allies while continuing to fight on the eastern front. To strengthen his argument, he claimed (probably knowing it to be untrue) that under cover of the Swiss talks the Germans were already switching their divisions from Italy to the eastern front.

Roosevelt, uncertain whether Stalin's letter required a reply, nevertheless signed a response prepared by Admiral Leahy and General Marshall on March 31. The president's telegram noted that the withdrawal of three German divisions (two of them were transferred to the eastern front) had occurred before the talks in Switzerland had even begun. The letter was also full of categorical denial of the very existence of negotiations. "No negotiations for surrender have been entered into," stated Roosevelt. "I must repeat that the meeting in Bern was for the single purpose of arranging contact with competent German military officers and not for negotiations of any kind." Again, the Americans and the British could not agree on their story. While Roosevelt continued to deny that negotiations had ever taken place, Field Marshal Alexander informed the Soviets of the meeting with Wolff on March 19.

Stalin was growing more and more suspicious. In his letter of April 3, sent the day after the receipt of Alexander's cable, Stalin changed his tone and suggested that the president was not "fully informed," implying that he did not trust Roosevelt. His next statement attested both to his paranoia and to his desire to put the Western Allies on the defensive. He referred to information in the possession of his "military colleagues," alleging that "negotiations did take place and that they ended in an agreement with the Germans, whereby the German commander on the Western Front, Marshal Kesselring, is to open the front to the Anglo-American troops and let them move east, while the British and Americans have promised, in exchange, to ease the armistice terms for the Germans."

Now it was the Americans' turn to be surprised. Secretary of War Henry Stimson advised his colleagues to be very careful in drafting a response, given the "astonishing situation in Stalin's mind and in the minds of his staff." FDR's next letter to Moscow was drafted by General Marshall and revised by Admiral Leahy. It conveyed the president's "astonishment" at receiving Stalin's earlier message and restated his denial of any negotiations in Switzerland, maintaining that the meetings there had "no political implications whatever." It also tried to shift responsibility for the misunderstanding between the Allies to the Germans. "I am certain that there were no negotiations in Bern at any time, and I feel that your information to that effect must have come from German sources which have made persistent efforts to create dissension between us to escape in some measure responsibility for their war crimes. If that was Wolff's purpose in Bern, your message proves that he has had some success." Roosevelt also questioned the reliability of Stalin's sources.

Stalin was more conciliatory in his next message, sent on April 7: "In my message of April 3 the point was not about integrity and trustworthiness. I have never doubted your integrity or trustworthiness." He still insisted on the right of the Soviets to be present at any negotiations on the western front. Supporting his earlier suggestion that the Germans and the Western Allies had made a deal, he indicated the fierce resistance of German troops in the East, as opposed to their lack of will to fight on the Anglo-American front. "As regards those who supply my information," he wrote, "I can assure you that they are honest and unassuming people who carry out their duties conscientiously and who have no intention of affronting anybody. They have been tested in action on numerous occasions." He forwarded to Roosevelt a copy of a letter from General Aleksei Antonov to General Deane noting erroneous intelligence information on German plans in the East supplied to the Soviet command by the Americans.[19]

Who were Stalin's "honest and unassuming people" who knew about the negotiations? Both the British and the Americans believed that the Germans had fed Stalin information about the Bern negotiations. Lord Beaverbrook, a confidant of Churchill's who shared that opinion, even advised the prime minister to ask Stalin to divulge what the Soviets knew about the negotiations. If Churchill had actually done so and Stalin had decided, for whatever reason, to satisfy Beaverbrook's curiosity, both the British and the Americans would have been in for a major surprise.

The authors of a Soviet TV blockbuster of the 1970s, *The Seventeen Moments of Spring,* which featured General Wolff's negotiations in Switzerland, credited a Soviet agent named Max Otto von Stirlitz with derailing the "separate talks" in Bern. That is what generations of Soviet and East European television viewers learned to believe. The truth was much more prosaic. Stirlitz's prototype was a Gestapo employee and gambling addict, Willy Lehmann, recruited by the Soviets in the late 1920s. He was uncovered and executed by German counterintelligence in 1942, long before the start of the Swiss negotiations. After Lehmann's arrest, the Soviets had no moles in the Nazi security apparatus who could report on German contacts with the West.[20]

The authors of the official history of the Russian intelligence services, issued after the disintegration of the Soviet Union, claim that the information on the Bern negotiations came from members of the Cambridge Five. On April 9 the NKGB reported that according to information received in London, before Kesselring was transferred to serve as commander of the western front, either he or two senior German officers had negotiated with the Allies regarding the surrender of German troops on the Italian front. The source of this information, an FBI agent, had heard about the negotiations from an employee of the OSS who had come to Britain from Italy. The Soviet agent had received confirmation of this rumor from Guy Liddell, a department head in British counterintelligence (MI5). Given that Anthony Blunt was then working in MI5 and was close to Liddell, it would be fair to assume that this information came to the Soviets from Blunt. It reflected the erroneous belief of many Allied officers not directly involved in the negotiations that the Allies were talking to Kesselring and correctly stated their goal: the surrender of German troops on the Italian front.[21]

This was not the first exploratory contact the Soviets had heard of. The Washington NKGB station reported in June 1944 on a meeting between Allen Dulles and Field Marshal Walther von Brauchitsch, as well as on the efforts of other German military officials to establish contact with him. The report indicated that Cordell Hull had told Dulles that there should be no negotiations with the Germans without the participation of the other Allies. The source of this information was in the State Department and may well have been Alger Hiss.[22]

If anything made Stalin anxious, it was the possibility of a separate peace between the Western Allies and Nazi Germany or, more realistically, a German opening of the western front to the Anglo-American armies, which would allow them to take control of Germany and perhaps some of Eastern Europe ahead of the Red Army. In Teheran, Stalin's main concern had been whether the Western Allies would open a second front; by now he worried that this front was moving too quickly. In late March 1945, speaking to a Czechoslovak delegation on a visit to the Kremlin, Stalin gave full expression to his distrust of the Western Allies. "We are fighting the Germans and will do so until the end," he declared. "But we must bear in mind that our allies will try to save the Germans and come to an arrangement with them. We will be merciless towards the Germans but our allies will treat them with kid gloves."[23]

The Bern crisis helped Stalin keep his allies on the defensive as he pushed ahead with his takeover of Eastern Europe. Dulles was ordered to break off all contacts with Wolff, and the German troops in northern Italy did not surrender to the Allies until May 2, two days after Hitler's death had released the German generals from their oath of loyalty to the führer. The Western Allies would now have to be particularly careful about any new approaches from the Germans. They could not be certain how much Stalin knew. Playing on Roosevelt's fears of a possible Soviet withdrawal from the not yet established United Nations, Stalin did not allow the Bern incident to interfere with the realization of those provisions of the Yalta agreements that served his own purposes. Among these was Soviet entry into the war with Japan, which was now imminent: the USSR denounced the neutrality pact with Japan on April 5.

In his last letter to Stalin, signed on April 11, 1945, President Roosevelt noted that the Bern incident had finally "faded into the past." It did so, but not without causing major damage to Allied relations and wiping out all vestiges of mutual trust remaining after the Yalta Conference. The Bern incident had inaugurated a new era in East-West relations that found full expression in the long decades of the Cold War—an era of competitive espionage fueled by geopolitical paranoia. In the course of the Cold War, as in March 1945, the secret services on both sides of the divide both calmed and inflamed the worst fears and suspicions of their political masters.[24]

30

STALIN DIGS IN

A t the height of the Bern crisis Andrei Gromyko informed the State Department that Molotov, who was supposed to head the Soviet delegation to the San Francisco conference, would stay in Moscow to attend a meeting of the Supreme Soviet. On March 24 Roosevelt appealed directly to Stalin, asking him to send Molotov at least to the opening sessions. "I am afraid that Mr. Molotov's absence will be construed all over the world as a lack of . . . interest on the part of the Soviet Government in the great objectives of this Conference," he wrote. Stalin was not moved—Molotov would stay in Moscow. "As regards various interpretations," wrote Stalin, "you understand, this cannot determine the decisions which are to be made."[1]

Stalin was displeased with Roosevelt and was prepared to undermine the single thing that mattered most to him. His decision to keep Molotov at home was made in the midst of another dispute between the Soviet embassy in Washington and the State Department, this one concerning the participation of the Soviet republics of Ukraine and Belarus in the San Francisco conference. On March 12 Gromyko informed the State Department that thirty members of the Ukrainian and Belarusian delegations would arrive in San Francisco to take part in the conference. The announcement came as a complete surprise to the Americans. Secretary of State Stettinius was outraged and later admitted he "had serious trouble with Gromyko over this matter." Speaking from notes prepared for his meeting with the Soviet ambassador, he stated that "it was clearly settled at the Crimean Conference that the two republics would not be invited to San Francisco." This was an overstatement. In fact, the Americans and Soviets left Yalta with different opinions of what had been decided.

Stettinius wanted Roosevelt to intervene personally with Stalin. Alger Hiss sent Stettinius a draft letter for Roosevelt that included a warning to Stalin: "Quite frankly the difficulties, both in relation to the effect on the American public support for the proposed organization and to the attitude of the other governments, seem to be far greater than I had realized." Hiss strongly advised Stettinius against sending such a letter. Citing the opinion of senior officers in the department, he warned that a number of other important issues had already been raised with Stalin or were about to be raised, and sending one more message would "rob this method of communication of its true importance." Old State Department hands tried to calm Stettinius, advising him to meet with Gromyko first. The tactic worked: no letter was sent to Stalin. Instead, on March 29 the secretary of state sent the ambassador a note indicating quite accurately that at Yalta "no obligation whatsoever was assumed in regard to the question of the presence of representatives of these republics at San Francisco."[2]

A diplomatic showdown had been avoided, but the Soviets did not change their position. When Undersecretary of State Joseph Grew read his government's note to Gromyko, the Soviet ambassador responded, "This is not our interpretation." Ultimately the Soviet interpretation won the day. By late March the commitment FDR had made to Stalin at Yalta had ceased to be secret: it was leaked to the press by members of the U.S. delegation to the San Francisco conference. The American public was outraged by its government's readiness to violate its declared principle of one nation, one vote. The administration quickly withdrew its own request for additional votes. The Ukrainians and Belarusians could now come without arousing suspicion: the secret deal was public knowledge.

If American politicians and diplomats found themselves engaged in soul-searching and finger-pointing as they tried to explain to the public how they could have been so unscrupulous, the Soviets had no such concern. In late April the two delegations, wearing brand-new "American suits" bought with funds allocated by the governments of Ukraine and Belarus, arrived in San Francisco and took part in the conference. As agreed, the two republics were admitted to membership in the United Nations with American and British support. In his memoirs Gromyko wrote that at the San Francisco conference "the Soviet representatives felt throughout that the western delegates were people from another world, thinking in another language."[3]

In March Stalin abruptly reversed his position on the dismemberment of Germany, motivated not by domestic opinion but by geopolitical considerations. This was a fundamental policy shift—nothing short of the surrender of one of the major concessions he had obtained from the Allies at Yalta, where he had insisted that the word "dismemberment" be added to the text of the surrender document presented to Germany.

The first meeting of the London commission on the dismemberment of Germany had taken place on March 7 and was attended by Anthony Eden; William Strang, the British ambassador to the European Advisory Commission; Fedor Gusev, the Soviet ambassador to London; and John G. Winant, the American ambassador to Britain. Eden's draft instructions for the commission suggested that it should begin by studying whether it was in fact necessary to dismember Germany, or whether it would suffice to establish control over German industry and disarm and demilitarize the country. Gusev sounded the alarm in a telegram sent on March 10 to Moscow. Six days later he drew Strang's attention to the contradiction between Eden's instructions and the decision made at Yalta. Strang agreed to revise the draft. On March 24, however, Gusev received a telegram from Molotov instructing him to accept the British language and to inform the commission that the USSR considered the Yalta decision on dismemberment a means of applying pressure on Germany should all other measures fail. The Allied diplomats were stunned; their relief was palpable.[4]

What had happened to account for this reversal? Memos prepared by Maxim Litvinov on the eve of the Yalta Conference show that the Soviet authorities regarded Germany's dismemberment as one of their goals. It was generally seen in Moscow as the main instrument for eliminating the German threat and giving the Soviet Union a breathing space of ten or twenty years, after which it would again be ready to confront the capitalist West. But such an approach had encountered unexpected resistance. After the conference, Eden's continued maneuvering in the London commission was a clear indication that even though the Soviets had won the battle at Yalta, the war was still going on. Winning without a clear commitment from the Western Allies to support dismemberment was practically impossible. And Stalin may have had second thoughts about not only its practicality but also its desirability.[5]

A strong central government would be necessary to ensure that reparations would be collected from all of Germany. Given that the country's industrial areas were in the Western Allies' zones of occupation, good relations were paramount if the Soviets were to get their hands on German industrial equipment. So Moscow decided to abandon dismemberment and score propaganda points instead. Molotov explained the sudden reversal of policy to Gusev as follows: "The English and the Americans, who first raised the question of dismembering Germany, now want to shift the blame for dismemberment to the USSR with the intention of defaming our state in the eyes of world public opinion." From now on, Stalin could tell Wilhelm Pieck and other German communists that dismemberment was a capitalist idea.

This became the official line for decades to come. The editors of the Soviet records of the Teheran and Yalta conferences went so far as to delete quite a few of Stalin's remarks in favor of dismemberment. Stalin made the task of censoring such statements relatively easy. Unlike Roosevelt and Churchill, he never suggested a specific plan for the dismemberment of Germany. Even at Yalta he allegedly raised the question only in order to "ascertain exactly what the intentions of the three governments are." On May 9, the official Soviet Victory Day, Stalin addressed his people, stating that the Soviet Union did not "intend to dismember or destroy Germany." The terms of surrender that the Allies finally offered Germany in June 1945 did not include a provision for dismemberment. It was a dramatic shift, but only one of many.[6]

As mounting East-West tensions caused the Soviets to abandon their original plan for Central Europe and persuaded them not to take full advantage of the agreements reached at Yalta on German dismemberment, they intensified their efforts to take the greatest possible advantage from the ambiguities of the Yalta agreements on Poland. The Moscow negotiations between Molotov, Harriman, and Clark Kerr were going nowhere, and in late March Roosevelt, with encouragement from Churchill, decided to appeal directly to Stalin. In a cable sent on March 31, FDR struck a very different tone from that of his address to Congress at the beginning of the month. "I cannot conceal from you the concern with which I view the development of events of mutual interest since our fruitful meeting at Yalta," he began. He lamented the "discouraging lack of progress made in the carrying out, which the world expects, of the political decisions which we reached at the Conference, particularly those relating to the Polish question." The president also expressed puzzlement that the provisions of the Declaration on Liberated Europe seemingly did not apply to Romania.

Turning to the work of the Molotov-Harriman-Kerr Commission in Moscow, Roosevelt questioned the right of the communist Poles to select or reject candidates for the future Polish government. Of course there was a problem of "reorganization," and the president tried to make the best of the ambiguous formula he had accepted at Yalta. "While it is true that the Lublin Government is to be reorganized and its members play a prominent role," he wrote, "it is to be done in such a fashion as to bring into being a new Government. This point is clearly brought out in several places in the text of the agreement. I must make it quite plain to you that any such solution which would result in a continuance of the present Warsaw regime would be unacceptable and would cause the people of the United States to regard the Yalta Agreement as a fraud." The president crossed out the last word and replaced it with "having failed." He insisted on the right of the Western ambassadors to invite their candidates to Moscow without restrictions, as well as on their right to travel to Poland.[7]

The letter was signed by Roosevelt, but its true promoter was Churchill, who reviewed the original draft and made his additions to the text of the cable. Throughout March, Churchill bombarded Roosevelt with messages encouraging him to intervene on Eastern Europe. He knew that without American support his own word would not mean much in the Kremlin, and on the issue of Romania he felt unable to address Stalin because, as he wrote to Roosevelt, the Soviet leader could tell him that he had not interfered in Greece and he would ask for the same freedom of action in Romania. The Soviet-British division of the Balkans into spheres of influence made a mockery of the Declaration on Liberated

Europe. It prevented Churchill from making the USSR accountable for its actions in Romania and hindered his freedom of maneuver with regard to Poland.[8]

Stalin took a week to answer Roosevelt's letter. "Matters on the Polish question have really reached a dead end," began Stalin. "What are the reasons for it? The reasons for it are that the Ambassadors of the United States and England in Moscow—members of the Moscow Commission—have departed from the principles of the Crimea Conference and have introduced into the matter new elements not provided by the Crimea Conference." Stalin restated his understanding of the Yalta formula on the Polish government as a decision to form a new government on the basis of the existing one, and he claimed that the ambassadors, Harriman in particular, were disregarding that government completely and trying to bring to Moscow Poles who either did not recognize the Yalta decisions or were unfriendly to the USSR. Stalin's solution was to insist that the new Polish government should be created on the basis of the old one.

His proposed "compromise" was to summon to Moscow eight Polish politicians, five from Poland and three from London, for consultations on the formation of the future government. "As regards the numerical correlation of old and new ministers in the composition of the Polish Government of national unity," wrote Stalin, "there could be established approximately a similar correlation which was realized in respect to the Government of Yugoslavia. I think that, taking into consideration the above-stated remarks, a harmonious decision on the Polish question can be reached in a short time." Churchill later pointed out that communists outnumbered pro-Western ministers in Yugoslavia twenty-five to six. As Stalin had told Molotov, the balance of forces on the ground would ultimately determine the fate of the decisions made at Yalta. In this case Stalin used his military muscle in Poland to impose his interpretation of the Yalta formula.

Stalin responded on April 7, but the president did not receive his reply until April 10 and never wrote back. "I would minimize the general Soviet problem as much as possible," he wrote to Churchill on April 11, concerning Bern, "because these problems, in one form or another, seem to arise every day and most of them straighten out as is the case of the Bern meeting. We must be firm, however, and our course thus far is correct." Despite his frustration with Soviet behavior after Yalta and deep dissatisfaction with Stalin, Roosevelt was not prepared to change course. The president saw no other option than to continue talking to Stalin and keeping things in perspective.[9]

While negotiations dragged on in Moscow, the Soviets took action in Poland to obtain the results they wanted. They went after the leaders of the Polish underground east and west of the Curzon Line. Reports received by the Polish government in exile in February 1945 and passed on to the British and American ambassadors in Moscow indicated that the NKVD was busy deporting Poles to the East: five thousand Poles from Hrodna, ten thousand from Białystok, and seventy-six thousand from Poznań. The Soviets were also arresting the commanders of the Polish Home Army and subjecting them to "harsh and brutal examination." In some areas, up to 20 percent of Home Army fighters were apprehended by the Soviets.

In March 1945 the NKVD initiated political consultations with the leaders of the Polish underground. It seemed that the Yalta agreements were finally working and that the Soviets were interested in reaching out to the opposition forces in preparation for the promised elections. But once the leaders of the Polish underground, headed by the commander in chief of the Polish Home Army, General Leopold Okulicki, showed up for a meeting with the Soviet authorities on March 27, they were arrested by their hosts, despite earlier guarantees of their personal safety. For Okulicki, it was his second arrest by the Soviets (the first one took place in 1941) and a major surprise, as in January 1945, during the weeks leading up to the Yalta Conference, he had ordered the dissolution of the Home Army so as not to provoke Soviet repressions against Polish society at large.

General Okulicki and fifteen other leaders of the Polish underground were taken to Moscow, where they were put on trial in June 1945. Okulicki, who had fought against Nazi Germany in 1939 and was one of the leaders of the Warsaw uprising in 1944, was accused of planning a military coalition with Germany against the USSR, espionage, terrorism, and belonging to a clandestine organization that was disbanded simply to provide a cover for further subversive activities. He was sentenced to ten years of imprisonment by Vasilii Ulrich, the notorious judge of the Moscow show trials of the 1930s. He was murdered in a Moscow prison in December 1946.[10]

On the other side of the Curzon Line, Kremlin representatives pushed through an aggressive Sovietization, eliminating all institutional links connecting that part of prewar Poland with the outside world. Their main target became the Ukrainian Greek Catholic Church, which, while preserving Orthodox rituals and traditions, was under the jurisdiction of Rome. On April 11, 1945, acting on instructions approved personally by Stalin, the Soviet secret police entered the residential premises of St. George's Cathedral in Lviv and arrested the head of the church, Metropolitan Yosyf Slipy, and his entourage. On that day they also arrested all the bishops of the church. Very few of them would survive long imprisonment in the Gulag, to which they were sent by their captors.[11]

In a highly bizarre twist, the arrests were an unintended consequence of Roosevelt's attempts to convince Stalin to treat the Catholic Church in Eastern Europe with due respect. The president's point man on the Catholics had been Edward Flynn. A friend of the president's since the early days of his political career, Flynn was nominated in 1943 as FDR's envoy to Australia. For the first time in almost forty-five years, however, Congress turned down a presidential appointment to a diplomatic post because of the opposition of Flynn's enemies in the Democratic Party. Flynn had no official function at Yalta, apart from being Roosevelt's guest and attending some of the official and private dinners at the conference. Roosevelt occasionally sent young State Department officials, including Alger Hiss, to brief Flynn about what was going on, as he believed that Flynn was "getting very bored." Hiss later recalled that with little to do, Flynn drank "more tea . . . than even an Irish American could wish for."[12]

Religion was never discussed in any detail at Yalta, but Stalin apparently repeated his famous saying about the pope: how many divisions has he got? Roosevelt, for his part, asked Molotov to let Flynn travel to Moscow to discuss religious policy with Soviet officials. Molotov agreed, and immediately after the conference Flynn, who was not especially perspicacious, went to Moscow as Averell Harriman's special guest. Kathleen had doubts about Flynn's diplomatic skills and questioned the prospects for the success of his mission. "Ed Flynn will remain with us a few weeks," she told her sister. "The Lord deliver us! However, he's not as bad as he sounds (remember the stink when Roosevelt appointed him Minister to Australia?). He is old and rather sweet and doesn't get in anybody's way—at least hasn't while here. Perhaps his common sense, something that he has a lot of, may keep him out of trouble in Moscow. His quest described at its worst is to make the Russians pray!"[13]

Flynn spent more than three weeks in the Soviet Union, from February 12 to March 10, visiting Soviet officials and attending the theater and dinners given in his honor. He never set down, either in his letters home or in his memoirs, exactly what he was trying to achieve, but leaks to the press gave his mission a three-point agenda: to persuade the Soviets to allow the Vatican to send Catholic clergy into Eastern Europe, to reopen Catholic institutions there, and to improve the plight of Italian prisoners of war in the USSR. All three were high on the Vatican agenda at the time.[14]

Before returning to the United States Flynn went to Rome to see the pope, who would have to be neutralized if Roosevelt was to avoid problems with his Catholic electorate over persecutions of the church in Eastern Europe. That logic was not lost on careful observers of the European scene, and in March 1945 there was probably no more diligent or interested observer than Joseph Goebbels. "Roosevelt has dispatched Flynn as special envoy to the Pope," he recorded in his diary on March 23. "Clearly Roosevelt wants to win the Catholic Church over to his side. The Pope is said to have been very displeased with the Anglo-Americans after the Yalta Conference."[15]

Pope Pius XII, who negotiated a concordat between Germany and the Holy See in 1933 and has often been accused of being too close to the Nazis during the war, left no doubt throughout his long term of office about his attitude toward communism. On numerous occasions since 1939, he had condemned the Soviet occupation of Poland and the atrocities committed under that occupation. Now he was trying to rally international support for the Catholics of

Poland. In December 1944 Kazimierz Papee, the representative of the Polish émigré government at the Vatican, informed his colleagues in Paris: "The mobilization of the Catholic world on behalf of Poland progresses and deepens continuously. . . . Cardinal [Jean-Marie-Rodrigue] Villeneuve [of Quebec] and Archbishop [Francis] Spellman [of New York] told me personally that Holy Father wanted from them full support of the Polish position."

Roosevelt knew how devastating the Vatican's open rejection of Yalta would be. On the eve of the conference, he sent Hopkins to Rome to placate the pope. In the fall of 1944, on the eve of presidential elections in the United States, Hopkins was upset by the Catholic Church's attempts to influence American domestic politics and U.S. policy toward Eastern Europe, but in January 1945 he was instructed to visit the pope en route to Yalta. Now Roosevelt wanted Flynn to serve as mediator between Stalin and Pius XII, a choice that made sense only if he was thinking about calming American Catholic opinion and the Vatican, and not about achieving the desired outcome of his negotiations.[16]

Whatever Flynn's aptitude, he was up against formidable odds. The Soviets had already made up their minds regarding the Vatican, and little could be done to change them. They were determined to link the pope and, by implication, the entire Catholic Church with fascism. In the eyes of the Kremlin, the Vatican was interfering in world affairs, throwing its support behind the Polish émigré government, opposing the transfer of German territories to Poland, and encouraging reactionary groups in Italy. Stalin was prepared to invoke a newfound Orthodox patriotism to discredit the pope as his armies entered Poland.[17]

Flynn was given the runaround in Moscow. "Their philosophy and outlook on life is more Asiatic so that it is not easy to come to decisions looking at it with western eyes," he wrote home. "They try to be cooperative and pleasant, but sometimes one has a feeling that they to say the least are not entirely frank." Flynn met with the newly elected patriarch Aleksii I of the Russian Orthodox Church, with Molotov, and with two secret-police colonels who were in charge of government bodies responsible for overseeing religious activities, but he did not get far. When Colonel Georgii Karpov, the head of the government committee responsible for relations with the Russian Orthodox Church, tried to convince Flynn that members of communist youth organizations could belong to the church and that some of them even wore crosses, Flynn's Soviet interpreter said under her breath, "Don't you believe it." Flynn was even more dissatisfied with his meeting with Ivan Poliansky, the official responsible for government relations with non-Orthodox denominations. "For a chairman of a commission," he wrote in his memoirs, "he seemed to know little or nothing about what was going on."[18]

On March 2, while Flynn was still making the rounds, Stalin and Molotov summoned Colonel Karpov and ordered him to prepare a memorandum on countering Vatican influences in the western borderlands of the USSR and on the world stage. Karpov's proposals were approved on March 16, before Flynn had reached Rome. The main victims were the members of the five-million-strong Ukrainian Greek Catholic Church, whose leaders were arrested on April 11. The church was officially abolished at a synod convoked by the NKVD in March of the following year. Its faithful were ordered to join the Russian Orthodox Church; those who did not were forced underground.[19]

Immediately after Yalta, the Soviets tried to be as accommodating toward Catholic institutions in Eastern Europe as could be expected, doubtless because of Roosevelt's attention. But that goodwill did not extend to Soviet territory. For the time being, Stalin's open assault on the Catholic Church ended at the borders assigned to the USSR at Yalta. Even the Transcarpathian region, which became part of the Ukrainian Soviet Socialist Republic in the summer of 1945, was not affected until 1949. The Greek Catholic Church also survived on territory west of the Curzon Line, which remained part of Poland.

Roosevelt's push for freedom of religion thus had the unintended consequence of reviving caesaropapism, an old imperial tradition according to which the Orthodox Church was administered as part of the Russian government. In preparation for the Teheran Conference, Stalin had not only ordered the dissolution of the Communist International, through which Moscow controlled Communist parties and communist-dominated movements throughout the world, but also allowed the election of an Orthodox patriarch for the first time since the 1920s. The persecution of the church by the atheistic state, which had been official policy since the Revolution of 1917, was temporarily suspended. The goal was to present an image of the Soviet Union as a country that respected its citizens' religious beliefs, making it easier for Western leaders to cooperate with their communist ally.

This was the image that Stalin was eager to project in conversation with a Polish Catholic priest from the United States, Father Stanisław Orlemański, in April 1944. His message was intended for Western governments and Poles in the United States, as well as in Poland. "We are not cannibals," Stalin told the priest. "We Bolsheviks have a point in our program that provides for freedom of religious convictions. From the first days of the existence of Soviet power, we set ourselves the goal of implementing that point. But the rebellious conduct of activists of the Orthodox Church deprived us of the possibility of implementing that point, and the government had to accept battle after the church laid a curse on Soviet power. Misunderstandings arose on that basis between representatives of religion and the Soviet government. That was before the war with the Germans. After the beginning of the war with the Germans, people and circumstances changed. War eliminated the differences between church and state, the faithful renounced their rebellious attitude, and the Soviet gov-ernment renounced its militant attitude with regard to religion."[20]

Stalin, the former Orthodox seminarian, was now prepared to make use of the church to achieve his international and domestic goals. After Yalta, as after the Molotov-Ribbentrop Pact, when he first laid hands on Western Ukraine, Western Belarus, and the Baltic states, Stalin was eager to use the church to secure the newly acquired territories and bind them more closely to Moscow. When the Soviet authorities put an end to the legal activities of the Greek Cath-olic Church in Ukraine, driving it underground, its parishes and flock were claimed by the Russian Orthodox Church. Stalin was following in the footsteps of the tsars, who had "reunited" the Ukrainian and Belarusian Catholics with the Russian Orthodox Church in the course of the nineteenth century. The tsars were unable to accomplish that goal in Galicia, which belonged to the Habsburgs, but after the war the dropout seminarian turned communist dicta-tor finally fulfilled this dream of the Romanovs.

As Yalta faded into the past, Stalin seemed to rely less and less on coopera-tion with the Allies, drawing new lines of demarcation in Europe without regard to the wishes of his Western partners. He was prepared to give ground on the issue of German dismemberment but determined to entrench him-self in Poland and the former Polish territories that he attached to the Soviet Union. Stalin undertook not only to move state boundaries but also to redesign civilizational fault lines that had divided the Orthodox East from the Catholic West for centuries. This religiously based repartition of Europe was intended to consolidate his hold on the newly acquired territories. Successful in the short term, the venture lacked staying power. The Greek Catholic Church went underground and was successfully revived in 1989 through the efforts of its flock and with the support of Pope John Paul II. Its revival coincided with the end of the Cold War and the disintegration of the communist bloc in Eastern Europe. If the state borders created at Yalta remained intact, the religious ones returned to their old positions.

31

AFTER ROOSEVELT

They began to assemble in the late morning. It was a pleasant spring day, and according to some estimates, half a million people lined Pennsylvania Avenue as a mile-long cortege made its way from Union Station to the White House. Thousands assembled in Lafayette Park, across from the White House, and the police were forced to push back the crowds. Some who had come less than three months earlier to witness the inauguration of Franklin Delano Roosevelt for an unprecedented fourth term had come again to see him laid to rest.

Roosevelt had died two days earlier, on April 12, 1945, at his retreat in Warm Springs, Georgia. He had gone there on March 29 after spending five days at his estate in Hyde Park in upstate New York. The president was exhausted, and his health was clearly in decline, but no one expected his sudden death. Eleanor Roosevelt, attending a benefit at the Sulgrave Club in Washington, was taken by surprise. So was Vice President Harry S. Truman, then sixty years old, who was summoned to the White House and learned the news from Eleanor. The visibly shaken Truman was sworn into office a few hours after Roosevelt's death. His first presidential act was to sign a proclamation declaring a day of national mourning. The president's body was brought by train to Washington at 10:00 a.m. After a 4:00 p.m. memorial service in the East Room of the White House, the casket was put back on the train. The nation was in mourning: two million people lined the railroad tracks to say good-bye to their president. The funeral took place the next day in Hyde Park.

In Washington, Roosevelt's friends and opponents tried to comprehend the loss. Roosevelt's Republican adversaries were as generous in their assessments of his accomplishments as were his Democratic allies. Senator Arthur Vandenberg of Michigan, a frequent critic of the Democratic administration, stated that the late president had "left an imperishable imprint on the history of America and of the world." Later a fierce critic of the Yalta decisions, Senator

Robert Taft of Ohio called Roosevelt "the greatest figure of our time," who died "a hero of the war, for he literally worked himself to death in the service of the American people."[1]

In Moscow a "deeply distressed" Stalin told Harriman, who delivered the news, that "President Roosevelt has died, but his cause must live on." That was also the message the new president was eager to send to the country and the world in the first hours of the transition. Truman authorized Edward Stettinius, who was the first to arrive at the White House following the news of the president's death, to make a statement to the press assuring the country and the world that his foreign policy would be carried on "without change of purpose or break in continuity." On the day the funeral train reached Washington the *New York Times* was already reporting that friends of the new president believed the new administration would take a course "a little right of center."[2]

Whatever that meant domestically, in the international arena it suggested a tougher stand with regard to Soviet policies and aspirations in Eastern Europe. On April 13, his first full day in office, Truman told Stettinius, upon hearing his report about the state of Soviet-American relations: "[W]e must stand up to the Russians at this point . . . we must not be too easy with them." Truman had little knowledge of foreign affairs and even less experience before assuming supreme office. He was well aware of this and did not hide his insecurity about guiding the ship of state at such a crucial point in history. Though ill equipped to continue the complex foreign-policy game so skillfully played by Roosevelt, he was determined to do his best. The new president sought to overcome his insecurity by being decisive, or trying to appear decisive, and preferred clarity to complexity as he responded on the basis of his gut feelings. Standing up to the Russians seemed like the right policy under the circumstances.[3]

Truman's new approach to the Soviet Union was a blessing for revisionists within the administration who had advocated a tougher policy but could not convince FDR to adopt it. As in the past, the revisionists came from the ranks of the State Department's "Russia hands" and were now led by Averell Harriman himself. After Roosevelt's death, Harriman promptly left Moscow for Washington for the sole purpose of meeting with the new president. "Frankly, one of the reasons that made me rush back to Washington," he told Truman on April 20, "was the fear that you did not understand, as I had seen Roosevelt understand, that Stalin is breaking his agreements." He warned Truman of a new "barbarian invasion of Europe."

Upset by unilateral Soviet actions in Poland and Molotov's stalling on negotiations leading to the formation of the new Polish government, Harriman was prepared to forget that the agreement reached at Yalta was vague at best. He himself had admitted at the end of the conference that it would have to be renegotiated in Moscow from the bottom up. On April 23, conferring with Truman and his closest advisers to formulate a position for the president's forthcoming meeting with Molotov, Harriman insisted that Stalin had violated the Yalta agreements. Secretary of War Henry Stimson attributed Harriman's tough stance to the fact that he and General John Deane had been "suffering personally from the Russians' behavior on minor matters for a long time." Stimson believed that the Soviets had kept their word on military affairs. Admiral Leahy also was not persuaded by Harriman's argument. He said that he had left Yalta convinced that the Soviets would not agree to a free government in Poland and that the Yalta agreements were open to multiple interpretations.[4]

Ultimately it was Harriman's interpretation that Truman took into his meeting with Molotov on the afternoon of April 23. After Roosevelt's death, Stalin changed his mind about the level of Soviet representation at the United Nations Conference and decided to send Molotov to the United States. This was a gesture of respect to the deceased president, who had cared so much about the UN, but also an attempt to size up his successor. In Washington, before seeing Truman, Molotov met with Stettinius and Anthony Eden, who was also visiting the U.S. capital. They fought over Poland. Eden and Stettinius tried to achieve what their ambassadors in Moscow had failed to do: to impress upon Molotov the need to bring representatives of Polish democratic parties to Moscow and include them in the new government. Their efforts proved unavailing. At Eden's suggestion, and with the encouragement of Harriman and other members of the administration, Truman then took the task upon himself and demanded that the Soviet foreign minister observe the Yalta agreements. The demand was made forcefully and repeatedly. According to Bohlen, who translated for the president, Molotov turned "ashy" in response.[5]

Truman recorded in his memoirs the exact words with which he rebuffed Molotov. "I have never been talked to like that in my life," Molotov allegedly said. "Carry out your agreements and you won't get talked to like that," Truman retorted. These words never made it into the American or the Soviet record of the meeting: whether they were actually spoken or not, the language used by the president at his meeting with Molotov was certainly far from ordinary. This was confirmed by Stettinius and others present, and Molotov remembered the conversation in his later years. "At our first meeting with Truman, he began talking to me in such an imperious tone!" he recalled in the early 1970s. "I thought, what kind of president is he? I said, 'I cannot talk with you if you take such a tone.' He stopped short a bit. Rather stupid to my mind. And he had a very anti-Soviet mindset. That's why he began in such a tone; he wanted to show who was boss."[6]

The exchange marked a turning point in the tone of Soviet-American relations but did not alter their course, nor did it have an immediate impact on the Soviet position with regard to Poland. Molotov refused to budge. Soviet decisions, after all, were made by Stalin, not by his foreign secretary. Truman had yet to learn this.

In the spring of 1945 Stalin had not yet developed a clear idea of what to do with his Eastern European conquests. He thought that the Soviet experience was unique, and that for the time being the countries west of the Soviet Union did not need a Soviet-type one-party state. He imagined that the Communist Party could coexist with other left-leaning parties in a so-called people's democracy. These transitional regimes would prepare the ground for a complete communist takeover of their respective states, perhaps ten or fifteen years in the future. In March 1945 he told Tito: "Today socialism is possible even under the English monarchy. Revolution is no longer necessary everywhere." He developed this idea at a meeting with Polish government leaders in May 1946: "In Poland there is no dictatorship of the proletariat, and you don't need it there. . . . The democracy that you have established in Poland, in Yugoslavia and partly in Czechoslovakia is a democracy that is drawing you closer to socialism without the necessity of establishing the dictatorship of the proletariat or a Soviet system."[7]

What Stalin did not doubt was that the new states must be linked politically and strategically with the Soviet Union and be under its exclusive spell. In the last months of the war, only Roosevelt, with his vocal opposition to the division of Europe into zones of interest and his promotion of the United Nations, seemed capable of keeping Stalin from declaring his intentions in Eastern Europe. It was only after the unexpected death of Roosevelt that Stalin decided to make his case to the new president with regard to the Soviet presence in Eastern Europe. On April 24, 1945, the day on which Red Army troops reached the suburbs of Berlin, Stalin sent a letter to Truman and Churchill bringing the situation in Poland to an open standoff.

> You evidently do not agree that the Soviet Union is entitled to seek in Poland a Government that would be friendly to it, that the Soviet Government cannot agree to the existence in Poland of a Government hostile to it. This is rendered imperative, among other things, by the Soviet people's blood freely shed on the fields of Poland for the liberation of that country. I do not know whether a genuinely representative Government has been established in Greece, or whether the Belgian Government is a genuinely democratic one. The Soviet Union was not consulted when those Governments were being formed, nor did it claim the right to interfere in those matters, because it realises how important Belgium and Greece are to the security of Great Britain. I cannot understand why in discussing Poland no attempt is made to consider the interests of the Soviet Union in terms of security as well. One cannot but recognize as unusual a situation in which two Governments—those of the United States and Great Britain—reach agreement beforehand on Poland, a country in which the U.S.S.R. is interested first of all and most of all, and, placing its representatives in an intolerable position, try to dictate to it.[8]

Churchill responded on April 28 with a long letter that began with a discussion of Soviet policy toward Poland and ended with a review of the status of the Balkan deal between Britain and the USSR. "I must . . . say that the way things have worked out in Yugoslavia certainly does not give me the feeling of a fifty-fifty interest as between our countries," wrote Churchill. "Marshal Tito has become a complete dictator. He has proclaimed that his prime loyalties are to the Soviet Union. Although he allowed members of the Royal Yugoslav Government to enter his government they only number six as against twenty-five of his own nominees. We have the impression that they are not taken into consultation on matters of high policy and that it is becoming a one-party régime."

Churchill also explained his understanding of the percentage deal: Western representatives should not be completely shut out of Romania and Bulgaria, countries with a predominant Soviet influence. "I recognise the consideration which you gave me when we had to intervene with heavy armed forces to quell the E.A.M.-E.L.A.S. attack upon the centre of government in Athens," wrote Churchill. "We have given repeated instructions that your interest in Roumania and Bulgaria is to be recognized as predominant. We cannot however be excluded altogether, and we dislike being treated by your subordinates in these countries so differently from the kind manner in which we at the top are always treated by you."

Churchill declared that in countries such as Greece, where British influence was dominant, the British were interested only in establishing order and conducting elections: they would live with any form of government established by the democratic process. That was what Britain and America expected for Poland. But the Soviet Union had stalled on consultations about the formation of a new government. "This provisional government," Churchill wrote, "was then, according to our joint decision at the Crimea, to pledge itself to hold 'free and unfettered elections as soon as possible on the basis of universal suffrage and secret ballot' in which 'all democratic and anti-Nazi parties shall have the right to take part and put forward candidates.' Alas! None of this has been allowed to move forward."

Moscow was also preventing Western representatives from visiting Poland, which, Churchill pointed out, was not the case with regard to Soviet representatives in countries occupied by British troops. Neither Britain nor America was prepared to accept anything less in Poland than a fully representative democratic government. "We could not however accept 'the Yugoslav model' as a guide to what should happen in Poland," Churchill wrote. "Neither we nor the Americans have any military or special interest in Poland. All we seek in material things is to be treated in the regular way between friendly States."[9]

Churchill and Stalin understood spheres of influence differently. The British prime minister saw them as zones of influence but not complete dominance. Stalin saw them as areas of exclusive control. Meanwhile the Americans completely rejected the idea of carving Europe into spheres of influence. This was their long-standing policy. But there was little that the new American president could do to stop a process that was already well under way. Eventually he would accept the policies of those members of his administration who concluded that establishing spheres of influence was the only way to deal effectively with the Soviets. That view became dominant in the American administration in the summer of 1945, but there was at least one State Department official who was prepared to embrace it even before Roosevelt's death.

His name was George Kennan. Left in charge of the U.S. embassy in Moscow during the Yalta Conference, he sent a letter to his friend Charles Bohlen in which he said he thought the Soviets would eventually be rewarded for their war effort at the expense of the nations of Eastern and Central Europe. "That would have been the best thing we could do for ourselves and for our friends in Europe, and the most honest approach we could have tried to restore life, in the wake of war, on a dignified and stable foundation." Kennan was even prepared to accept the partition of Germany and the creation of a West European federation along the lines proposed by some of his British colleagues. In mid-1944, in a long memorandum on changes in Soviet foreign policy over the past seven years, Kennan was indignant about what he saw as a Soviet attempt to create a zone of dependent states in Eastern Europe. By the time of Yalta he saw this as inevitable and, in fact, the best solution from both a moral and practical point of view.[10]

Churchill was the first to understand the dangers of an emerging world in which spheres of influence would be defined not by mutually agreed percentage deals but by immutable ideological and cultural divisions. He feared that cultural misunderstandings and miscalculations could lead to future conflicts. In his long letter to Stalin of April 28, he prophetically noted: "There is not much comfort in looking into a future where you and the countries you dominate, plus the Communist parties in many other States, are all drawn up on one side, and those who rally to the English-speaking nations and their Associates or Dominions are on the other."

The prime minister presented a vision of the future that he was trying to avoid: "It is quite obvious that their quarrel would tear the world to pieces and that all of us leading men on either side who had anything to do with that would be shamed before history. Even embarking on a long period of suspicions, of abuse and counter-abuse and of opposing policies would be a disaster hampering the great developments of world prosperity for the masses which are attainable only by our trinity. I hope there is no word or phrase in this outpouring of my heart to you which unwittingly gives offence. If so, let me know. But do not, I beg you, my friend Stalin, underrate the divergences which are opening about matters which you may think are small to us but which are symbolic of the way the English-speaking democracies look at life."[11]

In practice, the policies of both Britain and the Soviet Union were leading to the realization of a scenario similar to the one envisioned by Kennan. It was only a matter of time before the new leaders of the United States would embrace this reality and try to make the best of it.

As the war in Europe neared its end, the Grand Alliance encountered ever new problems. A clear indication of mounting difficulties between the Allies was their failure to agree on a day that would mark the official end of the war. The Western Allies declared victory on May 8, the Soviets on May 9. The consequences of this disagreement turned out to be more than diplomatic. Not having been informed that May 9 was Victory Day in the USSR, American and British ships in Murmansk harbor fired at Soviet barrage balloons deployed as part of the celebrations. The Soviet embassy in Washington later informed the State Department that one person was killed and several wounded by the Allies' friendly fire.[12]

That was by no means the end of inter-Allied misunderstandings and disagreements. By now Churchill was gloomily contemplating the possibility of another war, this time against the Soviets, and there was talk about the desirability of such a war among the American military. As Stanisław Kot, the former Polish ambassador to the Soviet Union, reported to Stanisław Mikołajczyk from the United Nations Conference in May 1945, "The idea of war with Russia is said to be gaining ground in influential US circles, particularly Army and Navy whose influence is strongly growing." Kot specifically mentioned the case of Catherine Nimitz, the wife of Admiral Chester Nimitz, who "is reputed not to be too bright herself and to be talking 'out of her husband's hat' and who is referred to as having said that 'America is now stronger than after any other war . . . whereas Russia is now considerably weakened. Now is the time to strike.'"[13]

Truman's decision to "stand up" to the Soviets during his meeting with Molotov was a personal victory for Harriman. He consolidated his success in a private meeting with the president on May 10, urging him to curtail Lend-Lease shipments to the Soviet Union as an indication of a tougher attitude now that hostilities in Europe were over. On the following day Truman signed a directive to that effect, and on May 12 the shipment of goods to the USSR was halted and ships already at sea were ordered to return to their ports. This policy, which affected not only the Soviets but also the British, turned out to be a public-relations disaster. Even Harriman did not advocate the immediate curtailment of supplies to a country that was about to enter the war in the Pacific on the side of the United States.

State Department officials were the first to hear the protests of their distressed allies. The Soviet chargé d'affaires, Nikolai Novikov, called Undersecretary of State

Joseph Grew to complain about the stoppage of shipments. Grew, who was one of the authors of the presidential order, denied any responsibility for the action. "I called the chargé back and told him that I had looked into the matter and had found that there was absolutely no truth in the rumor—we were not stopping the loading of Soviet ships," wrote Grew in a State Department memo. The order was reversed, shipments resumed, and the president decided to shift responsibility for the abrupt decision to government officials, including Grew. The pendulum had swung too far, and the hour of triumph for those proposing a tougher line against the Soviets was effectively over.[14]

After the Lend-Lease faux pas, Truman was prepared to seek advice outside his administration. He got it from Joseph Davies, the U.S. ambassador to the Soviet Union in 1937–38, who remained a steadfast Sovietophile despite having been in Moscow at the height of the Great Terror. Davies met Truman for the first time on April 30 and cautiously tried to curb his enthusiasm for "getting tough" with the Soviets in the wake of his meeting with Molotov. He found the president much more receptive on May 13, in the aftermath of the Lend-Lease fiasco. The Sunday-evening meeting in Truman's White House quarters lasted until almost midnight and left Truman convinced of the need to change course. He was now prepared to send Davies to Moscow for a meeting with Stalin in order to initiate a dialogue. The former ambassador declined the offer, citing his health, but began working on arrangements for a new Yalta—a meeting that would bring Truman and Stalin face-to-face to discuss the future of the world.[15]

The need to assure Stalin that Roosevelt's policy toward the Soviet Union remained in place was felt even by Truman's hard-line advisers, such as Harriman, who suggested Harry Hopkins, the embodiment of the "old regime" and its foreign-policy course, as Truman's personal emissary to the Soviet leader. Hopkins, by now gravely ill, rose almost from his deathbed to accompany Harriman to Moscow. During a series of meetings with Stalin in late May and early June, he was able to resolve the problem that had left the Molotov-Harriman-Kerr Commission in deadlock. But the solution would be adopted on Stalin's terms, according to his interpretation of the agreements. "At Yalta it had been agreed that the existing government was to be reconstructed and that anyone with common sense could see that this meant that the present government was to form the basis of the new," Stalin told Hopkins. "No other understanding of the Yalta agreement was possible. Despite the fact that they were simple people the Russians should not be regarded as fools, which was a mistake the West frequently made."

Stalin agreed to invite Poles from London, including Stanisław Mikołajczyk, and "democratic Poles" from Poland itself to Moscow for negotiations on the composition of the new Polish government. They approved a list of eight Western candidates that Hopkins cabled back to Washington. He could not secure the release of General Leopold Okulicki and fifteen other Polish underground leaders arrested by the Soviet authorities in late March—the Politburo would soon decide to put them on trial and make a political show of it. Still, Truman, Churchill, and Mikołajczyk accepted the deal brokered by Hopkins. Even George Kennan, whom Hopkins consulted in Moscow and who wanted no American involvement in the de facto Soviet sphere of influence, which would entail American responsibility for Soviet policies in Poland, admitted that Hopkins had managed to get the best deal possible.[16]

Soon after Hopkins left Moscow, the Polish democratic leaders on the list adopted by the two sides were flown to Moscow. Within days they reached an agreement on the composition of the new government. It was a long-awaited but inconclusive victory. Churchill complained in a letter to Truman that the deal brokered by Hopkins was "a milestone in a long hill we ought never have been asked to climb." In Truman's view, the Yalta agreements were working, and on July 5 the United States recognized the new provisional government of Poland. The major stumbling block to the final peace conference was thus removed. This was due to the policy of reconciliation advocated by Davies, and it would be Davies, not Harriman, who would accompany Truman to the next peace conference. The venue was Potsdam, a suburb of Berlin, deep within the Red Army's zone of occupation.[17]

Before leaving for Potsdam, Truman met with the Chinese foreign minister, T. V. Soong, whom he informed about the secret decisions made at Yalta. The president told his visitor that the United States needed the Soviet Union's help against Japan, implying that the Yalta agreements would be honored. China would be on its own if it sought to negotiate a better deal with the Soviet Union. The best Soong could do was to ask State Department officials "what was to be understood by the provision in the Yalta agreement that consideration should be given to Russia's predominant interest in Manchuria." Joseph Grew, who also met with him, had no answer. "I was not present at Yalta," he told Soong; "these things will be ironed out at the next meeting of the Big Three."[18]

Truman left for Potsdam on July 7. Before embarking on his first trans-atlantic journey as president, he paid a short visit to San Francisco to witness the signing of the United Nations Charter on June 26. The charter was brought to Washington by Alger Hiss on a special army plane in a fireproof safe with a parachute and delivered by the president to the Senate on July 2, upon his return to the capital. On the same day the Senate approved his nominee for the post of secretary of state, James Byrnes. His appointment was announced on June 30, after the country and the world learned that Edward Stettinius would become the first American representative to the United Nations. The new president had great respect for Byrnes, whose presence at Yalta qualified him as a foreign-policy expert in his eyes. Admiral William Leahy and Charles Bohlen, who had attended the Yalta Conference, joined Truman on board the heavy cruiser *Augusta* as he departed for Europe. Truman was surrounded by Roosevelt's advisers from Yalta and had the same question at the top of his agenda: Soviet participation in the war with Japan.[19]

For Truman the Potsdam Conference began on July 16, one day before its official opening, with a visit from Churchill. Unlike Roosevelt, Truman had no reservations about meeting privately with the prime minister. He wanted to establish good relations with Stalin but was not going to court him at the expense of the British prime minister. Churchill was eager to meet Roosevelt's successor and sized him up right away. He later told Lord Moran, "[H]e is a man of immense determination. He takes no notice of delicate ground, he just plants his foot down firmly on it." Churchill went out of his way to praise the world role of the United States. Impervious to Churchill's flattery, Truman was determined not to become a pawn in the more experienced politician's hands. They had corresponded extensively since his assumption of office, and Truman originally shared Churchill's attitude toward Soviet actions in Eastern Europe but eventually grew suspicious of his designs. Joseph Davies, whom Truman sent to London in late May to placate Churchill, warned him that the prime minister was playing the old game of balance of power in Europe and wanted America's help in securing the upper hand for Britain, even if that were to involve a new war.

The prime minister came to Potsdam more concerned about the Soviet threat than ever before and fully cognizant of Britain's limited power to influence the situation. His preconference efforts to enlist American support seemed to have been largely ineffective. Churchill's telegrams, in which he first used the metaphor he would later popularize of the "iron curtain" covering half of Europe, had little impact on Truman. Warned by his military, Truman was unreceptive to Churchill's suggestions that he link the withdrawal of American troops from the Soviet zone of occupation to cooperation on the Polish question. He also ignored Churchill's protests against the transfer of American forces from Europe to the Pacific. Churchill was becoming desperate. On his orders British military strategists prepared a contingency plan for war with the Soviet Union beginning on July 1. The name of the plan, "Operation Unthinkable," was appropriate indeed, given that the British army was not psychologically ready to fight a recent ally. The United States, meanwhile, was counting on Soviet military support in the Far East. With Germany defeated and the Soviet threat still only a theoretical possibility, there was less and less to keep the Western Allies together.

Churchill was in a bellicose mood and opposed every Soviet position at the Potsdam Conference, from German reparations and Poland's western borders (defending the stand he had taken at Yalta) to Stalin's attempts to establish a Soviet military base in the Dardanelles. He also rebuffed new and unsettling Soviet demands to remove the Franco regime from office in Spain and take over

Italian colonies in Africa. Stalin's appetite was growing, as was the geographical scope of Soviet aspirations. "I had not considered the possibility of the Soviet Union desiring to acquire a large tract of African shore," Churchill told Stalin. "If this is the case, it will have to be considered in relation to many other problems." He was also upset about Soviet policies in Eastern Europe and the growing division between the Soviet and Western zones of Germany. "The idea of Germany as a single unit has vanished. Instead we have Russian Germany divided from British Germany by a line drawn by God knows whom, on no economic or historic grounds," he complained privately to Lord Moran.

Truman backed Churchill but without vigor—Churchill suspected he was slow to grasp matters unfamiliar to him. He also grew to like Stalin, whom he considered a smart and honest man—one more victim of Stalin's great skill at manipulation. The Soviets were impressed by the new president's modesty but not by his intellect. "He talked modestly about himself," remembered Molotov. " 'There are millions like me in America, but I am the president.' He played the piano. Nothing special, of course, but not badly. He was far from having Roosevelt's intellect. A big difference." Truman did not try to play the honest broker, as Roosevelt had done at Yalta—that was beyond his diplomatic skills and would have introduced unwanted complexity into the task of achieving tangible results. Unlike Roosevelt, he had no ideological opposition to dividing Europe into spheres of influence, which improved the prospects of reaching an understanding with Stalin.[20]

The Truman-Churchill alliance at the conference came to an abrupt end with the news of Churchill's unexpected defeat in the British parliamentary elections. The main vote took place on July 5, allowing Churchill to leave for the conference, but a number of polls were delayed, and the results of the first general elections in Britain in ten years (there were no elections during the war) were not announced until July 26. The plenary sessions of the conference were suspended to allow Churchill and Eden to travel to London for the announcement of the results, but no one at Potsdam—least of all Churchill and Eden themselves—expected that they would not be coming back. By summer Churchill's worries about the outcome of the elections, which he had expressed so vividly at Yalta, seemed to fade away. He campaigned against Clement Attlee's Labour Party, suggesting that its program would require a Gestapo-like government body if it were to be implemented in Britain. Churchill ran on his wartime record, while his opponents looked to the future, promising full employment and state-run health care. The voters chose the future: after coming to power, Labour would establish the foundations of a welfare state.[21]

The news of Churchill's defeat came as a shock to both Truman and Stalin. Before leaving for London, Churchill told Byrnes that he "felt very confident of victory." For the Soviet leader it was a lesson in electoral democracy that he was eager to share with representatives of the "democratic" Eastern European regimes in his zone of influence. "One does not always succeed in being farsighted," he would tell the leaders of the Bulgarian government in January 1946. "Churchill is much more farsighted than your oppositionists, but during the Berlin conference he assured us that he would certainly obtain a majority in Parliament. Attlee, for his part, only expected to increase his vote but never thought that his party would gain a majority in Parliament. It's tough, but you can't see everything."[22]

Clement Attlee and Ernest Bevin, the leaders of the new Labour government, came to Potsdam and continued Churchill's policy, but the initiative now belonged to the Americans. Byrnes led the way with Truman's blessing, proposing a deal to Stalin that amounted to a division of Germany and of Europe itself into two spheres. In return for Soviet agreement to limit reparations in their zone of occupation, Byrnes offered Stalin and Molotov recognition of Poland's new western border on the Western Neisse and of Soviet puppet governments in Bulgaria, Romania, and Hungary. After some hesitation and bargaining, Stalin accepted the deal, which was also backed by the new masters in London. Molotov later explained the logic to a friend: "The main question at Potsdam was about reparations, but the Polish question was also of great importance. The Americans offered us a way out of the situation that reduced friction between us and our Western allies."[23]

The atomic bomb, which was successfully tested in the desert outside Los Alamos on July 16, had no apparent impact on American or Soviet behavior at the conference. Truman and Byrnes still wanted Soviet participation in the war with Japan. At the beginning of the conference, Stalin confirmed his Yalta pledge to enter that war without demanding any new concessions. Truman mentioned the powerful new weapon to Stalin, but Stalin did not react, and the matter was never discussed openly at the conference, which ended on August 2. Four days later, the first nuclear bomb was dropped on Hiroshima, and three days after that came the second nuclear strike at Nagasaki. On the day the bomb fell on Nagasaki, Soviet troops began their advance into Manchuria. Stalin hastened to claim his part of the booty before it was too late—at Potsdam he had said that the USSR would not be ready to enter the war before mid-August, and his commanders were even less optimistic.[24]

The Potsdam Conference did not bring the definitive end to the war that everyone had been hoping for. The new European borders would not be formally recognized by the international community, notably the government of the Federal Republic of Germany, for another thirty years, when the Helsinki Final Act was signed in August 1975. In the Far East Japan never signed a peace treaty with the Soviet Union or its successor, the Russian Federation, and part of the Kurile Islands remains a stumbling block to the full normalization of diplomatic relations. The Potsdam Conference never fully emerged from the shadow of Yalta, and many of its decisions, including those on the Polish borders and the de facto division of Germany and Europe, were retrospectively attributed to the earlier meeting. Potsdam was an attempt to continue Yalta, first without Roosevelt and then without Churchill. Its results were a mixed bag—but then, so was the Yalta Conference itself. Yalta has been praised for helping to end the war and putting together the elements of the subsequent peace. It has been criticized for laying the groundwork for the Cold War, which began in earnest three years later. Its true significance can be appreciated only by considering it in the context of its own time and peeling off the accretion of multiple layers of Cold War myth.

EPILOGUE

M ilitary guards welcomed the guests arriving at Livadia Palace on February 4, 2005, as they had done sixty years earlier. Aside from the guard of honor, and the return to Livadia of some of the soldiers and waitresses who had provided security and service sixty years earlier, there was little resemblance to February 1945. The organizers of this Yalta conference—a symposium entitled "Yalta 1945–2005: From the Bipolar World to the Geopolitics of the Future"—anxiously awaited but never received greetings from President Viktor Yushchenko of Ukraine, to which Yalta and the Crimea now belong, or from President Vladimir Putin of Russia, the legal successor to the Soviet Union. Nor were there greetings from the leaders of Britain or the United States. Each had his own reasons to overlook the anniversary of the conference that helped shape the modern world.[1]

Historians have often treated the events leading up to the disintegration of the Soviet bloc in Eastern Europe—the collapse of the USSR and the emergence of new nation-states—as a manifestation of "the revenge of the past." But the European borders established at Yalta generally survived the national resurgence of the late 1980s and early 1990s. Germany was reunited, but there was no adjustment to its eastern border. Czechoslovakia split into two states, but they retained the borders established immediately after the Second World War. Nor was there any change to the borders of Poland or the former Soviet republics of Lithuania, Belarus, and Ukraine, all of which "inherited" parts of interwar Poland. But while the Yalta borders generally remain intact, the historical and political consequences of its decisions continue to haunt the world's political elites.[2]

In October 2004 opposition parties in the German parliament raised questions about the continuing militarization of Kaliningrad Oblast, the part of the former East Prussia around Königsberg allocated to Russia by the Big Three in February 1945. They suggested calling an international conference and inviting representatives of the Germans who had been forcibly expelled from East Prussia to discuss the economic development of the region, which they referred to as "Königsberg oblast." They also suggested the creation of a Lithuanian-Polish-Russian region of cross-border cooperation to be called "Prussia." The Russian government was appalled. Stressing that the German government had no territorial claims against Russia, the Russian Foreign Ministry condemned those German politicians who had raised the question of the lost territories.[3]

In Japan there has always been a national consensus favoring the return of territories lost to Russia after the Second World War. The Japanese government never recognized the loss of the southern Kurile Islands, which were "awarded" to the Soviet Union by the Yalta Conference, and continues to insist on the return of the southern Kuriles, known in Japan as the "northern territories." In the spring of 2005 the Japanese parliament adopted a resolution increasing the number of islands that it wanted back from Russia. The return of these islands is regarded as a precondition for the signing of a peace treaty, the absence of which has clouded Russo-Japanese political, cultural, and economic relations ever since the end of the Second World War.[4]

In early 2005 Russia's neighbors to the west, the Balts and Poles, attacked the Russian government for its failure to apologize for Stalin's occupation of Eastern Europe. The attacks came in response to Russia's decision to invite world leaders to Moscow to celebrate the sixtieth anniversary of the victory over Nazi Germany in May. VE Day brought not only liberation from fascism but also Soviet occupation of Eastern and Central Europe, which lasted in one form or another for more than forty years. The leaders of the "captive" nations were now determined to remind the world of that episode and, in the process, to encourage Russia to face its Stalinist past and acknowledge the atrocities committed in Eastern Europe by the Soviet Union and its communist allies.

America's response to the growing international debate came in the form of a speech delivered by President George W. Bush in Riga on May 6, on his way to the Moscow celebrations. "As we mark a victory of six days ago—six decades ago, we are mindful of a paradox," stated Bush. "For much of Germany, defeat led to freedom. For much of Eastern and Central Europe, victory brought the iron rule of another empire. VE Day marked the end of fascism, but it did not end oppression. The agreement at Yalta followed in the unjust tradition of Munich and the Molotov-Ribbentrop Pact. Once again, when powerful governments negotiated, the freedom of small nations was somehow expendable. Yet this attempt to sacrifice freedom for the sake of stability left a continent divided and unstable. The captivity of millions in Central and Eastern Europe will be remembered as one of the greatest wrongs of history."[5]

Bush's critique of Yalta was in many ways a continuation of the historical argument advanced by leading figures in President Bill Clinton's administration. In March 1999 Secretary of State Madeleine Albright, the daughter of a

Czechoslovak diplomat who escaped to the West after the communist takeover, stated to representatives of Eastern European governments: "Never again will your fates be tossed around like poker chips on a bargaining table." In fact, Albright was developing an argument made earlier by her deputy, Clinton's classmate Strobe Talbott. "After World War II," he remarked in May 1997, "many countries in the east suffered nearly half a century under the shadow of Yalta. That is a place name that has come to be a codeword for the cynical sacrifice of small nations' freedom to great powers' spheres of influence, just as Versailles has come to signify a short-sighted, punitive, and humiliating peace that sows the seeds of future war."[6]

A U.S. administration official later revealed that President Bush's remarks in Riga were intended as an invitation for Putin to apologize for the Molotov-Ribbentrop Pact. If that was indeed the case, then the White House speechwriters clearly miscalculated. Bush scored points with leaders of the "new Europe," but he created unexpected problems for his administration at home. The speech, which linked Yalta, Munich, and the Molotov-Ribbentrop Pact, reignited the old debate between Republicans and Democrats over the role of Franklin Delano Roosevelt in what his critics called the "sellout" of Eastern Europe to Joseph Stalin. Conservative journalists and commentators praised Bush's remarks as a long overdue recognition of the "awful truth," while liberals accused the Republicans of reviving the spirit of Joseph McCarthy. The Democrats maintained that the Yalta Conference had done little more than recognize the reality on the ground: by the time of the Crimean summit Stalin had already gained control of Eastern Europe.[7]

New historical data that became available in the West after the fall of the Berlin Wall and the disintegration of the Soviet Union has made even more apparent the enormous price paid by Eastern Europe and, indeed, the entire world for the deal made in February 1945, but that knowledge has done little to raise the level of the 2005 debate on the Yalta Conference, as most arguments for and against are still informed by Cold War–era mythology.

"From Stettin in the Baltic to Trieste in the Adriatic an *iron curtain* has descended across the Continent. Behind that line lie all the capitals of the ancient states of Central and Eastern Europe. Warsaw, Berlin, Prague, Vienna, Budapest, Belgrade, Bucharest and Sofia; all these famous cities and the populations around them lie in what I must call the Soviet sphere, and all are subject in one form or another, not only to Soviet influence but to a very high and in some cases increasing measure of control from Moscow," declared Winston Churchill on March 5, 1946, slightly more than a year after the end of the Yalta Conference. The speech set the tone for the Cold War between East and West that would begin in earnest two years later. In the new international and political atmosphere, the Yalta agreements became a battleground between

Republicans and Democrats over the conduct of foreign policy. Disagreements gave rise to numerous myths about Yalta. Some blamed the conference participants for selling out Western interests to Stalin. Others tried to exonerate them. It became almost impossible to take a dispassionate view, or to distinguish myth from reality.[8]

The Yalta Conference was a contest between individual leaders and their conflicting agendas, but also a clash between two different approaches to international relations. FDR's policy was an embodiment of liberal internationalism, with its emphasis on international institutions and the spread of democratic values. At Yalta he was up against two veteran proponents of realpolitik. Stalin saw the world in terms of power interests, as did Churchill, despite his sincere commitment to democratic values.

The perception of the Yalta Conference as a diplomatic failure was largely based on the disappointments of the early Cold War. From the perspective of the late 1940s and early 1950s, the Yalta agreements failed to prevent the Soviet takeover of Eastern Europe and were accused of creating conditions for communist victory in China, where the Soviet Union was allocated a sphere of influence in Manchuria. And yet, if diplomacy is the art of the possible, and if one were to judge the results of Yalta according to the geopolitical and military situation at the time, one would conclude that the Western leaders achieved considerably more than they were subsequently credited with.

It is sometimes overlooked that Yalta was a wartime conference, and that the West was greatly indebted to the Soviet Union for the coalition's ultimate victory. The most devastating war in human history was far from over, and to achieve victory the Western leaders needed the Red Army and its commander in chief. Roosevelt, in particular, felt he needed the Red Army to help end the war in the Far East quickly and with as few American casualties as possible. He considered it essential to obtain Stalin's cooperation in establishing the United Nations Organization and believed that a secure and peaceful postwar world would depend on Soviet cooperation.

Both Roosevelt and Churchill realized that without a conference with Stalin, their influence on Eastern Europe would be nil. They did their best to make the summit happen. Churchill rushed to see Stalin in the fall of 1944 once the Soviet leader's reluctance to hold another tripartite conference made its proximate convocation all but impossible. Roosevelt made the greatest personal sacrifice, taking an exhausting journey despite his very poor health. The question of whether it was the trip that eventually killed him cannot definitely be answered, but few would deny that it was a contributing factor.

At Yalta, both Roosevelt and Churchill were in a poor bargaining position, as American and British forces were still recovering from the German counterattack in the Ardennes while the Red Army was securing bridgeheads on the

Oder River, a mere 70 kilometers from Germany's capital. Although the Western Allies had been providing technical assistance and air support for Soviet military operations against Germany since the fall of 1941, they did not put troops on the ground in Western Europe until the Normandy invasion of June 1944, and their numbers never reached even half of the Soviet deployment on the eastern front. The war in Europe was waged largely by the Red Army, with the obvious result that Stalin gained possession of most of Eastern Europe and would soon control a good deal of Central Europe as well.[9]

The situation in which the Western Allies found themselves on the eve of Yalta was best summarized by Anthony Eden: "[W]e had not very much to offer them, but . . . we required a great deal from them." The "not very much" that the West could offer Stalin included recognizing Soviet territorial acquisitions and allocating the lion's share of German war booty to the USSR. Given what the Western Allies had to offer and what they got in return, they did surprisingly well—especially the Americans. Roosevelt achieved his two main goals: a Soviet commitment to participate in the war with Japan and to join the world peace organization. These were the issues on which Stalin was interested in cooperating, or at least, as in the case of the United Nations, was prepared to meet Roosevelt halfway. He kept his promises, not fully realizing that he was helping to establish the foundations of a world order in which the United States would play a leading role.[10]

The British did reasonably well too, especially if one takes into account that the United States was in a position to offer most of the available incentives to the Soviets, while Britain wanted most from the USSR in the sensitive region of Eastern Europe. Churchill achieved one of his main objectives: to build up France to the status of a great power, obtaining a zone of occupation for his militarily weak ally and making it a member of the Allied Control Commission for Germany. Churchill was also able to block any decisions on reparations, thus forestalling the economic implosion of Central Europe. The British war cabinet was also pleased by the postponement of the final decision on the German-Polish boundary. The British managed to achieve this without sacrificing their strategic interests in Greece or Italy or undermining their control of overseas territories.

The Soviet Union, the main contributor to victory over Germany, had its own reasons to be satisfied with the results of the summit. At last its great-power status had been recognized, after years of international isolation. The Americans had promised that the lion's share of German reparations would go to the USSR. Germany would be divided into a number of states. Soviet control over Eastern Europe, with the notable exception of Poland, was not directly questioned by the Allies, and Stalin forced Roosevelt to accept his "political conditions" for entering the war with Japan, which gave the USSR territorial acquisitions and a sphere of influence in the Far East. Two additional seats for the Soviet Union in the United Nations seemed a good way of avoiding possible isolation in that body. Finally, the Soviets managed to elude questions they preferred not to discuss, such as the situation in Iran.

Then there was Poland. What was really at stake in the debates over Poland was the fate of Eastern Europe as a whole. The Soviets wanted a security zone along their western border—a belt of "friendly" states to replace the interwar cordon sanitaire designed to isolate the Soviet Union. Stalin was determined to control Poland, the country with the longest common border with the USSR and the keystone of his security arch. At Yalta he stressed the importance of Poland for Soviet security. Decades later, in connection with the rise of the Solidarity trade-union movement, Molotov gave expression to Stalin's and his own attitude toward Poland: "Poland has always been in a difficult situation. We had many conversations about Poland with Truman, Harriman. . . . We cannot lose Poland. If this line is crossed they will grab us too." The only way not to lose Poland, given that the average Pole regarded the Soviets as invaders, was to install a puppet government maintained by the Red Army and responsible to Stalin himself. The Soviet goals in the region were incompatible with free elections in which all democratic parties could compete on an equal footing. The West would accept nothing less because of domestic pressures, its commitment to democracy, and its desire for a foothold in the region.[11]

This was a clash of geopolitical vision, ideology, and culture that the Yalta Conference did very little to resolve. The deadlock favored the Soviets, whose troops were already deployed throughout Eastern Europe. Churchill and Roosevelt sought to put the best public face on their failure to obtain Soviet guarantees of democracy in the region. They did not consider this setback catastrophic, as Yalta was never intended to be the final peace conference. Another conference of the Big Three was indeed held in Potsdam. But it was Yalta that became a symbol of political failure once relations broke down and the Cold War set in. An important reason for that view of Yalta was the opposition manifested by Polish political circles in the West immediately after the publication of the Yalta decisions. From the Polish perspective, Yalta took away Polish territories; the Potsdam Conference would compensate Poland with lands in the west for the losses in the east.

"When I first came to Poland I kept hearing a very strange word," wrote Timothy Garton Ash in his award-winning book on the history of the Solidarity movement in Poland. "'Yowta,' my new acquaintances sighed, 'yowta!' and conversation ebbed into melancholy silence. Did 'yowta' mean fate, I wondered, was it an expression like 'that's life'?" In fact, "Yowta" is the Polish way of pronouncing the word "Yalta," and for generations that word meant betrayal, abandonment by the Western Allies of the first nation that rose up against

German aggression in September 1939. The negative legacy of Yalta, especially deeply felt in Poland, became part of political discourse in Soviet-controlled Eastern Europe throughout the Cold War.[12]

Could the Western Allies have done better at Yalta and spared Eastern Europe decades of subordination to the Soviet Union? The first answer that comes to mind is "Of course they could have." When one considers the long-term consequences for Poland and the rest of Eastern Europe, one cannot help but think that there could have been a better outcome. One need only recall the lack of specifics on the "reorganization" of the Polish government in the final documents of the conference. The devil is always in the details, and spelling out those details might have influenced Soviet behavior in the region. But could the Western democracies have stopped Stalin from doing what he wanted? Would words alone have changed his mind?

What strikes anyone looking for flaws in Western diplomacy at Yalta is the lack of unity between Roosevelt and Churchill, both in their approach to Stalin and in their handling of many questions at the negotiating table. The two Western leaders viewed the postwar world through different lenses. Roosevelt's agenda was global—the creation of a world peace organization, military victory in Europe and the Pacific, and the achievement of supremacy in America's global economic competition with the British Empire. Europe was of secondary interest—once the war in that theater was over, the United States would end its involvement in European affairs. Given this approach, Stalin emerged as a potential ally rather than a competitor. Churchill, by contrast, was keenly interested in Europe. He believed that securing control over the Mediterranean was vital to the continued existence of the British Empire, and that the independence of Eastern European states was essential to Britain's security, as it would prevent the Soviet Union from dominating the whole subcontinent. From Churchill's viewpoint, Stalin was a competitor and a potential enemy, by no means an ally.

As Stalin held the trump cards, the Western leaders found themselves competing for his favors. Churchill hastened to Moscow in October 1944 to make a deal behind Roosevelt's back, partitioning the Balkans into Soviet and British spheres of influence. At Yalta, Roosevelt paid him back by making a separate deal with Stalin on Asia and refusing to back Churchill fully on Poland and on the reparations issue. Churchill had every right to be unhappy with Roosevelt's treatment of him, which sometimes redounded to Stalin's benefit. But FDR had his reasons for the policies that he adopted at Yalta vis-à-vis Churchill and the British Empire.

Roosevelt played a key role as permanent chair of the plenary sessions. A skillful politician, he cast himself as an honest broker, as "Judge Roosevelt."

Despite his general agreement with Churchill on a number of goals, he preferred to attain them by applying his own tactics, and the results bore him out. Most of the concessions the Western Allies won from the Soviets were in cases where the two leaders presented a common front. Even so, they were mainly obtained by Roosevelt, not Churchill. Playing on disagreements between Stalin and Churchill, Roosevelt managed to secure results that a frontal attack could hardly have delivered.

Although Roosevelt avoided personal discussions with Churchill on Malta, he did not object to consultations between foreign secretaries and military commanders, who reached a high level of agreement on questions of diplomatic and military strategy. Nowhere was this more apparent than in the most contested issue of the conference, the fate of Poland and Eastern Europe. The Western leaders stood together in that battle through most of the conference, consulting on tactics and supporting each other in the plenary sessions. They diverged only on the sixth day of the conference, when FDR decided that diplomatic means had been exhausted.

There is the big question of what would have happened if Roosevelt had adopted a different policy, decided not to abandon Churchill in his stand on Poland, and insisted on a continuation of the discussion. The question cannot be answered with any degree of certainty. There is, however, no indication that Stalin would have been prepared to yield if the Roosevelt-Churchill alliance had held fast and the conference had continued beyond its actual terminus. Stalin was not opposed to such a continuation, but he was prepared to discuss the Black Sea Straits and German reparations, not Poland.

The main impediments to the success of the Yalta Conference were profoundly different geopolitical aspirations and underlying differences in political culture between the Eastern and Western Allies. Britain and the USSR had been in opposite camps for almost two years after the outbreak of the Second World War: it was only the German attack on the Soviet Union in June 1941 that brought Stalin into the Grand Alliance. In 1939 Stalin and the leaders of the Western democracies had conflicting goals; in 1941 they acquired a common enemy without changing their goals. At Yalta they faced the difficult task of agreeing to a new set of common goals once their enemy was defeated. Their differences extended to ideology and political culture and were exacerbated by diplomatic miscalculations and cultural misunderstandings. "The best friendships are those founded on misunderstandings," Stalin noted in Teheran. There were plenty of misunderstandings at Yalta, not all of which redounded to the benefit of friendship.[13]

Roosevelt, Churchill, and their shrewdest foreign-policy advisers believed or wished to believe that Stalin wanted greater cooperation with the West and was being bullied into unfriendliness by hard-liners in the Politburo such as Molotov and Lavrentii Beria. They could not have been more wrong. Raised in democratic systems, they never understood Stalin's role as puppet master in the Politburo, where some of his "hard-line colleagues" were working under threat of imminent arrest, having had family members executed and wives condemned to the Gulag. Roosevelt counted on good postwar relations with the USSR, thinking that the Soviet leadership would need American loans to rebuild its war-torn economy and alleviate the sufferings of its people. Again, he could not have been more wrong. From Stalin's perspective, the sufferings of his people were a small price to pay for the worldwide triumph of the Soviet model.

Churchill believed that he could trust Stalin and tried to address him in terms he would understand when he offered to divide the Balkans. He offered Stalin a 90 percent stake in Romania, which would still give Britain a foothold and some measure of influence. Stalin went along, but in reality he was never prepared to measure his control over territory in percentage points. Like the architects of the Peace of Augsburg (1555), which ended the war between the Catholics and the Lutherans in Germany, Stalin thought in theological terms about his new possessions: to ensure the victory of the true religion, the new communist faith, he would have to secure absolute sovereignty over his new realm. The Western leaders, dreaming of world government by consensus, could not accept the Augsburg principle of *cujus regio, eius religio*. Churchill was so disappointed by the outcome of Yalta that he refused to provide any substantial material of his own for the Yalta chapters of his memoirs. His Syndicate helpers had to put together the story from the official British records and the long list of anecdotes dictated by Churchill about his time at the conference.[14]

Stalin emerges from the pages of the formerly secret Soviet documents as the best informed and prepared of the three leaders. But knowledge of his opponents' position thanks to his extensive espionage networks and his own outstanding skills as a negotiator did not suffice to save him from misjudgments based on his dictatorial perspective. In the end, he misread his Western allies as much as they did him. There were, of course, some outright miscalculations. Like Roosevelt, Stalin believed that the United Kingdom would preserve and enhance its status as a great power after the war, and he thought of Britain as his main rival on the European subcontinent. There were ideological and cultural barriers that prevented him from understanding the motives of his guests at Yalta and anticipating their future actions. The master realpolitiker, who had sharpened his diplomatic teeth in contests with Hitler and Ribbentrop, never understood the nature of democratic government and the limitations that it places on political leaders.

Stalin was utterly baffled by Churchill's electoral defeat in the summer of 1945, which only served to deepen his mistrust of elections. He did not appreciate the power of public opinion over democratically elected politicians. He thought that the Western leaders, driven by their own interests, would agree to the division of Europe and ignore his suppression of the Polish democratic opposition, just as he had ignored the British suppression of communist resistance in Greece. Stalin and Molotov were genuinely upset when the Western governments protested against their actions in Poland. They had an even lower opinion of the vague Declaration on Liberated Europe that they were obliged to sign with "capitalist thieves" whom they had never trusted and had no intention of trusting in the future.

What alternatives were open to Roosevelt and Churchill when it came to Stalin's emerging empire in Eastern Europe? Their choice was stark. They could have condemned Stalin's actions, dissociated themselves from them, and repudiated him, denying him international legitimacy. Or they could continue the dialogue, seeking to make an incremental difference, never quite closing the door and keeping hope for democratic development of the region alive. The price for the second option was public silence about the most outrageous suppression of human freedom and giving a degree of legitimacy to Stalin's rule over Eastern Europe. The price for the first option is more difficult to calculate. Western leaders could have pursued it without endangering their military alliance and jeopardizing victory over Germany, but it would have spelled the end of any postwar relations with the Soviet Union. Roosevelt would have had to give up his dream of a new world built on the foundation of international institutions such as the United Nations. And it would have meant surrendering half of Europe to Stalin, leaving the West with no leverage to influence the situation, and initiating the Cold War before it became inevitable. The alternative—war with the Soviet Union, a plan prepared on Churchill's orders—was considered unrealistic even by the British military.

The Western Allies chose the second option, leaving the door open and continuing to try to turn the situation around. The sentiments of those who decided to take the risk and keep talking were later summarized by a member of the British delegation at Yalta and a Cold War–era ambassador to Moscow, Sir Frank Roberts: "We could have said 'no, we'll have nothing to do with it,' in which case the Russians would have gone ahead. There wouldn't even have been this, perhaps you may say, hypocritical possibility, by getting some Poles back into Poland, by having elections. . . . That was the alternative. We could have continued to recognize the Polish government in exile, and said everything was wrong. But I don't see that this would have been a better position. It would have, if you like, enabled us all to feel much nicer, if we hadn't given way to this terrible Stalin. But in practice I don't see how it would have helped anybody very much."[15]

In the end, the Western Allies succeeded in getting some of the democratic leaders and some elements of political pluralism back into Poland. Their hope of building on that modest success was not so naive as it appeared during the Cold War. Soviet archival evidence and recent research on the subject indicate that at the time of the Yalta Conference Stalin had not yet decided what to do with Eastern Europe. As late as May 1946, he advised the leaders of the Polish government: "Lenin never said there was no path to socialism other than the dictatorship of the proletariat; he admitted that it was possible to arrive at the path to socialism utilizing the foundations of the bourgeois democratic system such as Parliament."[16]

Closing all channels of communication in February 1945 and giving up all available levers of influence would have been an error much greater than any for which the Western architects of Yalta were ever criticized. One of the testimonies to Roosevelt's and Churchill's sound strategy at Yalta is that decades after the conference, with the benefit of hindsight, new archival findings, and tons of research, it is still very difficult to suggest any practical alternative to the course that they took.

There were of course other possibilities, but they had the potential of leading to a new war before the old one was over. Joseph Goebbels nourished high hopes of this as he followed the coverage of inter-Allied tensions in the Western media from his hideout in Berlin. If one were to take Stalin's fears as a guide to policy alternatives, then a separate peace with the dying Nazi regime or, more realistically, an armistice leading to the end of hostilities on the western front, could have been adopted instead of the policy that Roosevelt and Churchill followed at Yalta. These options could only be perceived as dead ends by the two Western leaders, who were committed to leading their nations and the long-suffering world toward peace. As Charles Bohlen wrote to George Kennan from Yalta, regarding his proposal to divide Europe in half, "Foreign policy of that kind cannot be made in a democracy."[17]

Cold War–era critics and proponents of the Yalta agreements raised a series of questions that continue to influence today's perception of the end of the Second World War. Was FDR too ill to conduct successful negotiations at Yalta? Did the Big Three decide behind closed doors to divide Europe into spheres of influence? Was it the selfish policy of the West, refusing to give the Soviet Union a security zone on its borders while taking control of Western Europe and maintaining empires of its own, that led to the failure of the Yalta agreements and the onset of the Cold War? These contradictory questions informed the often partisan historiography of the Cold War era. The end of the Cold War and the opening of the Soviet archives allow one to revisit the old debates. One can now approach these questions with a much better appreciation of what Stalin and his entourage knew about their allies from the vast Soviet intelligence network they maintained in the West, what they thought about their partners, what their geopolitical goals were, how they assessed the results of the negotiations, and whether they intended to honor their obligations.

President Roosevelt may have paid the ultimate price for his determination to carry on throughout the conference, but could America and Britain have done better if the United States had been represented by a younger, healthier, and more energetic leader? Roosevelt's associates at Yalta were in denial as to his health and remained so after the conference. For personal and political reasons they did not want to see what others who were not so close to the president or not vulnerable recognized immediately—signs of rapidly declining health. Most of what we know today about Roosevelt's failing capacities at Yalta comes from the British participants, who also were not entirely impartial, as the president's failing health offered a perfect rationalization for the cooling of British-American relations, whose decline is better understood as a result of the failing capacities of the British Empire.

The point on which most American and British observers of Roosevelt's actions at Yalta seem to agree is that despite his obvious fatigue, the president showed complete command of the major issues under discussion. Throughout the conference FDR demonstrated his trademark ability to make alliances, strike deals, and maneuver in order to achieve his main goals. There was no instance at Yalta when he yielded on an important issue spontaneously, in clear violation of his earlier position or without consulting his advisers. And there was a remarkable consistency between Roosevelt's positions at Yalta and in Teheran. He was clearly tired and pressed for the conference's early conclusion, but he did not leave Yalta before his main objectives had been achieved.

Another entrenched myth that should be further scrutinized, if not completely discarded, originated with supporters of General Charles de Gaulle, who maintained that the Big Three agreed at Yalta to the division of Europe into spheres of influence. Indeed, most of the negotiations at Yalta were conducted on the assumption that Stalin had the right to friendly governments in countries bordering on the Soviet Union. But both Roosevelt and Churchill emphatically rejected the "communization" of Eastern Europe and did all they could to prevent the emergence of what Churchill later called an "iron curtain"—the heavily policed border that shut out the West and eventually eliminated the last vestiges of democracy in the region. It was their inability to agree on the division of Eastern Europe that caused most of the tension during and after the conference, as is well attested by the conference protocols, Roosevelt-Churchill-Stalin correspondence, and the actions of the Allied diplomats.

If one is looking for high-level meetings to blame for the Cold War–era division of Europe, then Moscow and Potsdam come to the fore, not Yalta. It was in Moscow that Churchill and Stalin agreed to divide the Balkans in October 1944, while in Potsdam, at the prompting of James Byrnes, the new American president accepted the deal that divided Germany into distinct zones of occupation and offered Western recognition to Stalin's puppet governments in Eastern Europe. At Yalta Roosevelt and Churchill approved the establishment of a Soviet sphere of influence in northeastern China, but it was only in Potsdam that America and Britain tacitly accepted Stalin's control of Eastern Europe.

The Yalta deal on the Far East was originally criticized for its secrecy and betrayal of America's Chinese allies, but the most enduring criticism of the deal Roosevelt struck with Stalin at Yalta has been based on the belief that there was no need to bring the USSR into the war with Japan. That line of argument is largely based on the fact that by the time the Soviet Union entered the war in August 1945, the United States already possessed nuclear weapons and had dropped two on Japan. In February 1945, however, no one could have predicted whether the bomb would be produced, whether it would work, and how it might affect the conduct of the war. The American military estimated casualties in the forthcoming battle for Japan in the hundreds of thousands, and Truman left for Potsdam a few days before the first successful nuclear test still considering Soviet entrance into the war with Japan his first priority. Some historians today argue convincingly that the Soviet entrance into the war had at least as much effect as the atomic bomb on the Japanese decision to surrender.

A close reading of the Soviet, American, and British protocols of the Yalta Conference and the diaries and memoirs of its participants helps dispel another Cold War–era myth: that Stalin betrayed naive and trusting Western leaders and diplomats. Most participants at Yalta knew what many preferred to forget soon afterward: no satisfactory agreement had been reached on Poland. Roosevelt accepted the Soviet idea of the "reorganization" of the Polish government and, unable to ensure that this "reorganization" would lead to a democratic outcome, sought a formula to conceal that fact in the final documents of the conference. After Yalta, Stalin insisted on his interpretation of the document and the Western leaders on theirs.

By turning the Declaration on Liberated Europe from an instrument to prevent great-power meddling in the affairs of smaller European states into a mere statement of intentions, the Western leaders allowed Stalin to disregard its principles. The problem was that Stalin was not the only leader to disregard the declaration. With his policies in Italy and Greece, Churchill ignored the principles of the declaration, just as he ignored the Atlantic Charter in Iran and in the British imperial possessions overseas. The degree to which the British violated the declaration was different, but their disregard was plain for the world to see.

The opening of the Soviet archives and new research based on them help undermine one more Cold War–era myth, this one about conniving Western powers seeking to take advantage of naive Soviet leaders who asked only to be accepted as equals and were treated with suspicion despite their country's enormous sacrifice. This interpretation can hardly be sustained in light of the new evidence. Far from being a naive idealist striving for justice in the international arena, Stalin played his game in the most brutal way. He infiltrated Allied governments with his spies, read Allied diplomatic documents sometimes even before the Western leaders, played his partners off one against the other, and lied to them at every opportunity. Stalin was an imperial conqueror who never fully shed his revolutionary ideology. He regarded his allies as irreconcilable class enemies against whom any method of struggle was admissible. His sphere of influence would be secured by brute force and maintained through the intimidation, incarceration, and elimination of his opponents. Having perfected political control through terror in his own country, he was now determined to export his domination to the countries on his borders.

Finally, there is the question of Yalta's responsibility for the beginning of the Cold War. There is no doubt that Yalta was a stepping-stone to the insecure world of great-power tensions and the threat of nuclear annihilation. The disappointment that followed the initial excitement after the conference, whose results were oversold by its participants both at home and abroad, clearly marked a turning point in relations among the wartime Allies. But one should not overestimate the importance of an event that preceded the beginning of the Cold War by three years. That period witnessed such developments as Potsdam and Hiroshima, as well as the establishment of complete Soviet control over Eastern Europe. There were numerous, largely failed attempts at the highest levels to renegotiate relations among the great powers, now complicated by nuclear weapons.

Realities changed, as did the dynamics of the debate. Yalta left many unanswered questions and few alternatives open to world leaders, but the main decisions leading to the Cold War were made after the Yalta Conference. It would be wrong to assume that while the Western leaders at Yalta had limited but still viable alternatives to the actual policies adopted at the conference, their successors had none. The Yalta decisions were not carved in stone. Some of them were renegotiated or abandoned soon after the conference with the mutual agreement of the participants, as was the case with German dismemberment. It was the inability of the postwar leaders to negotiate a better deal than the one reached at Yalta that made the world point to Yalta as the final peace conference and the origin of many difficulties of the Cold War era.

With the passage of time, Yalta became much more important than its participants intended it to be, both as political reality and as historical mythology. In their minds the conference was in fact only a step on the long road to peace, which is almost always an arduous work in progress. That appears to have been Roosevelt's understanding not only during the difficult negotiations at Yalta but throughout the profound diplomatic crisis that followed. On April 11, 1945, the day before he died, he dictated to his secretary the text of a speech he was planning to deliver on April 13, Thomas Jefferson's birthday: "The work, my friends, is peace. More than an end of this war—an end to the beginnings of all wars. Yes, an end, forever to this impractical, unrealistic settlement of the differences between governments by the mass killing of peoples."[18]

There was probably no American president more eager to learn from the experience of Yalta than Richard Nixon. Yalta was very much on his mind when he returned from Moscow in June 1972, having signed the first strategic arms limitation treaty with Leonid Brezhnev. Nixon was the first American president to visit the Soviet Union after the Yalta Conference, and on his return he imitated Roosevelt by making a report to Congress. "[I]n Moscow we witnessed the beginning of the end of the era which began in 1945," Nixon told Congress on June 1, 1972. Shortly afterward, on June 16, as five burglars prepared to break into Democratic Party headquarters at the Watergate office complex, Nixon left for the Bahamas, taking with him Churchill's *Triumph and Tragedy*, the volume of memoirs that covered Yalta. He reflected on what he had read: "What we must not do is to repeat history. Yalta led to an improvement of relations but then to a sharp deterioration thereafter. Reading about Yalta gives one great pause because it was not what was agreed at Yalta, but the failure of the Soviets to keep the agreement, which led to all the troubles after that time."[19]

Unlike Republican critics of Yalta, Nixon knew how difficult it was to negotiate with the Soviets and was reluctant to blame FDR or his advisers at the conference. He basically accepted Churchill's interpretation of the Yalta agreements as a good deal broken by Stalin. He also learned the immediate political lesson of Yalta: do not oversell achievements when dealing with the Soviets, as the results could be catastrophic. But there is more to be learned from Yalta than political strategies to be employed in selling international agreements at home. Perhaps its main lesson lies in the realm of the moral implications of foreign-policy decisions.

While the two democratic leaders did their best with the few alternatives available to them at Yalta, the price they were forced to pay for the postwar peace was high not only in geopolitical terms but also in moral and human ones. Part of their sacrifice at Yalta lay in the realm of rhetoric, but another part was the very essence of their democratic beliefs. Both men—Roosevelt in particular—violated their own principles: they agreed to redraw international borders and forcibly resettle millions of people without consulting the governments and nations involved. They agreed to send Soviet prisoners of war home even if it meant their imprisonment or even death, as Churchill was well aware. Roosevelt preferred to pretend that he knew nothing about the partition of the Balkans into spheres of influence and was more than willing to grant the Soviet Union a sphere of influence in Asia. And, last but not least, he never overtly challenged Stalin's rule over Eastern Europe.

Roosevelt emerges from the pages of the documents pertaining to the history of the Yalta Conference as a true founder of the imperial presidency, running his own foreign policy by reducing the State Department to little more than an instrument for the implementation of policy devised in the White House. The result was not only the close association of U.S. foreign policy with FDR and his vision of the world but also the inability of anyone but the president himself to conduct the three-sided diplomatic exercise that inevitably came to an end after his sudden death. Roosevelt created a system in which the United States assumed the role of mediator and exercised a kind of influence on world affairs that it had not had before. With Roosevelt gone, the tripartite contest turned into a bipolar confrontation exacerbated by the implosion of the British Empire in the decade following the end of the war.

Like any war, any peace is never a one-act play. It has its beginning and its end, its ups and downs, its heroes and villains. It also has its price. As Yalta shows, no matter how hard democratic leaders try, there is always a price to be paid for making alliances with dictatorships and totalitarian regimes. If you support an ally of convenience and build up his power, it can then become difficult to keep him in check. Your enemy's enemy may well become your own enemy once the initial conflict is over, unless the alliance is based on common values and principles. The world is too complex and dangerous a place for anyone to entertain the notion that democracies should ally themselves only with democracies or that common values should serve as the sole foundation for future alliances. But Yalta shows that the unity of democratic states is essential to achieve their common goals. There will always be ideological and cultural differences not only between enemies but also between partners, as was the case at Yalta, and an appreciation of those differences is essential to making an alliance work and avoiding inflated expectations.

ACKNOWLEDGMENTS

My fascination with Yalta dates back to the early 1990s, when I was working on a scholarly article about the impact of the conference on Soviet religious policy. The Ukrainian Greek Catholic Church, created on the Orthodox-Catholic frontier of Eastern Europe in the late sixteenth century, was forcibly liquidated by the Soviet authorities in the aftermath of the Yalta Conference, and, after having studied the origins of the church, I felt an irresistible urge to take a close look at its dramatic descent into the catacombs in Stalin's Soviet Union. This venture in turn required a giant leap, frightening to any historian, from the early modern period to the mid-twentieth century. It is coming to completion with the publication of this book. In order to accomplish it, I drew on the support of the people and institutions I am happy to acknowledge here.

Bohdan Bociurkiw of Carleton University in Ottawa, an eminent authority on Soviet religious policy and a former prisoner of the Nazi concentration camp in Flossenburg, served as the reviewer of my first Yalta article. Although its main argument ran counter to many of his own ideas, Professor Bociurkiw helped improve it with advice on the sources and literature of a subject that was then still very new to me. At the University of Alberta, where I began my research on this book, Zenon Kohut and Frank Sysyn offered their support and advice. So did Roman Szporluk and John Coatsworth at Harvard during my visiting appointments there in 2002–5, and Terry Martin after I joined the Harvard faculty in 2007. The interest of Grace Kennan Warnecke and Anne Applebaum also helped advance my work. I am grateful for their encouragement and that of many others with whom I spoke about the Yalta Conference.

My research depended on the advice and generosity of many excellent scholars and individuals, some of whom I would never have come to know had it not been for this book. Serhiy Yurchenko of Livadia Palace in Yalta shared with me his knowledge of the sources and literature on the conference, Hennadiy Boriak in Kyiv helped with access to the Ukrainian archives, and A. I. Kokurin in Moscow advised on Yalta-related materials in the State Archive of the Russian Federation. At the State Archive, I am also indebted to M. V. Sidorova, who graciously furnished a number of invaluable images. My special thanks go to Antony Polonsky, who generously shared with me his photocopies of documents from the British archives. Norman Davies directed me to newly published cartographic materials on the Polish borders, and Dr. Tom Nary gave advice on the literature dealing with FDR's health problems at the time of the Yalta Conference. I avoided numerous pitfalls in my writing thanks to excellent advice from friends and colleagues who took on the daunting task of reading the entire manuscript before it went to the publisher. I owe a special debt in that regard to David Wolff, Mark Kramer, and Phil Bodrock. Chris Chappell at Palgrave Macmillan read a chapter of the book and gave me excellent advice on how to improve it. I am especially grateful to Antony Beevor, who, upon receiving the bound manuscript of the book, was generous enough to provide the publisher with a list of suggestions that helped me improve the text and avoid some errors.

Among the many discoveries I made while working on this book, one was of particular significance. I realized that writing for my colleagues is not the same as writing for a broader audience. I am very grateful to those friends and colleagues who introduced me to the art of academic belles lettres. Tim Colton at Harvard and Tim Snyder at Yale explained how the system of trade publishing works and helped me find a literary agent. I was extremely lucky to make the acquaintance of Steve Wasserman, who not only placed this book with an excellent publisher but also gave me my first lessons in the art of writing for a wider audience. At Viking I am grateful to Wendy Wolf for her original interest in the book and to Joy de Menil, who became my editor, for her devotion to the project. Joy's advice and meticulous editing not only improved this manuscript but also served as excellent training for future projects. Kristin Sprang and Chris Russell helped guide the manuscript through the editorial process, and the Viking copyediting and fact-checking team did a wonderful job. I owe a special debt to my friend of many years Myroslav Yurkevich, with whom I have worked on all my previous English-language books, and who this time around not only did an excellent job of smoothing out my prose but also helped formulate and sharpen my argument, especially in those cases where he did not agree with my judgment or my conclusions. Also of enormous help were the questions and comments of my students at Harvard who took the risk of enrolling in a research seminar on the Yalta Conference in the fall of 2008.

Finally, I would like to thank my family. My wife, Olena, encouraged my switch to writing for a broader audience and became fascinated with the topic, reading numerous versions of the manuscript, offering advice on how to improve it, and helping me input editorial corrections and revisions. As the book was submitted for copyediting, sad news came from Ukraine that my father, whom I had seen only a week earlier in apparent good health, had suddenly died of a heart attack. Like many of his generation, he was an avid reader of memoirs and historical literature on the Second World War. He lived through the horror of the Nazi occupation of Ukraine in 1941–43 and learned of the

Allied victory in Europe while working as a radio operator on the Kamchatka Peninsula, helping to deliver American Lend-Lease supplies to the Soviet Union. His fascination with the history of the war and the Grand Alliance helped shape my own interest in the period and eventually led to the writing of this book. I hoped that he would enjoy reading it when it appeared in one of its Slavic translations. It did not happen that way. Mindful of my debt to my father, I dedicate this book to my own children, Andrii and Olesia. For them, as for their generation, born in the last years of the Cold War, the history of that conflict—not to mention the demise of the Grand Alliance, which led to it—is the experience of their fathers and grandfathers, removed in time and emotionally distant. But this is experience of a kind that society at large, and we as individuals, cannot afford to forget.

NOTES

Chapter 1. The President's Journey

1 *Public Papers and Addresses of Franklin D. Roosevelt: Victory and the Threshold of Peace, 1944–45*, ed. Samuel I. Rosenman (New York, 1950), 523–25; Eleanor Roosevelt, *The Autobiography of Eleanor Roosevelt* (New York, 1992), 273; "For the Fourth Time," *Time*, January 29, 1945; Frank Freidel, *Franklin D. Roosevelt: A Rendezvous with Destiny* (Boston, 1990), 573–75.

2 Yalta Trip—Letters to Family, January 23, 1945, container 25, Edward J. Flynn Papers, Franklin D. Roosevelt Library; The President's Trip to Crimea Conference and Great Bitter Lake, Egypt, January 22 to February 28, 1945, Travel Log, Franklin D. Roosevelt Library.

3 Semiweekly news summary prepared for the secretary of state, January 13, 1945, series 8, clippings, Joseph Clark Grew Papers, MS Am 1687.7, Houghton Library, Harvard University.

4 Secret Service Records, Trips of the President, Yalta 1945, container 21, file 6-1, Franklin D. Roosevelt Library.

5 Anna Boettiger, Yalta Diary, 9, box 84, folder 11, Anna Roosevelt Halsted Papers, Franklin D. Roosevelt Library (hereafter cited as Boettiger, Yalta Diary); The President's Trip to Crimea Conference, Travel Log.

6 Doris Kearns Goodwin, *No Ordinary Time. Franklin and Eleanor Roosevelt: The Home Front in World War II* (New York, 1994), 573–75.

7 Yalta Conference: Miscellaneous, box 84, folder 8, Anna Roosevelt Halsted Papers; "FDR's Daughter," *Life*, March 5, 1945.

8 Edward R. Stettinius Jr., *Roosevelt and the Russians: The Yalta Conference* (Garden City, NY, 1949), 30.

9 Freidel, *Franklin D. Roosevelt*, 507–8; William D. Leahy, *I Was There: The Personal Story of the Chief of Staff to Presidents Roosevelt and Truman Based on His Notes and Diaries Made at the Time* (New York, 1950), 294, 297–98.

10 James F. Byrnes, *Speaking Frankly* (New York, 1947), 21–22; Stettinius, *Roosevelt and the Russians*, 69; Freidel, *Franklin D. Roosevelt*, 535–37.

11 Freidel, *Franklin D. Roosevelt*, 41–48, 512–17; Daniel Levy and Susan Brink, "A Change of Heart: FDR's Death Shows How Much We've Learned about the Heart," *US News and World Report*, February 12, 2005, 54–57; Eleanor Roosevelt, *Autobiography*, 273.

12 The President's Trip to Crimea Conference, Travel Log; Byrnes, *Speaking Frankly*, 22.

13 J. B. S. Hardman, ed., *Rendezvous with Destiny: Addresses and Opinions of Franklin Delano Roosevelt* (Whitefish, MO, 2005), 39–40; Jean Edward Smith, *FDR* (New York, 2007); H. W. Brands, *Traitor to His Class* (New York, 2008).

14 Norman Davies, *No Simple Victory: World War II in Europe, 1939–1945* (New York, 2007), 122–23; Danny Parker, *Battle of the Bulge: Hitler's Ardennes Offensive, 1944–45* (Cambridge, MA, 2004).

15 Geoffrey Roberts, *Stalin's Wars: From World War to Cold War, 1939–1953* (New Haven, CT, 2006), 61–164; Antony Beevor, *The Fall of Berlin, 1945* (New York, 2002), 39–55.

16 The President's Trip to Crimea Conference, Travel Log.

17 Leahy, *I Was There*, 292–93; Robert Maddox, "American Diplomacy before the Conference in the Crimea," in Paola Brundu Olla, ed., *Yalta: un mito che resiste* (Rome, 1988), 55–65.

18 Leahy, *I Was There*, 292–93; Stephen C. Schlesinger, *Act of Creation: The Founding of the United Nations* (Boulder, CO, 2003), 17–52; Freidel, *Franklin D. Roosevelt*, 577–78.

19 Mary E. Glantz, *FDR and the Soviet Union: The President's Battles over Foreign Policy* (Lawrence, KS, 2005), 15–87, 143–77; Barry M. Katz, *Foreign Intelligence: Research and Analysis in the Office of Strategic Services, 1942–45* (Cambridge, MA, 1989), 137–64.

20 Robert E. Sherwood, *Roosevelt and Hopkins: An Intimate History* (New York, 2001), 809; Eleanor Roosevelt, *Autobiography*, 273.

21 Byrnes, *Speaking Frankly*, 22–23; Stettinius, *Roosevelt and the Russians*, 72–73; Anthony Eden, *The Eden Memoirs: The Reckoning* (London, 1965), 512; Charles E. Bohlen, *Witness to History, 1929–1969* (New York, 1973), 171–72; Sherwood, *Roosevelt and Hopkins*, 811.

22 Boettiger, Yalta Diary, 9.

23 Letters to Family, postmarked in Washington on February 8, 1945, Edward J. Flynn Papers; The President's Trip to Crimea Conference, Travel Log; Stettinius, *Roosevelt and the Russians*, 68–69; Eden, *The Reckoning*, 511–12.

Chapter 2. Meeting on Malta

1 *Foreign Relations of the United States. Diplomatic Papers. The Conferences at Malta and Yalta, 1945* (Washington, DC, 1955), 26 (hereafter cited as *FRUS: Yalta*); Winston S. Churchill, *The Second World War: Triumph and Tragedy* (Cambridge, MA, 1953), 343.

2 Lord Moran, *Churchill at War, 1940–45* (London, 2002), 264–65.

3 Boettiger, Yalta Diary, 10; Sarah Churchill, *Keep on Dancing: An Autobiography* (London, 1981), 73.

4 Jon Meacham, *Franklin and Winston: An Intimate Portrait of an Epic Friendship* (New York, 2003), 298–302.

5 Moran, *Churchill at War*, 266; Stettinius, *Roosevelt and the Russians*, 70–72; Leahy, *I Was There*, 294.

6 Churchill, *Triumph and Tragedy*, 343; Eden, *The Reckoning*, 509; *The Diaries of Sir Alexander Cadogan O.M. 1938–1945* (New York, 1972), 701; Martin Gilbert, *Winston S. Churchill*, vol. 7, *Road to Victory, 1941–45* (Boston, 1986), 1168.

7 Carlo D'Este, *Warlord: A Life of Winston Churchill at War (1874–1945)* (New York, 2008).

8 Walter Reid, *Churchill 1940–1945: Under Friendly Fire* (Edinburgh, 2008), 3–16.

9 *FRUS: Yalta*, 3–5, 27–40; Churchill, *Triumph and Tragedy*, 344; Sherwood, *Roosevelt and Hopkins*, 812; S. V. Iurchenko, *Ialtinskaia konferentsiia 1945 goda: khronika sozdaniia novogo mira* (Simferopol, 2005), 28–32.

10 *FRUS: Yalta*, 6–10; Sherwood, *Roosevelt and Hopkins*, 844–45; Freidel, *Franklin D. Roosevelt*, 562–64.

11 *FRUS: Yalta*, 18–20; Sherwood, *Roosevelt and Hopkins*, 845; Meacham, *Franklin and Winston*, 253.

12 For the President from Harriman, December 6, 1944; From the President for Ambassador Harriman, no. 137, December 19, 1944, Map Room, Presidential Trips, Crimea Conference, box 21, Argonaut 1, section 1, Frankin D. Roosevelt Library; paraphrase of cable from Moscow dated December 21, 1944, special files, World War II, December 20–27, 1944, Averell Harriman Papers, Library of Congress.

13 Harriman's report on a conversation with Molotov, December 27, 1944, special files, World War II, December 20–27, 1944, Averell Harriman Papers, Library of Congress.

14 *FRUS: Yalta*, 21–40; Churchill, *Triumph and Tragedy*, 338, 342.

15 Eden, *The Reckoning*, 509; Yalta Conference: Notes, 10–11, Boettiger, Yalta Diary, 10–11; The President's Trip to Crimea Conference, Travel Log; Ernle Bradford, *Siege: Malta 1940–43* (New York, 1986).

16 Bohlen, *Witness to History*, 172; Eden, *The Reckoning*, 512.

17 *FRUS: Yalta*, 28–36.

18 Meacham, *Franklin and Winston*, 114–15; Bohlen, *Witness to History*, 172.

19 D'Este, *Warlord*, 319; David Carlton, *Churchill and the Soviet Union* (Manchester, UK, 2000), 4–134.

20 Anthony P. Adamthwaite, "British Diplomacy before the Conference in Crimea," in *Yalta: un mito che resiste*, 43–53.

21 Eden, *The Reckoning*, 513.

22 Ibid., 507; Cadogan, *Diaries*, 700; Moran, *Churchill at War*, 265; Sarah Churchill, *Keep on Dancing*, 73; Stettinius, *Roosevelt and the Russians*, 67–68.

23 Wilson D. Miscamble, *From Roosevelt to Truman: Potsdam, Hiroshima, and the Cold War* (New York, 2007), 61, 94–97.

24 Eden, *The Reckoning*, 510.

25 Cadogan, *Diaries*, 701; Stettinius, *Roosevelt and the Russians*, 63.

26 Eric Larrabee, *Commander in Chief: Franklin Delano Roosevelt, His Lieutenants and Their War*

(New York, 2004), 490; Ed Cray, *General of the Army: George C. Marshall, Soldier and Statesman* (New York, 1990), 501–4; Leonard Mosley, *Marshall: Hero for Our Times* (New York, 1982), 308–9.

27 Churchill, *Triumph and Tragedy*, 343–44; Sherwood, *Roosevelt and Hopkins*, 810–11; Leahy, *I Was There*, 295; *FRUS: Yalta*, 540–46.

28 Boettiger, Yalta Diary, 11–12.

29 Stettinius, *Roosevelt and the Russians*, 70–72, 74; Eden, *The Reckoning*, 512.

Chapter 3. The Tsar's Playground

1 The President's Trip to Crimea Conference, Travel Log; Boettiger, Yalta Diary, 13; Iurchenko, *Ialtinskaia konferentsiia*, 164–65; Al Eberhardt, "My Most Secret Mission: The Untold Story of Yalta," *Air Power History* 49 (Summer 2002): 40–51.

2 *FRUS: Yalta*, 39–40; Churchill, *Triumph and Tragedy*, 342; Michael F. Reilly as told to William J. Slocum, *Reilly of the White House* (New York, 1947), 210–11.

3 Iurchenko, *Ialtinskaia konferentsiia*, 164–65; Boettiger, Yalta Diary, 13.

4 Lord Moran, *Churchill at War*, 267; Yalta Conference: Notes, 13, Anna Roosevelt Halsted Papers; Arkadii N. Shevchenko, *Breaking with Moscow* (New York, 1985), 58–59.

5 Iurchenko, *Ialtinskaia konferentsiia*, 169–71; Bohlen, *Witness to History*, 173; Boettiger, Yalta Diary, 15; Reilly, *Reilly of the White House*, 212.

6 Reilly, *Reilly of the White House*, 212; *FRUS: Yalta*, 571; Boettiger, Yalta Diary, 14; Kathleen Harriman to Miss Marshall, Yalta, February 1, 1945, special files, World War II, February 1–5, 1945, Averell Harriman Papers.

7 Sarah Churchill, *Keep on Dancing*, 74; Boettiger, Yalta Diary, 16; Moran, *Churchill at War*, 267.

8 Sarah Churchill, *Keep on Dancing*, 74; Churchill, *Triumph and Tragedy*, 345; Bohlen, *Witness to History*, 173; Moran, *Churchill at War*, 268.

9 The President's Trip to Crimea Conference, Travel Log; Boettiger, Yalta Diary, 16; Reilly, *Reilly of the White House*, 212.

10 Trevor Royle, *Crimea: The Great Crimean War, 1854–1856* (New York, 2000).

11 N. Kalinin and M. Zemlianichenko, *Romanovy i Krym* (Simferopol, 2002), 39–63; Mark Twain, *The Innocents Abroad* (Hartford, 1869), 390–95.

12 "Notes on the Crimea," Secret Service Records, box 21, 6.I. Trips of the President, Yalta 1945, Franklin D. Roosevelt Library; N. Nikolaev, A. Kadievich, and M. Zemlianichenko, *Arkhitektor vysochaishego dvora* (Simferopol, 2003), 107–39.

13 Joseph E. Davies, *Mission to Moscow* (New York, 1943), 288–90.

14 "The Crimean Campaign," Memoirs of Jaroslaw Balan Sr., 56, private archive of Jars Balan, Edmonton, Canada; Charles Messenger, *The Last Prussian: A Biography of Field Marshal Gerd von Rundstedt, 1875–1953* (London, 1991).

15 A. H. Birse, *Memoirs of an Interpreter* (London, 1967), 179.

16 A. I. Kokurin, comp., "O spetsial'nykh meropriiatiiakh po Krymu. Priem, razmeshchenie i okhrana uchastnikov Krymskoi konferentsii 1945 goda," *Istoricheskii arkhiv* 1993, no. 5: 116–31.

17 Boettiger, Yalta Diary, 17; Iurchenko, *Ialtinskaia konferentsiia*, 46–52.

18 W. Averell Harriman and Elie Abel, *Special Envoy to Churchill and Stalin, 1941–1946* (New York, 1975), 393; Kathleen Harriman to Miss Marshall, Yalta, February 1, 1945, Averell Harriman Papers; Iurchenko, *Ialtinskaia konferentsiia*, 51.

19 Army cable for Deane from Harriman, January 25, 1945, special files, World War II, no. 176/7, February 21–27, 1945, Averell Harriman Papers; Harriman and Abel, *Special Envoy*, 393.

20 "On the completion of preparatory measures for the reception, accommodation, and security of the participants in the Crimean Conference," Gosudarstvennyi arkhiv Rossiiskoi Federatsii (hereafter cited as GARF), r-9401, op. 2, d. 94, fols. 15–27.

21 General Information Bulletin, Map Room, box 21 (Argonaut), sec. 2: Yalta (background), Franklin D. Roosevelt Library.

22 Boettiger, Yalta Diary, 17–18; Reilly, *Reilly of the White House*, 210–11.

23 "General Information Bulletin," no. 176/8, January 28–31, 1945, Averell Harriman Papers.

24 Churchill, *Triumph and Tragedy*, 347; David Reynolds, *In Command of History: Churchill Fighting and Writing the Second World War* (London, 2004), 466–86; Sarah Churchill, *Keep on Dancing*, 74–75; Cadogan, *Diaries*, 703.

25 Anthony Rhinelander, *Prince Michael Vorontsov: Viceroy to the Tsar* (Montreal, 1990); O. Iu. Zakharova, *Svetleishii kniaz' M. S. Vorontsov* (Simferopol, 2004).

26 Birse, *Memoirs of an Interpreter*, 180; "On the completion of preparatory measures," GARF, r-9401, op. 2, d. 94, fols. 1–18.

27 From Argonaut to Governor [of] Malta, January 31, 1945: Please pass to General Ismay from Miss Bright, box 337, book 10: Yalta Conference, group 24, folder 2, Harry Lloyd Hopkins Papers, Franklin D. Roosevelt Library; Birse, *Memoirs of an Interpreter*, 182; Sarah Churchill, *Keep on Dancing*, 74–75.

28 Boettiger, Yalta Diary, 19.

29 Kruglov's memorandum to Beria, January 27, 1945, GARF, r-9401, op. 2, d. 92, fols. 238–40; Eberhardt, "My Most Secret Mission," 4.

30 Kathleen Harriman to Miss Marshall, Yalta, February 1, 1945, Averell Harriman Papers.

31 "On the completion of preparatory measures," GARF, r-9401, op. 2, d. 94, fols. 25–27; Iurchenko, *Ialtinskaia konferentsiia*, 168–71; Felix Chuev and Albert Resis, *Molotov Remembers. Inside Kremlin Politics:* (Chicago, 1993), 19.

Chapter 4. The Red Host

1 N. G. Kuznetsov, *Kursom k pobede* (Moscow, 1975), 443; Iurchenko, *Ialtinskaia konferentsiia*, 163–64.

2 "On the completion of the preparatory measures," GARF, r-9401, op. 2, d. 94, fol. 27; Birse, *Memoirs of an Interpreter*, 178; *FRUS: Yalta*, 571; Kathleen Harriman to her sister Mary Harriman, Yalta, February 4–10, 1945, no. 176/9, February 1–5, 1945, Averell Harriman Papers.

3 Birse, *Memoirs of an Interpreter*, 178–79; "From I. M. Maisky's Diary," in O. A. Rzheshevskii, *Stalin i Cherchill'. Vstrechi. Besedy. Diskussii. Dokumenty i kommentarii, 1941–1945* (Moscow, 2004), 494; Kathleen Harriman to Mary, Yalta, February 4–10, 1945, Averell Harriman Papers.

4 "On the completion of preparatory measures," GARF, r-9401, op. 2, d. 94, fols. 16–25.

5 Felix Youssoupoff, *Lost Splendor: The Amazing Memoirs of the Man Who Killed Rasputin* (New York, 1954; repr. New York, 2007), chap. 26.

6 Ibid.; Francis Pridham, *Close of a Dynasty* (London, 1956).

7 Hiroaki Kuromiya, *Stalin* (New York, 2005); Simon Sebag Montefiore, *Young Stalin* (New York, 2007); Simon Sebag Montefiore, *Stalin: The Court of the Red Tsar* (New York, 2003); Anne Applebaum, *GULAG: A History* (New York, 2003).

8 "On the completion of preparatory measures," GARF, r-9401, op. 2, d. 94, fols. 16–25.

9 J. Otto Pohl, *The Stalinist Penal System: A Statistical History of Soviet Repression and Terror, 1930–1953* (Jefferson, NC, 1997), 112–18.

10 "Delo Evreiskogo antifashistskogo komiteta," *Al'manakh: Rossiia XX vek*, Mezhdunarodnyi Fond "Demokratiia," http://www.idf.ru/9/doc.shtml (visited January 10, 2008); Shimon Redlich, *War, Holocaust and Stalinism: A Documented History of the Jewish Anti-Fascist Committee in the USSR* (Luxembourg, 1995), 45–49; Yuri Slezkine, *The Jewish Century* (Princeton, 2004), 286–97.

11 Alexander Chubariyan and Vladimir Pechatnov, "Molotov 'the Liberal': Stalin's 1945 Criticism of His Deputy," *Cold War History* 1, no. 1 (August 2000): 135–36.

12 Terry Martin, *The Affirmative Action Empire: Nations and Nationalism in the Soviet Union, 1923–1939* (Ithaca, NY, 2001); Jan Gross, *Revolution from Abroad: The Soviet Conquest of Poland's Western Ukraine and Western Belorussia* (Princeton, 1987); Timothy Snyder, *The Reconstruction of Nations: Poland, Ukraine, Lithuania, Belarus, 1569–1999* (New Haven, CT, 2003).

13 Martin H. Folly, *Churchill, Whitehall and the Soviet Union, 1940–45* (New York, 2000), 44–45; Cadogan, *Diaries*, 597; Harriman and Abel, *Special Envoy*, 385; Frank Costigliola, "'I Had Come as a Friend': Emotion, Culture, and Ambiguity in the Formation of the Cold War, 1943–45," *Cold War History* 1, no. 1 (August 2000): 105.

14 Anatolii Gromyko, *Andrei Gromyko. V labirintakh Kremlia (vospominaniia i razmyshleniia syna)* (Moscow, 1997), 176; *Molotov Remembers*, 20, 45, 54; Milovan Djilas, *Conversations with Stalin* (New York, 1962), 73.

Chapter 5. Reunion of the Big Three

1 *Krymskaia konferentsiia rukovoditelei trekh soiuznykh derzhav—SSSR, SShA i Velikobritanii, 4–11 fevralia 1945 g. Sbornik dokumentov* (Moscow, 1979), 45–46; Charles Bohlen to John Martin, February 3, 1945, Livadia Palace, no. 176/9, February 1–5, 1945, Averell Harriman Papers; "Memorandum of Conversation. Present: Molotov, Pavlov, Harriman, Page," Moscow, January 18, 1945, no. 176/6, January 17–20,

1945, Averell Harriman Papers; "Memorandum of Conversation. Present: Harriman, Bohlen, Molotov, Pavlov," February 4, 1945, no. 176/9, February 1–5, 1945, Averell Harriman Papers.

2 *Krymskaia konferentsiia*, 46–48; The National Archives, Kew, UK (hereafter cited as TNA), Cabinet Papers, CAB 66/63, Record of the Political Proceedings of the "Argonaut" Conference held at Malta and in the Crimea from 1st February to 11th February 1945, Office of the War Cabinet, S.W. 1, 12th March 1945, copy no. 21, 9 (hereafter cited as Record of the Political Proceedings of the "Argonaut" Conference).

3 *Krymskaia konferentsiia*, 48–49; Churchill, *Triumph and Tragedy*, 347–49; Birse, *Memoirs of an Interpreter*, 182–83; Gilbert, *Winston S. Churchill*, 7:1173; British embassy memo on Map Room requirements, no. 176/5, January 11–16, 1945, Averell Harriman Papers; Freidel, *Franklin D. Roosevelt*, 507–8; Meacham, *Franklin and Winston*, 141–42.

4 Greg King, *The Court of the Last Tsar: Pomp, Power and Pageantry in the Court of Nicholas II* (Hoboken, NJ, 2006), 451–52.

5 *FRUS: Yalta*, 574; *Krymskaia konferentsiia*, 53; Kathleen Harriman to her sister Mary Harriman, Yalta, February 4–10, 1945, no. 176/9, February 1–5, 1945, Averell Harriman Papers.

6 Bohlen, *Witness to History*, 180; Boettiger, Yalta Diary, 21, box 84, folder 11, Anna Roosevelt Halsted Papers.

7 *Krymskaia konferentsiia*, 49–53; *FRUS: Yalta*, 570–73.

8 "Love of England," *Time*, February 5, 1945.

9 Yalta Conference: Notes, 18–19, 22, Anna Roosevelt Halsted Papers.

10 *FRUS: Yalta*, 570–73; Stettinius, *Roosevelt and the Russians*, 100; *Krymskaia konferentsiia*, 49–53.

11 Lord Hastings Ismay, *The Memoirs of General Lord Ismay* (New York, 1960), 387.

12 Laurence S. Kuter, *Airman at Yalta* (New York, 1955), 131.

13 Moran, *Churchill at War*, 272–77; Cadogan, *Diaries*, 704.

14 Andrew Cunningham, *A Sailor's Odyssey. The Autobiography of Admiral of the Fleet Viscount Cunningham of Hyndhope* (New York, 1951), 573; Kathleen Harriman to Mary, Yalta, February 4–10, 1945, Averell Harriman Papers; Bohlen, *Witness to History*, 178; Moran, *Churchill at War*, 273; Eden, *The Reckoning*, 514.

15 Cadogan, *Diaries*, 704; Kuter, *Airman at Yalta*, 135–36; Eden, *The Reckoning*, 514–15.

16 V. I. Trubnikov et al., eds., *Ocherki istorii Rossiiskoi vneshnei razvedki*, vol. 4 (1941–45) (Moscow, 1999), 163, 286, 618–62; Christopher Andrew and Vasilii Mitrokhin, *The Sword and the Shield: The Mitrokhin Archive and the Secret History of the KGB* (New York, 1999), 126.

17 John Earl Haynes and Harvey Klehr, *Venona: Decoding Soviet Espionage in America* (New Haven, CT, 1999), 8–56; Christopher Andrew and Oleg Gordievsky, *KGB: The Inside Story of Its Foreign Operations from Lenin to Gorbachev* (New York, 1992), 135–85; Andrew and Mitrokhin, *The Sword and the Shield*, 56–67.

18 Pavel Sudoplatov and Anatoli Sudoplatov, with Jerrold L. Schecter and Leona P. Schecter, *Special Tasks: The Memoirs of an Unwanted Witness—A Soviet Spymaster* (Boston, 1994), 222–23, 226.

Chapter 6. The Winter Offensive

1 *FRUS: Yalta*, 574; *Krymskaia konferentsiia*, 53; Gilbert, *Winston S. Churchill*, 7:1173–74.

2 Kathleen Harriman to her sister Mary Harriman, Yalta, February 4–10, 1945, no. 176/9, February 1–5, 1945, Averell Harriman Papers.

3 Kuznetsov, *Kursom k pobede*, 446; *FRUS: Yalta*, 573.

4 "Conversation between Mr. Page and General Ismay," Livadia, February 4, 1945, no. 176/9, February 1–5, 1945, Averell Harriman Papers; Boettiger, Yalta Diary, 21–22, Harriman and Abel, *Special Envoy*, 395.

5 *FRUS: Yalta*, 574–75; *Krymskaia konferentsiia*, 53–56; Kuznetsov, *Kursom k pobede*, 446.

6 *FRUS: Yalta*, 579; *Krymskaia konferentsiia*, 61–62.

7 Ivan Konev, "From the Vistula to the Oder," in Seweryn Bialer, ed., *Stalin and His Generals* (New York, 1969), 480–83; Konstantin Rokossovskii, *Soldatskii dolg* (Moscow, 1988), 295–96; Vasilii Chuikov, *Konets Tret'ego reikha* (Moscow, 1973), 102.

8 Andrei Gromyko et al., eds., *Correspondence between the Chairman of the Council of Ministers of the USSR and the Presidents of the USA and the Prime Ministers of Great Britain during the Great Patriotic War of 1941–1945*, vol. 1, *Correspondence with Winston S. Churchill and Clement R. Attlee (July 1941–November 1945)* (Moscow, 1957), 296–97.

9 "Memorandum of Conference with Marshal Stalin, January 15, 1945," no. 176/5, January 11–16, 1945, Averell Harriman Papers; *Molotov Remembers*, 45.

10 "Memorandum of Conference with Marshal Stalin, January 15, 1945," Averell Harriman Papers; *FRUS: Yalta*, 575, 579–80; *Krymskaia konferentsiia*, 57, 62–64; Cunningham, *A Sailor's Odyssey*, 627–28.

11 Lord Alanbrooke, *War Diaries, 1939–1945*, ed. Alex Danchev and Daniel Todman (London, 2001), 655; Cadogan, *Diaries*, 704; Kuznetsov, *Kursom k pobede*, 451–52.

12 Georgii Zhukov, *Vospominaniia i razmyshleniia*, vol. 2 (Moscow, 2002), 268–69; Antony Beevor, *The Fall of Berlin, 1945* (New York, 2002), 63–76; Otto Preston Chaney, *Zhukov* (Norman, OK, 1996), 106–326.

13 Beevor, *The Fall of Berlin*, 39–56; "Red Army book" of Vasyl Burlay (1907–64), in the author's possession; "Vospominaniia vypusknits Podol'skoi snaiperskoi shkoly," http://podol.ru/sharpshooter/memory.php#zhukova.

14 *FRUS: Yalta*, 578–79, 584–85; *Krymskaia konferentsiia*, 57–58, 61; Cray, *General of the Army*, 143–372; Kuznetsov, *Kursom k pobede*, 446; "Interpretative Report on Developments in Soviet Policy Based on the Soviet Press for the Period January 1945," February 15, 1945, 1–2, no. 176/8, January 28–31, 1945, Averell Harriman Papers.

15 Zhukov, *Vospominaniia i razmyshleniia*, 2:276–80; Chuikov, *Konets Tret'ego reikha*, 99–100.

16 *FRUS: Yalta*, 570, 581–82; Churchill, *Triumph and Tragedy*, 348; Robert Hopkins, "How Would You Like to Be Attached to the Red Army?" *American Heritage* 56, no. 3 (June–July 2005): 30–37; Beevor, *The Fall of Berlin*, 136–47.

17 Moran, *Churchill at War*, 273; Stettinius, *Roosevelt and the Russians*, 107; "Pendulum Swings," *Time*, February 5, 1945.

Chapter 7. The German Question

1 *SSSR i germanskii vopros, 1941–1949. Dokumenty iz arkhiva vneshnei politiki Rossiiskoi Federatsii* (Moscow, 1996), 597–600; *FRUS: Yalta*, 609–12; *Krymskaia konferentsiia*, 64–65.

2 "The Ghosts on the Roof," *Time*, March 5, 1945.

3 Maurice Paléologue, *An Ambassador's Memoirs*, vol. 1 (London, 1923), 91–95; Gifford D. Malone, "War Aims toward Germany," in Alexander Dallin et al., eds., *Russian Diplomacy and Eastern Europe, 1914–1917* (New York, 1963), 131–32.

4 *SSSR i germanskii vopros*, 118–19, 121–23.

5 Ibid., 126–31, 138; Eden, *The Reckoning*, 279–83.

6 *SSSR i germanskii vopros*, 236–44, 252–65, 296–301, 320–22; *Foreign Relations of the United States. Diplomatic Papers, 1943*, vol. 1 (Washington, DC, 1963), 545, 629–32, 723 [hereafter cited as *FRUS*].

7 "Stalin's Germans," *Time*, February 12, 1945; Bodo Scheuring, *Verräter oder Patrioten. Das Nationalkomitee "Freies Deutschland" und der Bund deutscher Offiziere in der Sowjetunion 1943–1945* (Berlin, 1993).

8 *Foreign Relations of the United States. Diplomatic Papers. The Conferences at Cairo and Teheran, 1943* (Washington, DC, 1943), 600–602 (hereafter cited as *FRUS: The Conferences at Cairo and Teheran*).

9 *SSSR i germanskii vopros*, 441–49.

10 Rzheshevskii, *Stalin i Cherchill'*, 476–81.

11 Churchill, *Triumph and Tragedy*, 350–51; Frank King, "Allied Negotiations and the Dismemberment of Germany," *Journal of Contemporary History* 16 (1981): 587–88.

12 *FRUS: Yalta*, 187; Diane Shaver Clemens, *Yalta* (London, 1970), 29–30; Russell D. Buhite, *Decisions at Yalta: An Appraisal of Summit Diplomacy* (Wilmington, DE, 1986), 21–28.

13 Record of the Political Proceedings of the "Argonaut" Conference, 12; *FRUS: Yalta*, 613; "Notes for the Conference with the President," box 337, book 10: Yalta Conference, no. 4, Hopkins Papers, Franklin D. Roosevelt Library.

14 *FRUS: Yalta*, 612–14; *Krymskaia konferentsiia*, 65–68; Record of the Political Proceedings of the "Argonaut" Conference, 11–14.

15 Memo for Stettinius, Livadia Palace, Yalta, February 5, 1945, NND 812006, record group 43: World War II Conferences, box 4: Big Three Meeting, National Archives and Records Administration (hereafter cited as NARA); Stettinius, *Roosevelt and the Russians*, 136–37.

16 Eden, *The Reckoning*, 515–16; *FRUS: Yalta*, 656–57, 660; *Krymskaia konferentsiia*, 87.

17 Bohlen, *Witness to History*, 182–83; *Krymskaia konferentsiia*, 68.

Chapter 8. Spoils of War

1 "From I. M. Maisky's Diary," in Rzheshevskii, *Stalin i Cherchill'*, 497.

2 "Communications Section News Bulletin, Argonaut Edition," Afternoon Press, February 6, 1945, box

337, book 10: Yalta Conference, group 24, folder 2, Hopkins Papers; *FRUS: Yalta*, 616–17; *Krymskaia konferentsiia*, 70–72; Record of the Political Proceedings of the "Argonaut" Conference, 14–16.

3 Clemens, *Yalta*, 42–44; *FRUS: Yalta*, 572; Reynolds, *In Command of History*, 454, 465; Jean Lacouture and Patrick O'Brian, *De Gaulle: The Rebel, 1890–1944* (New York, 1993).

4 Ambassador Caffery to the Secretary of State, January 28, 1945, box 337, book 10: Yalta Conference, group 24, folder 1, Hopkins Papers; Robert Gildea, *The Past in French History* (New Haven, CT, 1996), 130.

5 Clemens, *Yalta*, 43; Charles de Gaulle, *Complete War Memoirs* (New York, 1984), 754–55; Montefiore, *Stalin*, 477–78.

6 *FRUS: Yalta*, 617–18; Record of the Political Proceedings of the "Argonaut" Conference, 15.

7 *SSSR i germanskii vopros*, 396–97, 414–17.

8 Clemens, *Yalta*, 34–46; George F. Kennan, *Memoirs, 1925–1950* (Boston, 1967), 164, 168–71; *FRUS: Yalta*, 198–201.

9 *FRUS: Yalta*, 616–19, 634; *Krymskaia konferentsiia*, 70–75; Eden, *The Reckoning*, 516; Stettinius, *Roosevelt and the Russians*, 128.

10 "From I. M. Maisky's Diary," in Rzheshevskii, *Stalin i Cherchill'*, 497; Ivan Mikhailovich Maiskii, *Izbrannaia perepiska s rossiiskimi korrespondentami* (Moscow, 2005), 2:529.

11 Ivan Maiskii, *Memoirs of a Soviet Ambassador: The War, 1939–43* (London, 1967); Pavel Sudoplatov and Anatoli Sudoplatov, *Special Tasks*, 344–46; K. A. Zalesskii, *Imperiia Stalina. Biograficheskii entsiklopedicheskii slovar'* (Moscow, 2000).

12 "Memorandum of Conversation between Harriman and Maisky," January 20, 1945, no. 176/6, January 17–20, 1945, Averell Harriman Papers; Maisky to Harriman, January 21, 1945, no. 176/7, January 21–27, 1945, Averell Harriman Papers.

13 *Sovetsko-Amerikanskie otnosheniia, 1939–1945. Dokumenty*, comp. B. I. Zhiliaev and V. I. Savchenko, ed. G. N. Sevostianov, vol. 1 (Moscow, 2004), 615–18; "From I. M. Maisky's Diary," in Rzheshevskii, *Stalin i Cherchill'*, 493.

14 *SSSR i germanskii vopros*, 601–5; "From I. M. Maisky's Diary," in Rzheshevskii, *Stalin i Cherchill'*, 493–95.

15 "From I. M. Maisky's Diary," in Rzheshevskii, *Stalin i Cherchill'*, 497–98; "Notes for the Conference with the President," box 337, book 10: Yalta Conference, no. 4, Hopkins Papers; *FRUS: Yalta*, 620–21; *Krymskaia konferentsiia*, 76–78; Stettinius, *Roosevelt and the Russians*, 130.

16 *FRUS: Yalta*, 621; *Krymskaia konferentsiia*, 78–79; Record of the Political Proceedings of the "Argonaut" Conference, 16–17; "From I. M. Maisky's Diary," in Rzheshevskii, *Stalin i Cherchill'*, 498.

17 Margaret MacMillan, *Paris, 1919: Six Months That Changed the World* (New York, 2003), 180–93.

18 *FRUS: Yalta*, 622; "Notes for the Conference with the President," box 337, book 10: Yalta Conference, no. 4, Hopkins Papers; Harriman and Abel, *Special Envoy*, 403; Beevor, *The Fall of Berlin*, 24–39.

19 *FRUS: Yalta*, 621–23; *Krymskaia konferentsiia*, 79–82; Rzheshevskii, *Stalin i Cherchill'*, 499.

20 David Reynolds, *Summits: Six Meetings That Shaped the Twentieth Century* (New York, 2007), 129–33.

21 Geoffrey Roberts, "Stalin at the Teheran, Yalta and Potsdam Conferences," *Journal of Cold War Studies* 9, no. 4 (Fall 2007): 6–40.

Chapter 9. The Security Council

1 Sarah Churchill, *Keep on Dancing*, 75; Moran, *Churchill at War*, 275.

2 Stettinius, *Roosevelt and the Russians*, 137–38.

3 MacMillan, *Paris 1919*, 83–97; George G. Gill, *League of Nations, 1929–1946: International Cooperation towards Peace in the 20th Century* (Darby, PA, 1994).

4 Schlesinger, *Act of Creation*, 33–52; "Leo Pasvolsky," http://en.wikipedia.org/wiki/User:John_Z/drafts/Leo_Pasvolsky.

5 *FRUS: Yalta*, 60–61; Clemens, *Yalta*, 56; Rzheshevskii, *Stalin i Cherchill'*, 421–22.

6 Memorandum of Conversation, Harriman and Dekanozov, December 25, 1944, no. 175, Averell Harriman Papers; Paraphrase of embassy's telegram, December 28, 1944, no. 176, December 28–31, 1944, Averell Harriman Papers; cf. *FRUS: Yalta*, 63–66.

7 *FRUS: Yalta*, 66–68, 77.

8 Ibid., 589–90; Bohlen, *Witness to History*, 181.

9 Moran, *Churchill at War*, 276.

10 Stettinius, *Roosevelt and the Russians*, 138.

11 *FRUS: Yalta*, 660–61, 671–72; *Krymskaia konferentsiia*, 87–88; Record of the Political Proceedings of the "Argonaut" Conference, 23–24; *SSSR i germanskii vopros*, 334–35.

12 *FRUS: Yalta*, 661–63, 672–73, 682–83; cf. *Krymskaia konferentsiia*, 88–91, 104–5; Record of the Political Proceedings of the "Argonaut" Conference, 24–25; Stettinius, *Roosevelt and the Russians*, 139–45; Bohlen, *Witness to History*, 193; Clemens, *Yalta*, 218–20.

13 *FRUS: Yalta*, 554; Record of the Political Proceedings of the "Argonaut" Conference, 25; Cadogan, *Diaries*, 705.

14 Rzheshevskii, *Stalin i Cherchill'*, 421–22; *FRUS: Yalta*, 663–65; *Krymskaia konferentsiia*, 91–93; Record of the Political Proceedings of the "Argonaut" Conference, 26–27.

15 *FRUS: Yalta*, 665–67, 676–77; *Krymskaia konferentsiia*, 94–97; Record of the Political Proceedings of the "Argonaut" Conference, 27–28; Byrnes, *Speaking Frankly*, 36; George Scott, *The Rise and Fall of the League of Nations* (London, 1973), 310–12.

16 Byrnes, *Speaking Frankly*, 37; Moran, *Churchill at War*, 275–76.

Chapter 10. In the Führer's Shadow

1 *FRUS: Yalta*, 658–59.

2 Ibid., 666–67, 676, 925; *Krymskaia konferentsiia*, 96; Roberts, *Stalin's Wars*, 50–51.

3 Beevor, *The Fall of Berlin*, 74–75, 87–88.

4 Hugh Trevor-Roper, ed., *Final Entries 1945: The Diaries of Joseph Goebbels* (Barnsley, UK, 2007), 39, 102, 183; Ian Kershaw, *Hitler 1936–1945: Nemesis* (New York, 2000), 775–78.

5 *FRUS: Cairo and Teheran*, 599–600; *Molotov Remembers*, 53.

6 Hugh D. Phillips, *Between the Revolution and the West: A Political Biography of Maxim M. Litvinov* (Boulder, CO, 1992); Albert Resis, "The Fall of Litvinov: Harbinger of the German-Soviet Non-Aggression Pact," *Europe-Asia Studies* 52, no. 1 (2000): 33–56.

7 "The Molotov-Ribbentrop Pact and the Baltic States: An Introduction and Interpretation," *Lituanus: Lithuanian Quarterly Journal of Arts and Sciences* 35, no. 1 (Spring 1989): 8–46.

8 Djilas, *Conversations with Stalin*, 69–70; Valentin Berezhkov, *Kak ia stal perevodchikom Stalina* (Moscow, 1993), 221–26.

9 "Hitler and Molotov Meetings. Berlin, November 12 and 13, 1940. Official Transcripts," http://www.worldfuturefund.org/wffmaster/Reading/Germany/Hitler-Molotov%20Meetings.htm; G. L. Rozanov, *Stalin i Gitler* (Moscow, 1991), 167–79.

10 Rozanov, *Stalin i Gitler*, 180–81.

11 Paléologue, *An Ambassador's Memoirs*, 1: 91–95.

12 Berezhkov, *Kak ia stal perevodchikom Stalina*, 52, 56–57.

13 "Comrade Molotov's Visit," *Time*, November 25, 1940; Lloyd C. Gardner, *Spheres of Influence: The Great Powers Partition Europe from Munich to Yalta* (Chicago, 1993), 75–85.

14 *Molotov Remembers*, 14–20.

15 Ibid., 16; Winston S. Churchill, *The Second World War*, vol. 3: *The Grand Alliance* (Boston, 1950), 370; Ivan Maiskii, *Vospominaniia Sovetskogo posla: voina, 1939–1943* (Moscow, 1965), 139–74; Davies, *No Simple Victory*, 94–98, 160–65; Glantz, *FDR and the Soviet Union*, 59–87; Jonathan Fenby, *Alliance: The Inside Story of How Roosevelt, Stalin and Churchill Won One War and Began Another* (San Francisco, 2006), 64–76.

16 *SSSR i germanskii vopros*, 322–23; *Molotov Remembers*, 14–20.

Chapter 11. Dividing the Balkans

1 *FRUS: Yalta*, 103–6; Henry Kissinger, *Diplomacy* (New York, 1994), 17–55, 369–93.

2 Kathleen Harriman to her sister Mary Harriman, Moscow, January 13, 1945, no. 176/5, January 11–16, 1945, Averell Harriman Papers.

3 "Cordon Insanitaire?" *Time*, December 27, 1943.

4 Kennan, *Memoirs*, 519–21.

5 *SSSR i germanskii vopros*, 333–60.

6 Rzheshevskii, *Stalin i Cherchill'*, 418–26; Churchill, *Triumph and Tragedy*, 227; Gilbert, *Winston S. Churchill*, 7:992.

7 Churchill, *Triumph and Tragedy*, 73–79; Gardner, *Spheres of Influence*, 184–92; Reynolds, *In Command of History*, 458–60.

8 Churchill, *Triumph and Tragedy*, 208.

9 Hanson W. Baldwin, "British Move in Greece," *New York Times*, October 6, 1944; "Area of Decision," *Time*, October 9, 1944.

10 Churchill, *Triumph and Tragedy*, 227; Rzheshevskii, *Stalin i Cherchill'*, 418–26; Gilbert, *Winston S. Churchill*, 7:991–95; Reynolds, *In Command of History*, 458–60; Gardner, *Spheres of Influence*, 199.

11 Rzheshevskii, *Stalin i Cherchill'*, 429–35; Gilbert, *Winston S. Churchill*, 7:1001; Eden, *The Reckoning*, 483.

12 "Area of Decision," *Time*, October 9, 1944; cf. Whittaker Chambers, *Ghosts on the Roof: Selected Essays* (New Brunswick, NJ, 1996), 102.

13 "Translation of Article by G. Malinin," December 21, 1944, no. 176/2, Averell Harriman Papers; "Interpretative Report on Developments in Soviet Policy Based on the Soviet Press for the Period October 13–December 31, 1944," no. 9, 2, no. 176/4, January 6–10, 1945, Averell Harriman Papers; "Extract from Cable February 6, 1945, from the Acting Secretary to the Secretary of State," no. 176/10, February 6–9, 1945, Averell Harriman Papers.

14 Geoffrey Roberts, "Litvinov's Lost Peace, 1941–1946," *Journal of Cold War Studies* 4, no. 2 (Spring 2002): 23–54.

15 *SSSR i germanskii vopros*, 595–97; Alexei M. Filitov, "Problems of Post-War Construction in Soviet Foreign Policy Conceptions during World War II," in Francesca Gori and Silvio Pons, eds., *The Soviet Union and Europe in the Cold War, 1945–53* (Houndmills, UK, 1996), 3–22.

16 Bohlen, *Witness to History*, 174–76.

Chapter 12. *The Battle for Poland*

1 Arciszewski to Roosevelt, February 3, 1945, Map Room, box 21, Argonaut (2), Franklin D. Roosevelt Library; Arciszewski to Churchill, February 3, 1945, FO371/47577/2896, TNA.

2 Moran, *Churchill at War*, 268; *FRUS: Yalta*, 509; Eden, *The Reckoning*, 516.

3 *Krymskaia konferentsiia*, 47; *SSSR i germanskii vopros*, 595–97.

4 *FRUS: Yalta*, 667, 677; *Krymskaia konferentsiia*, 97.

5 Ivan Kozlovs'kyi, *Vstanovlennia ukraïns'ko-pol's'koho kordonu, 1941–1951 rr.* (Lviv, 1998), 50–56; Norman Davies, *White Eagle, Red Star: The Polish-Soviet War, 1919–20, and "The Miracle on the Vistula"* (London, 2003).

6 Harriman and Abel, *Special Envoy*, 369.

7 *FRUS: Yalta*, 509–10; 667–68.

8 "A general discussion on the Polish situation," CAB 65, WM (45) 74, C 1, January 22, 1945, TNA.

9 *FRUS: Yalta*, 508–9, 668.

10 *FRUS: Yalta*, 67–78, 667–70; *Krymskaia konferentsiia*, 47, 97–99; Record of the Political Proceedings of the "Argonaut" Conference, 9, 28–30; Stettinius, *Roosevelt and the Russians*, 88.

11 War Cabinet, WM (45) 10th Conclusions, Minute 1, Confidential Annex, January 26, 1945—12.30 p.m., FO371/47577/2896, 41, TNA; *FRUS: Yalta*, 508–11.

12 Frank Roberts's report on his conversation with O'Malley, March 2, 1943, FO371/34564/C2281, TNA; Kozlovs'kyi, *Vstanovlennia ukraïns'ko-pol's'koho kordonu*, 69.

13 Wojciech Materski, Anna M. Cienciala, and Natalia S. Lebedeva, eds., *Katyn: A Crime without Punishment* (New Haven, CT, 2008), 208–22; Krystyna Kersten, *The Establishment of Communist Rule in Poland, 1943–48* (Berkeley, 1992), 39–76.

14 Roman Buczek, *Stanisław Mikołajczyk*, 2 vols. (Toronto, 1996).

15 Norman Davies, *Rising '44: The Battle for Warsaw* (London, 2004), 243–432.

16 Rzheshevskii, *Stalin i Cherchill'*, 418–19, 439–58; Antony Polonsky and Bolesław Drukier, eds., *The Beginnings of Communist Rule in Poland* (London, 1980), 43–49, 261–401; Kersten, *The Establishment of Communist Rule in Poland*, 77–117.

17 WM (45) 12th Conclusions, Minute 3, Confidential Annex, January 29, 1945—5.30 p.m., FO371/47578/2896, TNA; report on conversation with Maurice Dejean, January 3, 1945, FO371/47575/2896, TNA.

18 Earl of Halifax, from Washington to Foreign Office, January 6, 1945, FO371/47575/2896, TNA; Polish-Russian Settlement, January 5, 1945, 1, FO371/47575/2896, TNA.

19 Note by Orme Sargent, January 8, 1945, FO371/47575/2896, 74, TNA.

20 Memo on conversation with Mikołajczyk, 24 January 1945, TNA, FO371/47576/2896, p. 206; "Memorandum," January 26, 1945, 1–11, FO371/47576/2896, TNA.

21 Record of conversation between Sir A. Cadogan and the Polish Minister of Foreign Affairs, January 26, 1945, 1–2, FO371/47577/2896, TNA; memo by C. F. A. Warner on his conversations with the Polish ambassador to the British government Count Edward Raczynski, January 30, 1945, 237–39, FO371/47576/2896, TNA.

22 Eden to Churchill, January 28, 1945, 97, FO371/47577/2896, TNA; "Memorandum on the Polish Situation" (note in pencil: "copy to prime minister"), no. 176/7, January 27, 1945, Averell Harriman Papers.

Chapter 13. "What Would the Ukrainians Say?"

1 "From I. M. Maisky's Diary," in Rzheshevskii, *Stalin i Cherchill'*, 506.

2 *FRUS: Yalta*, 679–80; *Krymskaia konferentsiia*, 100–101; cf. Robert Beitzell, ed., *Tehran, Yalta, Potsdam: The Soviet Protocols* (Hattiesburg, MS, 1970), 94.

3 *FRUS: Yalta*, 667–70.

4 Philipp Ther, "War versus Peace: Interethnic Relations in Lviv during the First Half of the Twentieth Century," in John Czaplicka, ed., *Lviv: A City in the Crosscurrents of Culture* (Cambridge, MA, 2004), 264–71; Serhy Yekelchyk, *Stalin's Empire of Memory: Russian-Ukrainian Relations in the Soviet Historical Imagination* (Toronto, 2004), 42–52; N. M. Pashaeva, *Ocherki istorii russkogo dvizheniia v Galichine XIX–XX vv.* (Moscow, 2001), 149–54.

5 Kathleen Harriman to her sister Mary Harriman, Moscow, January 19, 1945, and March 8, 1945, no. 176/5, January 11–16, 1945, and no. 177/9, March 7–10, 1945, Averell Harriman Papers; "Satire," *Time*, December 25, 1944.

6 Kozlovs'kyi, *Vstanovlennia ukraïns'ko-pol's'koho kordonu*, 56–62; Yekelchyk, *Stalin's Empire of Memory*, 47, 173; Dmytro Tabachnyk, *Istoriia ukraïns'koï dyplomatiï v osobakh* (Kyiv, 2004), 474–87.

7 British Ambassador to the Polish government Sir Owen St. Clair O'Malley to Anthony Eden, February 27, 1943, FO371/34564/C2281, TNA; I. A. Khrenov et al., eds., *Dokumenty i materialy po istorii sovetsko-pol'skikh otnoshenii* (Moscow, 1973), 7:351.

8 "Poland's Ukrainian Minority," February 23, 1945, 1–2, FO371/47788/N8723, TNA; Serhii Plokhy, *Unmaking Imperial Russia: Mykhailo Hrushevsky and the Writing of Ukrainian History* (Toronto, 2005).

9 William Taubman, *Khrushchev: The Man and His Era* (New York, 2003), 18–207.

10 G. A. Kumanev, *Riadom so Stalinym: otkrovennye svidetel'stva* (Moscow, 1999), 111–13; Yekelchyk, *Stalin's Empire of Memory*, 48–49; Nikita Khrushchev, *Vremia. Liudi. Vlast' (Vospominaniia)*, 4 vols. (Moscow, 1999), 1:568–69.

11 Reports on conversations with the Lviv professors Francis Groër and Jakub Parnas, a cousin of the historian Lewis Namier, and Sir Frank Roberts's comments on December 15, 1944, FO371/39501/C17269, TNA; V. Iu Vasil'ev et al., comps., *Politicheskoe rukovodstvo Ukrainy, 1938–1989* (Moscow, 2006), 98–99; Snyder, *The Reconstruction of Nations*, 154–201.

12 Report on conditions in Lviv based on an interview with Lieutenant Colonel Gibson, the head of the British prisoner-of-war mission, May 29, 1945, FO371/44649/N8568, TNA; "Dovidka pro pam'iatnyky mista L'vova," September 21, 1945, Tsentral'nyi derzhavnyi arkhiv vyshchykh orhaniv vlady Ukraïny (Kyiv) (hereafter cited as TsDAVOVU), fond 2, op. 7, no. 1929, fols. 44–46; lists of artifacts from Lviv and Kyiv collections preselected for transfer to Poland, June 18–December 12, 1945, TsDAVOVU, R-2, op. 7, vol. 3, 16–606.

13 Mr. Balfour, from Moscow to Foreign Office, no. 199, January 20, 1945, 113, FO371/47576/2896, TNA; Phillip Knightley, *The First Casualty: The War Correspondent as Hero and Myth-maker from the Crimea to Iraq* (Baltimore, 2004), 274–75.

14 Gross, *Revolution from Abroad*, 187–224; Jerzy Kochanowski, "Gathering Poles into Poland: Forced Migration from Poland's Former Eastern Territories," in Philipp Ther and Anna Siljak, eds., *Redrawing Nations: Ethnic Cleansing in East-Central Europe, 1944–48* (Lanham, MD, 2001), 135–54; Orest Subtelny, "Expulsion, Resettlement, Civil Strife: The Fate of Poland's Ukrainians, 1944–47," ibid., 155–72.

15 "Digest of Messages Received between July 19 and September 26, 1944, in London from Poland on the Soviet Authorities' Repressive Measures," Poland Ambasada (U.S.) records, box 107, folder 1, Hoover Institution Archives, Stanford University.

16 "Messages Received by Polish Government from Their Military Authorities in Poland," no. 177/8, March 3–6, 1945, Averell Harriman Papers; "Dear Brothers," a letter from Przemyśl, February 10, 1945, no. 177/1, February 10–12, 1945, Averell Harriman Papers.

17 Eden, *The Reckoning*, 516; Rzheshevskii, *Stalin i Cherchill'*, 507.

18 Andrei Gromyko, *Memoirs* (London, 1989), 118; Byrnes, *Speaking Frankly*, 29–30; Bohlen, *Witness to History*, 187.

19 Drew Pearson, "Merry Go-round," *Washington Post*, February 23, 1945.

20 *FRUS: Yalta*, 669–71, 686.

21 Ibid., 669, 671; *Krymskaia konferentsiia*, 103; Rzheshevskii, *Stalin i Cherchill'*, 507.

22 Bohlen, *Witness to History*, 188; Eden, *The Reckoning*, 517.

23 Bohlen, *Witness to History*, 188–90; *FRUS: Yalta*, 727–28; Draft of Roosevelt's letter to Stalin, February 7, 1945, 208–12, FO371/47577/2896, TNA.

24 *FRUS: Yalta*, 508.

Chapter 14. Counting Votes in the United Nations

1 *FRUS: Yalta*, 699; Stettinius, *Roosevelt and the Russians*, 161–62, 172.
2 *FRUS: Yalta*, 709; *Krymskaia konferentsiia*, 120.
3 *FRUS: Yalta*, 711–12; "From I. M. Maisky's Diary," in Rzheshevskii, *Stalin i Cherchill'*, 507.
4 Bohlen, *Witness to History*, 194; Byrnes, *Speaking Frankly*, 40; *FRUS: Yalta*, 48–49, 52, 75; Clemens, *Yalta*, 52–54.
5 *FRUS: Yalta*, 712; Stettinius, *Roosevelt and the Russians*, 187.
6 Vladyslav Hrynevych, "Iak Ukraïnu do vstupu v OON hotuvala stalins'ka 'konstytutsiina reforma' voiennoï doby," *Dzerkalo tyzhnia*, no. 41, October 22–28, 2005; "Puta na chornykh koniakh mystetstva. Pid sofitamy sekretnykh sluzhb (dokumenty z papky-formuliaru na O. P. Dovzhenka)," *Z arkhiviv VUChK-GPU-NKVD-KGB*, no. 1–2 (2/3), 1995.
7 Ivan Serov to Lavrentii Beria, "Report on the Reaction of Western Reporters to the Formation of the Provisional Government of the Polish Republic," GARF, r-9401, op. 2, d. 92, fols. 93–98.
8 "Puta na chornykh koniakh mystetstva."
9 *FRUS: Yalta*, 711–12; Byrnes, *Speaking Frankly*, 40.
10 Record of the Political Proceedings of the "Argonaut" Conference, 43.
11 *FRUS: Yalta*, 712–15, 729; Stettinius, *Roosevelt and the Russians*, 173–78.
12 Bohlen, *Witness to History*, 194; Cadogan, *Diaries*, 706; Leahy, *I Was There*, 306; Eden, *The Reckoning*, 517.
13 *FRUS: Yalta*, 729; *Krymskaia konferentsiia*, 124; Churchill, *Triumph and Tragedy*, 359.
14 Churchill, *Triumph and Tragedy*, 359–60.
15 Moran, *Churchill at War*, 276–77.
16 Eden, *The Reckoning*, 517; Churchill, *Triumph and Tragedy*, 359; *FRUS: Yalta*, 711.
17 "From I. M. Maisky's Diary," in Rzheshevskii, *Stalin i Cherchill'*, 508; Stettinius, *Roosevelt and the Russians*, 178–81; Moran, *Churchill at War*, 276–77.
18 Harriman and Abel, *Special Envoy*, 409; Stettinius, *Roosevelt and the Russians*, 186–88.
19 Stettinius, *Roosevelt and the Russians*, 196.
20 *FRUS: Yalta*, 35–37; *Krymskaia konferentsiia*, 131–34.
21 *FRUS: Yalta*, 746–47, 992.
22 Stettinius, *Roosevelt and the Russians*, 193–96; *Truman in the White House: The Diary of Eben A. Ayres*, edited with commentary by Robert H. Ferrel (Columbia, MO, 1991), 38.
23 Byrnes, *Speaking Frankly*, 40; Stettinius, *Roosevelt and the Russians*, 196–97; Allen Weinstein, *Perjury: The Hiss-Chambers Case* (New York, 1978), 359.
24 Byrnes, *Speaking Frankly*, 40; *FRUS: Yalta*, 773–76.
25 Leahy, *I Was There*, 310; Byrnes, *Speaking Frankly*, 40–41; Moran, *Churchill at War*, 277; Stettinius, *Roosevelt and the Russians*, 203.

Chapter 15. Stalemate on Poland

1 *FRUS: Yalta*, 718–19; *Krymskaia konferentsiia*, 116, 119–20.
2 *Krymskaia konferentsiia*, 120.
3 *FRUS: Yalta*, 716–19; Record of the Political Proceedings of the "Argonaut" Conference, 44–45; Stettinius, *Roosevelt and the Russians*, 181–84.
4 Gilbert, *Winston S. Churchill*, 7:1190; Churchill, *Triumph and Tragedy*, 375; Minutes of the War Cabinet meeting, WM (45) 16 C. A., TNA.
5 Cadogan, *Diaries*, 706; Eden, *The Reckoning*, 517.
6 Stettinius, *Roosevelt and the Russians*, 209–12; Eden, *The Reckoning*, 517–18.
7 *FRUS: Yalta*, 776–82; Record of the Political Proceedings of the "Argonaut" Conference, 55–60; G. P. Murashko et al., eds., *Vostochnaia Evropa v dokumentakh rossiiskikh arkhivov, 1944–1953*, vol. 1: *1944–1948* (Moscow and Novosibirsk, 1997), 117.
8 *FRUS: Yalta*, 716.
9 Malone, "War Aims toward Germany," 130–31; *Vostochnaia Evropa v dokumentakh rossiiskikh arkhivov*, 39–40; *FRUS: Cairo and Teheran*, 510–12, 594, 600–603; *FRUS: Yalta*, 669.
10 "Poland's western frontier," War Cabinet, W. P. (45) 48, January 23, 1945, CAB 66/61, TNA; WM (45) 10th Conclusions, Minute 1, Confidential Annex, January 26, 1945—12.30 p.m., FO371/47577/2896, 40, TNA; War Cabinet, W. M. (45) 1st Conclusions, Minute 6, Confidential Annex, January 2, 1945—5:30 p.m., Foreign Affairs, FO371/47575/2896, TNA; "General discussion on the Polish situation," Offices of the War Cabinet, W. 1, CAB 65, WM (45) 74. C 1, January 22, 1945, 33, TNA.
11 *FRUS: Yalta*, 510; Gilbert, *Winston S. Churchill*, 7:1167.

12 *FRUS: Yalta*, 717, 720; Record of the Political Proceedings of the "Argonaut" Conference, 45; Minutes of War Cabinet Meeting, W. M. (45) 16 C. A., TNA; "Excerpt from Churchill's Speech to the House of Commons, December 15, 1945," Poland Ambasada (U.S.) Records, box 7, folder 2: Transfer of population (Western border), Hoover Institution Archives.

13 Djilas, *Conversations with Stalin*, 87–97.

14 Memo by Francis B. Stevens, "Gleanings from Ehrenburg," January 13, 1945, no. 176/5, January 11–16, 1945, Averell Harriman Papers; "Press. Secretary of State, Washington," February 13, 1945, no. 177/2, February 13–17, 1945, Averell Harriman Papers; "Interpretative Report on Developments in Soviet Policy," February 15, 1945, 4, no. 176/8, January 28–31, 1945, Averell Harriman Papers; Andrew Nagorski, *The Greatest Battle: Stalin, Hitler, and the Desperate Struggle for Moscow That Changed the Course of World War II* (New York, 2008), 247.

15 Beevor, *The Fall of Berlin*, 106–10, 194–97.

16 *FRUS: Yalta*, 717, 720, 777, 787, 792–93, 869–70, 973–74; *Krymskaia konferentsiia*, 126–27, 152, 158–60, 250–51.

17 Eden, *The Reckoning*, 517.

Chapter 16. The Bombline

1 Churchill, *Triumph and Tragedy*, 360; Gilbert, *Winston S. Churchill*, 7:1186–87.

2 Alanbrooke, *War Diaries*, xi–xxx, 658; Lord Moran, *Churchill at War*, 276.

3 *FRUS: Yalta*, 562–67; Mark Stoler, *Allies and Adversaries: The Joint Chiefs of Staff, the Grand Alliance, and U.S. Strategy in World War II* (Chapel Hill, NC, 2000), 219–30.

4 *FRUS: Yalta*, 562–65; "Present Relations between the United States Military Mission, Moscow and the Soviet Military Authorities," January 22, 1945, no. 176/7, January 21–27, 1945, Averell Harriman Papers.

5 *FRUS: Yalta*, 571; *Krymskaia konferentsiia*, 51; John R. Deane, "Negotiating on Military Assistance, 1943–1945," in Raymond Dennett and Joseph E. Johnson, eds., *Negotiating with the Russians* (Boston, 1951), 4–8.

6 Alanbrooke, *War Diaries*, 656; *FRUS: Yalta*, 603; Kuter, *Airman at Yalta*, 151; To Deane from the Joint Chiefs of Staff, January 18, 1945, no. 176/6, January 17–20, 1945, Averell Harriman Papers.

7 *FRUS: Yalta*, 603–5.

8 Kuter, *Airman at Yalta*, 145; *FRUS: Yalta*, 645.

9 Kuter, *Airman at Yalta*, 150–51, 153, 169.

10 Michael Parrish, *The Lesser Terror: Soviet State Security, 1939–53* (Westport, CT, 1996), 178–80; Nikolai Vlasik, "On vnikal bukval'no vo vse (Iz dnevnikov nachal'nika lichnoi okhrany Stalina)," *Nash sovremennik*, no. 10 (October 2005).

11 Kuter, *Airman at Yalta*, 148; Leahy, *I Was There*, 301; Alanbrooke, *War Diaries*, 660; Vladimir Bulatov, *Admiral Kuznetsov* (Moscow, 2006).

12 John R. Deane, *The Strange Alliance: The Story of Our Efforts at Wartime Co-operation with Russia* (New York, 1947), 255.

13 Alanbrooke, *War Diaries*, 656; *FRUS: Yalta*, 643–45, 689–90; To Deane from the Joint Chiefs of Staff, January 18, 1945, Averell Harriman Papers.

14 Stewart Halsey Ross, *Strategic Bombing by the United States in World War II: The Myths and the Facts* (Jefferson, NC, 2003), 180; Frederick Taylor, *Dresden: Tuesday, February 13, 1945* (New York, 2005), 383–84; Air Force Historical Studies Office, Historical Analysis of the February 14–15, 1945, Bombings of Dresden, http://www.airforcehistory.hq.af.mil/PopTopics/dresden.htm.

Chapter 17. The Far Eastern Blitz

1 Gromyko, *Memoirs*, 114–16.

2 Geoffrey Jukes, *The Russo-Japanese War 1904–1905* (Oxford, 2002).

3 *SSSR i germanskii vopros*, 142–43.

4 *FRUS: Cairo and Teheran*, 554, 617–19; "Interpretative Report on Developments in Soviet Policy Based on the Soviet Press for the Period October 13–December 31, 1944," January 10, 1945, 7, no. 176/4, January 6–10, 1945, Averell Harriman Papers; *SSSR i germanskii vopros*, 347–48; Tsuyoshi Hasegawa, *Racing the Enemy: Stalin, Truman, and the Surrender of Japan* (Cambridge, MA, 2005), 14–33.

5 *FRUS: Yalta*, 378–79.

6 Ibid., 379–83, 385–88; Stettinius, *Roosevelt and the Russians*, 92; Hasegawa, *Racing the Enemy*, 34, 313.

7 Stettinius, *Roosevelt and the Russians*, 90; *FRUS: Yalta*, 396.
8 *FRUS: Yalta*, 396–400; Hasegawa, *Racing the Enemy*, 27–33; Cray, *General of the Army*, 497–98.
9 *FRUS: Yalta*, 379–83, 385–88, 564, 567, 593–94, 607–8, 651–55; Stettinius, *Roosevelt and the Russians*, 92; Kathleen Harriman to her sister Mary Harriman, Yalta, February 4–10, 1945, no. 176/9, February 1–5, 1945, Averell Harriman Papers; To Deane from the Joint Chiefs of Staff, January 18, 1945, no. 176/6, January 17–20, 1945, Averell Harriman Papers; Kuter, *Airman at Yalta*, 156–58.
10 *FRUS: Yalta*, 698–99; Kuznetsov, *Kursom k pobede*, 450–52.
11 *FRUS: Yalta*, 766–71; *Krymskaia konferentsiia*, 139–43; Bohlen, *Witness to History*, 196–97; Stettinius, *Roosevelt and the Russians*, 238.
12 *FRUS: Yalta*, 733–34, 898.
13 *FRUS: Yalta*, 757–60; Deane, *The Strange Alliance*, 255.
14 Leahy, *I Was There*, 307.

Chapter 18. "Allies Should Not Deceive"

1 Sarah Churchill, *Keep on Dancing*, 76; Cadogan, *Diaries*, 705–6.
2 Kuter, *Airman at Yalta*, 122–23; Cadogan, *Diaries*, 706.
3 Boettiger, Yalta Diary, 22.
4 Sarah Churchill, *Keep on Dancing*, 76; Cadogan, *Diaries*, 706–7.
5 Dinner menu, Yalta Conference, Miscellaneous, box 84, folder 8, Anna Roosevelt Halsted Papers; Stettinius, *Roosevelt and the Russians*, 219; Alger Hiss, *Recollections of a Life* (New York, 1988), 121; Sarah Churchill, *Keep on Dancing*, 76.
6 Sarah Churchill, *Keep on Dancing*, 76; Kathleen Harriman to her sister Mary Harriman, Yalta, February 9, 1945, no. 176/10, February 6–9, 1945, Averell Harriman Papers; Stettinius, *Roosevelt and the Russians*, 219; Alanbrooke, *War Diaries*, 660.
7 Gilbert, *Winston S. Churchill*, 7:1186, 1196; Reynolds, *Summits*, 146; Stettinius, *Roosevelt and the Russians*, 104–5.
8 Churchill, *Triumph and Tragedy*, 362–63.
9 Sarah Churchill, *Keep on Dancing*, 76–77; Stettinius, *Roosevelt and the Russians*, 221; Harriman and Abel, *Special Envoy*, 415–16; Kathleen Harriman to Mary, Yalta, February 9, 1945, Averell Harriman Papers; Montefiore, *Stalin*, 483.
10 Amy Knight, *Beria: Stalin's First Lieutenant* (Princeton, 1995).
11 Kathleen Harriman to Mary, Yalta, February 9, 1945, Averell Harriman Papers; cf. Harriman and Abel, *Special Envoy*, 416, and Montefiore, *Stalin*, 483.
12 Pavel Sudoplatov and Anatoli Sudoplatov, *Special Tasks*, 225–26; Sergo Beriia, *Moi otets–Lavrentii Beriia* (Moscow, 1994); cf. Sergo Beria, *Beria, My Father: Inside Stalin's Kremlin* (London, 2001), 104; cf. Reilly, *Reilly of the White House*, 205–6.
13 Reilly, *Reilly of the White House*, 210; Sergo Beria, *Beria, My Father*, 104.
14 Sergo Beria, *Beria, My Father*, 93.
15 Ibid.
16 Ibid., 69–132; Pavel Sudoplatov and Anatoli Sudoplatov, *Special Tasks*, 226; Andrew and Mitrokhin, *The Sword and the Shield*, 337–39; Gary Kern, "How 'Uncle Joe' Bugged FDR," *Studies in Intelligence* (unclassified edition) 47, no. 1 (2003): 19–31.
17 Cadogan, *The Diaries*, 707; Leahy, *I Was There*, 311; Alanbrooke, *War Diaries*, 660.
18 Stettinius, *Roosevelt and the Russians*, 221; Kathleen Harriman to Mary, Yalta, February 9, 1945, Averell Harriman Papers.
19 Churchill, *Triumph and Tragedy*, 361.
20 Moran, *Churchill at War*, 277; Gilbert, *Winston S. Churchill*, 7:1195.
21 Churchill, *Triumph and Tragedy*, 361.
22 Ibid., 364; Moran, *Churchill at War*, 278.
23 Churchill, *Triumph and Tragedy*, 362; *FRUS: Yalta*, 798–99.
24 Churchill, *Triumph and Tragedy*, 363.
25 *FRUS: Yalta*, 798; Hiss, *Recollections of a Life*, 120.
26 Stettinius, *Roosevelt and the Russians*, 219.

Chapter 19. A Polish Surrender

1 Hopkins, "How Would You Like to Be Attached to the Red Army?" 30–37; Alanbrooke, *War Diaries*, 660.
2 Iurchenko, *Ialtinskaia konferentsiia*, 267–68.

3 *FRUS: Yalta*, 803–4, 842; *Krymskaia konferentsiia*, 161, 173.

4 Stettinius, *Roosevelt and the Russians*, 223–24.

5 Ibid., 224–25; *FRUS: Yalta*, 803–7; Sergo Beria, *Beria, My Father*, 106; *Molotov Remembers*, 53.

6 *FRUS: Yalta*, 842–43, 846–48, 850–55; *Krymskaia konferentsiia*, 173–74, 177–81; Record of the Political Proceedings of the "Argonaut" Conference, 74–76; "Interpretative Report on Developments in Soviet Policy," February 15, 1945, 4, no. 176/8, January 28–31, 1945, Averell Harriman Papers.

7 Record of the Political Proceedings of the "Argonaut" Conference, 80–82; Eden, *The Reckoning*, 518; Cadogan, *Diaries*, 707–8.

8 Gilbert, *Winston S. Churchill*, 7:1198.

9 Stettinius, *Roosevelt and the Russians*, 251–52; *FRUS: Yalta*, 872–73; *Krymskaia konferentsiia*, 194–95; Record of the Political Proceedings of the "Argonaut" Conference, 84.

10 Gilbert, *Winston S. Churchill*, 7:1203.

11 *Krymskaia konferentsiia*, 207–10; Record of the Political Proceedings of the "Argonaut" Conference, 93.

12 Stettinius, *Roosevelt and the Russians*, 258; *FRUS: Yalta*, 973–74.

13 *FRUS: Yalta*, 898–99; *Krymskaia konferentsiia*, 213; Record of the Political Proceedings of the "Argonaut" Conference, 97; Stettinius, *Roosevelt and the Russians*, 270–71; "Observations concerning the Crimean Declaration," February 16, 1945, Poland, Ministerstwo spraw zagranicznych, box 98, folder 44, Hoover Institution Archives.

14 Bohlen, *Witness to History*, 192; Harriman and Abel, *Special Envoy*, 412–13; Stettinius, *Roosevelt and the Russians*, 215; Moran, *Churchill at War*, 283; Leahy, *I Was There*, 315–16.

Chapter 20. The Fate of Germany

1 *FRUS: Yalta*, 849–50, 854; *Krymskaia konferentsiia*, 182–83; Record of the Political Proceedings of the "Argonaut" Conference, 77–78.

2 Briefing papers for Stettinius from the War Department, no. 15, NND 812006, record group 43: World War II Conferences, box 3: The Big Three Meeting, NARA.

3 RU/US 2415 (OS) Okno TASS no. 1198, Hoover Institution Poster Collection.

4 Kuter, *Airman at Yalta*, 175.

5 *FRUS: Yalta*, 849, 856–57; *Krymskaia konferentsiia*, 181–82.

6 Moran, *Churchill at War*, 274–75; *FRUS: Yalta*, 555; Bohlen, *Witness to History*, 184–85; Byrnes, *Speaking Frankly*, 25.

7 Harriman and Abel, *Special Envoy*, 402.

8 *FRUS: Yalta*, 899–900, 908; *Krymskaia konferentsiia*, 214; Bohlen, *Witness to History*, 185; Moran, *Churchill at War*, 279–80.

9 Record of the Political Proceedings of the "Argonaut" Conference, 100; Ambassador Caffery to Harry Hopkins, February 15, 1945, box 337, book 10: Yalta Conference, no. 15, Hopkins Papers; Acting Secretary of State Grew to the President, February 3, 1945, Map Room, Presidential Trips, Crimea Conference, box 21, Argonaut 2, section 1A, Franklin D. Roosevelt Library; Bohlen, *Witness to History*, 184–85.

10 Rzheshevskii, *Stalin i Cherchill'*, 499; *FRUS: Yalta*, 702–4, 707, 807–9; *Krymskaia konferentsiia*, 163–64; Record of the Political Proceedings of the "Argonaut" Conference, 64–65; Stettinius, *Roosevelt and the Russians*, 229–32; Clemens, *Yalta*, 165–66.

11 *FRUS: Yalta*, 874–75, 885; *Krymskaia konferentsiia*, 195–96, 198–99; Gilbert, *Winston S. Churchill*, 7:1207; Record of the Political Proceedings of the "Argonaut" Conference, 85–86.

12 *Krymskaia konferentsiia*, 211; Record of the Political Proceedings of the "Argonaut" Conference, 94; Gilbert, *Winston S. Churchill*, 7:1205.

13 *FRUS: Yalta*, 901–3; Gromyko, *Memoirs*, 112–13; Stettinius, *Roosevelt and the Russians*, 265; Moran, *Churchill at War*, 280.

14 *FRUS: Yalta*, 901–3, 909, 915–16; *Krymskaia konferentsiia*, 215–16; Record of the Political Proceedings of the "Argonaut" Conference, 98–99; Stettinius, *Roosevelt and the Russians*, 264, 265.

15 Box 337, book 10: Yalta Conference, group 24, folder 1, 1–4, Hopkins Papers, Franklin D. Roosevelt Library; Moran, *Churchill at War*, 280–81.

16 *Krymskaia konferentsiia*, 216; Gromyko, *Memoirs*, 113.

17 "Interpretative Report on Developments in Soviet Policy Based on the Soviet Press for the Period February 1945," 7, March 15, 1945, no. 177, March 16–19, 1945, Averell Harriman Papers; "Krivenko and Kobulov to Beria," GARF, r-9401, op. 2, d. 9, fols. 227–29; Radio Bulletin no. 38, February 13, 1945, series 8, clippings, MS Am 1687.7, Joseph Clark Grew Papers.

18 Record of the Political Proceedings of the "Argonaut" Conference, 94; *Molotov Remembers*, 60; John Gimbel, *Science, Technology, and Reparations: Exploitation and Plunder in Postwar Germany* (Stanford, CA, 1990).

Chapter 21. Liberated Europe and the Balkan Deal

1 Kissinger, *Diplomacy*, 415.
2 *FRUS: Yalta*, 93–100; Stettinius, *Roosevelt and the Russians*, 88–89.
3 *FRUS: Yalta*, 860–62.
4 Ibid., 848–49, 853–57; *Krymskaia konferentsiia*, 156–57, 181–82, 186–89; Record of the Political Proceedings of the "Argonaut" Conference, 76–77; Bohlen, *Witness to History*, 191.
5 P. J. Stavrakis, *Moscow and Greek Communism, 1944–1949* (New York, 1989); David H. Close, ed., *The Greek Civil War, 1943–50: Studies of Polarization* (London, 1993).
6 "Mission to Athens," *Time*, January 8, 1945; Churchill, *Triumph and Tragedy*, 286–89; Moran, *Churchill at War*, 253.
7 "The Speech," *Time*, January 29, 1945; "Prime Minister Churchill's Address in Commons on Relations among Britain, the US and the USSR," *New York Times*, January 18, 1945.
8 Churchill, *Triumph and Tragedy*, 293; Earl of Halifax, from Washington to Foreign Office, January 6, 1945, FO371/47575/2896, TNA; "Press. Secretary of State, Washington," February 13, 1945, no. 177/2, February 13–17, 1945, Averell Harriman Papers.
9 "Memo by Francis B. Stevens: Gleanings from Ehrenburg," January 13, 1945, no. 176/5, January 11–16, 1945, Averell Harriman Papers.
10 *FRUS: Yalta*, 820–21, 845–46; *Krymskaia konferentsiia*, 157, 197, 205–7; Record of the Political Proceedings of the "Argonaut" Conference, 66, 73–74; Walter E. Roberts, *Tito, Mihailović, and the Allies, 1941–45* (Durham, NC, 1987), 297–320; Clemens, *Yalta*, 260–62.
11 *Molotov Remembers*, 51; *FRUS: Yalta*, 848–49, 854, 868, 873, 884, 899–900.

Chapter 22. Iran, Turkey, and the Empire

1 Byrnes, *Speaking Frankly*, x; *FRUS: Yalta*, 844; Record of the Political Proceedings of the "Argonaut" Conference, 73.
2 Gilbert, *Winston S. Churchill*, 7:1166.
3 Leahy, *I Was There*, 313; *FRUS: Yalta*, 844–45; Moran, *Churchill at War*, 278–79; Eden, *The Reckoning*, 514.
4 Stettinius, *Roosevelt and the Russians*, 236–38; Kuter, *Airman at Yalta*, 172.
5 Eden, *The Reckoning*, 514; *FRUS: Yalta*, 845.
6 *FRUS: Yalta*, 345; Yonah Alexander and Allan Nanes, eds., *The United States & Iran: A Documentary History* (Frederick, MD, 1980), 77–80; Richard A. Stewart, *Sunrise at Abadan: The British and Soviet Invasion of Iran, 1941* (New York, 1988).
7 *FRUS: Cairo and Teheran*, 749.
8 Stettinius, *Roosevelt and the Russians*, 180–81; Abbas Milani, "Hurley's Dream: How FDR Almost Brought Democracy to Iran," *Hoover Digest*, no. 3 (Summer 2003): 144–52.
9 Ronald W. Ferrier, *The History of the British Petroleum Company* (Cambridge, 1982), 252–53; Martin Sicker, *The Middle East in the Twentieth Century* (Westport, CT, 2001), 156–58; "Interpretative Report on Developments in Soviet Policy Based on the Soviet Press for the Period October 13–December 31, 1944," 7, January 10, 1945, no. 176/4, January 6–10, 1945, Averell Harriman Papers.
10 *FRUS: Yalta*, 339.
11 Ibid., 715.
12 "From I. M. Maisky's Diary," in Rzheshevskii, *Stalin i Cherchill'*, 508; *SSSR i germanskii vopros*, 608; Stettinius, *Roosevelt and the Russians*, 180.
13 *FRUS: Yalta*, 333, 345, 500–501; Stettinius, *Roosevelt and the Russians*, 65–66, 180–81; Eden, *The Reckoning*, 511.
14 *FRUS: Yalta*, 738–40; Rzheshevskii, *Stalin i Cherchill'*, 494–95.
15 *FRUS: Yalta*, 810, 819–20.
16 Ibid., 877.
17 Eden, *The Reckoning*, 515.
18 *FRUS: Yalta*, 982; Eden, *The Reckoning*, 515.
19 *Krymskaia konferentsiia*, 211–12; Gilbert, *Winston S. Churchill*, 7:1205.
20 Eden, *The Reckoning*, 507–9.
21 *FRUS: Yalta*, 910–11.

22 Clemens, *Yalta*, 258–60; *FRUS: Yalta*, 903–4, 909–10, 916–17; Record of the Political Proceedings of the "Argonaut" Conference, 101–2.
23 Michał Sokolnicki to London, January 16, 1945, Michał Sokolnicki Papers, box 3, File: Diplomatic Correspondence and Reports, January–August 1945, Hoover Institution Archives.
24 Trevor-Roper, *Final Entries 1945*, 191.
25 *Molotov Remembers*, 72–73.
26 Louise F. Estrange Fawcett, *Iran and the Cold War: The Azerbaijan Crisis of 1946* (Cambridge, 1992); Jamil Hasanli, *At the Dawn of the Cold War: The Soviet-American Crisis over Iranian Azerbaijan, 1941–46* (Lanham, MD, 2006).
27 "People," *Time*, July 16, 1945.

Chapter 23. Secret Agreements

1 *FRUS: Yalta*, 557; Iurchenko, *Ialtinskaia konferentsiia*, 277–78.
2 Richard Connaughton, *Rising Sun and Tumbling Bear: Russia's War with Japan* (London, 2007).
3 Averell Harriman, "Statement Regarding Our Wartime Relations with the USSR, Particularly Concerning the Yalta Agreement," in Richard F. Fenno, ed., *The Yalta Conference* (Boston, 1955), 60–71; Harriman and Abel, *Special Envoy*, 398–99; *FRUS: Yalta*, 894–97; Bohlen, *Witness to History*, 197–98.
4 *FRUS: Yalta*, 984; Harriman and Abel, *Special Envoy*, 399; Meacham, *Franklin and Winston*, 317.
5 Memorandum of conversation, June 11, 1945, Points in Yalta Agreements Affecting Far East, Conversations, MS Am 1687.3, vol. 7 (28), Joseph Clark Grew Papers.
6 *FRUS: Yalta*, 826; Churchill, *Triumph and Tragedy*, 390.
7 Churchill, *Triumph and Tragedy*, 388–90; Gilbert, *Winston S. Churchill*, 7:1205.
8 Eden, *The Reckoning*, 513–14.
9 Leahy, *I Was There*, 318; "President Roosevelt's Report to the Congress on the Crimea Conference," *New York Times*, March 1, 1945.
10 *FRUS: Yalta*, 966; Gilbert, *Winston S. Churchill*, 7:1208.
11 *FRUS: Yalta*, 557, 834, 857; Byrnes, *Speaking Frankly*, 40–41; Stettinius, *Roosevelt and the Russians*, 282; Moran, *Churchill at War*, 277.
12 *FRUS: Yalta*, 927; *Krymskaia konferentsiia*, 221.
13 *FRUS: Yalta*, 967–68; *Krymskaia konferentsiia*, 260.

Chapter 24. Prisoners of War

1 *Krymskaia konferentsiia*, 210–11; Record of the Political Proceedings of the "Argonaut" Conference, 93–94.
2 Montefiore, *Stalin*, 379, 445–46, 452–53.
3 Beria and Merkulov to Stalin and Molotov, January 1, 1945, GARF, r-9401, op. 2, d. 92, fols. 1–2; Berezhkov, *Kak ia stal perevodchikom Stalina*, 340–48, 355–56.
4 Berezhkov, *Kak ia stal perevodchikom Stalina*, 374; Gorbatiuk to Beria, March 5, 1945, GARF, r-9401, op. 2, d. 93, fol. 253.
5 Beevor, *The Fall of Berlin*, 73–74; Nikolai Tolstoy, *Victims of Yalta* (London, 1977), 25–41, 278–303; Marta Dyczok, *The Grand Alliance and Ukrainian Refugees* (Houndmills, UK, 2000), 17–22.
6 Deane, *The Strange Alliance*, 182–85.
7 Tolstoy, *Victims of Yalta*, 49–55, 62–63; Dyczok, *The Grand Alliance*, 23–25; Arieh J. Kochavi, "From Cautiousness to Decisiveness: Changes in Soviet Negotiation Tactics toward the British during World War II," *East European Quarterly* 26, no. 4 (January 2003): 488–90.
8 Eden, *The Reckoning*, 484–85; Kochavi, "From Cautiousness to Decisiveness," 490; Rzheshevskii, *Stalin i Cherchill'*, 476–77; Dyczok, *The Grand Alliance*, 39–40.
9 Deane, *The Strange Alliance*, 187–88; Tolstoy, *Victims of Yalta*, 80–82.
10 Deane, *The Strange Alliance*, 187–88.
11 "Interpretative Report on Developments in Soviet Policy Based on the Soviet Press for the Period October 13–December 31, 1944," 8, no. 9, January 10, 1945, no. 176/4, January 6–10, 1945, Averell Harriman Papers; Deane, *The Strange Alliance*, 187–88.
12 Memorandum of Conversation, January 11, 1945, Subject: Mistreatment of Soviet Citizens, Conversations, MS Am 1687.3, vol. 6 (12), Joseph Clark Grew Papers.
13 *FRUS: Yalta*, 413–16; Secstate to Amembassy, Circular, January 22, 1945, no. 176/7, January 21–27, 1945, Averell Harriman Papers; Memorandum of Conversation, January 5, 1945, Subject: Kravchenko

Case, Conversations, MS Am 1687.3, vol. 6 (12), Joseph Clark Grew Papers; Briefing papers for Stettinius from the War Department, 41 items, no. 1, Kravchenko case, NND 812006, record group 43: World War II Conferences, box 3, NARA; Kochavi, "From Cautiousness to Decisiveness," 492–94.

14 Deane, *The Strange Alliance*, 188–89.
15 *FRUS: Yalta*, 863–66; *Krymskaia konferentsiia*, 210–11; Record of the Political Proceedings of the "Argonaut" Conference, 93–94.
16 Cadogan, *Diaries*, 709; Tolstoy, *Victims of Yalta*, 93–97.
17 *FRUS: Yalta*, 863–65, 985–87; *Krymskaia konferentsiia*, 282–300.
18 Soviet note of March 23, 1945, MS Am 1687.3, vol. 6 (44), Joseph Clark Grew Papers; Tolstoy, *Victims of Yalta*, 97–99, 139–40, 176–98, 322–28.
19 Bohlen, *Witness to History*, 199; Deane, *The Strange Alliance*, 182–201.

Chapter 25. The Last Supper

1 Stettinius, *Roosevelt and the Russians*, 272; Cadogan, *Diaries*, 708; *FRUS: Yalta*, 855; Moran, *Churchill at War*, 280–82; Churchill, *Triumph and Tragedy*, 390–91; Gilbert, *Winston S. Churchill*, 7:1208.
2 Yalta Conference: Miscellaneous, box 84, folder 8, Anna Roosevelt Halsted Papers; Bohlen, *Witness to History*, illustrations between 178 and 179; Iurchenko, *Ialtinskaia konferentsiia*, 288; Gilbert, *Winston S. Churchill*, 7:1208.
3 *FRUS: Yalta*, 921; Churchill, *Triumph and Tragedy*, 391.
4 *FRUS: Yalta*, 921–22; Stettinius, *Roosevelt and the Russians*, 272–74.
5 Churchill, *Triumph and Tragedy*, 392.
6 Stettinius, *Roosevelt and the Russians*, 272–74.
7 *FRUS: Yalta*, 922–23.
8 Ibid., 922–25; Churchill, *Triumph and Tragedy*, 392–93; Gilbert, *Winston S. Churchill*, 7:1208–9.
9 Stettinius, *Roosevelt and the Russians*, 275–76.
10 Churchill, *Triumph and Tragedy*, 392–93; Moran, *Churchill at War*, 285.
11 Gilbert, *Winston S. Churchill*, 7:1208–9.
12 Churchill, *Triumph and Tragedy*, 393; Moran, *Churchill at War*, 285.

Chapter 26. Crossing the Finish Line

1 Moran, *Churchill at War*, 281.
2 *FRUS: Yalta*, 557–58, 925–33; *Krymskaia konferentsiia*, 220–23; Record of the Political Proceedings of the "Argonaut" Conference, 103–5; Moran, *Churchill at War*, 283; Leahy, *I Was There*, 319; Stettinius, *Roosevelt and the Russians*, 279; Gilbert, *Winston S. Churchill*, 7:1210; Iurchenko, *Ialtinskaia konferentsiia*, 292–96.
3 *FRUS: Yalta*, 926–29; *Krymskaia konferentsiia*, 220–23, 263–74.
4 *FRUS: Yalta*, plate 8, 929, 930; Cadogan, *Diaries*, 709–10.
5 Sarah Churchill, *Keep on Dancing*, 77–78.
6 *FRUS: Yalta*, 931–33; *Krymskaia konferentsiia*, 238–41; Stettinius, *Roosevelt and the Russians*, 284; Iurchenko, *Ialtinskaia konferentsiia*, 299.
7 Elliott Roosevelt, ed., *FDR: His Personal Letters* (New York, 1947), 4:1570; Boettiger, Yalta Diaries, 16; Harriman and Abel, *Special Envoy*, 417; *FRUS: Yalta*, 560; Moran, *Churchill at War*, 281; Reilly, *Reilly of the White House*, 215; "President Roosevelt's Report to Congress on the Crimea Conference," *New York Times*, March 2, 1945; Trevor-Roper, *Final Entries 1945*, 22.
8 Sarah Churchill, *Keep on Dancing*, 77–78; Moran, *Churchill at War*, 282–83; Mary Soames, ed., *Winston and Clementine: The Personal Letters of the Churchills* (Boston, 1999), 515; Gilbert, *Winston S. Churchill*, 7:1213–14.
9 Churchill, *Triumph and Tragedy*, 394; Moran, *Churchill at War*, 286; Gilbert, *Winston S. Churchill*, 7:1219; General Information Bulletin, no. 176/8, January 28–31, 1945, Averell Harriman Papers.
10 Kennan, *Memoirs*, 195–96.
11 Kathleen Harriman to Miss Marshall, Yalta, February 1, 1945, no. 176/9, February 1–5, 1945, Averell Harriman Papers; Maiskii, *Izbrannaia perepiska*, 2:156–57; A. V. Khanilo, "Uchastniki Krymskoi konferentsii v Chekhovskom dome," in S. V. Iurchenko et al., eds., *Ialta 1945–2005: Ot bipoliarnogo mira k geopolitike budushchego. Materialy mezhdunarodnogo nauchnogo simpoziuma* (Simferopol, 2005), 82–83.
12 Churchill, *Triumph and Tragedy*, 394–95; Moran, *Churchill at War*, 286; Kuznetsov, *Kursom k pobede*, 454–55.

13 V. N. Shustov, "Ialtinskaia konferentsiia v vospominaniiakh ee uchastnikov," in G. V. Saenko et al., eds., *Ialta, Potsdam, Vtoraia Mirovaia. Materialy trekh kruglykh stolov, posviashchennykh 60-letiiu Velikoi Pobedy* (Moscow, 2006), 55–61; Churchill, *Triumph and Tragedy*, 395; Moran, *Churchill at War*, 291; Rzheshevskii, *Stalin i Cherchill'*, 512–13; Gilbert, *Winston S. Churchill*, 7:1220–21.

Chapter 27. Days of Hope

1 Anton Chekhov, *The Lady with the Dog and Other Stories*, trans. Constance Garnett (New York, 1917), 12.
2 Moran, *Churchill at War*, 283; Sherwood, *Roosevelt and Hopkins*, 870; Harriman and Abel, *Special Envoy*, 399; Gilbert, *Winston S. Churchill*, 7:1220; Reynolds, *Summits*, 139.
3 Stettinius, *Roosevelt and the Russians*, 295; Bohlen, *Witness to History*, 200.
4 Lord Ismay, *Memoirs*, 388; Cadogan, *Diaries*, 708–9; War Cabinet, WM (45) 18th Conclusions, Minute 3, Confidential Annex, February 12, 1945—5.30 p.m., CAB, 65/51, TNA.
5 Cadogan, *Diaries*, 708–9; Sherwood, *Hopkins and Roosevelt*, 870; Hiss, *Recollections of a Life*, 97, 118–21, 125; Leahy, *I Was There*, 322; Bohlen, *Witness to History*, 200; Stettinius, *Roosevelt and the Russians*, 295–98.
6 Moran, *Churchill at War*, 284–85; Reynolds, *Summits*, 139.
7 *SSSR i germanskii vopros*, 608; Kuznetsov, *Kursom k pobede*, 448; Gromyko, *Memoirs*, 112.
8 *Molotov Remembers*, 53; Gromyko, *Memoirs*, 112–15.
9 Maiskii, *Izbrannaia perepiska*, 2:161; *SSSR i germanskii vopros*, 606–8.
10 Beria to Stalin, February 23, 1945, GARF, r-9401, op. 2, d. 93, fols. 135–82; A. I. Kokurin, "Okhrana i khoziaistvennoe obsluzhivanie Ialtinskoi konferentsii rukovoditelei SSSR, SShA i Anglii," in *Ialta 1945–2000: Problemy mezhdunarodnoi bezopasnosti na poroge novogo stoletiia*, ed. V. P. Kazarin (Simferopol, 2001), 130–32; Iurchenko, *Ialtinskaia konferentsiia*, 308–11.
11 Georgii Zhukov, *Vospominaniia i razmyshleniia*, vol. 3 (Moscow, 1969), 290–91; Vladislav Zubok and Constantine Pleshakov, *Inside the Kremlin's Cold War: From Stalin to Khrushchev* (Cambridge, MA, 1996), 27–35.
12 Hiss, *Recollections of a Life*, 120.
13 Gilbert, *Winston S. Churchill*, 7:1228–36; Cadogan, *Diaries*, 716; War Cabinet, WM (45) 23d Conclusions, Minute 2, Confidential Annex, February 21, 1945—6.30 p.m., CAB, 65/61, TNA.
14 Statement by Winston Churchill to the House of Commons, February 27, 1945, http://www.ena.lu/statement_winston_churchill_house_commons_27_february_1945-020002923.html; Churchill, *Triumph and Tragedy*, 399–402; Gilbert, *Winston S. Churchill*, 7:1235.
15 Susan Butler, ed., *My Dear Mr. Stalin: The Complete Correspondence of Franklin D. Roosevelt and Joseph V. Stalin* (New Haven, CT, 2005), 297.
16 Report to Congress by President Franklin D. Roosevelt on the Crimea Conference, March 1, 1945, http://www.teachingamericanhistory.com/library/index.asp?document=658.
17 Trevor-Roper, *Final Entries 1945*, 7, 16, 22–23, 58–60.

Chapter 28. Signs of Trouble

1 Joseph Stalin, Order of the Day, no. 5, http://www.ibiblio.org/pha/policy/1945/450223a.html; N. V. Novikov, *Vospominaniia diplomata. Zapiski 1938–1947* (Moscow, 1989), 280–83.
2 Butler, ed., *My Dear Mr. Stalin*, 298–99.
3 Deane, *The Strange Alliance*, 189–97; Abel and Harriman, *Special Envoy*, 419–20.
4 Butler, ed., *My Dear Mr. Stalin*, 300–302.
5 Deane, *The Strange Alliance*, 197–201; Abel and Harriman, *Special Envoy*, 420–23; Arthur M. Schlesinger Jr., "Foreword," in Butler, ed., *My Dear Mr. Stalin*, xv; Miscamble, *From Roosevelt to Truman*, 73–74.
6 Kathleen Harriman to her sister Mary Harriman, March 8, 1945, Moscow, no. 177/9, March 7–10, 1945, Averell Harriman Papers.
7 Protocol of conversation: Harriman, Kennan, Page, Molotov, Dekanozov, Pavlov, January 8, 1945, Subject: Hungarian Armistice Negotiations, 6, no. 176/4, January 6–10, 1945, Averell Harriman Papers; George Kennan memo to Averell Harriman, January 13, 1945, and Averell Harriman letter to Andrei Vyshinsky, January 13, 1945, no. 176/5, January 11–16, 1945, Averell Harriman Papers.
8 Biographical information on Vyshinsky in NND 812006 record group 43: World War II Conferences, box 3, NARA; Byrnes, *Speaking Frankly*, 49–53.
9 Pierre de Senarclens, *Yalta*, trans. Jasmer Singh (New Brunswick, NJ, 1987), 78–80.
10 Instructions to A. Clark Kerr, no. 177/3, February 18–22, 1945, Averell Harriman Papers; informa-

tion telegram, Grew to Harriman, February 15, 1945, no. 177/4, February 23–25, 1945, Averell Harriman Papers; *FRUS: Yalta*, 803–4, 973; Harriman and Abel, *Special Envoy*, 412.

11 Memorandum of Conversation, February 16, 1945, Subject: Crimean Conference, Conversations, vol. 6 (26), Joseph Clark Grew Papers.

12 To the Secretary of State from the Acting Secretary, February 14, 1945, no. 117/2, February 13–17, 1945, Averell Harriman Papers; "Fortnightly Survey of American Opinion on International Affairs," Survey no. 21, February: First Half, February 20, 1945, no. 117/3, February 18–22, 1945, Averell Harriman Papers.

13 Record of the conversation between Polish ambassador and minister of state, February 12, 1945, FO371/47578/2896, 132–33, TNA; minutes of the meeting between Field Marshal Sir Harold Alexander, Supreme Allied Commander, and Lieutenant-General W. Anders, Commander of Second Polish Corps, on January 17, 1945, FO371/47580/2896, 145–47, TNA.

14 Winston Churchill, "Poland," February 21, 1945, FO371/47579/2896, 137–38, TNA; "Letter from M. Mikołajczyk," *Daily Herald*, February 16, 1945; memo on Mr. Harvey's conversation with Mr. Romer, February 18, 1945, FO371/47579/2896, 218–20, TNA; Mr. Eden to Sir O. O'Malley, February 20, 1945, FO371/47579/2896, 125–26, TNA.

15 Churchill, *Triumph and Tragedy*, 399–402; Krystyna Kersten, *Jałta w polskiej perspektywie* (London, 1989), 105–6; Trevor-Roper, *Final Entries 1945*, 7, 16.

16 British memo of February 18, 1945, FO371/47579/2896, 4042, TNA; cf. no. 177/3, February 18–22, 1945, Averell Harriman Papers; *Correspondence between the Chairman of the Council of Ministers of the USSR*, 1:331–32, 339–44; Kersten, *Jałta*, 111.

17 *Ocherki istorii Rossiiskoi vneshnei razvedki*, 4:618–62.

18 Haynes and Klehr, *Venona*, 53–54; Robert Louis Benson and Michael Warner, eds., *Venona: Soviet Espionage and the American Response, 1939–1957* (Washington, DC, 1996), 419–21, http://www.nsa.gov/venona/venon00108.cfm#29.

19 "Minutes of First Meeting of Polish Commission, Kremlin, February, 1945," 1, no. 177/4, February 23–25, 1945, Averell Harriman Papers; From Harriman for the Acting Secretary, February 24, 1945, no. 177/4, February 23–25, 1945, Averell Harriman Papers; *FRUS: Yalta*, 973.

20 "A Possible Line of Approach to the Setting Up of the Poland Commission to Be 'Sold,' if Possible, to M. Molotov," February 22, 1945, no. 177/3, February 18–22, 1945, Averell Harriman Papers; Bohlen, *Witness to History*, 191–92; Kersten, *Jałta*, 114.

21 "Press. Secretary of State, Washington," February 13, 1945, no. 177/2, February 13–17, 1945, February 19, 1945, Averell Harriman Papers; To Secstate Washington, February 22, 1945, no. 177/3, February 18–22, 1945, Averell Harriman Papers.

22 Churchill, *Triumph and Tragedy*, 293–94.

Chapter 29. Spy Wars

1 Stettinius, *Roosevelt and the Russians*, 285–86; Edward Flynn to Helen Flynn, February 17, 1945, Moscow, Yalta Trip—Letters to Family, container 25, Edward J. Flynn Papers; Kathleen Harriman to her sister Mary Harriman, February 16, 1945, Moscow, special files, World War II, no. 177/2, February 13–17, 1945, Averell Harriman Papers.

2 Stettinius, *Roosevelt and the Russians*, 286–88.

3 Allen Weinstein and Alexander Vassiliev, *The Haunted Wood: Soviet Espionage in America—The Stalin Era* (New York, 2000), 269; Benson and Warner, *Venona*, 423; cf. http://www.law.umkc.edu/faculty/projects/ftrials/hiss/hissvenona.html; cf. Russian text of the message at http://homepages.nyu.edu/~th15/russianvenona.html, and its retranslation at http://homepages.nyu.edu/~th15/venonaretranslation.html.

4 Allen Weinstein, *Perjury* (New York, 1997), 182–84; Weinstein and Vassiliev, *The Haunted Wood*, 5–12, 40–44, summarized in Theodore Draper, "The Case of Cases," *New York Review of Books* 44, no. 18 (November 20, 1997): 13–18; no. 19 (December 4, 1997): 16; John Earl Haynes, Harvey Klehr, and Alexander Vassiliev, *Spies: The Rise and Fall of the KGB in America* (New Haven and London, 2009), 1–31.

5 "Chief Clerk," *Time*, April 16, 1945; "Cast of Characters," *Time*, May 28, 1945.

6 Whittaker Chambers, "The Ghosts on the Roof," *Time*, March 5, 1945; Schlesinger, *Act of Creation*, 105.

7 Sam Tanenhaus, *Whittaker Chambers* (New York, 1997), 188–93; Weinstein, *Perjury* (1978), 344–47.

8 Draper, "The Case of Cases"; G. Edward White, *Alger Hiss's Looking-Glass Wars: The Covert Life of a Soviet Spy* (New York, 2005).

9 Weinstein, *Perjury* (1997), 182–84; Weinstein and Vassiliev, *The Haunted Wood*, 5–12, 40–44; Eduard Mark, "Who Was 'Venona's' 'Ales'"? Cryptanalysis and the Hiss Case," *Intelligence and National Security* 18, no. 3 (Autumn 2003): 45–72; Eduard Mark, "*In Re* Alger Hiss: A Final Verdict from the Archives of the KGB," *Journal of Cold War Studies* 11, no. 3 (Summer 2009): 26–67.

10 Jerrold Schechter and Leona Schecter, *The Sacred Secrets: How Soviet Intelligence Operations Changed American History* (Washington, DC, 2002), 130–31.

11 Charles E. Bohlen, "Testimony Concerning Nomination as Ambassador to Russia," in Richard F. Fenno Jr., ed., *The Yalta Conference*, 2d ed. (Lexington, MA, 1972), 130–33; Bohlen, *Witness to History*, 194.

12 Susan Jacoby, *Alger Hiss and the Battle for History* (New Haven, CT, 2009).

13 Zhukov, *Vospominaniia i razmyshleniia*, 2:290–91.

14 Allen Dulles, *The Secret Surrender* (New York, 1966), 87–111.

15 Bradley F. Smith and Elena Agarossi, *Operation Sunrise: The Secret Surrender* (New York, 1979), 81–85.

16 Richard Breitman, "Record Group 263: Records of the Central Intelligence Agency. Records of the Directorate of Operations Analysis of the Name File of Guido Zimmer," http://www.archives.gov/iwg/declassified-records/rg-263-cia-records/rg-263-zimmer.html.

17 Smith and Agarossi, *Operation Sunrise*, 101–83.

18 Harriman and Abel, *Special Envoy*, 432–33.

19 *Correspondence between the Chairman of the Council of Ministers of the USSR and the Presidents of the USA and the Prime Ministers of Great Britain during the Great Patriotic War of 1941–1945*, vol. 2, *Correspondence with Franklin D. Roosevelt and Harry S. Truman (August 1941–December 1945)* (Moscow, 1957), 192–209; cf. Smith and Agarossi, *Operation Sunrise*, 108–11.

20 Mark Shteinberg, "Kto Vy, shtandartenfiurer Shtirlits?" http://www.russian-bazaar.com/cgi-bin/rb.cgi/f=mste&auth=1&n=29&y=2003&id=mste.2003.7.10.22.22.27.29.istina.15.37&back=1.

21 *Ocherki istorii Rossiiskoi vneshnei razvedki*, 2:648; cf. idem, 194–95.

22 Haynes and Klehr, *Venona*, 100–108.

23 Roberts, *Stalin's Wars*, 243.

24 Butler, ed., *My Dear Mr. Stalin*, 321.

Chapter 30. Stalin Digs In

1 Butler, ed., *My Dear Mr. Stalin*, 302–3, 321.

2 *FRUS: Yalta*, 990–92; Stettinius, *Roosevelt and the Russians*, 197–98; Clemens, *Yalta*, 223–40.

3 Memorandum of Conversation, March 29, 1945, Subject: Representation in World Organization, Conversations, MS Am 1687.3, vol. 6 (45), Joseph Clark Grew Papers; Tsentral'nyi derzhavnyi arkhiv vyshchykh orhaniv vlady ta upravlinnia Ukraïny, fond 1, op. 16, spr. 33 (Dokumenty San-Frantsys'koï konferentsiï), fond 4669, op. 1, spr. 21, "Plan besedy Manuilskogo s Korotchenko po khoziaistvennym voprosam Narkomata inostrannykh del SSSR," February 6, 1944; Leahy, *I Was There*, 341–42; Gromyko, *Memoirs*, 152.

4 King, "Allied Negotiations," 590–91; *SSSR i germanskii vopros*, 609–19, 626.

5 *SSSR i germanskii vopros*, 597–600.

6 Ibid., 626; Wilfried Loth, "Stalin's Plans for Post-War Germany," in Gori and Pons, eds., *The Soviet Union and Europe in the Cold War*, 24–25.

7 Butler, ed., *My Dear Mr. Stalin*, 310–12.

8 Kersten, *Jałta*, 116–21.

9 Butler, ed., *My Dear Mr. Stalin*, 318–21.

10 Information on the messages received by the Polish government, no. 177/8, March 3–6, 1945, Averell Harriman Papers; Kersten, *Jałta*, 121–24; Davies, *Rising '44*, 459–70.

11 Bohdan Bociurkiw, *The Ukrainian Greek Catholic Church and the Soviet State, 1939–50* (Edmonton, 1996); Jaroslav Pelikan, *Confessor between East and West* (Grand Rapids, MI, 1990).

12 Hiss, *Recollections of a Life*, 121–22.

13 Kathleen Harriman to her sister Mary Harriman, Yalta, February 10, 1945, no. 176/9, February 1–5, 1945, Averell Harriman Papers.

14 Serhii Plokhy, "In the Shadow of Yalta: International Politics and the Soviet Liquidation of the Ukrainian Catholic Church," in Serhii Plokhy and Frank E. Sysyn, *Religion and Nation in Modern Ukraine* (Edmonton, 2003), 66.

15 Trevor-Roper, *Final Entries 1945*, 212.

16 Report by Kazimierz Papee, Polish Ambassador in Vatican, December 4, 1944, Ambasada (France), box 5, file 2, Hoover Institution Archives; Harry Hopkins to John G. Winant, US Ambas-

sador to Great Britain, September 4, 1944, box 337, book 10: Growing Crisis in Poland, Hopkins Papers.

17 To the Secretary of State, Washington, from the Ambassador, Moscow, February 7, 1945 [English translation of Patriarch Aleksii's address], 3, no. 176/10, February 6–9, 1945, Averell Harriman Papers; To the Secretary of State, Washington, from the Ambassador, Moscow, February 13, 1945 [summary of Soviet press reports], February 13, 1945, no. 177/2, February 13–17, 1945, Averell Harriman Papers.

18 Yalta Trip—Letters to Family, March 10, 1945, container 25, Edward J. Flynn Papers; Memorandum of Conversation, February 22, 1945, Present: Karpov, Flynn, Melby, no. 177/3, February 18–22, 1945, Averell Harriman Papers; Edward Flynn, *You're the Boss* (New York, 1947), 190–95.

19 Plokhy, "In the Shadow of Yalta," 58–73.

20 *Vostochnaia Evropa v dokumentakh rossiiskikh arkhivov*, 37–38.

Chapter 31. After Roosevelt

1 Arthur Krock, "President Roosevelt Is Dead, Truman to Continue Policies," *New York Times*, April 13, 1945, 1; Smith, *FDR*, 633–36.

2 "War News Summarized," *New York Times*, February 14, 1945; "War News Summarized," *New York Times*, April 15, 1945; "Bugler: Sound Taps," *Time*, April 23, 1945; Conrad Black, *Franklin Delano Roosevelt: Champion of Freedom* (London, 2003), 1114–15.

3 Thomas M. Campbell and George C. Herring, eds., *The Diaries of Edward Stettinius, Jr., 1943–1946* (New York, 1975), 318–19.

4 Harriman and Abel, *Special Envoy*, 447–53.

5 Bohlen, *Witness to History*, 213.

6 Harry S. Truman, *Memoirs*, vol. 1, *Year of Decisions* (New York, 1955), 82; *Molotov Remembers*, 55; John Lewis Gaddis, *The United States and the Origins of the Cold War, 1941–1947* (New York, 2000), 203–5; Miscamble, *From Roosevelt to Truman*, 119–23.

7 Roberts, *Stalin's Wars*, 247.

8 *Correspondence between the Chairman of the Council of Ministers of the USSR*, 1:331–32.

9 Ibid., 1:339–44.

10 Bohlen, *Witness to History*, 175–76.

11 *Correspondence between the Chairman of the Council of Ministers of the USSR*, 1:343–44.

12 Memorandum of Conversation, June 5, 1945, Subject: Alleged Firing on Soviet Balloons by American Ships at Murmansk, Conversations, MS Am 1687.3, vol. 7 (25), Joseph Clark Grew Papers.

13 Stanisław Kot to Stanisław Mikołajczyk, from San Francisco, May 14, 1945, 18, box 166, file 14, Stanisław Mikołajczyk Papers, 18, Hoover Institution Archives, Stanford University.

14 Memorandum of Conversation, May 12, 1945, Conversations, MS Am 1687.3, vol. 7 (11), Joseph Clark Grew Papers; Harriman and Abel, *Special Envoy*, 460; Miscamble, *From Roosevelt to Truman*, 133–35.

15 Miscamble, *From Roosevelt to Truman*, 135–43.

16 *Vostochnaia Evropa v dokumentakh rossiiskikh arkhivov*, 222–23; Sherwood, *Roosevelt and Hopkins*, 894; Harriman and Abel, *Special Envoy*, 459, 463–75.

17 Kersten, *Jałta*, 124–73; Miscamble, *From Roosevelt to Truman*, 159.

18 Memorandum of Conversation, June 11, 1945, Points in Yalta Agreements Affecting Far East, Conversations, MS Am 1687.3, vol. 7 (28), Joseph Clark Grew Papers; Hasegawa, *Racing the Enemy*, 97–98.

19 Miscamble, *From Roosevelt to Truman*, 169–71; Schlesinger, *Act of Creation*, 109–11.

20 Lord Moran, *Churchill at War*, 336, 343; Byrnes, *Speaking Frankly*, 76–77; *Molotov Remembers*, 55; Miscamble, *From Roosevelt to Truman*, 180–202.

21 Gregor Dallas, *Poisoned Peace: 1945—The War That Never Ended* (London, 2005), 526–38; R. B. McCallum and Alison Readman, *The British General Election* (New York, 1964).

22 Byrnes, *Speaking Frankly*, 78; *Vostochnaia Evropa v dokumentakh rossiiskikh arkhivov*, 359.

23 Byrnes, *Speaking Frankly*, 79–87; *Molotov Remembers*, 53; Miscamble, *From Roosevelt to Truman*, 207–17.

24 Hasegawa, *Racing the Enemy*, 177–214.

Epilogue

1 Liudmila Obukhovskaia, "Imet' uvazhenie k proshlomu," *Krymskaia pravda*, February 9, 2005.

2 Ronald Grigor Suny, *The Revenge of the Past: Nationalism, Revolution and the Collapse of the Soviet Union* (Stanford, CA, 1993).

3 Evgenii Grigor'ev, "MID RF otstoial Kaliningrad," *Nezavisimaia gazeta*, November 16, 2004.

4 Artem Blinov, "Tokio daiut trubu, no ne ostrova," *Nezavisimaia gazeta*, January 17, 2005; Artem Blinov, "Ul'timatum proigravshego," *Nezavisimaia gazeta*, March 10, 2005.

5 For the text of Bush's Riga speech, see http://www.encyclopedia.com/doc/1G1=133371464.html.

6 Matt Welch, "When Men Were Men and Continents Were Divided," *Reason on Line*, May 10, 2005, www.reason.com/hitandrun/2005/05/when_men_were_m.shtml.

7 Elisabeth Bumiller, "In Row over Yalta, Bush Pokes at Baltic Politics," *International Herald Tribune*, May 16, 2005; Pat Buchanan, "Was WWII Worth It? For Stalin, Yes," WorldNetDaily, May 11, 2005, http://www.wnd.com/news/article.asp?ARTICLE_ID=44210; "Yalta Regrets," *National Review*, May 11, 2005, www.nationalreview.com/editorial/editorial2200505110923.asp; Arthur Schlesinger Jr., "Yalta Delusions," The Huffington Post, May 9, 2005, www.huffingtonpost.com/theblog/archive/2005/05/yalta-delusions.html; Jacob Heilbrunn, "Once Again, the Big Yalta Lie," *Los Angeles Times*, May 10, 2005.

8 "Winston Churchill's Iron Curtain Speech," http://www.historyguide.org/europe/churchill.html; Athan G. Theoharis, *The Yalta Myths: An Issue in U.S. Politics, 1945–1955* (Columbia, MO, 1970); Serhii Plokhy, "Remembering Yalta: The Politics of International History," in Serhii Plokhy, *Ukraine and Russia: Representations of the Past* (Toronto, 2008), 213–39.

9 Davis, *No Simple Victory*, 9–72.

10 *FRUS: Yalta*, 501.

11 *Molotov Remembers*, 54.

12 Timothy Garton Ash, *The Polish Revolution: Solidarity*, 3d ed. (New Haven, CT, 2002), 3.

13 Winston S. Churchill, *Closing the Ring* (New York, 1962), 332.

14 Reynolds, *In Command of History*, 466–86.

15 Leszek Kolakowski, Edward Mortimer, Antony Polonsky, and Frank Roberts, "Yalta & the Fate of Poland," *New York Review of Books* 33, no. 9 (May 29, 1986): 43–44.

16 *Vostochnaia Evropa v dokumentakh rossiiskikh arkhivov*, 457–58; Roberts, *Stalin's Wars*, 249.

17 Bohlen, *Witness to History*, 176.

18 Butler, ed., *My Dear Mr. Stalin*, 320–21.

19 Richard Nixon, *The Memoirs of Richard Nixon* (New York, 1978), 621; Reynolds, *Summits*, 273–76.

INDEX